Creative International Cookbook

Compiled by Beryl Frank
Edited by Charlotte Turgeon

Bonanza Books
New York

Contents

Introduction

The Creative International Cookbook provides a way to experience other countries without ever leaving your own kitchen. This comprehensive collection of over 1600 recipes features dishes that are commonly prepared in homes around the world. The foods of many countries are represented here—from everyday meals to holiday feasts.

You'll probably encounter a number of unfamiliar words and ingredients as you use this book. The Glossary on page 624 will provide definitions and helpful information about the foreign terms found in these recipes. It might be helpful to read through the Glossary before using the book and then refer to it when a particular recipe sounds foreign to you.

The book is divided into the following chapters: Appetizers; Soups; Salads; Eggs and Cheese; Poultry; Meats; Seafood; Tempura; Pasta, Rice, and Other Grain Dishes; Breads and Pancakes; Vegetables; and Desserts. Within each chapter, the recipes are organized by country. Recipes from European countries—France, Germany, Greece, Hungary, Ireland, Italy, Poland, and Spain—are found at the beginning of each chapter. Then, you'll find recipes from Scandinavia, the Middle East, China, Japan, and Mexico, in that order. To make the book even easier to use, running heads at the top of each page indicate the chapter and which countries are represented on that page.

This exciting cookbook offers a broad range of recipes, which should interest both novices and more experienced cooks. So discover and enjoy the challenge of preparing international foods.

Cheese, bacon & onion quiche

❧ Appetizers ❧

Cheese, bacon, & onion quiche

FRANCE

1 single-crust Basic Pastry
  (see Index; do not bake)
6 slices bacon, cut into 2-inch pieces
1 small onion, chopped
3 eggs
½ cup milk
½ cup heavy cream
1 cup shredded Swiss cheese
½ teaspoon salt
⅛ teaspoon pepper

Line quiche or pie pan with pastry.
Cook bacon until crisp. Drain; place in pie shell.
Sauté onion in bacon fat until lightly browned.
Drain off fat. Off heat, stir in the eggs, milk, cream, cheese, and seasonings. Pour into pastry-lined pan.
Bake in preheated 375°F oven 25 minutes or until a knife plunged into the custard comes out clean. Serve hot, warm, or cold.
MAKES 4 SERVINGS.

Oysters Rockefeller

FRANCE

2 tablespoons chopped green onion
2 tablespoons chopped celery
3 tablespoons chopped fennel (optional)
3 tablespoons chopped parsley
¼ pound butter
1 cup watercress or spinach
3 tablespoons bread crumbs
3 tablespoons Pernod or anisette
¼ teaspoon salt
⅛ teaspoon white pepper
Dash cayenne
2 dozen oysters on the half shell

Sauté onion, celery, and herbs in 3 tablespoons butter for 3 minutes. Add watercress or spinach; let it wilt. Place this mixture, remaining butter, bread crumbs, liqueur, and seasonings into blender or food processor. Spin for 1 minute.
Put 1 tablespoon mixture on each oyster. Place oyster shells on rock-salt beds; dampen the salt slightly.

Bake at 450°F about 4 minutes or until butter is melted and oysters are heated.
MAKES 4 SERVINGS.

Jellied-shrimp canapé

FRANCE

1 recipe Basic Aspic (see Index)
24 small cooked shrimp
24 slices white bread
1½ tablespoons butter

Place 1 teaspoon aspic in each of 24 muffin compartments. Chill. Dip shrimp in aspic; center each on top of chilled aspic. Add just enough aspic to cover shrimp. Chill again.
Meanwhile, cut out toast rounds with a biscuit cutter; butter each. Place on baking sheet.
Bake in 350°F oven about 30 minutes or until brown. Cool.
Remove jellied shrimp by running a spatula around edges of gelatin. Serve on cold buttered toast rounds.
MAKES 24 CANAPÉS.

Note: Toast rounds may be made ahead and frozen.

Chicken-liver pâté

FRANCE

2 tablespoons butter
½ pound chicken livers
2 eggs, hard-cooked
1 package (3-ounce size) cream cheese, softened
1 tablespoon finely chopped parsley
¾ teaspoon salt
⅛ teaspoon pepper
1 tablespoon cognac

Heat butter in medium frypan. Cook chicken livers, stirring occasionally, over medium heat 3-5 minutes or until tender. Drain. Chop livers and eggs in food grinder or food processor.
With wooden spoon, work cream cheese until light and fluffy. Mix cheese into liver mixture along with remaining ingredients. Refrigerate for several hours.
Serve pâté with hot toast or crackers.
MAKES 1¼ CUPS.

7

Country meat loaf

FRANCE

¾ pound sliced bacon,
    simmered 5 minutes
1 tablespoon salted butter
1 cup chopped onion
1 pound ground pork
½ pound ground veal
½ pound finely chopped
    chicken livers
2 cloves garlic, crushed
½ teaspoon salt
¼ teaspoon allspice
⅛ teaspoon ground cloves
⅛ teaspoon ground nutmeg
¼ teaspoon pepper
2 eggs, beaten
½ cup heavy cream
2 tablespoons sherry
½ pound boiled ham, sliced
    ¼ inch thick and cut into
    strips ¼ inch wide
1 bay leaf

Line a 2-quart mold, casserole, or 9 × 5 × 3-inch loaf pan with the parboiled bacon. Save 3 slices for the top.
Melt butter in small pan; cook onion until tender.
In a 2-quart bowl mix onion, ground meats, liver, seasonings, eggs, cream, and sherry. Beat several minutes to lighten. Place ⅓ of mixture into mold. Lay ½ of the ham over meat mixture. Add ⅓ more meat mixture, ham, and finish with meat mixture. Lay 3 bacon strips over loaf; place bay leaf on top. Cover tightly with aluminum foil and a lid. Place in a hot-water bath.
Bake in preheated 350° oven about 1½ to 2 hours. The juices will be clear when loaf is done. Place a weight on top of loaf to press out air. Cool loaf at room temperature. Refrigerate overnight. Unmold and serve loaf chilled.
MAKES 10-12 SERVINGS.

Roquefort cheese balls

FRANCE

¼ pound Roquefort cheese
3 tablespoons unsalted butter, softened
1 tablespoon minced green-onion tops
Freshly ground pepper to taste
2 teaspoons brandy
¼ cup bread crumbs
2 tablespoons finely minced parsley

Mash cheese in small bowl. Beat in butter to form a smooth paste. Blend in onion, pepper, and brandy. Shape into small balls, about ½ inch in diameter. Mix crumbs and parsley. Roll balls in crumb mixture. Chill, if made ahead. Serve cheese balls at room temperature, with crusty French bread.
MAKES 24 BALLS.

Marinated mushrooms

FRANCE

1 pound small whole
    mushrooms

marinade
1 cup chicken broth
1 cup dry white wine
2 tablespoons fresh lemon
    juice
¼ cup white vinegar
¼ cup vegetable oil
1 small onion, sliced
1 small carrot, sliced
1 stalk celery
1 clove garlic, peeled
¼ teaspoon rosemary
¼ teaspoon marjoram
¼ teaspoon thyme
⅛ teaspoon oregano
1 bay leaf
4 peppercorns
¼ teaspoon salt

Combine all ingredients except mushrooms in a 2-quart saucepan; bring to a boil. Simmer gently 30 minutes. Strain marinade, pressing juice from vegetables. Return to saucepan. Add mushrooms; simmer for 5 minutes.

Cool to room temperature, then chill at least 4 hours, preferably overnight.
MAKES 4 SERVINGS.

Stuffed mushrooms
FRANCE

1 pound mushrooms (caps should be 2 to 3 inches in diameter)
4 tablespoons butter, melted
3 tablespoons finely chopped onions
1 tablespoon butter
¼ cup Madeira
¼ cup fine, dry bread crumbs
¼ cup grated Swiss cheese
¼ cup grated Parmesan cheese
4 tablespoons minced parsley
½ teaspoon tarragon
¼ teaspoon pepper
2 tablespoons heavy cream

Remove stems from mushrooms. Brush caps with 2 tablespoons melted butter. Place hollow-side-up in roasting pan. Mince mushroom stems; squeeze in towel to remove moisture.

Sauté onions in tablespoon butter to soften. Add mushroom stems; cook over high heat, stirring frequently, about 5 minutes or until most moisture has disappeared. Add Madeira; boil until it has mostly evaporated. Remove from heat.

Mix in bread crumbs, cheeses, parsley, tarragon, and pepper. Bind together with cream. Fill mushroom caps with stuffing. (Mushrooms can be prepared ahead to this point. Refrigerate until ready to use.)

Just before baking, top with drops of melted butter. In preheated 375°F oven bake 15 minutes or until caps are tender and stuffing is slightly browned.
MAKES 6 TO 8 SERVINGS.

Stuffed tomatoes
FRANCE

4 medium tomatoes, peeled

cream-cheese stuffing
4 ounces cream cheese, softened
2 tablespoons light cream
1 teaspoon chopped chives

dressing
2 tablespoons wine vinegar
6 tablespoons vegetable oil
¼ teaspoon salt
Pepper to taste
1 teaspoon chopped chives

Cut a thin slice from bottom of each tomato. Reserve slices. From stem ends, scoop out the seeds and pulp with a spoon. Mix cream cheese, cream, and 1 teaspoon chives. Fill tomatoes with Cream-Cheese Stuffing.

Mix vinegar, oil, salt, pepper, and 1 teaspoon chives. Pour dressing over tomatoes. Chill up to 2 hours.

Serve on salad greens.

Use reserved tomato slices as hats for tomatoes.
MAKES 4 SERVINGS.

Note: To peel tomatoes, dip in boiling water 30 seconds, then rinse with cold water. Skins will slip off.

Fresh vegetables w/green mayonnaise
FRANCE

green mayonnaise
¼ teaspoon sugar
½ teaspoon dry mustard
¾ teaspoon salt
1 large egg yolk
2 tablespoons fresh lemon juice
¾ cup vegetable oil plus ¼ cup French olive oil or 1 cup vegetable oil
2 tablespoons chopped parsley
1 teaspoon fresh or frozen chives
1 teaspoon fresh or ½ teaspoon dried tarragon (optional)

Fresh vegetables for dipping, such as mushrooms, cherry tomatoes, cauliflower florets, zucchini sticks, green-pepper slices, cucumber slices, carrot sticks.

Mix sugar, mustard, salt, egg yolk, and 1 tablespoon lemon juice in 1-quart bowl. Using wire whisk, very slowly add oil, a drop at a time, until about ¼ cup is added. Once a thick emulsion has formed, oil can be added 1 teaspoon at a

9

time. When mixture is very thick, add remaining lemon juice. Slowly beat in remaining oil. Add herbs; mix well. Chill.

Arrange chilled vegetables attractively on a large platter, with mayonnaise in the center as a dip. MAKES 8 SERVINGS.

Note: If mayonnaise separates, place 1 teaspoon cold water or an egg yolk in a separate bowl. Slowly beat in mayonnaise. When emulsion is reformed, continue adding oil as above.

Artichoke hearts w/mushroom filling

FRANCE

mushroom filling
2 tablespoons butter
1 tablespoon minced shallots
½ pound finely chopped mushrooms
¼ teaspoon salt
Dash pepper
⅛ teaspoon tarragon
1 tablespoon flour
2 tablespoons brandy or sherry
½ cup heavy cream

6 artichoke bottoms (see Index, Boiled Artichokes)

Melt butter in small saucepan. Cook shallots several minutes. Add mushrooms; cook until all liquid is evaporated. Add seasonings; stir in flour. Add brandy and cream; heat until thickened.

Place about 2 tablespoons filling on each artichoke bottom. Place filled bottoms in greased casserole; cover.

Heat for 10 to 15 minutes in preheated 300°F oven. Serve hot.
MAKES 6 SERVINGS.

Artichoke appetizers

FRANCE

2 large artichokes, cooked according to basic directions (see Index, Boiled Artichokes)
6 ounces cream cheese, softened
½ teaspoon Tabasco sauce

¼ teaspoon garlic powder
¼ teaspoon salt
4 tablespoons half-and-half cream or milk
About ½ pound small shrimp, cooked

Gently remove leaves from prepared artichokes. Use leaves that are firm enough to handle and have a good edible portion.

Beat cream cheese, seasonings, and milk until smooth and creamy. Place about ½ teaspoon cream cheese on base of each leaf. Garnish with a shrimp on each leaf.

Arrange leaves on a large, round plate in a sunflower shape. Chill.
MAKES ABOUT 36.

Boiled artichokes

FRANCE

6 artichokes
6 quarts water
3 tablespoons salt
Hollandaise Sauce (see Index) or melted butter

Cut off artichoke stalks, pull off hard outer leaves, and trim off points of remaining leaves with scissors. Cut off about ¼ of the top, which removes many thorny pointed leaves. Place artichokes in boiling salted water; boil about 45 minutes or until base is tender but not mushy. Drain upside down.

Before serving, remove choke or hairy growth in center by opening top leaves and pulling out tender center or cone in one piece. Below this cone is the choke. Scrape off with a spoon to expose the tender artichoke heart. Discard choke. Replace cone upside down in center. Fill with Hollandaise Sauce, or serve butter separately.

Pull off each leaf, beginning at bottom. Dunk base of leaf in sauce; pull between the teeth to scrape off the tender flesh. Discard remainder of leaf. Continue this way until all leaves are eaten. Discard cone, cut base into wedges, and dip into remaining sauce.

Artichokes are also delicious served cold with French Dressing (Vinaigrette).
MAKES 6 SERVINGS.

Boiled artichokes

Stuffed clams

Stuffed clams

GREECE

2-dozen clams (little-neck or cherrystone)
¾ cup dry white wine
¼ cup water
½ teaspoon salt
3 tablespoons olive oil
½ cup chopped onion
½ cup raw long-grain rice
¼ teaspoon pepper
½ teaspoon allspice
¼ teaspoon cinnamon
3 tablespoons currants
3 tablespoons pine nuts
2 tablespoons chopped parsley

Scrub the clams and soak them in several changes of cold water to remove the sand. Place in a skillet with the wine, water, and salt. Cover and steam for 10 minutes, until the shells open. Discard any clams that do not open. Cool and then remove the clams from the shells. Save the shells and strain the pan juices.

In a medium saucepan heat the oil and sauté the onion until golden. Add the rice and 1 cup of the pan juices. Bring to a boil. Cover and reduce the heat to low. Cook for 15 minutes. Add the pepper, spices, currants, pine nuts, and parsley. Cook for 5 minutes. Cool.

Dice the clams and add to the pilaf. Stuff the shells with the rice mixture and chill. Serve as an appetizer.

MAKES 24 APPETIZERS.

Shrimp pies

GREECE

4 ounces cream cheese
1 egg yolk
1 tablespoon chopped parsley
1 tablespoon chopped green onions
½ teaspoon lemon juice
¼ teaspoon salt
1 6-ounce package small frozen shrimp, thawed and chopped
2 tablespoons grated Kafaloteri (or Parmesan) cheese
6 sheets phyllo
1 stick butter, melted

Whip the cream cheese with an electric mixer. Beat in the egg yolk. With a spatula mix in the parsley, green onions, lemon juice, salt, shrimp, and cheese. Chill for 1 hour.

Proceed as for Spinach and Cheese Pies (see Index), using the phyllo dough or substituting the puff pastry.

MAKES 30 APPETIZERS.

Caviar dip

GREECE

½ of an 8-ounce jar of tarama
1 small onion, finely grated
1 egg yolk
4 slices white bread (stale)
¼ cup lemon juice
½ cup olive oil

Place the tarama in a blender jar and whirl at low speed to a smooth paste. Add the onion and egg yolk and whirl to mix.

Remove the crust from the bread and soak the bread in water. Squeeze to dry. Tear it into pieces and add to the fish-roe mixture. Whirl until well-blended. Add the lemon juice and olive oil alternately while whirling at medium speed. Blend at high speed until well-combined. Chill and serve with melba toast, pita bread, or lavash (Arabic crisp flatbread) and crisp raw vegetables.

MAKES 1½ CUPS.

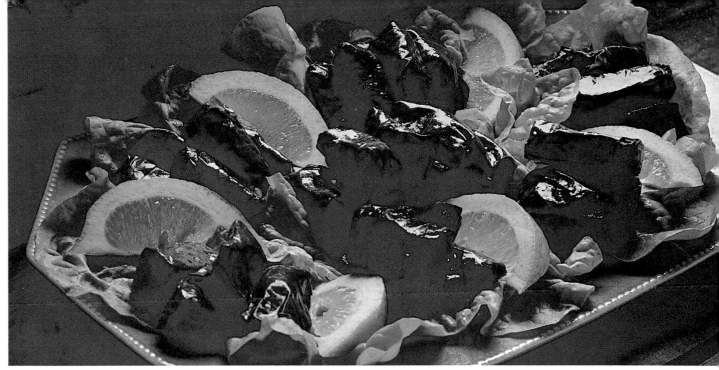

Stuffed grapevine leaves

Stuffed grapevine leaves

GREECE

1 1-pound jar vine leaves
1½ tablespoons olive oil
1 medium onion, finely chopped
½ cup pine nuts
¾ cup raw long-grain rice
½ cup golden raisins
2½ cups water
2 tablespoons finely chopped parsley
½ teaspoon salt
Freshly ground pepper
½ teaspoon cinnamon
2 medium tomatoes, peeled, seeded, and chopped
Juice of 1 lemon
¼ cup olive oil
Lemon wedges for garnish

Unfold the vine leaves and rinse them carefully under cold running water. Drain them. Heat the 1½ tablespoons of oil in a saucepan. Add the onion and sauté until limp. Add the pine nuts and cook over medium heat for 5 minutes. Add the rice, raisins, and 1½ cups of the water. Cover and cook for 20 minutes or until all liquid is absorbed. Stir in the parsley, salt, pepper, cinnamon, and tomatoes.

With the stem end of the leaf toward you, place approximately 1 tablespoon of filling on each vine leaf. Fold up the stem end to enclose the filling. Fold the sides to the center and roll to form a neat package. Do not try to secure the rolls with toothpicks, as they are fragile and will tear easily.

Place a thin layer of unfilled vine leaves in the bottom of a large, heavy saucepan. Tightly pack the rolls in the pan, seam-side-down, in layers. Sprinkle each layer with some of the lemon juice and part of the ¼ cup of oil. Add the remaining 1 cup of water and place a heavy kitchen plate on top of the rolls in the pan to weight them down. Cover the pan. Bring the rolls to a boil, then reduce the heat to simmer and cook for 30 minutes. Remove from the heat and cool. Carefully remove the stuffed leaves from the pan and serve them cold garnished with lemon wedges.

Stuffed leaves can be frozen in a covered container. Thaw it in the refrigerator for 24 hours before serving.

MAKES 6 SERVINGS.

Fried cheese hors d'oeuvres

Appetizer strudel

Eggplant dip

GREECE

1 large eggplant (1½ pounds)
2 cloves garlic, minced
2 tablespoons olive oil
2 tablespoons vinegar
½ teaspoon salt
⅛ teaspoon pepper
2 tablespoons chopped parsley
8 black olives
2 hard-cooked eggs, sliced
1 tomato, cut in wedges
½ cucumber, sliced

Pierce the eggplant several times with a fork. Bake at 350°F for 50 to 60 minutes or until tender. Skin while warm, and mash with a wooden spoon. Add the garlic, olive oil, vinegar, salt, pepper, and parsley. Chill.

Mound on a plate and garnish with the olives, eggs, tomato, and cucumber. Serve with crisp crackers or melba toast.

MAKES 2 CUPS.

Fried cheese hors d'oeuvres

GREECE

3 tablespoons butter
1 egg, well-beaten
1 teaspoon flour
½ pound Kasseri cheese, sliced ½ inch thick
3 tablespoons brandy
Juice of ½ lemon

Heat the butter in a large frying pan until melted and the foam has subsided. Beat the egg and flour together.

Dip the cheese slices in the egg mixture and fry until well-browned on both sides. Gently warm the brandy. Ignite it and pour it over the cheese in the skillet.

Squeeze the lemon juice over the cheese and serve with crusty bread and the sauce from the pan.

MAKES 4 SERVINGS.

Pickled onions

GREECE

1 pound small boiling onions
½ cup water
½ cup white wine
½ cup olive oil
Juice of 2 lemons
½ teaspoon salt
10 peppercorns
1 small bay leaf

Peel the onions and make an "X"-shaped cut in each end to keep them from splitting.

Combine the water, wine, oil, lemon juice, salt, peppercorns, and bay leaf in a medium-size saucepan. Bring to a boil, then reduce the heat and simmer for 5 minutes. Add the onions and cook over low heat for 25 minutes or until tender.

Cool the onions and serve them in a bowl with a small amount of the pan liquid. Serve with cocktail picks.

MAKES 6 TO 8 SERVINGS

Greek meatballs

GREECE

1 pound ground beef or a mixture of beef and lamb
½ cup fresh bread crumbs (1 slice bread)
1 teaspoon salt
½ cup finely chopped onion
1 tablespoon dried parsley flakes
1 small clove garlic, pressed
1 teaspoon crumbled dried mint
1 egg, beaten
¼ cup ouzo or anisette
¼ cup flour
4 tablespoons olive oil

Combine the meat, bread crumbs, salt, onion, parsley, garlic powder, mint, egg, and ouzo. Mix well. Form into meatballs and roll them in the flour. Place on a cookie sheet and chill for 1 hour.

Heat the oil in a large skillet and fry the meatballs over medium-high heat until done (about 10 minutes for cocktail meatballs or 15 to 20 minutes for larger meatballs). Serve them hot.
MAKES 16 LARGE OR 32 SMALL MEATBALLS.

Spinach & cheese pies

GREECE

1 egg
½ medium onion, finely chopped
¼ pound crumbled feta cheese
4 ounces cream cheese
5 ounces (½ of a 10-ounce package) frozen chopped spinach, thawed and drained
1 tablespoon chopped parsley
½ teaspoon dillweed
1 small clove garlic, pressed
6 sheets phyllo or 4 frozen patty shells (omit the butter when using the patty shells)
1 stick butter, melted

In a blender or mixer bowl combine the egg, onion, and feta cheese. Beat to combine. Add the cream cheese and combine well. Add the spinach and seasonings and mix just until blended. Chill for 1 hour.

If you use phyllo dough:
Phyllo must be handled with great care, since it is very delicate and dry to the touch. Carefully unroll as many sheets as you need and store the remainder immediately. Place the sheets not immediately in use between linen tea towels to prevent drying. If the weather is very hot and dry, sprinkle a little water on the towels.

Phyllo sheets are generally 16 × 22 inches. Stack 2 leaves together, cutting through both sheets. Cut strips 2 inches wide by 16 inches long. Brush with melted butter. Place a teaspoon of filling on one end of the strip. Fold one corner of the strip to the opposite side, forming a triangle and enclosing the filling. Continue folding as you would an American flag, to the end of the strip, maintaining the triangular shape. Brush with melted butter.

Place on an ungreased cookie sheet and bake at 375°F for 20 minutes. Serve hot.

If you use puff pastry dough:
Defrost the patty shells at room temperature for 15 to 20 minutes. Form each shell into a ball and roll on a floured pastry cloth to an 11 × 11-inch square. Cut into 16 individual squares. Place ½ teaspoon of filling on each square. Fold to form a triangle, and seal with milk.
Bake at 450°F for 12 minutes.
MAKES APPROXIMATELY 33 IF MADE WITH PHYLLO, APPROXIMATELY 64 SMALLER PASTRIES IF MADE WITH PUFF PASTRY DOUGH.

Note: These can be baked and then frozen. Reheat on a cookie sheet at 350°F for 15 minutes.

Mushroom turnovers

HUNGARY

1 cup butter
1 8-ounce package cream cheese
2 cups flour
½ teaspoon salt
1 egg, well-beaten

mushroom filling

2 tablespoons butter or margarine
½ cup sliced green onions
½ pound mushrooms, cleaned, chopped
½ teaspoon salt
⅛ teaspoon pepper
1 teaspoon lemon juice
1 teaspoon flour
½ cup sour cream

Allow butter and cream cheese to stand at room temperature 1 hour to soften. Place butter and cream cheese in mixing bowl; beat until light. Add flour and salt; mix well. Form into ball. Cover; chill overnight.

Prepare mushroom filling. Melt butter in heavy skillet. Add onions and mushrooms; cook until mushrooms are lightly browned and liquid has evaporated. Add salt, pepper, and lemon juice; stir well. Stir in flour and sour cream; cook over very low heat until thickened. Allow to cool before rolling dough.

Remove dough from refrigerator a few minutes before rolling. Divide into 3 parts. Roll 1 part at a time on lightly floured board to ⅛ inch thick. Cut into 2½ inch rounds. Place 1 teaspoon filling in center of each round. Moisten edges with water. Fold in half; crimp edges. Reroll trimmings. Place on ungreased baking sheet; brush with beaten egg. Bake in preheated 350°F oven 25 to 30 minutes.

Caraway biscuits w/ham filling

HUNGARY

1 10-ounce package pie-crust mix or enough homemade pie pastry for 2 crusts.
½ cup shredded Swiss cheese
4 tablespoons cold water (approximately)
1 egg, well-beaten
1 tablespoon caraway seeds

ham filling

1¼ cups ground or finely minced cooked ham
¼ cup mayonnaise
¼ cup finely minced celery
1½ teaspoons freeze-dried chives
½ teaspoon prepared mustard

Combine pie-crust mix (or homemade pastry) and Swiss cheese in mixing bowl; mix well. Sprinkle cold water over mix; stir with fork until mixture is just dampened. Form into ball. If mixture will not hold together, add small amount cold water. Divide dough into 2 parts; roll 1 part at a time on pastry cloth or lightly floured surface to ¼ inch thick. Cut into 1½-inch rounds (approximately 40). Place on ungreased cookie sheets. Brush half of rounds with egg; sprinkle lightly with caraway seeds. Bake in preheated 375°F oven 10 to 12 minutes or until lightly browned. Place on rack to cool.

Combine all filling ingredients; mix well. Place heaping teaspoons of mixture on plain pie-crust rounds; top each with caraway-seed-topped round. Arrange biscuits on platter; garnish with parsley and cherry tomatoes.

MAKES APPROXIMATELY 20.

Note: Pie-crust rounds can be made in advance and stored in air-tight container until ready for use.

Deviled eggs

HUNGARY

6 hard-cooked eggs
2 tablespoons mayonnaise
3 tablespoons tomato catsup
½ teaspoon dry mustard
½ teaspoon lemon juice
Few drops of Tabasco
¼ teaspoon salt
White pepper
Paprika
Finely chopped green onion

Peel eggs; cut in half lengthwise. Place yolks in small bowl. Add remaining ingredients, except paprika and onion; mix well. Spoon mixture into egg whites, or use decorating tube and pipe egg-

yolk mixture into whites. Sprinkle with paprika and onion. Refrigerate until serving time.
MAKES 4 SERVINGS.

Deviled eggs with bacon
Omit catsup; add 3 tablespoons sour cream and 2 slices crisp bacon, crumbled. Proceed as in above recipe.

Appetizer strudel
HUNGARY

3 tablespoons bacon fat or lard
3 cups shredded cabbage
1 small onion, grated
1½ teaspoons caraway seeds
Salt and pepper
3 sheets phyllo or strudel leaves (available in delicatessens)
3 tablespoons melted butter
1 tablespoon fine dry bread crumbs
1 egg yolk, well-beaten

Melt fat in large heavy skillet. Add cabbage and onion; cook, stirring, until limp. Add caraway seeds and salt and pepper to taste. Set aside.
Set out large clean linen towel. Remove strudel leaves from package; immediately cover with very lightly dampened towel and plastic wrap to prevent drying. Place 1 strudel leaf on towel, long side toward you. (Strudel leaves are usually rectangular in shape.) Brush with melted butter; sprinkle with ½ tablespoon bread crumbs. Top with second strudel leaf. Brush with butter; sprinkle with crumbs. Top with third strudel leaf; brush with butter. Arrange cabbage filling on dough in 3-inch-wide band, 1 inch from edge of dough, leaving 1½ inches free on both ends. Roll up like jelly roll, using towel to support dough.
Carefully transfer to lightly greased baking sheet. Turn ends under to seal. Cut several slits in top of dough. Brush with beaten egg. Bake in pre-heated 375°F oven 25 minutes or until golden. Carefully remove from cookie sheet; cut into 6 pieces.
MAKES 6 SERVINGS.

Variations: Can also be filled with mushrooms and sour cream or any leftover minced meat preparation, such as chicken paprikas. Take care not to use too much gravy.

Craibechan of the sea
IRELAND

"Craibechan" means any savory mixture of little bits and pieces.

3 tablespoons butter
1 clove garlic, peeled, chopped
1 leek, cleaned, sliced
1 medium onion, peeled, chopped
3 cups cooked seafood (Lobster, crab, and shrimp can be
  used, or salmon and cod make a good combination.
  Steam or poach fish; cool.)
Salt and pepper
Few drops of Tabasco
1 small head Bibb lettuce
1 lemon, cut into wedges
Radish roses

Melt butter in small skillet. Add garlic, leek, and onion; sauté until tender. Combine onion mixture and seafood; pass through food chopper. Season with salt, pepper, and Tabasco to taste. Refrigerate until serving time.
Line plates with Bibb lettuce; mound fish mixture in center of plate. Garnish with lemon wedges and radish roses.
MAKES 4 SERVINGS.

Cured trout
IRELAND

Smoked or cured salmon or trout is a traditional Irish appetizer. It is served very thinly sliced against the grain and served on lettuce with lemon wedges. Irish smoked salmon is truly a delicacy, but very expensive! Try the following version of cured trout as a substitute. Start early, as this recipe takes 7 days to make.

1 4-pound trout (or 2 2-pound trout), boned, butterflied,
  head removed
4½ teaspoons salt
½ teaspoon freshly ground pepper

½ teaspoon garlic powder
6 tablespoons olive oil
1 tablespoon brown sugar

On the day you begin the curing process, wash fish; pat dry with paper towels. Place on large nonmetallic platter. Combine salt and seasonings; place in a small shaker bottle. On day 1, rub fish with ⅓ of salt mixture. Cover with plastic wrap; refrigerate.

On day 2, drain any liquid from platter; rub fish with 2 tablespoons oil. Cover; refrigerate overnight. Rub fish with salt mixture on days 3 and 5 and with oil on days 4 and 6. On day 6 also rub fish with sugar.

On day 7 hang fish in cool, dry, breezy place 24 hours. Then, to serve, slice paper thin against the grain.

MAKES 10 TO 12 APPETIZER SERVINGS.

Oysters on the half shell

IRELAND

24 oysters
Beds of lettuce or crushed ice
Lemon wedges
Tabasco sauce

Wash oysters well to remove sand and grit. Prepare beds of lettuce or crushed ice. Open oysters with oyster knife just before serving. Discard top shell; loosen oyster from bottom of shell by cutting ligaments.

Serve oysters immediately. Garnish with lemon wedges; accompany with Tabasco. Pass lots of whole-wheat soda bread.

MAKES 4 SERVINGS.

Dublin prawn cocktail

IRELAND

1 pound large shrimp or prawns
½ cup water
½ cup vinegar
2 teaspoons seafood seasoning
1 teaspoon salt
1 small clove garlic, pressed

Wash shrimp under cold running water; drain.

Combine water, vinegar, seafood seasoning, salt, and garlic in large saucepan; bring to boil. Add shrimp; stir well. Return to boil; cover. Reduce heat to low; cook approximately 10 minutes or until shrimp are pink and firm. Drain; rinse in cold water. Peel and devein shrimp, leaving last joint of tail intact.

Arrange shrimp on bed of Bibb lettuce or on bed of crushed ice. Serve with Dublin Cocktail Sauce.

MAKES 3 TO 4 SERVINGS.

Dublin cocktail sauce

¼ cup tomato catsup
¼ cup whipping cream
1½ tablespoons prepared horseradish
½ teaspoon lemon juice

Combine all ingredients; mix well. Chill until serving time.

Marinated garbanzo beans

ITALY

2 16-ounce cans garbanzo (chick peas) beans
½ teaspoon salt
¼ teaspoon freshly ground pepper
½ teaspoon dried oregano, crumbled
¼ cup olive oil
Finely chopped parsley

Drain the garbanzo beans well. Place in a serving dish. Add the salt, pepper, oregano and oil and stir well. Garnish with parsley and refrigerate several hours before serving.

MAKES 6 SERVINGS.

Note: White beans (cannelli beans) or kidney beans can be substituted for the garbanzo beans. One 4-ounce can of drained, oil-packed tuna may also be added if cannelli beans are used. Hard-cooked eggs, peeled and sliced, and quartered tomatoes would make a tasty garnish.

Melon w/prosciutto

ITALY

½ of a large ripe honeydew or cantaloupe
¼ pound prosciutto, sliced paper thin
A pepper mill

Remove the seeds and rind from the melon and slice into crescents. Cut the ham slices in half and wrap a piece of ham around each piece of melon. Arrange on a platter and grind fresh pepper over the ham and melon just before serving. Lemon or lime wedges are a suitable garnish.
MAKES 4 TO 6 SERVINGS.

Figs & prosciutto

4 fresh ripe figs
¼ pound prosciutto, sliced thin

Chill figs thoroughly; peel. Cut pointed tips from figs; peel in sections by sliding knife under skins. Cut figs into quarters.
Arrange on small platter alternately with rolled prosciutto slices.

Eggs stuffed w/tuna

ITALY

6 hard-cooked eggs, peeled
1 4-ounce can oil-packed tuna, drained
1 tablespoon minced parsley
½ tablespoon capers, finely chopped
1 tablespoon mayonnaise
1 small clove garlic, pressed
¼ teaspoon freshly ground black pepper
Parsley
Pimiento slivers

Cut the eggs in half lengthwise and remove the yolks. Put the yolks in a small bowl and mash with a fork. Drain and finely chop the tuna. Add to the egg yolks along with the parsley, capers, mayonnaise, garlic powder, and pepper. Mix very well and stuff the egg whites with the yolk and tuna mixture and garnish with parsley and pimiento. Chill well.
Serve as part of an antipasto platter.
MAKES 6 SERVINGS.

Crab balls

ITALY

1 pound crab meat
4 tablespoons butter, or margarine
1 teaspoon salt
⅛ teaspoon cayenne pepper
1 teaspoon dry mustard
1 teaspoon dehydrated parsley flakes
2 teaspoons Worcestershire sauce
½ cup soft bread crumbs
2 egg yolks, lightly beaten
½ cup flour
Oil for frying

Pick over the crab meat and remove any bits of shell and cartilage. Flake the crab meat and place in a mixing bowl.
Melt the butter or margarine in a small saucepan. Add the seasonings and bread crumb mixture and egg yolks to the crab and mix well. Refrigerate for 2 to 3 hours or until stiff enough to be handled easily. Form into 35 small balls the size of a walnut. Dredge in flour.
Heat several inches of oil in a heavy saucepan or

Oysters on the half shell

deep-fat fryer to 360°F. Fry the crab balls until golden brown and serve hot. Garnish with parsley and lemon wedges.

MAKES 35 BALLS.

Antipasto

ITALY

Select one or several ingredients from each group:

Meat: Capocollo, Mortadella, Prosciutto, salami, pepperoni

Cheese: Mozzarella, Provolone, Caciocavallo

Fish: Oil-packed tuna (select the best grade available and an Italian brand if possible) garnished with capers, sardines, anchovies

Vegetables: Carrots, celery, cherry tomatoes, pearl onions, artichoke bottoms filled with tarragon-flavored mayonnaise, asparagus spears marinated in Italian

dressing and garnished with a chopped hard-cooked egg, green olives, ripe olives, black salt-cured olives

Commercially available products: Caponata (an eggplant relish from Sicily) served with toasted Italian bread, or melba toast, pickled mushrooms, marinated artichoke hearts, gardinera (assorted vegetables pickled in vinegar), pepperonata (hot pickled peppers)

Antipasto literally translated means before the meal. It is usually an assortment of cold appetizers, artfully arranged and garnished. Generally, it is a selection of cold meats and cheeses and a few pickles and vegetables. However, one or two hot items add variety, especially for a special meal or party. A selection of antipasto ingredients, plus a few hot appetizers, could compose a complete light, buffet meal on a warm summer night or be served at a cocktail party.

An eighth pound of assorted meats and cheeses

Antipasto

accompanied by several small portions of vegetable appetizers would generously serve one person. If hot appetizers or a large meal is planned, keep the antipasto small. Bread or bread sticks and an aperitif or a glass of wine make good accompaniments.

Above is a short list of possible ingredients from which to choose. The variety of ingredients is by no means limited to those on this list! Use your imagination and the ingredients you have on hand. Visit an Italian grocer or delicatessen and try several meats and cheeses as well as the pickled vegetables, olives and other items available.

Stuffed olives

ITALY

1 6-ounce can jumbo pitted black olives
1 2-ounce can anchovy fillets
2 tablespoons olive oil
1 clove garlic, minced
2 tablespoons finely chopped parsley
12 stemmed cherry tomatoes
½ of a medium green pepper, thinly sliced

Drain the olives. Drain the anchovy fillets and cut each one in half. Stuff each olive with ½ of an anchovy fillet. Place in a serving bowl. Combine the olive oil, garlic, and parsley and pour over the olives. Mix well. Chill several hours. Bring to room temperature before serving.
Garnish with the cherry tomatoes and green peppers. Be sure to provide cocktail picks for your guests to spear these nibbles.
MAKES 6 SERVINGS.

Italian vegetable dip

ITALY

½ cup olive oil
½ cup butter
4 garlic cloves, peeled and finely minced
1 2-ounce can anchovies, drained and finely chopped
Freshly ground pepper
10 to 12 cups assorted raw vegetables, peeled, trimmed and cut-up: cherry tomatoes, green peppers, celery, carrots, mushrooms, cauliflower, radishes, and zucchini
1 loaf crusty Italian bread, cut into slices

Italian vegetable dip

Heat the butter and olive oil together over low heat in a fondue pot or a ceramic bagna cauda pot (or heat in a skillet and pour into a casserole with a candle warmer). Heat gently so that the butter does not brown.
Add the garlic and anchovies and continue to cook until the anchovies dissolve and the mixture is bubbly. Reduce the heat so that the mixture stays warm but does not brown and serve with the vegetables and bread.
Provide your guests with forks so that they can spear the vegetables, swirl in the sauce, and eat holding the bread like a napkin under the vegetables to collect the delicious drippings.
MAKES 6 SERVINGS.

21

Mozzarella cheese sandwiches w/anchovy sauce

Mozzarella cheese sandwiches w/anchovy sauce

ITALY

anchovy sauce
¼ cup butter
2 anchovy fillets
1 tablespoon drained capers, chopped
2 tablespoons chopped parsley
Juice of ½ lemon

mozzarella cheese sandwiches
16 thin slices of Italian bread (½ inch thick)
8 thick slices mozzarella cheese (⅜ inch thick)
3 eggs
Salt to taste
½ cup dry bread crumbs
¼ cup butter or margarine

First, prepare the anchovy sauce. Melt the butter in a small skillet. Do not brown. Under cold running water, rinse the anchovies. Chop finely and add with the capers and parsley to the butter. Add the lemon juice and stir well. Keep warm.

Remove the crust from the bread. Lay one slice of cheese between two slices of bread and press together. In a small bowl beat the eggs and a pinch of salt. Dip the bread and cheese sandwiches in the egg and dredge in the bread crumbs. Heat the butter or margarine over moderate heat in a heavy skillet. Add the cheese sandwiches and cook until golden brown on one side and turn and cook on the other side. Serve immediately topped with the anchovy sauce.
MAKES 8 3-INCH SANDWICHES.

Clams casino

ITALY

2 dozen cherrystone clams
2 tablespoons olive oil
1 tablespoon butter
½ cup finely minced onion
¼ cup finely chopped green pepper
2 cloves garlic, peeled and chopped
1 cup dry bread crumbs
4 slices crisp bacon, crumbled
½ teaspoon dried oregano, crumbled
2 tablespoons grated Parmesan cheese
Parsley flakes and paprika
Olive oil

Wash and scrub the clams well to remove the grit. Place on a baking sheet and place in a 450°F oven until the shells open. Remove the meat from the shell and chop. Reserve the chopped clams and discard ½ of the shells.
Heat the oil and butter in a small skillet. Add the onion, pepper and garlic and sauté until tender. Remove from the heat and cool. Add the bread crumbs, bacon, oregano, Parmesan cheese, and the reserved clams and mix well. Fill the clam shells with the mixture. Sprinkle with the parsley flakes and paprika and drizzle with olive oil.
Bake in a 450°F oven until lightly browned (about 7 minutes). Serve hot.
MAKES 6 SERVINGS.

Fried cheese sticks

ITALY

1 pound mozzarella cheese
2 tablespoons flour
2 eggs
2 tablespoons water
1 cup Italian-style bread crumbs

sauce
1 tablespoon olive oil
2 tablespoons finely minced onion
1 (8-ounce) can tomato sauce
1 clove garlic, pressed
½ teaspoon crumbled oregano
Salt and pepper

Oil for deep frying

Cut cheese into ½-inch slices, then into fingers or wedges. Coat lightly with flour. Beat eggs and water together in shallow bowl. Dip cheese in egg mixture, then in crumbs; coat well. Refrigerate at least 1 hour uncovered.

Meanwhile, prepare the sauce. Heat oil in small saucepan. Add onion; sauté until tender. Add remaining sauce ingredients; stir well. Cover; simmer 30 minutes.

Heat 2 inches oil to 380°F. Fry breaded cheese fritters, a few at a time, until pale golden. Drain well on paper towels. Serve immediately accompanied by tomato sauce.
MAKES 6 SERVINGS.

Liver pâté on toasted bread rounds

ITALY

½ pound chicken livers
3 tablespoons butter
1 small onion, chopped
1 clove garlic, minced
2 tablespoons white wine
½ teaspoon crumbled sage
Salt and pepper
2 teaspoons minced capers
1 teaspoon anchovy paste
Rounds of Italian bread, sliced ½ inch thick

Trim livers; remove all membrane and fat. Rinse under cold water; pat dry on paper towels.

Melt butter in small, heavy skillet. Add livers, onion, and garlic; sauté until livers are lightly browned. Add wine and seasonings. Cover; simmer 10 minutes. Put mixture through food mill. Return to skillet. Add capers and anchovy paste, mix well. Simmer 5 minutes.

Toast bread slices in oven until crisp and golden; spread thickly with liver pâté.
MAKES 4 SERVINGS.

Note: Bread can also be toasted in hot garlic-flavored olive oil. This makes a richer, more highly seasoned appetizer.

Stuffed artichokes

ITALY

4 medium-size globe artichokes
¾ cup dry bread crumbs
3 tablespoons grated Parmesan cheese
1 tablespoon chopped parsley
1 small clove garlic, pressed
¼ teaspoon dried oregano, crumbled
¼ teaspoon pepper
2 tablespoons butter
2 tablespoons olive oil
1 cup boiling water

Remove the stems from the artichokes. Cut about ½ inch from the tips of the leaves with a pair of kitchen shears. Drop into boiling salted water and cook 5 minutes. Drain and shake to remove the water and cool.

Combine the bread crumbs, cheese, parsley, garlic, oregano and pepper and mix well. Tap the base of the artichokes on a flat surface to spread the leaves. Stuff each artichoke with ¼ of the bread crumb mixture, spooning it between the leaves.

Place the artichokes in a saucepan or stove-top casserole, placing them close together so that they do not tip over. Top each artichoke with ½ tablespoon of butter and ½ tablespoon of oil. Pour the boiling water into the dish or pan. Cover and cook over low heat 35 to 45 minutes or until the artichokes are tender.
MAKES 4 SERVINGS.

Asparagus w/mayonnaise sauce

ITALY

1 (10-ounce) package frozen asparagus spears, partially
   thawed
1 tablespoon melted butter
1 tablespoon dry sherry
2 teaspoons finely minced onion
¼ teaspoon salt
Dash pepper

mayonnaise sauce

1 egg
1 teaspoon dry mustard
1 teaspoon salt
Dash of cayenne pepper
1 cup olive oil
3 tablespoons lemon juice
Parsley
Paprika

Place asparagus in small casserole, separating
spears. Mix butter, sherry, and seasonings. Pour
over asparagus; cover. Bake at 350°F 25 minutes,
until crisp-tender. Cool; refrigerate.

In blender container combine egg, seasonings,
and ¼ cup oil. Cover; blend thoroughly. Remove center portion of blender cover. With
blender running, add ½ cup oil in small steady
stream. Slowly add lemon juice. Add remaining
¼ cup oil in thin steady stream. Blend until
thick and smooth. Scrape mayonnaise down
from sides of blender occasionally.

Arrange asparagus on beds of Bibb lettuce; coat
with mayonnaise. Garnish with parsley and paprika. Serve as first course.
MAKES 4 SERVINGS.

Stuffed mushrooms I

ITALY

1 pound medium or large mushrooms
1 cup dry bread crumbs
2 tablespoons dried parsley flakes
2 tablespoons grated Parmesan cheese
½ clove garlic, pressed
Salt and pepper
5 tablespoons olive oil, divided

sauce

1 small onion, chopped
2 teaspoons olive oil
1 8-ounce can tomato sauce
½ teaspoon sugar
¼ teaspoon oregano, crumbled
½ clove garlic, pressed
Salt and pepper

Wash the mushrooms well and remove the
stems. Hollow out the mushroom caps slightly by
scraping with a teaspoon. Drain well and pat
dry.

Combine the bread crumbs, parsley, Parmesan
cheese, garlic, salt and pepper, and 2 tablespoons olive oil and mix well. Fill the mushrooms with the crumb mixture. Pour 3 tablespoons of olive oil in the bottom of a shallow
baking dish. Tilt to coat the dish evenly. Place
the mushroom caps in the oiled baking dish.

Next prepare the sauce. Sauté the onion in the
oil in a small pan until tender. Add the remaining ingredients, stir well and simmer 10 minutes.
Pour the sauce evenly over the mushrooms. Bake
at 350°F for 30 minutes.
MAKES 4 SERVINGS.

Stuffed mushrooms II

ITALY

1 pound large mushrooms
1 pound bulk sausage
Salt and pepper
1 small clove garlic, pressed
2 eggs
¼ cup grated Parmesan cheese
¾ cup Italian-style bread crumbs
¼ cup olive oil

Wash the mushrooms and pat dry. Stem the
mushrooms and hollow the caps slightly with a
spoon. Chop the stems.

Brown the sausage in a heavy skillet until all the
pink has disappeared. Add the chopped mushrooms and cook 2 minutes. Drain well. Remove
from the heat and cool. Add the salt, pepper,
and garlic. Beat the eggs and cheese together and
add to sausage mixture along with the bread
crumbs; mix well.

Pour the oil into a 13 × 9 × 2 inch baking dish and tilt to coat. Dip the outside of the mushroom caps in the oil and turn to coat. Stuff with the sausage mixture and place side by side in the baking dish. Bake at 375°F for 20 minutes. Serve hot as part of an antipasto platter.
MAKES 4 TO 6 SERVINGS.

Stuffed mushrooms III

ITALY

12 medium mushrooms
5 tablespoons olive oil
2 tablespoons finely minced onion
¼ cup finely minced prosciutto
⅓ cup Italian-style bread crumbs
¼ cup freshly grated Parmesan cheese
2 teaspoons chopped parsley
⅛ teaspoon garlic powder
Salt and pepper
Chopped parsley
Grated Parmesan

Wash mushrooms. Remove stems; reserve for another use. Hollow out mushroom caps with teaspoon; drain well; pat dry. Place 2 tablespoons oil in bottom of small casserole. Dip outside of each mushroom cap in oil, swirling to coat.
In small skillet heat 3 tablespoons oil. Add onion; sauté until tender. Remove from heat. Add prosciutto, bread crumbs, cheese, and seasonings; mix well.
Fill mushrooms with bread-crumb mixture. Bake uncovered at 350°F 30 minutes.
MAKES 2 TO 4 SERVINGS.

Cream-cheese spread

POLAND

1 3-ounce package cream cheese
1 cup small-curd cottage cheese
½ teaspoon caraway seeds
1 teaspoon capers
1 tablespoon minced onion
1 loaf party rye bread

Soften cream cheese; place in blender or food processor. Add remaining ingredients; spin. Chill thoroughly.

To serve, spread on party rye bread slices.
MAKES 12 SERVINGS.

Pickled herrings

POLAND

2 pounds salt herring
2 cups water
⅓ cup cider vinegar
1 medium onion, sliced into rings
¼ cup granulated sugar
1 teaspoon pickling spices
½ teaspoon mustard seed

Skin herring; remove backbone. Cut fish into 1- to 2-inch pieces. Soak fish in cold water overnight to remove salt.
Next morning, drain water from fish; rinse fish in cold water. Combine remaining ingredients; pour over herring. Marinate fish overnight in refrigerator. Serve herrings chilled.
MAKES APPROXIMATELY 1 QUART.

Shrimp paste

POLAND

½ cup cooked shrimp
2 tablespoons chili sauce
2 tablespoons mayonnaise
2 tablespoons lemon juice
¼ teaspoon dillweed

Place ingredients in blender or food processor. Cover; spin for 30 seconds, scraping sides once during blending process.
Serve with crackers.
MAKES ¾ CUP.

Stuffed mushroom caps

POLAND

24 fresh mushroom caps
⅔ cup mayonnaise
¼ cup Parmesan cheese
½ small clove garlic, pressed

Wash mushroom caps; let dry on a paper towel. Combine mayonnaise, cheese, and garlic. Mix well.

25

Fill mushroom caps with cheese mixture; place under broiler 4 inches from flame. Broil approximately 5 minutes, or until cheese melts and mixture is golden brown and bubbly.
MAKES 24 MUSHROOM CAPS.

Quark snacks

POLAND

2 cups all-purpose white flour
3 teaspoons baking powder
1 teaspoon salt
¼ cup all-vegetable shortening
¾ cup milk (about)
2 egg yolks, beaten
3 tablespoons caraway seeds

cottage-cheese filling
1 cup dry-curd cottage cheese
2 tablespoons dried parsley flakes
1 teaspoon salt
2 tablespoons chopped pimiento

Combine dry ingredients; cut in shortening to resemble a coarse meal. Add milk to form a soft dough. Knead dough 6 times. Roll dough on floured surface to ¼ inch thickness. Brush half the biscuits with beaten egg yolks; sprinkle with caraway seeds. Bake biscuits at 450°F for 10 minutes or until golden brown.
Make Cottage-Cheese Filling by combining cottage cheese, parsley flakes, salt, and pimiento.
To serve, spread Cottage-Cheese Filling on plain biscuits and top with caraway-seed biscuits.
MAKES 20 SNACKS.

Cabbage dunking bowl

POLAND

1 small cabbage head
1 cup mayonnaise
1 tablespoon minced onion
1 tablespoon finely chopped Bread-and-Butter Pickles (see Index)
1 tablespoon anchovy paste
¼ teaspoon salt
¼ teaspoon white pepper

Clean and wash cabbage head. Hollow out center of cabbage for dip. Refrigerate until ready to serve. Put remaining ingredients into blender or food processor; spin.
Fill hollowed-out cabbage head with dip just before serving.
MAKES 1 CUP.

Blue-cheese dip

POLAND

Delicious served with potato chips.

1 ounce blue cheese
1 cup small-curd cottage cheese
¼ cup minced onions
¼ cup sour cream

Crumble blue cheese into cottage cheese; blend. Pour cheese mixture into blender or food processor, add remaining ingredients, and blend.
Chill before serving.
MAKES 1¼ CUPS.

Deviled crayfish dip

POLAND

½ cup crayfish or lobster meat
2 hard-cooked eggs
¼ teaspoon salt
⅛ teaspoon white pepper
2 tablespoons lemon juice
½ cup mayonnaise
1 sprig parsley

Chop crayfish (or lobster) and eggs. Add remaining ingredients (except parsley) to crayfish and egg mixture; blend. Chill. Serve garnished with parsley.
MAKES 1 CUP.

Green-olive dip

POLAND

6 ounces cream cheese
½ cup green-olive meat
¼ cup milk
¼ teaspoon salt
¼ teaspoon white pepper

Soften cream cheese; add remaining ingredients. Spin in a food processor or blender. If dip is too thick, more milk may be added to obtain desired consistency.
MAKES 1 CUP.

Egg and parsley dip

POLAND

8 hard-cooked egg yolks
1 tablespoon crushed parsley flakes
2 tablespoons wine vinegar
1 tablespoon minced onion
½ teaspoon seasoned salt
¼ teaspoon white pepper
¼ teaspoon dillweed
½ cup mayonnaise

Mash egg yolks. Add remaining ingredients to mashed egg yolks; blend well. Refrigerate before serving.
MAKES ¾ CUP.

Polish eggs in the shell

Steak toasts w/mushroom caps

POLAND

1 teaspoon salt
½ teaspoon black pepper, peppermill-ground
4 2-ounce filets mignons
¼ cup butter
1 cup fresh mushroom caps
¼ cup mayonnaise
2 teaspoons horseradish
4 slices toast
4 lemon slices
Dillweed

Salt and pepper both sides of filets. Melt butter in heavy skillet. Sauté steaks to desired doneness. Remove from skillet; add mushrooms. Sauté mushrooms until done.
Combine mayonnaise and horseradish. Spread each toast slice with mixture.
To serve, place steaks on toast slices and top each steak with ¼ cup mushrooms. Garnish with lemon slice and dillweed.
MAKES 4 SERVINGS.

Polish eggs in the shell

POLAND

4 hard-cooked eggs in the shells
½ bunch parsley, chopped fine
3 tablespoons butter
1 teaspoon salt
1 teaspoon paprika
¼ cup shredded Muenster cheese

Cut eggs in half with large, sharp knife; scoop eggs out of shells. Save shells. Chop egg whites fine; squeeze yolks fine with a fork.
Combine chopped eggs, parsley, butter, salt, and paprika. Mix well. Refill egg shells with egg mixture. Sprinkle with cheese. Bake 10 minutes at 400°F or until cheese melts and browns.
MAKES 4 SERVINGS.

Steak toasts w/mushroom caps

Pickled fish

Polish sausage links

POLAND

1½ cups all-purpose white flour
3-ounce package cream cheese, softened
½ cup butter
6 Polish sausage links
1 egg yolk, beaten

Combine flour, cream cheese, and butter; mix until a soft dough forms. Divide dough into 7 equal parts. Wrap each link in dough.

Cut remaining dough into crescent shapes. Place crescents on top of wrapped Polish links; press to secure. Brush each wrapped link with beaten egg yolk. Bake in 425°F oven 10 to 12 minutes or until golden brown. Slice to serve.

MAKES 6 SERVINGS.

Horseradish sour-cream dip

POLAND

1 cup sour cream
1 teaspoon prepared horseradish (more, if desired)
¼ teaspoon celery seed

Combine ingredients; mix well. Chill well before serving.

MAKES 1 CUP.

Polish sausage links

Mushroom & chicken-liver dip

POLAND

½ pound chicken livers
¼ cup butter
1 3-ounce can mushroom stems and pieces
2 tablespoons minced onion
2 tablespoons chopped parsley
½ cup mayonnaise
½ teaspoon salt
¼ teaspoon white pepper

Sauté livers in butter until brown. Drain; chop fine. Drain and chop mushrooms. Add to chicken livers. Add remaining ingredients; blend well.
MAKES 1½ CUPS.

Langostino w/garlic mayonnaise

SPAIN

A delicious summer dish served in Catalonia, the region known as "All Things in Season" because of its wide variety of fresh fruits, vegetables and seafood.

3 cups cooked langostino
1 cup mayonnaise
1 small clove garlic, pressed

Cut langostino into bite-size pieces; chill. Combine mayonnaise with garlic. (Use more or less garlic to taste.) Place garlic mayonnaise in small bowl. Arrange cold langostino around garlic mayonnaise. Serve with cocktail picks for dipping.
MAKES 3 CUPS.

Pickled fish

SPAIN

1 pound dressed freshly caught white fish fillets
1 cup lime juice, freshly squeezed
2 tomatoes
1 red pepper
1 green pepper
¼ cup pimiento-stuffed olives
2 tablespoons chopped onions
¼ cup olive oil

2 tablespoons wine vinegar
1 teaspoon oregano
1 teaspoon salt
½ cup slivered blanched olives

Wash fish well. Remove skin or bones; slice into small pieces. Place in small glass or stainless-steel bowl. Pour lime juice over fish; refrigerate 10 to 12 hours. Spoon juice over fish every 2 hours. Peel and seed tomatoes; slice into thin wedges. Core and seed peppers; slice into small strips. Slice olives. Add vegetables and remaining ingredients to fish 1 hour before serving time. Toss gently.
Serve fish arranged attractively on a platter with cocktail picks.
MAKES 8 SERVINGS.

Pickled beets

SPAIN

A tapa served with mixed drinks.

1 teaspoon salt
½ teaspoon pepper
1 cup olive oil
¼ cup red-wine vinegar
½ tablespoon chopped onion
2 teaspoons parsley
1 teaspoon garlic juice or pressed garlic
1 quart sliced beets, cooked

Combine all ingredients except beets in quart jar; shake until well mixed. Pour over beets. Cover; marinate 24 hours in refrigerator. Toss occasionally to mix sauce and beets.
Serve as an appetizer or as a salad mixed with sweet onion rings.
MAKES 1 QUART.

Spanish pickled cauliflower

SPAIN

2 quarts water
1 quart cider vinegar
½ cup noniodized salt
4 to 5 large heads cauliflower
1 tablespoon garlic powder
12 garlic cloves, peeled

31

24 dry red peppers
12 dill sprigs, dried

Combine water, vinegar, and salt in large saucepan; bring to boil. Clean cauliflower; break into florets. Soak in ice-cold water. (Cauliflower is soaked in ice cold water to retain its crispness when covered with the hot vinegar solution.) Sterilize 12 pint jars. Put ¼ teaspoon garlic powder, 1 garlic clove, 2 peppers, and 1 dill sprig in each jar. Fill each jar with cauliflower; cover to within ½ inch from top of jar with boiling vinegar mixture. Adjust lids. Process in boiling-water bath 15 minutes. Remove jars; cool slowly. Immediately use or reprocess jars that do not seal.
MAKES 12 PINTS.

Dates with ham

SPAIN

A delicious finger food.

16 small strips thinly sliced Italian or other smoked ham
16 dates with pits removed

Wrap ham slices around dates. Arrange on serving platter.
MAKES 16 APPETIZERS.

Almond-stuffed olives

SPAIN

24 whole almonds
24 large pitted green olives

Shell almonds. Drop into boiling water. Boil 2 to 3 seconds or until covering separates easily from almond meat.
For crisp almonds: Pull almond through hole in olive. Serve.
For soft almonds: Pull almond through hole in olive. Place stuffed olives back in olive juice; marinate at least 24 hours.
MAKES 24 STUFFED OLIVES.

Olive-ham turnovers

SPAIN

turnover pastry
2 cups flour
½ teaspoon salt
⅔ cup Garlic Mayonnaise (see Index)
Dash of cayenne
2 tablespoons cold water
turnover filling
⅔ cup ground Italian or other smoked ham
⅔ cup chopped ripe olives
3 to 4 tablespoons mayonnaise

Heat oven to 425°F.
Sift flour with salt. Add mayonnaise, cayenne, and water; mix. Turn onto lightly floured board; roll thin. Cut into 2½-inch squares.
Mix together filling ingredients. Put generous ½ teaspoon filling on each pastry square. Moisten edges with water; fold over into triangles; pinch edges to seal. Bake 15 minutes or until pastry browns.
MAKES 2½ DOZEN TURNOVERS.

Chick-pea fritters

SPAIN

2 cups cooked chick peas
¼ cup finely chopped onion
¼ teaspoon garlic powder or pressed garlic
½ teaspoon baking powder
1 teaspoon salt
Dash of pepper
½ cup diced Italian or other smoked ham
Olive oil for frying

Mash chick peas with masher. Add remaining ingredients; mix well. Shape mixture into small balls. Press ham cube in center of each ball, covering ham with the chick-pea mixture.
Heat oil to 375°F. Deep-fat-fry balls until golden brown. Serve hot. Or heat oil in fondue pot. Arrange fritters around pot; allow guests to cook their own fritters.
MAKES 16 APPETIZERS.

Tuna turnovers

SPAIN

Delicious tapa served in Madrid bars. Try them at your next party.

1 tablespoon chopped onion
1 3-ounce can mushrooms, drained (reserve liquid)
½ cup chopped pitted green olives
2 tablespoons butter
1 teaspoon flour
1 large clove garlic, pressed
¼ teaspoon salt
2 7-ounce cans tuna fish
1 2-crust pie pastry (homemade or mix)

Sauté onion, mushrooms, and olives in butter until onion is tender. Stir in flour, garlic powder, salt, and mushroom liquid; heat. Add tuna. Prepare pastry. Roll out; cut into 2½-inch circles. Place 2 teaspoons tuna mixture in center of each pastry circle. Fold pastry over. Dampen edges; seal. Bake in 450°F oven 7 minutes or until crust is golden brown.
MAKES ABOUT 2 DOZEN APPETIZERS.

Fried garlic croutons

SPAIN

1-pound loaf day-old bread
½ cup butter
¼ cup olive oil
1 clove garlic, pressed
½ teaspoon salt
2 tablespoons dried parsley flakes or fresh parsley

Cut bread into ½-inch cubes. Spread cubes evenly over cookie sheet. Let dry 2 days or until cubes lose moisture.
Heat butter and oil in large skillet until butter melts. Remove butter mixture from skillet; reserve. Add garlic, salt, and parsley to butter mixture; mix well.
Reheat skillet in which butter mixture was heated. Add croutons; distribute evenly over skillet surface. Pour butter mixture over croutons. Stir to distribute evenly. Fry croutons until golden brown and heated thoroughly. Cool; store up to 1 month in airtight container.
MAKES 2 QUARTS.

Cheese mold

SPAIN

The main ingredient of this dish is a rare cheese ripened in the mountain caves of Asturias. The taste somewhat resembles blue cheese.

6 ounces queso de cabrales or blue cheese
¾ cup butter
Dash of cayenne
Ground pistachio nuts

Soften cheese; cream until smooth. Cream butter until light and fluffy. Blend together cheese, butter, and cayenne.
Line small mold with 3 layers cheesecloth, overlapping at top. Press cheese into mold. Cover top of cheese with overlapping cheesecloth. Refrigerate 24 hours.
Lift cheese out of mold, using cheesecloth. Turn onto serving dish. Carefully remove cheesecloth. Smooth rough edges with damp metal spatula. Sprinkle with pistachio nuts. Serve with vegetables and/or crackers.
MAKES 1½ CUPS.

Liver loaf

DENMARK

1 pound calf or chicken livers
1 medium onion
¼ cup butter
¼ cup flour
½ cup heavy cream
½ cup chicken broth
¼ pound pork or beef fat, chopped
2 eggs
1 teaspoon salt
½ teaspoon pepper
5 anchovies or 2 tablespoons anchovy paste

Put the raw liver and onion through a food chopper.
In a large skillet melt the butter and blend in the flour. Pour in the cream and broth slowly while stirring, then add the chopped fat. When this mixture is thickened and smooth, add the rest of the ingredients. Blend all together thoroughly.
Grease a baking dish or loaf pan and pour the mixture into the prepared dish. Set this in a pan 33

of hot water and bake it in a 350°F oven for 1 hour or more. If needed, add more water to the hot-water bath. The liver is done when a testing knife comes out clean. Chill the loaf and serve it as is, or slice it for smorgasbord sandwiches.
MAKES 8 SERVINGS.

Eggs stuffed w/shrimp

DENMARK

1 4½-ounce can shrimps
6 to 8 hard-cooked eggs
2 tablespoons butter

Drain the shrimps, reserving the liquid.
Cut the cold, hard-cooked eggs in half lengthwise to make boats of the egg whites. Remove the yolks. In a bowl mash the egg yolks fine with softened butter. Add enough of the reserved shrimp liquid to make a smooth paste.
Fill the egg halves with the paste so that the whites are covered. Top each egg half with as many shrimps as it will hold. Chill the eggs and serve.
MAKES 12 TO 16 EGG HALVES.

Horseradish ham rolls

DENMARK

This makes an excellent appetizer for the smorgasbord table but is also tasty when used as the focal point of a meal.

½ cup heavy cream
1 teaspoon sugar
2 tablespoons prepared horseradish
½ cup cooked macaroni
6 to 8 slices cooked ham
¼ cup shredded Swiss cheese

Whip the heavy cream and, when stiff, add the sugar and horseradish. Gently fold in the cooked macaroni. Spread this mixture on the ham slices and roll them.
When arranged on the serving plate, sprinkle the ham rolls with cheese.
MAKES 6 TO 8 ROLLS.

Sandwich island

ICELAND

4 tablespoons lemon juice
8 flounder fillets, fresh or
    frozen (thawed)
6 tablespoons oil
1 teaspoon salt
3 tablespoons flour

sauce
1 medium cucumber
1 bunch dill
½ cup cream
1 teaspoon mustard
1 teaspoon lemon juice
Pinch of salt
Pinch of sugar

other ingredients
8 slices white bread
3 tablespoons butter
8 pieces green lettuce
½ bunch parsley

Add the lemon juice to the fish fillets and let them stand for 10 minutes.
Heat the oil in a pan. Salt the fillets and dip them in the flour. Fry the fillets to a golden brown on each side (about 2 minutes) and set them aside to drain on paper towels.
To make the sauce, peel the cucumber and dice it very fine. Chop the dill very fine. Beat the cream in a bowl until it is very stiff. Spice the cream with mustard, lemon juice, salt, and sugar. Add the cucumber and dill.
Remove the crusts from the bread and spread the bread with a thin layer of butter. Place the fish fillets on the bread and cover them thinly with sauce. Top each with another piece of bread, placing the buttered side to the bottom. Cut the bread in half. Set the sandwich on a piece of lettuce and garnish it with parsley.
MAKES 8 SERVINGS.

Dill & sardine sandwiches

NORWAY

Open-faced sandwiches are popular on the smorgasbord table as well as at any light meal.

Cheese mold

White or rye bread
Butter
Sardines, chopped
Dill pickle, chopped

Cut the bread into oblong shapes about 1 inch wide. Generously butter the bread strips. Mix the sardines with enough dill pickle to suit your taste. Spread this mixture on top of the buttered bread.

If these sandwiches are to be used for a light lunch, you may prefer to quarter the bread instead of making oblongs. Either way, the taste is a treat.

MAKE WHATEVER QUANTITY YOU NEED.

Pickled mackerel

SWEDEN

3 red onions
1 cup plus 1½ tablespoons vinegar
Dash of salt
20 peppercorns
2 bay leaves
4 whole mackerels
1 bunch dill, chopped

Peel the onions and slice them into rings. In a pot boil the vinegar, salt, peppercorns, and bay leaves. Set aside to cool. Wash, clean, fillet, and halve the mackerels. Cut each piece in half again. Dry them thoroughly.

Put the fillets into a glass pot. Cover them with onion rings. Spread the marinade on top of that.

Pickled mackerel

Let stand for at least 24 hours. Serve the mackerel with chopped dill.

MAKES 16 PIECES.

Swedish platter

SWEDEN

When dining in Sweden, one finds eating is a culinary art as well as a taste treat. The food looks as good as it tastes.

Choose from the following:
Marinated sardines
Marinated onion rings
Pickle slices
Apple slices
Cucumber slices
Kippers, halved
Eggs, scrambled
Smoked fish
Bread, thinly sliced or lightly toasted
Lemon juice
Salmon rolls
Baked ham
Bacon slices
Hard-boiled eggs
Caviar

The Swedish platter can be expanded to meet any number of guests and can use everything your kitchen and pocketbook allow. The main idea is to present the food in an attractive, appetizing manner.

Try marinated sardines with marinated onion rings, decorated with pickle slices. Many foods mix well with apple or cucumber slices. Serve halved kippers on top of scrambled eggs. Smoked fish goes well on thin slices of bread, topped with lemon juice. Try salmon rolls with horse-radish-sauce stuffing, baked ham or bacon slices with grilled tomato on top, or stuffed eggs with caviar. The possibilities are endless. Lightly browned toast or the bread of your choice complements the platter as well as the palate.

Swedish meatballs

SWEDEN

This recipe improves if made one day ahead of time.

1 pound ground beef
¼ pound ground veal
¼ pound ground pork

2 cups bread crumbs
½ cup milk
1 onion
2 tablespoons butter
2½ teaspoons salt
¼ teaspoon pepper
2 teaspoons nutmeg
2 teaspoons paprika
1 teaspoon dry mustard
3 beaten eggs
¼ cup butter

sauce
Fat left in skillet
¼ teaspoon pressed or
   minced garlic
5 tablespoons butter
2 teaspoons tomato paste
1 teaspoon beef concentrate
2 cups bouillon or beef stock
1 teaspoon aromatic bitters
   (optional)

Have all the meats ground together twice. Soak the bread crumbs in milk. Add the meat, and mix together.

Sauté the onion in about 2 tablespoons of butter. Mix the rest of the ingredients, except the ¼ cup of butter, with the onion; put all together with the meat. Mix well and form into 48 small balls. Brown the meatballs in ¼ cup butter. Remove the meatballs and set them aside.

To make the sauce, add the garlic and 1 tablespoon of the butter to the fat left in the skillet. Blend in the rest of the butter and the remaining ingredients. Stir this mixture over low heat until it thickens. Then pour the sauce into a casserole. Stir in 1 cup of sour cream.

Last, add the meatballs to the sauce. Heat the casserole in a moderate oven until it is hot.
MAKES 48 BALLS.

Jellied fish

SWEDEN

2 or 3 pounds fresh fish
1 bay leaf
5 allspices
Salt and pepper to taste
1 tablespoon gelatin in ½ cup cold water

Cut up the fish and boil it with the spices in enough water to cover for ½ hour. Remove all bones and skin. Add the gelatin to the fish and water; pour the mixture into a greased mold. Allow the jellied fish to set firmly before turning it out onto a platter. Garnish with parsley.
MAKES 8 OR MORE SERVINGS.

Marinated salmon in dill

SWEDEN

3 pounds center-cut fresh salmon, cleaned and scaled
1 large bunch fresh dill
¼ cup salt (coarse salt preferable)
¼ cup sugar
2 tablespoons crushed white pepper

Cut the fish in half lengthwise, and remove the backbone and small bones. Place half of the fish, skin side down, in a glass baking dish or casserole. Wash and shake dry the dill and place it on top of the fish. Combine the rest of the ingredients in a bowl and sprinkle this mixture over the dill, covering the whole piece of salmon. Place the other half of the fish, skin side up, on the top.

Cover the fish with aluminum foil; on top of that place a platter holding 3 or 4 cans to make weight. Refrigerate the fish like this for 48 hours. Morning and evening during this period, turn the fish over and baste it with the liquid that accumulates. Separate the halves of fish and baste inside as well. Put the platter with weights back in the refrigerator each time.

When ready to serve, remove the fish from its marinade, scrape away the seasonings, and pat it dry with paper towels. Slice each half of the fish, skin side down, on the diagonal, removing the slice from the skin. Serve the salmon as an appe-

Marinated salmon in dill

tizer or on sandwiches, with Mustard Sauce.
MAKES 8 TO 10 SERVINGS.

Mustard sauce

3 tablespoons Dijon mustard
1 teaspoon powdered mustard
3 tablespoons sugar
1 tablespoon light wine vinegar
3 tablespoons brine

Mix the mustard, powdered mustard, sugar, and vinegar together in a pot. Add the brine slowly, and beat it well into a thick sauce. Pour it over the salmon when ready to serve.

Anchovy sandwiches

SWEDEN

½ loaf day-old homemade-type bread, unsliced
10 anchovy fillets
4 tablespoons softened butter
2 tablespoons prepared mustard
4 hard-cooked eggs, finely chopped
¼ cup chopped dill or ¼ cup dill, parsley, and chives
    combined
Dash of freshly ground black pepper
Vegetable oil combined with butter for frying (about 2
    tablespoons of each)

Trim the crusts from the bread and slice it into 12 thin slices about ⅛ inch thick.

In a small bowl chop the anchovies and mash them together with the butter, mustard, finely chopped eggs, herbs, and pepper. Spread this smooth mixture on 6 slices of the bread. Top each slice with its covering piece of bread. Refrigerate them for up to 3 days.

When ready to serve, melt the combined oil and butter in a 12-inch skillet. Fry the sandwiches, 2 or 3 at a time, until they are golden brown. Drain the sandwiches, cut in quarters, and serve them hot.
MAKES 24 HORS D'OEUVRES.

Anchovy sticks

SWEDEN

10 slices bread, toasted and buttered
½ cup chopped green onions
½ cup chopped parsley
¼ pound butter
40 anchovy fillets

Cut each piece of buttered toast into 4 1-inch strips. Mix together the chopped onions and parsley. Sprinkle the mixture over the toast strips. Top with 1 anchovy fillet on each toast stick, and dot with butter.

Bake the sticks at 375°F just long enough to heat through. (The best way to be sure this appetizer is just right is to try one—but you may want to eat the whole batch!) Serve the sticks hot; allow 2 or 3 sticks per person.
MAKES 40 STICKS.

Fried cauliflower

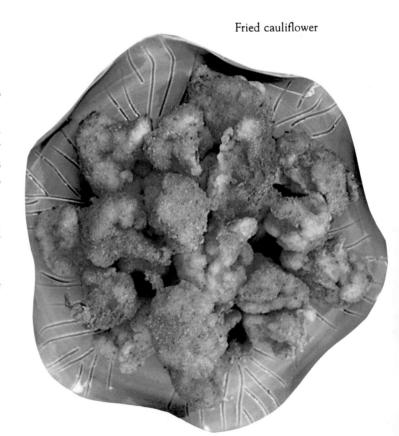

Herring rolls

SWEDEN

8 herring fillets
½ cup milk
½ cup mineral water
2 apples
2 tablespoons lemon juice
½ cup cream
1 small onion
½ cup sour cream
Pinch of cayenne or sharp paprika
Salt and pepper to taste
½ teaspoon sugar
8 teaspoons cranberry sauce
1 red onion
½ bunch dill
2 dill pickles

Place herring fillets in a bowl and sprinkle with milk and mineral water. Let them sit for at least 3 hours. Core the apples and slice them in 8 pieces. Sprinkle them with half of the lemon juice. Dry the fillets with a paper towel and roll them upright on the apple pieces. Place the rolls on a serving plate.

Beat the cream until stiff. Add the small onion, the rest of lemon juice, and the sour cream, sugar, and cayenne or paprika. Salt and pepper to taste. Spread the sauce over the herring rolls and crown each with a teaspoon of cranberry sauce.

Peel the red onion and cut it into rings. Garnish the herring rolls with onion rings, dill, and sliced pickles.
MAKES 8 PIECES.

Fried cauliflower

MIDDLE EAST

1 medium cauliflower, separated into florets
1 well-beaten egg seasoned with a pinch of salt
Oil for deep frying

Precook the cauliflower in ½ cup boiling water until almost tender, no more than 10 minutes. Drain and pat dry with towels. Heat cooking oil in skillet. Dip florets in the beaten egg mixture, a few at a time, and fry in the hot oil until golden on all sides. Drain on paper towels. When all are cooked, serve with garlic yoghurt sauce.
MAKES 4 TO 8 SERVINGS.

Garlic-yoghurt sauce

1 cup unflavored yoghurt
1 medium garlic clove, crushed
¼ teaspoon salt

Mix these ingredients together until well-blended. Taste to adjust seasonings if needed. Chill until ready to serve.

Manna cheese

MIDDLE EAST

1 cup cream cheese
½ cup cream
½ teaspoon coriander seed
Honey to taste

Soften the cream cheese and blend in the cream using your mixer. When the mixture is creamy, add the coriander seed followed by the honey. Add the honey one tablespoon at a time until the taste of the dip is as sweet as you like it. This is a matter of individual taste. Serve the dip at room temperature with your favorite crackers.
MAKES ENOUGH FOR A LARGE DIP DISH.

Mushroom-yoghurt dip

MIDDLE EAST

2 tablespoons butter
4 ounces finely chopped mushrooms
4 scallions, chopped using 2 inches of the greens
3 ounces cream cheese
½ cup unflavored yoghurt
1 small clove garlic, crushed
1 teaspoon salt
Parsley for garnish

Sauté the mushrooms and scallions in butter until golden-brown. Allow to cool to room temperature.

Cream the remaining ingredients in a bowl, blending until smooth. Add the mushroom and scallion mixture. Sprinkle with salt and mix

well, adjusting the seasonings if necessary. Mound onto your serving dish and refrigerate until well-chilled. Garnish with parsley.
MAKES ABOUT 2½ CUPS.

Cheese & herb spread

MIDDLE EAST

Serve this spread with party rye or any of the thin, Middle Eastern breads. Good for cocktails or as a first course.

6 ounces cream cheese at room temperature
1 cup finely crumbled Feta cheese
½ cup unflavored yoghurt
2 tablespoons finely chopped chives
2 tablespoons chopped fresh dill
2 tablespoons chopped fresh mint
Salt to taste
1 small clove garlic, crushed
Tomato slices
Cucumber slices
Black olives
Parsley sprigs

With a fork, mash cream cheese until fairly smooth. Add Feta cheese and yoghurt, stirring vigorously with a wooden spoon. When fairly light and fluffy, add the seasonings. Cover and chill the mixture for at least 2 hours.

When ready to serve, mound the cheese in the center of a dish. Arrange tomatoes, cucumbers, olives, and parsley around the cheese. Serve with your choice of bread or crackers.
MAKES 4 SERVINGS.

Hummus

MIDDLE EAST

This Middle Eastern delicacy is popular in the West as a dip. To keep up the flavor of the dish, serve it on triangles of pita bread.

1 or 2 cloves garlic, mashed
½ teaspoon salt
¼ teaspoon black pepper
¼ teaspoon paprika
⅛ teaspoon cayenne pepper

2 cups cooked garbanzo beans or chick peas (canned chick peas may be substituted, drained and rinsed and liquid reserved)
½ cup tahini (sesame seed paste)
¼ cup lemon juice
Reserved liquid from beans as needed
1 tablespoon olive oil
½ teaspoon paprika
Minced parsley

In a bowl, mash garlic, salt, black pepper, paprika, and cayenne pepper. Drain garbanzo beans, reserving the liquid; in a separate bowl mash thoroughly.

Gradually, add the garlic mixture along with tahini and lemon juice. Put in as much of the reserved liquid as needed to make a smooth purée, but not too runny. (Hummus should be a spreadable consistency.) Spoon into a serving bowl and pour olive oil and paprika on top. Sprinkle with parsley and your appetizer is ready.
MAKES 2 TO 2½ CUPS.

Middle Eastern pickled vegetables

MIDDLE EAST

This dish serves as a vegetable accompaniment to the meal or as an appetizer when forks are used. The nice part is it can be made well ahead of when you want to use it. It must be made at least 4 to 6 weeks ahead to taste the best.

1 head cauliflower, cut into florets
Celery, cut into 2-inch pieces
1 cabbage, cut into thin wedges
1 large bunch carrots, cleaned and quartered
Wide-mouth quart jars with new lids
1 clove garlic per quart jar
3 quarts water
2 cups white vinegar
1 cup coarse noniodized salt
6 to 8 crushed dried hot red peppers
2 teaspoons sugar
2 or 3 sprigs fresh dill

Clean and prepare the vegetables and set aside. Sterilize the quart jars and when cool, place 1 garlic clove into each jar.

In a large saucepan bring remaining ingredients to a boil and allow to continue boiling for 10 minutes. Pack some of each of the vegetables into the jars very tightly. Pour liquid or brine over the vegetables and seal the jars. Store for 4 to 6 weeks before serving.
MAKES AT LEAST 4 TO 6 SERVINGS.

Stuffed zucchini

MIDDLE EAST

This appetizer or first course can be arranged on its serving platter early in the day and run under the broiler at the last minute.

4 zucchini, about 4½ inches long
1 teaspoon salt
1 cup water
1 cup crumbled Feta cheese
⅓ cup grated gruyère cheese
2 tablespoons flour
1 tablespoon chopped fresh dill
1 teaspoon crushed garlic
Hearty dash of freshly ground black pepper
¼ cup bread crumbs
2 tablespoons butter

Cook zucchini in salted water until tender, about 15 minutes. Drain and let cool. Slice in half lengthwise and scoop out seeds.
Mix cheeses with flour, dill, garlic, and pepper. Arrange zucchini in an oven dish, cut-side up, and dust with pepper. Fill with cheese mixture, sprinkle with bread crumbs, and dot with butter. Broil for just a few minutes until cheese mixture is very hot. Serve at once.
MAKES 8 SERVINGS.

Turkish stuffed peppers

MIDDLE EAST

This is a delicious appetizer and a cook's delight since it can be made ahead and kept in the refrigerator until ready to eat.

⅓ cup olive oil
2 cups chopped onions
1 cup uncooked rice
¼ cup pine nuts
2¼ cups water
1 scant tablespoon tomato paste
1 teaspoon salt
½ teaspoon freshly ground black pepper
1 teaspoon sugar
1 teaspoon allspice
1½ tablespoons fresh chopped mint
2 tablespoons lemon juice
8 sweet green peppers, tops removed, seeded but kept whole
1 cup water
2 lemons, quartered

In a large skillet, sauté the onions in oil until light brown. Add the rice and cook for just 3 minutes, until rice is well-coated with oil. Stir in pine nuts for 1 minute more. Add water, tomato paste, salt, pepper, sugar, and allspice. When mixture is at a boil, cover and simmer for 30 minutes. With a large fork, toss rice gently and add mint and lemon juice, tossing again.
Stuff the prepared peppers with the rice and place in a large casserole dish, top-side up. Pour in 1 cup of water and cover the dish. Bake at 350°F for 1 hour or until the peppers are tender. Remove from the oven and allow to cool. Pour off any water that remains and chill the peppers overnight. Serve garnished with the lemon quarters.
MAKES 8 SERVINGS.

Egyptian shrimp pâté

MIDDLE EAST

½ pound cooked prawns of shrimp
¼ cup almonds, chopped, toasted, and blanched
1 tablespoon grated candied ginger
¼ teaspoon curry powder
1 mashed garlic clove
1 tablespoon fresh lemon juice
2 tablespoons finely chopped parsley
2 tablespoons melted butter
4 finely chopped Greek olives
Salt and pepper to taste

garnish
Whole cooked prawns
Lemon wedges
Greek olives

This mixture can be made with a food chopper but is easier in a food processor or blender. Purée all ingredients in order given and blend into a smooth paste. Form into a loaf and chill for at least 12 hours, overnight is even better.

When ready to serve, place loaf on serving dish and garnish with whole prawns, lemon wedges, and Greek olives. Serve with your favorite cracker or pita bread.

MAKES ONE LARGE LOAF.

Chopped liver pâté

MIDDLE EAST

¼ pound butter or chicken fat
1 large onion, finely chopped
1 pound chicken livers
1 tablespoon Worcestershire sauce
Salt and pepper to taste

Melt butter or chicken fat in medium skillet; lightly sauté chopped onion. Add chicken livers; cook until they are slightly pink at the center, about 5 minutes. Remove from heat.

Put entire mixture through a food mill or food processor so it is ground very smooth. If you use a colander instead of a food mill, you may want to put the liver mixture through twice to ensure a smooth texture. Last, add Worcestershire sauce and salt and pepper. Mix together well with a spoon.

Shape into a greased mold for a party. Turn out on a serving plate and surround with party crackers so that guests may help themselves.

MAKES 10 TO 16 SERVINGS.

Turkish meatballs

MIDDLE EAST

1 pound lean ground lamb or beef
1 medium onion, finely chopped
¼ cup uncooked rice
1 tablespoon salt
½ teaspoon freshly ground black pepper
2 cups water
1 cup olive oil or vegetable oil
2 lightly beaten eggs

Blend meat, onions, rice, salt, and pepper. When thoroughly mixed, form balls about 1 inch in diameter.

In a heavy skillet bring 2 cups of water to a boil. Add meatballs and return to boiling. Then simmer, uncovered, for 30 minutes, adding boiling water if needed. Remove meatballs to a plate.

Drain water from skillet and heat oil. Dip the waiting meatballs into the beaten egg and deep-fry for 5 minutes or until brown on all sides. Drain on paper towels and keep warm until ready to serve. These may be served on wooden skewers.

MAKES ABOUT 16 MEATBALLS.

Won ton

CHINA

½ pound pork, minced
¼ cup fresh mushrooms, minced
1 tablespoon scallion, minced
¼ teaspoon salt
⅛ teaspoon freshly ground black pepper
1 egg yolk
Won ton squares (bought)
Peanut oil

Mix minced pork, mushrooms, and scallion with salt, pepper, and egg yolk. Place ½ teaspoonful of the mixture in center of won ton square. Fold one corner up over the filling at an angle to make two askew triangles. Pull the bottom corners of the triangles gently down below their base. Overlap the tips of the two corners slightly and pinch them together.

Fry in hot peanut oil and drain. Serve with Chinese mustard or catsup mixed with a little horseradish.

MAKES APPROXIMATELY 120 WON TON.

Turkish meatballs

3 teaspoons salt
2¼ cups water
Oil

Beat eggs. Add cornstarch and salt. Beat in water. Heat oil in bottom of 8-inch frying pan or wok and pour about ¼ cup of batter into pan. Fry lightly, turn and fry on other side.
MAKES APPROXIMATELY 24 SKINS.

Egg rolls I

CHINA

You can purchase ready-made egg roll skins in supermarkets or Oriental specialty stores or make your own according to above recipe.

dipping batter
1 egg
1 tablespoon cornstarch
1½ teaspoons baking powder
1 cup flour
1 tablespoon sugar
2 teaspoons salt
1¼ cups milk
1¾ cups water

Chinese stuffed mushrooms

CHINA

24 large mushrooms, stems removed
1 pound ground meat
4 tablespoons chopped scallions
3½ tablespoons soy sauce, divided
⅛ teaspoon salt
Freshly ground black pepper to taste
1½ tablespoons flour
1¼ cups beef broth

Wash mushrooms and remove stems; put mushrooms aside. Chop together the meat and scallions, until fine. Add 1 tablespoon soy sauce, salt, pepper, and flour. Shape mixture into small balls and stuff mushrooms.
Heat large skillet to medium heat. Add remaining soy sauce and beef broth. Place mushrooms in skillet stuffed-side-up, cover, and let cook for about 20 minutes or until meat is done.
MAKES 24 STUFFED MUSHROOMS.

Egg-roll skins

CHINA

18 eggs
3 tablespoons cornstarch

Chopped liver pâté

Put egg-roll batter in pan until set.

Sauté filling ingredients and spoon about ½ cup filling into egg-roll skin.

Fold like an envelope and seal.

Fry in hot oil about 5 minutes.

filling

1 cup shredded bamboo shoots

½ pound bean sprouts, rinsed and well-drained

1½ cups shredded water chestnuts

3½ cups slivered cooked chicken

¾ cup slivered barbecued pork

¾ cup finely chopped fresh parsley

1 cup chopped fresh mushrooms

½ cup finely chopped scallion

Salt and freshly ground black pepper to taste

Oil

Beat egg slightly. Sift together dry ingredients. Mix with egg. Slowly stir in milk and water and stir until smooth.

All filling ingredients should be cut finely. Mix filling ingredients (except oil) together and sauté in a little oil for about 10 minutes, stirring occasionally. Let mixture cool. Spoon about ½ cup onto egg roll skin. Fold like an envelope. Dip in batter and fry in hot oil for about 5 minutes, turning carefully to brown both sides. Serve with Chinese mustard and/or duck sauce.
MAKES APPROXIMATELY 2 DOZEN.

Egg rolls II

CHINA

for dough

½ pound flour

1½ cups water

Salt

1½ teaspoons peanut oil

for filling

½ pound green cabbage

1 leek

1 medium onion

1 8-ounce can bamboo shoots

1 4-ounce can mushrooms

4 tablespoons oil

4 ounces ground beef

4 ounces ground pork

2 cups fresh bean sprouts

4 tablespoons soy sauce

2 tablespoons sherry

Salt

Cayenne pepper

Peanut oil

Beaten egg yolks

6 cups oil for deep frying

Place flour in a bowl. Slowly stir in water, making sure that you always stir in the same direction. Add salt and 1½ teaspoons peanut oil and cover bowl. Let rest for 30 minutes.

Meanwhile, prepare filling. Wash and drain cabbage and leek and cut into thin slices. Chop onion. Drain bamboo shoots and cut into fine strips. Drain and coarsely chop mushrooms. In skillet heat 4 tablespoons oil and add ground meats; cook until lightly browned. Stir in cabbage, leek, onion, and bamboo shoots. Cook for 5 minutes. Add mushrooms and bean sprouts and cook for an additional 2 minutes. Season to taste with soy sauce, sherry, salt, and cayenne pepper. Remove from heat and set aside.

Brush an 8-inch skillet with peanut oil. Pour in ⅛ of the egg roll dough; tilt skillet to spread batter evenly. Over low heat cook until set. Turn out onto moistened paper toweling. Cover with another moistened paper towel. Continue until all dough is used up.

Cut egg roll rounds into 6-inch squares. Divide filling among the eight egg rolls. Fold two opposite corners of egg rolls towards middle. Starting with corner closest to you, roll up egg roll. Brush inside of opposite corner with small amount of beaten egg yolk; seal egg roll.

Heat oil in deep frypan. Add rolls and fry until done. Put paper toweling on cake rack, place egg rolls on rack and drain. Keep them warm and serve on preheated platter.

MAKES 8 EGG ROLLS.

Egg rolls II

Vegetarian egg rolls

CHINA

Oil
Egg roll or won ton skins
Vegetables such as cabbage, bok choy, celery, carrots, fresh
  mushrooms, onions, scallions, green pepper, bean sprouts

Use as many of the above vegetables as you wish, in whatever amounts you desire. Shred or finely chop all the vegetables. Stir-fry quickly in small amount of oil. Add soy sauce to taste, garlic powder and some peanut butter.

Fill egg roll skins, or won ton skins (for cocktail size) and fry in oil in wok (or deep frypan). Serve immediately or freeze and warm in oven before serving.

Sauce

Apricot preserves
Plum preserves
Soy sauce
Dijon mustard
Peanut butter

Combine amounts of above ingredients to taste. Some prefer the sauce somewhat sweet, while others like it sharp.

Shrimp toast

CHINA

¼ teaspoon sesame-seed oil
¼ teaspoon soy sauce
Pinch of white pepper
Pinch of salt
½ pound uncooked shrimp, cleaned, deveined
8 slices 2-day-old white bread, sliced thin
1 quart vegetable oil

Add sesame-seed oil, soy sauce, pepper, and salt to shrimp; mix thoroughly. Cut 32 rounds from bread slices. Spread shrimp mixture evenly on 16 rounds. Top each circle with another round; press edges together.
Heat oil in deep pot until very hot. Drop each round into oil; turn to brown evenly. Takes approximately 2 minutes. Drain on paper toweling.
MAKES 16.

Mandarin shrimp hors d'oeuvres

CHINA

6 tablespoons oil
1 pound small cleaned shrimp
Salt to taste
1 tablespoon sherry, or to taste

Heat oil; stir-fry shrimp just until color changes. Drain; sprinkle with salt and sherry.
MAKES 6 SERVINGS.

Scallops Chinese-style

CHINA

1 cup soy sauce
1 tablespoon lemon juice
2 teaspoons fresh gingerroot, finely chopped, or powdered ginger
2 tablespoons sugar
1 pound scallops, cut into bite-size pieces

In large saucepan combine soy sauce, lemon juice, ginger, and sugar. Bring to a boil. Add scallops and cook over medium-high heat until all the liquid has evaporated.
MAKES 25 APPETIZERS.

Abalone appetizer

CHINA

1 teaspoon grated fresh gingerroot
1 tablespoon soy sauce
1 tablespoon sherry
1 can abalone, drained, cut into bite-size pieces

Mix together ginger, soy sauce, and sherry. Pour over abalone. Refrigerate several hours.
MAKES 5 OR 6 SERVINGS.

Baked chicken wings

CHINA

1 10-ounce bottle soy sauce
2 teaspoons freshly grated ginger, or 1 teaspoon powdered ginger
2 cloves garlic, minced
⅓ cup brown sugar
1 teaspoon dark mustard
24 chicken wings
Garlic powder

Mix together soy sauce, ginger, garlic, brown sugar, and mustard. Blend well. Marinate chicken wings in mixture for two hours or longer. Drain wings, reserving marinade.
Bake 1½ hours at 350°F, turning and basting with marinade frequently. Sprinkle with garlic powder and place under broiler to get crispy for a minute or two just before serving.
This can also be served as a main dish (serves 4-5).
MAKES 8 TO 12 SERVINGS.

Chicken wings in oyster sauce

CHINA

3 tablespoons oil
2 cloves garlic, crushed
8 chicken wings, each divided into 3 parts
2 tablespoons soy sauce
3 tablespoons oyster sauce
1 tablespoon sugar
½ cup water

Preheat wok. Coat bottom and sides with oil. Rub bottom and sides with garlic; discard garlic.

Add middles and tips of wings; brown on both sides. Add rest of wing pieces; brown.

Mix together soy sauce and oyster sauce; stir into chicken. Stir in sugar and water. Cover wok; cook over medium-low heat 15 minutes.
MAKES 4 SERVINGS.

Salted chicken
CHINA

1½ tablespoons salt
1 tablespoon rice wine
2 small slices gingerroot
2 scallions, cut into 1-inch pieces
1 whole chicken, 2½ to 3 pounds
Cold water
1 cup chicken stock
¼ teaspoon salt
1 tablespoon sesame oil

Mix together salt, wine, gingerroot, and scallions. Rub chicken with mixture; let stand 30 minutes. Place chicken in pot; cover with cold water. Bring to boil; simmer 40 minutes over medium heat. Remove from pot; chill. Remove skin; cut into pieces approximately 2 inches long and 1 inch wide.

Mix together stock, ¼ teaspoon salt, and sesame oil. Pour over chicken. Garnish with additional scallions if desired.
MAKES 12 SERVINGS.

Sweet-&-sour spareribs
CHINA

5 tablespoons soy sauce
2 tablespoons sherry
2 cloves garlic, minced
1 teaspoon sugar
1½ pounds spareribs
1 tablespoon cornstarch
1 tablespoon vinegar
1 teaspoon cornstarch
Oil for cooking

Combine 3 tablespoons soy sauce, 1 tablespoon sherry, garlic, and 1 teaspoon sugar; blend well.

Have butcher cut crosswise through bones of spareribs at about 1- to 1½-inch intervals. Cut bones apart. Pour soy-sauce mixture over spareribs. Let stand at room temperature 1 hour; baste occasionally. Blend in 1 tablespoon cornstarch. Blend together 2 tablespoons sugar, 2 tablespoons soy sauce, 1 tablespoon sherry, vinegar, and 1 teaspoon cornstarch together in saucepan. Cook over medium heat, stirring constantly, until thickened. Set aside.

Heat approximately 3 inches oil in deep pot. Drain marinade from spareribs. Add portion of meat at a time to hot oil; cook until well browned. Drain on paper toweling. Place cooked spareribs into cooked sauce; coat well. Cover; chill. Serve spareribs at room temperature.
MAKES ABOUT 24 TO 28 PIECES.

Oriental chicken livers
CHINA

8 ounces chicken livers, cut in half
⅓ cup soy sauce
½ cup flour
1 small onion, sliced, or onion flakes

Marinate chicken livers overnight in soy sauce. Remove livers from marinade and dredge in flour. Heat small amount of oil in frying pan and fry livers and onion until browned. Serve as an appetizer, or with rice as a main course.

This can also be served as a main course (serves 2).
MAKES APPROXIMATELY 4 SERVINGS.

Cucumber hors d'oeuvres
CHINA

2 tablespoons oil
3 small red chili peppers, seeded, cut into very thin slices
4 medium to large cucumbers, cut into 2-inch lengths, quartered, seeded
1 teaspoon soy sauce
2 tablespoons sugar
¼ teaspoon salt
1 tablespoon vinegar

Heat oil in skillet. Add chili peppers; stir-fry 4 seconds. Add cucumbers; stir-fry 30 seconds. Add soy sauce, sugar, and salt; stir until well blended.

Refrigerate at least 24 hours; remove cucumbers from liquid. Sprinkle with vinegar.
MAKES 6 SERVINGS.

Shrimp wrapped in bacon

JAPAN

8 cleaned large shrimp, intact
8 slices bacon

Wrap shrimp with bacon; fasten with toothpicks. Bake in 350°F oven for 15 to 20 minutes. Serve as an appetizer.
MAKES 4 SERVINGS.

Simple tuna appetizer

JAPAN

1 6-ounce can tuna
1 teaspoon soy sauce (more, if desired)
2 tablespoons chopped onion

Drain tuna. Mix with soy sauce and chopped onion; spread on rice crackers (or another cracker of your choice) as an appetizer.
MAKES 5 TO 6 SERVINGS.

Skewered fish meat

JAPAN

6 pieces white fish meat, each about 2 ounces
Salt
7 ounces white miso (soybean paste)
½ cup rice wine (or sherry)
2 tablespoons sugar

Sprinkle fish meat lightly with salt; refrigerate for 12 hours.

Mix soybean paste, rice wine (or sherry), and sugar together until well-blended. Drain fish, place in mixture, and refrigerate for 24 hours.

Thread fish on skewers; broil in oven, on grill, or on a hibachi.
MAKES 3 SERVINGS.

Chicken livers wrapped in bacon

JAPAN

8 slices bacon, cut in half
1 pound chicken livers, halved
1 6-ounce can whole water chestnuts, drained and sliced

Lay bacon slices flat, place chicken livers and water chestnuts on top, and roll up. Secure with toothpicks.

Place appetizers in small amount of hot oil in frying pan or wok; cook until bacon is browned.
MAKES 4 SERVINGS.

Fried chicken balls

JAPAN

½ large onion, chopped
1 cup finely chopped raw chicken
1 tablespoon sugar
1½ tablespoons mirin (sweet rice wine)
2 tablespoons soy sauce
1 egg
2 tablespoons oil
3½ tablespoons water
1½ tablespoons sherry

Soak chopped onion in water; squeeze out moisture. Combine chicken and onion with sugar, mirin (or sherry mixed with sugar: 1 part sugar to 2 parts sherry), 1 tablespoon soy sauce, and egg. Stir until thoroughly mixed. Roll into bite-size balls.

Heat oil in pan; brown meatballs on all sides. Combine water, sherry, and remaining 1 tablespoon soy sauce. Add to meat in pan; cook until liquid is almost evaporated.
MAKES 4 SERVINGS.

Chicken liver teriyaki

JAPAN

1 pound chicken livers
½ cup each of soy sauce, sugar, and water
Soy sauce or mustard for dipping

Marinate livers in mixture of soy sauce, sugar, and water. Skewer the livers; place on hibachi or grill, turning while cooking. When done, dip livers into soy sauce or mustard and enjoy.
MAKES 4 SERVINGS.

Roast beef w/horseradish

JAPAN

Horseradish, freshly grated or bottled
Water
4 slices roast beef, each about ⅛ inch thick

Mix horseradish with small amount of water until of spreading consistency. Spread beef with horseradish; roll it up. Spread horseradish as thick or thin as you prefer. Serve as a meal appetizer or cut into small pieces and spear with toothpicks.
MAKES 2 SERVINGS.

Beef roll-ups

JAPAN

Ground ginger
2 teaspoons soy sauce
8 ounces thinly sliced uncooked lean beef
½ carrot
1 scallion
1 pimiento
2 fresh mushrooms
2 tablespoons oil
2 tablespoons soy sauce
2 tablespoons mirin (sweet rice wine)

Mix a small amount of ginger with 2 teaspoons of soy sauce. Put beef in the mixture; let stand for 20 minutes.
Cut the carrot, scallion, and pimiento into thin slices. Slice the mushrooms thin also. Lay the beef out flat and fill it with the vegetables. Roll up the beef; fasten it with toothpicks.
Heat oil in skillet. Fry the beef rolls, turning on all sides. Add 2 tablespoons soy sauce and the mirin; turn heat higher for 1 minute. Remove toothpicks and cut roll-ups into bite-size pieces. If desired, garnish with lettuce leaves.

If you do not have mirin, you can use sherry mixed with sugar: 1 part sugar to 2 parts sherry.
MAKES APPROXIMATELY 2 SERVINGS.

Chili & cheese appetizers

MEXICO

1 dozen 6-inch corn tortillas
Oil for frying
6 pickled jalapeño peppers
1 cup refried beans (homemade or canned)
½ cup shredded sharp cheddar cheese

Cut each tortilla into quarters. Heat 1 inch of oil to 360°F in a small heavy skillet. Fry tortillas until crisp; drain on paper towels.
Carefully stem and seed peppers; cut each into 6 thin strips. Spread each chip with 1 teaspoon beans. Top with ½ teaspoon shredded cheese, and a thin pepper strip. Broil until cheese melts. Serve immediately.
MAKES 48 APPETIZERS.

Cheddar-cheese puffs

MEXICO

2 cups grated cheddar cheese
½ cup butter or margarine, softened
1 cup flour, sifted
½ teaspoon salt
½ teaspoon paprika
48 small green olives, stuffed with pimientos

Blend cheese with butter. Add sifted flour, salt, and paprika; mix well. Mold 1 teaspoon dough around each olive to cover. At this point you may refrigerate or freeze cheese puffs for up to 10 days.
Bake puffs at 400°F for 15 minutes. Serve hot.
MAKES 48 APPETIZERS.

Fiesta cheese ball

MEXICO

8 ounces cream cheese
1 pound sharp cheddar cheese, grated
¼ cup butter, softened
1 tablespoon chili powder

5 cups chopped black olives
½ cup dried parsley

Have cheeses and butter at room temperature before combining with an electric mixer. Beat cream cheese and butter until combined. Add cheddar and chili powder. Mix well. Add olives; mix lightly.

Form into 2 balls; roll balls in dried parsley. Chill well. (Cheese balls may be frozen for later use.) Serve cheese balls with assorted crackers.

As a variation omit the butter and chili powder and substitute 1 4-ounce can of chopped green chilies.
MAKES 2 BALLS.

Chili & cheese dip

MEXICO

2 tablespoons olive oil
1 medium onion, finely chopped
1 12-ounce can tomatoes, drained and chopped
1 4-ounce can chopped green chilies
1 pound pasteurized processed American cheese spread

Heat oil in medium skillet; sauté onion until golden. Add tomatoes and chilies. Reduce heat to simmer; cook mixture until almost dry, stirring occasionally.

Meanwhile, melt cheese over hot water in double boiler. Combine melted cheese and tomato mixture. Serve dip in chafing dish or fondue pot, so that dip remains warm. Serve with corn chips or tostadas.
MAKES 6 TO 8 SERVINGS.

Avocado dip

MEXICO

For raw vegetables or corn chips.

3 ripe avocados
1 tomato, peeled and seeded
1 small red onion, finely diced
1 tablespoon chopped hot jalapeño pepper
Dash of ground coriander
1 tablespoon lemon juice
1 tablespoon vinegar

2 tablespoons salad oil
1 teaspoon salt

Mince avocados and tomato. Stir in all other ingredients; spoon into individual dishes. You may use scooped-out avocado shells for serving dishes. If made ahead of time, put the avocado seeds in the mixture to keep it green.
MAKES 2 CUPS.

Bean dip

MEXICO

1 1-pound can refried beans
⅓ cup hot jalapeño relish (or more, to taste)
Sour cream (optional)
¾ cup grated Jack cheese

Combine beans with the jalapeño relish, stirring well. If mixture is too thick, add a small amount of sour cream; mix well. Place in three ramekins; sprinkle each with ¼ cup of cheese. Heat ramekins successively, as needed, at 350°F for 20 minutes. Serve dip hot with tortilla chips.
MAKES 6 SERVINGS.

Spicy dip

MEXICO

1 1-pound can tomatoes, drained and chopped
1 cup chopped scallions (onions and green stem)
1 teaspoon salt
1 4-ounce can green chili sauce

Mix tomatoes, scallions, and salt. Add green chili sauce to taste. Chill.
MAKES 1 CUP.

Shrimp dip

MEXICO

¼ cup chili sauce
2 teaspoons lemon juice
1 teaspoon prepared horseradish
¼ teaspoon salt
4 drops hot-pepper sauce
1 cup sour cream
1 4½-ounce can shrimp, drained and chopped (1 cup shrimp)

Combine chili sauce, lemon juice, horseradish, salt, and hot-pepper sauce. Fold in sour cream. Add chopped shrimp. Chill. Serve dip with crisp vegetables.
MAKES 1¾ CUPS.

Tortilla chips

MEXICO

1 dozen corn tortillas
Oil for frying
Salt

Defrost tortillas if they are frozen. Cut each tortilla into 8 wedges.
Use a small heavy skillet, electric skillet, or deep fryer to heat at least 1 inch of cooking oil to 360°F. Fry tortilla pieces, a few at a time, until crisp and lightly browned. Remove from oil with a slotted spoon. Drain chips on paper towels and salt lightly. Serve chips with dips or refried beans.
MAKES 8 DOZEN CHIPS.

Tortillas & beans

MEXICO

Beans and cheese are only the beginning of the list of possible burrito fillings. Leftover taco filling or other ground meat, chicken, and chili sauce, or just cheese, make a delicious sandwich.

4 large flour tortillas (7 to 8 inches in diameter or larger)
3 cups refried beans
½ cup grated cheddar cheese
¼ cup Green Chili Salsa

Lightly brush tortillas with water; heat briefly on griddle until warm and pliable.
Meanwhile, heat refried beans to serving temperature. Place ¾ cup beans down center of each tortilla. Top with 2 tablespoons grated cheese and 1 tablespoon Green Chili Salsa. Fold top and bottom edges of tortilla in 2 inches, then fold sides toward center, overlapping each other. At this point it is wisest to wrap a napkin around the sandwich to hold it shut.
MAKES 4 SERVINGS.

Stuffed eggs

MEXICO

8 hard-cooked eggs, chilled
1 tablespoon grated onion
1 tablespoon finely minced green pepper
¼ teaspoon chili powder
¼ teaspoon salt
2 to 3 dashes Tabasco
2 teaspoons lemon juice
1 tablespoon olive oil
16 small shrimp, cooked, peeled, and deveined
Parsley
Lettuce

Cut hard-cooked eggs in half lengthwise; remove yolks. Mash yolks with onion, green pepper, chili powder, salt, Tabasco, lemon juice, and olive oil. Stuff egg whites with egg-yolk mixture; garnish each egg with a shrimp and a tiny sprig of parsley.
Place eggs on a plate surrounded by fresh green lettuce. Refrigerate until serving time.
MAKES 4 OR MORE SERVINGS.

Crisp-fried burritos

MEXICO

These sandwiches are a California-Mexican treat and can be filled with any filling you wish. For example: leftover taco filling, chicken and chilies, or beans. One of these makes a more than ample lunch.

4 large flour tortillas (7 to 8 inches in diameter or larger)
2 cups grated extra-sharp cheddar cheese
1 4-ounce can chopped green chilies
Oil for frying
Chili con Carne (see Index)
Chopped white onion
Grated cheddar cheese

Lay tortillas briefly on a hot griddle, to make them pliable. Fill immediately with ½ cup cheese and 1 tablespoon chilies placed in center of each tortilla. Fold top and bottom edges in toward center 1 or 2 inches, then fold sides toward center, overlapping each other to form a tight package. Fasten with a toothpick.

Heat 1 inch oil to 360°F in an electric skillet. Fry burritos until golden brown, turning once. Drain on paper towels. Serve burritos topped with chili, onions, and grated cheese.
MAKES 4 SERVINGS.

Meat pies

MEXICO

These meat pies are large. They can be served as a substantial first course with a light supper, or cut into pieces and served. These would make a delicious luncheon dish, so make enough for leftovers!

1 10-ounce package frozen patty shells
1 cup diced cooked roast beef
1 onion, chopped
1 clove garlic, minced
2 tablespoons butter
½ teaspoon salt

¼ teaspoon pepper
¼ teaspoon thyme
¼ teaspoon cumin
¼ teaspoon chili powder
2 dashes Tabasco
1 tomato, peeled and chopped
¼ cup raisins
¼ cup sliced stuffed green olives
2 hard-cooked eggs, diced
Milk

Remove patty shells from freezer and allow to stand at room temperature until soft enough to roll.

Meanwhile, prepare the filling. In a small skillet sauté beef, onion, and garlic in butter over low heat 5 minutes. Add salt, pepper, thyme, cumin, chili powder, Tabasco, and tomato. Reduce heat to simmer; cook for 10 minutes. Soak raisins in boiling water until plump. Drain well. Combine meat mixture, raisins, olives, and eggs; set aside. Roll each patty shell on a floured pastry cloth to

Meat pies

a rectangle approximately 5 × 8 inches. Place ⅓ cup filling on one half of the rectangle. Fold to form a turnover. Seal with milk.

Preheat oven to 450°F. Place turnovers on an ungreased cookie sheet; brush with milk. Place in oven; immediately reduce heat to 400°F; bake for 20 to 25 minutes or until well-browned and puffed.

MAKES 6 SERVINGS.

"Little fat ones"

MEXICO

2 cups Masa Harina
½ cup sifted all-purpose flour
½ teaspoon salt
1½ cups warm water
3 tablespoons melted lard
Oil for frying
1 pound Mexican pork sausage
¼ pound cheddar cheese, grated
1 small onion, chopped
1 4-ounce can Green Chili Salsa

Combine Masa Harina, flour, and salt in a mixing bowl. Add water and melted lard. Mix well; knead until well-blended. Divide into 15 equal pieces. Flatten each piece into a 3-inch circle. Bake on ungreased griddle over medium heat until very slightly browned. While still warm, pinch up edges between your thumb and fingers to form a rim all around tortillas. Punch up small mounds in centers so that rounds look like small sombreros. Set aside until serving time.

At serving time, fry sausage; drain. Keep them warm.

In a small skillet heat 2 inches oil to 375°F. Fry in deep fat until golden brown. Drain. Fill brims of sombreros with sausage; top with grated cheese and onion; drizzle with a little of the Chili Salsa.

MAKES 15.

Pork tidbits

MEXICO

1½ pounds boneless pork (leg, shoulder, or loin)
Water
1 teaspoon salt
½ teaspoon coriander
½ teaspoon crumbled oregano
½ teaspoon crumbled dried cilantro (Italian parsley)
½ teaspoon pepper

Cut meat into thin finger strips approximately 2 inches long and ½ inch wide, with a little fat on each piece. Place meat in a large saucepan. Add enough water to cover ¾ of the meat. Add salt, coriander, oregano, and cilantro; stir well.

Bring to a boil over moderate heat; cook, stirring occasionally, until all water has evaporated. Reduce heat to low; slowly brown meat in its own fat. Sprinkle with pepper while browning.

Serve tidbits hot as an appetizer with sauces for dipping, such as Spicy Dip (see Index) or jalapeño sauce, or use as a filling for tacos.

MAKES 4 SERVINGS.

Mexican cocktail meatballs

MEXICO

Very different!

1 pound lean hamburger
1 large clove garlic, minced
1 12-ounce bottle chili sauce
1 10-ounce jar grape jelly

Mix hamburger with garlic powder and shape into small balls. Pan fry until well-cooked; drain. Mix chili sauce and grape jelly. Add meatballs; heat mixture. Serve sauce warm in chafing dish.

MAKES 12 SERVINGS AS AN APPETIZER.

❧ Soups ❧

Consommé

½ cup cold water
4 egg whites
1 quart Basic Stock, cold (see Index)
1 teaspoon salt
⅛ teaspoon pepper
Brown gravy
1 tablespoon Madeira
1 tablespoon cognac

Put water and egg whites into medium saucepan; beat to a foam. Add cold stock, salt, and pepper; heat to a boil. Just as mixture starts to boil, reduce heat and simmer for 8 to 10 minutes.
Pour liquid through wet cheesecloth. Do not break up egg whites. After straining, color with food coloring if beef stock is used. (Chicken consommé is not colored.) Flavor with Madeira and cognac. Serve consommé plain or with garnish.
MAKES 6 SERVINGS.

Asparagus soup

FRANCE

30 stalks asparagus (about 2 pounds)
4 quarts water
1 tablespoon salt
¼ cup minced onion
¼ cup minced parsley
1 teaspoon ground coriander
2 tablespoons butter
1 tablespoon flour
2 cups chicken broth, heated
½ cup heavy cream
1 tablespoon lemon juice
½ teaspoon salt
¼ teaspoon white pepper

Trim tough ends and peel asparagus stems with potato peeler. Tie together in 3 bunches; simmer in large pot of salted water until just tender. Lift bundles out; place in sink of cold water. When cool, drain on paper towels. Cut tips from stalks; reserve. Cut stalks into 1-inch pieces; reserve.
In medium saucepan, sauté onion and parsley with coriander and butter until vegetables are softened. Stir in flour; cook for 3 minutes. Remove pan from heat; stir in heated broth. Simmer mixture 5 minutes. Add reserved asparagus stalks. Puree mixture in blender, food processor, or food mill until smooth. Do this by batches. Return purée to saucepan; stir in cream and reserved asparagus tips; heat but do not boil. Stir in lemon juice. Add salt and pepper; adjust seasonings to taste. Serve soup hot or chilled.
MAKES 6 SERVINGS.

Fish soup Normandy

Fish soup Normandy

FRANCE

fish stock
½ pound fish (heads, bones, or trimmings)
4 cups hot beef bouillon
Juice of ½ lemon
1 small onion, sliced
1 stalk celery, sliced
1 carrot, sliced

fish dumplings
¾ pound cooked white fish (cod, haddock, etc.)
¼ teaspoon salt
⅛ teaspoon white pepper
1 tablespoon butter
1 egg
3 sprigs parsley, finely chopped
2 teaspoons lemon juice
3 tablespoons soft bread crumbs

soup ingredients
3 tablespoons vegetable oil
1 medium onion, sliced
5 carrots, sliced into ½ inch lengths
1 stalk celery, sliced into ½ inch lengths
2 sprigs parsley
2 cups hot beef broth
2 tablespoons tomato paste
1 4-ounce can sliced mushrooms, drained
3 small tomatoes, peeled and quartered
1 teaspoon curry powder
1 green pepper, sliced
1 4½-ounce can shrimp, deveined and drained
¾ cup white wine
Salt to taste
Dash cayenne pepper
Dash garlic powder
1 sprig parsley, chopped

Clean fish, trimming well. Place into large saucepan. Add bouillon, lemon juice, onion, celery, and carrot. Simmer over low heat 1 hour. Strain.

To prepare Fish Dumplings, put fish through meat grinder (fine blade). Season with salt and pepper. Blend in butter and egg. Add parsley, lemon juice, and bread crumbs. Mix well; set aside.

In large Dutch oven or saucepan, heat oil; add onion, carrots, celery, and parsley; while stirring constantly, cook until slightly browned. Gradually add beef broth. Cover; simmer over low heat 20 minutes. Add Fish Stock, tomato paste, mushrooms, tomatoes, curry powder, and green pepper. Continue simmering for 10 minutes. Moisten your hands; shape Fish Dumplings. Drop them into soup. Add shrimp; simmer for 15 minutes more. Pour in wine. Season to taste with salt, cayenne pepper, and garlic powder. Stir in chopped parsley. Serve.
MAKES 6 SERVINGS.

Carrot & potato soup

FRANCE

This soup is delicious hot or cold.

2 tablespoons butter
2 leeks, white part only, sliced
4 cups cubed potatoes
3 cups sliced carrots
6 cups chicken broth
2 teaspoons salt (only 1 teaspoon salt if canned broth is used)
⅛ teaspoon white pepper
2 cups half-and-half cream or milk
Shredded raw carrot

Melt butter in large saucepan; cook leeks several minutes. Add potatoes, carrots, broth, salt, and pepper. Bring to a boil, reduce heat, and simmer for 30 minutes, until vegetables are done.
Carefully purée hot soup in blender or food processor. Return purée to pan. Add half-and-half; heat to serving temperature. Garnish soup with shredded carrot. If desired, chill soup several hours to blend flavors, and serve as a cold soup.
MAKES 8 SERVINGS.

Sherry bisque

FRANCE

1 small ham hock
¾ cup split green peas
1 bay leaf
6 cups beef broth
6 slices bacon, diced
¾ cup chopped onion
1 stalk celery, diced
3 tablespoons flour
1 8-ounce can tomato purée
1 cup chicken broth
⅓ cup sherry
¼ cup butter
Freshly ground pepper to taste

Place ham hock, split peas, bay leaf, and 4 cups beef broth into 4-quart saucepan. Bring to a boil, reduce heat, and simmer.
Sauté bacon in frypan until fat is rendered. Add onion and celery; cook until tender. Stir in flour; mix to blend. Add remaining 2 cups beef broth;

cook until slightly thickened. Add onion mixture to split-pea mixture; continue to cook until split peas are soft, about 1½ hours.

When done, remove ham hock and bay leaf. Purée mixture in blender or food mill. Add tomato purée, chicken broth, and sherry. Add butter and pepper; stir until melted. Strain soup, if desired, before serving.

MAKES 8 TO 12 SERVINGS.

Cream of lettuce soup

FRANCE

¼ cup butter
1 leek or 2 green onions
½ cup chopped onion
1 quart shredded lettuce*
4 tablespoons flour
1 tablespoon chopped parsley
½ teaspoon salt
⅛ teaspoon nutmeg
6 cups chicken broth
2 egg yolks
½ cup heavy cream
Lettuce and parsley for garnish

Wash the leek or green onion well. Remove all but 2 inches of the green tops. Melt the butter in 3-quart saucepan. Add chopped onion and leek or green onions; sauté until tender. Add lettuce; cover; simmer for 5 minutes. Stir in flour. Add parsley and seasonings and chicken broth. Simmer gently 30 minutes. Purée soup in blender or food processor.

Mix egg yolks and cream in small bowl. Stir in ¼ cup hot soup. Gradually add egg mixture to hot soup, stirring constantly. Heat gently several minutes, until soup thickens. Garnish soup with shredded lettuce and parsley.

MAKES 8 SERVINGS.

Use Boston Bibb or romaine lettuce for best flavor. Do not use iceberg (head) lettuce.

Vichyssoise

FRANCE

3 to 4 leeks or green onions
1 medium onion, chopped
2 tablespoons butter
2 large potatoes, peeled and diced
½ teaspoon salt
3 cups chicken broth
1 cup milk
1½ cups heavy cream
1 drop Tabasco sauce (optional)
1 tablespoon minced parsley or chives

Thoroughly clean leeks or onions, halve lengthwise, and cut into thin slices. Heat butter. Add leeks or onions; cook until transparent. Add potatoes, salt, and chicken broth. Simmer mixture 35 minutes.

Purée in blender, food processor, or food mill; reheat. Pour in milk and 1 cup cream. Heat and stir until well-blended, but do not boil. Season with Tabasco sauce, if desired. Chill mixture.

Beat ½ cup cream until stiff; fold into soup. Adjust seasonings. Serve soup garnished with chopped chives or parsley.

MAKES 4 SERVINGS.

Onion soup

FRANCE

4 large onions, thinly sliced
1 tablespoon butter
1 tablespoon vegetable oil
¼ teaspoon sugar
2 tablespoons flour
6 cups beef broth
¼ cup dry white wine or vermouth
Salt and pepper to taste
4 slices French bread, cut ½ inch thick
2 teaspoons vegetable oil
1 clove garlic, peeled and cut
2 tablespoons cognac
1 cup grated Swiss cheese

In covered 4-quart saucepan or Dutch oven cook onions slowly with butter and oil for 15 minutes.

Stir occasionally. Uncover; increase heat to moderate. Add sugar; sauté onions, stirring frequently, about 30 minutes or until onions turn golden brown. Sprinkle onions with flour; stir over heat for 2 to 3 minutes. Blend in hot broth and wine; adjust seasonings. Simmer, partially covered, for 1 hour.

Meanwhile, place bread slices in 350°F oven 30 minutes or until lightly toasted. Halfway through the baking, baste each slice with ½ teaspoon oil, and rub with cut garlic glove.

Before serving, add cognac and divide soup into ovenproof bowls or casseroles. Sprinkle ½ cup cheese in soup. Float slices of French bread on top of soup; sprinkle with rest of cheese.

Bake in preheated 325°F oven 15 to 20 minutes, until hot, then set under broiler for 2 to 3 minutes, until cheese is golden brown. Serve immediately.

MAKES 4 SERVINGS.

Cream of mushroom soup

FRANCE

¼ cup butter
½ cup finely chopped onion
1 pound mushrooms
6 tablespoons flour
6 cups chicken broth
1 bay leaf
2 sprigs parsley
½ teaspoon salt
⅛ teaspoon pepper
2 tablespoons butter
1 tablespoon lemon juice
1 cup heavy cream or half-and-half cream
2 egg yolks
½ cup sour cream
Chopped parsley, if desired

Melt butter in 3-quart saucepan. Add onion and stems from mushrooms; cook until onion is tender. Stir in flour; add broth. Cook over medium heat, stirring constantly, until thickened. Add bay leaf, parsley sprigs, salt, and pepper. Simmer for 20 minutes. Strain; return to pan.

In small frying pan sauté sliced mushroom caps in 2 tablespoons butter and lemon juice. Add to strained broth; simmer for 10 minutes.

Blend cream and egg yolks. Slowly add small amount of soup to yolks, stirring constantly; then add yolks to soup, still stirring. Heat gently 2 minutes. Stir in sour cream. Serve soup hot. Garnish with chopped parsley.

MAKES 8 SERVINGS.

White bean soup

GERMANY

1 pound dried navy beans
3 quarts water
Smoked ham bone or ham hock
2 tablespoons chopped parsley
1 cup finely chopped onions
1 clove garlic, minced
2 cups finely chopped celery with green tops
1½ teaspoons salt
½ teaspoon pepper

Cover beans with water in large pot or soup kettle and soak overnight. Drain. Rinse beans well, drain, and return to pot with ham bone and 3 quarts water. Simmer uncovered for 2 hours.

Add parsley, onions, garlic, celery, salt, and pepper. Simmer uncovered for 1 hour or until vegetables are tender. Remove ham bone, dice the meat, and add meat to soup. Serve hot.

MAKES 8 SERVINGS.

Two-bean soup

GERMANY

1¼ cups dry white beans
¼ pound ham, cubed
1 cup cut green beans, fresh or frozen
¼ cup diced celery
1 green onion, diced
1 yellow onion, diced
1 potato, peeled and diced
1 tablespoon butter
2 tablespoons flour
¾ cup beef broth
½ teaspoon salt

¼ teaspoon pepper
1 sprig parsley for garnish

Cover white beans with cold water and soak overnight. Drain and place beans in a 2-quart saucepan. Add ham and enough cold water to cover beans by 1 inch. Bring water to a boil and simmer for about 1 hour or until beans are tender. Add green beans, celery, onion, and potato. Add enough water to cover the vegetables; simmer for 20 minutes.

In a frypan melt butter and stir in flour. Cook, stirring until lightly browned. Remove from heat and stir in heated beef broth. Cook mixture until smooth. Stir mixture into the soup and simmer until soup is thickened and vegetables are tender. Season with salt and pepper. Garnish with chopped parsley and serve immediately.
MAKES 4 TO 6 SERVINGS.

Bean soup w/frankfurters
GERMANY

1 pound dried navy beans
8 cups water
3 cups beef broth
1 carrot, chopped
1 celery stalk, chopped
4 strips bacon, cubed
2 small onions, chopped
1 teaspoon salt
¼ teaspoon white pepper
6 frankfurters, sliced
2 tablespoons chopped parsley

Soak beans in water overnight. In a 3-quart saucepan bring beans, water, and beef broth to a boil. Cool for about 1 hour. Add carrot and celery and continue cooking for 30 minutes.

In a separate frypan cook the bacon until transparent. Add the onions; cook until golden. Set aside.

Mash soup through a sieve or food mill or purée briefly in a food processor. Return to pan and add the bacon-onion mixture, salt and pepper. Add frankfurters; reheat about 5 minutes. Sprinkle soup with chopped parsley and serve.
MAKES 4 TO 6 SERVINGS.

German lentil soup
GERMANY

1 pound dried lentils
6 slices bacon, diced
1 cup chopped onion
½ cup chopped carrots
6 cups water
1½ teaspoons salt
½ teaspoon pepper
½ teaspoon thyme
2 bay leaves
½ cup grated potato
1 ham bone or 2 smoked pork hocks
2 tablespoons fresh lemon juice

Wash and sort lentils. Soak lentils overnight or bring to a boil and boil 2 minutes. Cover and let stand 1 hour. Drain lentils.

In 4- or 5-quart Dutch oven sauté bacon until crisp. Remove bacon. Sauté onions and carrots in bacon grease until onions are golden. Add lentils, 6 cups water, seasonings, potato, and ham bone or pork hocks. Simmer, covered, for 3 hours. Or, in a crock pot, cook on low for 6 hours.

To serve, remove bay leaves and ham bone. Skim fat. Remove any meat from ham bone or hocks. Mash lentils slightly to thicken soup. Just before serving, stir in lemon juice.
MAKES 3 QUARTS.

Kale & potato soup
GERMANY

4 medium potatoes
2 tablespoons vegetable oil
8 cups water
1 teaspoon salt
½ teaspoon pepper
2 pounds fresh kale
½ pound cooked, sliced smoked garlic sausage

Peel and chop potatoes. Combine with vegetable oil and water. Cook for 20 to 30 minutes or until potatoes are tender. Remove potatoes and reserve liquid. Mash potatoes through a sieve and

Onion soup

return to potato liquid. Add salt and pepper and simmer for 20 minutes.

Wash kale discarding all tough leaves, and cut into thin shreds. Add to potatoes and cook for 25 minutes. Add sausage. Simmer gently for 5 minutes. Serve.

MAKES 6 TO 8 SERVINGS.

Goulash soup

GERMANY

2 cups chopped onion
¼ cup shortening
3 green peppers, chopped
3 tablespoons tomato paste
1 pound lean beef, cut in 1-inch cubes
Dash red pepper
1 teaspoon paprika
2 cloves garlic, minced
½ teaspoon salt
6 cups beef broth, canned or homemade
1 tablespoon lemon juice
¼ teaspoon caraway seeds

Fry onions in hot fat until transparent. Add green peppers and tomato paste. Cover and simmer 10 minutes. Add meat and remaining ingredients. Simmer about 1½ hours, until meat is tender. (Add cubed potatoes if you like and simmer until potatoes are done.) Best when served the second day.

MAKES 6 SERVINGS.

Lentil soup w/frankfurters

GERMANY

1 cup dried quick-cooking lentils
6 cups water
2 slices lean bacon, diced
1 leek or green onion, finely chopped
1 large carrot, finely chopped
1 celery stalk, chopped
1 onion, finely chopped
1 tablespoon vegetable oil
2 tablespoons flour
1 tablespoon vinegar
4 frankfurters, thickly sliced
1 tablespoon tomato catsup
1 teaspoon salt
¼ teaspoon black pepper

Wash the lentils thoroughly. In a 2½-quart saucepan bring 6 cups water to a boil. Add the lentils, bacon, leek or green onion, carrot and celery. Simmer, partially covered, for 30 to 40 minutes.

Meanwhile in a frypan, sauté chopped onion in vegetable oil until soft. Sprinkle flour over onion, and stir. Lower heat, stir constantly, and cook until the flour turns light brown. Do not burn flour. Stir ½ cup of hot lentil soup into the browned flour; beat with a wire whisk until well-blended. Beat in vinegar.

Add contents of frypan to lentil pan and stir together. Cover and simmer for 30 minutes or until lentils are soft. Add the frankfurters and catsup. Cook to heat frankfurters through. Season with salt and pepper and serve hot.

MAKES 4 SERVINGS.

Cabbage soup

GERMANY

4 thick slices bacon, diced
2 onions, sliced
1 turnip, sliced
2 carrots, diced
2 potatoes, cubed
1 small head green cabbage, shredded
4 cups chicken stock or broth
2 cups water

6 parsley sprigs and bay leaf, tied together with thread
Salt and pepper to taste
¼ cup grated Parmesan cheese for garnish

In a 6-quart saucepan or pot, combine all ingredients except salt, pepper, and cheese. Simmer partially covered for 1½ to 2 hours. Discard the parsley bundle; season to taste.
Pour into hot soup plates and garnish with cheese.
MAKES 6 SERVINGS.

Greek lentil soup

Oxtail soup

GERMANY

1 2-pound disjointed oxtail or 2 veal tails
1 medium onion, sliced
2 tablespoons vegetable oil
8 cups water
1 teaspoon salt
4 peppercorns
¼ cup chopped parsley
½ cup diced carrots
1 cup diced celery
1 bay leaf
½ cup tomatoes, drained
1 teaspoon dried thyme
1 tablespoon flour
1 tablespoon butter or margarine
¼ cup Madeira

In a 4-quart Dutch oven brown oxtail and onion in hot oil for several minutes. Add water, salt, and peppercorns; simmer uncovered for about 2 hours. Cover and continue to simmer for 3 additional hours. Add the parsley, carrots, celery, bay leaf, tomatoes, and thyme; continue simmering, covered, for 30 minutes longer or until the vegetables are tender.
Strain stock and refrigerate for an hour or more. In a blender purée the edible meat and vegetables and reserve. Remove fat from top of stock and reheat.
In a large, dry frypan brown flour over high heat. Cool slightly. Add the butter or margarine; blend. A little at a time, add the stock and vegetables. Correct the seasoning and add Madeira just before serving.
MAKES 6 SERVINGS.

Fresh tomato soup

GERMANY

6 medium-size tomatoes or about 2 pounds Italian plum tomatoes well washed
1 onion, chopped
1 stalk celery, chopped
2 cups chicken broth
1 tablespoon tomato paste
½ teaspoon dried basil
¼ teaspoon freshly ground pepper
½ teaspoon salt
½ cup yoghurt

Cut tomatoes into wedges and place in 1½-quart saucepan with all ingredients except yoghurt. Simmer uncovered for 30 minutes. Strain to remove tomato skins and seeds. Adjust seasonings. Garnish with spoonfuls of yoghurt.
MAKES 4 TO 6 SERVINGS.

German potato soup

GERMANY

2 medium potatoes
1 medium-size onion
4 stalks celery with green leaves
2 tablespoons vegetable oil
Boiling water
1 small bay leaf
½ teaspoon salt
2 tablespoons butter
2 to 3 cups milk
Chopped parsley for garnish

Peel and thinly slice potatoes, onion, and celery. Sauté for 3 to 5 minutes in hot vegetable oil.

In a large pot, add enough boiling water to cover vegetables. Place bay leaf and salt in pot and boil vegetables until tender. Drain vegetables and reserve liquid.

Mash vegetables into vegetable stock; add butter. Thin soup with milk as desired; heat until warm. (Do not boil.) Ladle into soup bowls and sprinkle with chopped parsley.

MAKES 4 TO 6 SERVINGS.

Potato & cucumber soup

GERMANY

1 medium cucumber
4 medium potatoes, peeled and diced
1 teaspoon salt
2 cups cold water
¼ teaspoon white pepper
1 cup heavy cream
½ cup milk
1 green onion, grated
1 teaspoon dried dillweed (or 1 tablespoon chopped fresh dill)

Peel the cucumber and slice it lengthwise. Scoop out seeds with a spoon and discard. Dice cucumber.

In a heavy 2½-quart saucepan boil potatoes in salted water until the potatoes are very soft. Pour potatoes and cooking liquid into a sieve or food mill set over a large bowl. Force potatoes through. Return to saucepan. Stir in pepper, cream, milk, grated onion and the cucumber.

Simmer gently about 5 minutes or until the cucumber is tender. Add dill and season to taste. Serve hot.

MAKES 4 SERVINGS.

Egg & lemon soup

GREECE

2 10¾-ounce cans condensed chicken broth or 1½ quarts homemade chicken broth
2 soup-cans water
2 teaspoons dried parsley

⅓ cup raw long-grain rice
2 eggs
Juice of 1 fresh lemon

Combine the chicken broth, water, and parsley. Bring to a boil. Add the rice. Cover and cook for 25 minutes.

Meanwhile, beat the eggs well. Slowly add the lemon juice to the eggs while continuing to beat. Slowly pour 1 cup of the hot soup into the egg mixture while beating. Slowly pour the egg and soup mixture back into the soup pot while stirring vigorously. Cook over very low heat for a few minutes, stirring constantly, until slightly thickened. *Do not boil,* as the mixture will curdle.

The chicken-broth mixture can be made in advance and reheated, but do not add the egg and lemon-juice mixture until just before serving. This soup does not reheat well.

MAKES 4 SERVINGS.

Egg & lemon soup w/meatballs

GREECE

1 pound lean ground lamb or beef
¼ cup raw long-grain rice
¼ cup finely chopped onion
2 tablespoons finely chopped parsley
Salt and pepper
2 10½-ounce cans chicken broth or 1½ quarts homemade chicken broth
2 soup-cans water
2 eggs
⅓ cup lemon juice
Parsley for garnish

Combine the beef, rice, onion, parsley, and salt and pepper to taste. Shape into small meatballs, using a rounded teaspoon of the meat mixture for each one.

In a 3-quart saucepan, combine the chicken broth and water and heat to boiling. Add the meatballs, cover, and reduce the heat to simmer. Cook for 20 minutes.

Beat the eggs until thick and lemon-colored. Slowly beat in the lemon juice. Now add 1 cup of the soup broth slowly to the egg and lemon mixture, while continuing to beat. Add the mixture to the soup in the saucepan, and heat through. Garnish with parsley and serve immediately.

MAKES 6 SERVINGS.

Beef meatball soup

GREECE

soup stock

2 tablespoons olive oil	1½ quarts
½ cup chopped onion	homemade beef broth
1 clove garlic, minced	2 soup-cans water
2 10¾-ounce cans	½ cup red wine
condensed beef broth or	3 tablespoons tomato paste

meatballs

1 pound ground beef	½ teaspoon salt
¼ cup raw long-grain rice	¼ teaspoon pepper
1 egg, beaten	2 tablespoons chopped fresh
¾ teaspoon crushed dried mint	parsley for garnish

Heat the oil in a 3-quart saucepan. Add the onion and garlic and cook until limp. Add the beef broth, water, wine, and tomato paste. Bring the broth mixture to a boil slowly while making the meatballs.

Combine all the meatball ingredients, mixing well with your hands. Roll into small meatballs, using a rounded teaspoon of meat mixture for each one.

Drop the meatballs a few at a time into the boiling stock. Cover the saucepan and reduce the heat to low. Cook for 20 to 25 minutes or until the rice in the meatballs is thoroughly cooked. Garnish with the chopped parsley and serve.

MAKES 4 SERVINGS.

Greek lentil soup

GREECE

2 cups lentils
8 cups water
½ cup chopped onion
2 cloves garlic, minced
½ cup chopped carrots
½ cup chopped celery
¼ cup olive oil
1 teaspoon salt
½ teaspoon pepper
3 tablespoons tomato paste
2 bay leaves
½ teaspoon oregano
3 tablespoons wine vinegar

Wash and pick over the lentils. Soak them overnight in 2 cups of water.

In a Dutch oven or soup kettle sauté the onion, garlic, carrot, and celery in olive oil. Add the lentils, 6 cups of water, salt, pepper, tomato paste, bay leaves, and oregano. Bring to a boil and cook for 2½ to 3 hours or until the lentils are soft. Remove the bay leaves.

At this point the mixture may be puréed in the blender until smooth. Thin with water if necessary. Return the mixture to the soup pot and heat. Add the wine vinegar and serve.

MAKES 6 TO 8 SERVINGS.

Chilled cucumber soup

GREECE

¼ cup shelled walnuts
1 large clove garlic, peeled
3 tablespoons olive oil
1 tablespoon white wine vinegar
3 cups yoghurt
⅓ cup cold water
1 cucumber, peeled and chopped
Salt and pepper
Chopped fresh mint or parsley

Combine the walnuts, garlic, oil, and vinegar in a blender container or food processor and spin until smooth. The mixture may also be mashed together with a mortar and pestle.

Combine the yoghurt and water in a mixing bowl and add the walnut mixture. Stir until all the ingredients are well-mixed. Add the cucumber and salt and pepper to taste. Chill for several hours before serving. Garnish with fresh chopped mint or parsley.

MAKES 4 SERVINGS.

Greek tomato-rice soup

GREECE

4 tablespoons butter
½ cup chopped onion
½ cup chopped green pepper
5 fresh medium tomatoes, peeled, seeded, and chopped
½ cup raw rice or orzo
4 cups chicken stock or broth
¾ teaspoon salt
¼ teaspoon pepper
¼ teaspoon summer savory
½ cup finely chopped parsley
Sour cream or plain yoghurt and chopped green onions for garnish

Melt the butter in a large saucepan. Add the onion and green pepper and cook for 5 minutes over medium heat. Add the tomatoes and rice or orzo. Continue to cook for 5 more minutes. Add the chicken stock, salt, pepper, savory, and parsley. Bring to a boil. Reduce the heat to simmer and cook for 20 minutes or until the rice is tender.

Garnish with a dollop of sour cream or plain yoghurt and chopped green onions.

MAKES 4 SERVINGS.

Lamb broth w/vegetables

GREECE

lamb stock

2 to 3 lamb shanks or 2 pounds lamb neck slices
2 tablespoons butter
½ cup chopped onion
2 stalks chopped celery (including the tops)
3 carrots, peeled and sliced

¼ cup chopped parsley
1 tablespoon oregano
1 bay leaf
1 teaspoon salt
½ teaspoon pepper
2 quarts water

soup

½ 3-ounce can tomato paste
3 carrots, peeled and sliced
3 stalks celery, sliced
1 large onion, sliced

2 teaspoons salt
2 vegetable bouillon cubes
⅔ cup orzo or pastina

The day before serving: Brown the lamb shanks or neck slices in the butter in a large Dutch oven or soup kettle. Add the onion and brown. Add 2 stalks of celery, 3 carrots, parsley, oregano, bay leaf, 1 teaspoon salt, and ½ teaspoon pepper.

Add 2 quarts of water and simmer for 2½ hours. Strain the stock into a large bowl or pot and discard the vegetables. Remove the meat from the bones and chop. Refrigerate the meat and stock overnight.

To make the soup: Skim the fat on the surface of the stock.

In a large Dutch oven combine the tomato paste, stock, meat, 3 carrots, 3 stalks celery, 1 onion, 2 teaspoons salt, and bouillon cubes. Bring to a boil. Reduce the heat and simmer for 10 minutes. Add the orzo or pastina and cook 20 minutes longer. Taste, and adjust seasonings. Serve with crusty bread.

MAKES 6 SERVINGS.

Bean soup

HUNGARY

1 cup dried white beans
1 ham hock or ham bone
8 cups water
1 bay leaf
1 carrot, diced
2 stalks celery, sliced
1 clove garlic, mashed
1 tablespoon lard
1 medium onion, peeled, chopped
1 tablespoon flour
1½ teaspoons sweet paprika
½ pound smoked sausage (Debrecziner or Kielbasi are good choices)

Wash beans; pick over, removing foreign matter. Place in small bowl. Cover with water; soak overnight.

Following day place beans, remaining water, and ham bone in Dutch oven. Add 8 cups water and bay leaf. Bring to boil; cover. Reduce heat to low; cook, stirring occasionally, 2½ to 3 hours or until beans are tender. Remove ham hock. Take meat from bone; dice. Return meat to soup. Add carrot, celery, and garlic; cook 30 minutes.

Meanwhile melt lard in small heavy skillet. Add onion, cook until transparent. Add flour; reduce heat to very low. Cook, stirring, until flour is lightly and evenly browned. Remove from heat; stir in paprika. Ladle 1 cup soup into roux; mix well. Add mixture to soup; mix thoroughly. Add sausage; cook, stirring occasionally, until soup thickens. Taste; adjust seasonings if necessary. Pinched noodles (*csipetke*) can be added to this soup if desired.

Garnish soup with spoonful sour cream. Serve with crusty bread and chopped onions.
MAKES 6 SERVINGS.

Caraway soup

HUNGARY

4 tablespoons lard or bacon fat
1 tablespoon caraway seeds
4 tablespoons flour
1½ teaspoons salt
⅛ teaspoon pepper
6 cups water
1 egg, well-beaten

Melt lard in large saucepan. Add caraway seeds and flour; cook, stirring constantly, over low heat until lightly browned. Remove from heat. Add salt, pepper, and water; stir until well-blended. Return to heat; cook, stirring, until thickened.

Add ½ cup soup to egg; beat well. Add to pot; cook, stirring, 4 minutes. Serve soup in individual bowls; garnish with croutons.
MAKES 4 SERVINGS.

Garlic croutons

3 slices firm white bread (rye or black bread can be substituted)
3 tablespoons bacon fat or butter
1 clove garlic, peeled

Trim crusts from bread; cut into ½-inch cubes. Melt butter in small frying pan. Add garlic; sauté until lightly browned. Remove; discard. Add bread cubes; cook, stirring, until golden. Drain on absorbent paper. Set aside; keep warm.

Chicken & vegetable soup w/pinched noodles

HUNGARY

2 tablespoons butter or margarine
2 carrots, peeled, sliced
2 stalks celery, sliced
½ cup chopped green pepper
1 small onion, peeled, chopped
4 cups chicken broth or stock (preferably homemade, see Index)
1½ cups chopped cooked chicken or turkey
1 large tomato, peeled, chopped
Salt and pepper
½ cup frozen peas
½ recipe Pinched Noodles (see Index)

Heat butter in large saucepan. Add carrots, celery, green pepper, and onion; sauté 6 minutes, stirring occasionally. Add chicken broth, chicken, tomato, salt, and pepper; cook 20 minutes. Add peas; stir well. Cook 5 minutes. Add small pieces of noodles; cook 5 minutes, stirring occasionally.
MAKES 4 SERVINGS.

Note: Save carcass from roast chicken; use to make stock for above soup. Add leftover meat to broth.

Variation: Omit pinched noodles; add ¼ cup raw long-grain rice to soup when chicken broth is added.

Cold cherry soup

HUNGARY

1 pound fresh sour cherries
¾ cup sugar
4 cups water
1 cinnamon stick (3 inches long)
2 strips lemon rind
¼ teaspoon salt
½ cup cold water
2 tablespoons cornstarch
½ cup dry red wine
¾ cup sour cream

Wash cherries well. Remove the stems; pit cherries. Place in large saucepan with sugar, 4 cups water, cinnamon, lemon rind, and salt. Bring to boil over moderate heat; cover. Reduce heat to 65 low; cook 10 minutes. Remove cinnamon stick and lemon rind.

Combine cold water and cornstarch; mix well. Add slowly to soup; mix well. Cook, stirring, until slightly thickened. Remove from heat; stir in wine. Place sour cream in small bowl. Add 1 cup hot soup; mix well. Pour mixture into saucepan; mix thoroughly. Place in covered container; chill well. Serve soup in chilled bowls. Garnish with sour cream and sprinkle lightly with cinnamon.

MAKES 6 SERVINGS.

Sauerkraut soup

HUNGARY

This dish is traditionally considered a hangover cure and is served at the end of a New Year's Eve party.

2 tablespoons lard
½ pound lean boneless pork
1 medium onion, chopped
2 teaspoons Hungarian sweet paprika
4 cups water
Salt and pepper
1 16-ounce can sauerkraut
½ pound Polish sausage, sliced
2 tablespoons flour
2 tablespoons water
Sour cream

Heat lard in large saucepan. Add pork; cook over moderate heat until well-browned. Remove with slotted spoon; reserve. Add onion; cook until transparent. Remove from heat; add paprika, stirring well. Add water, salt, pepper, and reserved pork. Cover; bring to boil over moderate heat. Reduce heat to low; cook 1½ hours or until meat is tender. Add sauerkraut and sausage; cook 20 minutes. (Rinse sauerkraut if less-tart soup is desired.)

Combine flour and water; mix well. Add to soup; cook, stirring, until slightly thickened. Serve soup in individual bowls; top with dollop of sour cream.

MAKES 4 TO 5 SERVINGS.

Gulyas soup

HUNGARY

1 pound lean boneless stewing beef	Salt and pepper
2 tablespoons lard	1 16-ounce can tomatoes, broken up
2 medium onions, peeled, chopped	2 medium potatoes, peeled, diced
1 clove garlic, peeled, chopped	2 medium carrots, peeled, sliced
2 teaspoons Hungarian sweet paprika	2 red sweet peppers, cleaned, cut into chunks (green peppers may be substituted all or in part)
Dash of cayenne pepper	
3 cups beef stock or broth	2 tablespoons flour
2 cups water	2 tablespoons water
½ teaspoon caraway seeds	
½ teaspoon crumbled dried marjoram	Sour cream

Wipe beef with damp cloth; cut into 1-inch cubes. Melt lard in Dutch oven. Add beef; brown well on all sides. Remove from pan with slotted spoon; reserve.

Add onions and garlic to pan, cook 4 minutes, stirring occasionally. Add paprika, cayenne, stock, 2 cups water, caraway, majoram, salt, pepper, and reserved meat. Stir well. Bring to boil over moderate heat. Reduce heat to low and cook, covered, 45 minutes. Add tomatoes, potatoes, carrots, and red peppers. Stir well; return to boil. Cover; cook 30 minutes.

Combine flour and 2 tablespoons water; stir to form smooth paste. Add slowly to soup, stirring well. Cook over low heat, stirring until thickened. Serve soup in individual bowls; top with sour cream.

MAKES 4 TO 5 SERVINGS.

Hungarian potato soup

HUNGARY

3 tablespoons bacon fat or lard
1 medium onion, chopped fine
1½ tablespoons flour
1 stalk celery, chopped
1 carrot, peeled, chopped
½ cup minced green pepper
1 pound potatoes, peeled, diced
6 cups water or vegetable stock

Gulyas soup

Broth with liver dumplings

Broth w/liver dumplings

HUNGARY

4 chicken livers
½ small onion
1 tablespoon chicken fat or soft butter
1 egg, beaten
½ teaspoon crumbled dried marjoram
1 tablespoon chopped parsley
Salt and pepper
1 tablespoon flour
Approximately 3 tablespoons dry bread crumbs
5 cups beef or chicken broth

Put chicken livers and onion through food grinder, or chop in food processor. Add fat, egg, and seasonings; mix well. Add flour and bread crumbs; mix. Add enough bread crumbs to form stiff mixture. Refrigerate 1 hour.

Heat broth to boiling in medium saucepan. Form liver mixture into walnut-size dumplings. Drop into boiling soup; do not crowd. Cook 10 minutes or until dumplings float. Remove with slotted spoon; place in warm soup tureen. Continue until all dumplings are cooked. Strain broth over dumplings.

Serve soup garnished with chopped parsley.
MAKES 4 SERVINGS.

1 teaspoon Hungarian paprika
1½ teaspoons salt
Pepper

Heat fat in large saucepan or Dutch oven. Add onion; cook until transparent. Add flour; cook, stirring, until lightly browned. Add remaining ingredients; stir well. Bring to boil; cover. Reduce heat to low; cook 40 minutes or until vegetables are tender.

Pinched Noodles (see Index) or Dumplings (see Index) can be added to soup if desired, or several cut-up frankfurters can be added.
MAKES 4 SERVINGS.

Giblet soup

HUNGARY

½ cup flour	1 small onion, studded with 2 cloves
2½ teaspoons salt	2 celery stalks with leaves, chopped
¼ teaspoon pepper	
½ teaspoon paprika	2 tablespoons butter or margarine
½ teaspoon poultry seasoning	½ cup chopped onion
1 teaspoon parsley flakes	2 carrots, peeled, diced
½ pound chicken gizzards	2 stalks celery, chopped
¼ pound chicken livers	1 cup chopped tomatoes
1 pound chicken necks	Salt and pepper
4 tablespoons bacon drippings	
10 cups water	

Combine flour, ½ teaspoon salt, pepper, paprika, poultry seasoning, and parsley flakes. Wash chicken gizzards, livers, and necks. Dredge chicken parts well in flour mixture.

Balnamoon
skink

Heat bacon fat in Dutch oven. Fry chicken in fat until well-browned. Remove livers; reserve. Add water, onion, 2 stalks celery, and 2 teaspoons salt to pan; bring to boil. Cover; reduce heat to low; cook 1 hour. Add livers; cook 30 minutes. Strain broth. Cool gizzards, livers, and necks. Wash Dutch oven. Return to heat; melt butter. Add onion, carrots, and 2 stalks celery; cook until tender. Add broth, tomatoes, salt, and pepper; bring to boil. Cover; reduce heat to low; cook 30 minutes.

Meanwhile, finely mince gizzards and livers. Pick neck bones; chop meat. Add chopped chicken and giblets to soup; heat through.
MAKES 6 SERVINGS.

Balnamoon skink

IRELAND

2½- to 3-pound chicken
6 cups water
2 teaspoons salt
½ teaspoon pepper
1 celery root
1 leek, sliced
1 large carrot, peeled, sliced
2 tablespoons chopped parsley
1¼ cups frozen peas
¼ teaspoon ground mace
2 egg yolks
½ cup whipping cream
2 cups shredded leaf lettuce or outer leaves of an iceberg lettuce

Wash chicken well inside and out. Combine chicken, water, salt, and pepper in Dutch oven. Cover; bring to boil over moderate heat. Skim any scum from surface. Reduce heat to low; cook 1 hour.

Clean and cube celery root. Add celery root, leek, and carrot to soup; cook 15 minutes. Remove chicken; cool slightly. Skin; remove from bones; dice. Return chicken to soup. Add parsley, peas, and mace; simmer 8 to 10 minutes.

Beat egg yolks and cream together well in small bowl. Add some of soup to cream mixture; beat well. Add slowly to soup, mixing well. Cook over very low heat 3 minutes. Ladle soup into serving bowls; sprinkle each bowl with some lettuce.
MAKES 6 SERVINGS.

Hough soup

IRELAND

A hearty beef and vegetable soup.

stock

3 pounds sliced beef shin	1 cup broken-up canned tomatoes
1 pound beef bones (split marrow bone or neck bone)	1 stalk celery (including some leaves), chopped
1 onion, studded with 4 cloves	¼ cup chopped parsley
1 bay leaf	2 teaspoons salt
½ teaspoon crumbled dried thyme	10 cups water

soup

1 turnip, peeled, diced	¼ cup chopped parsley
1 large onion, thinly sliced	¼ medium cabbage head, shredded
3 large carrots, peeled, sliced	½ cup long-grain rice
2 stalks celery, sliced	
1 16-ounce can tomatoes, broken up	

The day before serving: Place beef shin and bones in shallow roasting pan. Roast in 400°F oven until browned. Place in Dutch oven with remaining stock ingredients. Bring to boil; skim if necessary. Cover with lid ajar; simmer 3 to 4 hours or until meat falls from bones. Remove meat; cool. Strain stock; refrigerate. Remove bones and any fat and gristle from meat; dice. Reserve meat for soup.

The following day: Combine stock, reserved meat, and soup ingredients in large Dutch oven or soup kettle. Bring to boil; cover. Reduce heat to low; cook 40 to 50 minutes, or until vegetables and rice are tender.
MAKES 8 SERVINGS.

Cottage broth

IRELAND

This soup makes a whole meal in itself, served with assorted hot breads, sliced cheese, and a green salad.

stock

2 lamb shanks (about 3 pounds)

7 cups water

1 onion, studded with 4 cloves

2 bay leaves

2 teaspoons salt

4 peppercorns

2 carrots, peeled, chopped

1 stalk celery, chopped

soup

3 tablespoons butter or margarine

2 leeks, cleaned, sliced

1 medium onion, chopped

2 turnips, peeled, diced

3 medium carrots, peeled, sliced

2 stalks celery, chopped

1/4 cup chopped parsley

1 teaspoon crumbled dried thyme

1/4 cup barley, soaked overnight in water to cover

The day before serving: Place lamb shanks in shallow roasting pan; roast at 400°F until well-browned (20 to 30 minutes). Place lamb and remaining stock ingredients in Dutch oven. Bring to boil. Cover; reduce heat to low. Simmer 2½ to 3 hours or until meat is very tender. Remove meat from broth. Strain stock. Discard vegetables. Refrigerate stock overnight. Remove lamb from shanks; dice. Reserve for soup.

The following day: Melt butter or margarine in large Dutch oven. Add vegetables, except parsley; cook over moderate heat, stirring occasionally, until tender.

Remove fat from soup stock; add to vegetables. Add parsley, thyme, barley (drained), and reserved lamb; mix well. Bring soup to boil; cover. Reduce heat to low; cook 1 to 1¼ hours or until barley is tender.

MAKES 8 SERVINGS.

Split-pea soup w/crubeens

IRELAND

2 cups split peas

Cold water

2 pigs' feet, split

½ cup chopped onion

1 cup chopped celery

½ cup chopped carrot

1 medium potato, peeled, chopped

1 bay leaf

1 teaspoon salt

¼ teaspoon crumbled dried thyme

Dash cayenne pepper

2 tablespoons butter

2 tablespoons flour

fried croutons

2 slices thick white bread

2 tablespoons butter or margarine

Rinse peas; pick over. Place in bowl; cover with water. Soak overnight. Drain any remaining liquid from peas; add water to make 10 cups of liquid. Combine peas and liquid in Dutch oven. Rinse pigs' feet under running water; add to peas. Bring to boil. Skim any foam. Reduce heat to low; cook 1½ to 2 hours. Remove pigs' feet. Add vegetables and seasonings; cook 1 hour more. When pigs' feet have cooled, remove skin, gristle, and bones; chop meat. Purée soup in electric blender or pass through sieve. Add chopped meat.

Melt butter in small saucepan. Add flour; cook until bubbly. Add small amount of soup to flour mixture, stirring well. Pour back into soup kettle. Stir well; cook 5 minutes.

Next make croutons (crubeens). Remove crusts from bread; cut into ½-inch cubes. Melt butter in heavy skillet; fry bread cubes over moderate heat until golden. Drain; serve sprinkled on soup.

MAKES 6 TO 8 SERVINGS.

Cream of potato soup

IRELAND

3 tablespoons butter or margarine

1 cup chopped onion

1 cup chopped celery

4 cups peeled, diced potatoes

1 10¾-ounce can chicken broth

1 soup-can water

1 13-ounce can evaporated milk

2 tablespoons flour

Chopped chives or crisp bacon for garnish

Melt butter or margarine in large saucepan. Sauté onion and celery until onion is transparent. Add potatoes, chicken broth, and water. Bring to boil. Reduce heat to low; cook, covered, 40 to 45 minutes or until vegetables are very tender. Purée soup in electric blender until smooth, or force through sieve. Return to saucepan. Add milk, reserving ¼ cup. Simmer 20 minutes.

Combine flour with reserved milk, mixing well. Add to soup; cook, stirring constantly, until soup is thick and creamy. Serve soup hot, garnished with chopped chives or crisp bacon curls.
MAKES 6 TO 8 SERVINGS.

Note: The flour can be omitted if a thinner soup is desired.

Aran scallop soup
IRELAND

This soup is a specialty of the Aran Islands.

fish stock

1½ pounds small fish, cleaned, or fish trimmings (heads, tails, and bones of mild ocean fish, or lobster and shrimp shells)
3 cups cold water
½ cup chopped onion
¼ cup chopped carrot

½ cup chopped celery
½ cup white wine
1 bay leaf
3 peppercorns
Several parsley sprigs
1 cup clam juice

soup

¾ pound fresh scallops
2 slices bacon, diced
2 cups peeled, diced potatoes
½ teaspoon salt
¼ teaspoon white pepper
1 tablespoon chopped parsley
½ teaspoon crumbled dried thyme

2 cups peeled diced tomatoes
1½ cups hot light cream
¾ cup crushed water biscuits or pilot crackers
Pats of butter
Ground mace
Chopped parsley

To make fish stock: Wash fish or trimmings in cold water; drain. Combine water, vegetables, and wine in heavy saucepan. Tie bay leaf, peppercorns, and parsley in small piece of cheesecloth; add seasonings and fish or trimmings to water and vegetables. Bring to boil over moderate heat; cook uncovered 20 to 30 minutes. Strain stock; add clam juice. Reserve.

To prepare soup: Wash scallops in cold water. If large, cut in half or quarter. Drain; reserve. Sauté bacon in large heavy saucepan 3 to 4 minutes or until it starts to brown. Add potatoes; cook until tender. Add salt, pepper, parsley, thyme, tomatoes, and reserved fish stock. Stir well; cook over moderate heat 15 minutes. Add scallops; bring to gentle boil. Cover; reduce heat

to low. Cook 10 to 12 minutes or until scallops are cooked through.

Stir in heated cream. Do not allow mixture to boil after adding cream. Slowly stir in water biscuits, while cooking over low heat, to thicken soup.

Ladle soup into bowls; float a pat of butter on each serving. Garnish with chopped parsley and a sprinkling of mace.
MAKES 4 SERVINGS.

Cock-a-leekie soup
IRELAND

This soup was served frequently in medieval times, when it was customarily garnished with prunes stuffed with hazelnuts.

½ cup pearl barley
1 2- to 3-pound chicken
1 veal knuckle (approximately ¾ pound)
2 quarts water
2 teaspoons salt
1 bay leaf
6 peppercorns
3 sprigs parsley
6 leeks (approximately 1 pound)

Cover barley with cold water; soak 12 hours. Rinse chicken inside and out; pat dry. Combine chicken, veal knuckle, 2 quarts water, and salt in large pot. Tie bay leaf, peppercorns, and parsley in piece of cheesecloth; add to soup kettle. Drain barley; add to other ingredients. Bring to boil over high heat; skim foam from soup. Reduce heat to moderate; cook 1½ hours.
Meanwhile, clean and slice leeks; add to soup. Remove chicken; cool. Remove veal knuckle; discard. Cook soup 30 minutes more. When chicken is cool enough to handle, skin it; remove meat from bones. Cut into 1-inch pieces; return to soup. Remove and discard cheesecloth bag of seasonings. Taste soup; add salt and pepper if necessary.
MAKES 4 TO 6 SERVINGS.

Dublin clam soup

IRELAND

Traditionally this soup would be made with cockles or mussels, which can be substituted for clams if available.

3 dozen clams
1 cup water
1 medium onion, chopped
1 bay leaf
2 tablespoons chopped parsley
3 tablespoons sweet butter
3 tablespoons flour
2 cups milk
1/2 cup heavy cream
1 egg yolk
1/4 teaspoon nutmeg
Salt and white pepper to taste
Chopped parsley

Scrub clams well; wash in cold running water to remove sand. Discard any clams with open or damaged shells.

Combine the water, onion, bay leaf, and parsley in large saucepan. Add clams; cover; bring to boil. Reduce heat to low; cook 5 to 10 minutes or until shells open. Remove clams from shells; reserve. If desired, discard only top shells, then place clams in soup bowl with bottom shell intact. Strain broth; reserve.

Melt butter in heavy saucepan. Add flour; cook until bubbly. Add milk; cook, stirring constantly, until thick. Add clam broth; heat through.

Beat cream and egg yolks together; add some of hot soup to mixture. Beat well; add to saucepan. Cook over low heat, stirring constantly, 3 minutes. Add nutmeg and salt and pepper to taste. Stir in clams. Heat 1 to 2 minutes. Serve immediately.

MAKES 4 TO 6 SERVINGS.

Split pea soup

ITALY

2 cups split peas
Water
1 large onion, finely chopped (about 1 1/2 cups)
1 clove garlic, peeled and minced
1 ounce salt pork, chopped
3 tablespoons olive oil
1 1/2 cups tomato sauce
1 teaspoon sugar
Salt and pepper
1 bay leaf
1 cup uncooked small shell macaroni
Grated Romano cheese

Pick over the split peas and rinse well. Place in a small bowl and cover with water. Soak overnight.

In a large saucepan, sauté the onion, garlic and salt pork in the olive oil until the onion is tender. Add the soaked peas, water to cover the peas, the tomato sauce, sugar, salt and pepper and bay leaf.

Simmer, covered, over low heat 1 1/2 to 2 hours or until the peas are tender. Remove the bay leaf and add the macaroni and additional water if the soup is too thick. Cover and simmer for 20 minutes. Serve hot, sprinkled with the grated Romano cheese.

MAKES 4 TO 5 SERVINGS.

Italian tomato-rice soup

ITALY

2 tablespoons butter
1/2 cup chopped onion
1/2 cup chopped celery
1 28-ounce can peeled tomatoes
1 1/2 cups chicken broth
1/2 teaspoon dried marjoram, crumbled
1/2 teaspoon dried sweet basil, crumbled
2 teaspoons sugar
Salt and pepper
1/3 cup long-grain rice
Grated Parmesan cheese

Melt the butter in a large saucepan. Sauté the onion and celery until limp. Combine the tomatoes, chicken broth, onions, celery, and butter in a blender jar or food processor and spin until smooth. Pour back into the saucepan. Add the marjoram, sweet basil, sugar, and salt and pepper to taste.

Bring the mixture to a boil over moderate heat. Add the rice, stir well and cover. Reduce the heat to low, and simmer 15 to 20 minutes or until the rice is tender. Serve garnished with Parmesan cheese.

MAKES 4 SERVINGS.

Pavian soup

ITALY

4 slices white bread
3 tablespoons melted butter
5 cups chicken stock or 2 13-ounce cans regular strength chicken broth
4 eggs
6 tablespoons shredded Parmesan cheese

Trim the crusts from the bread. Brush on both sides with the melted butter and place on a cookie sheet. Bake at 350°F for 30 minutes, or until golden.

Pour the stock into a large shallow saucepan and heat to boiling. Reduce the heat to low, then break the eggs one at a time into a saucer and slide into the liquid. Poach lightly. Remove with a slotted spoon and keep warm. Strain the stock, return to the pan and heat to boiling. Put one toasted bread slice in each soup bowl. Top with 1 poached egg. Ladle the soup over the egg. Sprinkle each bowl with 1½ tablespoons of cheese and serve.

MAKES 4 SERVINGS.

Green soup w/meatballs

ITALY

½ pound fresh spinach or beet greens
½ cup water
¼ teaspoon salt

soup
¾ pound lean ground beef
½ cup dry bread crumbs

¼ cup grated Parmesan cheese
1 egg, well beaten
½ cup parsley, finely chopped
Salt
White pepper
4 cups beef broth (homemade or canned)

Remove the stems from the spinach and rinse well. In a medium saucepan, heat the water and salt. Add the spinach, reduce the heat to low and cook for 3 minutes. Drain well and coarsely chop.

In a bowl combine the ground beef, bread crumbs, Parmesan cheese, egg, parsley, salt, and pepper. Mix well and form into walnut-sized meatballs. In a large saucepan, heat the beef broth to boiling. Add the spinach and meatballs and bring to a boil again. Reduce the heat to low, cover and simmer 15 minutes and serve.

MAKES 4 SERVINGS.

Clam soup

ITALY

2 dozen cherrystone clams in shells
3 tablespoons olive oil
2 cloves garlic, peeled, minced
4 cups peeled ripe tomatoes, coarsely chopped
¼ cup white wine
4 tablespoons chopped Italian flat-leaf parsley

Scrub clams well under cold running water. Soak 30 minutes in cold water to cover. Heat oil in large saucepan. Add garlic; sauté 1 minute. Add tomatoes and wine; bring to boil. Reduce heat to low; simmer 15 minutes. Keep warm.

In large frying pan or Dutch oven with close-fitting lid, bring 1 cup water to boil. Drain clams well; place in pan. Cover; steam 5 to 10 minutes, until clams open. (Discard any clams that will not open.)

Place clams in shells in warm soup bowls. Strain clam broth through cheesecloth; add to tomato sauce. Mix well; pour over clams in bowls. Sprinkle with parsley; serve with garlic toast.

MAKES 4 SERVINGS.

Pavian soup

Neopolitan minestrone

ITALY

1½ pounds beef shanks
1 onion, quartered
1 package soup greens (or 2 celery stalks, 1 carrot, 1
* potato, 1 turnip, and a sprig of parsley, all cleaned and*
* chopped)*
1 small bay leaf
2 whole peppercorns
1 clove
1½ teaspoons salt
6 cups water
1 celery root (celeriac)
¼ pound ham
2 ounces penne or elbow macaroni
3 tablespoons tomato paste
1 teaspoon dry chervil
4 tablespoons grated Parmesan cheese

In a large Dutch oven, combine the beef shanks, onion, soup greens, bay leaf, peppercorns, clove, and salt. Add the water and bring to a boil. Skim any foam. Reduce the heat to low and simmer covered 1½ to 2 hours. Remove the meat and cool. Strain the broth and skim the fat. Return the broth to the pot. Clean the celery root and cut into thin sticks. Dice the meat from the beef shanks and cut the ham into thin strips.

Boil the macaroni until tender in boiling salted water and drain. Bring the broth to a boil. Combine the tomato paste with 1 cup of the broth and stir until dissolved. Add to the broth in the pot along with the celery root, diced beef and the ham. Cover and cook 15 minutes. Add the macaroni and chervil and heat through. Sprinkle with the Parmesan cheese and serve.

MAKES 6 SERVINGS.

Neopolitan minestrone

Fish stew

Fish stew

ITALY

5 tablespoons olive oil
1 clove garlic, minced
1 pound (4 medium) potatoes, peeled, diced
1 pound firm-fleshed whitefish (flounder, cod, or snapper), cut into chunks
4 cups fish stock or 2 bottles (8 oz.) clam broth plus 2 cups water
1 (16-ounce) can Italian-style tomatoes, puréed or sieved
½ cup white wine
½ teaspoon crushed fennel seed
1 bay leaf
1 teaspoon salt
⅛ teaspoon crushed red pepper
Freshly gound black pepper
3 tablespoons chopped parsley

Heat oil in Dutch oven. Add garlic; sauté until well-browned; discard. Add potatoes; cook, stirring constantly, until lightly browned. Add fish, stock, tomatoes, wine, and seasonings. Bring to boil; reduce heat to low. Simmer 20 to 25 minutes, until fish and potatoes are tender.
Ladle into soup bowls; sprinkle with parsley. Serve with garlic toast.
MAKES 4 SERVINGS.

Butterball soup

ITALY

1½ tablespoons butter
1 egg yolk
3 tablespoons flour
1 tablespoon grated Parmesan cheese
⅛ teaspoon salt
White pepper
Dash of nutmeg
1 egg white, stiffly beaten
4½ cups clear beef broth

Thoroughly cream butter and egg yolk in small bowl. Add flour, cheese, and seasonings; mix well. Fold in egg white.
Bring broth to boil in large saucepan. Reduce heat to moderate; drop dough by teaspoons into boiling broth. Cover pan; simmer 10 minutes. Ladle into soup bowls. Garnish if desired with chopped parsley, or add cooked julienne-cut carrots and celery.
MAKES 4 SERVINGS.

Broth w/beaten egg

ITALY

4 cups clear broth (homemade or canned)
2 eggs
2 tablespoons freshly grated Parmesan cheese
1 tablespoon minced parsley
Freshly grated Parmesan cheese

Bring broth to boil in medium saucepan. Beat eggs, cheese, and parsley together. Add mixture to boiling broth, beating constantly with wire whisk. Cook, while beating, 1 minute. Serve immediately, garnished with additional grated cheese.
MAKES 4 SERVINGS.

Venetian minestrone

ITALY

1½ pounds, lean round steak
3 tablespoons olive oil
1 large onion, peeled, sliced
1 clove garlic, minced
6 cups beef stock or broth
4 tomatoes, peeled, chopped
1 teaspoon crumbled dried oregano
½ teaspoon crumbled dried thyme
1 teaspoon salt
½ teaspoon pepper
½ cup long-grain white rice
½ pound savoy cabbage, shredded
3 tablespoons chopped fresh parsley
Grated Parmesan cheese

Thinly slice round steak across grain.
Heat olive oil in Dutch oven. Add onion and garlic; sauté until tender. Remove with slotted spoon; reserve. Add round steak; brown well. Add beef broth, tomatoes, seasonings, onion, and garlic; bring to boil. Reduce heat to low; cover. Cook 1 hour, until meat is very tender. Add rice; simmer 20 minutes. Add cabbage; simmer 15 minutes. Add parsley; ladle into soup bowls. Sprinkle with Parmesan.
MAKES 4 TO 5 SERVINGS.

Quick minestrone

ITALY

soup

6 cups trimmed cut-up assorted fresh vegetables selected
  from the following list: broccoli, cauliflower, green beans,
  swiss chard, spinach, peas, and celery
6 tablespoons butter or margarine

Venetian minestrone

Roman-style vegetable soup

2 tablespoons olive oil
6 cups beef stock or canned beef broth
Salt and pepper

garnish

3 tablespoons olive oil
1 clove garlic, peeled
2 cups diced stale Italian bread
Grated Parmesan cheese

In a large kettle or Dutch oven, sauté the vegetables in the butter and olive oil until they begin to soften. Add the beef stock or broth and salt and pepper to taste. Cook over high heat for 20 minutes or until the vegetables are tender.

Meanwhile, prepare the garnish. Heat the oil in a small skillet with the garlic clove until the garlic is browned. Discard. Sauté the bread in the oil over moderate heat until golden. Serve the soup garnished with the bread cubes. Pass the Parmesan cheese.

MAKES 5 TO 6 SERVINGS.

Roman-style vegetable soup

ITALY

½ cup finely chopped salt pork
1 large onion, peeled, diced
1 clove garlic
3 carrots, peeled, diced
2 stalks celery, sliced
1 parsnip, peeled, diced
½ bunch parsley, chopped
2 large chopped tomatoes
1 quart beef broth
1 (16-ounce) can red kidney beans, drained
1 teaspoon crumbled sweet basil
Salt and pepper
1½ cups uncooked wide egg noodles
Grated Parmesan cheese

Render salt pork in large pan over moderate heat. Add onion and garlic; cook until tender. Add carrots, celery, parsnip, parsley, and tomatoes. Stir well; add beef broth, kidney beans, basil, salt, and pepper. Bring to boil; reduce heat

to low. Cover; cook 1 hour. Add noodles; simmer 15 minutes, until noodles are tender. Serve sprinkled with Parmesan cheese.
MAKES 4 GENEROUS SERVINGS.

Stuffed stewed chicken

This makes a beautiful 2-course dinner in a pot.

stuffing

2 tablespoons butter	1 egg
1 chicken liver	¼ cup dry bread crumbs
½ cup chopped onion	2 tablespoons grated
1 cup ground ham	Parmesan cheese
½ cup chopped fresh parsley	¼ teaspoon ground nutmeg
½ pound hamburger	Salt and pepper

soup

1 3-pound chicken	1 turnip, peeled and diced
8 cups water	1 bay leaf
2 carrots, peeled and sliced	½ teaspoon thyme
2 celery stalks, sliced	Salt and pepper
1 onion, sliced	Paprika
½ cup chopped fresh parsley	

First prepare the stuffing. Melt the butter in a small skillet and sauté the chicken liver and onion until the onion is lightly browned and the liver is cooked through. Add the onion and pan drippings to the remainder of the stuffing ingredients in a mixing bowl. Chop the chicken liver finely and add to the stuffing. Mix well.

Wash the chicken well and pat dry. Pack the stuffing into the chicken cavity and truss the openings shut. Tie the legs together and tie or pin the wings next to the body. Place the chicken in a large deep kettle (a Dutch oven will do). Add the water, vegetables and seasonings and bring to a boil. Reduce the heat to low, skim any foam from the surface of the water. Cover and simmer 2 hours or until the chicken is well done.

Remove the chicken from the pan and keep warm. Skim the fat from the broth. Add cooked noodles or rice if you wish and serve as a first course. Then, carve the chicken and serve the chicken and stuffing accompanied by rice or potatoes and the vegetables of your choice as the main course.
MAKES 4 SERVINGS.

Chicken broth w/filled pasta (cappelleti)

pasta
1 recipe Egg Noodles (see Index)

filling
¾ cup ricotta cheese
¼ cup grated Parmesan cheese
2 tablespoons chopped parsley
Salt and white pepper, to taste

soup
3 10¾-ounce cans condensed chicken broth
3 soup-cans water or
  8 cups homemade chicken stock

First make the pasta according to the recipe. Cover with plastic wrap and let stand 30 minutes. Meanwhile make the filling. In a small mixing bowl, thoroughly mix the ricotta and Parmesan cheese, parsley, and salt and pepper to taste.

On a lightly floured surface, roll the dough ¼ at a time, until paper thin, keeping the remainder of the dough tightly covered. If using a pasta machine, roll to slightly less than 1/16th of an inch. Cut into 2-inch rounds with a floured biscuit cutter. Reroll the scraps. To fill, top each round with ¼ teaspoon of the filling. Dampen the edge of the circle with a little water and fold into a half-moon shape. Place the filled pasta on a plate or tray and cover until all are completed. Will make 90 to 100 filled pasta if rolled by machine.

For the soup, combine the chicken broth and water in a large saucepan and bring to a boil over moderate heat. Add the filled pasta and cook for 5 to 10 minutes or until tender. Ladle into soup bowls and serve with grated cheese.

Cappelletti can be made in advance and frozen (uncooked) in a single layer on a cookie sheet. Transfer to a freezer bag and keep frozen until ready to cook. Frozen pasta will require slightly longer to cook.
MAKES 8 SERVINGS.

Note: To adjust this recipe for more or fewer servings, allow 1 cup of broth per person and 10 to 12 capelletti.

Sicilian sausage soup

ITALY

¼ pound sweet Italian sausage (with the casing removed)
½ cup finely chopped onion
¼ cup chopped peeled carrots
¼ cup chopped celery
2 tablespoons chopped parsley
1 16-ounce can Italian-style peeled tomatoes, broken up
* with a fork*
1 13¾-ounce can regular strength chicken broth or 1 pint
* homemade chicken broth*
½ teaspoon dried sweet basil, crumbled
¼ cup orzo (rice-shaped macaroni for soup, also called
* "soupettes")*
Salt and pepper

In a medium skillet, brown the sausage, breaking it up in small pieces as it cooks. Remove from the skillet with a slotted spoon and place in a large saucepan. Sauté the onion in the sausage drippings until tender. Remove the onion with a slotted spoon and add to the sausage. Add the vegetables, chicken broth, and sweet basil to the sausage mixture.

Bring the soup to a boil and stir well. Cook over moderate heat for 15 minutes. Stir in the orzo and salt and pepper to taste. Reduce the heat to low and simmer covered for 20 minutes or until the orzo is tender.

MAKES 4 SERVINGS.

Soup w/meatballs

ITALY

2 (10¾ ounce) cans condensed beef broth or 1½ quarts
* beef broth*
2 soup cans water
2 tablespoons tomato paste
1 teaspoon crumbled sweet basil
¼ cup raw long-grain rice
2 cups washed, coarsely shredded fresh spinach leaves

meatballs
½ pound lean ground beef
¼ pound ground pork or milk sausage
¼ cup fine dry bread crumbs
1 egg, lightly beaten
¼ cup finely chopped onion
Salt and pepper

Combine beef broth and water in large saucepan; bring to boil. Dissolve tomato paste in broth; add basil. Cover; keep hot.

In mixing bowl combine meats, bread crumbs, egg, onion, and seasonings; mix well. Form into meatballs; use 1 scant tablespoon meat mixture for each.

Drop meatballs one by one into boiling broth. Cover; cook 10 minutes. Add rice; stir gently. Cover; cook 20 minutes. Add spinach; cook 5 minutes. Garnish with chopped parsley, if desired. Serve with crust bread.

MAKES 4 SERVINGS.

Note: Swiss chard can be substituted for spinach if desired.

Chilled apricot soup

POLAND

A quick fruit soup for an impromptu dinner party.

2 No. 2½ cans apricot halves
1 cup sour cream

Chill apricot halves thoroughly. Drain. Blend drained apricot halves in blender. Add sour cream; continue to blend until well-mixed. Serve chilled.

MAKES 4 SERVINGS.

Sour-cream peach soup

POLAND

2 No. 303 cans peaches, sliced
1¾ cups peach juice and cold water
1 tablespoon cornstarch
1 teaspoon lemon juice
⅔ cup sour cream
½ teaspoon cinnamon (if desired)

Drain peaches; reserve liquid. Purée peaches. Set aside. Measure drained peach liquid. Add enough cold water to equal 1¾ cups liquid. Thicken ¼ cup peach juice and water with cornstarch. Add thickened juice to remaining liquid; heat until thickened, about 10 minutes.

Stir in lemon juice. Add puréed peaches and sour cream; blend well. Serve immediately. If desired, garnish with cinnamon before serving.
MAKES 4 SERVINGS.

Almond soup

SPAIN

A food processor or blender makes this soup simple to prepare.

1½ cups almonds
1 clove garlic
2 cups water
1 cup white wine
2 tablespoons olive oil
½ teaspoon salt
White grapes
4 red-rose petals

Blanch almonds by dropping them into boiling water about 5 minutes or until outer shells come off easily.
Place almonds and garlic in food processor or blender; process until a meal develops. With machine running, gradually add water, wine, oil, and salt. Process until soup develops smooth consistency; chill. Ladle soup into bowls; garnish with grapes and rose petals.
MAKES 4 SERVINGS.

Bean & sausage soup

SPAIN

By chilling the soup overnight, the flavors have a chance to blend.

1 pound dried white navy beans
1 pound chorizo or other garlic sausage
1 pound Italian or other smoked ham, diced
1 ham bone
1 pound potatoes, diced
½ cup diced carrots
1 cup sliced leeks
4 cups chopped cabbage
1 clove garlic, pressed
1 bay leaf and 2 peppercorns tied together in cheesecloth
1 teaspoon salt
1½ quarts beef stock

Cover beans with water; soak overnight. Drain. Combine beans with remaining ingredients in large pot; bring to boil.
Reduce heat; simmer 4 to 6 hours or until beans and vegetables are tender. Remove sausage; skin and dice. Return to soup. Chill overnight. Reheat soup to serve.
MAKES 20 SERVINGS.

Garlic soup

SPAIN

In the traditional soup, only olive oil is used. However, the butter gives the soup a slightly milder taste.

⅓ cup olive oil
¼ cup butter
8 garlic cloves, peeled
½ teaspoon paprika
Dash of cayenne
1 teaspoon salt
¼ teaspoon pepper
3 cups bread cubes
6 cups boiling water

Heat oil and butter in deep cast-iron skillet until butter melts. Add garlic; sauté until golden brown. Remove garlic; mash. Reserve. Stir in spices. Add bread cubes. Fry until golden brown. Remove; save.
Add water to oil. Using a little water, form a paste with garlic. Add to soup; bring to boil. Reduce heat; simmer 30 minutes. Ladle soup into serving bowls. Serve with bread cubes.
MAKES 8 SERVINGS.

Variation: Just prior to serving, beat 4 eggs. Slowly add to soup. Cook just long enough to set eggs.

Hominy soup

SPAIN

1 leftover ham bone
1 stewing chicken, cut up
2 onions, chopped
2 garlic cloves, chopped fine

2¾ quarts water
1 tablespoon salt
3 peppercorns
2 bay leaves
1 pound leftover ham, cubed
1 29-ounce can white hominy

Combine ham bone, chicken, onions, garlic, water, and spices in soup kettle; bring to boil. Reduce heat; simmer 2 hours. Add ham and hominy with its liquid; cook 1 hour. Remove ham bone, chicken, peppercorns, and bay leaves from soup with slotted spoon.

Remove meat from bones; re-add to soup. Refrigerate overnight to blend flavors. To serve, remove soup from refrigerator. Skim fat; reheat.
MAKES 8 TO 10 SERVINGS.

Gazpacho
SPAIN

The traditional Spanish soup.

8 tomatoes, peeled, seeded, chopped fine
1 cucumber, peeled, seeded, chopped fine
1 cup finely chopped onions
1 sweet green pepper, seeded, finely chopped
3 teaspoons salt
1 teaspoon garlic juice
¼ cup olive oil
¼ cup lemon juice
¼ teaspoon pepper
Dash of cayenne
2 cups tomato juice

Combine tomatoes, cucumber, onions, and green pepper; mix well. Sprinkle with salt. Let set at room temperature 1 hour to blend flavors. Add remaining ingredients; mix well. Chill thoroughly.

Put ice cube in each serving glass. Fill with soup mixture. Serve with Fried Garlic Croutons (see Index).
MAKES 6 TO 8 SERVINGS.

Quick gazpacho
SPAIN

1 large cucumber
1 teaspoon salt

1 quart tomato juice
2 teaspoons onion juice
Dash of hot sauce
½ teaspoon Worcestershire sauce
⅛ teaspoon white pepper
1 teaspoon sugar
1 tablespoon chopped fresh parsley
Juice of 1 lemon
Fried Garlic Croutons (see Index)

Peel and dice cucumber. Sprinkle with ½ teaspoon salt. Squeeze with your hands. Cover; let set 20 minutes. Drain. Combine cucumbers with remaining ingredients, except croutons. Mix thoroughly; chill thoroughly. To serve, ladle into chilled soup cups; garnish with croutons.
MAKES 4 SERVINGS.

Cold buttermilk soup
DENMARK

3 egg yolks
½ cup sugar
1 teaspoon lemon juice
½ teaspoon grated lemon rind
1 teaspoon vanilla
1 quart buttermilk

Beat the egg yolks lightly in a large bowl, gradually adding the sugar. Add the lemon juice, rind, and vanilla. Slowly add the buttermilk, continuing to beat (either with an electric beater on slow or with a wire whisk) until the soup is smooth. Serve the soup in chilled soup bowls.
MAKES 6 TO 8 SERVINGS.

Apple soup
DENMARK

1½ pounds tart apples
2½ quarts water
½ lemon, sliced thin
1 piece of stick cinnamon
4 tablespoons cornstarch
Sugar to taste
¼ cup wine (optional)

Wash, quarter, and core the apples. Do not peel them. Cook the apples until soft in 1 quart of water with the lemon and cinnamon stick. Put the apples through a coarse sieve. With the rest of the water, put the strained mixture into a pot and bring it to a boil.

Mix the cornstarch with ¼ cup of water and add it to the pot, stirring constantly. Add the sugar and wine. Serve the soup hot.

MAKES 8 SERVINGS.

Beer & bread soup

DENMARK

1 small loaf dark rye bread
3 cups water
3 cups dark beer or ale
½ cup sugar
1 whole lemon (both juice and grated rind)
Light or whipped cream for garnish

Break the bread in small pieces into a mixing bowl. Mix the water and beer and pour this over the bread. Allow it to stand for several hours.

When ready to serve, cook the mixture over a low flame, stirring occasionally, just long enough for it to thicken. (If the mixture is too thick, strain it through a coarse sieve.) Bring it to a boil and add the sugar, lemon juice, and lemon rind. Serve the soup with a spoonful of light or whipped cream on top.

MAKES 6 TO 8 SERVINGS.

Pea soup w/ham

DENMARK

3 medium onions
3 whole cloves
1 pound yellow peas
4 cups water
1 pound slice of ham
1 teaspoon marjoram
1 teaspoon thyme
Parsley for garnish

Dice 2 of the onions. Peel the third onion, but leave it whole. Stick cloves into the whole onion.

Put the diced onions, whole onion, peas, and water into a pot. Cook them for 20 minutes; add

Gazpacho

the ham. Add the marjoram and thyme and let it cook for at least 1½ hours. Remove the cloved onion and the ham. Cut the ham into thick slices. Season the soup with salt to taste. When ready to serve, place a slice of ham on top of each serving of soup; garnish with parsley.

MAKES 4 TO 6 SERVINGS.

Crab soup

DENMARK

1 bunch soup greens
2 tablespoons butter
1 onion, diced
½ pound perch fillets
1 quart water
½ pound frozen Greenland crab (thawed)
½ cup white wine
1 teaspoon salt
½ teaspoon white pepper
1 teaspoon curry
½ teaspoon herbs
1 bunch parsley

Clean, wash, and chop the greens very fine. Sauté them lightly in hot butter with the diced onion. Chop the fish fillets and add them and the water to the soup pot. Allow to simmer for 15 minutes.

83

Fish soup

Remove the fish pieces from the liquid mixture with a slotted spoon. Put the soup mixture through a sieve and pour the strained liquid with the fish back into the pot. Put in the fish pieces and add the crab meat. Pour in the white wine and add the salt, pepper, curry, and the herb mixture. Bring this to a boil but do not cook it. Serve the soup at once with parsley sprinkled on top.

MAKES 4 TO 6 SERVINGS.

Fish soup

DENMARK

1 pound fish fillets
2 tablespoons lemon juice
2 tablespoons aquavit
Chives
4 onions, peeled
1 leek
2 carrots
4 to 5 medium potatoes
3 slices bacon
4 cups beef broth or meat stock
Pinch of saffron
½ teaspoon basil
1 bay leaf
Salt and pepper to taste
Parsley for garnish

Drain the fish fillets and cut them into 1-inch pieces. Put them into a deep dish. Add the lemon juice and aquavit, and cover.

Finely chop the chives and peeled onions. Cut the leek in half and then into pieces. Peel and dice the carrots and potatoes.

Dice the bacon and put it into a pot, cooking it until it is just transparent. Add the onions and chives and cook for 3 minutes more. Let this mixture steam. Add the leek, carrots, and potatoes; steam for 1 minute more. Pour in the meat stock and add the saffron, basil, and bay leaf. Cover and cook for 15 minutes. Then add the fish mixture with its liquid and simmer slowly for 5 minutes more. Season the soup with the salt and pepper. Serve the soup in bowls or in a tureen. Garnish with parsley.

MAKES 4 TO 6 SERVINGS.

Carrot soup

FINLAND

4 or 5 large fresh carrots or 2 cups canned carrots with
    liquid
2 tablespoons butter
2 tablespoons flour
2 quarts milk
1 teaspoon salt
Sugar to taste
Parsley

Wash and scrape the carrots if you are using
fresh ones. Cook them in lightly salted water until they are soft. Mash the carrots with their
stock. (If using canned carrots, simply mash the
carrots as they come from the can, reserving the
stock for use in the soup.)

Melt the butter in a large saucepan. Add the
flour, stirring with a wooden spoon until
blended. Gradually add the milk (heat it first or
let it come to room temperature). Allow this to
simmer for 10 minutes, stirring occasionally.
Add the carrots and the stock, salt, sugar to
taste, and parsley. Serve the soup piping hot.
MAKES 6 TO 8 SERVINGS.

Beet soup

FINLAND

2 large raw beets
2 tablespoons butter
1 tablespoon flour
4 cups meat broth

Pea soup with ham

2 teaspoons sugar
1 tablespoon vinegar
½ teaspoon salt
1 small raw beet
Sour cream for garnish (optional)

Wash the 2 large beets and cook them in salted water until tender. Drain, peel, and cube them. In a 2-quart pot melt the butter, add the flour, and stir until very smooth. Add the hot meat broth. Stir the mixture until it comes to a boil. Add the sugar, cubed beets, vinegar, and salt. Cook the mixture over low heat for about 2 hours. Grate the small beet. Sprinkle it into the soup before serving. Top with a spoonful of whipped sour cream if desired.
MAKES 6 SERVINGS.

Finnish vegetable soup

FINLAND

1½ cups diced raw carrots
1 cup fresh green peas
1 cup cauliflower florets

½ cup diced new potatoes
½ cup fresh green beans, cut small
8 halves small red radishes
2 cups finely chopped fresh spinach
2 teaspoons salt
2 tablespoons butter
2 tablespoons flour
1 cup milk
1 egg yolk
¼ cup heavy cream
½ pound cooked, cleaned medium shrimps (optional)
Parsley or dill for garnish

Prepare the fresh vegetables as indicated in the list of ingredients. Put all vegetables except the spinach in a 3-quart pot. Cover them with cold water and add the salt. Boil them uncovered for 5 minutes or until the vegetables are tender. Add the spinach and cook for another 5 minutes. Remove the pan from the heat. Strain the liquid stock and put the stock and the vegetables into separate bowls.

Melt the butter in the soup pot over moderate heat. Remove it from the heat and stir in the flour. Slowly add the vegetable stock, then add the milk. Beat well with a wire whisk. Combine the egg yolk and cream in a small bowl. Gradually add 1 cup of the hot soup. Still using the whisk, add the mixture back into the soup. Bring it to a simmer. Add the vegetables and cooked shrimps; simmer uncovered for 3 to 5 minutes more. Add seasonings if necessary, such as more salt and pepper.

Pour the soup into a soup tureen or serve in individual bowls, garnishing each portion with the chopped parsley or dill.
MAKES 6 TO 8 SERVINGS.

Leek soup

FINLAND

3 whole potatoes
6 leeks
5 cups beef broth
Salt and white pepper to taste
2 egg yolks
6 tablespoons cream
Parsley for garnish

Leek soup

Peel and dice the potatoes. Clean, wash, and cut the leeks into thick strips.

Simmer the meat stock, and add the diced potatoes to it, and cook it for 15 minutes. Add the leeks. Simmer 5 more minutes, taking care that the leeks remain firm. Salt and pepper to taste. Remove 1 cup of the broth. To this add the egg yolks and cream. Slowly add this mixture to the soup. Heat, but do not cook any longer. Serve the soup in soup bowls with parsley garnish.
MAKES 6 SERVINGS.

Orange soup

ICELAND

1 tablespoon cornstarch
4 cups water
1½ cups orange juice
¼ cup sugar
Whipped cream for garnish
Thin orange slice for garnish

Mix the cornstarch in ¼ cup cold water. Bring the rest of the water to a boil. Add the cornstarch mixture to the boiling water to thicken slightly. Add the orange juice and sugar.

Serve either hot or cold, garnished with a spoonful of whipped cream and a thin orange slice. For a pudding, rather than a soup, add 4 tablespoons of cornstarch to thicken.
MAKES 6 SERVINGS.

Spinach soup

NORWAY

2 pounds fresh spinach or 2 packages frozen chopped
*   spinach*
2 quarts chicken stock
3 tablespoons butter
2 tablespoons flour
1 teaspoon salt
Dash of freshly ground pepper
⅛ teaspoon nutmeg
Hard-cooked egg for garnish (optional)

Thoroughly wash the spinach, then drain it. Chop it coarsely. If frozen spinach is used, thaw it completely and drain it. Bring the soup stock to a boil in a 4-quart pot and add the spinach. Simmer it uncovered for about 8 minutes. Strain the spinach from the stock into separate bowls. Press the spinach with a spoon to remove most of the liquid. If desired, chop the cooked spinach even finer.

Melt the butter in the soup pot, then remove it from heat. Stir in the flour, being careful to avoid lumps. Add the liquid stock, 1 cup at a time, stirring constantly. Return it to the heat and bring it to a boil. Add the spinach, salt, pepper, and nutmeg. The soup will thicken slightly. Simmer it for about 5 minutes more. Serve the soup, garnishing each serving with a few slices of hard-cooked egg, if desired.
MAKES 4 TO 6 SERVINGS.

Beef & cabbage soup

NORWAY

½ pound diced beef
½ cup shredded cabbage
2 quarts beef broth or water
4 small potatoes, diced
1 carrot, diced
1 parsnip, diced
1 stalk celery, sliced
1 leek, sliced
Salt and pepper to taste

Add the beef and shredded cabbage to the liquid bouillon. Cook this for 1 hour. Add all the vegetables to the soup and cook it until the vegetables are tender. Season with salt and pepper; serve.
MAKES 6 OR MORE SERVINGS.

Cauliflower soup

NORWAY

1 medium head cauliflower
1 teaspoon salt
6 cups water
2 tablespoons butter
2 tablespoons cornmeal
1 cube beef bouillon
1 egg, beaten well

1 cup cream
Parsley for garnish (optional)

Wash the cauliflower and break it into pieces. Cook it in salted water for about 10 to 15 minutes, until it is tender. Drain off the water into another pot.

Add the butter, cornmeal, and bouillon cube to the cauliflower water. Boil this for 3 minutes. Remove from heat. Add the egg and cream very gradually, stirring constantly. Last, put in the cauliflower pieces. Bring the soup to a boil but do not boil it. Serve the soup with or without parsley garnish.

MAKES 6 OR MORE SERVINGS.

Cold potato soup

NORWAY

4 potatoes
1 medium onion
2 cups milk
2 cups all-purpose (or whipping) cream
1/2 teaspoon salt
Dash of pepper, freshly ground
2 tablespoons butter
2 cups sour cream
1 teaspoon chopped chives

Cook the potatoes and onion together until well-done. Drain and mash them thoroughly. Slowly bring the milk and sweet cream to the boiling point. Add the mashed potatoes, onion, salt, pepper, and butter. Allow them to simmer for no longer than 5 minutes. Chill them thoroughly. When ready to serve, beat the mixture thoroughly with the sour cream. Serve the soup in individual cups, sprinkling the top of each with some chives.

MAKES 8 SERVINGS.

Fruit soup

NORWAY

This soup may be served for dessert, as a first course, or even for breakfast.

1/2 pound pitted prunes
1 1/2 cups currants
1 1/2 cups raisins

2 1/2 cups fresh apples
1/3 cup cooked rice
3 tablespoons tapioca
1/2 cup sugar
2 tablespoons lemon juice

Cover the fruit with cold water and bring it to a boil. Allow it to simmer until the fruit is soft but not mushy. Add the cooked rice to the fruit. Add the tapioca; cook until the mixture is clear. Add the sugar; cook for 2 minutes more. Set aside to cool.

When the mixture is thoroughly cooled, add the lemon juice.

MAKES 8 SERVINGS.

Note: If tapioca is not available, substitute 4 teaspoons of arrowroot dissolved in 4 tablespoons of cold water and cook just until thickened.

Blueberry soup

NORWAY

This soup is delicious served either hot or cold.

1 quart fresh blueberries, washed and drained
2 1/4 quarts cold water
1/2 cup sugar
Generous slice of lemon rind
4 tablespoons cornstarch

Place the blueberries, 2 quarts of the cold water, the sugar, and the lemon rind in a 3-quart pot. Cook this over low heat only until the fruit is soft. Stir in the cornstarch mixed with the remaining 1/4 cup of cold water. The mixture will thicken slightly.

MAKES 6 OR MORE SERVINGS.

Hot potato soup

NORWAY

3 tablespoons butter
3 leeks
4 large potatoes
3/4 cup water
1 quart milk
Salt and pepper to taste
Paprika

Melt the butter in a 2-quart pot. Wash and chop the leeks and sauté them in the butter. Peel and slice the potatoes and add them to the leeks. Add the water; cover. Cook until both potatoes and leeks are soft enough to put through a sieve. After the mixture has been put through the sieve, add hot milk to it, stirring constantly. Season with salt and pepper. Serve the soup with a dash of paprika on top of each portion.
MAKES 6 SERVINGS.

Norwegian yoghurt soup
NORWAY

1 cup yoghurt
½ cup sour cream
Salt
1 bunch dill or 1 tablespoon chopped dill
2 teaspoons brandy
½ pound crab meat
White pepper

Combine the yoghurt, sour cream, and salt to taste; beat them until foamy. Reserve several sticks of fresh dill for garnish; chop the rest. Add it to the liquid. Add the brandy and crab meat. Let the mixture sit in the refrigerator for at least 30 minutes, until chilled well. Season to taste and garnish with dill sticks. Serve the soup cold.
MAKES 6 SERVINGS.

Middle Eastern almond soup
MIDDLE EAST

2 tablespoons butter
1 small onion, chopped (about ½ cup)
2 tablespoons flour
1 quart boiling chicken stock
½ cup ground almonds
½ cup heavy cream
Salt and pepper to taste

Melt butter, add onions, and cook until onions are transparent. Stir in the flour. Continuing to stir, add the boiling soup stock. Simmer for 5 minutes. Stir in almonds and simmer for another 20 minutes. Last, add cream and allow all to

heat through. Season to taste and serve piping hot.
MAKES 4 TO 5 SERVINGS.

Lemon-curry chicken soup
MIDDLE EAST

Lemon is a popular flavoring in the Middle East and always available. This variation of chicken soup shows how much a lemon can improve an already good soup.

6 tablespoons rice
8 cups chicken stock
4 eggs
4 tablespoons lemon juice
½ teaspoon curry powder
1 tablespoon parsley

Bring rice and soup stock to a boil and then simmer for 20 minutes or until rice is tender. In a bowl, beat eggs, lemon juice, and curry. When well-blended, stir in 3 tablespoons of hot stock until that is also well-blended. Add the egg mixture to soup and stir for 5 minutes more. Ladle soup into serving bowls, sprinkle with parsley, and serve.
MAKES 4 TO 6 SERVINGS.

Lamb & egg soup
MIDDLE EAST

1½ pounds lamb or mutton
2 quartered onions
2 cleaned and diced carrots
2 teaspoons salt
½ teaspoon cayenne pepper
4 cups water
4 tablespoons butter or margarine
4 tablespoons flour
4 egg yolks
3 tablespoons lemon juice
4 tablespoons butter
1 teaspoon ground paprika

Remove bones from the meat and then place bones and meat in a heavy soup pot. Add onions, carrots, salt, and cayenne pepper with 4 or more cups water to cover all. Cook for at least 1

89

hour or until meat is tender. Add extra liquid as needed. When meat is fork-tender, strain off the liquid and reserve.

Mince the meat until fine or put through a meat chopper or food processor and then return it to the liquid on a low flame on the stove. Mix ½ cup of the liquid with the flour to form a paste. Slowly add this thickening to the soup, stirring all the while.

Beat the egg yolks with the lemon juice until frothy. This is best done with a whisk or a fork. Gradually add the egg mixture to the soup. Remove from heat and stir until well-blended.

Place 1 teaspoon of butter in each soup plate. Pour the soup on top of the butter. Sprinkle paprika into each dish and serve at once. This soup is popular in Turkey as a dish served at weddings but it makes a party anytime you serve it.
MAKES 4 TO 6 SERVINGS.

Turkish tomato soup
MIDDLE EAST

1½ cups unflavored yoghurt
1½ tablespoons olive oil
¼ cup lemon juice
1½ teaspoons curry powder
Pinch of thyme, optional
4½ cups tomato juice
Salt to taste
Chopped chives for garnish (optional)

Beat the yoghurt in a bowl until very smooth. Add olive oil, lemon juice, curry, and thyme. When well-mixed, gradually add the tomato juice. Season with salt, cover, and chill. When ready to serve, dish into individual bowls and garnish with chives.
MAKES 4 TO 6 SERVINGS.

Cold yoghurt & cucumber soup
MIDDLE EAST

Since it is not always possible to have fresh mint and fresh dill, this recipe calls for dried. If you are using the fresh leaves, double the amount called for here.

1 medium-size cucumber
2 cups yoghurt
2 teaspoons white vinegar
1 teaspoon olive oil
1 teaspoon dried mint
¼ teaspoon dried dill weed
1 teaspoon salt
Fresh mint leaves for garnish
Cucumber slices for garnish

Peel cucumber and slice in half lengthwise. Remove the seeds and discard. Coarsely chop or grate the cucumber.

Place yoghurt in a bowl and stir until it is very smooth. Add the remaining ingredients, continuing to blend well with your spoon. Be gentle as you mix the ingredients. Add extra salt if desired and refrigerate the soup for at least two hours. Serve in chilled soup bowls. Garnish with fresh mint leaves, if available and cucumber slices.
MAKES 2 TO 3 SERVINGS.

Yoghurt & noodle soup
MIDDLE EAST

3 cups unflavored yoghurt
1 beaten egg
3 cups chicken or beef broth
1 cup ¼-inch noodles broken into small pieces
1 teaspoon salt
3 tablespoons butter
1 medium onion, finely chopped
1 tablespoon crushed dried mint

In a saucepan, mix yoghurt and egg. Then bring almost to a boil, stirring constantly in one direction (to prevent curdling). Stir in broth, noodles, and salt. Bring to a boil, reduce heat, and simmer for 10 minutes or until the noodles are tender.

While the soup simmers, melt butter in a small pan. Add onions and sauté until lightly browned. Stir in the mint. Add this mixture to the cooked soup, stir, and serve hot.
MAKES 4 TO 6 SERVINGS.

Turkish tomato soup

Yoghurt soup

Cold yoghurt and cucumber soup

Middle Eastern yoghurt soup

MIDDLE EAST

1 cup cooked barley
3 tablespoons butter
1 cup finely chopped onion
2 pints plain yoghurt
1 egg
1 tablespoon flour
4 cups chicken broth
4 tablespoons butter
1 cup chopped fresh coriander (parsley or mint may be
    substituted)
Salt and pepper to taste
Chopped chives for garnish

Cook barley until tender and set aside. In a skillet, melt butter and brown onions lightly. Set aside.

Place yoghurt in a large soup pot over a very low flame. Gradually stir in the egg and the flour. Add the chicken broth, 1 cup at a time, stirring, until mixture comes to a boil. Add the reserved barley and onions and allow to simmer.

When ready to serve, sauté the coriander in butter and add to soup along with seasonings to taste. Stir well and ladle into soup bowls piping hot. Garnish with chives.

MAKES 6 TO 8 SERVINGS.

Yoghurt & rice soup

MIDDLE EAST

This soup only takes about 25 minutes to make, which means a good hot start to a meal for almost any cold night.

¼ cup uncooked rice
5 cups chicken or beef stock
1 tablespoon cornstarch
2 cups unflavored yoghurt
2 beaten egg yolks
2 tablespoons fresh, chopped mint
2 tablespoons melted butter

Place rice and stock in saucepan and cook for 20 minutes. In a small pan, make a paste of cornstarch mixed with 2 or 3 tablespoons yoghurt. When smooth, gradually add remaining yoghurt, then egg yolks with a few spoonfuls of hot stock, stirring constantly.

When the mixture has just come to a boil, add it to the simmering rice and cook for 2 more minutes. (If the soup is too thick, add a little water to make desired consistency.) Dish into serving bowls, sprinkle with mint and melted butter.
MAKES 4 TO 6 SERVINGS.

Matzo balls for soup

MIDDLE EAST

1 cup matzo meal
½ cup chicken stock
¼ teaspoon ground ginger
2 beaten eggs
4 tablespoons oil or melted chicken fat

Matzo balls for soup

Four hours before planning to serve, mix the ingredients together and refrigerate. This is to allow all moisture to be absorbed into the balls. Measure out 1 tablespoon of the mixture and roll into a ball, using wet hands for the rolling. Continue rolling balls the size you prefer and put on a plate until all are done. Drop the finished balls into the soup about 30 minutes before dinner is ready.

MAKES 4 TO 6 SERVINGS.

Watercress soup

MIDDLE EAST

4 medium-size potatoes, washed but not peeled
Water to cover
2 medium-size onions, chopped
3 tablespoons butter
2 bunches watercress, chopped
1 teaspoon salt
¼ teaspoon black pepper
1 cup milk
¾ cup yoghurt
Croutons for garnish

Soup with vegetables and meat dumplings

Cover potatoes with water and boil in the jackets until done. Reserve 2 cups of the potato water. Peel and dice the potatoes.

Fry onions in melted butter in a large saucepan until lightly browned, about 5 minutes. Add the potatoes, potato water, watercress, salt, and pepper. Cover and allow to simmer for 5 minutes. Just before serving, add milk and yoghurt and heat but do not boil. Ladle into soup dishes and garnish with croutons.

MAKES 4 TO 6 SERVINGS.

Cold fruit soup

MIDDLE EAST

1 cup pitted sour red cherries
1 cup sliced peaches
1 cup pitted plums
1 cup grated green apple
1 cup sugar
6 cups water
1 teaspoon lemon juice
1 stick cinnamon
4 whole cloves
¼ teaspoon salt
1½ tablespoons cornstarch
3 tablespoons water
1 cup light cream
3 tablespoons Sabra* or lemon juice
Sour cream

Combine and cook the first ten ingredients for 20 minutes. Be sure the fruit is tender. Discard cinnamon stick and cloves. Force the mixture through a coarse sieve or a food mill.

Dissolve the cornstarch in water and return fruit to pan. Stir in the cornstarch mixture until fruit is slightly thickened. Last, add cream and Sabra or lemon juice. Chill thoroughly and add more Sabra/lemon juice if needed to taste. Serve in chilled glass dishes topped with a generous spoonful of sour cream.

MAKES 6 SERVINGS.

*Sabra is a liqueur which comes from Israel but lemon juice is a good substitute.

Chilled melon soup

MIDDLE EAST

1 large cantaloupe
1½ pints half-and-half cream
1 small chicken breast, boiled, boned and finely minced
2 tablespoons sugar
¼ teaspoon salt
¼ teaspoon cinnamon
3 tablespoons cornstarch
1 cup Mandorcrema (Almond wine)
Yoghurt for garnish

Prepare melon by halving, removing seeds, and chopping the meat fairly fine. Combine melon meat in a saucepan with 1 pint cream, chicken meat, sugar, salt, and cinnamon. After mixture has come to a boil, simmer for 10 minutes. Then allow to cool and purée to a fine texture.

Dissolve cornstarch in remaining cream and add to the purée. Cook on a low flame until mixture is slightly thickened. Add wine and extra milk, if needed. Chill thoroughly and serve topped with a generous spoonful of yoghurt.

MAKES 4 TO 6 SERVINGS.

If Mandorcrema is not available, use Amaretto liqueur and reduce sugar to 1 tablespoon.

Middle Eastern lentil soup

MIDDLE EAST

1 tablespoon fresh coriander leaves (parsley or mint can substitute)
½ teaspoon salt
1 tablespoon cumin
6 cloves garlic
1 tablespoon oil
2 cups lentils (soaked overnight in cold water)
Boiling water to cover
4 cups chicken stock
¼ teaspoon black pepper
Pinch of cayenne pepper
1 tablespoon flour mixed with enough water to make a paste
2 sliced scallions
1 tablespoon chopped parsley

Crush coriander, salt, cumin, and garlic and sauté in hot oil. Add lentils and cover with boiling water. Cook until water evaporates and add

more boiling water as needed until lentils soften. Drain lentils. Put them in the soup pot with chicken stock. Season with black and cayenne peppers. Add the flour mixture and stir soup until it thickens. Add scallions to soup and serve. Sprinkle each soup bowl with parsley.

MAKES 4 TO 6 SERVINGS.

Orange & lemon soup

MIDDLE EAST

This soup peps up those who eat it because of the spicy flavor. It's a cook's favorite as well, since it can be put together in a matter of minutes.

1 large onion, finely chopped
2 tablespoons margarine or butter
2 cups tomato juice
1 chicken bouillon cube
2 cups orange juice
1 cup lemon juice
1 thinly sliced lime for garnish

In a large pan, sauté the onion in margarine. Add tomato juice and bouillon cube. Bring to a boil, stirring constantly until cube has completely dissolved. Add the remaining fruit juices and simmer for just 3 minutes. Serve at once, garnished with thin slices of lime.

MAKES 4 SERVINGS.

Mint soup

MIDDLE EAST

1 tablespoon olive oil
1 clove garlic, crushed
½ cup fresh mint leaves or 2 tablespoons dried mint
2 tablespoons cornstarch
½ cup cold water
4 cups chicken broth
Salt and pepper to taste
Dash of cayenne
3 beaten egg yolks

Heat the oil and sauté garlic and mint on a low heat for 8 to 10 minutes. Mash this through a fine sieve. Dissolve the cornstarch in water.

Put chicken soup stock in large saucepan and bring to a boil. Add the sieved mixture, corn-starch dissolved in water, and seasonings and cook for five minutes, allowing soup to thicken slightly. Add the egg yolks and stir until well-blended. Serve in individual soup bowls.
MAKES 4 SERVINGS.

Soup w/vegetables & meat dumplings

CHINA

meat dumplings

2 slices bread	White pepper
½ pound lean ground beef	5 cups beef bouillon
Salt	

soup

¼ head savoy cabbage (green cabbage can be substituted), sliced	1 small onion, chopped
	½ cup frozen peas
1 leek, sliced	4 ounces egg noodles
2 ounces fresh mushrooms, sliced	Salt
	White pepper
1 celery stalk, sliced	1 tablespoon soy sauce
1 tablespoon oil	3 tablespoons sherry

Soak bread in small amount of cold water. Squeeze as dry as possible and mix with ground beef and salt and pepper to taste. Bring bouillon to a boil. Using 1 teaspoon of meat mixture at a time, form little dumplings and drop into boiling broth. Reduce heat and simmer for 10 minutes. For soup, slice cabbage, leek, mushrooms, and celery. Heat oil in a large saucepan. Add onion and cook until golden. Add sliced vegetables and cook for 5 minutes. Remove dumplings from beef broth with a slotted spoon, drain on paper toweling, and keep warm. Strain broth and add to vegetables. Add peas and noodles and simmer for 15 minutes. Return dumplings to soup. Season with salt, pepper, soy sauce and sherry. Serve immediately.
MAKES 4 TO 6 SERVINGS.

Egg drop soup

CHINA

4 cups chicken broth, homemade or canned
1 tablespoon cornstarch
¼ cup cold water
1 tablespoon soy sauce
Pinch of grated fresh gingerroot, or a sprinkle of powdered ginger
Few sprinkles freshly ground pepper
2 eggs, slightly beaten
1 tablespoon fresh parsley, coarsely chopped
garnish
A few cooked pea pods, or a small amount chopped scallions

Bring chicken broth to a boil. Dissolve corn-starch in water, stir into broth and bring to a boil again. Add soy sauce, ginger, and pepper. Holding eggs above soup, slowly pour into soup in a slow steady stream while whisking eggs into soup to form long threads.
Turn off heat, add parsley, and garnish soup with pea pods or chopped scallions. If desired, warm chow mein noodles can be served with this soup.
MAKES 4 SERVINGS.

Sharks'-fin soup

CHINA

¾ pound dried sharks' fins (available in Chinese groceries)
1 tablespoon oil
2 tablespoons fresh gingerroot, sliced
¼ cup scallions, sliced
1 tablespoon sherry
3 quarts chicken broth, divided
2 tablespoons cornstarch
1 teaspoon soy sauce
¼ cup water
½ pound crab meat

Wash sharks' fins and cover with cold water. Drain, cover with fresh water and boil 3 hours. Drain, add fresh water and boil again for 3 hours. Drain and let dry.
Heat oil in large saucepan. Sauté the ginger and scallions for 3 minutes. Add the sherry, 1 quart of the chicken broth and the sharks' fins. Cook over medium-high heat 15 minutes. Drain off

any remaining liquid. Add the remaining broth; bring to a boil. Mix together the cornstarch, soy sauce, and water. Slowly stir into the soup. Stir in the crab meat. Heat through.
MAKES APPROXIMATELY 8 SERVINGS.

Crab soup

CHINA

2 tablespoons oil
½ pound crab meat
¼ teaspoon salt
2 medium tomatoes, chopped coarsely
1½ teaspoons fresh gingerroot, chopped
5 cups chicken broth
2 eggs, beaten
1½ tablespoons vinegar
1½ tablespoons sherry
1½ tablespoons soy sauce
3 scallions, sliced

In large pot heat oil. Sauté crab meat, salt, tomatoes, and ginger for 5 minutes. Add chicken broth and cook over low heat 10 minutes. Beat eggs, and add vinegar, sherry, and soy sauce. Pour into the soup slowly. Stir in the scallions and let soup simmer for about 3 minutes.
MAKES 4 TO 6 SERVINGS.

Oriental clam soup

CHINA

2 cups chicken broth
2 cups clam juice
2 cups minced clams
1 small onion, minced
2 tablespoons fresh parsley, minced
2 tablespoons soy sauce
1 tablespoon sherry

In large saucepan combine chicken broth and clam juice. Add clams and onion and bring to a boil. Simmer for 10 minutes. Add parsley, soy sauce, and sherry and heat through.
MAKES 5 TO 6 SERVINGS.

Chicken vegetable soup

CHINA

6 cups chicken broth
½ cup bean sprouts
¼ cup water chestnuts, thinly sliced
1 scallion, minced
½ cup bok choy, sliced (use leafy part also)
3 Chinese mushrooms, soaked and drained and sliced
½ cup snow pea pods
½ cup cooked, diced chicken
2 teaspoons soy sauce
1 tablespoon sherry
Pepper to taste

Bring chicken broth to boil in soup pot. Add vegetables and chicken and simmer about 1 minute. Add soy sauce and sherry. Add pepper to taste. If desired, cellophane noodles or very fine egg noodles may be added.
MAKES 4 TO 6 SERVINGS.

Egg-flower soup

CHINA

4 cups chicken broth
½ medium onion, chopped
½ cup celery, sliced
Pinch of salt
1 egg, beaten
½ cup chopped spinach

Place chicken broth in pot and bring to boil. Add onion, celery, and salt. Bring to boil again. Stir in beaten egg. Add spinach and let simmer for 1 minute.
MAKES 4 SERVINGS.

Black-mushroom soup

CHINA

¼ cup dried black mushrooms
1 clove garlic, crushed
1 tablespoon sesame oil
8 cups rich chicken broth
1 piece of gingerroot, size of hazelnut
2½ tablespoons soy sauce
½ cup finely diced cooked chicken

½ *cup finely diced cooked ham*
½ *cup diced bamboo shoots*
½ *cup finely chopped scallions*

Soak mushrooms in warm water until soft and spongy, about 10 minutes. Squeeze out liquid and chop very fine. Crush garlic and sauté in oil for 2 or 3 seconds, remove from oil and set aside. Sauté the mushrooms in the same pan for about 5 minutes.

In soup kettle bring chicken broth to boil. Add mushrooms, garlic, ginger, and soy sauce. Cover and simmer about 4 hours. Strain the broth and add chicken, ham, bamboo shoots, and scallions. Simmer just to heat through the added ingredients.
MAKES 8 SERVINGS.

Won ton soup

CHINA

dough for won ton squares
4 ounces flour
Salt
1 tablespoon milk
2 tablespoons oil
1 small egg
filling
4 ounces fresh spinach, chopped
4 ounces ground pork
½ *tablespoon soy sauce*
⅛ *teaspoon powdered ginger*
soup
5 cups chicken broth
2 tablespoons chopped chives

In bowl, stir together flour and salt. Add milk, oil, and egg. Knead dough until it is smooth. On a floured board roll out dough until it is paper thin. Cut into 3-inch squares. Cover with a kitchen towel while you prepare filling.
Thoroughly wash spinach; remove coarse stems. Place in bowl and barely cover with boiling water; let stand for 3 minutes. Drain well and coarsely chop. Add ground pork, soy sauce, and ginger. Blend thoroughly. Place 1 teaspoon of filling on each dough square, giving filling a lengthy shape. Fold over dough from one side

and roll up jelly-roll fashion. Press ends of roll together to seal.
Bring chicken broth to a boil. Add won tons and simmer over low heat for 20 minutes. Spoon soup into bowls. Garnish with chopped chives.
MAKES 6 SERVINGS.
Note: Won ton squares can be puchased in most markets.

Celery soup

CHINA

1 heaping tablespoon dried Chinese mushrooms
½ *pound pork shoulder*
2 small onions, minced
1 clove garlic, minced
2 small celeriac roots (celery stalks may be substituted)
4 tablespoons oil
3 cups hot chicken broth
1 ounce transparent noodles
2 tablespoons soy sauce
⅛ *teaspoon powdered ginger*

Soak Chinese mushrooms in cold water for 30 minutes. Cut pork into 1½-inch long, ½-inch-thick strips. Mince onions and garlic. Cut off celery tops and set aside. Brush celeriac roots under running cold water, peel and cut into ½-inch cubes.
Heat oil in saucepan. Add pork and brown on all sides while stirring constantly for about 3 minutes. Add onions, garlic and celeriac root and cook for 5 minutes more. Drain mushrooms and cut in halves or quarter if very large, and also add to saucepan. Pour in chicken broth, cover and simmer over low heat for 25 minutes.
Meanwhile, in another saucepan, bring salted water to a boil, add noodles, remove from heat immediately and let stand for 5 minutes. Drain noodles. Five minutes before end of cooking time of soup, add coarsely chopped celery leaves. Season to taste with soy sauce and ginger. Place noodles in soup tureen or 4 individual Chinese soup bowls, pour soup over noodles and serve.
MAKES 4 SERVINGS.

Celery soup

Chinese chicken soup

CHINA

1 fowl, about 4 to 5 pounds
2½ quarts water
2 small slices gingerroot
4 scallions
Salt to taste
1 tablespoon sherry (more if desired)

Combine chicken and water in pot; bring to boil. Add remaining ingredients. Cover; simmer over low heat about 3 hours or until chicken is tender. Remove chicken from soup; cut meat into small pieces. Strain soup; add chicken meat.
MAKES ABOUT 8 SERVINGS.

Noodle soup

CHINA

2 tablespoons dried Chinese mushrooms
½ pound boneless pork
2 tablespoons sherry
2 tablespoons soy sauce
Salt to taste
White pepper to taste
Pinch of ground ginger
1 quart salted water
½ pound transparent noodles
5 ounces bamboo shoots
2 quarts chicken broth
3 tablespoons vegetable oil
1 small can chicken meat, cut into 1-inch squares
5 ounces ham steak, cut into 1-inch squares
½ cup chopped watercress

Soak mushrooms 30 minutes; drain well. Set aside. Cut pork into 3-inch strips ⅛ inch thick. Combine sherry, soy sauce, salt, pepper, and ginger in bowl. Add pork. Let stand, covered, 1 hour.
Bring salted water to boil. Add noodles; cook 10 minutes. Drain well; set aside. Slice mushrooms and bamboo shoots. Add mushrooms, bamboo shoots, and noodles to chicken broth; simmer 2 minutes.
Remove pork from soy-sauce mixture; pat dry. Sauté pork in oil 2 minutes; remove. Add chicken, pork, and ham to broth. Add watercress. Spoon broth into individual soup bowls.
MAKES 6 SERVINGS.

Wonton soup

Homemade chicken broth

CHINA

Many Chinese recipes call for chicken broth. Canned broth is perfectly acceptable, but it is nice to use homemade broth at times. This can also be frozen.

1 stewing chicken, about 4 pounds
4 quarts water

Clean the chicken; remove excess yellow fat. Bring water to boil in large pot. Place chicken in pot; cover. Let come to boil again; reduce heat to simmer. Cook chicken 3 to 4 hours, occasionally skimming off fat. Remove from heat; let broth cool.

Discard skin and bones. Save meat for use in recipes. Store broth in covered glass jar in refrigerator. It will keep approximately 3 weeks if once a week it is brought to boil, cooled, and refrigerated again. If you prefer clear broth, strain before storing.

Mushroom soup w/"sizzling" rice

CHINA

2 cans (approximately 10½ ounces) chicken broth
¼ pound lean pork, finely diced
2 garlic cloves, minced fine
1 tablespoon soy sauce
½ cup sliced fresh mushrooms
¼ cup sliced water chestnuts
¼ cup tiny frozen green peas
"Sizzling" rice (see Index)

Pour broth into saucepan. Add pork, garlic, and soy sauce; simmer 15 minutes. Add mushrooms, water chestnuts, and peas; simmer 2 minutes. Turn into warm heatproof pitcher or bowl. Keep warm in 250°F oven.

Place half of rice into preheated serving bowl. Divide rest of rice among individual soup bowls; pour soup over. Serve rest of rice as accompaniment.

MAKES 4 OR 5 SERVINGS.

Easy egg-drop soup

CHINA

2 10½-oz. cans fat-free chicken broth
1 can water
2 tablespoons cornstarch
4 tablespoons cold water
2 eggs, beaten slightly
2 tablespoons chopped scallions

Heat chicken broth and water, covered, until boiling. Blend cornstarch with water. Slowly add to soup; turn off heat. Add eggs by pouring slowly into soup, stirring constantly. Divide scallions into 4 individual soup bowls; add soup.

MAKES 4 SERVINGS.

Chicken velvet soup

CHINA

1 chicken breast, cooked
1 teaspoon salt
2 egg whites, beaten until stiff peaks form
3 cups chicken broth
1 small can cream-style corn
1 tablespoon cornstarch
2 tablespoons cold water
1 teaspoon sherry
2 tablespoons minced beef, cooked

Remove chicken meat from bones; mince. Mix with salt. Fold into egg whites.

Bring broth to boil. Add corn, cornstarch mixed with cold water, and sherry. Cook 2 minutes over low heat. Stir in chicken mixture. Bring to boil; remove from heat. Garnish each bowl with beef.

MAKES 6 SERVINGS.

Mandarin soup

CHINA

1 tablespoon oil
½ pound pork, trimmed of fat, sliced into thin strips
1 cup chopped celery
½ cup diced carrots
1 cup sliced fresh mushrooms
6 cups chicken broth, homemade or canned
¾ cup finely chopped spinach

1 egg, beaten
2 tablespoons cornstarch
¼ cup cold water

Heat oil in pot. Sauté pork 10 minutes. Add celery, carrots, and mushrooms; sauté 5 minutes. Stir in chicken broth and spinach; bring to boil. Add egg, stirring constantly.
Mix together cornstarch and water. Stir into soup; stir until soup is thickened.
MAKES 6 SERVINGS.

Cabbage & bean-thread soup

CHINA

2 ounces pork, thinly sliced into small pieces
1¼ teaspoons soy sauce
1 teaspoon cornstarch
½ ounce transparent (cellophane) noodles
2 tablespoons oil
1 teaspoon salt
3 cups water
¼ cup thinly sliced Chinese cabbage
½ cup thinly sliced cucumber
1 tablespoon chopped green onion
¼ teaspoon freshly ground black pepper
½ teaspoon sesame-seed oil

Mix pork with 1 teaspoon soy sauce and cornstarch. Place noodles in bowl with enough hot water to cover. Let stand 5 minutes.
Sauté pork in oil over moderate heat until tender; remove. Add salt to water; bring to boil. Add noodles, pork, cabbage, and cucumber. Mix together onion, pepper, sesame oil, and ¼ teaspoon soy sauce. Add to soup; mix well. Heat through.
MAKES 6 SERVINGS.

Cabbage & ham soup

CHINA

½ pound sliced ham, rind removed, boned, cut into ½-inch cubes
6 cups cold water
1 teaspoon salt
1 Chinese cabbage, leaves separated, washed

Place ham and bone into deep pot. Add water. Sprinkle in salt. Cover; bring to boil over high heat. Turn heat to simmer; cook about 25 minutes.
Place leaf stalks of cabbage together; slice crosswise into thin slices. Add to ham mixture. Heat to boiling; simmer 10 minutes. Serve immediately.
MAKES 6 SERVINGS.

Hot-and-sour soup

CHINA

¼ cup cloud ears
¼ cup golden needles
¼ cup ground pork, shredded into 1½-inch-long strips
3 tablespoons cornstarch
2 teaspoons sherry
½ cup water
3 tablespoons white-wine vinegar (or to taste)
White pepper to taste
½ teaspoon hot oil
2 teaspoons sesame-seed oil
4 cups chicken stock
Salt to taste
1 tablespoon soy sauce
2 bean curds, each cut into 8 pieces
1 egg, beaten
2 scallions, chopped

Soak cloud ears and golden needles in hot water about 15 minutes or until noticeably increased in size; drain. Shred cloud ears. Cut golden needles in half.
Combine pork with 1 tablespoon cornstarch and sherry. Mix 2 tablespoons cornstarch with water; set aside. Combine vinegar, pepper, hot oil, and sesame oil in bowl; set aside.
Bring chicken stock, salt, and soy sauce to boil in large soup pot. Add pork; boil 1 minute. Add cloud ears, golden needles, and bean curds; boil 1 minute. Add cornstarch mixture; stir until thickened. Lower heat. Add vinegar mixture. Taste; adjust seasoning if necessary. Slowly stir in egg. Garnish with scallions.
MAKES 5 OR 6 SERVINGS.
Note: Cloud ears and golden needles are available in Chinese specialty stores.

Japanese meatball soup

JAPAN

½ pound ground beef or pork
2 eggs
1 tablespoon flour
2 teaspoons freshly grated ginger or 1 teaspoon ground
  ginger
5 cups beef or chicken stock
1 teaspoon soy sauce
Pinch of salt
3 carrots, parboiled and sliced ¼ inch thick
Very thin spaghetti, enough for 4 small servings, cooked and
  drained
4 sprigs of parsley

Mix together beef or pork, eggs, flour, and ginger. Set aside. Mix the stock with the soy sauce and salt. Bring to a boil. Add the carrots.

Make very small meatballs from the meat mixture, drop gently into the boiling soup, and boil gently for about 15 minutes.

Divide the spaghetti into 4 individual bowls; add the soup and meatballs. Garnish with parsley.
MAKES 4 SERVINGS.

Japanese vegetable soup

JAPAN

2 ounces dried mushrooms
Cold water
½ pound lean pork
1 carrot
4 ounces canned bamboo shoots
2 celery stalks
4 cups hot beef broth
4 ounces fresh spinach
3 tablespoons rice wine or sherry
1 tablespoon soy sauce
⅛ teaspoon ground ginger
3 drops Tabasco sauce

Soak mushrooms in a generous amount of cold water for 30 minutes, covering the bowl. Cut pork into very thin strips. Cut the carrot and bamboo shoots into matchstick-size pieces. Cut the celery into thin slices. Drain the mushrooms; cut them into halves or quarters, depending on size.

Bring beef broth to a boil. Add pork, mushrooms, and other vegetables. Cook over low heat for 10 minutes. Meanwhile, thoroughly wash the spinach; chop it coarsely.

Remove soup from heat, add spinach, and let stand for 3 minutes. Season soup with rice wine (or sherry), soy sauce, ginger, and Tabasco sauce. Return it to heat; heat through, but do not boil again. Serve soup in preheated soup bowls or cups.
MAKES 4 SERVINGS.

Chicken & vegetable balls

JAPAN

12 ounces leftover cooked chicken, chopped
2 bamboo shoots, cut into very thin strips
4 mushrooms, chopped
2 small carrots, chopped fine
1 egg, beaten
1 teaspoon soy sauce
1 teaspoon sugar
3 cups chicken stock
4 tablespoons soy sauce
1 tablespoon sugar

Combine chicken, bamboo shoots, mushrooms, carrots, egg, 1 teaspoon soy sauce, and 1 teaspoon sugar. Form into balls after mixing very well.

Drop meatballs into the boiling chicken stock to which 4 tablespoons soy sauce and 1 tablespoon sugar have been added. Simmer about 8 minutes. Serve meatballs hot or cold. The chicken-stock mixture is also served hot poured into individual bowls.
MAKES 2 TO 3 SERVINGS.

Fondue-pot Japanese-style chicken soup

JAPAN

½ uncooked boned chicken breast
8 fresh mushrooms
4 cups hot chicken broth
1 cup cooked rice
4 strips lemon peel

Cut chicken meat into thin slices. Wash and cut mushrooms into thin slices. Put chicken broth in fondue pot over medium-high heat, add chicken and mushrooms, and cook for 4 minutes.

Place ¼ cup of rice in each of 4 bowls; put 1 lemon-peel strip in each bowl. Spoon in the chicken-broth mixture and enjoy.
MAKES 4 SERVINGS.

Japanese chicken soup

JAPAN

5 cups chicken broth
1 4-ounce can mushroom stems and pieces, or slices (drain and reserve liquid)
2 teaspoons soy sauce
1 cup cooked fine noodles
1 chicken breast, cooked, boned, and thinly sliced
4 thin slices lemon with rind

Bring chicken broth to a boil. If there is not 5 cups of broth, add mushroom liquid to make 5 cups. Simmer, covered, for 5 minutes. Add mushrooms; heat through. Add soy sauce and noodles. Stir well; heat for 3 minutes.

Divide sliced chicken equally into 4 bowls. Pour soup into bowls. Garnish each with a lemon slice.
MAKES 4 SERVINGS.

Miso soup w/egg

JAPAN

4 cups chicken broth
¼ cup white miso (soybean paste)
¼ teaspoon salt
1 egg, beaten
2 teaspoons sherry or sweet rice wine (sweet sake)
Lemon-peel twists

Bring broth, miso, and salt to a boil. While slowly mixing the soup, gradually pour in the egg. Remove from heat; stir in the sherry or sake. Place a twist of lemon peel in each bowl before adding soup.
MAKES 4 SERVINGS.

Clear soup

JAPAN

This is a nice soup to start off with before enjoying a dinner of Sukiyaki or Tempura.

4 cups chicken broth
1 teaspoon soy sauce
1 teaspoon sugar
Pinch of salt
1 cup cubed chicken
1 scallion, chopped fine
Few sprigs of parsley

Combine chicken broth, soy sauce, sugar, and salt; bring to a boil. In each of 4 bowls put a few cubes of chicken, a few pieces of scallion, and parsley for garnish. Pour soup into bowls; serve without spoons.
MAKES 4 SERVINGS.

Egg-flower soup w/water chestnuts

JAPAN

1 quart chicken broth
½ cup finely chopped water chestnuts
2 eggs, beaten
¼ teaspoon pepper

Bring chicken broth to a boil. Add water chestnuts, cover, and simmer for 4 minutes. Add beaten eggs slowly while stirring soup. Add pepper, stir through once.
MAKES 6 SERVINGS.

Rice chowder

JAPAN

2 cups diced leftover cooked chicken
5 cups chicken stock
2 tablespoons soy sauce
2 tablespoons sherry
Pinch of salt
½ teaspoon ground ginger
4 cups leftover rice
4 chopped scallions

Add diced chicken to the boiling stock that has been mixed with the soy sauce, sherry, salt, and ginger. Simmer slowly for about 10 minutes. Add the leftover rice; heat through.

Put ¼ of the chopped scallions into each of 4 individual bowls. Pour in the soup; serve.

MAKES 4 SERVINGS.

Japanese clam soup

JAPAN

16 small clams
4 cups boiling water
½ teaspoon salt
¾ teaspoon rice wine or sherry
1 tablespoon soy sauce
Lemon slices for garnish

Thoroughly wash the clams. Put them into boiling water; boil them until the shells crack. Put in the salt, rice wine or sherry, and soy sauce. Serve the clam soup with a garnish of lemon slices.

MAKES 4 SERVINGS.

Lobster soup

JAPAN

6 ounces lobster meat
2¼ teaspoons salt
1½ teaspoons soy sauce
4½ cups dashi
2 medium cucumbers, sliced thin
8 dried mushrooms
4 pieces lemon rind

Mince the lobster meat, pour ½ teaspoon of the salt over it, and boil. Gradually add ¾ teaspoon of soy sauce and ¼ cup of dashi to the lobster. Peel and slice the cucumbers. Boil the mushrooms in ¼ cup of dashi and ¾ teaspoon salt. Into each of 4 bowls place pieces of boiled lobster, cucumbers, and mushrooms. Heat together 4 cups of dashi, ¾ teaspoon of salt, and ¾ teaspoon of soy sauce; pour some into each bowl. Garnish lobster soup with floating lemon rind.

MAKES 4 SERVINGS.

Oyster soup

JAPAN

8 ounces shucked oysters
4 cups dashi
¾ teaspoon cornstarch
Small amount of cold water
½ teaspoon Tabasco

Wash the oysters. Add them to the boiling dashi; cook until the oysters are done. Mix the cornstarch with enough cold water to make a smooth paste; add to soup. Flavor with the Tabasco.

MAKES 4 SERVINGS.

Oyster soup w/miso

JAPAN

8 ounces shucked oysters
3½ ounces miso (soybean paste)
4 cups dashi
¾ teaspoon cornstarch
Cold water
½ teaspoon red pepper

Wash oysters; set aside.

Blend the miso and dashi; bring to a boil. Gradually add oysters to the boiling mixture. Mix the cornstarch with enough cold water to make a smooth paste; add this to the oyster mixture, stirring constantly. Simmer until done. Flavor with red pepper.

MAKES 4 SERVINGS.

Mexican meatball soup

MEXICO

broth
2 10¾-ounce cans condensed beef broth
2 soup cans water
1 bay leaf
¼ cup dry sherry
½ cup tomato sauce

meatballs
¾ pound ground beef
¾ pound lean ground pork
⅓ cup raw long-grain rice
1½ teaspoons salt

1/4 teaspoon pepper
1 egg, slightly beaten
1 tablespoon chopped mint
2 tablespoons chopped parsley for garnish

Combine broth ingredients in large saucepan. Bring mixture to a boil over moderate heat. Meanwhile, combine meatball ingredients. Mix well; form into meatballs, using approximately 1 tablespoon meat mixture for each meatball. Add meatballs, a few at a time, to hot broth. When all meatballs have been added, cover saucepan; reduce heat to low. Cook for 30 minutes. Remove bay leaf. Garnish soup with parsley. Serve with crusty bread.

MAKES 4 TO 6 SERVINGS.

Mexican soup

MEXICO

1 clove garlic, peeled
3/4 teaspoon salt
4 tablespoons butter
1 medium onion, chopped
1 fresh hot green pepper, chopped
1/2 pound baked ham, chopped
1 cup chopped unpeeled zucchini squash
4 1/2 cups beef broth
1/4 teaspoon crumbled thyme
2 sweet red peppers, cleaned, seeded, and chopped
3 tablespoons tomato paste
1 16 1/2-ounce can whole-kernel corn
Salt and pepper
2 tablespoons chopped fresh parsley

On a cutting board sprinkle the garlic clove with 3/4 teaspoon salt; mash with blade of a knife. Melt butter in a Dutch oven; add garlic, onion, hot pepper, ham, and zucchini. Sauté over moderate heat for 10 minutes. Add beef broth and thyme; simmer for 15 minutes. Add sweet peppers, tomato paste, and corn (along with the liquid from the can); stir well. Cook for 15 minutes more. Season to taste with salt and pepper. Garnish soup with parsley.

MAKES 4 TO 6 SERVINGS.

Note: If fresh hot peppers are not available, substitute 1 canned green chili, chopped, for the hot pepper. Three canned pimientos (chopped) may be substituted for the red peppers if necessary, but first check the frozen-foods section of your local market. Frozen chopped red peppers are now available year round in some places.

Hominy soup

MEXICO

This soup is traditionally served in Mexican homes on Christmas Eve when the family returns from church.

3 pigs feet, split, or 2 large, fresh pork hocks
1 stewing chicken (about 4 pounds), cut up
1 pound lean pork (Boston butt), cut up
2 medium onions, finely chopped
2 cloves garlic, chopped
3 quarts water
1 tablespoon salt
4 red chili pods
1 29-ounce can white hominy, drained

garnish

1 cup sliced radishes
1 cup shredded lettuce
1/2 cup sliced green onions
1/2 cup shredded Jack cheese

In large kettle combine pigs feet or pork hocks, chicken, pork, onions, garlic, water, salt, and chili pods. Bring to a boil; reduce heat to low. Cook for 2 hours. Add hominy; continue cooking until meat starts to fall off bone (3 to 3 1/2 hours total cooking time). Remove meat from broth; cool meat and broth in refrigerator several hours or overnight.

Discard chili pods; remove meat from bones. Skim fat from surface of broth. At serving time, add meat to broth; heat. Serve soup hot in soup bowls with hot tortillas. Pass the garnishes in separate bowls, so that each diner can garnish his plate to his own taste.

MAKES 8 TO 10 SERVINGS.

Corn soup

MEXICO

4 cups fresh corn, cut from the cob
1 cup chicken stock
¼ cup butter
½ cup chopped green onions
3½ cups milk
½ teaspoon salt
3 tablespoons chopped green chilies
6 tablespoons sour cream
Tostadas
Chopped parsley

Combine corn and chicken stock in blender or food processor, spin to a smooth purée. Melt butter in large saucepan. Wilt green onions in butter. Add corn purée; simmer for 5 minutes or until thickened. Add milk and salt; cook 15 minutes over low heat.

Divide chilies among 6 soup bowls. Pour soup into bowls. Garnish each with a tablespoon of sour cream, a few tostadas, and a little chopped parsley. Serve.
MAKES 6 SERVINGS.

Mexican lentil soup

MEXICO

1 cup lentils
1 quart water
5 slices bacon, cut into squares
1 medium onion, chopped
½ cup sliced carrots
½ cup sliced celery
1 8-ounce can tomato sauce
3 medium tomatoes, chopped
1 teaspoon salt
1 bay leaf
1 beef bouillon cube

Soak lentils in water 30 minutes.

Sauté bacon and onion until bacon is crisp and onions are transparent. Add water, lentils, carrots, celery, tomato sauce, chopped tomatoes, salt, bay leaf, and bouillon cube. Simmer about 1½ hours.
MAKES 8 1-CUP SERVINGS.

Cold tomato & vegetable soup

MEXICO

8 large tomatoes, peeled and seeded
2 medium cucumbers, peeled and seeded
2 large green peppers, seeds and pith removed
1 cup finely chopped sweet onion
3 cloves garlic, peeled
⅓ cup olive oil
1 cup rich beef bouillon
½ tablespoon lemon juice
Salt and freshly ground black pepper

Finely chop about ⅔ of the tomatoes. Set aside in large bowl. Finely chop cucumbers, peppers, and onion, adding each vegetable with its juices to the large bowl.

Purée remaining tomatoes, garlic, and olive oil; pour over chopped vegetables along with bouillon and lemon juice. Add salt and pepper to taste. Refrigerate for several hours. Before serving, sample and adjust seasonings; add a little bouillon to thin the soup, if needed.
MAKES 6 SERVINGS.

Chicken soup w/vermicelli

MEXICO

6 cups chicken stock
1 whole chicken breast, split (about 1 pound)
¼ pound vermicelli
¼ cup vegetable oil
1 large tomato, peeled, seeded, and chopped
1 ripe avocado
2 hot green chilies, chopped
Salt and pepper to taste

Early in the day heat stock to boiling in large saucepan. Add chicken, reduce heat to low, and simmer for 25 minutes. Remove and cool chicken. Skin, remove from bones, and shred the meat.

At dinner time break vermicelli into 2-inch lengths. Heat oil in small skillet; lightly brown vermicelli. Drain on paper towels.

Meanwhile, again heat stock to boiling. Add vermicelli; cook until tender. Add tomato and

chicken shreds; heat through. Peel and seed avocado; cut into chunks. Add avocado, chilies, salt, and pepper. Heat through. Serve soup hot with tostadas.

MAKES 6 SERVINGS.

Avocado cream

MEXICO

1½ tablespoons butter or margarine
1½ tablespoons flour
2½ cups hot chicken stock
1 very ripe avocado (large)
2 tablespoons lime juice
¾ cup heavy cream
¼ cup sherry
½ teaspoon salt
Dash white pepper

Melt butter or margarine in large saucepan. Add flour, cook until bubbly. Add hot chicken stock slowly, stirring constantly, and cook over low heat until slightly thickened.

Peel avocado, remove 4 thin slices for garnish, and dip in lime juice. Mash remaining avocado and add remaining lime juice to keep it from turning brown. Add avocado pulp, cream, sherry, salt, and pepper. Serve cream hot, garnished with an avocado slice.

MAKES 4 SERVINGS.

Mexican rice I

MEXICO

In Mexico, this would be called a *sopa seca* (dry soup) and served as a separate course. However, it also makes a delicious accompaniment for meat or fowl.

3 tablespoons vegetable oil
½ cup chopped onion
1 clove garlic, minced
1 cup raw long-grain rice
¼ cup chopped red pepper
½ teaspoon salt
Dash cayenne pepper
2 cups boiling water
2 teaspoons chicken-broth granules

¾ cup frozen peas and carrots, thawed
1 small tomato, peeled, seeded, and chopped (about ⅓ cup)

Heat oil in heavy frying pan over medium heat. Add onion, garlic, rice, and red pepper; sauté until onion is limp and rice is opaque. Add salt, cayenne pepper, boiling water, and chicken-broth granules. Cover, cook 20 minutes or until liquid is absorbed.

Add peas and carrots and tomato. Cook, stirring, just until vegetables are heated through. Serve rice immediately.

MAKES 4 TO 6 SERVINGS.

Mexican rice II

MEXICO

3 tablespoons olive oil
1 cup raw long-grain rice
¼ cup chopped green onions
1 small clove garlic, pressed
2 cups chicken broth
3 tablespoons tomato paste
½ teaspoon ground cumin
¼ cup grated Jack cheese
Chopped green onions for garnish

Heat oil in 2-quart saucepan over moderate heat. Add rice; sauté until very lightly browned. Add onions, garlic, and chicken broth; stir well. Stir in tomato paste and cumin. Bring mixture to a boil. Cover, reduce heat to low. Cook for 20 minutes or until all liquid is absorbed.

Place rice mixture in small ovenproof (preferably earthenware) casserole. Top with grated cheese. Bake in 350°F oven until cheese melts. Garnish rice with green onions; serve.

MAKES 4 SERVINGS.

Cumin rice

MEXICO

3 tablespoons olive oil
1 green pepper, chopped
1 red pepper, chopped
½ cup chopped onion
1 clove garlic, chopped
1 cup raw long-grain rice

¾ teaspoon ground cumin
2 teaspoons chicken-broth granules
2 cups boiling water

Heat oil in ovenproof casserole. Add pepper, onion, garlic, and rice until rice is lightly browned and onion is limp. Add cumin, chicken-broth granules, and boiling water. Cover tightly; bake at 350°F for 30 minutes or until all liquid is absorbed. Serve rice as a side dish with meat, fish, or fowl.
MAKES 4 SERVINGS.

Dry soup w/vermicelli

MEXICO

½ pound chorizo (Mexican pork sausage)
6 tablespoons olive oil
½ pound vermicelli
1 small onion, chopped
1 cup canned tomatoes
2 cups chicken broth
Salt and pepper to taste
Parmesan cheese
Chopped parsley

Brown the chorizo; drain and set it aside.
Heat oil in heavy skillet. Sauté vermicelli over medium heat until golden. Drain; place in 2-quart casserole. Pour off all except 1 tablespoon oil. Sauté onion until limp. Add tomatoes, chicken broth, and salt and pepper to taste. Bring to a boil. Pour over vermicelli. Add chorizo; stir well. Cover and bake at 350°F for 15 minutes or until all liquid is absorbed. Sprinkle soup with Parmesan cheese and chopped parsley; serve.
MAKES 6 SERVINGS.

Spanish stew

MEXICO

This hearty vegetable and beef soup-stew is of Spanish origin, with a few Mexican additions!

2 pounds beef shanks
3 quarts water
2 cloves garlic, peeled and chopped
1 onion, sliced
1 tablespoon salt
8 peppercorns
6 tablespoons tomato purée
3 medium carrots, peeled and sliced
3 zucchini, sliced
3 cups fresh green beans, nipped and cut into 1-inch lengths
2 medium potatoes, peeled and sliced
3 ears of corn, cut into 1-inch pieces

Brown the beef shanks in a roasting pan in a 450°F oven. In a large soup pot combine browned beef, pan drippings, water, garlic, onion, salt, and peppercorns. Bring to a boil, reduce heat to low, cover, and cook 2½ hours or until meat is very tender. Remove meat. Strain broth and return it to kettle. Add tomato purée; bring to a boil. Add vegetables. Reduce heat to low; cook, covered, 30 to 45 minutes or until vegetables are tender.
Cut meat from bones; add to soup. Heat through. Serve stew with your favorite chili sauce.
MAKES 6 TO 8 SERVINGS.

❧ Eggs and Cheese ❧

Mushroom quiche

FRANCE

3 tablespoons butter
2 tablespoons minced shallots or green onions
1 pound sliced fresh mushrooms
1 teaspoon salt
1 teaspoon lemon juice
2 tablespoons Madeira (optional)
3 eggs
1½ cups heavy cream
1 9-inch pie shell, baked 5 minutes at 425°F
¼ cup grated Swiss Cheese

Melt butter in small frying pan. Sauté shallots a few minutes. Add mushrooms, salt, lemon juice, and Madeira. Cook for several minutes, until mushrooms are done and their juice has evaporated.

Beat eggs and cream until smooth. Add mushrooms; mix. Pour into pastry shell. Sprinkle cheese on top of quiche. Bake it in preheated 375°F oven 25 to 30 minutes, until a knife inserted in center comes out clean. Serve quiche hot.

MAKES 6 TO 8 SERVINGS.

Cheese soufflé

FRANCE

4 tablespoons butter
3 tablespoons flour
1 cup milk
½ teaspoon salt
Dash pepper
¼ teaspoon dry mustard
1 cup shredded sharp cheddar or Swiss cheese
4 eggs, separated
¼ teaspoon cream of tartar
1 tablespoon Parmesan cheese or fine bread crumbs

Melt 3 tablespoons butter in 1-quart saucepan. Stir in flour; heat for a few minutes. Add milk all at once. Cook and stir over medium heat until mixture thickens. Stir in salt, pepper, and mustard. Add cheese; cool slightly. Beat in egg yolks.

In medium-size bowl beat egg whites until frothy. Beat in cream of tartar; continue beating egg whites until soft peaks form. Stir ¼ of egg whites into cheese sauce. Gently fold in remaining whites.

Prepare a 1½- or 2-quart soufflé dish by greasing with 1 tablespoon butter and dusting with Parmesan cheese. Pour soufflé into dish; bake in preheated 375°F oven 25 to 30 minutes. Soufflé is done when it is puffed and golden and looks slightly dry, not shiny. Serve soufflé at once, with a sauce if desired.

MAKES 4 SERVINGS.

Spinach soufflé

FRANCE

5 tablespoons butter
1 tablespoon minced shallots or green onions
¾ cup chopped frozen spinach, thawed
Dash nutmeg
3 tablespoons flour
1 cup milk
½ teaspoon salt
Dash pepper
4 eggs, separated
¼ teaspoon cream of tartar
1 tablespoon Parmesan cheese or bread crumbs

Melt 1 tablespoon butter in small pan. Sauté shallots several minutes, until tender. Add spinach; cook a few minutes to remove moisture. Add nutmeg; set aside.

Melt remaining 3 tablespoons butter in 1-quart saucepan. Stir in flour; cook for several minutes. Add milk all at once. Add salt and pepper. Cook and stir over medium heat until sauce thickens. Stir in spinach. Cool sauce slightly, then add egg yolks. Mix well.

In medium-size bowl beat egg whites until frothy. Beat in cream of tartar; continue beating until soft peaks form. Stir ¼ of egg whites into spinach mixture. Gently fold in remaining whites.

Prepare 1½- or 2-quart soufflé dish by greasing with 1 tablespoon butter and dusting with Parmesan cheese. Pour soufflé into prepared dish.

Sausage omelet

Bake in preheated 375°F oven 25 to 30 minutes. Soufflé is done when golden, puffed, and somewhat dry, not shiny. Serve soufflé at once, with a sauce if desired.

MAKES 4 SERVINGS.

Note: To form a "high-hat" soufflé, use a knife perpendicular to edge of dish. Draw a circle through soufflé 1 inch from the edge and about 1 inch deep.

Crepes veronique

FRANCE

The term *veronique* always indicates green grapes.

4 ounces cream cheese
1 cup small-curd cottage cheese
1 tablespoon sugar
Dash salt
½ teaspoon grated lemon rind
12 Basic Crepes (see Index)
½ cup sugar
½ cup apple juice or cider
¼ cup butter
1 tablespoon lemon juice
½ teaspoon cinnamon
2 cups halved seedless grapes

Beat cream cheese, cottage cheese, 1 tablespoon sugar, salt, and lemon rind for filling. Fill crepes, using about 2 tablespoons filling for each. Roll crepes; place in greased baking dish. Bake in preheated 350°F oven 15 minutes.

Make sauce in small saucepan by combining ½ cup sugar, apple juice, butter, lemon juice, and cinnamon. Heat until sugar has dissolved. Add grapes; heat through. Pour sauce over hot crepes. Serve.

MAKES 6 SERVINGS.

Basic French omelet & fillings

FRANCE

2 eggs
2 tablespoons water
¼ teaspoon salt
Dash of pepper
1 tablespoon butter

omelet fillings

1 to 2 tablespoons grated Swiss or Parmesan cheese
1 tablespoon minced fresh herbs, such as parsley, chives, or tarragon
2 to 3 tablespoons sautéed ham or chicken livers, cooked shrimp or crab, cooked asparagus tips, etc.

In small bowl mix eggs, water, salt, and pepper with a fork. Heat butter in 8-inch omelet pan until just hot enough to sizzle a drop of water. Pour in egg mixture. Mixture should start to set immediately. With pancake turner draw cooked portions from edge toward center, so that uncooked portions flow to bottom. Tilt pan as you do this and slide pan back and forth over heat to keep mixture from sticking. Add one of the above fillings, if desired.

While top is still moist and creamy-looking, fold in half or roll with pancake turner. Turn out onto plate with a quick flip of the wrist. Omelets will take about 2 minutes from start to finish.

MAKES 1 SERVING.

German farmer's breakfast

GERMANY

A good lunch or dinner dish. Serve with a green salad and bread.

4 medium potatoes, cooked and peeled
4 strips bacon, cubed
3 eggs
3 tablespoons milk
½ teaspoon salt
1 cup cooked ham, cut into small cubes
2 medium tomatoes, peeled
1 tablespoon chopped chives

Slice potatoes. In a large frypan cook bacon until transparent. Add the potato slices; cook until lightly browned.

Meanwhile blend eggs with milk and salt. Stir in the cubed ham.

Cut the tomatoes into thin wedges; add to the egg mixture. Pour the egg mixture over the potatoes in the frypan. Cook until the eggs are set. Sprinkle with chopped chives and serve at once.

MAKES 3 TO 4 SERVINGS.

Baked spinach w/cheese
GERMANY

1 pound fresh spinach, washed and dried
¼ pound butter
1 large onion, diced
2 cloves garlic, minced
½ teaspoon salt
½ pound Emmenthaler cheese, grated
1 teaspoon paprika
⅛ teaspoon nutmeg
¼ teaspoon pepper

Cut spinach into strips. In a large Dutch oven heat butter until bubbly. Add onion and garlic; sauté for 2 to 3 minutes. Add the spinach. Sprinkle with salt. Cover and steam for 5 minutes. Remove from heat.

Grease an ovenproof casserole. Sprinkle half the cheese over the bottom of the casserole. Add the spinach. Sprinkle with paprika, nutmeg, and pepper. Top with remaining cheese. Bake at 350°F about 20 minutes or until cheese bubbles.
MAKES 4 SERVINGS.

Eggs in green sauce
GERMANY

This cold dish is perfect for summer dinners. Green sauce originated in Frankfurt and was Goethe's favorite dish. In Germany, this dish is served with potatoes boiled in their skins. The potatoes are peeled at the table and dunked into the sauce.

2 tablespoons mayonnaise
1 cup sour cream (part yoghurt can be used)
1 lemon, juiced
9 hard-cooked eggs
½ teaspoon salt
¼ teaspoon pepper
½ teaspoon sugar
1½ cups chopped fresh herbs (any combination of dill, chives, parsley, tarragon, or borage)

Blend mayonnaise, sour cream, and lemon juice. Finely chop 1 hard-cooked egg and stir into mayonnaise mixture. Season with salt, pepper, and sugar. Thoroughly rinse the herbs, pat dry, and chop. Blend with the sauce.

Slice rest of hard-cooked eggs in half and arrange in the sauce.
MAKES 4 SERVINGS.

Egg pouches
GREECE

2 tablespoons butter
3 eggs, well beaten
½ tomato, chopped
2 green onions, chopped
½ cup crumbled feta cheese
½ teaspoon salt
⅛ teaspoon pepper
2 pieces pita bread

Melt the butter in a small, heavy skillet. Combine the eggs, vegetables, cheese, salt, and pepper. Pour into the skillet and cook over low heat as you would scrambled eggs, until set.

Meanwhile, cut pockets in the bread with a sharp knife. If the bread is large, cut in half and gently separate the inside layers, being careful not to split open the sides. For smaller bread, cut a thin slice from the top edge of the bread and separate the inside layers with a sharp knife. Fill the bread with the egg mixture and serve with mayonnaise.
MAKES 2 SERVINGS.

Greek artichoke omelet
GREECE

4 tablespoons olive oil
1 clove garlic, minced
2 green onions, chopped
2 teaspoons chopped parsley
1 8½-ounce can artichoke hearts, drained and cut in half
4 eggs, well-beaten

Heat the oil in a medium-size skillet or 9-inch omelet pan. Add the garlic and green onions and sauté for 1 minute. Add the parsley and artichoke hearts and sauté for 3 minutes. Add the eggs. Lower the heat and cook until the eggs are set.

Serve with tomato sauce.
MAKES 2 SERVINGS.

Egg omelet w/green pepper

GREECE

4 eggs, well-beaten
1 tablespoon water
Salt and pepper
2 tablespoons butter
½ cup crumbled feta cheese

Beat the eggs with the water; add salt and pepper to taste.

In an 8-inch omelet pan or small skillet heat the butter over medium heat until it sizzles. Add the egg mixture and reduce the heat to low. As the eggs begin to set, carefully lift the edges of the omelet with a spatula and let the uncooked eggs flow to the bottom of the pan. When the omelet is almost done, sprinkle with the feta cheese.
Fold the omelet and serve topped with Tomato Sauce.
MAKES 2 SERVINGS.

Tomato sauce

2 tablespoons olive oil
1 green pepper, cut in slices
1 clove garlic, minced
1 8-ounce can tomato sauce

Heat the oil in a small saucepan or skillet. Add the pepper and garlic and sauté for 3 minutes. Add the tomato sauce and lower the heat to simmer. Simmer for 15 minutes.

Cheese pies

GREECE

6 ounces cream cheese
1 egg
1 cup crumbled feta cheese
1 tablespoon chopped parsley
1 10-ounce package frozen patty shells (6 individual shells)
2 tablespoons milk

Beat the cream cheese with an electric mixer to soften. Add the egg and beat well. Add the feta cheese and parsley and beat until well-combined. Chill the mixture for at least 1 hour.
Defrost the patty shells at room temperature for 15 to 20 minutes or until soft. Roll each patty shell into a rectangle approximately 4½ X 8½ inches on a floured pastry cloth.
Place ¼ cup of the cheese mixture on one half of the rectangle. Fold the top of the rectangle over the bottom to form a square pie. Seal with the milk and brush the tops of the pies with it. Preheat the oven to 450°F. Place the pies on a cookie sheet and place in the oven. Immediately reduce the heat to 400°F and bake for 20 to 25 minutes or until well-browned and puffed.
MAKES 6 PIES.

Spinach-cheese pie

GREECE

1½ pounds fresh spinach
¼ cup olive oil
¾ cup chopped green onions
½ pound crumbled feta cheese
1 cup ricotta or farmer cheese
2 tablespoons grated Kafaloteri or Parmesan cheese
2 tablespoons chopped parsley
4 eggs, beaten
¼ teaspoon nutmeg
Salt and pepper
1 stick sweet butter, melted
8 ounces phyllo sheets

Wash the spinach well, tear it into bite-size pieces, and discard the stem. Steam the spinach over boiling water for 8 minutes, until it wilts. Drain well and pat dry on paper towels.
Heat the olive oil in a small skillet and cook the green onions for 3 minutes or until limp. In a large bowl combine the spinach, onions (and the oil from the pan), feta cheese, ricotta, Kafaloteri cheese, parsley, eggs, nutmeg, and salt and pepper to taste. Stir well.
Brush a 13 X 9 X 2-inch baking dish with some of the melted butter. Brush 4 sheets of phyllo with butter, fold in half, and stack in the pan. Pour in the filling. Stack the remaining phyllo sheets, buttered and folded in half, on top of the filling. Brush the top of the pie with butter.
Preheat the oven to 375°F. Bake 1 hour or until golden brown and puffed. Cool the pie for 5 minutes and cut into squares.
MAKES 12 SERVINGS.

Feta-cheese sandwiches

GREECE

2 pita-bread rounds
8 ½-inch slices feta cheese
1 cup finely shredded lettuce
½ of a medium tomato, diced
¼ cup diced cucumber
2 tablespoons chopped green pepper
2 radishes, thinly sliced
3 tablespoons oil-and-vinegar salad dressing

Warm the pita bread. Cut in half and form a pocket in each. Place 2 slices of cheese in each pocket.

In a bowl combine the vegetables and salad dressing. Stuff each bread pocket with some of the salad mixture, and serve.
MAKES 2 SERVINGS.

Sausage omelet

HUNGARY

2 slices bacon, diced
1 small onion, peeled, sliced
¼ of large green pepper, cleaned, cut into strips
¼ of large red pepper, cleaned, cut into strips (all green pepper can be used if red pepper is unavailable)
¾ cup Hungarian sausage, sliced (or substitute linginica, Kielbasi, or any spicy smoked sausage)
3 eggs
1 tablespoon milk
Salt and pepper
2 tablespoons butter or margarine

Fry diced bacon in small heavy skillet until crisp. Remove with slotted spoon; reserve. Add onion, peppers, and sausage to skillet; cook until onion and sausage are lightly browned. Reduce heat to simmer; cover. Cook while making omelet.

Beat eggs, milk, salt, and pepper together until well-mixed. Heat butter in 10-inch heavy skillet until foam subsides. Add eggs; cook, lifting edges to let uncooked egg run to bottom of pan. Cook until bottom is lightly browned. Top with sausage mixture; fold. Transfer to warm platter.
MAKES 2 SERVINGS.

Note: In winter, substitute ½ cup frozen mixed green and red peppers; add toward end of cooking time for omelet filling.

German farmer's breakfast

Egg fritters w/tomato sauce

HUNGARY

6 hard-boiled eggs
1 raw egg, well-beaten
1 cup fine dry bread crumbs
Oil for deep-frying

tomato sauce
1 tablespoon butter or margarine
2 tablespoons minced onion
1 8-ounce can tomato sauce
2 tablespoons dry white wine
1 tablespoon chopped parsley

Peel eggs; pat dry with paper towel. Dip hard-boiled eggs, 1 at a time, in beaten egg, then in crumbs. Coat thoroughly; shake off excess. Chill while making sauce.

Heat butter in small saucepan. Add onion; sauté until limp. Add remaining sauce ingredients; simmer 15 minutes. Keep warm.

Heat 3 inches oil in deep heavy saucepan or French fryer to 350°F. Fry eggs 2 at a time 1 to 2 minutes or until golden. Remove; drain on absorbent paper. Serve fritters topped with sauce.
MAKES 3 TO 4 SERVINGS.

115

Bacon and eggs

Scrambled eggs & cauliflower

HUNGARY

1 small head cauliflower, trimmed, separated into florets
Boiling salted water
¼ cup butter
1 medium onion, peeled, chopped
4 eggs, lightly beaten
Salt and pepper
Chopped parsley

Cook cauliflower in boiling salted water to barely cover, until tender. Drain well; reserve.
Heat butter in heavy skillet until melted. Add onion; cook until lightly browned. Add cauliflower; heat gently 1 minute.
Combine eggs and salt and pepper to taste; pour over cauliflower in skillet. Cook, stirring occasionally, until eggs are set. Garnish with chopped parsley.
MAKES 3 SERVINGS.

Hungarian eggs farmer's-style

HUNGARY

4 slices bacon, diced
¼ cup finely minced onion
1½ cups cooked fine egg noodles
4 eggs
¼ cup milk
Salt and pepper
3 tablespoons butter or margarine
Chopped parsley

Cook bacon in small frying pan until crisp. Remove with slotted spoon; reserve. Add onion to skillet; cook until tender. Remove with slotted spoon.
Combine noodles and onion in mixing bowl; mix lightly. Beat eggs, milk, salt, and pepper together; add egg mixture and bacon to noodle mixture; gently mix.
Melt butter in large heavy skillet over moderate heat. When butter is bubbling and hot, add noodle mixture. Reduce heat to low; cook, stirring, until eggs are set. Place eggs on warm platter; garnish with parsley. Serve with crisp hot toast.
MAKES 4 SERVINGS.

Green-pepper omelet

HUNGARY

1 tablespoon lard or margarine
½ cup sliced onion
1 large green pepper, cleaned, cut into strips
2 tomatoes, peeled, chopped
¼ teaspoon Hungarian sweet paprika
Salt and pepper
2 tablespoons butter
6 eggs

Melt lard in small frying pan over moderate heat. Add onion; cook until lightly browned. Add green pepper; sauté 2 minutes. Add tomatoes, paprika, salt, and pepper; cook over low heat 15 minutes or until mixture is thick. Keep warm while preparing omelets.
Melt 1 tablespoon butter in 8-inch skillet or omelet pan. Beat eggs in bowl until well-mixed. Pour half of egg mixture into pan; tilt pan to cover evenly. Cook without stirring, lifting

cooked edges of omelet to let uncooked egg run under, until set. Top with half of pepper and onion mixture; fold omelet in half. Turn out onto heated platter; keep warm. Continue in same manner with remaining egg mixture.

Serve omelets immediately, garnished with parsley and accompanied by fried potatoes.
MAKES 2 TO 4 SERVINGS.

Sunday morning omelet

IRELAND

2 tablespoons butter or margarine
4 medium eggs, lightly beaten
Salt and pepper
½ cup chopped baked ham
1 tablespoon chopped chives
1 tablespoon chopped parsley

Melt butter in 10-inch skillet.

Meanwhile, beat eggs with salt and pepper to taste. Pour egg mixture into skillet; cook over low heat without stirring. As eggs cook, lift edges of omelet; allow uncooked egg to flow to bottom of pan. When eggs are set, loosen from pan; sprinkle with ham, chives, and parsley. Fold in half; heat through.

Slide omelet onto platter; garnish with parsley and sliced tomatoes. Serve with potato cakes.
MAKES 2 SERVINGS.

Bacon & eggs

IRELAND

½ pound thickly sliced bacon (country-cured if available)
4 (or more) large eggs
Salt and pepper

Trim rind from bacon. Fry in large, heavy skillet until crisp, 4 to 5 slices at a time. Keep warm. Pour off all fat; reserve.

Clean pan with paper towels, removing all browned bits. Pour 6 tablespoons fat into pan. Heat over moderate heat until few drops of water dance in fat. Break eggs into fat, 1 at a time. Reduce heat to low; cook until whites begin to set.

Baste yolks with hot bacon fat by tipping pan and spooning hot fat over yolks. Cook until whites are set and yolks are still soft, but glazed over in appearance.

Serve eggs immediately with bacon, hot mashed potato cakes, and freshly made toast.
MAKES 4 SERVINGS

Eggs wrapped in ham

IRELAND

8 thick slices bacon
4 slices boiled ham
4 large hard-boiled eggs, shelled
1 8-ounce can tomato sauce
½ teaspoon sweet basil
Salt and pepper
2 tablespoons melted butter
Parsley for garnish

Fry bacon in heavy skillet until lightly browned but not crisp. Drain on paper towels. Cut ham slices in half; trim so that pieces are same size as bacon. Slice hard-boiled eggs in half lengthwise.

Eggs wrapped in ham

Cheese turnovers

Place 1 slice of ham on slice of bacon; wrap around outside of 1 hard-boiled-egg half. Secure with toothpick. Follow same procedure with remaining egg halves. Place in 8- or 9-inch-square baking dish or equivalent, yolk facing up.

Combine tomato sauce, sweet basil, salt, and pepper; mix well. Pour around egg halves. Brush exposed egg yolks and white with melted butter. Bake eggs at 350°F 20 minutes. Serve eggs on toast with sauce spooned over.

MAKES 4 SERVINGS.

Egg collops

IRELAND

1 tablespoon butter
1 tablespoon finely chopped onion
2 tablespoons finely chopped green pepper
4 large hard-boiled eggs, chopped
½ cup cream of celery soup
Salt and pepper
Flour
1 egg, well-beaten
2 tablespoons water
Fine dry bread crumbs
Oil for deep frying

Melt butter in small saucepan. Add onion and green pepper; sauté until tender.

Combine eggs, vegetable mixture, soup, salt, and pepper in mixing bowl; mix well. Form into 8 croquettes. Dredge lightly in flour. Beat egg with 2 tablespoons water. Dip croquettes in egg wash, then in bread crumbs. Pat so that bread crumbs adhere thickly to croquettes. Place on a rack and refrigerate for 1 hour.

Heat oil in deep fryer to 365°F. Fry croquettes 2 at a time until golden. Drain well. Serve.

MAKES 4 SERVINGS.

Potato omelet

IRELAND

4 slices bacon
1½ cups peeled, thinly sliced potatoes
½ cup finely chopped onion
¼ cup finely chopped green pepper
4 eggs
Salt and pepper

Zucchini omelet

Cook bacon in heavy skillet until crisp. Drain; crumble; reserve. Add potatoes to hot bacon fat in skillet; sauté 5 minutes or until potatoes are just tender. Add onion and green pepper; sauté 3 minutes.

Beat eggs with salt and pepper; pour over potatoes in skillet. Sprinkle with bacon; cook over medium heat as you would an omelet, without stirring, until eggs begin to set. Cover; cook a few minutes longer, until eggs are completely set and bottom of omelet is browned.

Serve omelet cut in wedges, garnished with parsley and tomato wedges.

MAKES 2 SERVINGS.

Zucchini omelet

ITALY

¼ cup olive oil or cooking oil
1 medium zucchini squash, thinly sliced
¼ cup onion, finely chopped
1 large tomato, peeled and finely chopped
¼ teaspoon dried oregano, crumbled
Salt and pepper
6 eggs
½ cup grated provolone or mozzarella cheese (optional)

Heat the oil in a 10-inch skillet over medium-high heat. Add the zucchini and onion and sauté until lightly browned. Add the tomato, oregano, salt, and pepper and sauté to evaporate the liquid.

Beat the eggs together well. Pour over the vegetable mixture and cook as you would an omelet, lifting the cooked egg and allowing the uncooked egg to flow to the bottom of the pan, until the top is almost set and the bottom is lightly browned. Sprinkle with the cheese (if used), cover and cook over low heat until the top of the omelet is set and the cheese is melted.

Slide onto a platter, cut in wedges and serve.

MAKES 4 SERVINGS.

Cheese turnovers

ITALY

dough

2½ cups all-purpose flour
1 teaspoon salt
1 package active dry yeast
1 cup warm water
2 tablespoons olive oil

filling

1 (8-ounce) ball mozzarella cheese, shredded
1 cup finely minced prosciutto
½ cup chopped stuffed green olives
Pepper

1 egg
1 tablespoon water

Combine flour and salt in mixing bowl. Dissolve yeast in warm water. Add yeast mixture and oil to flour. Mix to form stiff dough. Turn out onto lightly floured surface; knead until smooth and elastic. Place in greased bowl. Rotate to grease surface of dough. Cover; let rise in warm place until double in bulk (1½ to 2 hours).

To prepare filling, combine cheese, ham, olives, and pepper to taste; mix well.

Punch dough down. Place on lightly floured surface; divide into 12 equal parts. Roll each part to 5-inch circle. Spoon about 2 heaping tablespoons filling on ½ of each round. Fold over; moisten edges lightly with water; seal. Place on lightly greased cookie sheets. Beat egg and water together; brush turnovers with mixture. Bake at 375°F 20 minutes, until golden. Makes 12 turnovers.

Note: Turnovers can also be deep-fried. Heat at least 1½ inches fat to 360°F. Do not brush turnovers with egg. Fry until golden; drain on paper towels.

Eggs in purgatory

ITALY

1 tablespoon olive oil
1 small clove garlic, minced
¼ cup onion, finely chopped
2 tablespoons chopped green pepper
1 tablespoon chopped parsley

Salt and pepper, to taste
1 can (16 ounces) peeled Italian plum tomatoes, broken up
8 eggs
4 large slices toasted buttered Italian bread

Heat the oil in a medium skillet. Sauté the garlic, onion and green pepper until limp. Add the parsley, and sauté 2 minutes. Add the salt, pepper, and tomatoes. Bring to a boil, then reduce the heat to simmer and cook for 15 minutes. Bring the mixture to a boil once again.

Break the eggs into a saucer, one at a time, and slide into the sauce mixture. Reduce the heat to low, cover the pan, and poach to the desired degree of doneness. Serve 2 eggs per serving on a slice of buttered, toasted Italian bread.
MAKES 4 SERVINGS.

Eggs—Florentine-style

ITALY

1 pound fresh spinach
A pinch of salt
3 tablespoons butter or margarine

cheese sauce
3 tablespoons butter
3 tablespoons flour
Salt
White pepper
1 cup hot chicken broth
½ cup light cream
¾ cup freshly grated Parmesan cheese

eggs
6 eggs
Boiling salted water
A few drops white vinegar

Wash the spinach, remove coarse stems and discard undesirable leaves. Place the wet spinach in a saucepan with a tight-fitting lid. Set aside.

Next, prepare the cheese sauce. Melt the butter in a medium saucepan. Add the flour, salt, and pepper and cook until bubbly. Add the chicken broth and cream and cook until thickened, stirring constantly. Remove from the heat and stir in the cheese. Keep the sauce warm.

Heat 1½ inches of salted water to boiling in a medium skillet. Add a few drops of vinegar and poach the eggs in the water to the desired degree of doneness. Meanwhile, sprinkle the spinach lightly with salt and steam over low heat 5 minutes. Drain. Place the spinach in a warm serving dish. Remove the eggs from the skillet with a slotted spoon and place on top of the spinach. Pour the sauce over the eggs and spinach. Serve immediately.
MAKES 3 TO 4 SERVINGS.

Italian eggs & sausage

ITALY

4 links Italian sausage (casing removed)
2 tablespoons chopped green pepper
2 tablespoons chopped onion
3 tablespoons butter or margarine
4 eggs
Salt and pepper

Fry the sausage in a skillet, breaking up with a slotted spoon. When lightly browned, remove from the pan.

In a 10-inch skillet, sauté the green pepper and onion in the butter until limp. Beat the eggs well, with salt and pepper to taste. Add the eggs and sausage to the skillet and cook over moderate heat, lifting the cooked egg occasionally with a spatula to let the uncooked egg flow to the bottom of the pan. When lightly browned and set, flip the omelet and cook until lightly browned. Slide onto a platter and cut in wedges to serve.
MAKES 4 SERVINGS.

Italian artichoke omelet

ITALY

¼ cup olive oil
1½ cups canned artichoke hearts, well-drained
1½ tablespoons lemon juice
6 eggs
½ teaspoon salt
Pepper
Parmesan cheese (optional)

Heat oil in large heavy skillet over moderate heat. Pat artichokes dry with paper towels; halve lengthwise. Sauté in hot oil until lightly browned. Sprinkle with lemon juice.

Beat eggs, salt, and pepper together well. Pour over artichoke hearts in skillet. Cook as you would omelet, lifting cooked egg with spatula and allowing uncooked egg to flow to bottom of pan. When top is almost set and bottom lightly browned, sprinkle with Parmesan cheese. Cook 2 minutes.

Cut into wedges; serve immediately.
MAKES 4 SERVINGS.

Spinach omelet

ITALY

1 10-ounce package frozen chopped spinach
3 tablespoons olive oil
¼ cup onion, finely chopped
1 clove garlic, minced
1 medium-size tomato, peeled and chopped
½ teaspoon dried sweet basil, crumbled
4 eggs
½ teaspoon salt
⅛ teaspoon pepper
3 tablespoons olive oil

Cook the spinach following the package directions. Drain very well. In a medium saucepan, heat the 3 tablespoons of oil and sauté the onion and garlic until tender. Add the tomato, spinach, and sweet basil and mix well. Cook, stirring constantly, over medium heat for 3 minutes.

Beat the eggs lightly until just mixed. Combine with the spinach mixture and salt and pepper and mix well. Heat the remaining 3 tablespoons of oil, in a 9-inch skillet with an ovenproof handle, until sizzling. Pour in the omelet mixture and cook covered for 10 minutes. The omelet should be fairly firm.

Place the omelet under a hot broiler for 1 or 2 minutes to cook the top of the omelet. Cut in wedges and serve.
MAKES 4 SERVINGS.

Fonduta

ITALY

Serve as a snack or hors d'oeuvre.

1 pound Fontina cheese (or Gruyère or Emmenthaler if Fontina is unavailable)
1 cup milk
4 eggs
Salt and white pepper, to taste
¼ cup white wine
1 canned white truffle, very thinly sliced (optional)
Bread sticks or 1 large loaf of crisp Italian bread, cut into chunks

Shred the cheese and place in a mixing bowl and stir in 1 cup of milk. Let stand 30 minutes.

Beat together the eggs, salt, and white pepper. Beat the wine into the egg mixture. Blend the egg mixture into the cheese, mixing well. Cook in the top of a double boiler over gently boiling water, stirring constantly until the cheese melts and the mixture is smooth and slightly thickened.

Pour into a chafing dish or fondue pot (turn the burner down as far as it will go without going out or the cheese will burn) and serve, garnished with the truffle if desired. Serve the bread in a basket with fondue forks so that your guests can dip in the manner of Swiss fondue.
MAKES 5 TO 6 SERVINGS.

Note: Fonduta may also be served in warm ramekins, surrounded by crisp toast triangles. This dish may also be served as a main course for 4 people, accompanied by cubes of ham and assorted raw vegetables.

Country pie

ITALY

2 tablespoons butter or margarine
½ cup chopped onion
1 10-ounce package frozen chopped spinach, thawed
1 pound ricotta cheese
½ cup grated Parmesan cheese
2 eggs, beaten
¾ teaspoon garlic salt
¼ teaspoon white pepper

¼ teaspoon ground nutmeg
1 9-inch unbaked pie shell

Heat the butter in a small skillet. Sauté the onion until tender.

Drain the spinach well in a sieve and press with a spoon to remove all the liquid. In a mixing bowl, combine the spinach, sautéed onions, ricotta, Parmesan cheese, eggs and seasonings and mix well. Pour into the pie shell and bake at 375°F for 45 minutes. Serve hot.

MAKES 4 TO 6 SERVINGS.

Fried cheese & rice balls

ITALY

2½ cups water
2 teaspoons chicken broth granules
1 cup long-grain white rice
¼ cup grated Parmesan cheese
1 tablespoon dehydrated parsley flakes
1 egg, lightly beaten
15 ½-inch cubes mozzarella cheese
½ cup dry bread crumbs
Oil for frying

Combine the water and chicken broth granules in a saucepan. Bring to a boil, add the rice, and stir well. Cover, reduce the heat to low, and cook 25 to 30 minutes or until all the liquid is absorbed and the rice is very tender and a little sticky. Cool for 1 hour in the refrigerator.

Combine the rice, Parmesan cheese, parsley flakes, and egg and mix well. Place a heaping tablespoon of the rice in the palm of your hand. Then place a cheese cube in the center of the rice. Add ½ tablespoon of the rice mixture on top of the cheese cube and form into a ball, pressing well to make sure it holds together. Roll in dry bread crumbs. Continue until all of the rice has been used; it should make about 15 balls.

Heat 3 inches of oil in a medium saucepan to 365°F. Fry the rice balls 3 or 4 at a time until golden. Drain on absorbent paper and place in a warm oven until all the rice balls are fried. Serve with tomato or marinara sauce if desired.

MAKES 4 SERVINGS.

Spanish scrambled eggs

SPAIN

8 eggs
1 teaspoon salt
1 tomato, peeled, seeded, chopped
2 tablespoons olive oil
1 clove garlic, peeled
¼ cup chopped onions
½ cup chopped Italian or other smoked ham
Chopped chives

Beat eggs with fork until frothy. Beat in salt.

Heat oil in shallow skillet. Add garlic; cook 5 minutes. Discard garlic. Add onions, tomato, and ham; sauté 5 minutes. Add eggs; cook, stirring frequently, until set. Spoon eggs onto heated serving platter; garnish with chives.

MAKES 4 SERVINGS.

Eggs w/sofrito

SPAIN

½ cup olive oil
1 onion, peeled, chopped
1 garlic clove, peeled, minced
1 cup diced green pepper
2 large tomatoes, peeled, seeded, chopped
Dash of hot sauce
6 eggs
¼ cup grated Swiss cheese
¼ cup sliced pimiento-stuffed Spanish olives

Heat ¼ cup oil. Add onion, garlic, and pepper; sauté until tender. Add tomatoes; cook until mixture thickens. Stir in hot sauce.

Heat remaining ¼ cup oil in large shallow skillet. Crack eggs into skillet one at a time. Fry until whites set. Sprinkle with cheese. Cover; fry 2 minutes. Put eggs on serving platter. Garnish with sofrito and olives.

MAKES 4 TO 6 SERVINGS.

Eggs with sofrito

Onion & potato omelet

SPAIN

This omelet is often eaten cold in Spain, served between 2 pieces of thick bread. It also is cut in squares and served with toothpicks.

¼ cup olive oil
1 large potato, washed, sliced thin
½ cup chopped onions
6 eggs
½ teaspoon salt
¼ teaspoon pepper

Heat 2 tablespoons oil in small shallow skillet. Add potato; sauté until tender. Add onions; sauté 2 minutes. Remove vegetables from skillet; drain.
Beat eggs until frothy. Add salt and pepper; mix well. Heat 1 tablespoon oil in skillet. Add half of egg mixture. Using fork, poke holes in center of omelet to allow uncooked egg mixture to run under cooked omelet. Cook 1 minute or until outside rim of omelet is formed. Add half of potato and onion mixture. Flip omelet; cook 1 minute or until omelet is set. Repeat process with remaining egg and potato mixture.
MAKES 4 TO 6 SERVINGS.

Supper omelet

SPAIN

A delicious late-night supper meal.

¼ cup olive oil
1 garlic clove, peeled
1 large onion, sliced into rings
1 green pepper, seeded, sliced into rings
1 red pepper, seeded, sliced into rings
1 tomato, peeled, seeded, sliced thin
1 large potato, peeled, sliced paper-thin
8 eggs
1 teaspoon salt
¼ teaspoon pepper

Heat 2 tablespoons oil in large shallow skillet. Add garlic; cook 5 minutes. Remove garlic; discard. Add onion and peppers; sauté until tender. Add tomato; sauté 3 to 4 minutes or until tomato begins to wilt but does not turn mushy. Remove vegetables from skillet. Keep warm,
Add remaining 2 tablespoons oil to skillet; heat. Add potato; fry until tender.
While potato is cooking, beat eggs, salt, and pepper until frothy. Add to potato. Cook until set. Do not flip. Place omelet on serving plate; cover with cooked vegetables. To serve, cut into 4 wedges.
MAKES 4 SERVINGS.

Eggs and Cheese

Spanish omelet w/sauce

SPAIN

sauce

2 tablespoons olive oil
½ cup chopped onion
1 clove garlic, peeled, chopped
1 green pepper, cleaned, seeded, cut into strips
1 red pepper, cleaned, seeded, cut into strips
1 8-ounce can tomato sauce

omelets

2 tablespoons olive oil
6 eggs
1 teaspoon salt
¼ teaspoon black pepper

To make sauce:

Heat oil in small cast-iron skillet until haze forms over skillet. Add onion, garlic, and peppers; cook until vegetables begin to wilt. Add tomato sauce; heat thoroughly. Keep warm.

To make omelets:

Heat 1 tablespoon oil in small skillet or omelet pan. Beat eggs until frothy. Beat in salt and pepper. Pour half of egg mixture into prepared pan; cook until set. Place omelet on warm serving plate. Cover half of omelet with sauce. Fold remaining half over top of sauce. Serve immediately. Prepare remaining omelet in same manner. MAKES 4 SERVINGS.

Potato & sausage omelet

SPAIN

¼ pound garlic-flavored sausage
3 tablespoons olive oil
2 potatoes, peeled, sliced
½ cup diced green-onion tops
6 eggs, lightly beaten with fork
Salt and pepper to taste

Place sausage in small skillet; cover with water. Bring to boil; boil 5 minutes. Drain. Peel sausage; dice.

Heat oil in skillet. Add sausage and potatoes; fry until browned. Stir in onion; sauté until wilted. Remove sausage and vegetables. Add eggs to skillet. Sprinkle with meat and vegetables. Cook over low heat without stirring. As eggs set on

Spanish omelet with sauce

bottom, lift edges and allow uncooked mixture to run underneath. Remove omelet from pan. Serve immediately.
MAKES 4 SERVINGS.

Bacon & egg cake

DENMARK

½ pound bacon
6 eggs
1 tablespoon flour
½ teaspoon salt
½ cup milk
3 tablespoons finely cut chives

Cut each slice of bacon in half. Fry it lightly (do not let it become crisp) in a 12-inch skillet. Drain and set it aside. Remove all but about 1 tablespoon of bacon fat from the skillet.
Combine the eggs, flour, and salt in a bowl. Gradually add in the milk.
Over moderate heat, warm the fat in the skillet. Pour in the egg mixture and turn the heat down to low. Do not stir. Let the eggs set firm, about 20 minutes. When the mixture is firm, remove it from the heat.
Arrange the bacon slices and chives on top and serve directly from the pan.
MAKES 4 SERVINGS.

Egg cake w/sausage

DENMARK

3 medium sliced boiled potatoes
1 8-ounce can cocktail sausages
2 tablespoons margarine
4 eggs, beaten well
¼ cup cream or water
Green peppers for garnish
1 or 2 tomatoes for garnish

Dice the potatoes and set them aside. Slice the cocktail sausages into the same bowl. Melt the margarine in a skillet and brown the potatoes and sausages together.

Add the eggs mixed with the cream or water. Cook the mixture over low heat until it sets firm in the center. Turn the egg cake out on a hot platter and garnish with the green peppers and tomato wedges.

MAKES 6 SERVINGS.

Danish eggs

DENMARK

6 eggs
3 tablespoons canned condensed milk
1 teaspoon salt
Dash of pepper
1 teaspoon dried beans
2 pickles, sliced or diced
3 tablespoons chives
8 ounces Danish cheese, diced
3 tablespoons butter
2 tomatoes
2 tablespoons chopped dill

In a bowl, mix the eggs with the condensed milk, salt, and pepper. Add the dried beans, pickles, 2 tablespoons of chives, and the cheese. Heat the butter in a large frypan. Add the egg mixture; cover. Simmer it on low heat for 10 minutes.

Coucou

While the eggs are cooking, wash, peel, and quarter the tomatoes.

When the egg mixture has set in the middle, place the tomatoes on top for decoration. Sprinkle with chopped dill and the remaining 1 tablespoon of chives.

MAKES 6 TO 8 SERVINGS.

Ham soufflé

DENMARK

2 cups cold cooked ham, minced fine
6 tablespoons butter or margarine
⅓ cup bread crumbs
¼ cup flour
1½ cups milk
3 eggs, separated
½ green pepper, minced fine
Salt to taste

Sauté the ham in 2 tablespoons of the butter or margarine until the butter or margarine is absorbed. Add the bread crumbs; blend well.

Melt the rest of the butter or margarine in another frying pan. Add the flour; stir until it is smooth. Add the milk slowly, stirring constantly. Remove from the heat and add the beaten egg yolks to the white sauce, beating vigorously. Next add the minced-ham mixture, green pepper, and salt to taste. Last, fold in the egg whites, stiffly beaten.

Pour the mixture into a well-greased baking dish. Bake it at 350°F for about 45 minutes or until it is firm.

MAKES 6 SERVINGS.

Baked eggs

SWEDEN

In addition to being a delicious light supper dish, this is an easy treat for an informal brunch.

6 eggs
1¼ cups milk
1 teaspoon salt
2 teaspoons sugar
1½ tablespoons flour
½ cup cooked ham (optional)

Beat the eggs until light. Measure the milk into a 2-cup measure. Add the salt, sugar, and flour to the milk. Mix this with the beaten eggs. Last, add the ham—finely diced. Pour the mixture into a buttered baking dish.

Bake the eggs at 425°F for 25 minutes or until the center is firm.

MAKES 4 SERVINGS.

Omelet w/anchovies

SWEDEN

3 tablespoons anchovy paste or 6 to 8 anchovy fillets
6 eggs
½ cup thin cream or milk

If anchovy fillets are used, line the bottom of a greased baking dish with the fillets. The egg mixture will be poured over them.

Separate the eggs, and beat the egg whites until stiff. Set them aside. Mix the anchovy paste with the egg yolks. Add the cream. Fold the egg whites into this mixture.

Bake the mixture at 325°F for 20 minutes or until it is set in the center. Serve at once.

MAKES 4 OR MORE SERVINGS.

Mushroom omelet

Scrambled eggs w/chicken

SWEDEN

8 eggs
1 cup diced cooked chicken
1 cup cream or milk
½ teaspoon salt
Dash of pepper
2 tablespoons butter
2 teaspoons chopped parsley or finely cut chives

Beat the eggs slightly. Add the chicken, cream, salt, and pepper. Melt the butter in a frying pan and add the egg mixture. Stir lightly with a large spoon until the eggs are set.
Place the eggs on a serving plate and garnish with the parsley or chives. Serve at once.
MAKES 4 OR MORE SERVINGS.

Poached eggs w/yoghurt

MIDDLE EAST

1 cup unflavored yoghurt
1 small garlic clove, finely chopped
1 teaspoon salt
4 large eggs
Salt to taste
Dash of pepper
2 tablespoons melted unsalted butter
1 teaspoon paprika

Combine yoghurt, garlic, and salt and divide into 4 ovenproof ramekins. Put the ramekins in a slow oven of 300°F.
Poach eggs on top of the stove and when done, set 1 egg in each ramekin. Sprinkle with salt and pepper to taste. Add paprika to melted butter and spoon some over each egg to add color. Serve at once.
MAKES 2 TO 4 SERVINGS.

Coucou

MIDDLE EAST

Variations of this egg dish, sometimes called kuku, are served all over the world—and it is tasty and delicious for any meal from brunch to a light supper.

3 tablespoons butter
⅔ cup chopped white of leeks
1 large onion, thinly sliced
1 large baking potato, peeled and thinly sliced
2 ripe tomatoes, peeled and thinly sliced
2 tablespoons basil
¼ cup minced parsley
¼ cup finely chopped green pepper
½ teaspoon salt
¼ teaspoon pepper
2 tablespoons butter, cut into bits
8 beaten eggs

Sauté the leeks and onion in butter until transparent. Lower the flame and then flatten leeks and onions on the bottom of the skillet. Layer the potatoes and tomatoes and cover with basil, parsley, green peppers, and seasonings. Dot this with butter.
Pour the beaten eggs over the vegetables and cover. Simmer slowly until eggs are set and top is lightly browned. Remove from fire and turn onto a heated platter.
MAKES 4 SERVINGS.

Mushroom omelet

MIDDLE EAST

Mushrooms grow profusely in the Middle East when the rains come—and here, they make the common egg into an omelet delicacy.

2 tablespoons butter
2 cups sliced mushrooms
1 teaspoon fat
4 beaten eggs
4 tablespoons milk
Salt and pepper to taste

Melt the butter and sauté the mushrooms for about 5 minutes.
Using another skillet, melt the fat. Mix the beaten eggs with milk and seasonings and pour into the skillet. Cook over a moderate flame until the eggs begin to set and are firm. Lay the mushrooms on half of the eggs and fold over on top of the other half. Remove to a heated platter and serve at once.
MAKES 3 TO 4 SERVINGS.

Squash omelet

MIDDLE EAST

2 yellow squash, about 6 inches long
4 eggs
4 tablespoons water
Generous dash of salt
3 tablespoons butter
1 medium onion, finely chopped
Salt and pepper to taste

Wash and dry squash and trim off the ends. Cut into ¼-inch slices and then cut slices in half.
In a bowl, beat eggs, water, and salt.
Use a medium skillet to sauté the onion in butter until onion is transparent. Add the squash and cook together for 15 minutes. Salt and pepper the squash. Pour the egg mixture over the squash and cook over low heat. Lift edges to allow uncooked egg to run out. When the omelet is set, cut into 4 sections and remove from the skillet to warmed plates. The omelet should be moist on top to be just right.
MAKES 4 SERVINGS.

Vegetable & herb omelet

MIDDLE EAST

6 well-beaten eggs
½ cup finely chopped spinach leaves
¼ cup chopped leek with some greens
¼ cup chopped scallions with some greens
1 cup finely chopped parsley
¼ cup chopped fresh dill
¼ cup fresh chopped mint
2 tablespoons finely chopped fresh coriander
2 tablespoons chopped walnuts
2 tablespoons currants
1 teaspoon salt
½ teaspoon black pepper
2 tablespoons butter
1 cup unflavored yoghurt

After the eggs are well-beaten, add remaining ingredients except for butter and yoghurt. Mix well.
Melt the butter in an ovenproof dish. Pour in the egg mixture. Bake covered at 350°F for 30 minutes. Uncover and bake until eggs are set, about 25 minutes. When the top forms a golden crust, dish and serve with yoghurt on the side.
MAKES 4 SERVINGS.

Egg foo yong

CHINA

Oil to cover bottom of skillet
½ pound fresh mushrooms, sliced
½ cup chopped celery
½ cup diced scallions
1 cup fresh bean sprouts, rinsed and drained
1 cup leftover cooked chicken, beef, or shrimp, cut into small pieces
4 eggs
Salt and pepper to taste

Sauté mushrooms, celery, and scallions for 5 minutes. Cool. Add bean sprouts and chicken, beef, or shrimp to sautéed mixture.
In large bowl, beat eggs well with salt and pepper. Combine other ingredients with eggs. Drop by spoonfuls into greased skillet. Cook over medium-high heat until browned on both sides. You may use a wok, and drop mixture by spoonfuls just to cover bottom of wok.
This can be served as a main course (serves 2) or as an appetizer.
MAKES 4 SERVINGS.

Simple egg foo yong

CHINA

These are simple and delicious. Leftover chicken, beef, shrimp, etc., may also be added to rest of ingredients.

Oil for cooking
½ cup celery, thinly sliced diagonally
½ cup diced scallions
½ cup sliced fresh mushrooms
4 eggs
Salt and pepper to taste
1 cup fresh bean sprouts

Heat oil in skillet (or wok, preferably), and sauté celery for 2 minutes. Add scallions and mushrooms and sauté another minute. Remove vegetables from skillet.

Beat eggs in bowl with seasonings and add sautéed vegetables and bean sprouts. Add more oil to skillet or wok, if necessary, and add egg mixture to skillet by spoonfuls; or, if cooking in wok, add enough egg mixture just to cover bottom of wok. Cook over medium-high heat until brown, turn and brown other side. Serve with duck sauce, as a main course or as an appetizer. MAKES 2 TO 4 SERVINGS.

Shrimp egg foo yong

CHINA

1 cup chopped fresh bean sprouts
¼ cup chopped white onions
¼ cup chopped fresh mushrooms
¼ cup finely chopped cooked shrimp
1 teaspoon soy sauce
Pinch of salt
4 eggs
¼ cup crisp noodles
Oil for frying

Mix together sprouts, onions, mushrooms, shrimp, soy sauce, and salt. Add eggs; mix. Mix in noodles. Shape mixture into hamburger-size patties.
Heat oil (small amount) in frying pan. Cook each patty about 2 minutes on each side. Can be served with Sweet-and-Sour Sauce (see Index). MAKES 4 SERVINGS.

Scrambled eggs w/shrimp

CHINA

½ pound shrimp, cooked
1 teaspoon rice wine or sherry
½ teaspoon cornstarch
Salt (about ½ teaspoon)
2 tablespoons oil
6 eggs, beaten lightly
Salt to taste

Marinate shrimp in mixture of wine or sherry, cornstarch, and salt for 15 minutes. Heat oil in large skillet and sauté shrimp over medium-high heat for approximately 2 minutes. Remove from skillet.

Add salt to taste to beaten eggs and add shrimps to egg mixture. Add more oil to skillet if necessary; heat to medium-high. Pour in egg-shrimp mixture and cook and stir until done to taste. MAKES 3 TO 4 SERVINGS.

Green pepper scrambled eggs

CHINA

4 eggs
½ teaspoon salt
Freshly ground black pepper to taste
½ cup finely chopped green pepper
Oil for cooking, enough to cover bottom of pan

Beat eggs with salt and pepper. Add green pepper. Heat oil in skillet and cook mixture over medium-high heat until desired doneness. (Don't cook until dry.) MAKES 2 SERVINGS.

Oriental scrambled eggs

CHINA

3 tablespoons chopped scallions
2 tablespoons butter
½ cup sliced water chestnuts
2 cups fresh bean sprouts
6 eggs
½ teaspoon salt
¼ teaspoon freshly ground black pepper
2 teaspoons soy sauce (or to taste)

Sauté scallions in butter until tender. Add water chestnuts and bean sprouts, mixing gently.
Combine eggs with salt, pepper, and soy sauce; beat slightly. Pour egg mixture over vegetables in pan. Cook over medium heat, stirring occasionally, until eggs are done as desired. MAKES 3 OR 4 SERVINGS.

Japanese scrambled eggs

JAPAN

4 fresh mushrooms, sliced
2 scallions, cut into ½-inch pieces
1 tablespoon butter or oil

4 eggs, lightly beaten
Few sprinkles of soy sauce

Slice mushrooms and scallions; sauté in butter or oil for 2 minutes.

Beat eggs, add a few sprinkles of soy sauce, and scramble in skillet with mushrooms and scallions until sufficiently cooked. If desired, add ½ teaspoon sherry to the eggs before cooking.
MAKES 2 SERVINGS.

Zucchini & mushroom omelet

JAPAN

1 zucchini, sliced thin
12 fresh mushrooms, sliced
¼ cup chopped onions
Butter or oil
Salt
Pepper
6 eggs, beaten

Slice zucchini; set it aside. Slice mushrooms; set them aside. Chop onions; combine with zucchini.

Heat butter or oil in skillet; sauté the zucchini and onions until just tender. Add the mushrooms; cook for about 30 seconds more. Add salt and pepper to season. Add beaten eggs to mixture in skillet. Cook on medium heat until bottom is browned. Carefully turn omelet, cover, and cook until browned on other side.
MAKES APPROXIMATELY 4 SERVINGS.

Chicken & mushrooms in eggs

JAPAN

¼ pound chicken meat
¼ pound fresh mushrooms
2 onions

sauce
½ cup chicken stock
4 tablespoons soy sauce
4 tablespoons rice wine or sherry

4 eggs
4 cups rice

Thinly slice chicken meat, mushrooms, and onions.

Combine the chicken stock, soy sauce, and rice wine or sherry. Bring to boil. Add chicken, mushrooms, and onions to sauce. Cook this mixture slowly for about 15 minutes. Place ¼ of the cooked mixture in a small frying pan. Pour a lightly beaten egg over this; cook until almost firm. Remove from pan and serve over rice. This is repeated 3 more times to serve 4 people.
MAKES 4 SERVINGS.

Japanese omelet

JAPAN

4 ounces white fish meat, finely minced
2½ tablespoons flour
½ teaspoon salt
6 eggs, beaten
3 tablespoons sugar
Oil for frying

Mix together fish, flour, and salt. Add beaten eggs; mix well. When thoroughly blended, add sugar.

Heat oil in pan; when hot, pour in egg mixture. Cover; simmer for 15 minutes or until bottom is browned. Turn; cook other side. If desired, sprinkle with finely chopped scallion.
MAKES 4 SERVINGS.

Rolled fish omelet

JAPAN

6 ounces white fish such as sole, flounder, etc.
6 eggs, lightly beaten
3 tablespoons soy sauce
3 tablespoons sugar
3 tablespoons water
3 tablespoons mirin or sherry
Salt
Dash freshly ground pepper
Oil

Chop fish fine; mix with eggs, soy sauce, sugar, water, mirin (if sherry is substituted, add 1½ tablespoons more sugar), salt to taste, and pepper. Cook half of this mixture in pan on medium heat, turning to cook both sides. Remove from pan; roll it up like jelly roll. Serve omelet hot.
MAKES APPROXIMATELY 4 TO 5 SERVINGS.

Eggs w/avocado sauce

MEXICO

8 eggs, hard-boiled and peeled
2 tablespoons butter
2 tablespoons minced onion
1 tablespoon flour
1 tablespoon minced green chili
½ cup milk
2 ripe avocados
½ teaspoon salt
2 tomatoes, cut in wedges

Keep eggs warm by placing them in hot water while preparing the sauce.

Melt butter; cook onion until limp. Add flour; cook until bubbly. Add green chili; mix well. Add milk; cook, stirring constantly, until thickened. Purée avocados in blender; add with salt to sauce.

Drain and halve eggs. Place 4 egg halves on each serving plate, top with some of the sauce, and garnish with tomatoes.

MAKES 4 SERVINGS.

Ranch-style eggs

MEXICO

sauce

2 tablespoons olive oil
¼ cup chopped onion
1 clove garlic, minced
1 1-pound can tomatoes
2 tablespoons chopped green chilies
½ teaspoon dried cilantro
½ teaspoon salt

Oil for frying
4 tortillas
2 tablespoons butter
8 eggs
1 small ripe avocado

First prepare the sauce. Heat oil in small skillet; sauté onion and garlic until lightly browned. Add tomatoes, green chilies, cilantro, and salt; simmer until thick. Keep sauce warm while cooking eggs.

Heat 1 inch vegetable oil in small cast-iron skillet over moderate heat. Soft-fry tortillas 1 at a time until they are just beginning to crisp. Drain and keep them warm. Melt butter in heavy skillet; fry eggs sunny-side-up to desired degree of doneness.

Put a tortilla on each plate. Top with 2 eggs and some of the sauce. Peel and slice the avocado; garnish the eggs with it.

MAKES 4 SERVINGS.

Mexican eggs & sausage

MEXICO

2 tablespoons oil
1 small onion, finely chopped
¼ pound chorizo, homemade (see Index) or commercial, with the casings removed
8 eggs, lightly beaten
Salt and pepper to taste
1 large tomato, peeled, seeded, and chopped

Heat oil in large heavy skillet. Fry onion in oil until lightly browned. Add chorizo, breaking it up with a fork as it cooks. Cook until chorizo is lightly browned. Add eggs, salt and pepper, and tomato; reduce heat to low. Stir well. Continue to cook as you would scrambled eggs, until eggs are set and fairly dry.

Serve with warm tortillas and sliced oranges with cinnamon sugar.

MAKES 4 SERVINGS.

Mexican scrambled eggs

MEXICO

8 eggs
2 tablespoons milk
1 large tomato, peeled, seeded, and chopped
1 tablespoon chopped green pepper
1 tablespoon chopped parsley
3 tablespoons butter
½ cup chopped ham
2 tablespoons chopped chives

Beat eggs in mixing bowl with milk. Add tomato, green pepper, and parsley; stir well to combine. Melt butter over low heat in large, heavy skillet; sauté ham 3 minutes. Pour in egg

Mexican scrambled eggs

mixture; cook, stirring frequently with a spatula, until set.

Sprinkle eggs with the chives and serve with hot, buttered tortillas for brunch.

MAKES 4 SERVINGS.

Scrambled eggs w/zucchini sauce

MEXICO

2 medium zucchini, sliced diagonally
5 tablespoons butter
1 8-ounce can tomato sauce
1 teaspoon seasoned salt
¼ teaspoon pepper
8 eggs
½ cup milk
1 cup shredded cheddar cheese
Chopped chives (for color)

Sauté zucchini in 2 tablespoons butter. Stir in tomato sauce, salt, and pepper. Simmer for 8 to 10 minutes.

Beat eggs with milk. Cook eggs in 3 tablespoons melted butter. When partially cooked, stir in ½ cup shredded cheese. Finish cooking.

Place servings of egg in individual dishes, with zucchini sauce on top. Sprinkle with chives and the remaining shredded cheese.

MAKES 4 SERVINGS.

Stuffed chili w/cheese casserole

MEXICO

1 4-ounce can California green roasted chilies (or 4 roasted, peeled Poblano chilies)
¼ pound sliced sharp cheddar cheese
4 eggs, separated
4 teaspoons flour
4 teaspoons water
½ teaspoon celery salt
¼ teaspoon salt

Lightly oil a 1½- to 2-quart glass or ceramic casserole; set aside.

Rinse and seed chilies. Fill chilies with cheese slices, folding and cutting cheese so that chili pepper completely encases cheese. Place in a single layer in bottom of oiled casserole.

Combine egg yolks, flour, water, and celery salt in a small mixing bowl; beat on low speed until well-blended.

In another small mixing bowl, beat egg whites until foamy. Sprinkle with salt; continue beating until stiff but not dry. Fold egg-yolk mixture lightly but thoroughly into stiffly beaten egg whites. Pour batter over chilies; bake at 325°F for 40 minutes or until puffed and lightly browned. Serve with heated stewed tomatoes with onion and green pepper or with the following sauce.
MAKES 4 SERVINGS.

sauce

½ cup finely chopped onion
1 clove garlic, minced
1 tablespoon olive oil
2 tablespoons tomato paste
1 cup chopped canned peeled tomatoes (10½ oz.)
1 can chicken broth, regular strength
1 teaspoon sugar
½ teaspoon salt
1 teaspoon vinegar
1 tablespoon flour
1 tablespoon water

Sauté onion and garlic in oil in small saucepan until lightly browned. Add tomato paste and chopped tomatoes; stir well. Add broth, sugar, salt, and vinegar. Cook on very low heat 1 to 1½ hours or until tomatoes are soft. Force through a sieve or whirl in blender or food processor until smooth. Return to saucepan and heat until almost boiling.
Combine flour and water to form a smooth paste. Slowly stir flour paste into tomato mixture. Simmer until thickened.

Cheese enchiladas

MEXICO

8 6-inch corn tortillas
Oil for frying
2½ cups grated sharp cheddar cheese
¾ cup chopped onion
1 6-ounce can ripe olives, drained and chopped
1 recipe Red Chili Sauce or 2 10-ounce cans Enchilada
    Sauce
1 cup grated Jack cheese
Ripe olives

Soften tortillas in hot oil in small skillet until pliable (not crisp).
Combine cheese, onion, and olives; toss well to combine. Place heaping ½ cup cheese mixture in center of each tortilla; roll up to form a tubular shape. Place enchiladas side by side in ovenproof 13 X 9 X 2-inch pan. Top with Red Chili Sauce or Enchilada Sauce. Sprinkle with Jack cheese; garnish with additional black olives. Bake, uncovered, at 350°F for 30 minutes or until hot and bubbly.
MAKES 4 SERVINGS.

Red chili sauce

½ cup chopped onion
1 clove garlic, minced
3 cups canned Italian plum tomatoes, drained
½ teaspoon salt
½ teaspoon oregano
2 tablespoons vegetable oil
3 tablespoons flour
3 tablespoons chili powder
1 cup water

Combine onion, garlic, tomatoes, salt, and oregano in blender or food processor. Spin until smooth. Heat vegetable oil in small skillet. Add tomato mixture; simmer 20 minutes.
Combine flour and chili powder in large saucepan; add enough water to make a smooth paste. Slowly stir in cooked tomato purée and 1 cup water; combine well. Cook over moderate heat, stirring constantly, until thickened. Reduce heat to low; simmer 20 minutes.

Mexican fondue

MEXICO

1 pound (4 cups) shredded cheddar cheese
1 pound (4 cups) shredded Monterey Jack cheese
¼ cup all-purpose flour
2 teaspoons chili powder
1 clove garlic, halved
1 12-ounce can beer
1 4-ounce can hot green chili peppers, seeded and chopped
Amounts as desired: French bread, cubed cooked ham,
    peeled cooked shrimp, cherry tomatoes, green pepper
    strips, avocado slices

133

Combine cheeses with flour and chili powder in large bowl until well-blended.

Rub the garlic half along the inside of a ceramic fondue pot; add beer and heat slowly, just until beer begins to bubble. Gradually add cheese mixture, a handful at a time, stirring constantly, until cheese has melted and is smooth; add hot peppers. Serve fondue warm. Select desired dippers and arrange tray around fondue pot.
MAKES 8 SERVINGS.

Tortilla omelet

MEXICO

1 tortilla
3 tablespoons oil
3 eggs, well-beaten
2 tablespoons milk
Salt and pepper
1 green onion, finely chopped
3 tablespoons Queso Blanco (or Jack cheese)

Cut tortilla into eighths. Heat oil over moderate heat in 8-inch skillet or omelet pan. Fry tortilla pieces briefly to a light golden color (not as crisp as tortilla chips).

Meanwhile, beat eggs, milk, salt and pepper to taste, and green onion together. Pour egg mixture over tortillas; immediately reduce heat to low. Cook as you would an omelet, lifting cooked egg and allowing uncooked egg mixture to flow to bottom of pan. When omelet is lightly browned and almost done, sprinkle with cheese; allow to melt. Fold or cut in wedges. Serve omelet with fried chorizo (see Index) and rolls.
MAKES 2 SERVINGS.

Tortilla & cheese casserole

MEXICO

½ cup chopped onion
1 clove garlic, peeled and minced
2 tablespoons olive oil
1 10-ounce can Mexican green tomatoes (tomatillos)
2 jalapeño peppers, stemmed and seeded
1 teaspoon dried cilantro
1 teaspoon salt
¼ teaspoon pepper
½ teaspoon sugar
12 tortillas, cut in ½-inch strips
Oil or lard for frying
1 pound Monterey Jack cheese, grated
½ cup heavy cream

Sauté onion and garlic in olive oil until limp. Drain tomatillos, reserving liquid. In blender or food processor combine tomatillos and ½ cup of reserved liquid, the jalapeño peppers, cilantro, salt, pepper, and sugar; whirl until smooth. Add to onions and garlic in skillet; simmer 10 minutes.

Heat 2 to 3 tablespoons oil or lard in skillet and fry tortilla strips a few at a time on both sides, without browning. Drain on paper towels. Add more fat to skillet as needed while frying tortillas.

Grease 2-quart casserole. Arrange a layer of tortilla strips on bottom of casserole. Top with a layer of sauce and a layer of cheese. Continue layering until all ingredients are used, ending with a layer of cheese. Pour heavy cream over top; bake at 350°F for 35 minutes.
MAKES 6 SERVINGS.

Note: If tomatillos are unavailable, use 2 cups of canned tomatoes and substitute cheddar cheese for the Jack cheese. Omit the heavy cream. Serve topped with sour cream.

❧ Salads ❧

Green salad

FRANCE

The only salad recognized in France is a mixture of crisp, dry greens, served with a light dressing.

2 quarts lettuce leaves, such as romaine, escarole, Bibb, or Boston, washed, dried, and chilled

salad dressing

⅔ cup peanut oil
⅓ cup fresh lemon juice
½ teaspoon sugar
¼ teaspoon pepper
½ teaspoon salt
1 clove garlic, crushed (optional)
¼ teaspoon dry mustard

Place lettuce in large wooden serving bowl. Mix remaining ingredients for salad dressing.
A very light flavor of garlic can be obtained by rubbing salad bowl with cut garlic clove.
Pour dressing over lettuce; toss to coat leaves. Use only enough dressing to coat leaves lightly. Serve at once.
MAKES 8 SERVINGS.

Nicoise salad

FRANCE

A delicious picnic dish in France or the United States.

8 small potatoes, cooked and still hot
½ cup finely chopped onion
1 pound fresh green beans, cooked and still hot

salad dressing

¾ cup olive oil
⅓ cup red wine vinegar
¼ teaspoon salt
⅛ teaspoon pepper
¼ teaspoon dry mustard
4 tomatoes, peeled and quartered
4 hard-cooked eggs, quartered
16 large ripe olives
1 small can anchovy fillets (optional)
2 lemons, cut into wedges
1 or 2 7-ounce cans tuna, drained

Slice potatoes into large bowl with a cover. Add onion and green beans.

Mix oil, vinegar, salt, pepper, and mustard. Pour ⅓ cup dressing over hot vegetables. Cover; let cool to room temperature. Refrigerate for several hours.
To serve salad, place potatoes and green beans on large platter. Carefully arrange tomatoes, eggs, olives, anchovies, lemons, and tuna on platter. Serve with dressing separate.
MAKES 6 SERVINGS.

Basic salad dressing

FRANCE

This dressing keeps well.

¾ cup olive oil or ½ cup peanut oil plus ¼ cup olive oil
¼ cup red wine vinegar
1 teaspoon salt
1 teaspoon sugar (optional)
½ teaspoon dry mustard
⅛ teaspoon cayenne pepper

Combine all ingredients; shake well (use a jar with a lid).
MAKES 1 CUP.

Green-bean salad

GERMANY

1 pound fresh green beans, cut lengthwise
Boiling salted water
¼ cup stock reserved from green-bean cookery
3 tablespoons vinegar
3 tablespoons vegetable oil
2 medium onions, thinly sliced
½ teaspoon dried dillseed
1 teaspoon sugar

Cook beans in boiling salted water until just tender. Reserve ¼ cup of the cooking liquid and drain off the rest.
Prepare sauce by combining vinegar, oil, reserved vegetable stock, onions, dill, and sugar; stir until blended. Pour mixture over beans; marinate several hours before serving.
MAKES 4 TO 6 SERVINGS.

Red-beet salad

GERMANY

2 bunches red beets

marinade

2 tablespoons water

¼ cup vinegar

2 teaspoons caraway seeds

1 teaspoon sugar

2 tablespoons minced onion

1 teaspoon horseradish

¼ teaspoon ground cloves

½ teaspoon salt

¼ teaspoon pepper

5 tablespoons vegetable oil

Wash beets and trim off greens; place in medium saucepan and cook, without peeling, in salted water to cover, until beets are tender. Peel and slice.

Prepare marinade dressing by combining remaining ingredients. Pour over beets and let stand for several hours before serving. Stir beets occasionally.

MAKES 6 SERVINGS.

Cabbage fruit salad w/sour-cream dressing

GERMANY

2 cups shredded raw cabbage

1 red apple, diced (do not peel)

1 tablespoon lemon juice

½ cup raisins

¼ cup pineapple juice

1½ teaspoon lemon juice

¼ teaspoon salt

1 tablespoon sugar

½ cup sour cream

Prepare cabbage and apple. Use 1 tablespoon lemon juice to wet diced apples to prevent darkening. Toss cabbage, apples, and raisins.

Mix fruit juices, salt, and sugar. Add sour cream; stir until smooth. Add to salad and chill.

MAKES 4 SERVINGS.

Red-cabbage salad

GERMANY

5 slices bacon

1 teaspoon sugar

2 tablespoons vinegar

¼ cup red or white wine

½ head red cabbage, shredded

2 tablespoons vegetable oil

½ teaspoon salt

¼ teaspoon pepper

1 teaspoon caraway seeds

Fry bacon in medium-size frypan until crisp. Remove and reserve bacon.

Add sugar, vinegar, and wine to bacon fat; stir and cook until sugar is dissolved. Pour this hot mixture over the cabbage. Toss with vegetable oil, salt, pepper, and caraway seeds. Sprinkle crumbled bacon over mixture. Serve at room temperature.

MAKES 4 TO 6 SERVINGS.

Cucumber relish salad

GERMANY

2 medium cucumbers

1½ tablespoons sugar

1½ tablespoons cider vinegar

½ teaspoon salt

⅛ teaspoon pepper

½ cup sour cream

1 tablespoon minced fresh parsley

Slice cucumbers paper-thin. Sprinkle slices with sugar, vinegar, salt, and pepper. Marinate for 20 minutes, drain off liquid, and toss lightly with sour cream. Top with minced parsley.

MAKES 4 SERVINGS.

Bavarian potato salad

GERMANY

4 cups potatoes, peeled and sliced ¼-inch thick

2 cups chicken broth, canned or homemade

½ teaspoon salt

¼ cup vegetable oil

⅓ cup chopped onion

½ teaspoon sugar

2 tablespoons lemon juice
Pepper, as desired

Boil potatoes in broth with ¼ teaspoon salt for 5 to 8 minutes, until tender. Drain. Toss warm potatoes with vegetable oil and onions.

Dissolve remaining ¼ teaspoon salt and the sugar in lemon juice. Pour over potatoes. Marinate salad 1 to 2 hours before serving. Serve at room temperature.
MAKES 4 TO 6 SERVINGS.

Potato salad w/beer dressing

GERMANY

6 medium potatoes
4 slices bacon
1 tablespoon chopped onion
1 stalk celery, chopped
1 teaspoon salt
2 tablespoons butter
2 tablespoons flour
½ teaspoon dry mustard
1 tablespoon sugar
1 cup beer
½ teaspoon Tabasco sauce
2 tablespoons chopped fresh parsley

Boil potatoes in medium-size saucepan until just tender. Peel and slice.

Fry bacon until crisp. Break into small pieces and mix with onion, celery, and salt; set aside.

Stir melted butter and flour in a small saucepan until blended. Add mustard and sugar. Slowly stir in beer and Tabasco sauce. Bring to boil, stirring constantly. Pour over potato mixture. Sprinkle with parsley. Toss lightly and let stand 1 hour. Add bacon mixture; toss gently.
MAKES 4 SERVINGS.

Cold potato salad

GERMANY

6 large potatoes, peeled and quartered
Boiling water
½ teaspoon salt
1 medium onion, minced
3 tablespoons vinegar
½ teaspoon prepared mustard

1 teaspoon sugar
2 teaspoons dillseed

In medium saucepan cook potatoes in boiling salted water until tender. Drain, reserving ¾ cup of potato water. Dice potatoes. Add oil and minced onion; toss gently.

In a small saucepan bring the ¾ cup potato water to a boil; pour over potatoes and onion. Keep at room temperature for 2 to 3 hours. Stir in vinegar, mustard, sugar, and dillseed. Potato salad will be creamy. Serve at room temperature.
MAKES 6 SERVINGS.

Hot potato salad

GERMANY

3 medium potatoes, boiled in skins
3 slices bacon
¼ cup chopped onion
1 tablespoon flour
2 teaspoons sugar
¾ teaspoon salt
¼ teaspoon celery seeds
¼ teaspoon pepper
⅜ cup water
2½ tablespoons vinegar

Peel potatoes and slice thin.

Sauté bacon slowly in a frypan, then drain on paper towels. Sauté onion in bacon fat until golden brown. Blend in flour, sugar, salt, celery seeds, and pepper. Cook over low heat, stirring until smooth and bubbly. Remove from heat. Stir in water and vinegar. Heat to boiling, stirring constantly. Boil for 1 minute. Carefully stir in the potatoes and crumbled bacon bits. Remove from heat, cover, and let stand until ready to serve.
MAKES 4 SERVINGS.

Herring salad

GERMANY

1 8-ounce jar pickled herring, drained
½ green pepper, seeded and diced
1 tart apple, cored and diced
1 orange, sectioned and diced

137

2 teaspoons grated onion
2 tablespoons vegetable oil
1 tablespoon vinegar
Lettuce cups

Combine ingredients and marinate in refrigerator for at least 1 hour. Serve on cupped lettuce leaves.
MAKES 4 SERVINGS.

Herring salad w/sour cream
GERMANY

sour-cream sauce
1 cup sour cream
½ cup yoghurt
Juice of ½ lemon
¼ teaspoon sugar

salad
2 small onions
2 tart apples
8 marinated herring fillets
2 teaspoons fresh dill or ½ teaspoon dried dillweed

To prepare sauce, blend thoroughly sour cream, yoghurt, lemon juice, and sugar.
Peel onions and cut into thin slices. Peel and quarter apples, remove cores, and cut into thin wedges. Blend onions and apples with sauce.
In a dish arrange herring and apple-onion mixture in layers. Cover tightly and marinate in refrigerator 5 hours. Sprinkle with dill before serving.
MAKES 4 TO 6 SERVINGS.

Hamburg City fish salad
GERMANY

1 tablespoon butter
1 pound white fish fillets, fresh or frozen (cod, turbot, or haddock)
½ cup hot water
4 hard-cooked eggs
2 dill pickles
1 tablespoon capers

sauce
2 tablespoons mayonnaise
2 tablespoons sour cream
2 teaspoons lemon juice

1 teaspoon Dijon-style mustard
½ teaspoon salt
¼ teaspoon white pepper

garnish
1 hard-cooked egg
4 slices canned beets

Melt butter in a frypan. Place fish in frypan and pour hot water over fish. Bring to a boil, cover, lower heat, and simmer gently for 10 minutes. Meanwhile, slice 4 hard-cooked eggs and the pickles. Drain fish, cool, and cut into cubes. Prepare salad sauce by blending mayonnaise, sour cream, lemon juice, mustard, salt, and pepper.
In a separate bowl gently mix fish cubes, egg and pickle slices, and capers. Arrange fish mixture in individual dishes and spoon salad sauce over tops. Chill for 30 minutes. To garnish, cut remaining egg into eight pieces and chop beet slices. Arrange garnish on each serving. Serve immediately.
MAKES 4 SERVINGS.

Fruit salad w/nuts
GERMANY

1 small honeydew melon	Lettuce leaves
2 oranges	12 walnut halves
1 cup blue grapes	

dressing

1 8-ounce container yoghurt	2 tablespoons evaporated milk
1 tablespoon lemon juice	Dash of salt
1 tablespoon orange juice	Dash of white pepper
1 tablespoon tomato catsup	

Scoop out melon with melon baller. Cut peel from oranges, remove white membrane, and slice crosswise. Cut grapes in half and remove seeds. Line a glass bowl with lettuce leaves; arrange melon balls, orange slices, grapes, and walnuts in layers on top of lettuce.
Mix and blend well all ingredients for the dressing. Adjust seasonings. Pour dressing over the fruit. Let salad ingredients marinate for 30 minutes. Toss salad just before serving.
MAKES 4 TO 6 SERVINGS.

Herring salad with sour cream

Hamburg City fish salad

Tomato salad

GERMANY

5 medium tomatoes, chopped

1 tablespoon sugar

1 teaspoon salt

1 teaspoon dried basil

¼ teaspoon dried thyme

¼ teaspoon freshly ground pepper

½ cup vegetable oil

6 tablespoons vinegar

1 tablespoon Worcestershire sauce

1 large onion, diced

Blend all ingredients together and chill for 1 hour before serving. Serve on lettuce.

MAKES 4 SERVINGS.

Bavarian sausage salad

GERMANY

½ pound knockwurst, cooked and cooled

2 small pickles

1 onion

3 tablespoons vinegar

1 teaspoon strong mustard (Dijon or Gulden)

2 tablespoons vegetable oil

½ teaspoon salt

Fruit salad with nuts

¼ teaspoon pepper
¼ teaspoon paprika
¼ teaspoon sugar
1 tablespoon capers
1 tablespoon chopped parsley

Cut the knockwurst into small cubes. Mince the pickles and onion.

Mix together the vinegar, mustard, and oil. Add salt, pepper, paprika, and sugar. Adjust seasonings if desired. Add the capers; mix well. Stir in the chopped knockwurst, pickles, and onions. Just before serving, garnish with chopped parsley.

MAKES 4 SERVINGS.

Sauerkraut salad w/ham

GERMANY

1 16-ounce can sauerkraut
½ pound blue grapes
6 ounces cooked ham

dressing

½ cup yoghurt
¼ teaspoon salt
¼ teaspoon white pepper
1 teaspoon honey

Rinse and drain sauerkraut; chop coarsely. Wash grapes and cut in half; remove seeds if desired. Cut ham in julienne strips. Gently mix these 3 ingredients.

Blend dressing ingredients and stir into sauerkraut mixture. Marinate for 10 minutes; adjust seasoning before serving, if necessary.

MAKES 4 SERVINGS.

Seafood salad w/mayonnaise

GREECE

3 cups cooked seafood (any one or a combination of crab, shrimp, or lobster)
½ cup chopped celery
½ cup sliced green onions
½ teaspoon dried dillweed
2 tablespoons olive oil
2 tablespoons lemon juice
4 medium tomatoes
2 hard-cooked eggs, sliced
Lemon wedges
Lettuce

Sauerkraut salad with ham

Greek country salad

caper mayonnaise
1 egg
½ teaspoon mustard
½ teaspoon salt
Dash cayenne pepper
½ teaspoon sugar
1 cup olive oil
3 tablespoons lemon juice
2 tablespoons capers, chopped

In a mixing bowl combine the seafood, celery, onions, dill, 2 tablespoons olive oil, and 2 tablespoons lemon juice. Mix well. Refrigerate until ready to use.

Slice the tops off the tomatoes. Scoop out the pulp and reserve for another purpose, leaving a shell approximately ½ inch thick. Drain.

Next, make the Caper Mayonnaise. In a blender container combine the egg, mustard, salt, pepper, sugar, and ¼ cup of the oil. Blend thoroughly. With the blender running, very slowly add ½ cup more oil. Then add the lemon juice gradually and the remaining ¼ cup of oil. Blend until thick, occasionally scraping the sides of the blender jar. Transfer to a serving bowl and fold in the capers.

Arrange the lettuce on individual plates. Place one tomato shell on each plate and stuff with seafood mixture. Garnish with hard-cooked eggs and lemon wedges and serve with Caper Mayonnaise.

MAKES 4 SERVINGS.

Cabbage salad

GREECE

4 cups finely shredded cabbage
1 medium green pepper, shredded
2 tablespoons grated onion
1 teaspoon sugar
¼ cup vinegar
½ teaspoon salt
¼ teaspoon pepper
1 cup yoghurt
½ cup mayonnaise
Green-pepper rings

Combine the cabbage, green pepper, and onion and toss well. Add the sugar, vinegar, salt, and pepper. Toss again and allow to stand for a few minutes.

Combine the yoghurt and mayonnaise and add to the salad. Mix well and garnish with green-pepper rings.

MAKES 4 SERVINGS.

Spinach salad w/feta cheese

GREECE

1 pound raw spinach
2 hard-boiled eggs, sliced
1 tomato, cut in wedges
½ medium onion, thinly sliced
½ cup crumbled feta cheese

141

Cucumbers with yoghurt

salad dressing
6 tablespoons olive oil
2 tablespoons wine vinegar
½ teaspoon oregano
½ teaspoon salt
¼ teaspoon pepper

Wash the spinach well. Pick it over and discard any brown or damaged leaves. Remove the stems and break into pieces in a large salad bowl. Add the eggs, tomato, onion, and feta cheese.

Combine the dressing ingredients and shake well. Pour the dressing over the salad, toss well, and serve.

MAKES 4 TO 6 SERVINGS.

Artichoke and tomato salad

Tomato & cucumber salad w/feta cheese
GREECE

1 large tomato, thinly sliced
½ medium cucumber, peeled and thinly sliced
½ cup thinly sliced Bermuda onion
3 ounces feta cheese, sliced or cubed
¼ cup olive oil
¼ cup wine vinegar
½ teaspoon crumbled marjoram
½ teaspoon seasoned salt

Arrange the tomato, cucumber, onion, and cheese in a small salad bowl. Combine the olive oil, wine vinegar, marjoram, and seasoned salt and pour over the vegetables. Let the salad stand at least 1 hour before serving.

MAKES 4 SERVINGS.

Greek country salad
GREECE

½ head garden lettuce
2 tomatoes, cut into wedges
½ medium onion, sliced and separated into rings
½ cucumber, sliced
¼ pound feta cheese, cut into ¾-inch chunks
3 anchovy fillets
½ cup calamata olives

salad dressing
⅓ cup olive oil
⅓ cup wine vinegar
2 tablespoons water
½ teaspoon dried dillweed

Break the lettuce into bite-size pieces and place in the bottom of a salad bowl. Top with the tomatoes, onion rings, sliced cucumber, cheese, anchovies, and olives.

Combine the dressing ingredients in a shaker bottle or plastic container and shake well. Pour the dressing over the salad and toss just before serving.

MAKES 4 SERVINGS.

Cucumbers w/yoghurt

GREECE

2 medium cucumbers
1 medium red onion, sliced
¾ cup yoghurt
1 teaspoon lemon juice
1 clove garlic, minced
¾ teaspoon salt
1 tablespoon chopped fresh mint

Score the skins of the cucumbers with the tines of a fork, and slice very thin. Place in a salad bowl with the red onion.

Combine the yoghurt, lemon juice, garlic, and salt. Pour the mixture over the cucumbers and garnish with fresh mint. Chill for 1 hour before serving.

MAKES 4 SERVINGS.

Zucchini salad

GREECE

3 medium zucchini
1 medium onion, sliced and separated into rings
Juice of 2 lemons (3 tablespoons)
½ cup olive oil
¼ teaspoon oregano
¾ teaspoon salt
Chopped parsley

Wash the zucchini well under cold running water. Trim off the stem and slice very thin. Place in a large bowl. Cover with boiling water and let stand for 5 minutes. Drain well. Return to the bowl and add the onion rings. Combine the lemon juice, oil, oregano, and salt and pour the mixture over the zucchini. Mix gently and marinate for several hours before serving. Garnish with chopped parsley.

MAKES 4 SERVINGS.

Artichoke & tomato salad

GREECE

2 4-ounce jars marinated artichoke hearts
½ cup sauterne
Juice of lemon
1 whole fennel

6 medium tomatoes, sliced
2 small onions, diced
1 clove garlic
½ teaspoon salt
¼ teaspoon white pepper
½ cup warm beef broth

Drain the artichoke hearts, reserving the marinade. Cut the artichoke hearts in half and place in a large salad bowl. Combine the reserved marinade, wine, and lemon juice and pour over the artichoke hearts.

Clean the fennel, wash and slice, and add to the artichoke hearts. Add the tomatoes and onions. Mash the clove of garlic with the salt and pepper and add to the beef broth. Mix well and pour over the vegetables. Marinate for at least 10 minutes. Serve with crusty bread.

MAKES 6 TO 8 SERVINGS.

Note: If fennel is unavailable, substitute 1 small bunch of celery, cleaned and sliced.

Marinated beef salad

HUNGARY

2 cups diced cooked roast beef
1 large red pepper, cleaned, cut into chunks
2 tomatoes, diced
1 small onion, finely minced

dressing

1 clove garlic
½ teaspoon salt
3 tablespoons oil
2 tablespoons wine vinegar
Freshly ground pepper
1 head Boston lettuce
¼ cup chopped parsley

Combine beef, red pepper, tomatoes, and onion in mixing bowl; mix well.

Prepare dressing. Peel garlic clove; mash with salt. Combine garlic, oil, vinegar, and pepper to taste in small bowl. Pour over meat and vegetables; mix well. Refrigerate several hours before serving.

Arrange Boston lettuce on chilled serving plates; top with beef salad. Garnish with parsley. Serve with rye bread and sweet butter.

MAKES 2 TO 4 SERVINGS.

Marinated cabbage salad

HUNGARY

1½ cups shredded green cabbage
1½ cups shredded red cabbage
¾ cup slivered green pepper
¾ cup peeled seeded cucumber, sliced thin
¼ cup thinly sliced onion
Salt
4 tablespoons water
2 tablespoons white vinegar
1 tablespoon sugar
½ teaspoon celery seed
Salt and pepper
¼ cup shredded carrots

Place each vegetable (except carrots) in separate small dish; sprinkle with salt. Let stand 1 hour. Meanwhile combine water, vinegar, sugar, celery seed, salt, and pepper in small saucepan. Bring mixture to boil over moderate heat, stirring constantly. Allow to cool.

Place vegetables in sieve; press to remove excess water. Combine cabbage, green pepper, cucumber, onion, and shredded carrots in small casserole; toss well. Add dressing; stir well. Chill 3 hours, stirring occasionally.

MAKES 6 SERVINGS.

Beet & apple salad

HUNGARY

1 1-pound can crinkle-cut beets (or plain, sliced beets),
* drained*
1 large tart apple, peeled, diced
2 tablespoons finely minced onion
2 tablespoons oil
2 tablespoons apple-cider vinegar
1½ teaspoons sugar
Salt and pepper

Combine beets, apple, and onion in 1-quart casserole; mix lightly.

Combine oil, vinegar, sugar, salt, and pepper; beat well. Add to salad; mix well. Cover; refrigerate 3 to 4 hours before serving. Serve salad on beds of lettuce.

MAKES 4 SERVINGS.

Salami salad

HUNGARY

2 tart apples, peeled, diced
2 teaspoons lemon juice
¾ pound salami or other flavorful sausage (fully cooked),
* cut into thin strips*
4 medium tomatoes, diced
2 tablespoons pimiento, drained (cut into strips, if canned
* whole)*
1 fresh green pepper, cleaned, diced
dressing
3 tablespoons mayonnaise
3 tablespoons sour cream
1 teaspoon Hungarian sweet paprika
2 tablespoons finely minced onion
Salt
garnish
2 hard-cooked eggs, peeled, quartered
8 small sardine fillets

Toss apples and lemon juice so that apples are coated and will not turn brown. Combine salami, apples, tomatoes, pimiento, and pepper in salad bowl; toss lightly. Chill.

Combine dressing ingredients; mix well. Chill several hours.

Garnish salad bowl with hard-cooked egg wedges. Top each hard-cooked egg wedge with rolled sardine fillet. Top with dressing.

MAKES 4 LUNCHEON SERVINGS.

Pickled red cabbage

IRELAND

Delicious served with meat or poultry.

1 medium red cabbage (3 pounds)
⅓ cup coarse salt
1 quart malt vinegar
¼ cup sugar
2 tablespoons mixed pickling spices
2 bay leaves
½ teaspoon peppercorns

Core cabbage; discard any coarse leaves. Wash well; drain. Finely shred cabbage. Place in large stainless-steel or glass bowl. Add salt; stir well. Let stand in cool place 2 days, stirring well several times a day. On the third day drain cabbage well; squeeze dry in old towel. Place in canning jars.

Combine remaining ingredients in large saucepan. Bring to boil; cook, stirring, 5 minutes. Cool; strain. Pour over cabbage in jars. Cover; refrigerate. Allow to age 3 days before serving. Will keep 6 weeks in refrigerator.
MAKES 4 PINTS.

Pickled beets

IRELAND

2 bunches beets
Boiling salted water
1 medium onion, peeled, sliced, separated into rings
1/2 cup vinegar
1/2 cup water
2 tablespoons sugar
1/8 teaspoon ground cloves
1/2 teaspoon salt
3 peppercorns
1/2 bay leaf

Wash beets well. Leave root ends intact; cut off all but 2 inches of tops. Cook in boiling salted water until fork-tender. Cooking time will depend on size of beets, but allow at least 15 minutes. Alternately, beets may be wrapped in foil and baked in 375°F oven until tender (45 minutes to 1 hour). Cool beets 15 minutes; peel. Slice or quarter beets. Place beets and onion rings in canning jar.

Combine remaining ingredients in small saucepan; bring to boil. Remove from heat; pour over beets. Cover; refrigerate several days before use.
MAKES 2½ TO 3 CUPS.

Note: Liquid from pickled beets can be reserved and used to pickle hard-cooked eggs, a favorite of beer drinkers!

Old-fashioned salad

IRELAND

1 small head lettuce
1 hard-boiled egg
salad dressing
2 hard-boiled eggs, very finely chopped

2 teaspoons malt vinegar
2 teaspoons dry mustard
1 large tomato, cut in wedges
1/4 cup finely sliced onion
2 teaspoons sugar
1/2 cup sour cream
1/2 cup mayonnaise
Salt and pepper

Clean lettuce; tear into bite-size pieces. Dry with paper towel. Peel and slice hard-boiled egg; arrange with tomato and onion on lettuce in salad bowl. Refrigerate until serving time.

Thoroughly mix hard-boiled eggs, vinegar, mustard, and sugar. Add sour cream, mayonnaise, and salt and pepper to taste; mix well. Refrigerate 1 hour before serving. Pour dressing over prepared salad. Serve.
MAKES 4 SERVINGS.

Luncheon salad

IRELAND

1 cup water
Salt
1 10-ounce package frozen green beans
1 pound small new potatoes, peeled
Boiling water
1/2 teaspoon salt
1/2 pound boiled ham, cut into strips
4 tomatoes, quartered
10 pimiento-stuffed olives, sliced
salad dressing
6 tablespoons olive oil
3 tablespoons malt vinegar
1/2 teaspoon garlic salt
1 teaspoon sugar
1/2 teaspoon pepper
1 head Boston lettuce

Bring 1 cup water and salt to boil in medium saucepan. Add green beans; cook, covered, over low heat 7 to 10 minutes. Drain.

Meanwhile, place potatoes in large saucepan; barely cover with boiling water. Add ½ teaspoon salt; bring to boil. Cover; cook 15 to 20 minutes or until tender. Drain. Steam in pot a few minutes; cool. Slice.

Combine green beans, sliced potatoes, ham, to- 145

matoes, and olives in large salad bowl; mix gently. Combine all salad dressing ingredients in blender or food processor; spin 1 minute. Pour dressing over salad; mix. Refrigerate several hours before serving.

Line individual serving bowls with Boston lettuce; add salad. Serve.

MAKES 3 TO 4 SERVINGS.

Tomato salad w/basil dressing

ITALY

dressing
½ cup olive oil
3 tablespoons red wine vinegar
1 teaspoon dried sweet basil, crumbled
½ teaspoon garlic salt
Freshly ground pepper

salad
1 head romaine lettuce
3 medium tomatoes, peeled and thickly sliced
1 medium onion, peeled and sliced
1 8-ounce ball mozzarella cheese

Combine the dressing ingredients in a screw-top jar or bottle and shake well. Clean the romaine and place on a serving platter. Arrange overlapping slices of tomato, mozzarella, and onion on the platter. Refrigerate until serving time. Then, shake the dressing well. Pour over the salad. Serve immediately.

MAKES 4 SERVINGS.

Pepper & tomato salad

ITALY

2 medium green peppers
3 medium firm ripe tomatoes
½ cup olive oil
2 tablespoons red wine vinegar
½ teaspoon dried sweet basil, crumbled
1 tablespoon dehydrated parsley flakes
Salt and pepper, to taste

Clean the green pepper and cut in thin lengthwise slices. Core the tomatoes and cut into thin slices. Arrange in a serving dish. Combine the olive oil, vinegar and seasoning and combine

well. Pour over the vegetables and refrigerate several hours before serving.

SERVES 4 OR 5.

Green salad w/croutons

ITALY

croutons
1 clove garlic, peeled and sliced
1 cup cubed stale Italian bread, with the crust removed (save for bread crumbs)
2 tablespoons olive oil

salad
1 medium head iceberg or Boston lettuce
1 medium head romaine lettuce or endive
¼ cup grated Parmesan cheese

dressing
½ cup olive oil
¼ cup red wine vinegar
½ teaspoon dried oregano, crumbled
½ teaspoon salt
¼ teaspoon pepper

First, prepare the croutons. Heat the olive oil in a small skillet and sauté the garlic in the oil over moderate heat until lightly browned. Remove the garlic with a slotted spoon and discard. Add the bread cubes and sauté, stirring frequently, until golden brown. Drain on paper towels.

Combine the dressing ingredients in a bottle or screw-top jar and shake well. Allow to stand at room temperature. Clean the lettuce and pat dry. Tear into bite-size pieces and place in a salad bowl. Refrigerate until serving time.

To serve, sprinkle the salad with the cheese and croutons. Shake the dressing well and pour over the salad. Toss well and serve immediately.

MAKES 4 TO 6 SERVINGS.

Cold macaroni & bean salad

ITALY

2 cups cooked, drained macaroni
1 16-ounce can red kidney beans, drained
1 medium green pepper, cleaned and chopped
½ cup finely chopped onion
½ cup finely chopped celery

Beet and apple salad

¼ cup salad oil
¼ cup wine vinegar
1 clove garlic, minced
½ teaspoon dried sweet basil, crumbled
½ teaspoon dried oregano, crumbled
Salt and pepper
¾ cup mayonnaise
Green pepper rings
Sliced hard-cooked eggs

In a bowl, combine the macaroni, beans, and vegetables, mixing well. Combine the salad oil, vinegar, garlic, sweet basil, oregano, salt, and pepper and mix well. Pour the dressing over the salad and mix well.

Refrigerate, covered, for several hours. Add the mayonnaise and mix well. Garnish with the green pepper rings and hard-cooked egg slices.
MAKES 6 SERVINGS.

Marinated bean salad w/tuna

ITALY

2 (16-ounce) cans cannelli beans, drained
1 (7-ounce) can white solid-pack tuna, drained; broken into chunks
¼ cup finely chopped onion
¼ cup finely chopped celery
¼ cup olive oil
2 tablespoons wine vinegar
½ teaspoon crushed dried sweet basil
Salt and pepper

In large bowl combine beans, tuna, and vegetables; mix gently. Combine olive oil, vinegar, and seasonings; mix well. Pour over salad; mix gently. Cover; refrigerate at least 4 hours.
Serve on bed of lettuce with sliced tomatoes, black olives, and sliced hard-boiled egg; or serve as part of mixed antipasto tray.
MAKES 6 SERVINGS.

Luncheon salad

147

Pepper and tomato salad

Cold potato & beet salad

ITALY

2 fresh beets
2 medium potatoes
½ cup chopped green onion
¼ cup olive oil
3 tablespoons wine vinegar
1 teaspoon dried sweet basil, crumbled
½ teaspoon dry mustard
Salt and pepper
1 head Boston lettuce, cleaned

Do not remove the stalks from the beets. Just wrap them well in aluminum foil. Wash the potatoes and prick with a fork. Preheat the oven to 450°F. Bake the beets for 1 hour. Place the potatoes in the oven and continue baking 1 hour more. Remove the beets and potatoes from the oven and allow to cool.

Remove the skins from the beets and potatoes and cut into ½-inch-thick slices. Combine the beets, potatoes, and onions and mix gently. Combine the olive oil, wine vinegar, sweet basil, mustard, salt, and pepper and mix well. Pour over the beets and potatoes and mix gently. Refrigerate for several hours, covered, to mellow the flavors. Serve at room temperature in a bowl garnished with the Boston lettuce.
MAKES 4 SERVINGS.

Cauliflower salad

ITALY

1 small head cauliflower
¼ cup chopped red pepper or pimiento
2 tablespoons chopped fresh parsley (Italian flat leaf if
  available)

¼ cup sliced black olives
1 tablespoon capers, chopped
1 tablespoon wine vinegar
3 tablespoons olive oil
½ teaspoon dried oregano, crumbled

Wash the cauliflower, clean it, and separate it into flowerettes. Slice the flowerettes into thick slices. Cook in boiling water until crisp, but tender. Drain well.

Gently mix the cauliflower, pepper, parsley, olives and capers in a serving bowl. Combine the wine vinegar, olive oil and oregano and mix well. Pour over the salad and refrigerate 1 hour before serving. This salad may be garnished with anchovies if you wish.

MAKES 4 SERVINGS.

Green salad with croutons

Note: Other cooked vegetables — for example, beets, broccoli, or green beans — may be substituted in this recipe.

Marinated vegetable salad

ITALY

2 quarts water
2 teaspoons salt
1 (10-ounce) package Italian beans, partially defrosted
1 (10-ounce) package cauliflower
2 carrots, peeled, thinly sliced
1 medium zucchini, sliced ¼ inch thick
2 cloves garlic
1 teaspoon salt
¼ cup white wine vinegar

Macaroni salad with salami

6 tablespoons olive oil
¼ teaspoon pepper
½ cup sliced ripe olives
1 medium onion, peeled, sliced, separated into rings

Combine water and salt in Dutch oven; bring to boil. Add beans, cauliflower, and carrots. Cook 4 minutes. Add zucchini; cook 3 minutes. Drain in colander.
Peel garlic cloves; place on wooden board. Sprinkle with salt; mash well with side of knife. Combine garlic, vinegar, oil, and pepper in bottom of salad bowl; mix well. Add vegetables, olives, and onion; mix gently. Cover; refrigerate several hours or overnight before serving.
MAKES 6 SERVINGS.

Pickled green-bean salad

ITALY

1 (16-ounce) can green beans, drained
2 tablespoons chopped onion
2 tablespoons chopped celery
2 tablespoons chopped green pepper
¼ cup olive oil
2 tablespoons wine vinegar
½ teaspoon crumbled sweet basil
Salt and pepper

In mixing bowl combine green beans, onion, celery, and green pepper. Mix oil, vinegar, and seasonings; pour over vegetables. Mix gently. Refrigerate at least 4 hours before serving. Serve on beds of lettuce or in lettuce cups.
MAKES 4 SERVINGS.

Macaroni salad w/salami

ITALY

1 cup cooked tubetti or other short macaroni
½ cup chopped green pepper
¼ cup chopped celery
½ cup cooked frozen peas, drained (undercook slightly so they retain their shape)
½ cup salami strips
2 sweet pickles, finely chopped

salad dressing

½ cup mayonnaise or salad dressing
3 tablespoons milk
1 tablespoon lemon juice
Salt, pepper, and cayenne

garnish

2 hard-cooked eggs, peeled, quartered
2 medium tomatoes, peeled, quartered
2 tablespoons chopped parsley

Cucumbers in sour cream

In mixing bowl lightly combine tubetti, pepper, celery, peas, salami, and pickles. Combine mayonnaise, milk, and lemon juice in a small bowl. Season to taste with salt, pepper, and cayenne. Pour over salad; mix gently. Place in serving bowl; chill well.

Garnish with eggs and tomatoes; sprinkle with parsley.

MAKES 4 SERVINGS.

Raw mushroom salad

ITALY

¼ cup olive oil
1 tablespoon lemon juice
1 clove garlic, peeled, minced
½ teaspoon salt
½ pound fresh mushrooms
3 scallions
3 small heads Bibb or Boston lettuce
1 tablespoon capers, drained

Combine olive oil, lemon juice, garlic, and salt; mix well. Wipe mushrooms with damp cloth; trim; thinly slice. Wash, trim, and thinly slice green tops of scallions. Combine mushrooms and scallions in small bowl. Pour dressing over mushrooms; marinate several hours.

Clean lettuce; crisp in refrigerator. Place lettuce in large salad bowl. Add mushrooms and capers. Toss; serve immediately.

MAKES 6 SERVINGS.

Mixed seafood salad

ITALY

2 dozen mussels
2 dozen small clams
3 tablespoons olive oil
2 pounds small squid
½ cup white wine
1¼ pounds medium shrimp

dressing
4 tablespoons olive oil
2 tablespoons lemon juice
1 teaspoon Dijon mustard
Salt
Freshly ground pepper

2 tablespoons finely chopped parsley
Lettuce
Lemon wedges

Scrub mussels and clams well under cold running water. Heat 3 tablespoons oil in large skillet with tight-fitting lid. Add mussels and clams; cover. Cook over medium-high heat, shaking pan occasionally, until shellfish open (approximately 10 minutes). Remove clams and mussels from shells; cool. Reserve juices; strain through sieve lined with cheesecloth, to remove sand.

Wash squid; remove tentacles. Remove head, chitinous pen, and viscera; wash mantle well.

In large saucepan combine reserved juices from shellfish and white wine. Bring to boil over moderate heat. Add squid bodies and tentacles; cover. Simmer 20 minutes. Add shrimp; cook 5 minutes. (Squid should be tender and shrimp cooked through and pink.) Drain well. Shell shrimp; slice squid bodies into thin rings. In large bowl combine clams, mussels, squid, and shrimp.

For dressing, combine oil, lemon juice, mustard, salt, and pepper. Pour dressing over seafood; mix well. Sprinkle with parsley; marinate in refrigerator 2 hours. Serve on beds of lettuce, garnished with lemon wedges.

MAKES 4 SERVINGS.

Spiced apple salad

POLAND

1 cup granulated sugar
1 cup cold water
1 cup red hots (red cinnamon candies)
6 tart medium apples
1 cup creamed cottage cheese, small curd
½ cup finely chopped English walnuts
12 large lettuce leaves

Combine sugar, water, and cinnamon candies in saucepan. Cook over low heat until candy dissolves. Pare and core apples. Place them in the syrup; cover and cook very slowly until apples are tender but not broken. Turn apples several times during cooking period, so they will be even in color. Remove apples from syrup; drain and chill them thoroughly.

151

Mix cottage cheese and walnuts. Fill apple centers with cheese and nut mixture. To serve, arrange filled apples on lettuce beds.
MAKES 6 SERVINGS.

Bacon & spinach salad bowl

POLAND

8 slices bacon
1 pound raw spinach
3 hard-cooked eggs, chopped fine
2 tablespoons minced parsley

Fry bacon until crisp. Drain bacon on brown paper bag; crumble. Tear spinach into bite-size pieces; place in salad bowl. Add bacon pieces and chopped eggs; toss lightly. Serve salad with your favorite dressing.
MAKES 6 SERVINGS.

Beet & pickle salad

POLAND

2 cups cooked sliced beets
½ cup beet juice
½ cup bread-and-butter pickle juice
1 cup Bread-and-Butter Pickles (see Index)
¼ cup mayonnaise

Place beets, beet juice, and pickle juice in saucepan. Cover pan; simmer beets for 30 minutes. Remove from heat; add Bread-and-Butter Pickles. Chill mixture 24 hours.
To serve salad, drain and place in individual salad bowls; garnish with mayonnaise.
MAKES 6 SERVINGS.

Eggs stuffed w/mushrooms

POLAND

6 hard-cooked eggs
¼ teaspoon salt
½ teaspoon prepared mustard
½ teaspoon lemon juice
1 tablespoon mayonnaise
¼ teaspoon white pepper
1 3-ounce can mushroom stems and pieces
2 tablespoons chopped pimiento

Peel, halve, and place yolks in a bowl. Mash yolks until smooth. Add salt, mustard, lemon juice, mayonnaise, and white pepper. Mix well. Drain and chop mushrooms. Add mushrooms to egg-yolk mixture; mix well. Fill egg whites with egg-yolk and mushroom mixture; garnish each filled egg half with chopped pimiento.
MAKES 6 SERVINGS.

Pickled eggs

POLAND

1 quart water
½ cup granulated sugar
1 cup cider vinegar
1 teaspoon salt
1 tablespoon pickling spices
12 eggs

Combine water, sugar, vinegar, salt, and pickling spices. Bring to a rolling boil. Cook for 10 minutes. Cool to room temperature.
Hard-cook eggs. Peel and place them into a large container with a cover. Add cooled brine; marinate for 2 to 7 days, depending on taste preference.
MAKES 12 EGGS.

Red eggs

POLAND

6 eggs
1 quart juice from pickled beets

Hard-cook eggs. Peel and place in large container with a cover. Add pickled-beet juice; marinate for 24 to 48 hours, depending on taste preference.
MAKES 6 PICKLED RED EGGS.

Bread & butter pickles

POLAND

2½ gallons cucumbers, unpeeled and sliced paper-thin
2 large Spanish onions, peeled and sliced paper-thin
3 large sweet green peppers, cleaned and sliced into
    paper-thin strips

¼ *cup pickling salt**
4 *cups cider vinegar*
4 *cups granulated sugar*
2 *tablespoons mustard seed*
1½ *teaspoons turmeric*
½ *teaspoon whole cloves*

In a 6-gallon container layer cucumbers, onions, green peppers, and pickling salt. Cover with crushed ice; let stand 4 hours. Drain; rinse in ice-cold water.

Combine vinegar, sugar, mustard seed, turmeric, and cloves to form pickling brine. Stir to dissolve sugar. Bring pickling brine to a boil. Add drained vegetables; again bring mixture to a boil. Remove from heat immediately.

Pack vegetables into sterilized pint jars. Cover with pickling brine to ½ inch from jar rim. Seal jars; process in a boiling-water bath for 15 minutes.

MAKES 12 PINTS.

**Do not use table salt; it will make your pickling brine cloudy.*

Dilled croutons

POLAND

A delicious and economical addition to a tossed salad.

1-*pound loaf day-old bread*
1 *cup butter*
2 *teaspoons onion salt*
2 *tablespoons dried parsley flakes*
1 *teaspoon dried dillweed*

Cube bread into ½-inch cubes. Spread cubes evenly over a cookie sheet; let dry for 2 days or until cubes lose their moisture and become hard. Melt butter in large skillet. Remove butter from skillet; reserve. Add onion salt, parsley flakes, and dillweed to melted butter. Mix well.

Reheat skillet in which butter was melted. Add croutons; distribute evenly over skillet surface. Pour melted-butter mixture over croutons. Stir to distribute evenly. Fry croutons until golden brown and heated thoroughly. Cool. Store up to 1 month in airtight container.

MAKES 2 QUARTS.

Cauliflower & green-pepper mix

POLAND

1 *small head cauliflower, sliced thin*
½ *cup thinly sliced green pepper*
¼ *cup diced celery hearts*
1 *teaspoon salt*
1 *cup commercial French dressing*
8 *lettuce cups*

Gently toss cauliflower, green pepper, and celery hearts. Combine salt and French dressing; pour over mixed vegetables. Mix well. Chill and marinate salad 2 hours.

To serve, arrange lettuce cups on salad plates and fill each cup with salad mixture.

MAKES 8 SERVINGS.

Cottage-cheese-stuffed tomatoes

POLAND

4 *large tomatoes*
½ *teaspoon salt*
1 *cup small-curd cottage cheese*
½ *cup tomato pulp*
¼ *cup minced onions*
4 *sprigs parsley*

Wash and peel tomatoes. Remove cores, cut into quarters almost to the base, and spread apart. Salt tomatoes. Chill them thoroughly.

Mix cottage cheese with tomato pulp and minced onions. To serve, fill tomatoes with cottage-cheese and vegetable mixture. Garnish with parsley.

MAKES 4 SERVINGS.

Cucumbers in dill vinegar

POLAND

4 *small cucumbers (pickling size)*
1 *teaspoon salt*

dill vinegar
¼ *teaspoon dillweed*
¼ *teaspoon white pepper*
¼ *cup cider vinegar*
½ *cup cold water*

Wash and slice cucumbers into thin circles. Do not peel. Place cucumbers in shallow serving dish; sprinkle with salt. Stir cucumbers to distribute salt evenly over surfaces of slices. Let set 1 hour.

Prepare Dill Vinegar by combining dillweed, pepper, vinegar, and cold water. Pour Dill Vinegar over salted cucumbers. Refrigerate 1 hour before serving, to chill.

MAKES 4 SERVINGS.

Sweet & sour cucumbers

POLAND

4 medium-size cucumbers
2 teaspoons salt
½ cup half-and-half
2 tablespoons cider vinegar
2 tablespoons granulated sugar

Peel cucumbers. Using a potato peeler, slice cucumbers paper-thin. Sprinkle salt over cucumbers; squeeze with your hands to remove juice from cucumbers. After juice has formed, let cucumbers set in their own juice at room temperature 1 hour.

Add cream, vinegar, and sugar to cucumbers. Mix well. Chill.

MAKES 4 SERVINGS.

Sour cucumbers w/bread

POLAND

4 medium-size cucumbers
2 teaspoons salt
½ cup cream
¼ cup cider vinegar
4 slices white bread
½ teaspoon black pepper, peppermill-ground

Peel cucumbers. Using a potato peeler, slice cucumbers paper-thin. Sprinkle salt over sliced cucumbers. Squeeze cucumbers with your hands to remove juice. After juice has formed, let cucumbers and juice stand at room temperature 1 hour to wilt cucumbers.

Add cream and vinegar to cucumbers. Mix well.

Chill before serving. Serve cucumbers over bread slices. Garnish with pepper.

MAKES 4 SERVINGS.

Cucumbers in sour cream

POLAND

4 cucumbers, garden-fresh
1 cup sour cream with chives
1 small bunch leaf lettuce, cleaned
1 tablespoon parsley

Wash cucumbers thoroughly; slice into small wedges. Combine sour cream and cucumbers. Mix to coat cucumbers.

To serve, arrange lettuce leaves in salad bowls and pour ½ cup cucumber mixture on top of lettuce bed. Garnish with parsley before serving.

MAKES 4 SERVINGS.

Tongue & potato salad

POLAND

2 cups diced cooked potatoes
1 small onion, chopped fine
2 cups diced cold cooked tongue
2 hard-cooked eggs, chopped
2 tablespoons chopped fresh parsley
¾ cup commercial Russian salad dressing
4 lettuce cups

Combine potatoes, onion, tongue, eggs, and parsley; toss gently to mix. Pour salad dressing over potato mixture; mix well. Chill thoroughly.

To serve, arrange lettuce cups on salad plates and fill with tongue and potato salad.

MAKES 4 SERVINGS.

Sauerkraut salad

POLAND

4 cups drained sauerkraut
¼ cup minced onion
2 hard-cooked eggs, chopped
⅓ cup salad oil
2 tablespoons wine vinegar
⅓ cup sauerkraut juice
1 teaspoon dry mustard

Fresh garden salad

2 teaspoons granulated sugar
¼ teaspoon white pepper

In salad bowl, combine sauerkraut, onion, and hard-cooked eggs. Mix. Combine remaining ingredients in a jar; shake vigorously. Add dressing mixture to kraut mixture; toss lightly.
MAKES 6 SERVINGS.

Fresh garden salad

POLAND

2 cucumbers
½ cup white vinegar
½ cup water
1 teaspoon salt
12 cherry tomatoes, sliced into circles
1 green pepper, sliced thin
1 small sweet onion, peeled and cut into rings
1 tablespoon chopped parsley for garnish

Peel cucumbers; slice them crosswise. Combine vinegar, water, and salt. Pour over cucumbers; marinate at room temperature 2 hours. Drain. Add remaining vegetables to cucumbers; toss lightly. Chill before serving.
To serve, arrange on salad plates and garnish with parsley.
MAKES 4 SERVINGS.

Mushroom & sour-cream salad

POLAND

2 cups canned mushroom slices, drained
½ cup wine vinegar
Boston lettuce
½ cup sour cream
1 tablespoon chopped fresh parsley

Combine mushroom slices and vinegar; marinate in refrigerator 24 hours. Drain.
Arrange lettuce on salad plate. Place ½ cup marinated mushrooms in center of lettuce bed; garnish with 2 tablespoons sour cream and fresh parsley.
MAKES 4 SERVINGS.

Mushroom and sour-cream salad

Sliced-mushroom salad

POLAND

1 cup canned sliced mushrooms
¼ cup finely chopped onions
⅓ cup salad oil
¼ cup tarragon vinegar
Boston lettuce
¼ teaspoon black pepper, peppermill-ground

Drain liquid from mushrooms; pour into quart jar. Add onions, oil, and vinegar to mushrooms in quart jar. Cover; marinate for 24 hours, mixing occasionally.

Arrange lettuce on salad plates. Drain mushrooms; arrange ¼ cup marinated mushrooms on each lettuce bed. Garnish with black pepper.
MAKES 4 SERVINGS.

Hot bacon potato salad

POLAND

4 medium potatoes
2 slices bacon
½ cup chopped onions
¼ cup finely chopped celery
1 tablespoon flour
½ cup water
¼ cup wine vinegar
½ teaspoon salt
¼ teaspoon black pepper
1 tablespoon honey
¼ teaspoon dried dillweed

In a large saucepan cover potatoes with cold water; bring to rapid boil. Reduce heat; continue cooking for 20 minutes or until potatoes can be punctured easily with a dinner fork. Drain. Peel potatoes and slice into small pieces.

While potatoes are cooking, fry bacon in a large skillet until crisp. Remove bacon from skillet; drain on a paper towel to remove excess grease. Sauté chopped onions and celery in hot bacon grease until wilted. Stir in flour; stir to blend. Add water and vinegar; stir and cook until liquid is thickened. Add salt, pepper, honey, dillweed, and potatoes. Stir just enough to mix, being careful not to mash potatoes.

Crumble cooked bacon and use it to garnish potato salad just before serving.
MAKES 4 SERVINGS.

Cold Polish potato salad

POLAND

6 medium potatoes, cooked

marinade
¼ cup salad oil (olive oil may be used)
¼ cup cider vinegar
1 teaspoon dry mustard
1 teaspoon salt
½ teaspoon white pepper
1 tablespoon caraway seeds
1 medium onion, chopped fine
½ cup salad dressing
2 hard-cooked eggs, chopped
1 teaspoon paprika

Dice cooked potatoes into large bowl.

For marinade pour oil, vinegar, mustard, salt, white pepper, and caraway seeds into a jar. Seal jar; shake vigorously. Pour marinade mixture over potatoes; marinate for 1 hour. Add onion, salad dressing, and chopped eggs. Toss just enough to mix. Place potato salad in serving bowl and garnish with paprika.
MAKES 8 SERVINGS.

Warsaw salad

POLAND

2 medium-size cucumbers
6 large white radishes
2 Delicious apples
½ cup sour cream
2 tablespoons lemon juice
1 tablespoon finely chopped fresh parsley
1 teaspoon black pepper, peppermill-ground

Wash cucumbers and radishes thoroughly; slice them paper-thin. Combine. Wash and core apples; slice into thin slices. Add to vegetables; toss to mix. Combine sour cream and lemon juice.

To serve, place vegetables and fruit mixture in serving bowl; top with dressing. Garnish salad

Warsaw salad

with chopped parsley and freshly ground black pepper.
MAKES 4 SERVINGS.

Herring dinner salad

POLAND

8 ounces salt-herring fillets
4 medium potatoes
1 cup chopped pickled beets
¼ cup chopped dill pickles
4-ounce can mushroom slices, drained
½ cup mayonnaise
¼ cup milk
¾ teaspoon salt
½ teaspoon white pepper
¼ teaspoon garlic powder
¼ teaspoon nutmeg
4 hard-cooked eggs
2 teaspoons mayonnaise
¼ teaspoon mixed Italian spices
2 sprigs parsley, chopped

Soak the herring filets in cold water overnight. Boil potatoes in their jackets. Chill. Peel and cube potatoes. Remove herring from water; dry thoroughly. Dice herring into bite-size pieces; add to potatoes. Add beets, pickles, and mushroom slices. Toss fish and vegetables to mix.
Mix ½ cup mayonnaise with milk. Add ½ teaspoon salt, ¼ teaspoon white pepper, garlic powder, and nutmeg. Beat until well-blended. Pour mayonnaise mixture over herring and vegetables; mix gently. Refrigerate for 1 hour.
Peel hard-cooked eggs; cut in half. Remove yolks from whites; force yolks through a sieve. Season yolks with 2 teaspoons mayonnaise, ¼ teaspoon salt (optional), and ¼ teaspoon white pepper. Mix well.
Fill egg-white halves with egg-yolk mixture; sprinkle with Italian seasonings. Remove herring and vegetables from refrigerator; arrange filled eggs on top of salad. Garnish with parsley before serving.
MAKES 4 SERVINGS.

Fresh-fruit salad

Creamy fruit dressing

POLAND

1 cup creamed small-curd cottage cheese
½ cup sour cream
¼ teaspoon salt
½ cup maraschino cherry juice
1 tablespoon lemon juice

Force cottage cheese through a sieve or purée in a blender or food processor; fold in sour cream. Add salt, cherry juice, and lemon juice; blend well. Chill before serving.
MAKES 1¾ CUPS.

Fresh raw-spinach salad

POLAND

½ pound raw spinach
¼ cup chopped green pepper
½ Bermuda onion, cut into rings
1½ tablespoons lemon juice
1 tablespoon salad oil
½ teaspoon salt
¼ teaspoon black pepper, peppermill-ground
3 hard-cooked eggs
¼ cup anchovies

Thoroughly wash spinach, drain it, and wrap it in clean towel to dry. Tear spinach leaves into bite-size pieces; put into large salad bowl. Add green pepper, onion rings, lemon juice, salad oil, salt, and pepper. Toss lightly, just enough to mix.

To serve, garnish with hard-cooked eggs and anchovies.

MAKES 6 SERVINGS.

Liverwurst salad

POLAND

1 cup diced liverwurst
¼ cup finely chopped onion
¼ cup diced celery
¼ cup finely chopped green pepper
½ head lettuce, torn into medium-size pieces
½ cup shredded carrots

salad dressing

⅓ cup salad oil
⅓ cup salad vinegar
⅓ cup chili sauce
1 tablespoon prepared horseradish
½ teaspoon salt

Combine liverwurst, onion, celery, green pepper, lettuce, and carrots in salad bowl. Chill mixture thoroughly. Combine dressing ingredients in a jar; shake vigorously. Chill.

To serve, place vegetable and meat mixture in individual salad bowls. Pour dressing mixture into a small pitcher and pass to guests.

MAKES 6 SERVINGS.

Cottage-cheese salad dressing

POLAND

¼ cup lemon juice
¾ cup olive oil
1 teaspoon salt
¼ teaspoon white pepper
½ teaspoon dry mustard
2 tablespoons small-curd cottage cheese
1 tablespoon sweet pickle relish
1 tablespoon chopped parsley

Mix lemon juice, olive oil, salt, white pepper, and dry mustard in a glass jar; cover tightly, and

shake until thoroughly blended. Add cottage cheese, pickle relish, and chopped parsley. Mix well. Chill before serving.

MAKES 1¼ CUPS.

Sour-cream salad dressing

POLAND

3 egg yolks, hard-cooked
½ cup sour cream
¼ cup half-and-half cream
1 tablespoon vinegar
¼ teaspoon dillweed
½ teaspoon salt
¼ teaspoon black pepper
2 tablespoons chopped fresh parsley
3 egg whites, hard-cooked

Mash hard-cooked yolks until they resemble a fine meal. Stir in sour cream, half-and-half, and vinegar. Mix thoroughly. Add dillweed, salt, pepper, and parsley. Mix well.

Chop hard-cooked egg whites into fine pieces. Stir egg whites into cream mixture. Chill thoroughly before serving.

MAKES 1½ CUPS.

Garbanzo bean salad

SPAIN

A delicious salad in its own right or an ingredient in a tossed salad.

1 15-ounce can garbanzo beans, drained
½ teaspoon minced garlic or ¼ teaspoon garlic powder
2 tablespoons olive oil
2 tablespoons tarragon vinegar
¾ cup chopped celery
½ cup sliced pitted green olives
¼ cup chopped pimientos
3 scallions, chopped
½ teaspoon salt
Dash of pepper

Combine ingredients; mix well. Cover; marinate 24 hours in refrigerator. Serve salad in lettuce cups.

MAKES 4 SERVINGS.

Lettuce wedge w/chunky tomato sauce

SPAIN

1 head iceberg lettuce
2 tomatoes
¼ cup chopped green pepper
¼ cup chopped onion
2 tablespoons olive oil
1 tablespoon lemon juice
½ teaspoon minced garlic or ¼ teaspoon garlic powder
½ teaspoon crushed coriander leaves
½ teaspoon salt
Dash of cayenne

Core head of lettuce; cut into 6 wedges. Peel, seed, and chop tomatoes.

Combine all ingredients except lettuce. Beat with electric mixer on low speed 3 to 4 minutes or until tomatoes start to form their own juice. Let stand in refrigerator 3 hours to allow flavors to combine before serving. To serve, place lettuce wedge on salad plate. Pour tomato sauce over wedge.

MAKES 6 SERVINGS.

Mixed salad

SPAIN

2 cucumbers, peeled, sliced into rings
1 dozen small tomatoes, sliced into circles
1 green pepper, seeded, sliced into strips
1 red pepper, seeded, sliced into strips
1 Spanish onion, peeled, cut into rings

Combine all ingredients; toss lightly. Arrange salad on individual serving plates. Top each salad with 2 tablespoons dressing.

MAKES 4 SERVINGS.

Salad dressing

¼ cup olive oil
3 tablespoons wine vinegar
½ teaspoon salt
¼ teaspoon white pepper
1 teaspoon garlic juice or pressed garlic
¼ teaspoon crushed oregano
1 tablespoon chopped fresh parsley

Combine all ingredients; mix well.

Scalded salad

SPAIN

2 cups shredded leaf lettuce
1 onion, peeled, sliced into thin rings
1 green pepper, seeded, sliced into thin rings
5 bacon slices
1 small clove garlic, pressed, or dash of garlic powder
Salt and pepper to taste

Toss lettuce, onion, and green pepper together. Dice bacon. Fry until crisp. Remove bacon with slotted spoon. Add spices to hot bacon grease. Pour hot grease over salad greens, tossing as you pour. Sprinkle with bacon pieces. Serve immediately.

MAKES 4 TO 6 SERVINGS.

Savory salad

SPAIN

½ head lettuce
1 tomato
1 green pepper
¼ cup pitted green olives
2 celery stalks
5 radishes
½ cup canned tuna fish
1 can anchovies
6 canned sardines

Tear lettuce into bite-size pieces. Slice tomato and pepper into thin strips. Slice olives; dice celery; cut radishes into slices.

Place vegetables and tuna fish into large bowl; toss gently. Fill 6 individual salad bowls with tossed salad. Garnish each salad with anchovies and sardines. Pour dressing over individual salads or pass and let guests pour their own.

MAKES 6 SERVINGS.

Salad dressing

¼ cup olive oil
2 tablespoons lemon juice
¾ teaspoon salt
¼ teaspoon pepper
1 teaspoon oregano
1 small clove garlic, pressed, or ¼ teaspoon garlic powder

Combine ingredients; mix well.

Fresh-fruit salad

SPAIN

1 fresh pineapple
2 oranges
½ Spanish melon
1 pound green seedless grapes
2 Delicious apples

Peel pineapple. Cut into ¾-inch slices; remove rind and eyes. Cut into cubes, discarding center core. Peel and section oranges. Remove seeds from melon; slice into wedges. Wash grapes; remove from stems. Slice in half. Peel and dice apples.

Gently mix fruit in large bowl. Serve salad with Honey Dressing on the side.
MAKES 8 TO 10 SERVINGS.

Honey dressing

¾ cup mayonnaise
⅓ cup honey
¼ cup orange juice
⅛ teaspoon grated onion

Combine ingredients; mix well.

Melon salad

SPAIN

1 Spanish melon
1 cup fresh strawberries
1 orange
2 tablespoons honey
½ cup whipped cream
Pistachio nuts

Slice ¼ of top off melon; remove seeds. Scoop the flesh from melon, using melon-ball scoop; save melon shell. Place balls in large bowl. Wash and remove stems from strawberries. Add to melon balls. Peel orange, slice into sections by cutting between membranes. Add to melon balls.

Drizzle honey over fruit. Toss gently. Fill melon shell with honeyed fruit. Garnish with whipped cream and pistachio nuts; chill.
MAKES 4 TO 6 SERVINGS.

Poached oranges

SPAIN

4 oranges
1 cup sugar
½ cup sherry

Peel and remove all white membrane from oranges. Place oranges in saucepan; cover with water. Bring to boil. Reduce heat; simmer 15 minutes. Remove from water. Add sugar to water. Bring to slow boil; boil until thin syrup forms. Place oranges in syrup; simmer 5 minutes. Remove oranges from syrup; drizzle with wine. Chill oranges before serving.
MAKES 4 SERVINGS.

Cole slaw & ham
w/sour-cream dressing

DENMARK

½ cup thick sour cream
¼ teaspoon salt
2 teaspoons sugar
2 teaspoons lemon juice or vinegar
1 cup shredded cabbage
½ cup chopped celery
½ cup diced apple
8 slices boiled or baked ham

Whip together the sour cream, salt, sugar, and lemon juice. Mix the dressing with the cabbage, celery, and apple. (The apple may be peeled or not, depending on your preference. The peel adds color as well as flavor.) Spread this mixture on a ham slice, and roll it.
MAKES 8 SERVINGS.

Stuffed cucumbers

DENMARK

1 or 2 large salad cucumbers
5 tablespoons vinegar
4 tablespoons oil
½ teaspoon salt
Dash of pepper

filling

¼ *pound smoked salmon*
⅛ *pound herring fillets*
1 *hard-cooked egg*
2 *teaspoons horseradish*

Wash the cucumbers and cut each into about 8 round pieces. (Leave skins on to add color.) Mix the vinegar, oil, salt, and pepper, and marinate the cucumber pieces for 15 minutes. Remove the cucumber. Drain and dry it.

Finely chop the smoked salmon and herring. Dice the shelled egg fine. Mix this with the marinade from the cucumbers. Add the horseradish. Hollow out enough of the cucumber pieces to put the filling in. Garnish with parsley and surround with tomato wedges.

MAKES 8 SERVINGS.

Egg salad

DENMARK

1 *package frozen peas*
¼ *pound crab meat*
6 *hard-cooked eggs*
¼ *pound smoked salmon*

marinade

2 *tablespoons mayonnaise*
½ *cup sour cream*
1 *teaspoon salt*
Dash of pepper
1 *teaspoon sugar*
1 *teaspoon lemon juice*
½ *bunch parsley*

Cook the frozen peas according to package directions. Let them cool, then drain them. Drain the crab meat. Shell the eggs and cut them in small pieces. Cut the smoked salmon in strips. Mix all ingredients carefully.

Mix the mayonnaise and sour cream until lightly foamy. Add the rest of the seasonings and the chopped parsley. Pour the marinade over the salad, mixing gently. Refrigerate the salad for 10 to 15 minutes. Garnish with tomatoes and parsley and serve.

MAKES 6 SERVINGS.

Fresh mushroom salad

FINLAND

1 *cup water*
1 *tablespoon lemon juice*
½ *pound fresh mushrooms*
¼ *cup heavy cream*
1 *tablespoon grated onion*
1 *teaspoon sugar*
Salt
Pepper
Lettuce leaves

Bring the water and lemon juice to a boil. Wash the mushrooms and slice them thin. Add the mushrooms to the water and simmer them for 3 minutes. Remove them from the heat and drain them.

In a slightly chilled bowl combine the cream, onion, sugar, salt, and pepper. Mix the dressing with a spoon. Add the drained mushrooms and coat them thoroughly with the dressing. Serve the salad on lettuce leaves.

MAKES ABOUT 4 SERVINGS.

Cabbage salad

NORWAY

2 *cups cabbage, finely shredded*
1 *medium onion*
½ *cup chopped parsley*
3 *tablespoons sugar*
1 *teaspoon salt*
3 *tablespoons vinegar*
2 *tablespoons water*

Wash, shred, and drain the cabbage. Thinly slice the onion and separate it into rings. In a salad bowl toss the cabbage, onion rings, and parsley to mix.

In a small bowl dissolve the sugar and salt in the vinegar and water. Stir well until all the sugar is dissolved. Chill it well. Add the chilled liquid to the cabbage when ready to serve. Toss together gently so that all the cabbage absorbs the flavor of the dressing.

MAKES 4 SERVINGS.

Melon salad

Ham salad

SWEDEN

1 cup macaroni	**marinade**
4 cups salted water	½ cup sour cream
2 cups diced cooked ham	2 tablespoons mayonnaise
1 banana	1 tablespoon lemon juice
2 tablespoons lemon juice	Salt and pepper to taste
1 stalk celery	Pinch of sugar
½ small honeydew melon	
1 small bunch Concord grapes	
1 cup small peas	

Place the macaroni in boiling water for 12 to 15 minutes. Drain the macaroni, cool it with cold water, and let it stand to dry. Mix the cold macaroni and the diced ham in a large bowl.

Peel and slice the banana and let it stand with half of the lemon juice. Chop the celery and mix it with the rest of the lemon juice. Remove the seeds from the melon and cut it into bite-size pieces. Seed and halve the grapes. Drain the liquid from the peas. Mix all the fruit and the peas with the banana and celery, then combine this with the macaroni and ham.

Sardine & beet salad

NORWAY

8 sardines, chopped
2 large boiled beets, diced
1 medium onion, minced
4 tablespoons oil
4 tablespoons vinegar
1 teaspoon salt
Dash of cayenne pepper
Chopped parsley for garnish

Put together the sardines, beets, and onion in a large bowl. Mix the oil, vinegar, salt, and pepper together until well-blended. Pour this over the sardine mixture. Garnish with parsley on top.
MAKES 6 SERVINGS.

Cucumber salad

NORWAY

3 tablespoons boiling water
½ cup vinegar
3 tablespoons sugar
½ teaspoon salt
½ teaspoon freshly ground pepper
3 cucumbers

Combine all ingredients except the cucumbers in a saucepan. Bring them to a boil. Thinly slice, but do not peel, the cucumbers. Pour the liquid over the cucumbers. Allow them to cool. Serve the salad garnished with parsley.
MAKES 6 TO 8 SERVINGS.

Ham salad

Mix the sour cream and mayonnaise well. Add the rest of the ingredients. Spread the marinade over the salad and cover it. Refrigerate the salad for at least 60 minutes before serving.
MAKES 6 TO 8 SERVINGS.

Salmon & cucumber salad

SWEDEN

2 cucumbers, washed
½ cup French dressing
1 can (16 oz.) salmon
⅓ cup thick mayonnaise
1 tablespoon juice from salmon
Salt
Chopped parsley or chives for garnish

Cut the cucumbers in half lengthwise. Scoop out the seeds and some of the flesh to form a shell. Discard the seeds, but chop the cucumber taken out into small pieces. Marinate them in some of the French dressing for ½ hour.
Drain the salmon, reserving the salmon juice. Remove the skin and bones and flake the salmon into small pieces. Pour the remaining French dressing over the salmon and let it marinate for ½ hour in the refrigerator.
Thin the mayonnaise slightly with salmon juice. Drain the marinated salmon and mix it with the mayonnaise. Salt the cucumber shells lightly and sprinkle them with chopped chives or parsley. Fill them with the salmon salad. Spread the marinated cucumber over the top. Sprinkle this with chives and top with a line of thick mayonnaise.
MAKES 4 SERVINGS.

Salmon & macaroni salad

SWEDEN

1 teaspoon cream	*2 cups cooked macaroni*
1 teaspoon vinegar	*1 cup cooked peas*
½ teaspoon sugar	*1 cup diced celery*
1 cup mayonnaise	*1 cup cooked diced carrots*
1 can salmon	*Lettuce leaves*

Add the cream, vinegar, and sugar to the mayonnaise, stirring until all are well-mixed.
Remove the bones and skin from the salmon and flake it into small pieces. Add the macaroni and vegetables. Last, pour the mayonnaise mixture over the vegetable, macaroni, and salmon mixture; toss until they are covered. Serve the salad on crisp lettuce leaves.
MAKES 6 OR MORE SERVINGS.

Mixed-vegetable salad

SWEDEN

2 cups finely shredded raw cabbage
2 cups finely shredded raw carrots
2 cups finely shredded raw beets
2 cups seeded, finely shredded raw cucumbers
1½ cups thinly sliced radishes
1½ cups tomatoes
1½ cups French dressing

Crisp the cabbage, carrots, beets, cucumbers, and radishes in bowls of saltwater. Skin, seed, and shred the tomatoes.
Drain all vegetables and fruit when they are firm and crisp. Arrange them in a deep salad bowl in circular heaps so that the colors add to the eye-appeal of the salad. Just before serving, pour the French dressing over all.
MAKES 8 OR MORE SERVINGS.

Beet, nut, olive, & egg salad

SWEDEN

2 cups cooked, diced beets
1 cup chopped nuts
¼ cup sliced stuffed olives
French dressing
Lettuce leaves
4 hard-cooked eggs
Whole stuffed olives for topping

Mix the beets, nuts, and olives together. Add the French dressing and toss until all ingredients are well-coated. Arrange this on lettuce leaves.
Separate the egg whites from the yolks. Chop the whites fine and use them as a garnish around the mound of vegetables and fruit. Press the egg yolks through a fine sieve and sprinkle them on top of the vegetable mixture. Top the salad with a whole stuffed olive.
MAKES 4 SERVINGS.

Christmas salad

ICELAND

½ medium head red cabbage
1 tablespoon red currant jelly
1 tablespoon preserves or jam
Juice of 1 lemon (2 tablespoons)

Shred the cabbage and put it under a weight for several hours. (A plate with tin cans on top can be the weight.) Drain the cabbage and put it in a large bowl.

Add the jelly and preserves to the lemon juice, mixing well. Toss this mixture with the cabbage until it is well-mixed. It will be a color symphony on any table.

MAKES 4 TO 6 SERVINGS.

Egyptian-style white beans

MIDDLE EAST

This vegetable is listed as a salad as it is usually served chilled. Whatever you call it, it is filling and tasty on a warm evening.

1½ cups dried white beans
Water to cover
3 thinly sliced scallions
1 large cucumber, peeled and thinly sliced
½ cup olive oil
¼ cup lemon juice
2 finely minced garlic cloves
2 teaspoons salt

Wash beans, cover with water and soak for at least 12 hours; overnight is fine. Drain, place in a pot, and cover with fresh water. Boil for 2 hours or until the bean skins are split. Drain thoroughly and allow to cool.

In a bowl, place beans and remaining ingredients, stirring well to mix all of the flavors. Chill for several hours before serving.

MAKES 4 TO 5 SERVINGS.

Bulgur salad

MIDDLE EAST

1 pound bulgur (cracked wheat)
Enough water to cover

¼ cup chopped mint leaves
¼ cup chopped parsley
1 bunch chopped scallions
Salt and pepper to taste
½ cup olive oil
6 tablespoons lemon juice
Lettuce or grape leaves
2 tomatoes for garnish (optional, but good)

Wash and drain the bulgur and soak in water to cover for 1 hour. Drain again.

Add the remaining ingredients (except for lettuce) in order given, mixing thoroughly. Spoon onto a bed of lettuce or grape leaves and chill until served. Garnish with tomato wedges, if desired.

MAKES 6 SERVINGS.

Cheese salad

MIDDLE EAST

1 small cucumber
Salt
½ cup small-curd cottage cheese
½ cup crumbled Feta cheese
1 small onion, grated and drained (about ¼ cup)
1 tablespoon minced green pepper
¼ cup lemon juice
¼ cup olive oil
Salt and pepper to taste
Sprigs of fresh mint for garnish

After peeling the cucumber, cut in half lengthwise and score with a fork. Sprinkle with salt and set aside for ½ hour.

Mix thoroughly the two cheeses, grated onion, green pepper, lemon juice, and oil. Season to taste with salt and pepper. Then, drain, rinse, and cube the cucumber. Mix into the cheese until well-blended. Divide into individual portions and decorate with the fresh mint. Refrigerate for at least 30 minutes before serving.

MAKES 4 SERVINGS.

Easy chick-pea salad

MIDDLE EAST

2 10-ounce cans chick-peas
½ cup olive oil

165

3 tablespoons vinegar
1 tablespoon lemon juice
Salt and pepper to taste
1 finely minced garlic clove
1 medium onion, chopped
1 cup chopped vegetables (celery, tomatoes, peppers)
2 tablespoons diced pimientos for garnish
Parsley for garnish

Heat the chick-peas and drain. Mix the oil with vinegar, lemon juice, salt, and pepper. Add garlic and onions. Toss all with the chick-peas. Last, add the vegetables, tossing very gently. Decorate the salad with pimientos and sprinkle all with parsley.
MAKES 4 SERVINGS.

Eggplant salad

MIDDLE EAST

1 large eggplant
1 garlic clove, cut in half
1 grated onion
3 tablespoons minced parsley
2 tablespoons minced fresh mint
2 tablespoons vinegar
¼ cup olive oil
Salt and pepper to taste
2 ripe tomatoes, cut in eighths
Garnish of fresh sprigs of mint

Hold the eggplant over an open flame until the skin is crisp and the inside soft to the touch. Remove and discard the skin and drain pulp. Dice the drained eggplant.
Rub the salad bowl with garlic. Put diced pulp in bowl. Add onion, parsley, mint, vinegar, olive oil, salt, and pepper. Mix together gently. Chill. Before serving, toss in tomato wedges. Then garnish with mint. The salad is ready and delicious.
MAKES 4 TO 6 SERVINGS.

Leek salad

MIDDLE EAST

1 pound leeks, cleaned, rinsed, and drained
Water to cover
1 teaspoon salt
1 tablespoon cornstarch

2 tablespoons lemon juice
2 tablespoons olive oil

Cover leeks with water and add salt. Cook for 15 to 20 minutes or until tender. Drain off liquid and set leeks aside.
Add cornstarch to 2 cups of the drained liquid, stirring until mixture thickens. Add lemon juice and oil. When blended, pour over the waiting leeks. Allow to cool and then chill thoroughly. The leeks may look like onions, but they taste like asparagus.
MAKES 3 TO 4 SERVINGS.

Pea-cheese salad

MIDDLE EAST

½ pound diced mild cheddar cheese
½ cup mayonnaise
⅓ cup sweet pickles
2 cups drained, canned peas

Thoroughly coat the cheese with mayonnaise in a large bowl. Add the pickles and peas and mix lightly until all are blended but not broken. Marinate for several hours before serving.
MAKES 4 SERVINGS.

Fruited rice salads

Radish salad

MIDDLE EAST

1 tablespoon lemon juice
6 tablespoons olive oil
½ teaspoon hot mustard
4 to 5 cups thinly sliced radishes, white or red
8 to 10 thinly sliced black olives
1 cup crumbled Feta cheese
2 tablespoons minced fresh parsley
1 thinly sliced small red onion
Freshly ground black pepper to taste
Salt to taste

Combine lemon juice, oil, and mustard and mix well. (A small jar is good for this. Shake vigorously to mix.)
Place radishes, olives, Feta cheese, parsley, and onion in salad bowl. Add dressing and black pepper and toss well. Add extra salt if needed. Chill for 2 to 4 hours and serve. This salad is a great help when there is a large crop of fresh garden radishes to use up.
MAKES 6 TO 8 SERVINGS.

Cold spinach salad

MIDDLE EAST

2 large bags fresh spinach, washed and coarsely chopped
1 large onion, grated
¼ cup water
2 cups well-beaten plain yoghurt
2 tablespoons olive oil
1 tablespoon lemon juice
½ teaspoon salt
¼ teaspoon black pepper
1 finely minced garlic clove
½ cup chopped walnuts
1 tablespoon toasted sesame seeds
2 tablespoons minced fresh mint
Lemon wedges for garnish
Extra yoghurt, if desired

Place spinach, onion, and water in a large saucepan and cover. Steam for just 5 minutes. Strain through a colander and place spinach mixture in a salad bowl. Add the yoghurt, olive oil, lemon juice, salt, pepper, garlic, and walnuts and mix thoroughly. Adjust seasonings to taste and chill.

When ready to serve, sprinkle salad with sesame seeds and mint and garnish with lemon wedges. Extra yoghurt may be served with the salad for those who prefer more.
MAKES 4 TO 6 SERVINGS.

Tahina-cheese salad

MIDDLE EAST

¼ cup prepared tahina
1 finely chopped green onion
½ pound creamed cottage cheese
2 tablespoons sour cream
Salt and pepper to taste
6 medium cucumbers
Dash of paprika
Lettuce
Tomato slices for garnish

Blend tahina, onion, cottage cheese, sour cream, and seasonings. Set aside.
Slice the cucumbers in half lengthwise. Scoop out the seeds with a teaspoon, chop, and add to the cheese mixture. Fill the cucumber boats with the cheese mixture and sprinkle with paprika. Serve on lettuce and garnish with tomato slices.
MAKES 12 SERVINGS.

Fruited rice salads

CHINA

2 tablespoons butter
½ cup celery, diced
¼ cup onion, minced
2 teaspoons grated orange rind
1 cup orange juice
1 cup water
½ teaspoon poultry seasoning
1 cup long-grain rice
⅓ cup golden raisins
6 orange shells

Heat the butter in medium-size saucepan and sauté the celery and onion until tender. Stir in the orange rind, juice, water, poultry seasoning, rice, and raisins. Bring to a boil. Stir well, reduce heat and cover. Simmer until liquid is absorbed and rice is tender, about 30 minutes. Remove from heat.

When cool, refrigerate for several hours. Serve in orange shells.
MAKES 6 SERVINGS.

Mandarin salad

CHINA

1 teaspoon soy sauce
¼ cup French dressing
2 cups diced cooked veal (ham can be substituted)
¼ cup chopped onion
2 cups fresh bean sprouts
¼ cup sweet pickle relish
¾ cup mayonnaise
½ teaspoon salt
Dash of freshly ground black pepper

Combine soy sauce and French dressing. Marinate veal in mixture 45 minutes; chill. Add remaining ingredients; toss lightly. Serve on bed of lettuce.
MAKES 4 SERVINGS.

Mandarin-orange gelatin

CHINA

1 11-ounce can mandarin oranges, drained; reserve ½ cup liquid
3 tablespoons sauterne
2 3-ounce packages orange-flavored gelatin
1 envelope unflavored gelatin
2 cups hot water
1 cup cold water

Combine oranges with 2 tablespoons sauterne. Combine orange-flavored and unflavored gelatin in large bowl; mix well. Add hot water; stir until gelatin is dissolved. Stir in 1 tablespoon sauterne, reserved mandarin-orange liquid, and cold water. Chill until gelatin is thick and syrupy. Pour about ½ cup gelatin into 1½-quart mold rinsed in cold water. Arrange orange segments petal-fashion in gelatin. Chill until set.
Spoon about 1-inch layer thickened gelatin over oranges. Arrange layer of orange segments around edge of mold. Chill until set. Spoon another layer of gelatin over oranges. Repeat layers. Chill until set.
MAKES 6 SERVINGS.

Marinated bean sprouts

CHINA

This is an excellent salad to serve with meat or fish. It has a unique flavor. Try it for guests who like to sample something a little unusual.

1 pound fresh bean sprouts

marinade
3 tablespoons chopped scallion (green and white parts)
2 tablespoons sesame-seed oil
2 tablespoons soy sauce
1 tablespoon vodka
1 tablespoon vinegar

Place bean sprouts in colander; cook in rapidly boiling water for 1 minute. Immediately rinse with cold water; drain well.
Combine marinade ingredients in large bowl. Place bean sprouts in mixture; marinate at room temperature 1 hour. Refrigerate at least 3 hours before serving.
MAKES 4 SERVINGS.

Cucumber salad

CHINA

2 large cucumbers
⅓ cup white rice vinegar or white vinegar diluted with a little water
3½ teaspoons sugar
¾ teaspoon salt
2 slices fresh gingerroot, finely chopped

Cut cucumbers in half lengthwise and remove seeds; peel and slice crosswise into very thin slices. Mix together vinegar, sugar, salt, and ginger. Place sliced cucumbers in marinade and refrigerate for at least 2 hours before serving.
MAKES 4 TO 6 SERVINGS.

Cole slaw w/sesame dressing

CHINA

This is an unusual and tasty salad to go along with your Chinese meal.

3 cups shredded cabbage
2 medium carrots, shredded
½ medium onion, grated

sesame dressing
¼ cup sesame seeds, toasted
1½ tablespoons lemon juice
1½ tablespoons vinegar
1 teaspoon sugar
1 tablespoon soy sauce
¼ cup peanut oil

Combine cabbage, carrots, and onion.
Place sesame seeds in ungreased skillet over low heat and stir until lightly browned. Grind toasted seeds in blender. Add lemon juice, vinegar, sugar, and soy sauce, and blend into smooth paste. Combine mixture with peanut oil and blend well. Mix thoroughly with cabbage mixture.
MAKES 4 SERVINGS.

Asparagus salad
CHINA

1 tablespoon soy sauce
½ teaspoon red-wine vinegar
2 teaspoons sesame oil
1 teaspoon sugar
1 pound asparagus, tough ends broken off, sliced into 2-inch lengths

Combine soy sauce, vinegar, oil, and sugar; stir until sugar dissolves. Bring pot of water to boil. Drop asparagus into water; cook 1 minute. Drain; rinse with cold water. Toss asparagus with soy-sauce mixture; chill.
MAKES ABOUT 4 TO 5 SERVINGS.

Honan-style chicken salad
CHINA

1 pound chicken meat, shredded (leftover chicken is fine)
3 cucumbers, cut into matchstick pieces
1 leek, white part only, cut into small thin pieces
1 tablespoon minced fresh gingerroot
2 tablespoons soy sauce
2 tablespoons red-wine vinegar
2 tablespoons sugar
1 teaspoon crushed red pepper
1 tablespoon sesame oil
1 tablespoon sesame seeds, toasted in hot frying pan

Mix chicken with cucumbers; place in serving dish. Sprinkle with leek and gingerroot; chill in refrigerator.
Mix together soy sauce, vinegar, sugar, red pepper, and oil; blend thoroughly. Stir in sesame seeds. Just before serving, toss with chicken mixture.
MAKES ABOUT 4 SERVINGS.

Vegetable salad
JAPAN

1 large cucumber
2 carrots
1 large white radish
Salt
½ pound fresh mushrooms
10 ounces fresh shrimp
2 tablespoons chopped parsley
1 tablespoon chopped fresh dill

salad dressing
2 eggs
Salt
Pinch of sugar
3 tablespoons melted butter
2 tablespoons wine vinegar
1 teaspoon paprika

garnish
1 peach, sliced
1 mandarin orange or 1 tangerine, sectioned
½ orange, sliced

Grate unpeeled cucumber, carrots, and radish. Sprinkle with salt; let stand for 30 minutes. Drain off as much liquid as possible. Thinly slice mushrooms; mix with vegetables. Add shrimp and chopped fresh herbs. Toss; set aside for 15 minutes.
Meanwhile, prepare dressing by placing eggs, salt, sugar, and melted butter in top of double boiler. Beat over hot water until creamy. Remove from heat. Gradually add vinegar, beating constantly until dressing has cooled off. Season to taste with paprika.
Pour dressing over salad. Garnish with peach slices, mandarin orange or tangerine sections, and orange slices.
MAKES 6 SERVINGS.

Quick & easy salad

JAPAN

1 large cucumber, sliced
2 scallions, sliced in 1-inch pieces

salad dressing
1½ teaspoons soy sauce
2½ tablespoons sugar
6 tablespoons vinegar

Slice cucumber (do not peel). Slice scallions; toss with cucumber.

Mix together soy sauce, sugar, and vinegar. You may want to adjust the amounts to suit your taste. Pour dressing over vegetables. Toss well; serve. If you desire, you can sprinkle a few sesame seeds on top.
MAKES 2 SERVINGS.

Japanese egg salad

JAPAN

7½ ounces canned tuna fish
1 can mandarin oranges, approximately 11 ounces
16 stuffed olives
4 hard-boiled eggs

salad dressing
2 tablespoons oil
2 scant tablespoons lemon juice
2 tablespoons soy sauce
Salt
Pepper
Pinch of sugar
Parsley sprigs for garnish

Drain tuna fish; tear into bite-size pieces with a fork. Drain mandarin oranges and olives. Slice olives and hard-boiled eggs. Toss all ingredients lightly.

To prepare dressing, combine oil, lemon juice, soy sauce, salt, pepper, and sugar; stir until well-blended. Pour dressing over salad. Refrigerate for 10 minutes or longer. Divide among 4 individual glass bowls and garnish with parsley sprigs.
MAKES 4 SERVINGS.

Cauliflower salad

JAPAN

1 small cauliflower
3 tablespoons peanut butter
Water
Pinch of salt
Chopped peanuts

Boil cauliflower; separate into florets. Mix peanut butter with enough water to make a thin sauce. Season with salt. Mix in with the cauliflower. Sprinkle a little chopped peanuts over the top.
MAKES 4 SERVINGS.

Fresh spinach salad

JAPAN

10 ounces fresh spinach
4 ounces fresh mushrooms
¼ cup chopped scallion
Small amount of soy sauce
Sesame seeds (optional)

Thoroughly wash spinach; tear up larger pieces. Drain well. Slice mushrooms; add to spinach. Add chopped scallion; toss well. Sprinkle with the amount of soy sauce desired; toss lightly. Sprinkle each portion with sesame seeds.
MAKES 4 SERVINGS.

Rice salad

JAPAN

2 cups water
Salt
4 ounces long-grain rice
1 ounce dried mushrooms
8 ounces bean sprouts, canned or fresh
8 ounces canned bamboo shoots
4 ounces cooked ham
1 medium cucumber
4 tablespoons rice wine or brandy

salad dressing
5 tablespoons oil
5 tablespoons lemon juice

3 tablespoons rice wine or sherry
2 tablespoons soy sauce
Salt

garnish
1 small head Boston lettuce
1 lemon
Salt

Bring salted water to a boil. Add rice; cook for 15 minutes. Place rice in sieve. Pour cold water over it; drain thoroughly.

Chop mushrooms, place in small bowl. Cover with boiling water; let soak for 20 minutes. Drain bean sprouts, if canned. If using fresh bean sprouts, blanch, rinse with cold water, and drain them. Drain the bamboo shoots; cut bamboo shoots into ¼-inch-wide strips. Cut ham into ¼-inch-wide, 2-inch-long strips. Cut unpeeled cucumber in half, then into thin slices lengthwise, and finally into 2-inch-long thin strips. Drain the mushrooms.

To prepare salad dressing, combine oil, lemon juice, rice wine or sherry, soy sauce, and salt to taste; stir until well-blended. Add rice, bean sprouts, bamboo shoots, ham, cucumber, and mushrooms to dressing; toss thoroughly. Cover; refrigerate for 30 minutes to let flavors blend.

Meanwhile, wash lettuce and pat it dry. Tear it into large pieces. Line a serving platter with it. Arrange rice salad on top. Cut off both ends of lemon until pulp is visible. Place on platter. Sprinkle top of lemon with salt. Heat rice wine or brandy, pour it over lemon, and ignite. Serve immediately. (Lemon is only garnish, it is not eaten).
MAKES 4 SERVINGS.

Molded avocado ring

MEXICO

1½ cups mashed avocado (about 2 avocados)
2 tablespoons lemon juice
1 package lemon gelatin
¾ cup boiling water
1 cup sour cream
¾ cup mayonnaise
1 tablespoon onion juice or scraped onion
Dash cayenne pepper

2 tablespoons finely chopped green pepper
Mayonnaise
Paprika

Peel and seed avocados, sprinkle with lemon juice, and mash well. Force them through a sieve, or purée in a blender or food processor. Dissolve gelatin in boiling water. Add avocado, sour cream, mayonnaise, onion juice, cayenne pepper, and green pepper.

Lightly oil ring mold; pour in mixture. Chill it overnight. Unmold onto a large plate. Garnish with whole black olives, cherry tomatoes, and Bibb lettuce. Place a small bowl in the center of the ring; fill it with mayonnaise dusted with paprika.
MAKES 6 SERVINGS.

Chili w/salad

MEXICO

1 small head lettuce, in chunks
3 cups corn chips
1 large tomato, chopped
1 avocado, sliced
4 ounces chorizo or other garlic sausage, cooked and crumbled
¼ cup sliced ripe olives
½ cup shredded cheddar cheese
1 16-ounce can chili con carne with beans

Place lettuce chunks in bowl. Sprinkle with all other ingredients except chili. Heat chili and pour over all other ingredients. Serve at once.
MAKES 6 SERVINGS.

Cumin salad

MEXICO

2 medium tomatoes, diced
½ cup chopped onion
½ cup sliced ripe olives
¼ cup chopped fresh parsley
2 cups sliced iceberg lettuce

salad dressing
¼ cup olive oil
2 tablespoons lemon juice
Salt and pepper to taste
½ teaspoon ground cumin

Marinated beef salad

1 teaspoon crumbled dried sage leaves
⅛ teaspoon garlic salt

Layer tomatoes, onion, olives, parsley, and lettuce in salad bowl. Combine olive oil, lemon juice, salt and pepper, cumin, sage, and garlic salt, mixing well. Pour over salad. Refrigerate 1 hour before serving.
MAKES 4 SERVINGS.

Orange & onion salad

MEXICO

This salad can be prepared several hours ahead of the meal.

4 large oranges
1 Bermuda onion, sliced
1 medium cucumber, sliced
1 small green pepper, peeled, seeded, and chopped

salad dressing
⅓ cup vegetable oil
¼ cup wine vinegar
1 teaspoon sugar
½ teaspoon salt
¼ teaspoon chili powder

Peel oranges, removing as much white membrane as possible. Slice; remove seeds. Arrange oranges, onion, and cucumber in alternating layers in a serving dish. Sprinkle with green pepper. Pour dressing over all; garnish with endive. Refrigerate until serving time.
MAKES 6 SERVINGS.

Exotic fruit salad

MEXICO

salad
1 head Bibb lettuce
½ cup sliced radishes
½ medium cucumber, thinly sliced
2 small tomatoes, sliced
1 green pepper, cleaned, seeded, and cut into slivers
1 cup diced fresh pineapple
1 cup fresh strawberries, cut in half
½ cup drained mandarin oranges
½ ripe avocado
1 large peach
2 tablespoons lemon juice

salad dressing
½ cup finely minced onion
½ teaspoon prepared mustard
6 tablespoons lemon juice
Salt
White pepper
3 tablespoons vegetable oil
¼ cup chopped parsley
2 tablespoons chopped fresh dill
½ teaspoon crumbled dried tarragon

First prepare dressing. Combine onion, mustard, lemon juice, salt and white pepper to taste, oil, parsley, dill, and tarragon. Mix well. Let stand at least ½ hour to blend flavors.
Wash lettuce, dry, break into bite-size pieces, and place in large salad bowl. Add radishes, cucumber, tomatoes, green pepper, pineapple, strawberries, and mandarin oranges.

Mixed green salad

Just before serving, peel avocado half and peach, cut in wedges, and dip in lemon juice. Add to salad. Mix dressing; pour over salad. Toss and serve.

MAKES 6 SERVINGS.

Melon salad

MEXICO

1 tablespoon horseradish
⅛ teaspoon finely crushed red chilies
½ teaspoon salt
1 teaspoon sugar
½ cup olive oil
¼ cup mild fruit vinegar (preferably pineapple, pear, or apple)
½ ripe medium cantaloupe
½ medium head lettuce

In blender or food processor combine horseradish, chilies, salt, sugar, oil, and vinegar; blend. Let stand 20 minutes.

Peel cantaloupe; slice into thin wedges. Shred lettuce and arrange on serving plates. Top with cantaloupe wedges. Blend dressing again; pour it over salads.

MAKES 4 SERVINGS.

Mexican potato salad

MEXICO

4 medium potatoes
1 small onion, chopped
½ cup sliced ripe olives
½ cup chopped parsley
¼ cup olive oil
3 tablespoons red wine vinegar

173

½ teaspoon chili powder
½ teaspoon salt
¼ teaspoon pepper
2 hard-cooked eggs, chopped

Scrub potatoes and cook unpeeled in boiling salted water 30 to 40 minutes or until tender. Cool, peel, and dice. Gently combine potatoes, onion, olives, and parsley.

Mix together olive oil, vinegar, chili powder, salt, and pepper. Add dressing and eggs to salad; toss gently. Chill. Serve salad on lettuce leaves, garnished with tomatoes.

MAKES 4 SERVINGS.

Maximilian's salad

MEXICO

1 large head lettuce (or 8 cups mixed salad greens)
1 medium Bermuda onion, sliced
1 clove garlic, peeled
1 teaspoon salt
1 tablespoon sugar
½ teaspoon paprika
½ cup olive oil
¼ cup lemon juice
1 3-ounce package Roquefort cheese, crumbled

Clean lettuce, removing any brown or damaged leaves. Wash well; drain. Shake dry; tear into bite-size pieces. Combine lettuce and sliced onion in large salad bowl. Sprinkle garlic clove with salt; mash with blade of a knife. In blender or food processor combine mashed garlic, salt, sugar, paprika, olive oil, and lemon juice; whirl until blended. Pour over salad; toss. Sprinkle salad with Roquefort cheese. Serve with toasted tortillas.

MAKES 6 SERVINGS.

Pickled corn salad

MEXICO

½ cup chopped onions
½ cup diced green peppers
4 tablespoons chopped pimiento
3 tablespoons sugar
¾ teaspoon salt

½ teaspoon celery salt
½ teaspoon dry mustard
½ cup cider vinegar
½ cup water
3 cups frozen whole-kernel corn

Combine all ingredients except frozen corn; bring to a boil. Lower heat, cover pan, and simmer for 12 minutes; stirring occasionally. Add frozen corn; raise heat. When boiling resumes, lower heat; simmer until corn is just tender (2 or 3 minutes). Drain. Serve salad hot, or refrigerate and serve on lettuce leaves.

MAKES 4 TO 6 SERVINGS.

Salad Monterey-style

MEXICO

1 pound zucchini squash
1 avocado
2 tablespoons chopped onion
2 whole roasted peeled California chilies, seeded and chopped
¼ cup salad oil
2 tablespoons vinegar
1 teaspoon salt
⅛ teaspoon pepper
¼ teaspoon chili powder
¼ teaspoon sugar
1 3-ounce package cream cheese
Lettuce
1 tomato, cut in wedges
Pimiento-stuffed olives

Clean zucchini; slice into ½-inch-thick slices. Cook in boiling salted water until just tender. Drain. Peel and cube avocado; combine with zucchini, onion, and chilies.

Combine salad oil, vinegar, salt, pepper, chili powder, and sugar; pour over vegetables. Mix gently. Refrigerate for 20 to 25 minutes.

Cut cream cheese into ½-inch cubes. Place lettuce in serving bowl. Combine salad mixture with tomato wedges and cream cheese. Place in serving bowl; garnish salad with sliced olives.

MAKES 6 SERVINGS.

Peppers filled w/shrimp salad

MEXICO

4 large green peppers
2 cups cooked medium shrimp
1 tablespoon lemon juice
2 tablespoons chopped green pepper
2 tablespoons chopped red pepper (or substitute pimiento)
½ cup chopped celery
¼ cup finely chopped onion
1 tablespoon chopped fresh cilantro
½ teaspoon salt
¼ teaspoon pepper
¼ cup mayonnaise
¼ cup sour cream
4 thin lemon slices

At least 2 hours prior to serving, prepare and chill salad. First place peppers upright on cutting board. Slice down on each side of the stem, cutting away ⅓ of pepper. Reserve the piece of pepper to chop for the salad or for later use. Remove seeds and membrane from inside peppers. Blanch peppers in 1 inch boiling water 4 minutes. Immediately plunge them into ice water; drain well.

Meanwhile, toss together shrimp, lemon juice, green pepper, red pepper, celery, onion, cilantro, salt, and pepper. Mix together mayonnaise and sour cream. Add to shrimp mixture; blend well. Chill shrimp salad and peppers until serving time.

To serve, stuff pepper shells with shrimp mixture; garnish with a lemon slice.
MAKES 4 SERVINGS.

Marinated beef salad

MEXICO

This salad is a cool and imaginative way to use leftover roast beef.

salad
3 cups cubed cooked lean beef
½ cup chopped onion
2 tablespoons chopped parsley
1 sweet red pepper, seeded and chopped
1 medium tomato, chopped

salad dressing
½ cup olive oil
¼ cup wine vinegar
½ teaspoon salt
¼ teaspoon pepper
½ teaspoon crumbled oregano
½ teaspoon prepared mustard

garnish
1 head Boston lettuce
1 large tomato, cut in wedges

Combine beef, onion, parsley, red pepper, and tomato, tossing well. Combine olive oil, vinegar, salt, pepper, oregano, and mustard; pour over salad, tossing well. Refrigerate at least 3 hours.

At serving time line serving dish with lettuce leaves, fill with salad, and garnish with tomato wedges. Serve with plenty of crusty bread.
MAKES 4 SERVINGS.

Mixed green salad

MEXICO

1 head Bibb lettuce (or ½ head iceberg lettuce)
2 green peppers, cleaned, seeded, and cut into strips
4 small tomatoes, sliced
2 small onions, sliced and separated into rings
2 hard-cooked eggs, sliced
½ cup sliced stuffed green olives
½ medium cucumber, peeled, seeded, and cut into chunks

salad dressing
4 tablespoons olive oil
3 tablespoons tarragon vinegar
½ teaspoon salt
¼ teaspoon fresh ground pepper
1 clove garlic, crushed
¼ teaspoon crushed oregano
1 tablespoon chopped fresh parsley

Wash lettuce; clean, dry, and tear into bite-size pieces. Place in salad bowl, add peppers, tomatoes, onions, eggs, olives, and cucumber. Refrigerate.

Combine all dressing ingredients; mix well. At serving time toss salad at the table with prepared dressing.
MAKES 4 SERVINGS.

Poultry

Chicken veronique

FRANCE

⅓ cup flour
½ teaspoon salt
⅛ teaspoon freshly ground pepper
1 3- to 4-pound broiler-fryer, cut up, or 6 pieces chicken
¼ cup vegetable oil
¼ cup dry white wine
⅓ cup orange juice
4 tablespoons honey
¼ teaspoon salt
1 tablespoon chopped parsley
2 teaspoons grated orange rind
1 cup halved seedless green grapes
Orange slices

Mix flour, salt, and pepper. Dredge chicken in flour mixture. Shake off excess flour. Heat oil in large frying pan or Dutch oven. Brown chicken pieces on all sides. Drain off oil, if desired. Add wine, juice, honey, salt, parsley, and orange rind. Cover; simmer over low heat 45 minutes, until chicken is done. Remove chicken to serving platter.
Add grapes to pan juices. Heat gently 2 minutes to heat grapes. Pour sauce over chicken. Garnish with orange slices and additional green grapes.
MAKES 4 TO 6 SERVINGS.

Chicken-filled crepes

FRANCE

8 Basic Crepes (see Index)
3 tablespoons butter
¼ cup flour
¼ teaspoon salt
1 cup milk
2 tablespoons sherry
2 tablespoons chopped green onion, including tops
1½ cups finely chopped cooked chicken
½ cup chopped pecans
½ cup mayonnaise
2 egg whites, stiffly beaten
2 tablespoons grated Parmesan cheese

In advance: prepare and make the crepes.
Melt butter in 1-quart saucepan. Stir in flour and salt. Add milk all at once; cook and stir until thickened. Stir in sherry, green onion, chicken, and pecans.
Fill each crepe with filling. Roll up; place in greased baking dish. Before serving, fold mayonnaise into egg whites. Spread over tops of crepes. Sprinkle with cheese. Bake in preheated 375°F oven for 10 minutes or until bubbly.
MAKES 4 SERVINGS.

Chicken crepe soufflé

FRANCE

8 to 10 Basic Crepes (see Index)
bechamel sauce
2 tablespoons butter
¼ cup flour
2 cups cold milk
½ teaspoon salt
⅛ teaspoon white pepper
5 cups cooked chicken, chopped
1 pound mushrooms, sliced and sautéed
1 lemon, juiced
2 eggs, lightly beaten
Dash of cayenne
½ cup heavy cream
8 to 10 Basic Crepes (see Index)

Prepare the crepes.
To make sauce, melt butter and blend in flour. Cook for 3 minutes, stirring constantly. Add milk, salt, and pepper; cook until thickened. Reserve ½ cup sauce. Add chicken, mushrooms, lemon juice, eggs, cayenne, and cream to remaining sauce. Mix well.
Butter a round soufflé mold or ovenproof bowl; place crepes on bottom and sides. Fill with chicken mixture; place crepes on top. Bake in moderate (350°F) oven 30 minutes. Unmold onto warm platter. Serve with extra Bechamel Sauce.
MAKES 6 TO 8 SERVINGS.

Roast chicken

FRANCE

4 tablespoons butter
½ teaspoon salt
1 3-pound roasting chicken

1 tablespoon dried tarragon leaves
1 carrot, cut up
1 onion, peeled and quartered
1 tablespoon vegetable oil
½ tablespoon minced shallots
½ cup chicken broth
2 tablespoons brandy

Spread 1 tablespoon butter and the salt in cavity of chicken. Truss chicken; rub skin with 1 tablespoon of remaining butter. Place chicken in shallow roasting pan; surround with tarragon, carrot, and onion. Place in 325°F oven.

Melt remaining butter; add oil. Use this mixture to baste chicken. Baste every 15 to 30 minutes. Chicken will require about 1¼ to 1½ hours cooking time. Bird is done when juices of inner thigh are clear yellow when pricked with a fork. Remove chicken; allow to stand 15 to 20 minutes before carving.

To make sauce, remove vegetables and all but 2 tablespoons fat. Add shallots; sauté until tender. Add broth and brandy; boil rapidly to reduce stock. Serve with chicken.
MAKES 4 SERVINGS.

Poached chicken w/vegetables

FRANCE

1 small onion	4 small turnips, peeled and quartered
2 cloves garlic, peeled	
3 sprigs parsley	4 small leeks, cleaned and blanched 5 minutes in boiling water (green onions may be used)
1 teaspoon tarragon	
1 3-pound chicken	
1½ cups dry white wine	
1 cup chicken broth	2 tablespoons flour
1 teaspoon salt	½ cup heavy cream
4 carrots, peeled	2 egg yolks
	2 to 3 teaspoons horseradish

Place onion, garlic, parsley, and tarragon in cavity of chicken; truss. Place chicken in large Dutch oven. Add wine, broth, and salt; bring to a boil. Cover; place in preheated 325°F oven. Bake chicken 45 minutes. Add vegetables. Cover; bake for 30 minutes longer. When chicken and vegetables are done, remove to serving platter.

Whisk flour into cream. Skim any fat from pan juices. Beat in cream; heat until thick. Add small amount of gravy to egg yolks, then add egg yolks to pan. Stir and heat through. Add horseradish. Serve sauce with chicken.
MAKES 4 SERVINGS.

Chicken in wine

FRANCE

1 3- to 4-pound chicken, cut into serving pieces	⅛ teaspoon pepper
	3 strips bacon, cut into 2-inch strips
⅓ cup vegetable oil	
¼ cup cognac	1 4-ounce can button mushrooms, drained, or ¾ cup small mushrooms, quartered
2 medium onions, quartered	
1 clove garlic, minced	
3 cups Burgundy wine	1 tablespoon butter, softened
¼ teaspoon thyme	1 tablespoon flour
½ tablespoon tomato paste	1 or 2 parsley sprigs
1 bay leaf	2 slices white bread, toasted (optional)
½ teaspoon salt	

In large Dutch oven brown chicken in hot oil. Drain fat. Pour in cognac; carefully ignite. When flames subside, add onions, garlic, wine, thyme, tomato paste, bay leaf, salt, and pepper. Bring mixture to a boil; simmer, covered, for 1 hour. Skim off fat; correct seasonings. Discard bay leaf.

Meanwhile, place bacon in frypan; cook until done. Remove bacon; sauté mushrooms in hot fat. Drain off fat. Keep bacon and mushrooms warm until needed.

Blend butter and flour together to a smooth paste (*beurre manié*). When chicken is done, add paste to hot liquid. Stir and simmer for a minute or two. Arrange chicken in casserole or serving dish. Baste with sauce. Garnish with bacon, mushrooms, and parsley. Add toast if desired.
MAKES 4 SERVINGS.

Stuffed chicken breasts w/sherry sauce

FRANCE

2 whole chicken breasts, split, boned, and skinned
4 tablespoons butter
1 tablespoon chopped chives
1 tablespoon parsley

½ clove garlic, minced
½ teaspoon salt
⅛ teaspoon pepper
4 slices Swiss cheese
2 tablespoons vegetable oil
2 tablespoons flour
1 cup water
¼ cup dry sherry
2 teaspoons chicken-seasoned stock base

Pound each half chicken breast with flat side of meat mallet to ¼ inch thick. Form butter into 4 balls. Roll balls in mixture of chives, parsley, garlic, salt, and pepper. Place 1 seasoned ball on each slice of Swiss cheese. Place cheese on chicken breasts; roll so butter is completely enclosed. Secure with toothpicks.

Heat oil in frypan; brown the chicken rolls about 8 minutes. Place into covered shallow baking dish. Preheat oven to 350°F.

To make sauce, stir flour into drippings in frypan; stir and heat until smooth. Remove from heat. Mix water, sherry, and stock base. Stir into drippings; heat to boiling, stirring constantly. Spoon sauce over chicken; cover. Bake for 30 minutes. Remove toothpicks. Serve.
MAKES 4 SERVINGS.

Chicken w/Hunter sauce

FRANCE

½ cup flour
¼ teaspoon salt
Dash pepper
3-pound frying chicken, cut up
2 tablespoons vegetable oil
2 tablespoons butter
2 shallots or green onions
½ pound sliced mushrooms
½ cup white wine
¼ cup brandy
1 cup Basic Brown Sauce (see Index)
1 tablespoon tomato paste
¼ teaspoon thyme
½ teaspoon tarragon
1 tablespoon flour

Mix ½ cup flour, salt, and pepper. Dredge chicken in seasoned flour. Heat oil and 1 table-spoon butter in Dutch oven or large frypan. Add chicken pieces; cook until lightly browned. Remove chicken.

Add shallots and mushrooms to pan. Sauté until liquid from mushrooms has evaporated. Add chicken, wine, brandy, Brown Sauce, and tomato paste. Sprinkle with herbs. Cover; simmer gently until chicken is done, about 30 minutes. Mix flour and 1 tablespoon butter; add to hot sauce to thicken, if desired. Serve sauce separately.
MAKES 4 SERVINGS.

Mediterranean chicken

FRANCE

4 pounds fresh tomatoes, peeled, seeded, and chopped
2 tablespoons vegetable oil
2 tablespoons butter
½ teaspoon salt
⅛ teaspoon freshly ground pepper
8 whole boneless chicken breasts, skin removed
¼ cup vegetable oil
2 medium onions, thinly sliced
4 cloves garlic, crushed
½ teaspoon thyme
2 bay leaves
2 tablespoons tomato paste
1 cup dry white wine
½ teaspoon sugar
Pastry and olives for garnish

Cook tomatoes in 2 tablespoons oil and butter about 5 minutes. Add salt and pepper.

In large skillet brown chicken on both sides in ¼ cup hot oil. Add onions, garlic, thyme, bay leaves, and tomato paste. Cook until onions are softened. Add wine; cook rapidly to reduce to about half. Add tomatoes and sugar. Cover; simmer gently 15 minutes. Garnish with parsley and olives. Serve.
MAKES 8 SERVINGS.

Duck w/orange sauce

FRANCE

1 6- to 7-pound duck or 2 3- to 4-pound ducks

Chicken in wine

Roast chicken (next pages)

½ teaspoon salt

⅛ teaspoon pepper

orange sauce

2 tablespoons sugar

2 tablespoons vinegar

Brown Sauce (see Index for recipe, but omit Madeira and cognac)

2 tablespoons frozen orange-juice concentrate

1 teaspoon lemon juice

1 tablespoon cornstarch

1 tablespoon Madeira

2 tablespoons cognac

2 tablespoons Grand Marnier

2 oranges, sectioned

Clean duck; remove giblets. Sprinkle cavity with salt and pepper. Truss; scald with boiling water to open pores so fat will drain out during cooking. Also make small knife slits through skin in thigh, back, and lower breast areas. Roast both sizes of duck at 425°F for 1 hour. Reduce heat to 325°F; cook 6- to 7-pound duck 1 more hour or 3- to 4-pound duck 30 minutes more. If duck is not browned sufficiently, increase heat to 425°F for a few minutes.

Meanwhile, make Orange Sauce. Combine sugar and vinegar; boil briefly to caramelize (brown). Cool, add Brown Sauce, and heat to dissolve. Stir in orange and lemon juices; simmer for 8 to 10 minutes. Thicken slightly by mixing corn-

starch with Madeira and adding to sauce. Simmer for 1 to 2 minutes. Finish sauce with cognac, Grand Marnier, and orange sections.

When duck is roasted, let stand about 10 minutes before carving. Spoon some hot sauce over carved duck; serve rest of sauce separately.

MAKES 4 SERVINGS.

Grandma's chicken

GERMANY

2 very small chickens

¼ cup vegetable oil

1 teaspoon salt

½ teaspoon white pepper

2 teaspoons paprika

6 medium potatoes

4 slices bacon

4 to 6 small onions

¼ cup hot beef bouillon

Parsley sprigs for garnish

Clean chickens. Heat oil in a large Dutch oven. Add chickens; brown well on all sides for about 10 minutes. Season with salt, white pepper, and paprika. Continue cooking for another 10 minutes, turning often.

Meanwhile, peel potatoes and cut into 1-inch cubes. Cut bacon into 1-inch pieces. Add pota-

Oregano chicken

toes and bacon to chicken. Cook for 5 minutes. Dice onions and stir in with hot beef bouillon. Cover and bake in a preheated 350°F oven about 45 minutes. Remove cover and bake another 5 minutes to brown the chickens. Arrange on a preheated platter and garnish with parsley.
MAKES 4 SERVINGS.

Chicken livers w/apples & onion

GERMANY

3 tablespoons flour
1/2 teaspoon salt
1/4 teaspoon pepper
1/8 teaspoon cayenne pepper
3 medium apples
1/4 cup vegetable oil
1/4 cup sugar
1 large onion, thinly sliced

Rinse chicken livers and drain on paper towels. Coat livers evenly with a mixture of flour, salt, pepper, and cayenne pepper. Set aside.
Wash and remove cores from apples. Cut apples into 1/2-inch slices, to form rings. Heat 2 tablespoons vegetable oil in a frypan over medium heat. Add sliced apples and cook until lightly brown. Turn slices carefully and sprinkle with sugar. Cook uncovered over low heat until tender. Remove from pan and reserve.

Heat remaining 2 tablespoons vegetable oil over low heat. Add chicken livers and onion rings. Cook over medium heat, turning mixture often to brown all sides. Transfer to a warm serving platter. Serve with apple rings.
MAKES 4 SERVINGS.

Chicken w/artichokes

GREECE

2 tablespoons butter
2 whole chicken breasts (about 1 1/2 pounds), split
1 clove garlic, minced
1/2 teaspoon salt
1/4 teaspoon white pepper
1/2 cup chicken broth
1/4 cup white wine
1 10-ounce package frozen artichoke hearts, thawed
1 tablespoon cornstarch mixed with 1 tablespoon cold water
3 eggs
2 tablespoons lemon juice
2 tablespoons chopped parsley

Melt the butter in a heavy skillet. Brown the chicken breasts. Add the garlic and sauté for 3 minutes more. Add the salt, pepper, chicken broth, and wine. Cover and simmer for 30 minutes. Add the artichoke hearts and continue to cook for 10 minutes.
Drain off the broth and keep the chicken warm. Measure the broth. One cup is needed for the sauce. Add canned chicken broth if necessary.

Heat the broth in a small saucepan and thicken with the cornstarch mixed with cold water.

Beat the eggs well. Slowly add the lemon juice while continuing to beat the mixture. Slowly beat in the hot broth and then return the mixture to the saucepan. Cook over very low heat, stirring constantly, until thickened. Taste for seasoning. Arrange the chicken and artichokes on a platter. Pour the sauce over the chicken and garnish with parsley.

Oregano chicken

GREECE

3 pounds fryer-chicken parts
1 large freezer bag
½ cup olive oil
¼ cup lemon juice
2 cloves garlic, minced
½ teaspoon salt
1 teaspoon crumbled dried oregano
½ teaspoon freshly ground pepper
2 tablespoons butter, melted

The day before cooking: Wash the chicken parts and pat dry. Place in the freezer bag. Combine the oil, lemon juice, garlic, salt, oregano, and pepper and pour over the chicken. Tie the bag shut and turn the bag several times to coat the chicken with the marinade. Refrigerate for 24 hours, turning the bag occasionally.

To cook: Remove the chicken from the bag, reserving the marinade. Grill, 5 inches from white-hot charcoal, for 30 minutes, turning once. Brush frequently with the reserved marinade combined with the melted butter.
MAKES 4 TO 5 SERVINGS.

Variation: Substitute 1 3-pound roasting chicken for the chicken parts. Marinate in the same manner. Drain the chicken, reserving the marinade. Mount on a rotisserie spit, and cook for 1½ hours on an indoor unit or over charcoal. Baste frequently with the marinade mixed with the melted butter.

Roast chicken

GREECE

2 frying chickens, about 3 pounds each
1 teaspoon salt
1 teaspoon freshly ground pepper
2 cloves garlic, crushed
5 tablespoons melted butter
6-8 medium potatoes, peeled and cut in lengthwise wedges
2 medium onions, peeled and cut in wedges
⅓ cup lemon juice
½ cup water

Wash the chickens and pat dry. Rub with the salt, pepper, and garlic. Place in a large roasting pan, breast-side-up, and brush on all surfaces with 3 tablespoons of the melted butter.

Roll the potatoes in the remaining 2 tablespoons of melted butter and place in the pan with the chicken, along with the onions. Roast at 425°F for 25 minutes. Reduce the heat to 325°F and continue roasting 45 to 50 minutes longer or until the leg joint moves easily.

Pour the lemon juice over the chicken and remove the chicken, potatoes, and onions to a platter and keep them warm. Skim the fat from the pan juices. Add the water and bring to a boil. Pour into a gravy boat. Slice the chicken and serve.
MAKES 6 TO 8 SERVINGS.

Stuffed chicken breast Athenian

GREECE

4 split chicken breasts, skinned and boned
2 tablespoons crumbled feta cheese
1 tablespoon chopped walnuts
1 tablespoon chopped parsley
¾ cup flour
½ teaspoon salt
¼ teaspoon pepper
1 egg
2 tablespoons milk
2 tablespoons olive oil
2 tablespoons butter

Cut a small pocket in each chicken cutlet by making a slit in each piece that does not go all the way through the cutlet. Mix the feta cheese, walnuts, and parsley. Put 1 tablespoon of stuffing in each cutlet and seal the edges by pressing together.

Mix the flour, salt, and pepper. Dredge the cutlets in the flour mixture. Mix the egg and milk. Dip cutlets in the egg mixture and then again in the flour mixture. Refrigerate until ready to cook.

Heat the olive oil and butter in a large, heavy skillet, over medium heat, until the foam subsides. Cook the cutlets over medium-high heat until brown. Turn the cutlets over and reduce the heat. Cook until brown and cooked through. Do not cover, as the chicken will lose its crispness and the cheese will begin to ooze out of the cutlet. Serve the chicken with Rice Pilaf (see Index) and topped with Kima Sauce.

MAKES 4 SERVINGS.

Kima sauce

3 tablespoons olive oil
¼ cup chopped onion
¼ cup chopped carrots
¼ cup chopped celery
1 clove garlic, chopped
1 8-ounce can tomatoes, drained and chopped
2 tablespoons chopped parsley
¼ cup white wine
¼ teaspoon sugar
¼ teaspoon oregano

Heat the olive oil in a small, heavy skillet. Cook the onion, carrots, celery, and garlic until limp. Add the drained tomatoes, parsley, wine, sugar, and oregano; simmer for 20 minutes or until thick.

Broiled chicken w/cucumber sauce

GREECE

¼ cup olive oil
¼ cup lemon juice
1 cup dry white wine
1 teaspoon crumbled dried oregano
1 broiler-fryer (approximately 2½ pounds), split and quartered

Combine the oil, lemon juice, wine, and oregano and pour over the chicken in a baking dish. Marinate at room temperature for 3 hours. Broil in the oven 4 inches from the heat source, turning once, and basting with the marinade, until done (may also be broiled over charcoal). Serve with Cucumber Sauce.

MAKES 4 SERVINGS.

Cucumber sauce

1 cup plain yoghurt
⅓ cup olive oil
1 garlic clove, peeled and crushed
1 teaspoon salt
1 cucumber, peeled, seeded, and finely chopped

Combine the yoghurt, olive oil, garlic, salt, and cucumber and serve over the chicken.

Greek chicken

GREECE

1 5-pound roasting chicken
3 teaspoons dried oregano
2 large cloves garlic, pressed, or 1½ teaspoons garlic powder
¾ teaspoon salt
½ teaspoon pepper
1 30-inch piece heavy-duty aluminum foil

Wash and dry the chicken. With a sharp knife slash the chicken at 1-inch intervals on all skin surfaces, down to the bone if possible. This ensures penetration of the herbs into the meat. Combine the oregano, garlic powder, salt, and pepper. Rub the chicken cavity and skin with the herb mixture, using all of it.

Place the chicken in the center of the aluminum foil. Bring the 2 ends of the foil together over the chicken and fold together several times to seal. Seal the ends of the foil. Do not fold the foil tightly around the chicken, as juice will accumulate in the package. Place the package in a roasting pan. Roast at 400°F for 1½ hours.

Remove the chicken from the oven and carefully open a corner of the foil. Pour the juices into a measuring cup or gravy boat. Undo the foil and slice the chicken. Serve the juices and Rice Pilaf (see Index) with the chicken.

MAKES 6 SERVINGS.

Chicken kampama

GREECE

3 pounds chicken parts
2 tablespoons butter
2 tablespoons olive oil
2 medium onions, chopped
2 cloves garlic, minced
1 cup canned tomatoes
½ of a 6-ounce can tomato paste
2 sticks cinnamon
¼ teaspoon ground allspice
½ teaspoon sugar
¼ cup red wine

In a large skillet brown the chicken on all sides in the butter and olive oil. Remove from the pan.
Brown the onions and garlic. Add the tomatoes, tomato paste, seasonings, and wine. Bring to a boil. Add the chicken. Reduce the heat to simmer and cook for 1 to 1½ hours or until tender. Serve with Macaroni Athenian-Style (see Index).
MAKES 4 TO 5 SERVINGS.

Chicken w/yoghurt

GREECE

3 pounds fryer-chicken parts
Juice of 1 lemon
Salt and pepper
6 tablespoons butter
2 cloves garlic, minced
2 medium onions, sliced
½ cup white wine
1 cup chicken broth
1 teaspoon crumbled rosemary
1 cup plain yoghurt
2 tablespoons flour

Rub the chicken with the lemon juice, salt, and pepper. Melt the butter in a large, heavy skillet. Brown the chicken on all sides. Add the garlic and onions and brown them lightly. Add the wine, chicken broth, and rosemary. Reduce the heat to low, cover, and cook for 30 minutes or until the chicken is tender.
Combine the yoghurt and flour and mix well.

Remove the skillet from the heat and allow to cool for 10 to 15 minutes. Add the yoghurt and flour slowly, mixing well. Cook, stirring constantly, over very low heat until slightly thickened. Pour the sauce over the chicken and serve.
MAKES 4 SERVINGS.

Gala stuffed turkey

GREECE

1 16-pound turkey, thawed
  if frozen
¼ cup lemon juice
Salt and pepper

stuffing

1 stick butter
1 pound ground beef
Liver from the turkey,
  chopped
1 clove garlic, minced
1 cup chopped celery
1 cup chopped onion
¼ cup chopped parsley
1 teaspoon salt
½ teaspoon pepper
½ teaspoon ground
  cinnamon
1 cup long-grain raw rice
2 cups water
1 8-ounce can tomato sauce
½ cup currants
½ cup dry white wine
½ cup chopped walnuts
¼ cup pine nuts
½ cup butter, melted

Wash and dry the turkey. Remove the giblets. Reserve the liver for the stuffing. Sprinkle the turkey inside and out with the lemon juice, salt, and pepper.
Next prepare the stuffing. Melt the butter in a large Dutch oven. Brown the ground beef and turkey liver. Add the vegetables, and cook a few additional minutes. Add the seasonings and rice. Add the water and tomato sauce. Cover and cook 20 to 25 minutes or until the rice is tender. While the rice cooks, soak the currants in the wine. When the rice is tender, add the currants and nuts and mix well. Cool.
Stuff the turkey with the prepared stuffing, and truss. Brush with the melted butter and roast in an open pan for 5 hours at 325°F, brushing frequently with the butter, or until a meat thermometer inserted in the thigh of the turkey registers 185°F Let stand 15 minutes before carving.
MAKES 12 TO 14 SERVINGS.

Chicken livers & eggplant

GREECE

1 eggplant (1 pound) peeled and sliced ½ inch thick
¾ cup flour
1 teaspoon salt
½ teaspoon pepper
2 eggs, well-beaten
¼ cup olive oil
2 tablespoons butter
1 medium onion, sliced
1½ pounds chicken livers, washed, drained, and cut in half
2 tablespoons flour
1 cup chicken broth
2 tablespoons white wine
¾ cup canned tomatoes, drained and chopped
2 tablespoons chopped fresh parsley

Soak the eggplant in salted water for 15 minutes. Drain and pat dry. Combine the flour, salt, and pepper. Dip the eggplant in the beaten eggs and then in the seasoned flour, coating well. Heat the oil in a large skillet. Add the eggplant slices and fry over medium-high heat until crisp and brown. Drain on paper towels and keep them warm.

Melt the butter and fry the onion and chicken livers until well-browned. Add the flour, and mix well. Add the chicken broth, wine, tomatoes, and oregano. Cover and simmer 10 minutes.

Arrange the eggplant to form a border around the edge of a large round plate. Put the chicken livers and sauce in the center and top with the parsley. Serve with Rice Pilaf (see Index).
MAKES 4 SERVINGS.

Roast stuffed chicken

HUNGARY

1 4-pound roasting chicken
6 tablespoons butter
1 cup chopped onion
1 cup sliced mushrooms
7 thin slices white bread, crusts removed, cubed
¼ cup minced fresh parsley
1 egg, lightly beaten
Salt and pepper
2 tablespoons melted butter

½ teaspoon Hungarian sweet paprika
1 tablespoon dry sherry

Wash chicken; pat dry. Remove liver from giblet pack. Wash well; set aside. Reserve remaining giblets for another use. Melt 6 tablespoons butter in heavy skillet. Add onion and liver; sauté 3 minutes. Add mushrooms; cook, stirring, until liver is well-browned and onion transparent. Remove pan from heat. Finely chop chicken liver. Combine bread cubes, onion, mushrooms, butter, liver, parsley, egg, salt, and pepper in mixing bowl; mix well. Stuff chicken with mixture; truss. Secure neck opening with skewer. Combine 2 tablespoons melted butter, paprika, sherry, salt, and pepper; mix well.

Place chicken in roasting pan; brush well with butter mixture. Roast at 350°F 1¼ to 1½ hours or until juices run clear when breast is pierced with sharp knife. Baste several times with butter mixture while cooking. Remove stuffing, carve chicken, and serve. Thicken pan juices for gravy if desired.
MAKES 4 TO 5 SERVINGS.

Chicken paprikas

HUNGARY

1 3-pound frying chicken, cut up
½ cup flour
Salt and pepper
4 tablespoons butter or margarine
1 medium onion, peeled, sliced
½ pound mushrooms, sliced
1 tablespoon Hungarian sweet paprika
1 cup chicken broth
½ cup dry white wine
2 tablespoons flour
½ cup sour cream

Wash chicken well; pat dry. Combine flour, salt, and pepper in plastic bag. Add chicken pieces a few at a time; shake to coat. Melt butter in Dutch oven or kettle over moderate heat. Add chicken; brown well on all sides. Remove from pan.

Add onion to kettle; cook until lightly browned. Remove from pan with slotted spoon; reserve. Add mushrooms to pan; cook until tender. Remove pan from heat; add paprika. Stir in chicken broth and wine; add onion and chicken. Return to heat. Bring mixture to boil over moderate heat; cover. Reduce heat to low; cook 50 to 60 minutes or until chicken is tender.

Combine flour and sour cream; stir well. Remove chicken from pan; keep warm. Stir sour-cream mixture into pan juices; cook over very low heat until thickened. Pour sauce over chicken. Serve with rice, noodles, or dumplings.
MAKES 4 SERVINGS.

Chicken livers paprikash
HUNGARY

1 pound chicken livers
4 tablespoons butter or margarine
1 cup thinly sliced onions
1 clove garlic, peeled, mashed
1 tablespoon Hungarian sweet paprika
Salt and pepper
1 cup chicken broth
¼ cup sour cream
1 tablespoon flour

Rinse livers; drain very well. Remove fat or connective tissue. Melt butter in large heavy skillet over moderate heat. Add onions and garlic;

Stuffed chicken breast Athenian

Roast goose with apple-sausage stuffing

cook, stirring, until browned. Remove from heat. Add livers, paprika, salt, and pepper; stir well. Add chicken broth; cover. Bring to boil. Reduce heat to low; cook 15 to 20 minutes or until livers are done to taste.

Combine sour cream and flour; stir well. Add slowly to liver mixture, stirring well. Cook over very low heat until thickened. Serve livers with Buttered Noodles (see Index) or dumplings; garnish with chopped parsley.

MAKES 4 SERVINGS.

Roast turkey w/chestnut dressing

HUNGARY

1 10- to 12-pound turkey,
thawed if frozen

chestnut dressing

¼ cup butter or margarine	*½ teaspoon Hungarian*
1 large onion, peeled,	*sweet paprika*
chopped	*6 cups soft bread cubes*
2 stalks celery, chopped	*¼ cup chopped parsley*
¼ pound ground veal	*1 pound chestnuts, roasted,*
¼ pound ground pork	*skinned, chopped*
1 turkey liver, chopped	*1 egg, well-beaten*
¾ teaspoon salt	*5 slices bacon*
Freshly ground black pepper	

Wash turkey well; drain. Remove giblet pack; save liver for dressing. Lightly salt cavity of turkey; set aside while preparing dressing.

Melt butter or margarine in large skillet. Add onion and celery; sauté until tender. Using slotted spoon, transfer to large mixing bowl. Add veal, pork, and liver to skillet; sauté until lightly browned. Season with salt, pepper, and paprika; add to celery and onion mixture. Add remaining stuffing ingredients; mix well.

Stuff turkey with mixture; truss. Place in roasting pan, breast-side-up. Lay bacon strips in single layer over turkey. Roast at 325°F approximately 4 hours or to an internal temperature of 185°F. Allow to stand, tented with aluminum foil, 20 minutes before carving. Make your favorite gravy with pan drippings.

MAKES 6 TO 8 SERVINGS.

Chicken pie

Roast goose w/apple-sausage stuffing

HUNGARY

¾ pound sausage, hot or mild

5 tablespoons butter

1 medium onion, chopped

2 stalks celery, chopped

5 cups toasted white bread cubes

1 large apple, peeled, chopped

½ teaspoon crumbled dried marjoram

3 teaspoons salt

½ teaspoon pepper

1 8-pound goose

1 lemon

giblet stock

Goose giblets and liver (including neck if available)

4 cups water

2 celery tops

1 small onion

2 cloves

Salt and pepper

gravy

6 tablespoons rendered goose fat or drippings

6 tablespoons flour

Salt and pepper

1 teaspoon brown-gravy seasoning

4 cups giblet stock

Fry sausage in heavy skillet until well-browned, breaking into bite-size pieces as it cooks. Drain well; reserve. Melt butter in skillet. Add onion and celery; cook until tender. Combine sausage, onion, celery, butter, bread cubes, apple, marjoram, 1 teaspoon salt, and pepper in mixing bowl; mix well. Set aside.

Remove giblet pack from goose; set aside. Remove and discard loose fat in body cavity; reserve for rendering, or discard. Wash goose well; pat dry.

Squeeze lemon. Rub goose inside and out with the lemon juice and 2 teaspoons salt. Stuff neck cavity loosely; skewer shut. Spoon remaining stuffing into body cavity; truss. Be sure to tie wings and legs closely to bird. Place goose on rack, breast-side-up; prick well on breast and thighs so that fat will drain. Roast at 325°F 3 to 3½ hours or until meat thermometer registers 185°F when inserted into breast.

While goose cooks, prepare broth. Combine giblets, water, celery, onion, and seasonings in small saucepan; bring to boil. Cover; simmer 30 minutes. Remove liver; cook 30 minutes. Strain broth; cool. Chop liver and giblets; reserve.

Remove goose to platter when done; tent with aluminum foil while making gravy. Combine goose drippings and flour in medium saucepan; cook over low heat, stirring constantly, until lightly browned. Add salt, pepper, and gravy seasoning. Slowly stir in giblet stock; cook, stirring constantly, over low heat until thickened. Add reserved giblets; heat through.

Carve goose; spoon dressing into serving dish. Serve with gravy and red cabbage or sauerkraut and applesauce.

MAKES 6 SERVINGS.

Duck w/cherry sauce

HUNGARY

1 5- to 6-pound domestic duckling

1 medium onion, peeled, quartered, studded with 2 cloves

2 stalks celery, cut into thirds

cherry sauce

1 16-ounce can bing cherries or sweet black cherries

½ cup reserved juice from cherries

Grilled paprika chicken

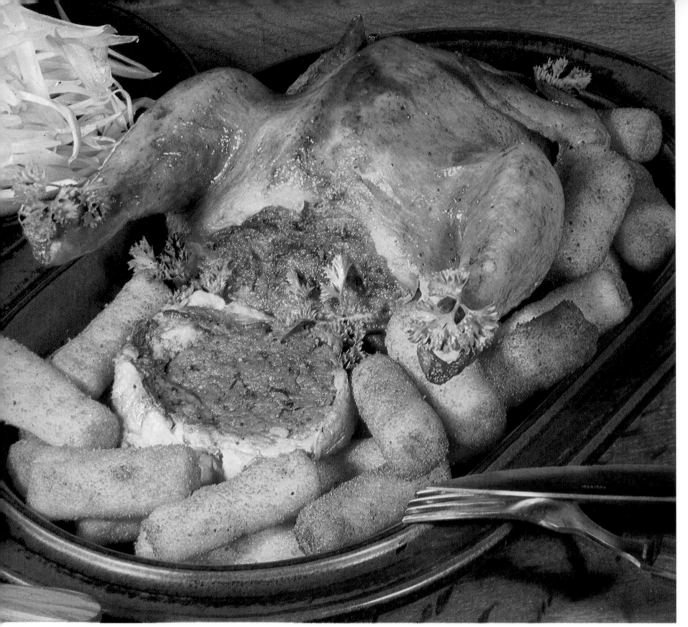

Goose with potato stuffing

½ cup Tokay wine
2 tablespoons cornstarch
2 tablespoons cherry brandy

Wash duckling; pat dry. Stuff body cavity with onion and celery. Place duckling on rack in roasting pan. Preheat oven to 450°F. Place roasting pan in oven; immediately reduce temperature to 350°F. Bake 1¾ to 2 hours or until juices run clear when breast is pierced with knife.

Meanwhile prepare Cherry Sauce. Drain cherries well; reserve ½ cup cherry juice. Heat cherry juice to boiling in small saucepan. Thoroughly mix wine and cornstarch. Stir into cherry juice; cook, stirring constantly, until thickened. Add cherries and brandy; heat through. Discard vegetables from duck cavity. Carve duck; top with Cherry Sauce.

MAKES 4 SERVINGS.

190

Grilled paprika chicken

HUNGARY

3 tablespoons lemon juice	1 teaspoon Hungarian sweet paprika
3 tablespoons melted butter	Freshly ground pepper
1 clove garlic, crushed	1 3-pound broiler-fryer, cut up
1 teaspoon salt	

sauce

3 tablespoons butter or margarine	2 teaspoons Hungarian sweet paprika
1 small onion, peeled, diced	1 cup chicken broth
¼ cup chopped green pepper	½ cup tomato sauce
¼ cup chopped mushrooms	2 tablespoons dry sherry
1½ tablespoons flour	

Combine lemon juice, butter, garlic, salt, paprika, and pepper in glass mixing bowl or heavy-duty plastic bag; mix well. Wash chicken; pat dry. Add to marinade; turn to coat with marinade. Cover or tie plastic bag shut; marinate overnight in refrigerator.

Drain chicken; reserve marinade. Arrange chicken on broiler pan, skin-side-down. Broil 6 inches from heat source, basting occasionally with marinade. Turn; cook 15 minutes, basting twice.

Meanwhile, make sauce. Melt butter in medium saucepan. Add onion; cook until tender. Add green pepper and mushrooms; sauté until tender. Add flour; stir well. Cook until bubbly. Remove from heat; stir in paprika; return to heat. Add chicken broth and tomato sauce; cook, stirring constantly, until thickened. Add sherry; stir well. Serve chicken accompanied by sauce, rice, and green salad.

MAKES 4 SERVINGS.

Chicken pie

IRELAND

1 2- to 2½-pound chicken	2 tablespoons chopped parsley
2 cups water	1½ cups mushrooms, cleaned, quartered
½ cup white wine	
1 stalk celery, sliced	3 tablespoons butter
1 carrot, peeled, sliced	3 tablespoons flour
1 shallot, peeled, chopped	2 cups reserved stock
½ teaspoon salt	Salt and pepper
½ teaspoon poultry seasoning	3 tablespoons cream
4 slices crisp bacon, crumbled	2 frozen puff pastry shells (from 10-ounce package), defrosted
2 hard-boiled eggs, peeled, quartered	1 egg yolk
1 medium onion, peeled, diced	

Wash chicken; pat dry. Place in large saucepan with water, wine, celery, carrot, shallot, ½ teaspoon salt, and poultry seasoning. Bring to boil; reduce heat to low. Cook 40 minutes or until cooked through. Strain; reserve stock. Cool chicken. Skin, bone, and cut chicken into 1-inch pieces. Combine chicken, bacon, eggs, onion, parsley, and mushrooms in 9½-inch pie plate; set aside.

Melt butter in medium saucepan. Add flour; cook, stirring constantly, until bubbly. Add 2 cups stock, salt, and pepper; cook, stirring constantly, until thickened. Stir in 2 tablespoons cream; pour over chicken mixture.

Lightly flour pastry cloth. Staff puff pastry shells one on top of other; flatten with heels of your hands to 4-inch circle. Very carefully roll with floured rolling pin to 9½-inch circle; place on top of pie. Turn edge of crust under; do not attach to pie pan. Cut small circle from center of crust to serve as steam vent. Roll any scraps for decoration. Cut into leaf shapes; place on crust. Beat together egg yolk and 1 tablespoon cream; brush crust well. Preheat oven to 425°F; bake pie 10 minutes. Reduce heat to 375°F; cook 20 minutes. If crust begins to brown too quickly, cover lightly with foil. Serve hot.

MAKES 4 TO 6 SERVINGS.

Chicken 'n cabbage

IRELAND

1 2½- to 3-pound chicken, cut up
Juice of ½ lemon
3 tablespoons butter
Salt and pepper
¾ cup white wine
3 tablespoons bacon fat
1 medium onion, finely chopped
3 cups shredded cabbage
1 cup diced celery
¼ cup diced green pepper
2 cups diced tomatoes
¼ teaspoon garlic powder
Salt and freshly ground pepper

Wash chicken; pat dry. Sprinkle with lemon juice. Heat butter in heavy skillet until melted. Add chicken; cook over moderate heat until well-browned. Season with salt and pepper. Add wine; reduce heat to low. Cover; simmer 45 minutes or until chicken is tender.

Melt bacon fat in separate skillet over moderate heat. Add onion; cook 3 minutes, stirring constantly. Add cabbage, celery, green pepper, and tomatoes; mix well. Season with garlic powder, salt, and pepper. Cover. Reduce heat to low; cook 10 minutes. Vegetables should be crisp-tender.

Place cabbage in serving dish; top with chicken. Serve immediately.

MAKES 4 SERVINGS.

Chicken w/brandy cream

3 tablespoons butter, divided
1 tablespoon oil
1 cup slivered onion
½ pound mushrooms, cleaned, sliced
¼ cup flour
Salt and pepper
4 chicken breast fillets (1 pound total) or bone and skin 1½
    pounds split chicken breasts
2 tablespoons brandy
1 cup heavy cream
½ teaspoon crumbled dried tarragon
1 egg yolk

Heat 2 tablespoons butter and the oil in heavy skillet over moderate heat. Add onion; sauté until tender. Add mushrooms; sauté 3 minutes, stirring occasionally. Remove from pan with slotted spoon; reserve.

Combine flour, salt, and pepper; dredge chicken breasts in mixture. Add remaining 1 tablespoon butter to skillet; melt over moderate heat. Add chicken; brown well on both sides. Warm brandy. Ignite; pour over chicken. Add cream and tarragon; heat through.

Beat egg yolk well. Add some of hot sauce to egg yolk; beat. Add to chicken; mix well. Add mushrooms and onions. Cook, stirring frequently, until thickened. Serve immediately. (Take care not to boil mixture after adding cream.)

MAKES 4 SERVINGS.

Roast Cornish game hens
w/savory stuffing

4 Cornish game hens, approximately 1 pound each
8 thick slices home-style white bread
1½ tablespoons parsley flakes
¾ teaspoon salt
½ teaspoon poultry seasoning
¼ teaspoon freshly ground pepper
¾ cup butter
1 cup finely chopped onions
4 livers from Cornish hens

Salt and pepper
3 tablespoons melted butter

Remove giblet packs from hens; reserve livers. Wash Cornish hens; pat dry.

Cut crusts from bread; cut into ½-inch cubes. Place bread cubes on cookie sheet. Bake at 350°F until golden, stirring occasionally. Remove from oven; combine with parsley, ¾ teaspoon salt, poultry seasoning, and pepper; set aside.

Melt ¾ cup butter in heavy skillet. Add onions and livers; cook until livers are lightly browned and onions are tender. Remove livers; chop. Add livers, cooked onions, and butter from pan to bread cubes. Toss to mix well. Cool completely.

Salt and pepper hens lightly. Pack stuffing tightly into birds; truss. Place in ovenproof baking dish, breast-side-up; brush with melted butter. Roast at 375°F. Turn birds every 15 minutes; baste with any remaining butter and pan juices. Cook a total of 45 minutes to 1 hour or until juices run clear when tip of knife is inserted in bird. Serve hens hot with wild rice and a green vegetable.

MAKES 4 SERVINGS.

Goose w/potato stuffing

1 8- to 9-pound young goose, thawed if frozen

potato stuffing
3 medium potatoes (approximately 1 pound), peeled
1½ teaspoons salt
¼ pound lean salt pork, diced
¼ cup finely chopped onion
¼ pound bulk sausage
¼ cup butter or margarine
1 egg
½ teaspoon pepper
1 teaspoon crumbled sage leaves

Remove giblets from goose; wash well. Pat dry with paper towels. Salt lightly inside and out; set aside while making stuffing.

Place potatoes in medium saucepan. Cover with cold water; add ½ teaspoon salt. Bring to boil over moderate heat. Cover; cook on low 20 to 30 minutes or until tender. Drain. Place tea towel over pan; steam gently a few minutes. Meanwhile, cook salt pork in heavy skillet over moderate heat until lightly browned. Remove with slotted spoon; reserve. Add onion to skillet; cook until tender. Remove with slotted spoon; add to salt pork. Add sausage to skillet; cook until lightly browned, breaking into small chunks as sausage cooks. Remove with slotted spoon; add to salt-pork mixture.

Put potatoes through ricer or mash with potato masher. Combine salt-pork mixture, potatoes, and remaining stuffing ingredients; mix well. Allow to cool.

Stuff goose with potato mixture; truss bird. Place in open roasting pan, breast-side-up, on rack or trivet. Prick goose well on legs and wing joints to release fat. Roast in preheated 325°F oven 2 to 2½ hours or until leg joint moves easily. Allow to stand 15 to 20 minutes before carving. Carve goose; remove dressing to serving dish. Serve with applesauce.
MAKES 6 SERVINGS.

Baked chicken w/marinara sauce

ITALY

1 2½- to 3-pound broiler-fryer chicken, cut up
½ cup all-purpose flour
1 teaspoon salt
¼ teaspoon pepper
3 tablespoons butter or margarine
1 15½-ounce can marinara sauce or 2 cups homemade marinara sauce
1 teaspoon dried dillweed
2 tablespoons grated Parmesan cheese

Combine the flour, salt, and pepper in a brown paper bag. Add the chicken a few pieces at a time and shake until coated with the flour mixture.

Place the chicken in a single layer in a shallow baking dish. Dot with the butter. Bake at 450°F for 25 minutes. Remove from the oven. Pour the sauce over the chicken. Sprinkle with the dillweed and cheese. Reduce the heat to 350°F and bake 25 minutes more. Serve hot or cold. This makes a great picnic dish.
MAKES 4 SERVINGS.

Chicken w/garlic & oil

ITALY

1 2½- to 3-pound frying chicken, cut-up
½ cup olive oil
4 medium potatoes
6 medium carrots
1 medium onion
2 cloves garlic, peeled and chopped
Juice of 1 lemon
Salt and freshly ground black pepper

Wash the chicken well and pat dry. Pour the olive oil into the bottom of a 14 × 10 × 2½-inch pan or other large roasting pan. Dip the chicken pieces into the oil and turn to coat. Turn the chicken skin-side-up and distribute evenly in the pan.

Peel the potatoes, quarter and cut into ½-inch-thick wedges. Arrange around the chicken. Peel the carrots, cut in half lengthwise and then into sticks. Add to the pan. Peel the onion and sliver. Distribute among the vegetables in the pan. Sprinkle the garlic and lemon juice over all. Salt lightly and grind fresh pepper over the whole pan. Bake at 350°F for 1 hour, basting every 15 minutes, or until the chicken is cooked through and the vegetables are tender.
MAKES 4 SERVINGS.

Chicken—Lake Como-style

ITALY

1 3-pound broiler-fryer chicken
1 tablespoon olive oil
1 clove garlic
½ teaspoon salt
½ teaspoon leaf sage, crumbled
3 thin slices salt pork
Juice of 1 fresh lemon
¼ teaspoon freshly ground pepper

Wash the chicken well in cold water and pat dry. With kitchen string, tie the legs together.

193

Place another piece of string around the chicken and tie the wings so that they stay close to the sides of the bird. Rub the outside of the chicken with olive oil. Place the chicken in a shallow baking dish, breast-side-up.

Peel the clove of garlic and sprinkle with the salt. Crush with the side of a heavy kitchen knife. Rub the chicken with the garlic and the crumbled sage. Lay the slices of salt pork over the chicken. Preheat the oven to 350°F. Roast for 1 hour. Remove from the oven and pour the lemon juice mixed with the pepper over the chicken. Return to the oven and roast for 30 minutes more, basting occasionally. The chicken is done when the skin is well browned and the leg joint moves easily when pulled. Remove to a platter, cut and remove the strings and carve. Serve with the pan juices.
MAKES 4 SERVINGS.

Variations: Pan-roasted potatoes are an excellent accompaniment to this dish! Peel four small potatoes and rub with olive oil. Place around the chicken at the beginning of the roasting time. If you prefer green vegetables, try artichoke hearts with this dish. Defrost a 9-ounce package of artichoke hearts and place around the chicken when the lemon juice and pepper are added to the chicken. Baste when you baste the chicken.

Chicken in the style of Florence

ITALY

1 2½- to 3-pound chicken
2 tablespoons olive oil
1 medium onion, chopped
1 clove garlic, minced
4 large fresh tomatoes, peeled and chopped (canned tomatoes may be substituted if drained and chopped)
4 large, chopped green olives
½ teaspoon dried sweet basil, crumbled
½ teaspoon dried oregano, crumbled
½ teaspoon celery salt
¼ teaspoon pepper
4 bay leaves

Wash the chicken, drain, and pat dry. Cut the chicken into quarters. Cut 4 (10-inch) pieces of aluminum foil and grease with olive oil. Place a piece of chicken in the center of each piece of foil.

Combine the onion, garlic, tomatoes, green olives, sweet basil, oregano, celery salt, and pepper. Mix well. Spoon some of the sauce over each piece of chicken. Add 1 bay leaf to each package. Place on a cookie sheet and bake at 425°F for 40 minutes. Serve from the packages with a green salad and garlic bread.
MAKES 4 SERVINGS.

Fried chicken, Italian-style

ITALY

2½ pounds chicken parts (drumsticks, thighs, breasts and wings)
⅓ cup flour
½ teaspoon seasoned salt
¼ teaspoon pepper
2 eggs
2 tablespoons milk
⅔ cup dry bread crumbs
⅓ cup grated Parmesan cheese
Oil for frying
Parsley
Lemon slices

Wash the chicken and pat dry. Combine the flour and seasoned salt and pepper in a paper bag and shake the chicken a few pieces at a time in the flour mixture until lightly coated. Beat the eggs and milk together in a shallow bowl. On a piece of waxed paper combine the bread crumbs and Parmesan cheese. Dip the floured chicken pieces in the egg and then the bread crumb mixture, coating well.

Heat 1½ inches of oil in a heavy skillet over moderate heat. Fry the chicken a few pieces at a time until golden brown. Drain on paper towels. Place on a baking sheet and bake at 350°F for 15 to 20 minutes or until the juices run clear when pierced with a knife. Garnish with parsley and lemon slices and serve with basil flavored tomato sauce if you wish.
MAKES 4 SERVINGS.

Chicken breasts, Piedmont-style

ITALY

4 chicken breast halves (about 1½ pounds total)
2 tablespoons flour
¾ teaspoon salt
¼ teaspoon pepper
3 tablespoons butter or margarine
½ cup sliced fresh mushrooms
4 thin slices Fontina or Swiss cheese

Skin and bone the chicken breasts. Place between sheets of waxed paper and flatten with a heavy skillet on a hard surface. Combine the flour, salt, and pepper and coat the chicken with the mixture. Heat 2 tablespoons of the butter in a heavy skillet. Sauté the chicken in the butter 5 to 6 minutes on each side or until golden and cooked through.

Meanwhile, in a small skillet, sauté the mushrooms in 1 tablespoon of butter until tender. Place the chicken in a single layer in a small ovenproof casserole. Top with the mushrooms and then the cheese. Broil just until the cheese is melted.

MAKES 4 SERVINGS.

Breast of chicken with Italian ham

Chicken livers & vegetables

ITALY

2 tablespoons butter or margarine
1 medium onion, peeled and sliced
1 clove garlic, minced
1 medium green pepper, cleaned and cut into chunks
¼ pound mushrooms, sliced
½ cup prosciutto, cut into strips
1 pound chicken livers
¼ cup flour
Salt and pepper
¼ cup butter or margarine
2 tablespoons dry sherry
½ cup chicken broth
2 tablespoons finely chopped parsley

In a small skillet heat the butter over moderate heat until the foam subsides. Add the onion, garlic, green pepper, mushrooms, and prosciutto and sauté over low heat while preparing the chicken livers.

Drain the chicken livers well in a colander. Combine the flour, salt and pepper on waxed paper. Dip the chicken livers in the flour mixture to coat well. Heat the ¼ cup of butter in a large skillet. Add the chicken livers and cook over moderate heat until browned. Drain the fat from the pan. Add the sherry and chicken broth. Cover and cook over low heat for 5 minutes. Place the chicken livers in a serving dish. Top with the vegetables and sprinkle with parsley. Serve with rice.

MAKES 4 SERVINGS.

Breast of chicken w/Italian ham

ITALY

4 individual chicken breasts, (about ½ pound each),
    skinned, boned
Salt and pepper
1 teaspoon crumbled dried leaf sage
¼ pound prosciutto, thinly sliced
4 tablespoons butter
1 small onion, minced
1 clove garlic, minced
½ pound mushrooms, cleaned, sliced

Chicken canalones

¼ cup chicken broth
¼ cup white wine
2 tablespoons chopped fresh parsley

Place chicken between sheets of waxed paper; pound with flat side of cleaver or bottom of heavy bottle to form cutlets of even thickness. Remove waxed paper. Season with salt and pepper; sprinkle with sage. Evenly distribute ham atop chicken. Fold in half; secure with toothpick.

Melt butter in heavy skillet. Add chicken; cook over moderate heat, turning until lightly browned. Remove from pan. Add onion and garlic to pan; cook 1 minute. Add mushrooms; cook until mushroom liquid evaporates. Return chicken to skillet; spoon mushrooms over them. Add chicken broth and wine. Cover; simmer 20 minutes.

Transfer to platter; cover chicken with mushrooms. Pour over pan juices; sprinkle with parsley; serve.
MAKES 4 SERVINGS.

Chicken in foil

Chicken croquettes

ITALY

4 tablespoons butter or margarine
4 tablespoons flour
¼ teaspoon salt
⅛ teaspoon pepper
1 cup milk
2 cups finely chopped cooked chicken
½ cup finely minced ham
3 tablespoons freshly grated Parmesan cheese
2 teaspoons dried parsley flakes
⅛ teaspoon nutmeg
¼ teaspoon poultry seasoning
½ cup flour
1 egg
1 tablespoon water
¾ cup fine dry bread crumbs
Oil for deep frying

Melt butter in heavy saucepan. Add 4 tablespoons flour, salt, and pepper; cook, stirring constantly, until bubbly. Add milk all at one time; cook, stirring constantly, until thick. Remove from heat. Add chicken, ham, Parmesan, parsley, nutmeg, and poultry seasoning; stir well. Chill 2 hours.

Form into round croquettes 1½ inches in diameter. Lightly coat with ½ cup flour. Beat egg and water together in shallow bowl or pie plate. Place bread crumbs on sheet of waxed paper. Dip croquettes in egg; roll in crumbs. Chill 1 hour. Heat several inches oil to 375°F in deep-fat fryer. Fry croquettes a few at a time until golden. Drain on paper towels; serve immediately.
MAKES 4 SERVINGS.

Stuffed chicken

ITALY

1 (6-pound) capon or roasting chicken
½ pound hot or sweet Italian sausage (either bulk or links with casing removed)
2 tablespoons olive oil
½ cup finely chopped onion
1 clove garlic, peeled, chopped
1 cup raw long-grain rice
2 cups boiling water

1 cup cleaned sliced fresh mushrooms (or substitute a
   4-ounce can drained mushrooms)
1 teaspoon chicken-broth granules
¼ teaspoon crumbled dried sweet basil
Salt and pepper
Olive oil for rubbing
6 medium potatoes, peeled

Wash chicken; pat dry.

In small skillet sauté sausage in oil until lightly browned. Add onion and garlic; sauté until lightly browned. Add rice; cook, stirring, until opaque. Add water, mushrooms, broth granules, and seasonings; cover tightly. Reduce heat to low; cook 15 to 20 minutes, until tender. Cool completely.

Stuff chicken with mixture. Truss body cavity shut. Stuff neck cavity; skewer shut. Pin wings close to body; tie legs together. Rub liberally with oil, salt, and pepper.

Grease roasting pan; place chicken in pan. Roast at 350°F (25 minutes to the pound). One hour before chicken is done, add potatoes to roasting pan. Baste occasionally with pan juices.
MAKES 6 SERVINGS.

Chicken hunter's-style

ITALY

1 (3-pound) frying chicken, cut up
½ cup flour
Salt and pepper
⅓ cup olive oil
1 medium onion, peeled, sliced
1 green pepper, cleaned, sliced lengthwise
1 clove garlic, minced
1 (16-ounce) can plum tomatoes
¼ cup dry white wine
½ pound mushrooms, cleaned, sliced

Wash chicken well; pat dry. Combine flour, salt, and pepper; dredge chicken well. Heat oil in large skillet. Add chicken; brown well on all sides. Remove from pan. Add onion, green pepper, and garlic; sauté until tender. Drain off fat remaining in pan.

Break tomatoes into pieces with fork; add to skillet. Add wine; stir well. Bring mixture to boil over moderate heat. Add chicken; cover. Reduce heat; simmer 45 minutes. Add mushrooms; cook 15 to 20 minutes, until chicken and mushrooms are tender.
MAKES 4 SERVINGS.

Chicken w/sausage

ITALY

2 pounds cut-up frying-chicken parts
3 tablespoons olive oil
4 sweet Italian sausage links (½ pound)
1 medium onion, peeled, sliced
1 large green pepper, cleaned, sliced
1 cup sliced fresh mushrooms
1 (16-ounce) can Italian-style plum tomatoes, broken up
   with fork
3 tablespoons tomato paste
½ cup red wine
1 teaspoon crumbled sweet basil
Pinch of sugar
Salt and pepper

Wash chicken parts; pat dry. Heat oil in heavy skillet. Fry chicken, few pieces at a time, until golden, turning frequently. Remove from skillet; drain well. Add sausages to skillet; prick with fork. Fry until well browned. Remove from pan. Discard all but 3 tablespoons drippings.

Add onion, pepper, and mushrooms; sauté until tender. Add tomatoes, tomato paste, wine, and seasonings; stir well. Bring to boil. Add chicken and sausage. Cover; reduce heat to low. Cook 35 to 40 minutes. Serve with plain pasta.
MAKES 4 SERVINGS.

Chicken shoemaker's-style

ITALY

1 2½ - 3-pound frying chicken
2 tablespoons olive oil
3 tablespoons butter
Salt and pepper
1 clove garlic, minced
2 tablespoons chopped green onion
1 cup sliced fresh mushrooms
½ teaspoon crumbled dried tarragon
½ cup chicken broth
½ cup dry white wine

¼ *pound chicken livers*
1 *tablespoon chopped parsley*

Cut up chicken, bones and all. Cut into quarters. Remove legs, thighs, and wings. Cut each quarter into 3 or 4 parts. Cut each wing or thigh in half. Wash chicken; pat dry. Heat oil and 2 tablespoons butter in large skillet over moderate heat. Add chicken; sauté until browned. Season with salt and pepper. Remove from pan.

Sauté garlic, onions, and mushrooms until tender. Add tarragon, broth, wine, and browned chicken pieces. Bring to boil; reduce heat to low. Cover; cook 30 minutes.

Melt remaining butter in small skillet. Sauté livers 5 minutes, until almost cooked through. Add to chicken; simmer 5 minutes. Garnish with parsley; serve.
MAKES 4 SERVINGS.

Turkey tetrazzini

ITALY

6 *tablespoons butter or margarine*
3 *tablespoons olive oil*
½ *pound fresh mushrooms, cleaned and sliced*
4 *tablespoons flour*
2 *cups chicken broth*
1 *cup heavy cream*
2 *tablespoons dry sherry*
¾ *cup grated Parmesan cheese*
⅛ *teaspoon ground nutmeg*
3 *cups cubed cooked turkey*
½ *pound spaghetti or vermicelli, cooked and drained*
¼ *cup Italian-style bread crumbs*

In a large saucepan heat 4 tablespoons of the butter and oil. Add the mushrooms and sauté for 5 minutes. Remove the mushrooms with a slotted spoon and reserve. Add the flour to the pan juices and stir to form a roux. Cook until bubbly. Slowly add the chicken broth and cook until thickened.

Remove from the heat and add the cream, sherry, Parmesan, and nutmeg and stir until the cheese melts. Add the turkey and reserved mushrooms and stir well. Combine with the cooked spaghetti and turn into a greased 13 × 9 × 2-inch baking dish (or use the 3-quart baking dish of your choice). Melt 2 tablespoons of butter and toss with the bread crumbs. Sprinkle over the casserole. Bake at 375°F for 25 to 30 minutes.
MAKES 6 SERVINGS.

Mixed-meat brochettes

ITALY

½ *cup white wine*
¼ *cup olive oil*
1 *clove garlic, crushed*
½ *teaspoon crumbled sage leaves*
2 *pounds raw turkey-breast meat, cut into 1½-inch cubes*
1 *pound Italian sweet sausage links*
24 *mushroom caps*
2 *green peppers, cleaned, cut into chunks*

In glass bowl or casserole combine wine, oil, garlic, and sage; mix well. Add turkey; stir to combine. Cover; let marinate 1 hour.

Prick sausages; simmer, in water to cover, 15 minutes. Drain; cool. Cut each sausage into 1½-inch pieces.

Grease 6 skewers. Alternately thread meats and vegetables on skewers. (Reserve turkey marinade for basting.) Grill or broil brochette about 8 inches from heat 20 minutes, until meats are cooked through. Baste occasionally, brushing with marinade. Serve at once with rice, noodles, or polenta.
MAKES 6 SERVINGS.

Turkey-breast cutlets w/lemon & wine sauce

ITALY

2 *tablespoons flour*
3 *tablespoons freshly grated Parmesan cheese*
½ *teaspoon salt*
¼ *teaspoon white pepper*
¼ *teaspoon nutmeg*
1 *egg, well beaten*
½ *cup milk*
1 *pound raw boneless turkey breast*
Flour

4 tablespoons sweet butter
⅓ cup dry white wine
Juice of ½ lemon
Chopped fresh parsley for garnish
Lemon wedges

In shallow bowl combine flour, cheese, salt, pepper, and nutmeg. Add egg and milk; beat until well blended.

Skin turkey breast; cut crosswise into 6 slices. Pound with meat mallet until thin. Dredge lightly in flour; shake off excess. Heat butter in large heavy skillet over moderate heat until foam subsides. Dip 2-3 pieces of turkey in batter; fry until golden. Remove from pan; keep warm. Repeat the process with remaining cutlets.

When all turkey is cooked, add wine to skillet. Cook over low heat 2 minutes, stirring to loosen browned bits from pan. Add lemon juice; mix well. Strain sauce over turkey cutlets; sprinkle with chopped parsley. Serve immediately with lemon wedges.
MAKES 4 SERVINGS.

Roast guinea hen
POLAND

2 2- to 3-pound dressed guinea hens
1½ teaspoons salt
1 lemon, quartered
2 small onions
4 slices country-style bacon, sliced
2 cups Dilled Croutons (see Index)
Tomato Cups with Peas (see Index)

Rub guinea hens inside and out with salt and lemon wedges. Insert an onion in each hen. Place bacon over back of hen. Roast in 325°F oven 40 minutes. Turn hens over in roasting pan; rearrange bacon over breasts of hens. Continue cooking for 35 to 40 minutes or until hen is fork-tender. Place bird on a hot platter and garnish with Dilled Croutons and Tomato Cups with Peas (see Index).
MAKES 4 SERVINGS.

Chicken in dill sauce
POLAND

2 chicken fryers, cut in pieces
1½ quarts boiling water
1 onion, quartered
2 celery stalks with leaves, chopped
3 peppercorns
5 tablespoons flour
⅓ cup cold water
1 teaspoon salt
2 tablespoons finely chopped fresh dill
½ cup sour cream

Cover chicken with boiling water; add onion, celery, and peppercorns. Cover; simmer for 2½ hours or until meat is fork-tender. Remove chicken from stock; keep it warm.
Strain stock; measure out 2¼ cups. Reheat the 2¼ cups stock. Form a paste with flour and water. Slowly stir flour paste into heated stock; stir until stock thickens. Add salt, dill, and sour cream to thickened stock; stir to blend. To serve, pour sauce over chicken pieces.
MAKES 6 SERVINGS.

Chicken bread pies
SPAIN

3 tablespoons olive oil
½ cup chopped onion
½ cup chopped green pepper
½ cup chopped Italian ham
1½ cups peeled, chopped tomatoes
½ cup chick-peas
½ teaspoon garlic powder
½ teaspoon salt
Dash of cayenne
1 box hot-roll mix
1 cup warm water
1 egg, beaten
1 egg white, unbeaten

Heat oil in skillet. Add onion and green pepper; sauté until tender. Add ham, tomatoes, chick-peas, garlic powder, salt, and cayenne. Simmer until mixture thickens and holds its shape in spoon.
Dissolve yeast from hot-roll mix in warm water as directed on package. Add beaten egg; blend 201

well. Add flour mixture to yeast mixture; blend well. Cover; let rise in warm place until double in bulk.

Punch down dough; place on well-floured surface. Roll out to 16 × 20-inch rectangle. Cut into 4-inch squares. Fill each square with heaping tablespoon of chicken mixture. Bring corners together; pinch edges together. Place on greased cookie sheet, pinched-edges-down. Let rise 30 minutes. Brush with egg white. Bake at 350°F 30 minutes.

MAKES 6 SERVINGS.

Chicken canalones
SPAIN

canalone dough
3 cups all-purpose flour
½ teaspoon salt
3 eggs
2 tablespoons olive oil
5 tablespoons water

chicken filling
2 garlic cloves, minced
2 onions, chopped fine
1 pound cooked chicken, diced
2 tablespoons tomato paste
½ cup dry red wine
1 tablespoon snipped fresh parsley
1 teaspoon salt
Dash of black pepper
1 teaspoon oregano

sauce
¼ cup olive oil
1 onion, chopped
2 garlic cloves, minced
1 green pepper, seeded, chopped
1 cup tomato sauce
¼ cup tomato paste
3 tablespoons dry red wine
1 teaspoon salt
Dash of pepper
1 tablespoon sugar

garnish
¼ cup Parmesan cheese

To make dough:
Sift flour and salt into large bowl. Make well in center. Add remaining ingredients; blend together, using pastry blender. When dough forms into ball, knead 5 minutes. Cover dough; let rest 5 minutes. Roll dough out on floured surface into 16 4½ × 5-inch paper-thin rectangles.

To make filling:
Mix together ingredients. Place some of filling in center of each pasta rectangle. Roll firmly; seal seams and ends, moistening with water to fasten. Drop filled pasta into boiling salted water; cook 10 minutes. Remove with slotted spoon; place seam-side-down in greased shallow baking dish.

To make sauce:
Heat oil. Add vegetables; sauté until limp. Add remaining ingredients; cook 20 minutes or until mixture thickens and holds its shape in spoon. Spread sauce over pasta. Garnish with Parmesan cheese. Bake in 400°F oven 15 minutes.

MAKES 4 TO 6 SERVINGS.

Chicken w/peppers, tomatoes, & olives
SPAIN

3 cups cooked chicken or turkey
2 large onions
1 red sweet pepper
1 green pepper
½ cup tomato sauce
1 tablespoon tomato paste
1 16-ounce can stewed tomatoes
1 teaspoon salt
½ teaspoon garlic powder
¼ teaspoon pepper
10 pitted black olives, sliced
10 pitted green olives, sliced

Cut chicken into slices. Peel and slice onions. Core, remove seeds, and slice peppers into strips. Layer chicken, onions, and peppers in greased baking dish.

Combine tomato sauce, tomato paste, tomatoes, salt, garlic powder, and pepper in saucepan. Heat to boiling. Pour sauce over layered chicken and vegetables; cover. Bake in 350°F oven 30 minutes. Uncover casserole; sprinkle with olives. Bake 15 minutes more.

MAKES 4 TO 6 SERVINGS.

Rice w/chicken
SPAIN

2 chicken breasts
3 chicken legs and thighs
½ cup olive oil
2 tablespoons sherry
½ cup chopped onions
1 green pepper, chopped
1 cup long-grain rice

1½ cups chicken broth, boiling
1 teaspoon garlic powder
1 bay leaf
½ teaspoon salt
¼ teaspoon pepper
Pinch of saffron
2 medium tomatoes, peeled, seeded, quartered
¼ cup freshly grated Parmesan cheese

Rinse chicken. Pat dry. Heat oil in skillet until haze forms above skillet. Reduce heat; brown chicken well on all sides. Remove chicken from pan; drizzle with sherry.

Add vegetables to oil; cook until limp. Add rice; sauté until opaque and well-coated with oil. Add boiling chicken broth and seasonings; return to boil.

Pour rice mixture into 2½-quart greased casserole. Top with browned chicken. Cover; bake in 350°F oven 45 minutes. Place tomato quarters on top of chicken. Sprinkle with Parmesan cheese. Bake 15 minutes.
MAKES 4 SERVINGS.

Chicken cooked in foil

SPAIN

4 chicken quarters
¼ cup olive oil
1 teaspoon salt
¼ teaspoon pepper
1 teaspoon garlic powder
1 small Spanish onion, chopped
½ cup finely chopped green pepper
2 teaspoons dried parsley
2 fresh tomatoes, peeled, chopped

Rinse chicken; pat dry with paper towel. Cut 4 10-inch squares of heavy-duty foil. Pour 1 tablespoon oil on each sheet of foil; spread to cover foil. Place chicken on foil squares. Sprinkle with salt, pepper, and garlic powder.

Combine onion, green pepper, parsley, and tomatoes; toss. Spoon vegetable mixture evenly over chicken quarters. Fold and seal foil. Place foil packs on cookie sheet; bake at 425°F 40 minutes. Serve chicken from foil packets. Be careful when opening packets: Steam is trapped inside.
MAKES 4 SERVINGS.

Chicken Seville style

SPAIN

¼ cup olive oil
3 chicken legs and thighs
1 Spanish onion, peeled, sliced
½ cup diced Italian or other smoked ham
1 tablespoon tomato paste
2 cans stewed tomatoes
1 large clove garlic, pressed, or 1 teaspoon garlic powder
1 teaspoon salt
¼ teaspoon pepper
¼ teaspoon thyme
¼ cup sliced pitted black olives
¼ cup sliced stuffed Spanish olives

In large, deep skillet, heat oil until haze forms above skillet; reduce heat. Add chicken pieces; brown evenly on all sides. Remove chicken.
Add onion and ham to skillet; cook until onion slices wilt and ham begins to brown, about 5 minutes. Drain excess oil from skillet. Add chicken, tomato paste, tomatoes, and spices. Turn heat to high; cook until mixture boils. Reduce heat to simmer; cover. Cook 30 minutes or until chicken is fork-tender; uncover. Add olives; cook 5 minutes. Serve chicken from skillet.
MAKES 4 SERVINGS.

Paella

SPAIN

6 rock lobster tails	¼ cup tomato sauce
12 large raw shrimp	3 cups long-grain rice
6 cherrystone clams	⅛ teaspoon saffron powder
6 mussels	1 teaspoon salt
½ pound chorizos or other garlic-flavored sausage	1 large clove garlic, pressed, or 1 teaspoon garlic powder
⅔ cup olive oil	¼ teaspoon pepper
½ pound pork cubes	1½ quarts boiling water
4 chicken breasts, thighs, and legs	1 cup frozen peas
	1 fresh tomato, peeled, seeded, diced
1 onion	
1 green pepper	

With kitchen shears, break center of ribs on belly side of lobster shell. Loosen meat from shell with fingers, leaving meat attached near tail fins. Shell and devein shrimp. Scrub clams and mus-

203

Paella

sels. Soak mussels in cold water 30 minutes to remove salty taste. Discard any that open their shells while soaking; drain.

Place sausage in shallow skillet. Cover with water; bring to boil. Boil 5 minutes; drain. Remove skin from sausage; cut into ¼-inch rounds. Heat ⅓ cup oil. Fry sausage until browned on each side. Remove from skillet; drain. Add pork to heated oil. Fry until brown on all sides and no longer pink. Remove from skillet; drain.

Add chicken to skillet. Fry 45 minutes or until golden brown and meat is cooked. Remove from skillet; drain. Add lobster to skillet; fry just until shells start to turn pink. Remove from skillet; drain.

204 Add remaining oil to skillet; heat thoroughly.

Peel and chop onion. Sauté in skillet 10 minutes or until tender.

Remove seeds and membranes from pepper; dice. Add to onions; sauté 5 minutes. Stir in tomato sauce; simmer until mixture thickens and holds its shape in spoon. Add rice, saffron, salt, pressed garlic or garlic powder, and pepper; mix well. Add boiling water; mix well. Bring mixture to boil; reduce heat to simmer.

Arrange lobster, shrimp, clams, mussels, sausage, pork, and chicken on top of rice mixture. Scatter peas and tomato over rice and meat; cover. Simmer 30 to 45 minutes or until rice is tender, shrimp and lobster meat turns white, and mussels and clams pop open. Remove from heat. Cover; let rest 10 minutes for flavors to mingle. Serve paella directly from pan.
MAKES 6 TO 8 SERVINGS.

Curried chicken

DENMARK

2 small chickens about 3 pounds each
1 medium onion, chopped
⅓ cup butter or margarine
1 light tablespoon curry powder
3 cups boiling water
2 teaspoons salt
¼ cup flour

Cut each chicken into pieces. Brown the onion in the margarine. Remove the onion and brown the chicken parts in the same fat. Replace the onion and add the curry powder. Pour the 3 cups of boiling water over the chicken and add the salt. Simmer until the chicken is tender.

Mix the flour with a little water and add it to the chicken liquid. Stir until it is thick and smooth. Serve the chicken piping hot.
MAKES 6 OR MORE SERVINGS.

Chicken cutlets

SWEDEN

2 tablespoons flour
2 cups chicken stock
3 egg yolks, beaten
3 cups finely diced cooked chicken
12 mushrooms, finely diced
Salt and pepper to taste
1 whole egg, beaten
Bread or cracker crumbs
Fat for deep-frying

Mix the flour with ¼ cup of the chicken stock. Add this to the rest of the heated stock. Stir until it is thickened. Add the egg yolks to the sauce very gradually, stirring vigorously. Add the chicken, mushrooms, and seasonings. Stir constantly as the mixture cooks for 5 minutes. Cool and then chill the mixture for several hours so it becomes stiff.
Shape the mixture into cutlets. Dip each cutlet into the beaten whole egg and then into the bread crumbs. Chill again. Fry the cutlets in deep fat, and serve.
MAKES 6 SERVINGS.

Cinnamon stick chicken

MIDDLE EAST

The hidden ingredient in the tasty sauce is cinnamon. It makes chicken taste like a party.

1 3-to-3½ pound chicken cut into pieces
Salt
Dash of freshly ground pepper
4 tablespoons butter
1½ cups finely chopped onions (2 medium onions)
1 tablespoon chopped garlic
6 plum tomatoes, peeled, seeded and finely chopped or
1 cup canned plum tomatoes, chopped and drained
2 tablespoons tomato paste
½ cup chicken stock
2 cinnamon sticks

Season chicken pieces with salt and pepper. Melt butter in a large skillet. Add chicken, skin-side down and turn until brown on all sides. Brown a few pieces at a time. When all are done, set aside.
Pour off most of the fat and add onions and garlic, stirring until onions are lightly browned. Add remaining ingredients with more salt and pepper if needed. When liquid has come to a boil, add the chicken, being sure that each piece is basted in the sauce. Cover and reduce heat. Simmer for 30 minutes, remove chicken to platter, and spoon the sauce over it. Serve at once.
MAKES 4 SERVINGS.

Stuffed roast chicken

MIDDLE EAST

4 tablespoons butter
½ cup finely chopped onions
Giblets (liver, heart, and gizzard) of the chicken, coarsely chopped
2 tablespoons pine nuts
1 cup uncooked long-grain white rice
2 cups water
1 tablespoon dried currants
2 tablespoons salt
Freshly ground pepper to taste
4 tablespoons melted butter
3- to 3½-pound roasting chicken
3 tablespoons yoghurt

Melt butter in a large saucepan; add onions and cook until transparent, about 5 minutes. Add giblets and pine nuts and stir together for 2 minutes more. Then stir in rice until the grains are covered with butter. Add water, currants, 1 tablespoon salt, and pepper and allow all to come to a boil. Reduce heat, cover, and simmer for 30 minutes or until rice has absorbed all of the liquid. Remove from the heat and stir in the melted butter, lifting gently with a fork.
Thoroughly dry the chicken inside and out and stuff with 1 cup of the rice mixture. Close all openings and truss the chicken securely. (Set aside the remaining rice to be heated and served when the chicken is finished cooking.)
Combine yoghurt with remaining tablespoon of

salt. Use half of this mixture to coat the chicken thoroughly. Place chicken, breast-side-up, on roasting pan and roast at 400°F for 15 minutes. Baste chicken again with remaining yoghurt mixture and continue cooking, lowering oven to 350°F, for 1 hour. When chicken is done, put on a heated serving platter and serve along with the heated rice bowl.

MAKES 4 TO 6 SERVINGS.

Chicken w/rice & cherries

MIDDLE EAST

1 3-pound chicken cut into serving pieces
Salt and pepper to season chicken
4 tablespoons olive oil
2 medium onions, finely sliced
½ cup chicken stock
2-pound can stoned black cherries, drained
¼ cup sugar
2 tablespoons water
¼ pound melted butter
2 cups cooked long-grain rice

Sprinkle the chicken with salt and pepper. Heat oil in large skillet and brown chicken pieces, a few at a time. Transfer cooked chicken to a heated plate. Then sauté onions in oil until lightly browned, about 5 minutes. Return chicken to skillet, add chicken stock, and bring to a boil. Reduce heat, cover, and simmer for 30 minutes. Transfer chicken to a plate, reserving liquid.

Make a sauce of cherries, sugar, and water, simmering for 5 minutes and stirring frequently. Remove from the heat and set aside.

Add half the melted butter to the reserved liquid. Put in half of the rice on a low heat and cook for about 5 minutes until rice is evenly coated. Transfer rice mixture to a casserole dish. Cover with chicken pieces and about half the cherries. Add rest of rice and melted butter and pour remaining cherries and their liquid over all. Bake covered, at 350°F for 20 minutes or until all are piping hot. Serve at once.

MAKES 4 TO 6 SERVINGS.

Chicken w/sesame seeds

MIDDLE EAST

½ cup flour
Salt and pepper to taste
1 teaspoon paprika
2 3-pound chickens cut into pieces
3 tablespoons oil
2 tablespoons light brown sugar
½ teaspoon ground ginger
1 cup dry red wine
2 tablespoons soy sauce
⅓ cup sesame seeds

Combine flour, salt, pepper, and paprika in a brown paper bag and coat the chicken pieces thoroughly by shaking them in the bag. Heat the oil in a skillet and brown the chicken, setting each piece in a casserole when done.

To the remaining fat, add brown sugar, ginger, wine, and soy sauce. Stir and, when well-blended, pour over the waiting chicken. Sprinkle with sesame seeds which have been lightly toasted in a dry skillet. Bake at 350°F for 1 hour.

MAKES 6 TO 8 SERVINGS.

Moroccan chicken

MIDDLE EAST

¼ cup olive oil
1 4-pound chicken, skinned and cut into serving pieces
1 medium-size onion, thinly sliced into rings
2 crushed garlic cloves
1 teaspoon salt
1 teaspoon black pepper
½ teaspoon oregano
1 bay leaf
2 tablespoons lemon juice
1¼ cups chicken stock
1 teaspoon cornstarch

Heat oil over moderate heat and brown the chicken pieces, turning them to brown on all sides. When chicken is nicely browned, drain on paper towels. Cook only as many pieces as the pan will hold. Do not crowd.

Pour off all but 2 tablespoons of oil. Add onion and garlic and cook until onion is golden, stirring occasionally. Add remaining seasonings and chicken stock. When liquid has come to a boil, return chicken to pan. Cover and simmer for 1½ hours or more until chicken is tender.

Transfer chicken to a heated platter. Strain the remaining liquid into a small saucepan, pressing the seasonings down to extract all the liquid. Dissolve cornstarch in ¼ cup of the liquid and add. Stir constantly until the mixture has thickened; pour over the chicken pieces. Serve on a bed of plain noodles with a salad.

MAKES 4 TO 6 SERVINGS.

Lemon-flavored chicken wings
MIDDLE EAST

2 pounds chicken wings (about 12 wings)
2 cups lemon juice
1 teaspoon salt
½ teaspoon black pepper
4 tablespoons butter or margarine

Cut off the smallest wing tip of the chicken wings and save for soup. You will only use the meaty pieces of the wings here. Make a marinade of lemon juice, salt, and pepper and place wings in a bowl with marinade covering. Marinate the chicken for 24 hours, stirring from time to time so that all pieces are covered.

When ready to cook, drain chicken on paper towels. Place in pan and rub each piece liberally with butter. Broil for 15 to 20 minutes or until crisp, or place in a hot oven at 500°F for ½ hour to 45 minutes.

MAKES 4 TO 6 SERVINGS.

Baked rice w/chicken
MIDDLE EAST

4 tablespoons softened butter
3 cups uncooked white rice
4 boned and halved chicken breasts
Salt and pepper
1½ cups milk
1 cup heavy cream
4 cups chicken stock
2 tablespoons butter, cut into pieces for dotting

Heavily grease the bottom and sides of a 3-quart casserole or baking dish. Use all 4 tablespoons of the butter. Spread 1½ cups uncooked rice in the dish. Place chicken, skin-side-up, on top of rice and season with salt and pepper.

In a saucepan, bring milk, cream, and 2 cups of stock to a boil. Pour over the chicken. Cover with remaining rice and dot with butter. Bake uncovered in a 400°F oven for 15 minutes. Simmer the remaining 2 cups of stock. Pour 1 cup over the casserole and bake for 15 minutes more. Pour in the remaining stock and bake for 30 minutes.

Remove casserole from oven and cover tightly, allowing to stand at room temperature for 20 minutes. Use a sharp knife around the inside edges of the casserole to loosen and allow to rest for 10 minutes more. Place a heated serving platter over the top of the casserole and invert. The molded rice will slide out easily.

MAKES 6 TO 8 SERVINGS.

Chicken liver pilaf
MIDDLE EAST

5 tablespoons butter
1 tablespoon olive oil
1 large onion, sliced
½ pound chicken livers
10 small scallions, cut into ½-inch lengths
1 tablespoon pine nuts
1 tablespoon raisins
1½ teaspoons salt
½ teaspoon black pepper
2 cups long-grain rice, soaked in cold water for 30 minutes
2 teaspoons sugar
2 teaspoons lemon juice
1 tablespoon tomato purée
1 teaspoon dried dill
2¾ cups boiling water

In a skillet melt 2 tablespoons butter and oil. Add onions and stir for 4 minutes. Add chicken livers and sauté until liver is brown on all sides, stirring constantly. Stir in scallions, nuts, raisins, salt, and pepper. Cook for 3 minutes more. Remove from the pan and set aside.

Melt remaining butter in a large saucepan. Add

rice and stir until well-coated, about 5 minutes. Add the remaining ingredients in order given. When all comes to a boil, reduce heat and cover. Cook for 20 minutes or until rice is tender with all liquid absorbed. Serve while hot.
MAKES 4 SERVINGS.

Chicken w/mandarin oranges & almonds

CHINA

2 ounces seedless raisins
1 jigger Madeira
1 large chicken, 3½ to 4 pounds, cut into serving pieces
2 teaspoons paprika
1 teaspoon white pepper
5 tablespoons oil
1 11-ounce can mandarin oranges, drained
1 clove garlic, minced
½ cup hot beef bouillon
1 tablespoon cornstarch
1 tablespoon soy sauce
½ teaspoon powdered ginger
½ cup heavy cream, lightly beaten
1 tablespoon butter
2 tablespoons sliced almonds

Cover raisins with Madeira and soak. Cut chicken into 6 serving pieces. Mix together paprika and pepper, and rub chicken with this mixture. Heat oil in skillet or Dutch oven. Add chicken and fry until golden on all sides, about 10 minutes. Drain mandarin oranges, reserving juice. Measure ½ cup of juice and pour over chicken. Add minced garlic. Pour in beef bouillon, cover and simmer for 30 minutes. Drain raisins and add, cook for another 5 minutes.
Remove chicken with slotted spoon and arrange on preheated platter and keep warm. Blend cornstarch with small amount of cold water; add to sauce, stirring constantly until thickened and bubbly. Season with soy sauce and powdered ginger. Add mandarin oranges and lightly beaten heavy cream. Heat through, but do not boil. Heat butter in small skillet. Add sliced almonds and cook until golden. Pour sauce over chicken and top with almonds.
MAKES 6 SERVINGS.

Chicken w/pineapple

CHINA

1 chicken approximately 2½ to 3 pounds, boned
marinade
2 tablespoons cornstarch
3 tablespoons oil
4 tablespoons soy sauce
1 tablespoon sherry
Salt
Pepper
2 tablespoons oil
1 cup pineapple chunks, drained, reserving pineapple juice
gravy
1 tablespoon oil
1 clove garlic, minced
½ cup pineapple juice
2 tablespoons sherry

Bone chicken and cut meat into bite-size pieces. Combine ingredients for marinade and blend thoroughly. Pour over chicken pieces, cover and refrigerate for 30 minutes.
Heat 2 tablespoons oil in heavy skillet. Drain chicken, reserving marinade. Add chicken to skillet and brown for about 5 minutes while stirring constantly. Add drained pineapple chunks. Cover skillet and simmer over low heat for 12 minutes. Remove chicken and pineapple chunks with slotted spoon. Arrange on preheated platter and keep warm.
Add additional 1 tablespoon oil to pan drippings. Stir in minced garlic and cook for 5 minutes. Blend pineapple juice with reserved marinade and sherry. Pour into skillet and heat through. Strain sauce through sieve, spoon over chicken and pineapple and serve immediately.
MAKES 4 SERVINGS.

Chicken cantonese

CHINA

½ pound white meat of chicken sliced in strips, about 1½ inches long and ½ inch wide
½ pound snow peas, strings removed
¼ cup peanut oil
¼ cup bamboo shoots
1 cup bok choy, sliced

1 cup fresh mushrooms, sliced
1 cup celery, sliced diagonally
¼ cup water chestnuts, sliced
4 cups chicken stock
2 tablespoons cornstarch mixed with ½ cup cold water

Slice chicken and set aside. Wash snow peas, remove strings, and set aside. Heat oil in skillet or wok and stir-fry chicken for about 10 seconds. Add bamboo shoots, bok choy, mushrooms, celery, and water chestnuts and stir-fry for another 10 seconds. Add chicken stock, bring to a boil, cover, and simmer for about 1 minute. Stir in cornstarch mixture and mix thoroughly. Serve immediately.
MAKES 3 TO 4 SERVINGS.

Chinese chicken w/rice
CHINA

2 tablespoons oil
2 medium onions, diced
1 green pepper, diced
2 cups cooked rice
2 cups cooked chicken breast, diced
Soy sauce to taste
Dash of ginger

Heat oil in large skillet and brown onions. Add remaining ingredients and stir frequently while cooking over moderate heat 20 minutes.
MAKES 2 SERVINGS.

Mandarin chicken
CHINA

3 tablespoons soy sauce
½ teaspoon dried dillweed
1 whole chicken breast, skinned, boned, cut into bite-size pieces
3 tablespoons peanut oil
½ cup thinly sliced celery
1 8-ounce can water chestnuts, drained, sliced thin
1 11-ounce can mandarin-orange sections, drained, liquid reserved
1 tablespoon cornstarch

Combine 2 tablespoons soy sauce and dillweed. Pour over chicken; let stand 30 minutes.

Heat 1 tablespoon oil in wok or large skillet. Add celery and water chestnuts. Stir-fry 2 minutes or until celery turns bright green. Remove from wok; set aside. Heat 2 tablespoons oil in wok. Add chicken mixture; stir-fry about 3 minutes or until chicken is very tender. Return vegetables to wok.
Blend liquid from mandarin-orange sections with cornstarch and 1 tablespoon soy sauce. Slowly stir into wok; cook until bubbly. Add orange sections; cook 1 minute or until heated through.
MAKES 2 SERVINGS.

Sesame chicken
CHINA

1 chicken, cut up, about 2½ to 3 pounds
Flour mixed with salt and pepper
2 eggs, beaten
2 tablespoons milk
1 cup flour mixed with ½ cup sesame seeds, ½ teaspoon salt, and ¼ teaspoon pepper
Peanut oil for frying

cream sauce
4 tablespoons flour
4 tablespoons butter, melted
½ cup half-and-half cream
1 cup chicken stock
½ cup whipping cream
½ teaspoon salt or onion salt, if desired

Wash chicken and pat dry. Dust with flour mixed with salt and pepper. Mix beaten eggs with milk and dip chicken into this mixture. Then roll in the sesame-seed mixture. Fry in oil until light brown and tender.
To prepare the sauce, blend the flour into the butter over low heat, stirring constantly. Mix together the half-and-half, chicken stock and whipping cream. Gradually add to the butter and flour, stirring constantly. When smooth, stir in the salt or onion salt. Serve immediately with the chicken.
MAKES 3 TO 4 SERVINGS.

Chicken with pineapple

Chicken with mandarin oranges and almonds
(pages 212-213)

Chicken chow mein

Chicken balls in oyster sauce

CHINA

2 raw chicken breasts, skin and bones discarded
2 scallions
1 teaspoon salt
1 tablespoon cornstarch
1 tablespoon sherry
2 tablespoons water
Oil for frying
½ cup onions, thinly sliced
1 teaspoon sugar
½ teaspoon fresh gingerroot, chopped
2 tablespoons oyster sauce
¼ cup chicken broth
Freshly ground black pepper to taste

Chop the chicken and scallions together until very fine. Mix in the salt, cornstarch, sherry, and water. Shape into small balls. Heat oil in skillet, and fry the balls until browned on all sides. Pour off the oil. Add the onions, sugar, ginger, oyster sauce, and chicken broth. Cook and stir over low heat 5 minutes. Sprinkle with pepper.
MAKES 4 SERVINGS.

Roast chicken Chinese-style

CHINA

4 scallions, chopped
2 small pieces fresh gingerroot
1 cup soy sauce
½ cup sherry
1 teaspoon sugar

¼ teaspoon salt
4 cups water
1 whole chicken, about 3 pounds
Scallions for garnish

Mix together chopped scallions, gingerroot, soy sauce, sherry, sugar, and salt. Add water to stew pot. Mix in scallion mixture. Bring to a boil. Wash chicken, place in pot, cover, and simmer for 30 minutes.

Remove chicken from pot and place on roasting rack in pan. Roast 45 minutes, or until chicken is tender and browned, in 350°F oven. Split chicken in half, and cut each half into 5 to 6 pieces. Arrange, skin-side-up, on serving platter. Garnish with scallions. Serve the broth as a dipping sauce.
MAKES 4 SERVINGS.

Chinese lemon chicken

CHINA

1 3-pound chicken
1½ teaspoons salt, divided
2 tablespoons soy sauce
2 tablespoons brandy
5 tablespoons safflower oil
½ teaspoon powdered ginger
1 cup chicken broth
¼ cup lemon juice
½ teaspoon sugar

Rub inside of chicken with 1 teaspoon of the salt. Rub the outside with the soy sauce. Place in a deep bowl and pour the brandy over the chicken. Marinate for 6 hours, turning the chicken frequently.

Drain and reserve marinade. In a wok over medium-high heat, combine the oil and ginger. Brown the chicken on all sides. Reduce the heat to low and add the marinade, chicken broth, lemon juice, sugar and remaining ½ teaspoon salt. Cover wok and simmer for about 25 minutes, or until the chicken is tender. Place on serving platter, cut into pieces, and pour juices in wok over chicken.

MAKES 4 SERVINGS.

Chicken chow mein

CHINA

1 green sweet pepper, cut into slices	1 4-ounce can sliced mushrooms, drained
1 red sweet pepper, cut into slices	8 ounces cooked chicken breast, cut into bite-size pieces
1 cup boiling water	6 cups water
1½ tablespoons butter	8 ounces egg noodles
1 small onion, chopped	Salt
2 stalks celery, sliced	1 tablespoon butter
1 tablespoon flour	Oil for frying
1 cup chicken broth	4 ounces sliced almonds, toasted and slightly salted
2 tablespoons soy sauce	
Freshly ground pepper to taste	

Cut green and red peppers into slices. Blanch in boiling water for 5 minutes. Remove and drain. Heat 1½ tablespoons butter in saucepan. Add onions and celery and sauté until onions are transparent. Sprinkle with flour, pour in chicken broth and bring to a boil while stirring constantly. Simmer for 10 minutes. Season with soy sauce and pepper. Add pepper slices, drained mushrooms, and chicken pieces. Cover and simmer for 15 minutes.

Meanwhile, bring 6 cups of slightly salted water to a boil and add noodles and cook for 15 minutes. Drain and rinse with cold water. Set aside ⅓ of the noodles. Place rest of noodles in heated bowl, add 1 tablespoon butter, cover and keep warm.

Heat oil in skillet until very hot. Cut noodles that were set aside into approximately 2-inch-long pieces. Add to hot oil and fry until golden. Drain on paper towels. To serve, spoon chicken mixture over buttered noodles; top with fried noodles and toasted almonds.

MAKES 4 SERVINGS.

Oriental chicken I

CHINA

⅓ cup flour
¼ teaspoon nutmeg
¼ teaspoon grated gingerroot
2 chickens, cut up
Oil for cooking
1 can sliced pineapple, 20 ounces; drain and reserve juice
¼ cup soy sauce
2 tablespoons sugar
2 cloves garlic, crushed
Rice

Blend flour, nutmeg, and gingerroot. Coat chicken with this mixture and brown well in oil in skillet. Transfer chicken to casserole dish and cover with sauce made from pineapple juice, soy sauce, sugar, and garlic. Bake, lightly covered, at 350°F for 1 hour. Brown pineapple slices in skillet and arrange on serving platter with chicken. Serve with rice.

MAKES APPROXIMATELY 6 SERVINGS.

Oriental chicken II

CHINA

4 ounces almonds, slivered
3 tablespoons peanut oil
¾ cup chopped onion
4 chicken breasts, boned, sliced thin
2 cans (approximately 6 ounces each) sliced bamboo shoots, drained
1 can water chestnuts, drained, sliced
1 cucumber, unpeeled, sliced thin
2 teaspoons sherry
¼ teaspoon ground ginger
1 teaspoon soy sauce
½ teaspoon cornstarch
1 tablespoon cold water
Salt to taste
Freshly ground pepper to taste

Brown almonds in 400°F oven about 10 minutes. Watch closely. Set aside.

Pour oil into large frying pan or wok; heat to medium-high heat. Add onion; cook until limp. Remove onion from pan (push up side, if using wok). Add chicken to pan; toss gently about 1 minute. Add bamboo shoots and water chestnuts; toss gently 1 minute. Add cucumber; cook 1 minute. Combine stock, sherry, ginger, and soy sauce. Add to pan; cook 1 minute.

Combine cornstarch and water in small dish. Stir slowly into hot mixture. Season with salt and pepper. Cook until liquid is thickened. While cooking, return onions to mixture. Serve chicken with rice and browned almonds.

MAKES 4 SERVINGS.

Oriental chicken w/vegetables

CHINA

¼ cup soy sauce
¼ cup chicken broth
2 whole chicken breasts, skinned, boned, meat cut into
    bite-size pieces
4 tablespoons peanut oil
1 clove garlic, minced
2 small yellow squash, sliced thin
1 medium zucchini, sliced thin
1½ cups snow-pea pods, fresh or frozen
½ pound fresh mushrooms, sliced
Boiled rice

Mix soy sauce with broth in shallow bowl. Marinate chicken in mixture at least 1 hour. Heat 2 tablespoons oil in wok until sizzling. Add garlic; cook 2 minutes. Drain chicken; reserve marinade. Cook chicken in wok, stirring constantly, 2 minutes. Remove from wok; keep warm.

Add 2 tablespoons oil to wok; heat. Add squash and zucchini; stir-fry until coated with oil. Push to one side. Add pea pods and mushrooms; toss to coat with oil. Add chicken and soy-sauce mixture; cover. Reduce heat; simmer 5 minutes or until vegetables are tender but still crispy. Serve with rice.

MAKES 4 SERVINGS.

Bean sprouts w/chicken

CHINA

1½ pounds shredded raw chicken meat
2½ teaspoons rice wine or sherry
1½ teaspoons salt
1 egg white
1 tablespoon cornstarch
Oil for frying
12 ounces fresh bean sprouts
½ teaspoon sesame oil
1 teaspoon cornstarch
1 teaspoon water

Mix chicken with 1½ teaspoons wine, salt, and egg white. Coat with 1 tablespoon cornstarch. Deep fry chicken in oil in wok or deep skillet until color changes. Remove from oil; drain.

Leave 1 tablespoon oil in pan. Stir-fry bean sprouts. Add chicken, 1 teaspoon wine, sesame oil, and cornstarch mixed with water. Stir until all ingredients are heated through.

MAKES 5 TO 6 SERVINGS.

Chicken w/dates

CHINA

1 chicken, approximately 3 to 3½ pounds
Salt
Pepper
Curry powder
2 tablespoons oil
1 medium onion, chopped
2 green peppers, cut into thin strips
1 cup beef bouillon
½ pound rice
1 teaspoon cornstarch
12 dates, pitted, cut into halves
1 cup yoghurt
3 tablespoons toasted sliced almonds

Divide chicken into 8 pieces. Remove all except wing and leg bones. Rub chicken with salt, pepper, and curry powder. Heat oil in heavy skillet. Add chicken; cook until golden on all sides. Add onion; cook until golden. Add green peppers. Pour in bouillon; simmer over low heat 30 minutes.

Meanwhile, cook rice until just tender.

Remove chicken from sauce; keep warm. Strain sauce. Blend cornstarch with small amount cold water. Slowly stir into sauce: cook until thick and bubbly. Add dates.

Beat yoghurt with fork; stir into sauce. If necessary, correct seasonings. Heat through, but do not boil. Spoon rice into bowl or platter; arrange chicken on top. Pour sauce over chicken; top with almonds.

MAKES 4 OR 5 SERVINGS.

Chicken velvet

CHINA

Meat from 2 chicken breasts, minced
2 teaspoons cornstarch
¼ cup cold water
Pinch of salt
3 egg whites, beaten until stiff peaks form
Vegetable oil for frying
½ cup snow-pea pods, cut in half
1 tablespoon oil

sauce

1 teaspoon cornstarch
1 teaspoon cold water
½ cup chicken broth
1 tablespoon sherry
1 tablespoon vegetable oil

Mix chicken with cornstarch, water, and salt. Fold mixture into egg whites. Drop by teaspoonfuls into hot oil; cook until lightly browned. Drain on paper toweling.

Sauté pea pods in 1 tablespoon oil until well-coated. Mix cornstarch with cold water in small saucepan until smooth. Add rest of ingredients; bring to boil. Add sauce and chicken to snow peas. Bring to boil.

MAKES 2 SERVINGS.

Paper-wrapped chicken

CHINA

1 pound chicken meat, sliced very thin
2 tablespoons soy sauce
1 tablespoon dry sherry
½ teaspoon brown sugar

½ teaspoon salt
1 scallion, sliced thin
1 teaspoon grated fresh gingerroot
16 pieces cooking parchment; if unavailable, use foil, approximately 4 inches square
Vegetable oil for frying

Combine chicken, soy sauce, sherry, brown sugar, salt, scallion, and ginger. Marinate 30 minutes. Divide chicken mixture into 16 portions. Wrap each portion in piece of cooking parchment; fasten well.

Heat oil in wok to 375°F. Deep-fry packages a few at a time 3 minutes. Drain on paper toweling; keep hot. Serve wrapped to keep in juices. Each is unwrapped just before eating.

MAKES 4 SERVINGS.

Chicken w/walnuts

CHINA

1 pound raw white chicken meat, cut into 1-inch cubes
1 teaspoon salt
1 teaspoon sugar
1 tablespoon soy sauce
3 tablespoons sherry
2 tablespoons cornstarch
1 egg, beaten
½ cup peanut oil
1 cup walnuts
2 teaspoons minced fresh gingerroot
3 garlic cloves, minced
½ cup boiling water
1 cup sliced bamboo shoots

Combine chicken in bowl with salt, sugar, soy sauce, and sherry; mix well. Let stand 30 minutes. Drain; reserve marinade. Dip chicken pieces into cornstarch, then into egg.

Heat oil in wok or deep skillet; brown walnuts. Remove walnuts; pour off all but 2 tablespoons oil. Brown chicken, ginger, and garlic. Add water, bamboo shoots, and marinade. Cover; cook over low heat 10 minutes. Add walnuts; mix through.

MAKES 4 SERVINGS.

Kang pao chicken

CHINA

12 ounces boned chicken, cut into ½-inch squares
1 egg white
2 teaspoons cornstarch
2 tablespoons brown bean sauce
1 tablespoon hoisin sauce
2 teaspoons sherry
1 teaspoon sugar
1 tablespoon white rice-wine vinegar
2 tablespoons water
2 teaspoons minced garlic
1 cup peanut oil
1¼ teaspoons crushed red pepper (or as desired)
½ cup roasted peanuts

Combine chicken with egg white and cornstarch in bowl. Mash bean sauce in separate bowl. Add hoisin sauce, sherry, sugar, vinegar, water, and garlic.
Heat wok over high heat. Add oil. When oil is very hot, add chicken; stir 30 seconds or until chicken changes color. Remove from wok; set aside. Drain off all but 2 tablespoons oil. Reheat wok. When oil is very hot, add red pepper; stir 25 seconds or until pepper darkens. Add chicken, bean-sauce mixture, and peanuts to wok; stir 1 minute or until heated through.
MAKES 2 OR 3 SERVINGS.

Cashew chicken

CHINA

2 tablespoons oil
½ teaspoon salt
1 cup sliced raw chicken breast meat
¾ cup pea pods
½ cup bamboo shoots
½ cup sliced fresh mushrooms
1 cup chicken broth
½ cup cashew nuts (or as desired)
¼ teaspoon sugar
½ teaspoon cornstarch
1 teaspoon water

Coat preheated wok with oil (swirl around) Sprinkle in salt. Stir-fry chicken 2 minutes. Add pea pods bamboo shoots, mushrooms, and chicken broth. Cover wok; cook 2 minutes.

Carefully stir in nuts and sugar. Mix cornstarch with water; stir into chicken mixture until thickened.
MAKES 4 SERVINGS.

Chicken go wan

CHINA

2 whole chicken breasts, boned, cut into ½-inch cubes
¾ cup soy sauce
2 cups long-grain rice
4½ cups chicken stock
1 cup sliced fresh mushrooms

Combine chicken and soy sauce in mixing bowl; let stand 1 to 2 hours to marinate. Combine rice, stock, and mushrooms in Dutch oven; mix lightly. Spoon chicken and soy sauce over top. Cover; cook over low heat approximately 30 minutes or until chicken and rice are tender.
MAKES 4 TO 6 SERVINGS.

Chicken w/sweet peppers

CHINA

2 whole chicken breasts, boned, cut into 1-inch pieces	1 red pepper, seeds and membrane removed, cut into 1-inch pieces
2 cloves garlic, pressed	8 green onions, cut into ½-inch pieces
4 tablespoons olive oil	3 celery stalks, cut into ½-inch pieces
3 tablespoons soy sauce	
½ teaspoon salt	¼ teaspoon sugar
¼ teaspoon freshly ground black pepper	¼ cup cold water
2 teaspoons cornstarch	
2 green peppers, seeds and membrane removed, cut into 1-inch pieces	

Combine chicken, garlic, 1 tablespoon oil, 2 tablespoons soy sauce, salt, pepper, and 1 teaspoon cornstarch in mixing bowl; mix well. Let marinate at least 30 minutes.
Heat 3 tablespoons oil in wok. Add peppers; stir-fry 3 minutes. Add onions and celery; stir-fry 2 minutes. Using slotted spoon, remove vegetables; keep warm. Place chicken in hot oil in wok; stir-fry 5 minutes.
Combine 1 tablespoon soy sauce, 1 teaspoon

cornstarch, sugar, and water. Pour over chicken. Add vegetables; combine carefully, cooking over low heat about 2 minutes or until heated through.

MAKES ABOUT 4 SERVINGS.

Oven barbecued chicken

CHINA

¼ cup soy sauce

2 cloves garlic, minced

2 teaspoons salt

¼ teaspoon freshly ground black pepper

1 teaspoon five-spice

1 teaspoon sugar

2 tablespoons oil

1 roasting chicken, approximately 4 pounds, whole, washed, dried

Mix together soy sauce, garlic, salt, pepper, five-spice, sugar, and oil. Rub into inside and outside of chicken. Let stand 1 hour. Place chicken on rack in shallow roasting pan. Roast in 425°F oven 2½ hours or until chicken is tender and nicely browned. Turn and baste often.

To serve, chicken can be cut up with bones left on (American-style), or meat can be taken off bones and cut into pieces about 1 inch square (Chinese-style).

MAKES ABOUT 4 SERVINGS.

Deep-fried sweet-&-sour chicken

CHINA

2 tablespoons cornstarch

2 tablespoons soy sauce

1 teaspoon salt

2 eggs

Oil for cooking

1 4-pound cooked chicken, boned, skinned, meat cut into 1-inch cubes

Combine cornstarch and soy sauce; mix well. Combine salt and eggs in mixing bowl; beat with whisk until light. Stir in cornstarch mixture until just mixed.

Heat oil in deep-fryer to 375°F or until small ball

of flour mixed with water dropped into oil floats to top immediately. Dip chicken into egg mixture; drain slightly. Drop chicken, several cubes at a time, into oil. Fry until lightly browned; drain on paper toweling. Place chicken in individual serving dishes. Spoon Sweet-and-Sour Sauce over chicken.

MAKES 4 TO 6 SERVINGS.

Sweet-and-sour sauce

¾ cup sugar

2 tablespoons soy sauce

1 tablespoon dry white wine

3 tablespoons wine vinegar

3 tablespoons catsup

2 tablespoons cornstarch

½ cup water

Combine sugar, soy sauce, wine, vinegar, and catsup in saucepan; bring to boil. Dissolve cornstarch in water; add to sauce. Cook over low heat, stirring, until sauce has thickened. Makes 1 to 1¼ cups.

Chicken with dates

Poultry / China

Orange duck (preceding pages)

Deep-fried sweet-and-sour chicken

Cornish hen w/hot sauce

CHINA

1 Cornish hen, about 1½ pounds
1 teaspoon finely chopped gingerroot
1 teaspoon finely chopped scallion
1 tablespoon soy sauce
1 teaspoon sesame oil
1 teaspoon dark vinegar
1 tablespoon Tabasco sauce
1 teaspoon sugar
Parsley for garnish

Cook hen in boiling water until tender. Remove; cool. Cut meat into bite-size pieces. Place on serving platter. Mix together rest of ingredients; pour over chicken. Garnish with parsley if desired.

MAKES 2 SERVINGS.

Peking duck

CHINA

4 to 5 pound duck
6 cups water
¼ cup honey
4 slices of fresh gingerroot, about 1 inch in diameter and ⅛ inch thick
2 scallions, sliced

sauce

¼ cup hoisin sauce
1 tablespoon water
1 teaspoon sesame-seed oil
2 teaspoons sugar
12 scallion brushes
Mandarin Pancakes

Wash the duck thoroughly with cold water, and dry. Tie a cord tightly around the neck skin and suspend the duck in an airy place to dry the skin (about 3 hours).

Bring water to boil. Add honey, gingerroot, and sliced scallions. Lower the duck by its string into the boiling liquid and moisten the duck's skin thoroughly, using a spoon. Suspend the duck by its cord until it is dry (about 3 hours).

Make the sauce by combining all the sauce ingredients in a small pan; stir until the sugar dissolves. Bring to a boil. Then simmer for 3 minutes. Set aside to cool. Cut scallions to 3-inch lengths and trim off roots. Stand each scallion on end and make 4 intersecting cuts 1 inch deep into its stalk. Repeat at other end. Place scallions in ice water and refrigerate until cut parts curl. Preheat oven to 375°F.

Untie the duck and cut off any loose neck skin. Place duck, breast-side-up, on a rack and set in a roasting pan. Roast for 1 hour. Lower heat to 300°F, turn the duck on its breast, and roast for 30 minutes longer. Raise the heat to 375°F, return the duck to its back, and roast for 30 minutes. Transfer to carving board.

With a small, sharp knife and using your fingers, remove the crisp skin from the breast, sides, and back of duck. Cut the skin into 2- by 3-inch rectangles and arrange them in a single layer on a platter. Cut the wings and drumsticks from the duck, and cut all the meat away from the breast and carcass. Slice the meat into pieces 2½ inches long and ½ inch wide, and arrange them on another platter.

Serve the duck with Mandarin pancakes, sauce, and the scallion brushes. Dip a scallion brush into the sauce and brush a pancake with it. The scallion is placed in the middle of the pancake with a piece of duck skin and a piece of meat. The pancake is rolled around the pieces and eaten like a sandwich.

MAKES APPROXIMATELY 6 SERVINGS.

Mandarin pancakes

2 cups sifted all-purpose flour
¾ cup boiling water
1 to 2 tablespoons sesame-seed oil

Make a well in the sifted flour in bowl and pour the water into it. Mix with a wooden spoon until it is a soft dough. Knead the dough gently on a lightly floured surface for 10 minutes. It should be smooth. Let it rest under a damp kitchen towel for 15 minutes. On lightly floured surface roll dough to thickness of about ¼ inch thick.

With a 2½-inch glass, cut as many circles as you can. Use the scraps of dough, kneading them again and cutting out more circles. Brush half of the circles lightly with the sesame-seed oil, and place an unoiled circle on top of an oiled one. 223

Flatten each pair, with a rolling pin, to a diameter of about 6 inches. Turn it once to roll both sides, trying to keep its circular shape. Cover the pancakes with a dry towel.

Heat an 8-inch skillet (ungreased) to high heat. Reduce heat to moderate and cook the pancakes, one at a time, turning them over as little bubbles and brown specks appear. Cook about 1 minute on each side. As each pancake is cooked, gently separate the halves and stack them on a plate.
MAKES APPROXIMATELY 24 PANCAKES.

Crispy duck

CHINA

1 duck, about 4 pounds
6 small slices fresh gingerroot
3 tablespoons salt
4 scallions, chopped fine
1 teaspoon Szechwan peppercorns
1 tablespoon rice wine or sherry
4 star anise
3 tablespoons soy sauce
Oil for deep frying

Coat duck well with mixture of gingerroot, salt, scallions, peppercorns, rice wine, and star anise. Let stand 30 minutes. Steam duck about 1 hour or until very tender. Remove; rub with soy sauce. Deep-fry until golden brown. Cut meat into bite-size pieces. Arrange on serving platter.
MAKES ABOUT 3 SERVINGS.

Pineapple duck

CHINA

1 duck, about 4 pounds
4 slices canned pineapple
1 large green pepper, cut into 1-inch squares
2 tablespoons oil
1 teaspoon salt
¼ teaspoon pepper
1 tablespoon soy sauce
1 tablespoon cornstarch mixed with 2 tablespoons cold water

Clean and quarter duck. Cover with boiling water and simmer gently until tender. Remove from broth and let duck drain. Reserve broth.

Cut each slice of pineapple into 8 pieces. Cut pepper into squares. Preheat skillet and add oil. Place pieces of duck in skillet, along with salt and pepper. Brown gently, turning frequently. When browned, add the pineapple and green pepper and stir-fry a few seconds. Add the broth and soy sauce. Cover and simmer about 10 minutes. Thicken slightly with cornstarch mixture. Serve with rice.
MAKES 3 SERVINGS.

Szechwan duck

CHINA

4 slices fresh gingerroot, minced
4 scallions, chopped fine
2 tablespoons salt
1 tablespoon Szechwan peppercorns
1 duck, 4 to 5 pounds, washed, cleaned
1 quart vegetable oil
Lotus-Leaf Rolls
2 tablespoons salt mixed with 1 teaspoon peppercorns, roasted in oven 10 minutes

Mix together gingerroot, scallions, salt, and peppercorns. Rub inside and outside of duck with mixture. Press on breastbone of duck; break to flatten it. Refrigerate overnight.

Steam duck 2 hours; cool thoroughly. Heat oil in wok or deep pot to 375°F. Deep-fry duck about 7 minutes or until golden brown and crisp. Serve with Lotus-Leaf Rolls. Diner takes meat off bones (comes off easily with chopsticks), dips it into roasted salt-and-peppercorn mixture, then makes sandwich on Lotus-Leaf Roll.
MAKES 4 SERVINGS.

Lotus-leaf rolls

1 cup flour
2 teaspoons sugar
2 teaspoons baking powder
½ cup milk (water can be substituted)
Oil

Mix flour with sugar and baking powder. Slowly add milk; stir with fork until soft dough. Knead 5 minutes. Cover with clean, dry cloth; let stand 15 minutes. Knead 2 minutes. Make rolls 1 inch in diameter and 1 inch thick. Brush with small amount oil; fold over. Use fork to make indentations all around edge. Steam 8 minutes over medium-high heat.

Salt duck (cold)

CHINA

3 tablespoons Szechwan peppercorns
½ cup kosher salt
1 duck, approximately 5 pounds
3 tablespoons sherry
½ cup chopped coriander for garnish (optional)

Mix peppercorns with salt. Toast mixture in pan over low heat, shaking pan occasionally. When peppercorns have nice aroma, remove from heat; cool. Crush peppercorns.

Wipe duck with paper towels; rub inside and outside with salt mixture. Cover; refrigerate overnight. Before cooking duck, rinse thoroughly with cold water.

To cook duck, put in heatproof bowl. Rub outside of duck with sherry. Cover bowl; place on trivet in bottom of large pot. Put water in pot, enough to reach halfway up bowl. Bring water to boil; lower heat to simmer. Cook 1 hour and 45 minutes, adding water if necessary. Let duck reach room temperature. Remove from bowl; drain excess liquids from inside duck into bowl. Chop duck meat into bite-size pieces. Arrange on serving platter. Pour liquid over duck; refrigerate 2 hours before serving. Garnish with coriander.

MAKES 4 SERVINGS.

Orange duck

CHINA

2 cups sherry
½ cup honey
2 tablespoons soy sauce
2 tablespoons candied ginger, finely chopped
2 teaspoons powdered mustard

1 teaspoon sesame seeds
1 duck, 3 to 4 pounds
Salt
2 tablespoons margarine

orange sauce
6 oranges
1 piece of candied ginger, approximately size of a walnut, chopped
2 to 3 tablespoons sugar

¼ cup sherry
1 teaspoon cornstarch
1 11-ounce can mandarin orange sections
1 banana

garnish
1 orange, sliced
2 maraschino cherries
Parsley sprigs

Blend thoroughly sherry, honey, soy sauce, finely chopped ginger, mustard, and sesame seeds. Pour over duck in large bowl, cover and refrigerate for 3 hours, turning duck occasionally. Remove duck and drain well on paper toweling. Reserve marinade.

Salt inside of duck lightly. Heat margarine in large skillet or Dutch oven. Add duck and brown well on all sides. Place duck in preheated 350°F oven and cook for 1 hour and 10 minutes, basting occasionally with reserved marinade.

To prepare sauce, pare half an orange and cut rind into thin strips. Now squeeze oranges. Blend orange juice, sliced rind, and chopped ginger. Add sugar and half the sherry. Heat mixture in saucepan. Blend rest of sherry with cornstarch, and slowly add to Orange Sauce, stirring constantly until thick and bubbly. Drain mandarin orange sections and slice banana. Add half of the fruit to sauce. Place duck on preheated platter. Garnish with rest of mandarins, banana and orange slices, cherries and parsley. Serve sauce separately.

MAKES APPROXIMATELY 4 SERVINGS.

Japanese fried chicken

JAPAN

2½ to 3 pound fryer, cut into pieces
marinade
4 tablespoons soy sauce
2 teaspoons mirin or sherry
Juice of 1 lemon
Salt
Paprika
4 tablespoons (approximately) cornstarch
Oil for frying

After cutting up chicken, wash and pat it dry. Mix together soy sauce, mirin (if substituting sherry, add 1 teaspoon sugar), lemon juice, dash of salt, and dash of paprika. Marinate chicken pieces in marinade for at least 2 hours; drain off excess liquid. Sprinkle chicken thoroughly with cornstarch.

Fry in oil on medium temperature for about 15 to 20 minutes, or until chicken is nicely browned. Drain on paper towels.
MAKES 4 SERVINGS.

Chicken teriyaki

JAPAN

1 broiler chicken, 2½ to 3 pounds, cut up

marinade
¾ cup soy sauce
¼ cup sugar
¼ cup sherry or sake
2 teaspoons grated fresh gingerroot
1 large clove garlic, crushed

Wash chicken; pat dry. Mix together marinade ingredients. Place chicken in marinade. Cover and refrigerate for several hours, turning occasionally.

Drain chicken, reserving marinade. Place skin-side-down in greased baking pan. Bake in 450°F oven for 15 minutes. Turn chicken; bake for another 15 minutes. Reduce oven temperature to 350°F. Pour off and reserve liquid in pan. Continue baking for approximately 30 minutes or until chicken is tender, brushing occasionally with reserved marinade. Broil (if desired) about 6 inches from heat until well-browned.
MAKES 4 SERVINGS.

Chicken breasts teriyaki

JAPAN

2 chicken breasts, halved, boned, and skin removed
4 tablespoons oil
4 tablespoons soy sauce
4 tablespoons sugar
½ teaspoon freshly grated ginger or ¼ teaspoon ground ginger

Parboil chicken breasts for only about 30 seconds. Drain. Heat oil medium high; brown the chicken. Pour off the oil. Add the soy sauce, sugar, and ginger to the pan; cover, and simmer until sauce is like syrup. Serve chicken with rice, if desired.
MAKES APPROXIMATELY 2 TO 3 SERVINGS.

Baked chicken legs w/fruit

JAPAN

1 teaspoon paprika
½ teaspoon ground ginger
1 teaspoon seasoned salt
¼ cup flour
6 chicken legs, disjointed, using thigh and leg
¼ cup shortening
1 29-ounce can or jar fruits-for-salad
3 oranges, peeled and cut into bite-size pieces
1 tablespoon brown sugar
2 teaspoons soy sauce
1 tablespoon cornstarch

Mix together paprika, ginger, seasoned salt, and flour. Place in small paper or double-plastic bag. Drop chicken in bag, one piece at a time, until well-coated. Set aside.

Heat shortening in skillet to low-medium heat. Brown chicken on all sides. Tear 6 pieces of heavy-duty aluminum foil large enough to hold chicken and fruit. On each piece of foil, place 1 thigh and 1 leg. Drain fruits, reserving liquid. Mix the canned fruit with the orange pieces; place 1/6 of fruit on each piece of foil, along with chicken pieces.

Into small saucepan place 1 cup of fruit syrup, brown sugar, soy sauce, and cornstarch. Mix well; bring to a boil. Simmer for 3 minutes. Spoon sauce over chicken and fruit. Fold foil; seal, by double-folding edges. Place packages in pan; bake at 425°F for 1½ hours or until chicken is tender.
MAKES 6 SERVINGS.

Chicken w/sesame seeds

JAPAN

This may also be made with pork or beef.

12 ounces boned chicken wings or breast meat
2 tablespoons rice wine or sherry
½ teaspoon (scant) salt
½ teaspoon oil
2 teaspoons sesame seeds

Sprinkle chicken with rice wine or sherry and salt. Set aside for 30 minutes. Heat oil in frying pan, brown meat on both sides, and remove to preheated platter. Heat sesame seeds in frying pan; sprinkle on the chicken.
MAKES 2 SERVINGS.

Skewered chicken pieces

JAPAN

marinade

1 cup soy sauce
1 cup sake (rice wine) or sherry
3 tablespoons sugar, or little less
2 teaspoons freshly ground pepper
1½ to 2 pounds skinless and boneless raw chicken meat,
cut into large cubes

Mix together soy sauce, sake or sherry, sugar, and pepper, bring to a boil. Marinate the chicken in the marinade for 30 minutes, put chicken pieces on skewer, and broil; or, put on grill or hibachi. Brush with extra marinade during cooking, turning to brown well on all sides.
MAKES 4 TO 5 SERVINGS.

Chicken patties

JAPAN

¾ cup chopped leftover cooked chicken
2 cups mashed potatoes
2 eggs
Bread or cracker crumbs
Oil for frying

Combine chicken, potatoes, and eggs. Mix well. Roll in bread or cracker crumbs; fry in hot oil. Dip patties in soy sauce, if desired.
MAKES 4 TO 6 SERVINGS.

Chicken sukiyaki

JAPAN

2 cups chicken stock
1 cup sugar
1 cup soy sauce
1 pound (2 cups) boneless and skinless chicken meat, cut
into bite-size pieces
8 large mushrooms, sliced
3 carrots, sliced diagonally and parboiled
6 scallions, cut into 2-inch lengths

Boil chicken stock that has been mixed with sugar and soy sauce. Add the chicken; simmer about 12 minutes. Add remaining ingredients; simmer another 3 minutes. Serve this with rice.
MAKES 3 TO 4 SERVINGS.

Oriental chicken livers

JAPAN

8 ounces chicken livers, cut in half
⅓ cup soy sauce
½ cup flour
Oil for frying
1 small onion, sliced, or onion flakes

Marinate chicken livers overnight in soy sauce. Remove livers from marinade; dredge in flour. Heat small amount of oil in frying pan; fry livers and onions until browned. Serve livers as an appetizer, or with rice as a main dish.
MAKES 2 TO 3 SERVINGS.

Simmered chicken livers

JAPAN

1 pound chicken livers
1 cup soy sauce
3 tablespoons white wine
1½ cups water
3 tablespoons sugar
1 tablespoon freshly grated ginger or ½ tablespoon ground
ginger
8 scallions, cut into 1-inch pieces

Cut the chicken livers in half. Mix together the soy sauce, wine, water, sugar, and ginger. Bring this mixture to a boil; add the livers to it. Boil

slowly until most of the liquid is absorbed. Add scallions; cook for another 2 minutes. Use as an appetizer, serving 4, as well as a main dish.
MAKES 2 SERVINGS.

Chicken cooked w/corn

MEXICO

1 2½- to 3-pound broiler-fryer chicken
4 tablespoons butter or margarine
Salt and pepper
1 16½-ounce can whole-kernel corn, drained, and the liquid reserved
½ cup chopped green chilies (optional)

sauce
3 tablespoons butter or margarine
2 tablespoons flour
1 cup half and half
2 eggs, separated
Salt and white pepper
¼ teaspoon nutmeg
2 tablespoons bread crumbs
2 tablespoons butter

Wash chicken, pat dry, and cut into quarters. Heat butter or margarine in heavy skillet. Brown chicken on all sides. Place in an ovenproof casserole. Season chicken with salt and pepper to taste. Add corn and chilies (if used) to juices in skillet along with ¼ cup reserved corn liquid. Stir well; pour over chicken.

Next make the sauce. Melt butter or margarine in saucepan. Add flour; cook until evenly and lightly browned, stirring constantly. Add half and half all at once; cook over medium heat, stirring, until slightly thickened.

Beat egg yolks, salt, pepper, and nutmeg together. Add some hot sauce to egg yolks; beat well. Pour egg-yolk mixture into saucepan; mix well. Remove from the heat. Beat egg whites until stiff but not dry; fold into sauce. Pour sauce over chicken, sprinkle with bread crumbs, and dot with butter. Bake in a preheated 350°F oven for 45 minutes.
MAKES 4 SERVINGS.

Tablecloth stainer

MEXICO

2 tablespoons butter or margarine
2 tablespoons cooking oil
1 pound boneless pork, cut into 1-inch chunks
1 roasting chicken (4 to 5 pounds), disjointed
½ cup flour

sauce
1 tablespoon blanched, slivered almonds
2 teaspoons sesame seeds
1 medium onion, chopped
1 green pepper, seeded and chopped
1 16-ounce can tomatoes, broken up with a fork
2 cups chicken stock
½ cup white wine
¼ cup sugar
1½ teaspoons cinnamon
1 tablespoon chili powder
3 cloves
1 bay leaf
1 sweet potato, peeled and cut into cubes
1 medium apple
1 cup pineapple chunks, drained
2 medium bananas (optional)

Heat butter and oil together in Dutch oven. Sauté pork until well-browned. Dredge chicken in flour; brown well. Reserve meats while making sauce.

Add 1 tablespoon of oil to pan, if necessary. Sauté almonds, sesame seeds, onion, and pepper until lightly browned. Add tomatoes; simmer for 10 minutes. Purée sauce in blender or food processor.

In Dutch oven combine puréed sauce, chicken stock, wine, sugar, cinnamon, chili powder, cloves, and bay leaf. Add chicken and pork. Bring to a boil. Reduce heat to low; cook for 30 minutes. Add sweet potato; cook 15 minutes more.

Peel, core, and dice apple. Add apple and pineapple to stew; heat through. Serve stew in bowls. Peel and slice bananas into individual bowls as the stew is served.
MAKES 6 SERVINGS.

Chicken w/orange juice

MEXICO

1½ pounds chicken breasts, split (4 chicken pieces total)
½ cup flour
½ teaspoon salt
¼ teaspoon pepper
¼ cup vegetable oil
¼ cup sherry or golden rum
½ cup crushed pineapple in natural juice
¾ cup orange juice
¼ cup seedless raisins
¼ teaspoon ground cinnamon
⅛ teaspoon ground cloves
2 tablespoons butter
¼ cup blanched slivered almonds

Rinse chicken; pat dry. Combine flour, salt, and pepper. Dredge chicken breasts thoroughly, shaking off excess flour. Heat oil over moderate heat in heavy skillet. Brown the chicken pieces on all sides until golden. Place chicken pieces in shallow pan.

Combine the sherry, pineapple, orange juice, raisins, cinnamon, and cloves. Pour mixture over chicken. Bake uncovered at 350°F for 30 minutes, basting frequently.

In a small saucepan melt the butter. Add the almonds and sauté over moderate heat until golden. Pour the almonds and butter over the chicken. Serve chicken with rice.

MAKES 4 SERVINGS.

Chicken with tomatoes and olives

Company chicken & rice casserole

MEXICO

3 tablespoons olive oil
½ cup chopped onion
1 cup raw long-grain rice
2 cups chicken broth
3 tablespoons dry sherry
1 bay leaf
Salt and pepper
1 teaspoon dried cilantro (dried coriander leaves)
2 cups cooked chicken, boned, skinned, and shredded
¾ cup sour cream
½ cup sliced stuffed green olives

Heat oil in large, heavy skillet. Sauté onion until limp. Add rice; cook, stirring occasionally, until lightly browned. Add chicken broth, sherry, bay leaf, salt and pepper to taste, cilantro, and chicken. Stir well. Bring mixture to a boil. Cover, reduce heat to simmer, and cook for 20 minutes or until all liquid is absorbed.
Uncover; stir in sour cream. Over very low heat, cook just long enough to heat through. Top chicken with the sliced olives, and serve.
MAKES 4 SERVINGS.

Chicken & taco chips casserole

MEXICO

9 taco shells or 1 12-ounce bag taco chips
2 whole chicken breasts, cooked and chopped
1 10½-ounce can chicken and rice soup
2 cups grated sharp cheddar cheese
1 10-ounce can tomatoes and green chilies

Crush taco chips in a bowl. Place a layer of crushed chips in bottom of greased 1-quart casserole. Sprinkle a layer of chopped chicken over chips. Pour several spoonfuls of condensed chicken and rice soup over the chicken layer. Sprinkle with a layer of grated cheese. Pour several spoonfuls of tomato and green chili mixture over cheese layer. Repeat process of layering chips, chicken, soup, cheese, and chilies until all ingredients are used. Top casserole with additional grated cheese if desired. Bake for 25 minutes at 350°F.

This may be prepared ahead and refrigerated before baking. It freezes well before and after baking.
MAKES 4 TO 6 SERVINGS.

Sour-cream chicken enchiladas

MEXICO

enchilada sauce
1 clove garlic, minced
2 small onions, chopped
3 tablespoons oil
2 tablespoons flour
1¾ cups chicken bouillon
2 5-ounce cans green chilies, drained and chopped
2 cups canned tomatoes, drained well and chopped (2 28-ounce cans)

enchiladas
12 corn tortillas, fresh or frozen (thawed)
1 pint sour cream
½ pound New York White Cheddar, shredded
4 cups cooked and shredded chicken
Extra cheese (shredded) and black olive slices for topping (if desired)

To make the sauce, sauté garlic and onions in oil. Add flour; stir in bouillon. Cook, stirring constantly, about 5 minutes, until thickened. Add chilies and tomatoes; allow to simmer for 5 to 10 minutes. Makes 3½ to 4 cups of sauce.
To assemble the enchiladas, dip tortillas in hot oil to soften. Drain well on paper towels. Mix sour cream, shredded cheese, and chicken. Place filling in center of each tortilla; roll them up. Use approximately ½ cup filling per tortilla. Place rolled enchiladas side-by-side in a large baking dish; pour sauce over them. Sprinkle with extra cheese and sliced black olives if desired. Bake at 350°F for about 30 minutes, until bubbly and hot.
MAKES 6 SERVINGS.

Mexican chicken livers

MEXICO

1 pound chicken livers
½ cup flour
½ teaspoon salt
⅛ teaspoon pepper
6 tablespoons butter
5 scallions, sliced
½ pound fresh mushrooms, sliced
¼ cup sherry (more as desired)

Coat chicken livers with flour mixed with salt and pepper. Melt butter; sauté chicken livers until golden brown. Add scallions and mushrooms; cook until tender. Add desired amount of sherry; simmer for 5 minutes. Serve livers on toast or rice.

MAKES 4 SERVINGS.

Open-faced tortilla sandwiches (tostadas)

sauce
½ cup onion
2 tablespoons olive oil
1½ cups drained and cut-up canned tomatoes
3 tablespoons chopped canned green chilies

2 tablespoons chopped cilantro
(2 4-ounce cans taco sauce may be substituted for the sauce)

tostadas
Vegetable oil for frying
8 corn tortillas (6 to 7 inches in diameter)
2 cups Refried Beans (see Index)
1½ cups grated Jack cheese

3 cups cubed cooked chicken breast
3 cups shredded iceberg lettuce
1 large ripe avocado
2 tablespoons lemon juice

First make the sauce. Sauté onion in hot oil until lightly browned. Add tomatoes and chilies; cook over low heat until thick. Add cilantro; cool.

To assemble the tostadas, heat oil over moderate heat in heavy 8-inch frying pan until quite hot. Fry tortillas, one at a time, flat, until crisp; drain on paper towels. Spread tortillas with beans; sprinkle with cheese, chicken, and lettuce. Peel and slice avocado. Dip slices in lemon juice; place on top of tostadas. Top with sauce. Serve.

MAKES 4 SERVINGS.

Variation: Spread tortillas with beans and serve the rest of the ingredients in small bowls on the table so that each person can assemble his own tostada.

Fiesta turkey in mole sauce

1 10- to 12-pound turkey, disjointed
¼ cup cooking oil
1 teaspoon salt
Water

mole sauce
6 dried Ancho chilies
Boiling water
2 tablespoons oil
1 medium onion, chopped
2 cloves garlic, minced
½ teaspoon crushed chilies
1 cup chopped canned Italian plum tomatoes
¾ teaspoon ground cinnamon
½ teaspoon ground cloves

¼ teaspoon ground coriander
¼ teaspoon anise
¼ teaspoon cumin
1 dry tortilla, cut into pieces
¼ cup sesame seeds
¼ cup raisins
2 cups chicken broth
2 squares (1 ounce each) semisweet chocolate, grated

Wash turkey; pat dry. Heat oil in Dutch oven; brown the turkey well on all sides, adding more oil if necessary to keep the turkey from sticking. Add salt and enough water to cover. Bring to a boil. Cover; reduce heat to low. Cook 1 hour or until tender. Set aside.

Meanwhile, prepare the sauce. Stem and seed red chilies under cold running water. Tear chilies into pieces; soak in boiling water to cover for 30 minutes. Drain; reserve ¼ cup soaking liquid. Heat oil in skillet. Sauté onion and garlic until limp.

In blender or food processor combine Ancho chilies, reserved liquid, onion, garlic, crushed chilies, tomatoes, and spices; purée until smooth. Add tortilla, sesame seeds, and raisins; purée, scraping blender container frequently. Heat skillet in which onion was cooked over moderate heat for several minutes. Pour purée into skillet; add chicken broth, stirring well. Simmer for 10 minutes. Remove from heat and add chocolate. Stir until chocolate melts.

Drain broth from turkey. Pour sauce over turkey; heat through. Serve turkey garnished with sesame seeds.

MAKES 8 TO 10 SERVINGS.

Note: The turkey could be roasted unstuffed, sliced, and served with the mole sauce if you prefer. Mole sauce is a long and complicated business. It is available in Latin American grocery stores and specialty stores canned and as a powder. It is reconstituted with broth before serving. Chicken and pork are also served with this sauce.

Braised duck in green mole sauce

MEXICO

1 5- to 6-pound duckling
1 clove garlic, mashed
¾ teaspoon salt
½ teaspoon pepper
3 tablespoons butter or
    margarine

green mole sauce

3 tablespoons olive oil
1 slice white bread
½ cup raw shelled pumpkin
    seeds (raw pepitas)
¼ cup blanched slivered
    almonds
1 10-ounce can Mexican
    green tomatoes (tomatillos)

1 4-ounce can peeled green
    chilies
3 tablespoons chopped
    cilantro
1½ cups chicken broth
Salt and pepper

Wash duck, clean thoroughly, and pat dry. Singe any pinfeathers. Rub with garlic, salt, and pepper. In large Dutch oven or stove-top casserole, heat butter or margarine over moderate heat until lightly browned. Brown duck well on all sides, pricking to release some fat from duck. Cover, reduce heat to low, and cook without liquid 25 to 35 minutes or until done through.

Meanwhile, make the sauce. Heat 2 tablespoons oil in skillet; fry bread until golden brown on both sides. Drain on paper towels. Add remaining oil to skillet; brown pumpkin seeds and almonds. Drain. Drain green tomatoes. Seed and chop green chilies. Combine green tomatoes, fried bread (torn into pieces), nuts and seeds, green chilies, cilantro, ½ cup chicken broth, and salt and pepper; purée.

Heat skillet over moderate heat. Pour sauce into skillet; stir in remaining chicken broth. Simmer for 5 to 10 minutes. Carve the duck and serve topped with the sauce.

MAKES 3 TO 4 SERVINGS.

Chicken w/tomatoes & olives

MEXICO

4 breast quarters of frying chicken
½ cup flour
2 tablespoons butter
2 tablespoons olive oil
1 clove garlic, chopped
1 cup chopped onion
¼ cup chopped carrots
¼ cup chopped celery
2 cups broken-up canned tomatoes
½ cup white wine
1 teaspoon chili powder
½ teaspoon ground cumin
½ teaspoon salt
¼ teaspoon pepper
¾ cup cut-up black olives

Wash chicken; pat dry. Dredge chicken in flour, shaking off excess. Heat butter and oil together in deep skillet or Dutch oven. Brown chicken well on all sides. Remove chicken from pan. Lightly brown garlic, onion, carrots, and celery in pan drippings.

Force tomatoes through a sieve, or purée in blender or food processor. Add tomatoes and wine to vegetables in pan or skillet. Add the seasonings; stir well. Place chicken in sauce. Simmer over low heat 30 minutes or until chicken is tender. Add olives; heat through. Serve chicken with rice, crusty bread, and a green salad.

MAKES 4 SERVINGS.

❧ Meats ❧

Beef in red wine sauce

FRANCE

3 tablespoons vegetable oil

12 small white onions, peeled

2 pounds lean stewing beef, cubed

1 tablespoon flour

2 cups dry red wine

1 cup beef bouillon

1 cup water

1 clove garlic, minced

1 tablespoon tomato paste

¼ teaspoon thyme

1 bay leaf

½ teaspoon parsley

1 teaspoon salt

½ teaspoon pepper

½ pound fresh mushrooms, quartered

Heat oil in large frypan. Sauté onions lightly; remove from pan. Add beef cubes; sauté until brown. Sprinkle cubes with flour; toss to coat meat. Cook for 2 minutes, stirring often. Add wine, bouillon, garlic, tomato paste, and seasonings. Stir well, cover, and simmer slowly about 3 hours or until meat is tender. Add more bouillon if necessary.

The last hour of cooking, add onions. Add mushrooms the last 15 minutes. If sauce is too thin, reduce it by boiling rapidly or by adding Sauce Thickener (see Index). Adjust seasonings. Serve.
MAKES 4 TO 6 SERVINGS.

Beef & chicken pot-au-feu

FRANCE

2 pounds beef chuck or rump roast

2 teaspoons salt

2 medium onions, stuck with 3 cloves each

6 carrots, peeled and cut in half

4 stalks celery (with leaves)

8 cups beef broth

4 sprigs parsley

1 bay leaf

½ teaspoon thyme

2 cloves garlic

8 peppercorns

1 2 to-3-pound chicken, whole or selected pieces

½ head cabbage, cut in wedges

4 turnips or potatoes, peeled and quartered

In large Dutch oven or roaster (at least 5-quart) place beef, salt, onions, 2 carrots, celery, and broth. Make a bouquet garni by tying parsley, bay leaf, thyme, garlic, and peppercorns in cheesecloth. Add to stew. Simmer gently 1 hour.

If using a whole chicken, add to meat after 1 hour of cooking; cook ½ hour more. Add vegetables. If using chicken pieces, cook beef 1½ hours, then add chicken and remaining vegetables. After adding vegetables, cook 30 to 45 minutes longer, until vegetables are done and beef is tender. Remove bouquet garni.

To serve, place broth in soup bowls. Serve as a first course, with rice or noodles if desired. Place meat, chicken, and vegetables on a large platter. Pour over a small amount of broth. Serve.
MAKES 8 SERVINGS.

Filet steaks w/herb butter

FRANCE

herb butter

4 ounces softened butter

1 tablespoon finely chopped parsley

1 tablespoon finely chopped chives

1 teaspoon dried chervil

1 teaspoon dried tarragon

1 tablespoon grated shallots or onion

Dash of pepper

4 filets mignons steaks

2 tablespoons vegetable oil

½ teaspoon salt

⅛ teaspoon pepper

4 lemon slices

Watercress

French-fried potatoes (cut very thin, dried on towels, and deep-fried)

Make Herb Butter first by blending all ingredients. Spoon onto sheet of waxed paper; shape into a roll about 1½ inches in diameter. Chill butter in freezer while steak is prepared. Cut in 4 thick slices just before serving.

Brush steaks with oil. Depending on thickness, broil about 5 minutes on each side or to desired doneness. Season with salt and pepper. Arrange steaks on preheated platter. Place 1 lemon slice on each steak; top with slice of Herb Butter. Garnish with watercress and potatoes.
MAKES 4 SERVINGS.

Steak Diane

FRANCE

3 tablespoons chopped scallions
3 tablespoons vegetable oil
3 tablespoons finely chopped chives
3 tablespoons finely chopped parsley
1 tablespoon Worcestershire sauce
1/2 teaspoon salt
1/4 teaspoon pepper
4 beef steaks, fillets, or rib-eye steaks
1/4 cup brandy, warmed

Sauté scallions in 1 tablespoon hot vegetable oil a minute or two. Add chives, parsley, Worcestershire sauce, salt, and pepper. Remove from heat.

In second frypan sauté steaks with remaining 2 tablespoons hot vegetable oil until done. (Time depends on thickness of steak.) Top each steak with some scallion mixture. Pour warmed brandy over the steaks. Touch with a lighted match. Spoon the juices over steaks until the flames subside. Serve.

MAKES 4 SERVINGS.

Stuffed flank steak

FRANCE

2 pounds flank steak, scored, or 2 pounds round steak, thinly sliced
2 tablespoons Dijon-style mustard
1/4 teaspoon thyme

spinach stuffing

1/2 package frozen spinach, cooked and drained
1/2 cup chopped onions
1 tablespoon bacon fat or vegetable oil
1/2 cup raw sausage meat

1/2 teaspoon salt
1/8 teaspoon allspice
1 egg
1/8 teaspoon pepper
1 clove garlic, crushed
1/4 cup dry bread crumbs

6 slices bacon
1 onion, chopped
1 carrot, chopped
1/2 cup dry white wine
1 can beef broth

Spread meat with mustard; sprinkle with thyme. Squeeze all water from spinach. Sauté 1/2 cup onions in fat or oil. Add spinach; toss. Add sausage, egg, salt, allspice, pepper, garlic, and crumbs to spinach mixture. Mix well.

Spread stuffing on meat; roll up jelly-roll fashion. Tie with string. Cook bacon in Dutch oven until partly done. Remove.

Add meat roll to Dutch oven; brown on all sides. This takes about 10 minutes. Lay bacon over meat. Add onion, carrot, wine, and broth. Bring to a simmer. Place in 325°F oven about 1 hour or until tender.

Place meat on platter. Strain juices, pressing hard on vegetables. If desired, thicken with 1 tablespoon cornstarch dissolved in water. Slice meat; serve with pan juices.

MAKES 4 TO 6 SERVINGS.

Steak w/wine sauce

FRANCE

2 tablespoons butter
2 tablespoons vegetable oil
4 8-ounce steaks, tenderloin, boneless rib, or other tender steak
2 tablespoons chopped shallots
1/2 pound mushrooms, sliced
1/2 cup dry red wine
1 tablespoon chopped parsley
1 teaspoon lemon juice
Salt to taste
Pepper to taste
2 tablespoons butter
4 slices toasted French bread, 1 inch thick

Using heavy frying pan, heat 2 tablespoons butter and oil. On medium heat sauté steaks, turning only once, until done as preferred (about 4 minutes for medium rare). Remove steaks; keep them warm.

Add shallots and mushrooms to remaining oil and butter. Sauté for several minutes, until tender. Add wine; boil rapidly 2 minutes. Add remaining ingredients, beating to mix well. To serve, place hot steaks on bread slices; top with a little sauce. Serve remaining sauce separately.

MAKES 4 SERVINGS.

Beef braised in red wine

FRANCE

3 to 4 pounds boneless beef roast (rump, sirloin tip, or top round)
1/2 teaspoon salt
1/4 teaspoon freshly ground black pepper

Filet steaks with herb butter

marinade

3 cups red wine
1 cup water
½ cup sliced onions
¼ cup sliced carrots
1 clove garlic, minced

1 bay leaf, crumbled
2 teaspoons chopped fresh parsley
1 teaspoon thyme

braising ingredients

2 tablespoons vegetable oil
2 strips lean bacon, cubed
1 ounce brandy, warmed
1 veal or beef knuckle
1 tomato, peeled and quartered
1 tablespoon chopped fresh parsley

1 bay leaf
3 green onions, chopped
1 cup beef bouillon
½ teaspoon salt

vegetables

10 small white onions, peeled
8 carrots, peeled and shaped like small balls

2 tablespoons flour
2 tablespoons butter

Parsley for garnish

3 tablespoons Madeira
2 tablespoons cognac

Rub beef roast with salt; sprinkle with pepper. Blend all marinade ingredients. Pour marinade into glass or ceramic bowl. Add beef roast; turn it several times, so that all sides are coated with marinade. Cover; marinate in refrigerator 12 to 24 hours. Turn roast occasionally. Remove roast from marinade; drain; pat dry with paper towels. Strain and reserve marinade.

Heat oil in large Dutch oven. Add bacon; cook until transparent, then add roast. Brown well on all sides. Drain off fat. Pour warm brandy over meat; ignite; wait until flames die down. Add remaining braising ingredients. Cover pan. Place in preheated 350°F oven. During cooking, occasionally pour some reserved marinade over roast. Cook roast 3 hours.

Meanwhile, prepare vegetables. Add onions and carrots to Dutch oven; braise for 1 hour more. When meat and vegetables are tender, remove meat from oven; place on preheated platter. Surround with onions and carrots. Garnish with parsley. Keep food warm.

Strain sauce through fine sieve. Skim off fat, if necessary. Cream together flour and butter. Thicken pan sauce with all or part of this. Stir and heat to boiling 1 to 2 minutes. Add Madeira and cognac. Adjust seasonings. Spoon some sauce over meat; serve the rest separately.

MAKES 6 SERVINGS.

235

Beef braised in red wine

Braised beef w/madeira sauce

FRANCE

marinade

1 6-ounce can frozen orange juice, thawed	1 teaspoon salt
½ cup water	½ teaspoon pepper
1 tablespoon grated orange peel	½ teaspoon ground cloves
2 medium onions, chopped	1 teaspoon ground coriander
	¼ teaspoon ground cumin
3 pounds boneless roast, round or chuck	2 tablespoons butter, softened
1 tablespoon vegetable oil	2 tablespoons flour
1 tablespoon butter or margarine	2 oranges, sectioned
Orange slices for garnish	⅓ cup Madeira

Place orange juice, water, orange peel, onions, salt, pepper, cloves, coriander, and cumin in blender or food processor. Spin until well-mixed (1 to 2 minutes). Place meat in large bowl. Pour marinade over meat. Marinate in refrigerator 4 to 6 hours. Turn meat once or twice.

Remove meat from marinade; scrape off and reserve marinade. In Dutch oven sauté beef in oil and 1 tablespoon butter until brown on all sides. Pour reserved marinade over meat; heat to a simmer; cook, covered, for 2½ hours or until meat is tender. Remove meat to preheated platter; keep it warm.

Make *beurre manie* for thickening sauce by creaming butter and flour thoroughly. Blend into juices in Dutch oven by chopping in small pieces of the mixture and whisking until smooth and thickened. Cook over medium heat 5 minutes; stir often. Add orange sections and Madeira; simmer another 5 minutes.

Slice meat; arrange on platter. Spoon sauce over meat. Garnish with orange slices. Serve rest of sauce separately.

MAKES 6 TO 8 SERVINGS.

Beef braised in beer

FRANCE

½ cup flour

2 teaspoons salt

¼ teaspoon pepper

3 pounds beef chuck or rump, sliced in pieces about 2 × 4 × ⅜ inch thick

3 tablespoons peanut oil

4 cups sliced onions

2 cloves garlic, peeled

1 bay leaf

2 tablespoons tomato paste

2 tablespoons brown sugar

½ teaspoon thyme

2 tablespoons chopped parsley

1 cup broth

2 cups beer

Mix flour, salt, and pepper. Dredge beef to coat evenly with flour.

Heat oil in large Dutch oven; brown the meat. Add remaining ingredients; bring to a simmer.

Cover tightly. Place in preheated 325°F oven; bake for 2 hours or until meat is tender. Before serving, remove garlic and bay leaf. Serve beef with boiled potatoes.
MAKES 6 SERVINGS.

Cold beef in gelatin

FRANCE

Leftover roast beef or Beef Braised in Red Wine (see Index)
Basic Aspic (see Index)
Parsley or watercress for garnish

Place meat in bowl slightly larger than meat. Pour Basic Aspic over meat. Cover; refrigerate until gelatin is set. Remove from bowl by placing bowl in sink of cold water to loosen gelatin.
Slice and serve. Garnish platter with parsley or watercress.

Braised leg of lamb mirabeau

FRANCE

4 pounds leg of lamb	*4 tablespoons anchovy paste (found in gourmet section of supermarket)*
½ teaspoon salt	
⅛ teaspoon pepper	
1 quart buttermilk	*¼ cup heavy cream*
¼ cup vegetable oil	*1 tablespoon butter*
2 large carrots, sliced	*18 flat anchovy fillets, rinsed in cold water*
2 large onions, sliced	
2 cups dry white wine	*18 stuffed green olives, cut in half*
2 cups beef bouillon	
1 whole clove garlic	*2 tablespoons fresh chopped tarragon (or 2 teaspoons dried)*

Rince meat under cold running water; pat dry with paper towels. Rub with salt and pepper. Pour buttermilk into large bowl that will hold the lamb. Add lamb; marinate for 10 hours or overnight. Drain meat; pat dry with paper towels.
Heat oil in large Dutch oven. Add lamb; brown on all sides about 15 minutes. Remove to a platter. Brown carrots and onions for 2 to 3 minutes. Remove with slotted spoon to platter.
Pour out browning oil. Add white wine and reduce it to half by boiling; scrape up coagulated particles. Place lamb, fattiest-side-up, in Dutch oven. Surround with vegetables. Pour in enough bouillon to

Braised leg of lamb mirabeau

come two-thirds of the way up the meat. Add garlic; bring liquid to simmer on top of range. Cover; place in 350°F oven 2½ hours. Turn and baste meat every half hour.
Remove meat; keep it warm. Strain and degrease cooking liquid. Correct seasoning. Blend anchovy paste and cream; stir into liquid. Add butter; stir until melted. Garnish meat with anchovy fillets and olives; sprinkle with tarragon. Serve sauce separately.
MAKES 8 SERVINGS.

Pork & lamb cassoulet

FRANCE

1 pound Great Northern beans	*1 pound boned lamb (shoulder or leg), cut into 2-inch chunks*
6 cups water	
2 medium onions, chopped	
½ teaspoon salt	*½ pound pork, cut into 1½-inch chunks*
¼ teaspoon pepper	
1 bay leaf	*1 stalk celery, thinly sliced*
3 whole cloves	*1 carrot, thinly sliced*
2 tablespoons butter	*2 green onions, chopped*
1 tablespoon vegetable oil	*½ pound Polish sausage, thinly sliced*

1 cup red wine

2 tablespoons tomato paste

2 cloves garlic, minced

3 tablespoons chopped parsley

Dash cayenne pepper

1 to 2 cups beef bouillon

2 tablespoons packaged bread crumbs

Wash beans. Place beans in pan with 6 cups water. Bring to a boil; boil for 2 minutes; remove from heat; let stand, covered, for 1 hour. Add onions, salt, pepper, bay leaf, and cloves to beans in their soaking liquid. Cover; cook for 1 hour. When done, drain beans; reserve liquid.

Meanwhile, heat 1 tablespoon butter and oil in frypan; fry lamb and pork until brown. Add celery, carrot, onions, and sausage to meat mixture. Pour in wine; simmer for 40 minutes. Stir in tomato paste, garlic, and parsley. Season with cayenne. Simmer again for 5 minutes, stirring occasionally. Add drained beans; mix thoroughly.

Grease ovenproof casserole and spoon in *cassoulet*. Add enough bean liquid or bouillon to come to top of bean-meat mixture. Sprinkle with bread crumbs and dot with 1 tablespoon butter. Bake in preheated 375°F oven 1 hour. Serve with chunks of French bread and red wine.

MAKES 6 SERVINGS.

Sauerkraut w/pork chops & sausage

FRANCE

This mild-flavored sauerkraut dish is from the region of Alsace.

½ pound thickly sliced bacon

3 cups chopped onions

2 large cans sauerkraut (No. 2½ size) or 4 pounds bulk

2 cloves garlic, peeled

20 juniper berries (or ½ cup gin)

2 bay leaves

½ teaspoon salt

6 peppercorns

2 cups dry white wine

8 smoked pork chops or 8 fresh pork chops

2 Polish sausages, cut into 8 pieces

8 frankfurters

Cook bacon in large Dutch oven until fat is rendered. Add onions; sauté until transparent.

Thoroughly rinse sauerkraut in cold water. Squeeze out moisture. Add to onions, along with juniper berries, bay leaves, salt, peppercorns, and wine. Cover; bake in preheated 325°F oven 2 hours. Check for liquid; add more wine if needed.

After cooking for 2 hours, add fresh pork chops. Cook for 30 minutes more. Add sausage and frankfurters. If smoked pork chops are used, cook sauerkraut 2½ hours, then add chops along with other meats. Cook another 30 to 45 minutes, until all meats are done. Serve with boiled potatoes.

MAKES 8 SERVINGS.

Stuffed roast pork

FRANCE

6 pounds center-cut loin of pork

bacon stuffing

6 strips bacon, diced

2 tablespoons brandy

1 cup chopped prunes

2 cups coarse bread crumbs from French bread

1 teaspoon grated lemon rind

3 tablespoons lemon juice

1 cup chicken broth

¼ teaspoon marjoram

½ teaspoon salt

⅛ teaspoon pepper

¼ teaspoon thyme

Cut a pocket in pork roast along ribs. Fry bacon until crisp; set aside. Add 2 tablespoons brandy to chopped prunes; let stand 30 minutes. Mix bread crumbs, lemon rind, lemon juice, broth, and seasonings. Add bacon and drippings and prunes with liquid.

Use stuffing to fill pocket in pork. Skewer the opening closed. Roast in shallow pan at 325°F about 2½ to 3 hours, until 180°F on a meat thermometer. Serve pork with braised hearts of celery as garnish.

MAKES 6 SERVINGS.

Pork and lamb cassoulet

Pork w/red cabbage

FRANCE

4 strips bacon, diced
1 carrot, thinly sliced
1 large onion, sliced
2 tablespoons butter
2 pounds red cabbage, cut into ½-inch strips
2 tart apples, diced
1 clove garlic, mashed
1 bay leaf
⅛ teaspoon clove
⅛ teaspoon nutmeg
½ teaspoon salt
¼ teaspoon pepper
2 cups red wine
2 cups beef bouillon
3 pounds boneless roast of pork
2 tablespoons vegetable oil

Simmer diced bacon in 1 quart water about 10 minutes. Drain. Over low heat, cook bacon, carrot, and onion in butter in covered ovenproof casserole 10 minutes. Do not brown. Stir in cabbage strips; mix well with other vegetables. Cover; cook slowly 15 minutes. Stir in all remaining ingredients except meat and vegetable oil. Simmer for 2 to 3 minutes on top of range. Cover; place in preheated 325°F oven. Cabbage should simmer slowly about 3 hours.

Just before cabbage is finished cooking, brown pork roast in hot oil. Place pork in casserole with cabbage. Cover; continue simmering for 2 additional hours or until pork is done. Correct seasonings. Serve.

MAKES 6 SERVINGS.

Braised veal rolls

FRANCE

6 veal chops or slices
1 onion, chopped
4 tablespoons vegetable oil
4 ounces mushrooms, minced (about 1 cup)
1 clove garlic, minced
1 cup red wine
1 cup chicken broth
1 tablespoon tomato paste
½ teaspoon salt

⅛ teaspoon pepper
⅛ teaspoon thyme
20 small pitted green olives
8 large fresh mushrooms, quartered
2 tablespoons Madeira

Pound veal slices to tenderize and flatten. In large frypan sauté onion in 1 tablespoon hot oil several minutes; add minced mushrooms. Continue cooking for 5 minutes. Spread onion-mushroom mixture on each slice of meat. Roll up; tie with string. Brown veal rolls in 2 tablespoons hot oil. Remove and reserve. Drain excess oil.

Add garlic, wine, broth, tomato paste, salt, pepper, and thyme to frypan. Heat to a simmer; add veal rolls. Cover; simmer for 1½ hours.

Meanwhile, place olives in pan of water; bring to a boil. (This removes some of the salt.) Sauté olives and quartered mushrooms in 1 tablespoon hot oil 3 to 4 minutes.

When veal is done, remove it from pan; keep it warm. Strain sauce into clean pan; reduce by boiling, to concentrate flavors and thicken it. Add Madeira, olives, and mushrooms. Heat through. Remove strings from veal rolls. Glaze meat with sauce; garnish with olives and mushrooms.

MAKES 6 SERVINGS.

Veal w/artichokes

FRANCE

1 clove garlic
1 tablespoon vegetable oil
1 pound veal round, cut into bite-size pieces and pounded
½ teaspoon salt
⅛ teaspoon pepper
1 cup canned tomatoes
¼ cup sherry
¼ teaspoon oregano
1 10-ounce package frozen artichoke hearts

In large frypan sauté garlic in hot oil. Remove garlic; discard. Season veal with salt and pepper. Brown in oil. Add tomatoes, sherry, and oregano; mix well. Add artichoke hearts. Cover; simmer for 1 hour or until meat is tender.

MAKES 4 SERVINGS.

Veal w/mushrooms

FRANCE

2 pounds boneless, thinly sliced veal cutlet or fillet
½ cup flour
1 teaspoon salt
¼ teaspoon pepper
2 tablespoons vegetable oil
3 tablespoons butter
1 pound sliced mushrooms
6 tablespoons wine
2 tablespoons lemon juice
Lemon slices for garnish

Gently pound veal into very thin pieces. Mix flour, salt, and pepper. Lightly flour veal. Melt oil and butter in 10-inch frying pan. Sauté veal until golden brown, about 3 minutes on each side. Remove; keep veal warm.

Add sliced mushrooms to frypan; cook several minutes. Add wine and lemon juice; boil rapidly to reduce sauce slightly. Pour sauce over veal, garnish with lemon slices, and serve.
MAKES 6 SERVINGS.

Veal w/orange slices

FRANCE

2 oranges
2 teaspoons grated orange rind
12 thinly sliced veal cutlets
2 tablespoons vegetable oil
2 tablespoons brandy, warmed
½ cup beef bouillon
½ teaspoon salt
⅛ teaspoon white pepper
¼ cup orange juice

Grate 2 teaspoons peel from oranges. Cut away remaining peel on oranges; remove any white membrane. Slice orange into thin rounds. Place in covered baking pan in warm (200°F) oven while preparing rest of dish.

In large frypan sauté veal in hot oil until lightly browned. Add warmed brandy; flame until alcohol is completely burned off. Stir in bouillon, salt, pepper, orange juice, and orange rind. Simmer, covered, for 8 minutes. Remove lid; raise heat to reduce sauce for 4 additional minutes.

Serve veal on heated serving platter; cover with sauce and garnish with warm orange slices.
MAKES 6 SERVINGS.

Sautéed calves liver

FRANCE

1 pound fresh calves liver, ⅜ inch thick
½ cup flour
½ teaspoon salt
⅛ teaspoon pepper
3 tablespoons butter
2 tablespoons vegetable oil
1 tablespoon chopped shallots or green onions
2 tablespoons brandy
⅓ cup beef broth

Gently remove membrane surrounding liver. Mix flour, salt, and pepper. Coat liver with flour, shaking off any excess. Melt butter in large frying pan. Add oil; heat until hot. Add liver in one layer; cook over medium heat. Liver must cook 3 to 4 minutes on each side. Turn liver as needed to prevent burning. When done, liver is only faintly pink. Remove liver to heated plate; keep it warm. Add shallots to frying pan; cook until tender. Add brandy; ignite. When flame has died out, add beef broth. Boil rapidly several minutes to reduce sauce. Scrape all browned bits from bottom of pan.

Pour sauce over liver. Serve liver hot with oven-browned potatoes.
MAKES 4 SERVINGS.

Ragout a la berghoff

GERMANY

¾ cup butter
3½-pound boneless round steak, cut into thin strips
1 cup chopped onion
1½ cups chopped green pepper
1 pound mushrooms, sliced
½ cup flour
2 cups beef broth, canned or homemade
1 cup dry white wine
1 teaspoon salt
1 teaspoon Worcestershire sauce
Few drops Tabasco sauce (to taste)

Melt ½ cup butter in large frypan. Brown meat over medium-high heat. Remove browned meat. In remaining butter sauté onion for 2 minutes. Add green pepper and mushrooms. Cook an additional 3 minutes.

Melt ¼ cup butter and add flour. Slowly add beef broth; cook until thickened. Stir in wine and seasonings. Add meat and mushroom mixture. Cover and simmer 45 minutes to 1 hour, until meat is tender. Serve with buttered noodles or dumplings.
MAKES 8 SERVINGS.

Beef goulash

GERMANY

3 tablespoons vegetable oil
1 pound round steak, cubed
3 medium onions, chopped
½ teaspoon salt
¼ teaspoon pepper
1 clove garlic, pressed, or ½ teaspoon garlic salt
1 teaspoon paprika
¼ teaspoon sugar
2 cups hot water
1 tablespoon flour
¼ cup cold water
½ cup heavy cream

Heat vegetagle oil in a large frypan or Dutch oven. Add meat cubes and brown well, approximately 10 minutes. Stir in onions; cook until soft. Sprinkle with salt, pepper, garlic salt, paprika, and sugar. Blend thoroughly. Pour in hot water; cover and simmer gently about 1½ hours. In a small jar or container shake or blend flour with cold water. Be sure to break up all lumps. Add to meat about 7 minutes before the end of cooking time. Stir constantly until sauce is thickened and bubbling. Remove from heat; stir in cream.

Serve with noodles, accompanied by a tomato salad if desired.
MAKES 4 SERVINGS.

Steaks esterhazy

GERMANY

¼ pound mushrooms, diced
1 small carrot, diced
1 shallot or green onion, minced
2 tablespoons butter
1 teaspoon paprika
½ teaspoon salt
1 cup sour cream
1 teaspoon Worcestershire sauce
4 servings beef sirloin, T-bone, or fillet steaks

Sauté mushrooms, carrot, and shallot or green onion in butter. Add paprika, salt, sour cream, and Worcestershire sauce. Simmer for 2 minutes but do not boil. Broil steaks and top with sauce.
MAKES 4 SERVINGS.

German beefsteaks

GERMANY

1 large, dry hard roll
½ cup water
4 tablespoons vegetable oil
1 medium onion, chopped
1 pound lean ground beef
½ teaspoon salt
¼ teaspoon pepper
4 medium onions, sliced

In a small bowl soak roll in water. Heat 2 tablespoons vegetable oil in a frypan; cook chopped onion until lightly browned. Transfer onion to a bowl. Squeeze roll as dry as possible and mix roll with onions. Add ground beef; blend well. Season with salt and pepper. Shape meat into 4 patties.

Heat 2 tablespoons vegetable oil in a frypan. Add ground-beef patties; cook about 5 minutes on each side or to desired doneness. Remove and keep warm.

Add sliced onions to pan drippings; cook until lightly browned. Arrange beefsteaks on a platter and top with onion rings.
MAKES 4 SERVINGS.

Beef roast with mushroom stuffing

Beef rolls

Beef rolls

GERMANY

4 pieces steak roll or sandwich steaks, each about 6 ounces
2 teaspoons Dijon-style mustard
½ teaspoon salt
¼ teaspoon pepper
2 large pickles, cut into long, thin strips
2 ounces salt pork (or 2 strips bacon), cut into thin strips
1 large onion, chopped

¼ cup vegetable oil
1½ cups hot beef broth
4 peppercorns
½ bay leaf
1 tablespoon cornstarch

Lay steaks on a flat surface. Spread each with mustard; sprinkle with salt and pepper. Divide pickles, salt pork (or bacon), and onion among the steaks as shown. Roll up steaks jelly-roll fashion; secure with beef-roll clamps, toothpicks, or thread.

Heat oil in a heavy saucepan, add the steak rolls, and brown well on all sides, about 15 minutes. Pour in hot beef broth, peppercorns, and bay leaf. Cover and simmer for 1 hour and 20 minutes. Remove beef rolls, discard clamps, and arrange on a preheated platter.

Blend cornstarch with a small amount of cold water, stir into gravy, and bring to a boil, until thick and bubbly. Correct seasonings and serve separately.

MAKES 4 SERVINGS.

Divide pickles, salt pork (or bacon), and onion among the steaks.

244

Bamberger meat and cabbage casserole

Beef strips & carrots

GERMANY

1 pound carrots
⅔ cup carbonated soda water
1 cup white wine
1 teaspoon salt
¼ teaspoon sugar
1 pound sirloin steak
2 tablespoons vegetable oil
2 small onions, diced
¼ teaspoon white pepper
½ cup heavy cream
1 tablespoon chopped parsley

Peel carrots and cut into thin slices (crosswise at a slant). Place in a saucepan with the soda water, wine, ½ teaspoon salt, and sugar. Cover and simmer for 25 minutes or until tender.
Meanwhile cut the meat into very thin slices. Heat the vegetable oil and sauté the onions about 5 minutes. Add the beef slices; cook for 5 minutes, stirring often. Season with ½ teaspoon salt and ¼ teaspoon pepper. Add the meat and onions to the carrots. Mix carefully. Stir in the cream. Heat through but do not boil. Correct seasonings if necessary.
Sprinkle with chopped parsley and serve.
MAKES 4 SERVINGS.

Sauerbraten

GERMANY

4 pounds boneless beef roast
1 cup water
1 cup wine vinegar
2 onions, sliced
1 teaspoon salt
6 peppercorns
2 bay leaves
2 cloves
2 tablespoons vegetable oil
1 medium tomato, peeled and chopped
2 tablespoons flour
2 teaspoons sugar
¼ cup water

Place meat in a large container (not metal). In a saucepan bring water, vinegar, onions, salt, peppercorns, bay leaves, and cloves to a boil. Simmer for 10 minutes. Cool marinade to room temperature. Pour marinade over meat. Refrigerate for 2 to 3 days, turning several times each day. Remove meat from marinade, and dry. Brown meat in hot vegetable oil in a Dutch oven. Add the tomato and marinade liquid. Cover and simmer gently 1 to 2 hours, until meat is tender. The meat could also be placed in a 325°F oven and baked, or it could be cooked on low in a slow cooker 3 to 4 hours.
Remove meat from juices. Also remove peppercorns, cloves, and bay leaves. Mix flour and sugar with water until lumps disappear. Add to pan juices and cook until thickened. Serve with boiled potatoes and red cabbage.
MAKES 6 TO 8 SERVINGS.

Sauerbraten w/gingersnap gravy

GERMANY

4-pound beef rump roast	*½ cup cider vinegar*
2 onions, thinly sliced	*¼ cup vegetable oil*
8 peppercorns	*½ teaspoon salt*
4 cloves	*2 cups boiling water*
1 bay leaf	*10 gingersnaps*
1 cup mild white vinegar	*½ cup sour cream*
1 cup water	*1 tablespoon flour*

Place the beef roast in a deep ceramic or glass bowl. Add onions, peppercorns, cloves, and bay leaf. Pour white vinegar, water, and cider vinegar over the meat; chill, covered, for 4 days. Turn meat twice each day. Remove the meat from the marinade, dry it well with paper towels, and strain the marinade into a bowl. Reserve the onions and 1 cup of marinade.
In a Dutch oven brown the meat on all sides in hot vegetable oil. Sprinkle meat with salt. Pour boiling water around the meat, sprinkle in crushed gingersnaps, and simmer, covered, for 1½ hours. Turn often. Add 1 cup of reserved marinade and cook meat 2 hours or more, until tender. Remove the meat and keep it warm. Strain the cooking juices into a large saucepan.
In a small bowl mix sour cream with flour. Stir it into the cooking juices and cook, stirring, until sauce is thickened and smooth. Slice the meat in

¼-inch slices; add to the hot gravy. Arrange meat on a heated platter and pour extra sauce over it.
MAKES 8 TO 10 SERVINGS.

Beef roast w/mushroom stuffing

GERMANY

½ teaspoon salt
¼ teaspoon white pepper
2 pounds flank steak

1 teaspoon Dijon-style mustard

mushroom stuffing
2 tablespoons vegetable oil
1 small onion, chopped
4-ounce can mushroom pieces, drained and chopped
¼ cup chopped parsley

2 tablespoons chopped chives
1 tablespoon tomato paste
¼ cup dried bread crumbs
¼ teaspoon salt
¼ teaspoon pepper
1 teaspoon paprika

gravy
3 strips bacon, cubed
2 small onions, finely chopped
1 cup hot beef broth

1 teaspoon Dijon-style mustard
2 tablespoons tomato catsup

Lightly salt and pepper flank steak on both sides. Spread one side with mustard.

To prepare stuffing, heat vegetable oil in a frypan, add onion, and cook for 3 minutes, until lightly browned. Add mushroom pieces; cook for 5 minutes. Stir in parsley, chives, tomato paste, and bread crumbs. Season with salt, pepper, and paprika. Spread stuffing on mustard side of flank steak, roll up jelly-roll fashion, and tie with thread or string.

To prepare gravy, cook bacon in a Dutch oven until partially done. Add the meat roll and brown on all sides, approximately 10 minutes. Add the onions and sauté for 5 minutes. Pour in beef broth, cover Dutch oven, and simmer for 1 hour. Remove meat to a preheated platter. Season pan juices with mustard. Salt and pepper to taste; stir in catsup. Serve the gravy separately.
MAKES 6 SERVINGS.

German beef stew

GERMANY

¼ cup shortening
3-pound boneless rump roast
2 cups sliced onions
¼ cup flour
2 tablespoons salt
2 tablespoons sugar
Pepper to taste
2 teaspoons dry mustard
½ teaspoon celery seed
¼ cup water
1 1-pound can tomatoes

Melt shortening in a Dutch oven. Add the meat and brown on all sides. Place the onions on top of the meat.

Mix the flour and seasonings with ¼ cup water. Blend with the tomatoes and add the mixture to the Dutch oven. Bake at 325°F about 2 hours, until meat is fork-tender. Serve with oven-browned potatoes.
MAKES 6 SERVINGS.

Bamberger meat & cabbage casserole

GERMANY

1 small head cabbage (about 1 pound)
1 tablespoon vegetable oil
2 medium onions, chopped
½ pound lean pork, cubed
1 pound lean ground beef
1 teaspoon caraway seeds
½ teaspoon salt
½ teaspoon pepper
½ cup dry white wine
1 teaspoon vegetable oil
3 to 6 strips thickly sliced bacon

Remove outer, wilted cabbage leaves and core. Place cabbage in a large pot of boiling water and simmer gently for 10 minutes. Remove and drain. Gently pull off 12 leaves and set aside. Finely chop the rest of the cabbage.

Heat 1 tablespoon vegetable oil; add onions, pork, and ground beef. Cook until lightly browned. Drain off excess fat. Add the chopped

247

cabbage, caraway seeds, salt, and pepper. Pour in the white wine. Cover and simmer the mixture for 10 minutes, stirring often.

Grease an ovenproof dish with 1 teaspoon of vegetable oil; line the dish with half the cabbage leaves. Spoon in the meat mixture; cover with the rest of the cabbage leaves. Cut bacon strips in half and arrange on top. Place in preheated 350°F oven; bake for approximately 45 minutes.
MAKES 4 SERVINGS.

False rabbit meatloaf
GERMANY

½ pound lean ground beef	1 teaspoon prepared mustard
½ pound lean ground pork	2 tablespoons chopped parsley
1 medium onion, chopped	3 hard-cooked eggs, peeled
3 tablespoons bread crumbs	4 strips bacon
3 tablespoons cold water	4 tablespoons vegetable oil
2 eggs	1 cup beef broth
½ teaspoon salt	
1 teaspoon paprika	

sauce

¼ cup hot water	¼ cup water
1 teaspoon cornstarch	½ cup sour cream

Thoroughly mix ground meats, onion, bread crumbs, 3 tablespoons cold water, and eggs. Flavor with salt, paprika, mustard, and parsley. Blend ingredients thoroughly. Flatten out meat mixture in the shape of a square (8 by 8 inches). Arrange whole hard-boiled eggs in a row along the middle of the meat. Fold sides of meat pattie over the eggs. Shape meat carefully into a loaf resembling a flat bread loaf. Occasionally rinse hands in cold water to prevent sticking.

Cube 2 strips bacon; cook in a Dutch oven about 2 minutes. Carefully add the vegetable oil; heat. Place meatloaf in the Dutch oven and cook until browned on all sides. Cut remaining bacon strips in half and arrange over the top of the meatloaf. Place uncovered Dutch oven in a preheated 350°F oven for about 45 minutes. While meat is baking, gradually pour hot beef broth over the top of the meatloaf; brush occasionally with pan drippings. When done, remove meat to a preheated platter and keep it warm.

Add ¼ cup of hot water to pan and scrape all particles from the bottom. Bring to a gentle boil and add cornstarch that has been mixed with ¼ cup water. Cook until bubbly and thick. Remove from heat and stir in sour cream. Reheat to warm. Season with salt and pepper if desired. Serve the sauce separately.
MAKES 4 SERVINGS.

Meatloaf w/cauliflower
GERMANY

1 pound ground beef
1 egg
¼ cup milk
⅓ cup dry bread crumbs
½ cup chopped onion
½ teaspoon salt
1 teaspoon Worcestershire sauce
¼ teaspoon pepper
1 small head cauliflower
1 cup grated sharp cheddar cheese
1 cup evaporated milk
3 tomatoes, halved

Mix beef, egg, milk, crumbs, onion, and seasonings to make a meatloaf. Mold into ring in 2-quart round baking dish.

Parboil cauliflower 5 minutes. Place in center of meatloaf. Mix cheese and milk; pour over cauliflower. Bake at 350°F for 45 minutes to 1 hour. Last 5 minutes of baking, place tomatoes on top of meatloaf.
MAKES 4 SERVINGS.

Sauerbraten meatballs
GERMANY

1 pound lean ground beef
¼ cup milk
¼ cup dry bread crumbs
⅛ teaspoon ground cloves
⅛ teaspoon ground allspice
½ teaspoon salt
Pepper to taste
2 tablespoons vegetable oil
1 cup plus 2 tablespoons water
½ cup vinegar

¾ teaspoon ground ginger
1 bay leaf
4 tablespoons brown sugar
2 tablespoons flour

Mix beef, milk, crumbs, cloves, allspice, salt, and pepper. Form into meatballs. Brown meatballs in hot oil. Drain off fat. Add 1 cup water, vinegar, ginger, bay leaf and brown sugar. Cover and simmer ½ hour. Skim off fat. Remove meatballs and keep them warm.

Mix flour and 2 tablespoons water. Slowly stir into the pan juices to make gravy. Pour gravy over meatballs. Serve with buttered noodles.
MAKES 4 SERVINGS.

Meatballs Königsberg-style

GERMANY

meatballs
1 roll
¾ cup water
1 pound lean ground beef
1 strip bacon, diced
4 anchovy fillets, diced

1 small onion, chopped
1 egg
½ teaspoon salt
¼ teaspoon white pepper

broth
6 cups water
½ teaspoon salt
1 bay leaf

1 small onion, peeled and halved
6 peppercorns

gravy
1½ tablespoons butter or margarine
1½ tablespoons flour
1 tablespoon capers
Juice of ½ lemon

½ teaspoon prepared mustard
1 egg yolk
¼ teaspoon salt
¼ teaspoon white pepper

Soak the roll in the water for about 10 minutes. Squeeze it dry; place in mixing bowl with the ground beef. Add the bacon, anchovy fillets, onion, egg, salt, and pepper. Mix thoroughly.
Prepare the broth by boiling the water, seasoned with salt, bay leaf, onion, and peppercorns.
Shape the meat mixture into balls about 2 inches in diameter. Add to the boiling broth and simmer over low heat for 20 minutes. Remove meatballs with a slotted spoon, set aside, and keep warm. Strain the broth through a sieve. Reserve broth and keep warm.
To prepare gravy, heat butter in a frypan and stir

in flour. Cook for 3 minutes, stirring constantly. Slowly blend in 2 cups of reserved broth. Add the drained capers, lemon juice, and mustard. Simmer for 5 minutes. Remove a small amount of the sauce to blend with the egg yolk. Stir egg yolk back into the sauce. Season with salt and pepper. Place reserved meatballs into the gravy and reheat if necessary. Serve on a preheated platter.
MAKES 4 SERVINGS.

Grilled bratwurst

GERMANY

6 bratwursts
1 can beer
1 medium onion, chopped
6 peppercorns
4 cloves
6 hard rolls

Place bratwursts, beer, onion, peppercorns, and cloves in a 3-quart saucepan. Simmer for 20 minutes. Drain.
Grill bratwursts 2 to 5 inches from charcoal about 10 minutes, until browned. Sprinkle with water to form crisp skin. Serve in hard rolls with Dusseldorf-style mustard.
MAKES 6 SERVINGS.

Roast pork w/madeira sauce

GERMANY

3 to 4-pound pork roast, boneless
Peel from 1 lemon
2 bay leaves
½ teaspoon salt
⅛ teaspoon white pepper
1 tablespoon vinegar
1 cup dry white wine
2 tablespoons flour
¼ cup Madeira wine

Place roast in roasting pan. Place lemon peel and bay leaves in bottom of pan. Mix salt, pepper, vinegar, and white wine. Pour over meat. Roast meat at 325°F until internal temperature reaches 170°F (about 2 to 2½ hours). Baste meat with

249

pan juices about every ½ hour. When roast is done, remove from pan. Degrease pan juice.
Mix flour with Madeira wine; gradually add to juices, stirring constantly with wire whisk. Cool until gravy thickens.
Slice meat and serve with gravy and spaetzle, potatoes, or noodles.
MAKES 6 TO 8 SERVINGS.

German hunter's stew

GERMANY

1½ cups minced onions
¼ pound mushrooms, sliced
2 tablespoons vegetable oil
1 pound lean ground beef
1 cup beef broth
⅝ teaspoon nutmeg
½ teaspoon Worcestershire sauce
1 teaspoon salt
½ teaspoon pepper
3 medium potatoes
3 tablespoons butter
2 eggs
4 tart apples
½ cup fine dry bread crumbs

In a frypan sauté onions and mushrooms in vegetable oil until soft. Add ground beef; sauté mixture 3 to 4 minutes. Stir in broth; bring to a simmer. Add ½ teaspoon nutmeg, Worcestershire sauce, ½ teaspoon salt, and ¼ teaspoon pepper.
Peel the potatoes and boil them in salted water until tender, about 30 minutes. Drain, and put through a food mill or grinder. Beat in 2 tablespoons butter, ½ teaspoon salt, and ¼ teaspoon pepper. Adjust seasonings to taste. Beat in eggs and remaining nutmeg.
Peel, core and slice apples. Layer mixtures in a 1½-quart buttered baking dish. Spread ⅓ of potatoes on bottom of dish. Top with ½ of the meat mixture and ½ of the apples. Continue with layers, ending with a layer of potatoes. Sprinkle the top with bread crumbs, and dot with remaining butter. Bake at 375°F for 45 minutes and then at 400°F for 10 minutes more.
MAKES 4 SERVINGS.

Hunter's stew w/cabbage

GERMANY

6 cups thinly sliced cabbage (about 2 pounds)
1 1-pound, 12-ounce can sauerkraut
1½ teaspoons salt
2 bay leaves
8 pork loin chops
1½ cups water
1 pound smoked sausage or frankfurters, sliced ½ inch thick
2 8-ounce cans tomato sauce

In advance: Spread cabbage in the bottom of a large roaster. Cover with sauerkraut. Sprinkle with salt. Add bay leaves. Place pork chops on top and add water. Cover and bake at 325°F for 1 hour.
Add sausage and tomato sauce. Continue baking until meat is tender. This is better if cooked and reheated the next day. Serve with boiled potatoes.
MAKES 8 SERVINGS.

Stuffed cabbage

GERMANY

12 outer leaves from cabbage
8 strips bacon
1 medium onion, chopped
¾ pound ground beef
2 cups cooked rice
Pinch paprika
½ teaspoon salt
¼ teaspoon pepper
1-pound can sauerkraut, drained
1 8-ounce can tomato sauce
½ can undiluted tomato soup
2 teaspoons sugar

Blanch cabbage leaves in boiling water 5 minutes. In a frypan sauté 4 strips of bacon and the onion until bacon is crisp. Mix ground meat, rice, and seasonings with bacon and onion. Place 2 tablespoons filling on each cabbage leaf. Roll up, folding in ends, and secure with toothpicks. Place sauerkraut in bottom of a 2-quart casserole. Place cabbage rolls on top of sauerkraut. Mix tomato sauce and soup and pour over cabbage rolls. Lay remaining 4 strips of bacon over top.

Pork chop and rice casserole

Sprinkle with sugar. Cover casserole and bake 1 hour in preheated 325°F oven. If sauce is too thin, uncover last ½ hour of baking.
MAKES 6 SERVINGS.

Pork chops in onion sauce

GERMANY

4 pork chops
½ teaspoon salt
¼ teaspoon pepper
1½ tablespoons flour
1½ tablespoons vegetable oil
4 small (or 2 medium) onions, thinly sliced
½ cup beer
½ cup hot beef broth
1 teaspoon cornstarch

Season pork chops with salt and pepper; coat with flour. Heat oil in a heavy frypan. Add pork chops; fry for 3 minutes on each side. Add onions; cook for another 5 minutes, turning chops once. Pour in beer and beef broth; cover and simmer, for 15 minutes. Remove pork chops to a preheated platter. Season sauce to taste.
Blend cornstarch with a small amount of cold water. Stir into sauce and cook until thick and bubbly. Pour over pork chops. Serve with brussel sprouts and boiled potatoes.
MAKES 4 SERVINGS.

Pork chops in onion sauce

Veal breast with herb stuffing

Pork chop & rice casserole

GERMANY

tomato sauce
¼ cup vegetable oil
3 medium ripe tomatoes, sliced
2 medium onions, chopped
2 garlic cloves minced
½ teaspoon salt
¼ teaspoon white pepper
¼ teaspoon dried oregano leaves

rice
1 cup uncooked long-grain rice
Water and salt (according to package directions)

chops
4 pork chops
½ teaspoon salt
¼ teaspoon white pepper
¼ teaspoon paprika
2 tablespoons vegetable oil
Margarine to grease casserole
3 tablespoons grated Emmenthal or Swiss cheese
1 tablespoon butter

To prepare sauce, heat vegetable oil in a frypan; sauté tomato slices, onions, and garlic for about 5 minutes, stirring constantly. Season with salt, pepper, and oregano. Cover and simmer tomatoes in their own juices for about 20 minutes. Strain through a sieve and return purée to the frypan. Cook until liquid is reduced to two-thirds, stirring frequently. Set aside.

Meanwhile, prepare rice according to package directions. Set aside.

Season pork chops with salt, pepper, and pa-prika. Heat oil in a frypan, add chops, and fry for 5 minutes on each side. Generously grease an ovenproof dish. Cover bottom with half the rice and pour half the tomato sauce over the rice. Arrange 2 pork chops on top, and sprinkle with half the grated cheese. Repeat layers. Dot with butter. Place in a preheated 350°F oven; bake for 30 to 40 minutes.

MAKES 4 SERVINGS.

Baked pork chops

GERMANY

6 pork chops
1 clove garlic, minced
1 teaspoon crushed caraway seeds
2 teaspoons mild Hungarian paprika (available at gourmet and specialty stores)
½ teaspoon salt
Pepper as desired
1 cup dry white wine
1 cup sour cream (optional)

Place the pork chops in an ovenproof casserole. Mix the remaining ingredients, except sour cream, and pour over the chops. Marinate the chops 2 to 3 hours in the refrigerator.

Bake the chops, uncovered, in the marinade in a preheated 325°F oven for 1 hour or until tender. 253

Add more wine if needed. Stir sour cream into pan juices and heat through but do not boil. Serve with sour-cream gravy and buttered noodles or dumplings.
MAKES 6 SERVINGS.

Pork chops dusseldorf
GERMANY

8 pork chops
2 tablespoons vegetable oil
½ cup chopped onion
1 cup dry white wine
1½ tablespoons Dusseldorf-style mustard
1¼ cups canned beef broth
2 tablespoons cornstarch
4 small sour gherkins, cut in half

In a large frypan brown the chops in hot oil. Remove the browned chops; sauté the onion until transparent. Carefully pour in the wine; stir to remove the browned particles.
Mix the mustard with the beef broth. Place the chops in the pan with the onion mixture; pour 1 cup beef broth over top. Cover and bake in a preheated 325°F oven 30 to 45 minutes, until tender. Remove chops to a heated platter. Keep them warm.
Mix the cornstarch with remaining ¼ cup beef

broth. Blend into the juices to make gravy. Heat until thick and bubbly. Pour gravy over the meat; garnish with sliced gherkins.
MAKES 4 SERVINGS.

Stuffed pork chops
GERMANY

6 slices boiled ham
6 slices Swiss cheese
12 boneless pork chops, pounded ¼-inch thick
1 cup milk
1 cup flour
3 eggs, beaten
1½ cups dry bread crumbs
¼ cup vegetable oil

Place 1 slice of ham and 1 slice of cheese between two slices of pork, pounded (as thin as possible.) Secure with toothpicks or string. Dip each in milk, then in flour. Shake off excess flour; dip into eggs, then into crumbs. Place in refrigerator at least ½ hour to dry coating.
Brown chops in hot oil in ovenproof frypan or covered casserole. Place in 350°F oven and bake, covered, about 30 minutes, until done. If chops are very thin, they can be fried in oil, about 5 to 8 minutes on each side, and served immediately.
MAKES 6 SERVINGS.

Veal cutlets with capers

Pork ribs & sauerkraut

GERMANY

1-pound, 12-ounce can sauerkraut
1 cup chopped onion
1-pound, 12-ounce can tomatoes
¾ cup firmly packed brown sugar
3 pounds country-style pork ribs

Layer ingredients in a large casserole or roaster as listed, starting with sauerkraut and ending with ribs. Do not stir. Cover and bake at 325°F for 3 hours. Uncover last 45 minutes of baking.
MAKES 6 SERVINGS.

Spareribs & sauerkraut

GERMANY

2 16-ounce cans sauerkraut
3 pounds country-style spareribs
2 teaspoons paprika
6 bouillon cubes
½ teaspoon caraway seeds
½ teaspoon pepper
10 slices bacon, rolled in flour

Rinse and drain the sauerkraut. Place sauerkraut in large 4- or 6-quart casserole. Add 2 quarts hot water. Add uncooked spareribs, paprika, bouillon cubes, caraway seeds, and pepper. Cook, covered, over low heat 3 to 4 hours.
Fry floured bacon slices. Break bacon into sauerkraut. Remove bones from the sauce before serving. Serve with dark bread and steins of beer.
MAKES 4 TO 6 SERVINGS.

Bavarian veal

GERMANY

1 pound veal, cut into 4 thin slices
½ teaspoon salt
⅛ teaspoon sugar
½ teaspoon white pepper
1 tablespoon Dijon mustard
4 slices bacon
4 hard-cooked eggs
2 tablespoons vegetable oil
1 onion, diced
¾ cup beef bouillon, heated
1 tablespoon tomato paste
2 tablespoons flour
¼ cup red wine

Dry veal on paper towels. Roll in a mixture of salt, sugar, white pepper, and mustard. Place a bacon slice on top of each piece of veal. Place an unsliced egg on top of the bacon. Roll up each slice of veal (jelly-roll fashion) and tie together with string.
Heat oil in a frypan and brown veal rolls well on all sides. Add onion; sauté for 3 minutes. Add the hot bouillon; cover and simmer gently 25 minutes. Remove the veal from the pan. Remove the strings from the veal and keep veal warm on a serving platter.
Add tomato paste to the pan drippings; stir. Thoroughly mix flour and red wine to remove all lumps. Add to sauce and cook until mixture thickens. Add warm veal rolls and heat through. Before serving, place veal rolls on a platter, pour sauce over the rolls, and serve with puréed potatoes, if desired.
MAKES 4 SERVINGS.

Bavarian veal w/asparagus

GERMANY

2 pounds veal cubes
2 tablespoons vegetable oil
1 large onion, chopped
1 cup chopped carrots
1 tablespoon chopped parsley
¼ cup fresh lemon juice
2 cups beef broth
3 tablespoons flour
½ teaspoon salt
Freshly ground pepper to taste
2 10-ounce boxes frozen asparagus tips and pieces or 2 pounds fresh, cleaned and cut into 1-inch pieces

In a Dutch oven brown the veal in hot oil. Add onion and carrots. Cook until onion is transparent. Stir in parsley. Mix lemon juice, broth, flour, and seasonings until well-blended. Pour over meat. Cover and bake in preheated 325°F oven 1½ hours or until meat is tender. Add more broth, if needed.

Cook asparagus until tender-crisp. Stir into veal and serve immediately.
MAKES 6 SERVINGS.

Veal steaks w/lemon & curry

GERMANY

1 pound veal cutlets, sliced thin
½ teaspoon salt
¼ teaspoon pepper
¾ teaspoon curry powder
3 tablespoons vegetable oil
2 onions, diced
2 tablespoons evaporated milk
2 tablespoons tomato paste
1 lemon, juiced
10 sprigs parsley, chopped
2 tablespoons cognac or brandy

Season veal with salt, pepper, and ½ teaspoon curry. Heat oil; brown veal slices on both sides. Remove meat and reserve.
Add onions; sauté until softened. Add evaporated milk and tomato paste. Cook until bubbly. Add lemon juice, rest of curry, and chopped parsley. Return the veal slices to the sauce. Add the cognac or brandy; heat through. Serve on a warmed platter.
MAKES 4 SERVINGS.

Stuffed veal breast

GERMANY

½ pound lean ground beef
¼ pound ground pork
1 egg
1 cup soft bread crumbs
1 tablespoon lemon juice
⅛ teaspoon nutmeg
½ teaspoon salt
Pepper to taste
4-pound breast of veal with brisket on
3 tablespoons shortening
2 teaspoons paprika
2 bay leaves
6 cloves
½ teaspoon rosemary
½ teaspoon basil
2 cups water

Mix ground meats, egg, bread crumbs, lemon juice, nutmeg, salt, and pepper for stuffing. Stuff pocket of veal breast. Sew closed or use toothpicks or skewers.
Brown roast in melted shortening in ovenproof casserole. To the drippings add paprika, bay leaves, cloves, rosemary, basil, and 2 cups water. Bake in a covered casserole at 325°F for 2 hours or until veal is tender. Slice veal and serve immediately.
MAKES 4 SERVINGS.

Veal steaks w/yoghurt

GERMANY

1 pound veal, sliced thin
½ teaspoon salt
¼ teaspoon pepper
3 tablespoons vegetable oil
3 to 4 medium apples, peeled and sliced
½ cup evaporated milk
1 small container yoghurt

Rub veal steaks with salt and pepper. Heat oil and cook veal slices about 2 minutes on each side. Place veal in an ovenproof casserole. Add apples.
Blend evaporated milk and yoghurt together. Spread over apples. Place in a preheated 325°F oven; cook just until bubbly, about 20 to 30 minutes.
MAKES 4 SERVINGS.

Veal rounds w/vegetables

GERMANY

Salt to taste (about ½ teaspoon)
Pepper to taste (about ¼ teaspoon)
Paprika to taste (about ¼ teaspoon)
4 veal fillets, cut ¼ inch thick
4 tablespoons butter
4 whole stewed tomatoes
12 canned white asparagus spears
¼ pound fresh mushrooms, sliced

Sprinkle salt, pepper, and paprika over the veal slices. Sauté in butter until browned. On each fillet place 1 stewed tomato, 3 spears asparagus, and a heaping tablespoon mushrooms. Cook gently. Pour cooking juices over the fillets while cooking. Cook, uncovered, until mushrooms are just tender.

Serve with puréed potatoes and a salad.
MAKES 4 SERVINGS.

Veal breast w/herb stuffing

GERMANY

herb stuffing

3 strips bacon	1 teaspoon dried basil leaves
1 medium onion	½ pound lean ground beef
1 4-ounce can mushroom pieces	½ cup dried bread crumbs
¼ cup chopped fresh parsley	3 eggs
1 tablespoon chopped fresh dill	⅓ cup sour cream
1 teaspoon dried tarragon leaves	½ teaspoon salt
	¼ teaspoon pepper

veal

3 to 4 pounds boned veal breast or boned leg	1 tablespoon vegetable oil
½ teaspoon salt	2 cups hot beef broth
¼ teaspoon pepper	2 tablespoons cornstarch
	½ cup sour cream

To prepare stuffing, dice bacon and onion. Cook bacon in a frypan until partially cooked; add onion and cook for 5 minutes. Drain and chop mushrooms, add to frypan, and cook for another 5 minutes. Remove mixture from heat, let cool, and transfer to a mixing bowl. Add herbs, ground beef, bread crumbs, eggs, and sour cream. Mix thoroughly. Season with salt and pepper.

With a sharp knife, cut a pocket in the veal breast or leg. Fill with stuffing; close opening with toothpicks. (Tie with string if necessary.) Rub outside with salt and pepper.

Heat oil in a Dutch oven. Place meat in the pan and bake in a preheated 350°F oven about 1½ hours. Baste occasionally with beef broth. When done, place meat on a preheated platter.

Pour rest of beef broth into the Dutch oven and scrape brown particles from the bottom. Bring pan drippings to a simmer. Thoroughly blend cornstarch with sour cream and add to pan drippings while stirring. Cook and stir until thick and bubbly.

Slice veal breast and serve sauce separately.
MAKES 6 SERVINGS.

Veal cutlets w/capers

GERMANY

4 lean veal cutlets, about 6 ounces each
2 tablespoons lemon juice
½ teaspoon salt
⅛ teaspoon pepper
½ teaspoon paprika
1 tablespoon vegetable oil
½ small jar capers, drained
¼ cup dry white wine
1 bay leaf
3 tablespoons evaporated milk
Sliced pickled beets for garnish
4 lettuce leaves for garnish

Sprinkle cutlets with lemon juice and season with salt, pepper, and paprika. Heat oil in a frypan and fry cutlets for 3 minutes on the first side. Turn cutlets over and add drained capers to pan. Fry again for 3 minutes; remove cutlets and arrange on a preheated platter.

Pour wine into pan, scraping loose any brown particles from bottom of frypan. Add bay leaf, simmer liquid 3 minutes. Remove bay leaf. Blend in evaporated milk and adjust seasonings. Pour sauce over cutlets. Cut beets into strips and arrange on lettuce leaves as a garnish.
MAKES 4 SERVINGS.

Veal cutlets w/cherry sauce

GERMANY

4 lean veal cutlets, about 6 ounces each
1 tablespoon vegetable oil
½ teaspoon salt
⅛ teaspoon white pepper
¼ cup red wine
2 tablespoons evaporated milk
1 16-ounce can tart cherries, drained
Parsley for garnish

Pat cutlets dry with paper towels. Heat oil in a frypan and brown cutlets on each side approximately 3 minutes. Season with salt and pepper. Remove cutlets from pan and keep them warm.

Blend wine and evaporated milk in pan and simmer for 3 minutes. Add cherries; heat through and adjust seasonings. Return cutlets to sauce and reheat, but do not boil. Arrange cutlets on preheated platter, pouring cherry sauce around them. Garnish with parsley.
MAKES 4 SERVINGS.

Marinated rabbit

GERMANY

1 3-pound rabbit, cut into serving pieces	¼ teaspoon pepper
1 teaspoon salt	3 tablespoons vegetable oil

marinade

2 cups red wine	2 bay leaves
2 cups chicken broth	1 teaspoon thyme
1 teaspoon allspice	

sauce

1 dozen pickled white onions (cocktail size)	½ pound fresh mushrooms, sliced
1 dozen stuffed green olives, sliced	2 tablespoons butter or margarine

Rub rabbit with salt and pepper; put into a large bowl. Mix together marinade ingredients, add to rabbit, and refrigerate overnight. Drain the pieces of rabbit, but do not pat dry. Strain and reserve the marinade.

In a large frypan over high heat, quickly brown all sides of rabbit pieces in hot vegetable oil. When brown, pour in reserved marinade and simmer over low heat 1 hour or until rabbit is tender.

Just before rabbit is done, sauté onions, olives, and mushrooms in hot butter or margarine. Add to rabbit mixture. Serve with boiled potatoes.
MAKES 6 SERVINGS.

Black Forest stew

GERMANY

marinade

1 cup chopped onions	¼ teaspoon rosemary
½ cup chopped carrot	¼ teaspoon thyme
½ cup chopped celery	1 bay leaf
1 clove garlic, minced	6 cranberries
2 whole cloves	5 peppercorns

1 tablespoon chopped parsley	¼ cup red wine vinegar
½ teaspoon salt	½ cup vegetable oil
3 cups dry red wine	

stew

3 pounds venison stew meat	¼ cup flour
½ teaspoon marjoram	1 cup beef broth
¼ cup butter or margarine	¼ teaspoon pepper
1 cup chopped onions	1 cup sour cream

Place marinade ingredients into a 2-quart saucepan. Bring marinade to a boil. Reduce heat and simmer 10 minutes. Cool. Place venison and marjoram in a large casserole. Pour cooled marinade over meat. Cover and refrigerate for 24 hours, stirring occasionally. Drain meat, reserving marinade. Pat meat dry.

In a large saucepan melt the butter. When hot, add the meat; brown, stirring to prevent burning. Remove meat and brown remaining 1 cup onions. Stir in flour; mix until well-blended. Add broth and 2 cups reserved marinade. Add pepper. Bring stew to a boil, stirring until slightly thickened. Add meat, cover, and simmer about 1 hour, until meat is tender. Skim off fat. Add sour cream and heat through.
MAKES 8 SERVINGS.

Savory pot roast

GREECE

1 4-pound roast
½ teaspoon salt
¼ teaspoon pepper
2 tablespoons flour
4 tablespoons butter
3 onions, sliced
3 carrots, peeled and sliced
2 stalks celery, sliced
½ cup tomato sauce
2 cups water
1 bay leaf
½ cup red wine

Wipe the meat with a damp cloth. Combine the salt, pepper, and flour. Rub into the surface of the pot roast. Melt the butter in a Dutch oven. Brown the pot roast on all sides. Add the onions and brown them. Add the carrots, celery, tomato sauce, water, bay leaf, and red wine. Cover and simmer for 3 hours.

Slice the meat and serve with the pan juices, accompanied by rice or potatoes.

MAKES 8 SERVINGS.

Steak in the Greek style

GREECE

2 pounds sirloin steak (1 inch thick)
½ teaspoon freshly ground pepper
1 clove garlic, crushed
2 tablespoons lemon juice
½ teaspoon salt
1 teaspoon oregano

Rub the meat with pepper and garlic. Broil or barbecue over medium-hot coals until done to your liking (15 minutes for medium). Sprinkle with lemon juice, salt, and oregano. Slice across the grain and serve with the juices from the platter.

MAKES 4 TO 5 SERVINGS.

Meat pies

GREECE

dough
2 cups flour   ⅓ cup shortening
2½ teaspoons baking powder   ¾ cup milk
1 teaspoon salt

filling
½ cup chopped onion   1 medium tomato, peeled,
¼ cup chopped green pepper   seeded, and chopped
2 tablespoons butter   2 tablespoons chopped
1½ cups finely chopped   parsley
    leftover cooked beef or   ½ teaspoon salt
    lamb   ¼ teaspoon pepper
2 hard-cooked eggs, peeled   1 egg beaten with 2
    and chopped   tablespoons of milk

In a mixing bowl combine the flour, baking powder, and salt. Cut in the shortening until the mixture resembles coarse meal. Add the milk and stir with a fork to form a soft dough. Wrap the dough in plastic wrap and refrigerate it while making the filling.

Sauté the onion and green pepper in butter until limp. Add the meat, hard-cooked eggs, tomato,

Veal cutlets with cherry sauce

parsley, salt, and pepper and mix well. Remove from the heat.

On a pastry cloth roll out the dough ¼ inch thick and cut it into 3½ × 5-inch pieces. Should make about 12 small pies. Top with 3 tablespoons of filling and fold like a turnover. Seal with the egg mixture and place on an ungreased cookie sheet. Brush the tops with the egg and milk mixture. Bake at 400°F for 15 minutes or until well-browned. Serve with garlic-flavored yoghurt.

MAKES 3 TO 5 SERVINGS.

Note: Frozen puff pastry can be used for this recipe. Use the method for making Cheese Pies (see Index) and fill with the meat mixture given above.

Onion & beef stew

GREECE

1¼ pounds stew beef, cut in 1-inch pieces
¼ cup olive oil
2 cups sliced onions or 2 cups small pearl onions, peeled
2 cloves garlic, minced
½ teaspoon salt
½ teaspoon pepper
½ teaspoon allspice
½ teaspoon sugar
1 2-inch piece cinnamon stick
1⅓ cups dry red wine
1 8-ounce can tomato sauce

Onion and beef stew

Brown the meat in hot olive oil in a heavy skillet. Remove the meat from the pan. Brown the onions and garlic. Add the other ingredients and stir well. Add the browned meat and bring the mixture to a boil. Reduce the heat to simmer, and cover. Cook, stirring occasionally, for 2 hours or until the meat is very tender.
Serve with Macaroni Athenian-Style (see Index) and a green salad.
MAKES 4 SERVINGS.
Note: This stew can easily be done in your slow cooker. Brown the meat, combine with other ingredients, and cook on low heat as the manufacturer directs for any stew.

Macaroni-meat bake

GREECE

3 tablespoons butter
½ cup chopped onion
1 clove garlic, minced

1 pound ground beef
¾ teaspoon salt
⅛ teaspoon pepper
¾ teaspoon cinnamon
¼ teaspoon sugar
4 tablespoons tomato paste
½ pound macaroni, cooked
¼ cup grated Romano cheese
1 egg

Melt the butter in a large, heavy skillet. Add the onion and garlic and cook until tender. Add the ground beef and brown it. Cover and simmer for 20 minutes. Add the salt, pepper, cinnamon, sugar, and tomato paste. Cook for 10 minutes.
Combine meat mixture, cooked macaroni, and Romano cheese. Stir well. Add the egg and stir to combine.
Turn the mixture into a greased 13 × 9 × 2-inch baking dish. Pack it down and make the surface level. Top with Custard Topping and dust with additional Romano cheese and cinnamon. Bake at 375°F for 30 minutes or until the

Macaroni casserole with eggplant

custard is set. Let stand for several minutes and cut into 8 squares to serve.
MAKES 8 SERVINGS.

Custard topping
¼ cup butter
¼ cup flour
2 cups milk, warmed
2 eggs, beaten

Melt the butter and add the flour and stir until bubbly. Remove from the heat. Add the warm milk slowly, stirring well. Return the mixture to the heat, and cook, stirring constantly, until the mixture starts to thicken.

Slowly add the hot mixture to the beaten eggs while continuing to beat. Pour the mixture back into the saucepan and cook over low heat, stirring constantly, until the mixture becomes thick, like custard. If the mixture should form lumps, pour it through a fine sieve or purée it in a blender or food processor and then return it to the saucepan.

Macaroni casserole w/eggplant

GREECE

1 eggplant (1 pound)	8 ounces whole or elbow
4 medium tomatoes	macaroni
5 tablespoons oil	3 quarts boiling, salted water
2 cloves garlic, chopped	3 tablespoons olive oil
½ teaspoon salt	1 pound meatloaf mixture
¼ teaspoon pepper	2 medium onions, chopped
1 stick cinnamon	¼ cup grated Kafaloteri
¼ teaspoon allspice	cheese
½ cup red wine	2 tablespoons butter
3 tablespoons tomato paste	

Clean the eggplant and dice into 1-inch cubes. Peel and quarter the tomatoes. Heat the 5 tablespoons of oil in a large skillet. Sauté the eggplant, tomatoes, and garlic for 5 minutes, stirring occasionally, to prevent sticking. Add the salt, pepper, cinnamon stick, allspice, wine, and tomato paste. Simmer for 15 minutes.

Meanwhile, cook the macaroni in 3 quarts of boiling, salted water until done. Drain and rinse

261

in warm water. Heat the remaining 3 tablespoons of oil. Brown the meat and onions. Combine with the vegetable mixture. Remove the cinnamon stick.

Grease a 13 × 9 × 2-inch casserole. Place the macaroni in the casserole. Add one half of the cheese, and mix. Top with the vegetable mixture and remaining cheese. Dot with butter. Bake at 350°F for 30 minutes.

MAKES 6 SERVINGS.

Tomato-meat sauce w/macaroni

GREECE

3 tablespoons butter
1 cup chopped onion
2 cloves garlic, minced
1 pound ground beef
1 6-ounce can tomato paste
2 cups water
¼ cup red wine
1 teaspoon salt
¼ teaspoon pepper
1 2-inch cinnamon stick
¼ teaspoon ground allspice
Dash ground cloves

Meat pies

Melt the butter in a large skillet. Add the onion, garlic, and beef and cook over medium heat, stirring occasionally, until the meat loses its pink color.

Combine the tomato paste and water and add to the meat mixture. Add the wine, salt, pepper, cinnamon stick, allspice, and cloves. Bring to a boil and then reduce the heat to simmer. Cook for 1 hour. Remove the cinnamon stick.

Serve over macaroni with grated cheese. This can also be served as a side dish (6-8 servings).

MAKES 4 SERVINGS.

Eggplant mousaka

GREECE

1 medium eggplant (1½ pounds)
1 pound ground beef (or lamb)
6 tablespoons vegetable oil
½ cup chopped onion
1 clove garlic, minced
1 8-ounce can tomato sauce
¼ teaspoon cinnamon
½ teaspoon salt

Peel eggplant and slice ¼ inch thick. Soak in salted water for ½ hour.

Brown the ground meat in 2 tablespoons of the oil and remove from the pan with a slotted

spoon. Brown onion and garlic in the drippings. Add tomato sauce, cinnamon, salt, and the cooked meat. Simmer on low heat for 10 minutes. Set aside.

Drain the eggplant and dry it with paper towels. Place on a broiler pan in a single layer and brush with 2 tablespoons oil. Broil until brown. Turn and brush with remaining 2 tablespoons oil and brown under the heat source.

Layer the eggplant and meat sauce in a 2-quart casserole, ending with the meat sauce. Top with Rich Cheese Sauce and bake for 45 minutes at 350°F. Leftovers are great reheated and served in pita bread pouches as a sandwich.
MAKES 4 SERVINGS.

Rich cheese sauce
2 tablespoons butter
2 tablespoons flour
¼ teaspoon nutmeg
1 5¾-ounce can evaporated milk
¼ cup water
½ teaspoon chicken-broth granules
1 egg, beaten
1 cup cottage cheese, small curd
¼ cup Parmesan cheese

Melt the butter, and add the flour and nutmeg. Cook and stir until bubbly. Stir in the milk, water, and chicken-broth granules. Cook, stirring constantly, over low heat, until the mixture thickens and boils, about 1 minute.

Add 1 cup of the sauce slowly to the beaten egg and beat well. Then beat back into the mixture in the saucepan. Cook, stirring constantly, for 1 minute. Remove from the heat, stir in the cottage cheese and Parmesan cheese, force the mixture through a fine sieve, and use to top mousaka.

Pocket sandwiches
GREECE

2 tablespoons olive oil
1 pound ground beef or lamb
½ cup chopped onion
¼ cup chopped green pepper
½ cup tomato sauce
½ teaspoon salt
¼ teaspoon pepper
½ teaspoon crumbled dried oregano
4 pieces pita bread

Heat the olive oil in a medium-size skillet. Add the ground meat and sauté for 5 minutes. Add the onion and green pepper and sauté for 3 more minutes. Drain off the fat. Add the tomato sauce and seasonings. Cover and simmer for 5 minutes. With a knife split the pita-bread pieces one-fourth of the way around and make a pocket. Stuff the bread with the meat mixture.
MAKES 4 SERVINGS.

Stuffed cabbage leaves
GREECE

1 large head cabbage
½ pound ground beef
½ pound ground lamb
1 medium onion, chopped
1 clove garlic, minced
½ cup plain yoghurt
½ cup raw long-grain rice
½ teaspoon crushed oregano
½ teaspoon salt
¼ teaspoon pepper
1 8-ounce can tomato sauce
2 bay leaves, crushed
1 10¾-ounce can beef broth
1 soup-can water
½ cup yoghurt or sour cream mixed with chopped mint (for garnish)

Core the head of cabbage and place under running water. Peel off 12 large cabbage leaves. Save any leaves that break. Put 1 inch of boiling water in a Dutch oven. Add the cabbage leaves and cover the pan. Steam over medium heat for 10 minutes or until the cabbage leaves are limp. Drain.

Mix the meats, onion, garlic, yoghurt, rice, oregano, salt, and pepper. Fill the cabbage leaves with ¼ cup of the filling. Fold the 2 sides toward the center and roll tightly. Fasten with 2 wooden toothpicks.

Place the rolls in a large Dutch oven or skillet. Place any broken cabbage leaves on the bottom of the pot or slice any remaining cabbage and place under the cabbage rolls. Layer the rolls, placing tomato sauce and crushed bay leaf over each layer (there should be 2 layers). Pour the beef broth and water over the rolls. Cover the kettle and simmer for 1 hour. Serve the cabbage rolls hot, garnished with yoghurt or sour cream mixed with chopped mint.

MAKES 4 SERVINGS (12 CABBAGE ROLLS).

Stuffed grape leaves w/egg & lemon sauce

GREECE

⅓ cup olive oil
½ cup chopped onion
1 pound ground beef or lamb
¾ cup raw rice
1 tablespoon dried mint leaves
½ teaspoon salt
¼ teaspoon pepper
1 cup water
1 jar (1 pound) grape leaves
2 cups beef broth (approximately)

Heat the oil in a large skillet and sauté the onion until golden. Add the ground meat and sauté until it loses its pink color. Add the rice, seasonings, and water. Simmer covered for 10 minutes or until the water is absorbed. Remove from the heat and cool for 30 minutes before stuffing the grape leaves.

Drain the brine from the grape leaves and rinse under cold running water. Drain and pat dry. With the stem end facing you, place 1 tablespoon of the meat filling on the leaf. Fold the stem end up to cover the filling. Fold the sides in and roll.

Line a large skillet or saucepan with broken, unfilled vine leaves. Pack the rolls tightly into the pan, seam-side-down, in layers. Pour the beef broth over the rolls until they are just covered with liquid; weight with a heavy plate to keep the rolls from opening. Cover and bring to a boil. Reduce the heat to simmer and cook for 30 minutes.

Pour off 1 cup of broth and use to make Egg and Lemon Sauce (see Index). Serve warm with the sauce poured over.

MAKES 6 SERVINGS.

Stuffed zucchini

GREECE

4 medium zucchini squash (about 2 pounds total)
1 pound ground beef
¼ cup olive oil
2 cloves garlic, minced
1 medium chopped onion
½ cup chopped green pepper
1 teaspoon crushed dried mint
1 cup fresh bread crumbs
1 tablespoon chopped parsley
1¾ cups tomato sauce
¼ cup grated Kafaloteri cheese
Salt and pepper

Slice the zucchini in half lengthwise. Scoop out the pulp and chop. Sauté the ground beef in the olive oil until it loses its pink color. Add the garlic, onion, and green pepper and cook for 5 more minutes. Remove from the heat. Add the zucchini pulp, mint, bread crumbs, parsley, ¼ cup tomato sauce, cheese, and salt and pepper to taste.

Stuff the squash shells with the mixture. Put the squash in a 13 × 9 × 2-inch baking dish, and pour the remaining 1½ cups of tomato sauce over the squash. Bake at 350°F for 40 minutes.

MAKES 4 SERVINGS.

Roast leg of lamb bandit-style

GREECE

1 leg of lamb (4 to 5 pounds), boned, rolled, and tied
2 cloves garlic, cut in slivers
Salt and pepper
2 tablespoons butter
1 3-foot section heavy-duty aluminum foil
2 pounds pearl onions, peeled and parboiled
2 tablespoons chopped parsley
1 teaspoon dried dillweed
½ cup white wine
¼ cup olive oil
Juice of 1 lemon

Cut slits in the fat on the outside of the lamb roast and insert the garlic slivers. Rub with the salt and pepper. Heat the butter in a deep skillet. Brown the lamb well on all sides. Place the lamb on the aluminum foil.

Add the onions to the skillet and brown them. Add the parsley and dill, then spoon the mixture around the lamb roast. Pour the wine, olive oil, and lemon juice over the lamb. Fold the foil around the lamb and seal tightly. Place the package in a large roasting pan. Bake at 375°F for 3 hours.

Serve with Braised Potatoes (see Index) and Tomatoes with Feta Cheese (see Index).
MAKES 6 TO 8 SERVINGS.

Hamburger steaks in the Greek style

GREECE

1¼ pounds meatloaf mix
½ teaspoon salt
¼ teaspoon pepper
¼ teaspoon thyme
¼ cup chopped parsley
2 tablespoons chopped celery leaves
1 medium onion, chopped
½ cup cooked rice
3 tablespoons butter
3 tablespoons tomato paste
1½ tablespoons flour
½ cup hot beef broth
¼ cup red wine
¼ cup sour cream
2 thin slices boiled ham

Combine the meatloaf mix, salt, pepper, thyme, parsley, celery leaves, and onion. Mix well with your hands or a fork. Add the rice and mix to combine. Form into 8 hamburger patties.

Melt the butter in a large skillet and add the hamburger patties. Cook over medium-high heat for 3 minutes on each side. Remove from the pan and keep them warm.

Add the tomato paste to the pan drippings. Then sprinkle with the flour and stir until smooth. Slowly add the broth and red wine, stir-

ring constantly. Cook over low heat until thickened. Remove from the heat, and stir in the sour cream. Add the patties to the gravy and simmer for 10 minutes.

Cut the boiled ham into thin strips. Arrange the patties and gravy on a serving dish and garnish with ham strips.
MAKES 4 SERVINGS.

Lamb shanks w/rice & green grapes

GREECE

2 tablespoons olive oil
4 lamb shanks, cracked
½ cup chopped onion
3 cups chicken broth
½ teaspoon salt
¼ teaspoon pepper
1 bay leaf
3 tablespoons butter
1 cup raw long-grain rice
2 cups green seedless grapes

Heat the olive oil in a heavy skillet and brown the lamb shanks. Place them in a 3-quart casserole. Brown the onion and add to the lamb shanks. Pour the chicken broth into the casserole and add the seasonings. Cover and cook at 375°F for 2 to 2½ hours or until the meat is fork-tender. Pour off the liquid and keep the lamb warm.

Melt 1 tablespoon of butter in a 1½- to 2-quart saucepan and brown the rice lightly. Add 2½ cups of lamb broth. Cover tightly. Reduce the heat to simmer and cook 20 to 25 minutes or until all the liquid is absorbed.

Meanwhile, melt the 2 remaining tablespoons of butter in a heavy skillet. Just before serving, cook the grapes in the butter, over medium-high heat, until bright green. Arrange the rice in a large dish, top with the lamb shanks, spoon the grapes and butter over the lamb, and serve.
MAKES 4 SERVINGS.

Lamb & green beans

GREECE

2 tablespoons flour
1 teaspoon salt
¼ teaspoon pepper
6 lamb shoulder chops (2 to 2½ pounds)
2 tablespoons olive oil
1 large onion, sliced
1 clove garlic, crushed
1½ cups chicken broth
1½ pounds green beans, ends nipped and cut in 1-inch
    sections
1 pound small new potatoes, scrubbed and a 1-inch strip
    removed around the middle
2 eggs
¼ cup lemon juice
Parsley
Lemon wedges

Mix the flour, salt, and pepper. Coat the chops and shake off the excess. Heat the oil in a Dutch oven and brown the chops evenly on both sides. Remove from the pan.

Sauté the onion and garlic until soft. Stir in the chicken broth and bring to boiling. Arrange the chops, green beans, and potatoes in the pan. Cover and reduce the heat to low. Cook, basting occasionally, for 45 to 50 minutes or until done. Arrange the chops and vegetables in a large bowl or deep platter and keep them warm.

Beat the eggs until foamy. Add the lemon juice while continuing to beat. Gradually beat in the pan juices and return the sauce to the pan. Cook over very low heat, stirring constantly, until thickened. Pour the sauce over the chops and garnish with parsley and lemon wedges.

MAKES 6 SERVINGS.

Variation: Substitute a 2½- to 3-pound cabbage, cut into 6 wedges, for the green beans. Follow the cooking method as given above.

Lamb chops

GREECE

4 loin or lean shoulder lamb chops (about 1¼ pounds)
1 clove garlic
½ teaspoon salt
¼ teaspoon pepper

4 tablespoons olive oil
3 shallots, peeled and chopped
½ cup retsina or dry white wine
½ teaspoon dried dillweed
1 tablespoon yoghurt
Salt and pepper
1 tablespoon parsley, chopped

Wipe the lamb chops dry with a damp cloth. Peel the garlic clove, sprinkle with the salt, and mash with the blade of a knife. Rub the chops with the garlic and pepper.

Heat the oil in a heavy frying pan and brown the chops well on both sides. Add the shallots and cook until glossy. Slowly add the wine a little at a time. Sprinkle the chops with the dill. Simmer the meat for 10 minutes on each side. (Reduce the time if the lamb chops are very thin.)

Remove the lamb chops to a heated platter and keep them warm. Add the yoghurt to the liquid in the pan, and stir. Season to taste with salt and pepper. Add the parsley to the gravy, pour over the lamb chops, and serve.

MAKES 4 SERVINGS.

Lamb stew w/white beans

GREECE

2 tablespoons olive oil
1 pound boneless lamb for stew, cut in 1½-inch pieces
1 cup chopped onion
2 cloves garlic, chopped
1 small stalk celery, chopped
2 medium carrots, sliced
1 teaspoon salt
¼ teaspoon pepper
1 bay leaf
½ teaspoon oregano
½ cup water
1½ cups canned tomatoes
2 tablespoons tomato paste
2 1-pound cans white beans, drained
2 tablespoons chopped parsley

Heat the oil in a Dutch oven. Brown the lamb on all sides. Add the onion and garlic and continue to cook for 5 minutes, until the onion and garlic are limp. Add the celery, carrots, seasonings, water, tomatoes, and tomato paste. Cover and cook over low heat for 1½ hours.

Add the beans and cook for 1 hour or until the lamb is tender. Garnish with chopped parsley and serve with crusty bread.
MAKES 4 TO 6 SERVINGS.

Rice w/lamb

GREECE

¼ cup butter or margarine
½ cup chopped onion
1½ cups raw long-grain rice
3 cups boiling water
3 teaspoons instant chicken broth, granulated
1 teaspoon dried mint
2 cups cubed cooked lamb
½ cup golden raisins
2 tablespoons chopped parsley

Melt the butter or margarine in a large saucepan. Add the chopped onion and cook until limp. Add the rice and cook 4 to 5 minutes or until lightly colored, stirring frequently. Add the boiling water, instant chicken broth, and dried mint. Cover, reduce the heat to simmer, and cook 15 minutes.

Add the lamb and raisins; continue cooking 5 more minutes or until all the liquid is absorbed. Fluff and serve garnished with the parsley.
MAKES 4 SERVINGS.

Stuffed zucchini

Skewered lamb

Skewered lamb

GREECE

¼ cup minced onion
1 clove garlic, minced
3 tablespoons olive oil
3 tablespoons lemon juice
1 teaspoon salt
¼ teaspoon pepper
½ teaspoon crumbled dried oregano
1½ pounds leg of lamb or lamb shoulder meat, cut into
   2-inch cubes
16 small boiling onions, peeled
16 mushrooms, cleaned and stems removed
2 red peppers, cut into chunks

Combine the onion, garlic, olive oil, lemon juice, salt, pepper, and oregano in a glass bowl or casserole. Add the lamb cubes and stir well. Cover and marinate for 3 to 4 hours (or longer in the refrigerator), stirring occasionally.

Parboil the onions in salted water for 10 minutes. Drain and cool.

Drain the lamb, reserving the marinade. Skewer the vegetables and lamb alternately (lamb cube, onion, mushroom, and then a pepper chunk; repeat). Cook over charcoal or in the broiler about 15 minutes, brushing frequently with the marinade. Serve with rice.

MAKES 4 SERVINGS.

Variation: Substitute cherry tomatoes and green peppers for the red peppers. Skewer the onions and meat alternately. Skewer the vegetables separately, and brush them with marinade. Tomatoes

Bandit pork

Veal with vegetables

can be grilled only a short time or they will fall off the skewer before the meat is done. Start the meat first and add the skewered vegetables 5 minutes before the meat is finished.

Cabbage rolls w/sauerkraut

GREECE

1 pound ground pork
1 medium onion, chopped
2 tablespoons olive oil
½ cup raw long-grain rice
1 teaspoon crushed dried mint
½ teaspoon salt
¼ teaspoon pepper
1 large head cabbage
1 1-pound can sauerkraut
2 large tomatoes, peeled and chopped
2 cups beef broth
Sour cream or yoghurt

Brown the pork and onion in the olive oil in a large skillet. Add the rice, mint, salt, and pepper. Set aside.

Core the cabbage head and, under running water, carefully remove 12 to 15 leaves (depending on the size of the leaves). Discard the limp or damaged leaves. Bring 2 inches of water to a boil in a Dutch oven. Add the cabbage leaves and steam until limp (about 10 minutes). Drain. Place 2 to 3 tablespoons of filling on each cabbage leaf (according to the size of the leaf) and fold the sides to the center and roll. Secure with toothpicks if desired. Shred any remaining cabbage from the cabbage head.

Place the sauerkraut in the bottom of the Dutch oven and add any shredded cabbage, the cabbage rolls, tomatoes, and broth. Place a heavy plate on the cabbage rolls (this weights them down so that they stay under the liquid in the pot as they cook). Cover and cook over low heat for 1 hour. Serve topped with the cabbage and sauerkraut from the cooking pot and a dollop of sour cream or yoghurt.

MAKES 4 SERVINGS.

Lamb stew

GREECE

1 tablespoon olive oil
2 tablespoons butter or margarine
1¼ pounds lamb for stew, cut in 1½-inch cubes
1 medium onion, quartered and separated into sections
1 cup tomato purée
½ cup white wine
¼ cup water
½ teaspoon oregano
½ teaspoon salt
¼ teaspoon pepper
3 carrots, peeled and sliced
1 medium zucchini, sliced
½ of a 9-ounce package frozen cut green beans

Measure the oil and butter or margarine into a heavy skillet or 3-quart saucepan and place over medium-high heat until the butter melts. Add the lamb and brown on all sides.

Remove the lamb from the pan and add the onion and cook until limp. Add the tomato purée, wine, water, oregano, salt, pepper, carrots, and the browned meat; mix well. Reduce the heat to simmer and cook for 1½ hours or until the lamb is tender. Add the zucchini and green beans. Cook for 30 minutes more or until the vegetables are tender.

MAKES 4 SERVINGS.

Lamb & cucumber stew

GREECE

2 pounds lamb shoulder
¼ cup olive oil
2 onions, chopped
1 cup canned whole tomatoes
2 cups beef broth
½ teaspoon salt
¼ teaspoon pepper
2 medium cucumbers
2 teaspoons vinegar
1 teaspoon sugar
1 tablespoon fresh dill, chopped, or ½ teaspoon dried
    dillweed

Wipe the meat with a damp cloth. Remove the meat from the bones and cut into 1-inch cubes. Heat the oil in a Dutch oven. Add the meat and brown it on all sides. Add the onions and cook until glossy. Add the tomatoes and broth. Season with salt and pepper. Cover and cook over low heat for 45 to 50 minutes or until the meat is tender.

Wash and pare the cucumbers. Cut them in half lengthwise. Remove the seeds and cut the cucumbers in cubes. Add to the stew, and cook 5 minutes. Add the vinegar, sugar, and dill. Stir to combine, and serve.

MAKES 4 SERVINGS.

Liver piquant

GREECE

1 pound calves' liver
1/4 cup flour
1/2 teaspoon salt
1/4 teaspoon pepper
2 tablespoons olive oil
2 tablespoons butter
2 cloves garlic, minced
1/2 teaspoon crumbled rosemary
2 tablespoons lemon juice
1/4 cup white wine
1 tablespoon chopped fresh parsley

Pat the liver dry. Combine the flour, salt, and pepper and dredge the liver in the mixture, shaking off the excess.

In a heavy skillet heat the oil and butter together over medium heat. Add the garlic and brown lightly. Remove with a slotted spoon and reserve for the sauce. Fry the liver in the same skillet until brown. Be sure not to overcook it. The liver should be very slightly pink inside. Remove the liver from the pan and keep it warm. Remove the pan from the heat and add the garlic, rosemary, lemon juice, and wine. Warm the sauce over low heat, scraping any browned bits from the bottom of the pan. Pour the sauce over the liver and sprinkle with chopped parsley. Let stand a few minutes before serving to combine the flavors.

MAKES 4 SERVINGS.

Bandit pork

GREECE

4 pieces heavy-duty foil, each 15 inches long
4 medium potatoes, peeled and thinly sliced
4 loin pork chops (1 to 1 1/4 pounds total)
2 onions, sliced and separated into rings
4 carrots, peeled and sliced
2 stalks celery, sliced
2 medium zucchini squash, sliced
1/2 teaspoon garlic powder
1 teaspoon salt
1/2 teaspoon pepper
3/4 teaspoon oregano
Juice of 1/2 fresh lemon
3/4 cup grated Kasseri cheese
2 tablespoons butter

On each of the sheets of foil, arrange 1/4 of the sliced potatoes. Top with 1 chop and 1/4 of the onions, carrots, celery, and squash. Sprinkle with the garlic, salt, pepper, oregano, and lemon juice. Top with cheese and dot with butter. Bring up the edges of the foil and fold to enclose the meat and vegetables. Fold the ends to seal. Place the packets on a cookie sheet and bake at 350°F for 1 1/2 hours.

Open the packets and serve.

MAKES 4 SERVINGS.

Marinated pork roast

GREECE

1 1/2 cups red wine
2 tablespoons lemon juice
1 clove garlic, minced
1 medium onion, chopped
1/2 teaspoon pepper
1 teaspoon crushed coriander
1 4-pound loin pork roast, boned, rolled, and tied
3 tablespoons olive oil
2 tablespoons cornstarch mixed with 2 tablespoons cold
    water (optional)

Combine the wine, lemon juice, garlic, onion, pepper, and coriander. Pour into a glass or deep ceramic container about the size of the pork roast. Add the pork roast and marinate, covered, for at least 8 hours. Turn frequently. Drain and pat dry.

271

Heat the oil in a Dutch oven. Add the roast and brown on all sides. Add the marinade. Cover and roast in the oven at 375°F for 2 hours. Uncover and bake for ½ hour more.

Strain the pan juices and thicken, if desired, with 2 tablespoons cornstarch mixed with 2 tablespoons cold water. Slice the roast and serve with fried potato slices.

MAKES 8 SERVINGS.

Veal w/vegetables

GREECE

2 tablespoons flour	Flour
3 tablespoons Kafaloteri or Parmesan cheese	6 tablespoons butter
½ teaspoon salt	1 eggplant, 1½ pounds
¼ teaspoon pepper	2 tablespoons olive oil
¼ teaspoon nutmeg	4 tomatoes, peeled and quartered
1 egg, beaten	Salt and pepper
½ cup milk	½ teaspoon rosemary
1 pound thinly sliced leg of veal, cut into serving-size pieces	Juice of 1 lemon
	2 tablespoons chopped parsley

Combine the flour, cheese, salt, pepper, and nutmeg. Add the egg and milk and beat until well-blended.

Wipe the veal with a damp cloth and dredge in flour. Melt 3 tablespoons of the butter in a skillet until it sizzles. Dip the veal in the flour and egg batter. Fry in the butter until golden. Turn and fry the other side. Remove to a platter and keep it warm.

Trim the stem and cap from the eggplant. Leaving the skin on the eggplant, slice it ¼ inch thick. Pour boiling water over the eggplant and let stand a few minutes. Drain.

Heat the oil in a medium-size skillet. Add the eggplant, tomatoes, salt and pepper to taste, and the rosemary. Steam 10 minutes or until the eggplant is tender. Stir several times. Arrange the vegetables in a serving dish. Arrange the veal on top of the vegetables.

Melt the remaining butter in the pan in which the veal was cooked until it foams. Add the lemon juice and parsley. Pour over the veal. Serve with Rice Pilaf (see Index).

MAKES 4 SERVINGS.

Braised veal

GREECE

2 pounds boneless veal cubes
¼ cup flour
½ teaspoon salt
¼ teaspoon pepper
4 tablespoons butter
½ cup sliced onions
1 green pepper, sliced
½ cup sliced mushrooms
¼ teaspoon rosemary
⅔ cup white wine
1 tablespoon lemon juice
½ teaspoon sugar
2 cups canned tomatoes, broken up with a fork

Dredge the veal cubes in the flour, salt, and pepper. Heat the butter in a heavy skillet. Brown the veal on all sides. Remove from the pan.

Add the onions, pepper, and mushrooms to the skillet and cook until lightly browned. Add the rosemary, wine, lemon juice, sugar, and tomatoes; stir well, and bring to a boil. Add the veal. Cover, and reduce the heat to simmer. Cook for 1 to 1½ hours or until the veal is tender. Serve with rice or macaroni.

MAKES 4 SERVINGS.

Rabbit w/sour cherry sauce

GREECE

2½ pounds frozen white meat of rabbit (or 1 whole rabbit, 2½ to 3 pounds, disjointed)

marinade

½ cup water	5 peppercorns
1 cup red wine	1 bay leaf
¼ cup chopped onion	3 cloves

gravy

4 tablespoons flour	¼ teaspoon crumbled rosemary
6 tablespoons oil	
½ cup chopped onion	1 cup hot stock (or beef broth)
2 cloves garlic, minced	
¾ cup sliced celery	½ cup reserved marinade
1 medium carrot, chopped	⅓ cup coarsely chopped walnuts
¾ teaspoon salt	
¼ teaspoon pepper	½ cup sour cherries, canned
	3 tablespoons cherry juice

Skin the rabbit and cut into small, serving-size pieces. Combine the marinade ingredients in a glass or ceramic container. Add the rabbit and marinate for 24 hours. Drain the rabbit, pat dry, and reserve the marinade. Dip the pieces in flour.

Heat the oil in a large skillet. Brown the rabbit on all sides. Add the onion, garlic, celery, and carrot; cook for 3 minutes. Season with salt, pepper, and rosemary. Add the broth and ½ cup reserved marinade. Cover and simmer 1 hour. Remove the meat and purée the gravy in a blender, or strain it. Combine the meat, nuts, cherries, and juice, and add to the gravy and reheat. Taste and season with additional salt and pepper if desired.

MAKES 4 TO 5 SERVINGS.

Stuffed cabbage rolls

HUNGARY

1 pound lean ground beef
1 medium onion, chopped
½ cup raw long-grain rice
½ cup sour cream
½ teaspoon garlic powder
Salt and pepper
1 large head cabbage
1 1-pound can sauerkraut (do not drain)
1 16-ounce can tomatoes, puréed or sieved
1 bay leaf
Sour cream

Combine beef, onion, rice, ½ cup sour cream, garlic powder, salt, and pepper in mixing bowl; mix well. Set aside.

Core cabbage; under running water, remove 12 to 15 leaves (depending on size of leaves). Discard limp or damaged leaves. Bring 2 inches of water to boil in Dutch oven. Add cabbage leaves; steam until limp (about 10 minutes); drain well. Place 2 to 3 tablespoons filling on each cabbage leaf. Fold sides of cabbage leaf to center; roll. Secure with wooden picks.

Shred any cabbage remaining from cabbage head. Place sauerkraut in bottom of Dutch oven. Add shredded cabbage; top with cabbage rolls. Combine tomatoes, salt, and pepper; pour over cabbage rolls. Add bay leaf. Place heavy plate on cabbage rolls. (This weights down cabbage rolls so they stay under liquid as they cook.) Cover; bring to boil. Reduce heat to low; cook 1 hour. Top rolls with sour cream; serve with sauerkraut and cabbage.

MAKES 4 SERVINGS.

Beef steak esterházy

HUNGARY

1½ pounds beef round steak, cut into 4 pieces
2 tablespoons lard
1 medium onion, peeled, chopped
1 carrot, peeled, chopped
1 stalk celery, chopped
1 parsnip, peeled, chopped
1½ cups beef broth or stock
½ teaspoon grated lemon rind
1 bay leaf
Salt and pepper
2 tablespoons butter or margarine
1 carrot, peeled, cut into matchstick strips
1 stalk celery, cut into matchstick strips
1 parsnip, peeled, cut into matchstick strips
2 tablespoons boiling water
1 teaspoon sharp prepared mustard
2 tablespoons flour
½ cup heavy cream

Wipe steaks with damp cloth. Heat lard in large heavy skillet. Brown beef well on both sides. Remove from pan. Add chopped vegetables to pan; sauté until tender. Add broth, lemon rind, bay leaf, salt, and pepper; mix well. Add steaks. Bring to boil; cover. Reduce heat to low; cook 1¼ to 1½ hours or until the steak is tender.

Meanwhile, melt butter in medium saucepan. Add vegetable strips and 2 tablespoons boiling water; cover. Cook over low heat until tender, adding more water if needed; reserve.

Transfer steak to platter; keep warm. Remove bay leaf from pan; discard. Purée broth and chopped vegetables in electric blender, or force through sieve; return to pan. Stir in mustard; cook over moderate heat until bubbly.

Mix flour with 2 tablespoons water to form smooth paste. Stir into gravy; cook, stirring constantly, until thickened. Remove from heat; stir in cream. Cook over very low heat 3 to 4 minutes. Pour sauce over steaks; garnish with matchstick vegetables.

MAKES 4 SERVINGS.

Beef gulyas

HUNGARY

3 slices bacon, diced
½ cup chopped onion
1½ pounds stew beef, cut into 1½-inch cubes
2 to 3 teaspoons Hungarian sweet paprika
½ teaspoon crushed caraway seeds
Salt and pepper
2 cups beef broth
2 cups frozen small pearl onions
1½ tablespoons flour
1½ tablespoons water

Cook bacon in large heavy skillet until crisp. Remove with slotted spoon; reserve. Add onion to skillet; cook until tender. Reserve. Add beef to skillet; brown well on all sides. Remove from heat.

Add paprika, caraway seeds, salt, and pepper; stir well. Add reserved onion and broth. Return to heat. Cover; bring to boil over moderate heat. Reduce heat to low; cook 1½ hours. Add pearl onions and bacon; cook 45 minutes to 1 hour or until tender.

Combine flour and water; stir to form smooth paste. Slowly stir into stew; cook, stirring constantly, until thickened. Garnish gulyas with sour cream or sautéed green peppers; accompany with buttered noodles.

MAKES 4 SERVINGS.

Robber's meat

HUNGARY

2 pounds lean lamb, cut into 1½-inch cubes

marinade
¼ cup chopped onion
1 clove garlic, crushed
3 tablespoons cooking oil
1½ tablespoons red wine vinegar
½ teaspoon crumbled dried marjoram
Salt and pepper

2 green peppers, cleaned, cut into chunks
2 onions, peeled, cut into chunks
½ pound fresh mushrooms, cleaned, stems removed

Wipe meat with damp cloth; place in glass bowl or casserole. Combine all marinade ingredients;

pour over meat. Mix well; cover. Refrigerate overnight.

Lightly oil 4 long skewers. Drain meat; reserve marinade. Thread meat and vegetables alternately on skewers. Brush with marinade.

Build standard charcoal fire in outdoor barbecue. When coals are white-hot, grill meat 4 inches from coals; allow approximately 10 minutes per side. Brush occasionally with marinade. Slide off skewers. Serve meat with crisp cabbage salad and fried potatoes.

MAKES 4 SERVINGS.

Note: Beef or pork or any combination of these meats can be used for Robber's Meat.

Stuffed kohlrabi

HUNGARY

8 medium kohlrabi
2 tablespoons butter or
  margarine
½ cup chopped onion
½ pound ground veal
½ pound ground pork
1 egg, well-beaten
2 tablespoons bread crumbs
1 tablespoon chopped parsley
½ teaspoon crumbled dried
  marjoram
Salt and white pepper
2 cups hot chicken broth

sauce
3 tablespoons butter
3 tablespoons flour
Salt and white pepper
¼ cup heavy cream
2 tablespoons chopped fresh
  parsley

Wash kohlrabi. Cut off leaves and stems; reserve. Peel root. Cut ½-inch slice (reserve slice); scoop out pulp, leaving ¼-inch shell. Chop pulp. Select tender leaves; shred. Place leaves and pulp in Dutch oven.

Melt butter in small saucepan. Add onion; sauté until tender. Combine veal, pork, egg, bread crumbs, parsley, and seasonings in mixing bowl. Add onion; mix well. Pack mixture into kohlrabi shells, mounding slightly. Top with slice removed in first step.

Place in Dutch oven. Pour broth over kohlrabi; bring to boil. Cover; reduce heat to low. Simmer 30 to 40 minutes or until shells can be pierced with fork. Transfer kohlrabi to baking dish. Strain broth; reserve. Place cooked kohlrabi leaves around stuffed kohlrabi; keep warm.

Prepare sauce. Melt butter in medium saucepan. Add flour, salt, and pepper; cook, stirring, until bubbly. Add 1½ cups reserved broth; cook over low heat until thickened. Remove from heat; stir in cream. Pour over kohlrabi; sprinkle with parsley. Broil in oven until sauce is lightly browned. Serve immediately.
MAKES 4 SERVINGS.

Lecsó w/meat

HUNGARY

¾ pound veal shoulder, cut into 1½-inch cubes
¾ pound pork shoulder, cut into 1½-inch cubes
4 slices bacon, diced
1 large onion, peeled, chopped
1 tablespoon Hungarian sweet paprika
1½ cups beef broth
Salt and pepper
2 tablespoons raw long-grain rice
1 16-ounce can peeled tomatoes, broken up
2 green peppers, seeded, cut into strips

Wipe meat with damp cloth; cut off excess fat. Cook bacon in large saucepan until crisp. Remove from pan; drain well. Crumble; reserve. Add meat cubes to pan; brown on all sides. Remove meat.

Add onion to pan; sauté until tender. Remove from heat; stir in paprika. Add beef broth, salt, pepper, and meat cubes; stir well. Bring to boil; cover. Reduce heat to low; cook 1 hour. Add rice, tomatoes, green peppers, and reserved bacon; stir well. Simmer 40 minutes. Serve with crusty bread and red wine.
MAKES 4 SERVINGS.

Pork chops w/ham & capers

HUNGARY

4 loin pork chops, 1 inch thick
2 tablespoons lemon juice
Salt and pepper
2 tablespoons lard
½ cup chicken broth
¼ cup white wine
2 ounces boiled ham, cut into julienne strips
2 tablespoons finely chopped sweet pickle
1 tablespoon coarsely chopped capers
½ cup sour cream
1 tablespoon flour

Wipe pork with damp cloth. Rub with lemon juice, salt, and pepper; let stand 10 minutes.

Stuffed kohlrabi

Heat lard in heavy skillet. Add chops; brown well on both sides over moderate heat. Add broth and wine; cook, covered, over low heat 30 to 35 minutes or until done through. Remove to platter; keep warm.

Add ham, pickle, and capers to liquid in skillet; cook 3 minutes. Combine sour cream and flour; stir well. Add to sauce, stirring constantly. Cook over very low heat until thickened. Pour sauce over the chops.

MAKES 4 SERVINGS.

Pork & sauerkraut goulash

HUNGARY

1¼ pounds lean pork, cut into 1½-inch cubes
¼ cup flour
¾ teaspoon salt
¼ teaspoon pepper
¼ cup lard or bacon drippings
1 medium onion, peeled, chopped
1 green pepper, cut into strips
1½ teaspoons Hungarian sweet paprika
1 cup beef broth
1 16-ounce can sauerkraut, drained
Sour cream for garnish

Trim pork of excess fat; wipe with damp cloth. Combine flour, salt, and pepper. Dredge meat in

mixture. Heat lard in large heavy saucepan or Dutch oven. Brown meat well on all sides. Remove with slotted spoon; reserve.

Add onion and green pepper to fat; cook until onion is tender. Drain off remaining fat. Add paprika, broth, and browned pork; bring to boil. Reduce heat to low; cook, covered, 50 minutes. Add sauerkraut; cook 45 minutes. Garnish with sour cream; serve with noodles.

MAKES 4 SERVINGS.

Stuffed breast of veal

HUNGARY

1 3- to 4-pound veal breast with pocket cut next to bone for stuffing
8 slices stale bread
Milk
5 tablespoons butter or margarine
1 small onion, finely minced
½ cup chopped mushrooms
1 egg, well-beaten
2 tablespoons chopped parsley
½ teaspoon crumbled dried tarragon
Salt and pepper
1 cup beef broth or stock
½ cup white wine
1 bay leaf

Liver goulash

Rinse veal in cold water; pat dry. Set aside.
Cut crusts from bread; save for bread crumbs.
Place bread in bowl. Add small amount of milk;
let stand few minutes. Melt 2 tablespoons butter
in small saucepan. Add onion; sauté 2 minutes.
Add mushrooms; sauté until tender. Squeeze liquid from bread. Combine bread, onion, mushrooms, egg, parsley, and seasonings in mixing
bowl; mix well.

Lightly salt pocket in veal breast. Fill with stuffing mixture; skewer shut. Rub outside of veal
with salt and pepper. Melt 3 tablespoons butter
in Dutch oven. Add veal breast; brown well on
all sides. Add broth, wine, and bay leaf; cover.
Bake in 350°F oven 2½ hours, basting with pan
juices every 30 minutes.

Remove from pan; let stand 15 minutes before
slicing. Cut into ½-inch-thick slices, using very
sharp knife. Thicken pan juices and serve with
roast if desired.

MAKES 6 SERVINGS.

Veal fricassee

HUNGARY

1½ pounds cubed veal shoulder or leg
4 tablespoons butter
½ cup chopped onion
Salt and pepper
2 cups water
2 teaspoons instant chicken-broth granules
2 carrots, peeled, sliced
2 stalks celery, sliced
¾ cup sliced fresh mushrooms
1 tablespoon chopped parsley
2 tablespoons flour
1 tablespoon lemon juice

Wipe veal with damp cloth. Melt 2 tablespoons
butter in heavy saucepan. Add veal; brown
lightly on all sides. Push meat to side of pan.
Add onion; cook until lightly browned. Add
salt, pepper, water, and chicken-broth granules;
bring to boil. Cover; cook over low heat 1 hour.
Add carrots and celery; cook 15 minutes. Add
mushrooms and parsley; cook 10 minutes.
Meanwhile, melt 2 tablespoons butter in small

saucepan. Add flour; cook over low heat, stirring to form lightly browned roux.

Remove meat and vegetables from heat. Drain liquid from stew; add enough hot water (if necessary) to make 1½ cups. Add liquid slowly to roux, stirring well; cook over low heat until thickened. Stir sauce and lemon juice into meat and vegetables. Serve veal with rice or boiled potatoes.

MAKES 4 SERVINGS.

Note: Any combination of vegetables can be substituted for carrots and celery in this recipe. Cauliflower or peas are often used.

Liver goulash

HUNGARY

1 pound liver (beef, calves, or pork), unsliced
3 tablespoons lard or bacon fat
2 medium onions, peeled, sliced
1 green pepper, cleaned, cut into strips
3 tablespoons flour

Salt and pepper
2 tablespoons tomato paste
1½ cups hot beef broth
1 teaspoon crumbled dried marjoram

Put liver in freezer 10 minutes or until ice crystals start to form. Remove from freezer; cut into 1-inch cubes. Place in colander to drain for few minutes.

Heat lard in heavy skillet. Add onions; cook over moderate heat until lightly browned. Remove from pan with slotted spoon. Add green pepper to pan; sauté until crisp-tender. Remove; reserve.

Combine flour, salt, and pepper; mix well. Dredge liver in flour mixture, coating well. Reserve excess flour. Add liver to hot fat; cook, stirring, until browned. Dissolve tomato paste in hot broth; pour over liver. Add onions, green pepper, and marjoram; cover. Cook over low heat 10 minutes.

Combine 1 tablespoon reserved flour mixture with 1 tablespoon water. Stir into liver mixture; cook, stirring, until thickened.

MAKES 4 SERVINGS.

Rabbit w/onions & apple

HUNGARY

1 2½ to 3-pound rabbit, disjointed
4 slices bacon
6 tablespoons flour
Salt and pepper
1 large onion, peeled, sliced
1 large tart apple, peeled, cut into slices
1 12-ounce can beer
¼ teaspoon crumbled dried thyme
1 teaspoon sugar
2 tablespoons water

Wash rabbit; pat dry. Cook bacon in Dutch oven until crisp; drain. Crumble; reserve. Combine 4 tablespoons flour, salt, and pepper; dredge rabbit in mixture, coating well. Brown in hot bacon drippings. Remove rabbit from the pan.

Add onion to pan; sauté over moderate heat until tender. Add apple, beer, seasonings, and ba-

Corned beef and cabbage

con; stir well. Add rabbit; bring to boil over moderate heat. Cover; reduce heat to low. Cook 1 to 1½ hours or until rabbit is fork-tender. Transfer rabbit to platter; keep warm.

Combine 2 tablespoons flour and water; mix well. Add to gravy; cook over low heat, stirring, until thickened. Serve rabbit with gravy and bread or Potato Dumplings (see Index).
MAKES 4 SERVINGS.

Beef 'n beer stew

IRELAND

3 tablespoons flour
¾ teaspoon salt
¼ teaspoon pepper
1½ pounds stew beef, cut into 1-inch cubes
3 tablespoons vegetable oil
3 medium onions, peeled, thickly sliced (2½ cups)
½ teaspoon crumbled dried thyme
¾ cup beer or stout
½ teaspoon dry mustard

Combine flour, salt, and pepper. Dredge meat in flour mixture, shaking off excess.

Heat oil in heavy skillet. Add onions; cook over moderate heat until lightly browned. Remove with slotted spoon; reserve.

Brown meat in oil in 2 batches, stirring occasionally to ensure even browning. Return meat and reserved onions to pan. Add thyme, beer, and mustard. Cover; bring to boil. Reduce heat to low; cook 1½ to 2 hours or until meat is very tender. Serve stew with mashed potatoes or boiled new potatoes tossed with parsley butter.
MAKES 4 SERVINGS.

Corned beef & cabbage

IRELAND

1 3-pound corned-beef brisket
Cold water to cover
1 small onion, peeled, studded with 4 whole cloves
1 clove garlic, peeled, crushed
1 bay leaf
4 peppercorns
1 medium head cabbage

Wipe beef with damp cloth. Place in Dutch oven; cover with cold water. Add onion, garlic, bay leaf, and peppercorns. Bring to boil over moderate heat. Skim any foam; cover. Reduce heat to low; cook approximately 3 hours or until tender. Remove meat; keep warm.

Wash cabbage; cut into 4 wedges. Cut out core; remove any damaged outside leaves. Tie each wedge with kitchen string as you would a package.

Bring meat stock to boil. Add cabbage; cook 12 to 15 minutes or until cabbage is tender. Drain well; dress with butter, salt, and pepper. Slice corned beef. Serve with cabbage and boiled potatoes. The following horseradish sauce is a spicy addition.

Horseradish sauce

½ cup sour cream
½ cup mayonnaise
2 tablespoons (or more) prepared hot horseradish
1 tablespoon chopped parsley

Mix all ingredients together, adding horseradish to taste. Let stand at least 1 hour before serving.

Corned-beef hash

IRELAND

4 tablespoons butter or margarine
1 small onion, minced
1 16-ounce can corned beef (or 2 cups chopped leftover corned beef)
3 medium potatoes, peeled, diced
¾ cup water
2 tablespoons catsup
1 teaspoon Worcestershire sauce
¼ teaspoon garlic powder
Salt and pepper
4 eggs (optional)

Melt butter in large, heavy skillet. Add onion; sauté until tender. Add remaining ingredients, except eggs; stir well. Bring to boil over moderate heat. Reduce heat to low; cook, covered, 45 minutes, stirring occasionally.

Make 4 wells in hash. Break eggs into wells. Cover; cook on low 10 to 12 minutes or until whites of eggs are set. Serve hash garnished with 279 parsley. Accompany with sliced tomatoes with French dressing.

MAKES 4 SERVINGS.

Hamburger steaks baked w/cream

IRELAND

1½ pounds lean ground beef
½ cup dry bread crumbs
3 tablespoons chopped onion
1 teaspoon Worcestershire sauce
1 egg
Salt and pepper
2 tablespoons butter or margarine
1 medium onion, peeled, chopped
2 carrots, peeled, chopped
2 stalks celery, chopped
1 tablespoon flour
1 cup light cream
1 10¾-ounce can cream of celery soup
2 tablespoons chopped parsley

Combine ground beef, bread crumbs, onion, Worcestershire sauce, egg, salt, and pepper in mixing bowl; mix well. Form into 8 patties. Melt butter in heavy skillet over moderate heat. Fry meat patties until well-browned on both sides. Remove to 13 × 9 × 2-inch baking dish.

Add onion, carrots, and celery to pan drippings; sauté until tender. Add flour; stir until well-blended.

Combine cream and cream of celery soup. Add to vegetables. Reduce heat to low; cook until mixture is hot and well-blended. Pour over hamburgers in casserole. Cover tightly with aluminum foil. Bake at 350°F 1 hour. Serve hamburgers with mashed potatoes, garnished with chopped parsley.

MAKES 4 SERVINGS.

Slumgullion

IRELAND

1½ pounds ground lamb or beef
1 large onion, peeled, finely chopped
3 large potatoes, peeled, cubed
4 carrots, peeled, chopped
Water to cover
Salt and pepper to taste
1 tablespoon Worcestershire sauce

Brown meat in large skillet over moderate heat. Add onion as meat begins to color. Stir occasionally; break up large chunks of meat with spoon. Drain off fat. Add remaining ingredients; mix well.

Bring to boil. Reduce heat to low; cook 1 hour. Stir occasionally. Mixture should be thick when done; vegetables should be tender. Serve slumgullion over mashed potatoes.

MAKES 4 TO 5 SERVINGS.

Roast leg of lamb w/accompaniments

IRELAND

1 5-pound whole leg of lamb or sirloin half leg of lamb
4 tablespoons butter or margarine
1 teaspoon crumbled dried rosemary
1 clove garlic, minced
Freshly ground pepper
6 to 8 medium potatoes
1 pound carrots, peeled, trimmed
8 brown-skinned onions

Wipe lamb with damp cloth; place in roasting pan. Melt butter. Add rosemary, garlic, and pepper to taste. Brush lamb well with butter mixture. Roast at 325°F 2 hours. Add potatoes and carrots to pan; brush well with butter mixture. Return to oven.

Do not peel or clean onions; just place on oven shelf next to roasting pan. Place small drip pan on shelf below. Roast 1 hour more or until lamb has reached an internal temperature of 180°F and vegetables are easily pierced with fork.

Carve lamb; place vegetables in serving bowl. Peel back brittle brown skins on onions. Remove cooked onion inside; serve with plenty of butter, salt, and pepper. Serve lamb with pan gravy or Mint Sauce.

MAKES 6 TO 8 SERVINGS.

Mint sauce

¼ cup water
2 tablespoons granulated sugar
1 tablespoon dried mint (¼ cup chopped fresh mint)
3 tablespoons distilled white vinegar

Combine water, sugar, and mint in small saucepan; bring to boil, stirring constantly. Remove from heat; cover. Cool completely. Thirty minutes before serving, add vinegar; stir well.

Irish stew

IRELAND

1½ pounds boneless lamb for stew
2 large onions, peeled, thickly sliced
5 medium potatoes, peeled, quartered, cut into chunks
2 stalks celery, sliced
1 turnip, diced
Salt and pepper
1½ cups chicken broth
1 bay leaf
Chopped parsley

Cut lamb into 1-inch cubes, removing large pieces of fat. Wipe meat with damp cloth or paper towels. Layer vegetables and meat in 2½-quart lightly greased casserole, beginning and ending with vegetables. Salt and pepper each layer lightly. Add chicken broth and bay leaf; cover tightly. Bake at 325°F 2 hours.
Stir; sprinkle with parsley. Remove bay leaf before serving.
MAKES 4 SERVINGS.

Shepherd's pie

IRELAND

1 cup peeled, sliced carrots
1 medium onion, peeled, sliced
3 cups diced cooked roast lamb or beef
½ cup frozen peas, slightly thawed
Salt and pepper
1 cup leftover gravy (or 1 cup canned gravy)
2 cups thick mashed potatoes
1 egg
2 tablespoons milk

Place carrots in small saucepan. Barely cover with water; cook until fork-tender. Drain. Meanwhile, in separate saucepan cook onion, barely covered with water, until tender; drain.
Combine lamb, vegetables, and salt and pepper to taste in 2-quart casserole; mix well. Heat gravy; thin with boiling water if it has become very thick. Pour gravy over meat and vegetables; stir to combine. Bake, uncovered, at 350°F 20 minutes.
Place potatoes in pastry bag and pipe over top of meat mixture, or mound over top of casserole with spoon. Beat egg and milk together; brush potatoes with mixture. Return to oven; bake 20 minutes. Turn on broiler unit; cook until potatoes are lightly browned. Serve hot.
MAKES 4 SERVINGS.

Creamed ham & potatoes

IRELAND

3 tablespoons butter or margarine
¼ cup finely chopped onion
4 cups peeled, diced potatoes
2 cups milk
2 cups diced cooked ham
1 tablespoon flour
1 tablespoon water
Salt and pepper
½ cup shredded sharp cheddar cheese
Chopped parsley

Melt butter in large, heavy saucepan over moderate heat. Sauté onion until tender. Add potatoes and milk; stir well. Bring to low boil over moderate heat. Reduce heat to low; cook 10 minutes. Add ham; simmer 10 minutes or until potatoes are tender.
Combine flour and water; stir into potato mixture. Cook until thickened. Season to taste with salt and pepper. Spoon mixture into individual serving dishes; top with cheese and chopped parsley.
MAKES 4 SERVINGS.

Pork chops w/apple cream gravy

IRELAND

6 center-cut pork chops, cut ½ inch thick (about 1½ pounds)
5 tablespoons flour
Salt and pepper
3 tablespoons butter or margarine
½ cup slivered onion
1 cup light cream (or half-and-half)
½ cup apple cider
1 large apple, peeled, cored, sliced ¼ inch thick
¼ teaspoon ground mace

Wipe pork chops with damp cloth. Combine 3 tablespoons flour with salt and pepper to taste on piece of waxed paper. Dredge chops with flour mixture.

Melt butter in heavy skillet. Sauté onion in butter until tender. Remove with slotted spoon; reserve. Brown pork chops in remaining butter. Reserve.

Add 2 tablespoons flour to pan drippings; stir well. Cook 2 minutes or until bubbly but not brown. Reduce heat to low; gradually add cream, stirring constantly. Stir in apple cider and salt; cook until bubbly. Stir in onions. Arrange chops in gravy; top with apple slices. Sprinkle with mace; cover. Cook on low 15 minutes. Serve chops hot with mashed potatoes.
MAKES 4 TO 6 SERVINGS.

Beer-braised pork roast

IRELAND

1 5-pound pork loin roast
2 tablespoons vegetable oil
2 medium onions, peeled, sliced
1 teaspoon salt
½ teaspoon pepper
1 12-ounce can or bottle Guiness stout or dark beer

Wipe meat with damp cloth. Heat oil in Dutch oven over moderate heat. Brown meat on all sides. Remove to platter. Add onions to pan; sauté until tender.

Place pork roast in Dutch oven; spoon onions over roast. Sprinkle with salt and pepper. Add beer. Cover; bring to boil over moderate heat. Reduce heat to low; cook approximately 2½ hours or until roast is fork-tender.

Remove roast to warm platter; thicken pan juices if desired. Slice roast. Serve with applesauce.
MAKES 5 SERVINGS.

Dublin coddle

IRELAND

1 pound large pork-sausage links
4 to 6 thick slices bacon (approximately ½ pound), cut into 2-inch pieces
¾ pound onions (3 medium)
1½ pounds potatoes (4 medium)
Black pepper
Finely chopped parsley

Prick sausages in several places. Place sausage and bacon in skillet; barely cover with water (about 3 cups). Bring to boil. Cover; simmer 10 minutes. Drain; reserve liquid.

Peel and slice onions. Peel and thinly slice potatoes. Layer sausage, bacon, onions, and potatoes in 2½-quart casserole. Lightly pepper layers. Pour broth from sausages into casserole to barely cover meat and vegetables (about 2½ cups).

Cover casserole with foil; bake at 350°F 1 hour or until potatoes are tender. Sprinkle dish with parsley. Serve.
MAKES 4 TO 5 SERVINGS.

Pork ciste

IRELAND

pastry crust

1 cup flour	3 tablespoons lard
½ teaspoon salt	2 to 3 tablespoons cold water

pork and apple filling

1½ pounds lean pork, cut into 1-inch cubes	½ cup milk
1 cup water	¼ cup flour
½ cup chopped onion	2 large tart apples, peeled, cored, sliced
1 teaspoon crumbled dried sage leaves	1 tablespoon sugar
¾ teaspoon salt	1 egg yolk
	1 tablespoon milk

First prepare pastry crust. Combine flour and salt, mixing well. Cut in lard until mixture resembles coarse meal. Add water a tablespoon at a time, while stirring with a fork, just until mixture holds together. Form into ball. Cover with plastic wrap; refrigerate.

Brown pork in large saucepan over moderate heat, stirring frequently. Add water, onion, sage, and salt; mix well. Cover; simmer over low heat 30 minutes or until meat is tender.

Combine milk and flour; stir to form smooth mixture. Add to pork mixture in saucepan, stirring constantly to prevent lumps from forming. Cook over low heat until thickened and bubbly. Pour ½ of pork mixture into 1½-quart lightly greased casserole. Top with apples; sprinkle with sugar. Add remaining pork mixture.

Roll pastry crust. Turn out dough onto lightly floured board; roll to fit casserole dish. Place over meat mixture. Turn under small margin of pastry around edge of casserole; crimp edge. Cut several steam vents in pastry.

Beat egg yolk and milk together; brush crust well with egg wash. Bake at 450°F 10 minutes. Reduce heat to 350°F; bake 25 minutes more. Serve hot.

MAKES 4 TO 5 SERVINGS.

Hamburger steaks baked with cream

Venison stew

IRELAND

3 pounds venison, cut into
   1½-inch cubes

marinade

¾ cup red wine	1 bay leaf
2 tablespoons olive oil	1 clove garlic, peeled,
1 medium onion, chopped	crushed
3 juniper berries, crushed	6 peppercorns

stew

¼ pound salt pork, diced	1 cup beef broth
¼ cup chopped shallot (or	1 teaspoon crumbled dried
onion)	thyme
½ cup chopped celery	½ cup port wine
½ cup chopped carrot	3 tablespoons currant jelly
Flour	

Wipe venison with damp cloth; place in large casserole or glass dish. Combine all marinade ingredients; pour over venison. Cover tightly; marinate in refrigerator 24 hours, stirring 3 or 4 times. Drain meat; reserve marinade.

Fry salt pork in Dutch oven until lightly browned. Remove with slotted spoon; reserve. Add shallot, celery, and carrot to pan drippings; sauté until tender. Remove from pan; reserve.

Pat venison dry with paper towels; dredge lightly in flour. Brown in salt-pork fat, turning to ensure even browning. Add reserved vegetables, salt pork, beef broth, and thyme.

Strain marinade; add to pan. Stir well. Cover; bring to boil. Reduce heat to low; cook 2 to 2½ hours or until meat is tender. Stir in port wine and currant jelly; simmer 15 minutes. Serve venison stew with boiled new potatoes.

MAKES 6 SERVINGS.

Rabbit cooked in stout

IRELAND

1 2½- to 3-pound rabbit, disjointed
½ cup flour
¼ teaspoon paprika
Salt and pepper
¼ pound salt pork, diced
1 pound pearl onions, cleaned, peeled
½ pound button mushrooms, cleaned, stems removed
1½ cups stout or dark beer
2 tablespoons chopped parsley
1 bay leaf
½ teaspoon crumbled dried thyme
2 tablespoons butter
2 tablespoons flour

Wash rabbit; pat dry. Combine flour, paprika, salt, and pepper on piece of waxed paper. Dredge rabbit in flour mixture; shake off excess.

Cook salt pork in heavy skillet until lightly browned. Remove with slotted spoon; reserve. Add rabbit to pan drippings; brown well on all sides. Place rabbit in large casserole. Add onions, mushrooms, and salt pork to casserole. Combine stout, parsley, bay leaf, thyme, salt, and pepper; pour over rabbit. Cover; bake at 350°F 1½ hours.

Knead butter and flour together until well-blended. Place rabbit in warm serving dish; keep warm while thickening sauce. Place casserole on burner if it is stove-top safe, or transfer pan juices to small saucepan. Cook over low heat 2 to 3 minutes. Add butter and flour mixture in small balls to sauce, stirring well. Cook over low heat 5 minutes, stirring constantly. Pour over rabbit. Serve.

MAKES 4 TO 5 SERVINGS.

Steak w/tomato sauce

ITALY

This recipe is excellent for disguising a less-tender steak.

sauce
2 tablespoons olive oil
1 small onion, peeled, minced
2 cloves garlic, peeled, minced
1 (16-ounce) can Italian-style tomatoes
1 teaspoon crumbled oregano
Salt and pepper

2 tablespoons olive oil
3 pounds T-bone, porterhouse, or sirloin steak, 1 inch thick

To prepare sauce, heat oil in small skillet. Add onion and garlic; sauté until tender. Break up tomatoes with fork to form small chunks. Add tomatoes, oregano, salt, and pepper to skillet; stir well. Cover; simmer 15 minutes, until sauce begins to thicken.

In large heavy skillet heat remaining oil until very hot. Add steak; brown quickly on both sides, turning several times. Pour tomato sauce

Irish stew

over steak. Cover; cook over low heat approximately 10 minutes (until done to taste). Remove steak from skillet; carve. Serve topped with tomato sauce.

MAKES 4 SERVINGS.

Beef braised w/cloves

ITALY

1 (4-pound) beef rump or bottom-round roast
12 cloves
Salt and freshly ground pepper
3 tablespoons olive oil
1/2 cup chopped onion
1/4 cup chopped celery
1/4 cup chopped carrot
1 clove garlic, peeled, chopped
1/2 cup dry red wine
2 cups beef broth
1/2 cup tomato sauce
1 teaspoon crumbled oregano
1 bay leaf
4 slices bacon

Wipe roast with damp cloth. Stud with cloves; rub with salt and pepper. Heat oil in Dutch oven. Brown meat well on all sides. Remove from pan and drain off excess fat.

Add to the juice onion, celery, carrot, and gar-

Shepherd's pie

lic; sauté until tender. Add wine, broth, tomato sauce, oregano, and bay leaf. Bring to boil. Reduce heat to low; place roast in pan. Place bacon on roast. Cover; simmer 3 hours. Slice meat; serve with pan juices, accompanied by plain pasta or potatoes.

MAKES 8 SERVINGS.

Rabbit cooked in stout

Beef stew—Florentine-style

Italian beef stew

ITALY

2 tablespoons olive oil
2 slices bacon, chopped
½ cup chopped onion
½ cup sliced celery
1 clove garlic, minced
1¼ pounds lean stew beef,
    cut in 1-inch cubes
2 tablespoons chopped
    parsley
1 16-ounce can peeled
    tomatoes, broken up
½ cup water

1 teaspoon beef-broth
    granules
½ teaspoon dried sweet
    basil, crumbled
Salt and pepper
½ teaspoon sugar
3 medium carrots, peeled
    and sliced
3 medium potatoes, peeled
    and diced
¼ cup red wine
1½ cups sliced zucchini
    squash (unpeeled)

Heat the oil in a Dutch oven. Add the bacon and
sauté until crisp. Remove the bacon from the pan
with a slotted spoon and reserve. Add the onion,
celery, and garlic and sauté 5 minutes. Remove
with a slotted spoon and reserve.

Add the stew beef and cook over moderate heat
until well browned on all sides, stirring occasionally. Add the reserved ingredients, parsley, tomatoes, water, beef-broth granules, and seasonings
and cook covered over low heat for 1 hour. Add
the carrots and potatoes and stir well. Cover and
cook for 45 minutes. Add the wine and zucchini
and stir well. Cook 15 more minutes or until the
vegetables are tender.

MAKES 4 SERVINGS.

Beef stew—Florentine-style

ITALY

Many Northern Italian dishes begin with what is
called "battuto," which means to chop together.
In the American kitchen, if a recipe calls for onion and garlic, we chop each ingredient separately and add it to the skillet. In Italy, a number of vegetables and salt pork or bacon are
chopped together so that each takes flavor from
the other. This method is used here to make a
delicious beef stew.

2 ounces salt pork
1 medium onion
1 clove garlic, peeled
1 medium carrot
1 celery stalk with leaves
2 sprigs parsley
2 tablespoons oil
1½ pounds lean beef cubes
1 cup red wine (preferably Chianti)
½ cup tomato sauce
1 bay leaf
1 teaspoon crumbled oregano
Salt and pepper

Roughly chop pork, onion, garlic, carrot, celery,
and parsley; combine. Mince together on wooden
board until all ingredients are very finely
chopped. Place "battuto" in Dutch oven or large
heavy frypan. Add oil; sauté until pork is lightly
browned and vegetables limp.

Wipe beef cubes with damp cloth; add to pan. Brown on all sides. Drain off excess fat. Add wine, tomato sauce, and seasonings; bring to boil. Reduce heat to low; cook 2 hours, until meat is very tender. Garnish with chopped parsley if desired.

MAKES 4 SERVINGS.

Stuffed peppers

ITALY

4 medium bell peppers
1 pound ground beef
½ cup chopped onion
1 small clove garlic, minced, or ½ teaspoon garlic powder
1 teaspoon mixed Italian herbs, crumbled
Salt and pepper
1 16-ounce can stewed tomatoes
1 8-ounce can tomato sauce
¼ cup water
1 cup instant rice (or quick-cooking)
2 ounces thinly sliced mozzarella cheese

Cut the tops off of the peppers and remove the seeds and membranes. Parboil the peppers for 5 minutes and drain.

Sauté the ground beef, onions and garlic until lightly browned in a large skillet, adding a little oil if the meat is very lean. Add the garlic powder if used, Italian herbs, salt and pepper, tomatoes, ½ of the can of tomato sauce, water and rice. Stir well. Bring to a boil, reduce the heat to low and cook, covered, 15 minutes.

Place the peppers in a 2-quart casserole. Stuff with the meat mixture and spoon the remaining meat mixture around the peppers. Top with the remaining tomato sauce. Cover and cook 30 minutes, at 350°F. Uncover, top with the cheese and cook 10 more minutes.

MAKES 4 SERVINGS.

Meatloaf—Italian-style

ITALY

1½ pounds meatloaf mix (ground beef, pork, and veal) or
    1½ pounds lean ground beef
1 egg, lightly beaten
½ cup Italian-style bread crumbs
¼ cup chopped onion
½ teaspoon dried sweet basil, crumbled
½ teaspoon dried oregano, crumbled
Salt and pepper to taste
1 10½-ounce can pizza sauce with cheese
2 ounces thinly sliced mozzarella cheese

In a large bowl, combine the meat, egg, bread crumbs, onion, seasonings, and one half of the can of pizza sauce. Mix well. Form into a large round loaf, and place in a 3-quart round casserole. Pour the remaining pizza sauce over the meatloaf. Bake at 350°F for 1¼ hours. Top with the sliced cheese and bake 5 more minutes. Remove from the oven and let stand 5 minutes before slicing.

MAKES 4 TO 6 SERVINGS.

Stuffed zucchini

ITALY

4 medium zucchini squash (about ¾ pound each)
1 pound ground beef (or ½ pound beef and ½ pound
    sausage)
¼ cup olive oil
1 clove garlic, chopped
1 medium onion, chopped
½ cup green pepper, chopped
1 tablespoon chopped parsley
½ teaspoon dried oregano, crumbled
Salt and pepper
1 cup fresh bread crumbs from French or Italian bread
1¾ cups tomato sauce (divided)
¼ cup grated Parmesan cheese

Slice the zucchini in half lengthwise. Scoop out the pulp and chop. Sauté the ground beef (and sausage if used) in the olive oil until it loses its pink color. Add the garlic and onion and green pepper and cook 5 more minutes.

Remove from the heat and add the squash pulp, parsley, oregano, salt and pepper, bread crumbs and ¼ cup of the tomato sauce. Mix well and stuff the squash shells with the mixture. Place in a shallow baking dish. Top with the remaining 1½ cups of tomato sauce and sprinkle with the cheese. Bake at 350°F for 40 minutes.

MAKES 4 SERVINGS.

Pizza burgers

ITALY

1½ pounds ground beef
½ cup chopped onion
1 clove garlic, pressed, or ¾ teaspoon garlic salt
¼ teaspoon pepper

sauce

2 cups peeled Italian-style tomatoes, broken up with a fork
1 8-ounce can tomato sauce
¼ cup chopped canned mushrooms
1 teaspoon dried oregano, crumbled
6 large French rolls, split (or small individual French bread loaves)
8 ounces mozzarella cheese, sliced

Combine the ground beef, onion, garlic salt and pepper and form into 6 patties the size and shape of the rolls. Combine the tomatoes, tomato sauce, mushrooms, and oregano in a saucepan and heat. Broil the hamburgers until done to your liking.

Place the hamburgers on the bottom half of the rolls. Top with some of the sauce, the sliced cheese and then garnish with an additional tablespoon of the sauce. Return to the broiler until the cheese melts. Serve open face or topped with the other half of the roll.

MAKES 6 SERVINGS.

Beef rolls w/tomato gravy

ITALY

1¼ pounds very thinly sliced top round of beef (¼ inch thick)
¼ cup olive oil
1 medium onion, finely chopped
¾ cup Italian-style bread crumbs
3 tablespoons olive oil
2 tablespoons chopped onion
1½ cups canned Italian-style peeled plum tomatoes, broken up
½ cup tomato sauce
½ tablespoon dehydrated parsley flakes
½ teaspoon sugar
½ teaspoon oregano
Salt and pepper

Pound the meat well and cut into rectangular pieces approximately 4 × 6 inches. You should have 8 pieces, so vary the measurements accordingly.

In a small skillet, heat the olive oil and sauté the onion until it is tender. Remove from the heat and add the bread crumbs and stir well. Place 2 tablespoons of the bread crumb mixture on each piece of steak and roll jelly-roll fashion to enclose the stuffing. Fasten with toothpicks.

Heat the olive oil in a heavy skillet and brown the steak rolls. Place in a shallow baking dish. Add the onion and brown lightly. Add the remaining ingredients and stir well. Simmer for 15 to 20 minutes or until thickened. Pour over the steak rolls, cover and bake at 350°F for 1 hour. Serve with mashed potatoes.

MAKES 4 SERVINGS.

Mixed boiled meats w/green sauce

ITALY

meat pot

1 pound beef pot roast or brisket	1 teaspoon salt
1 pound veal shoulder	½ teaspoon sugar
2 whole chicken legs	4 peppercorns
2 marrow bones, cracked	½ teaspoon thyme
Water	4 carrots, peeled and cut in half lengthwise
2 bay leaves	2 leeks, cleaned and cut in half lengthwise
1 onion	
2 cloves	½ pound cooked beef tongue
1 clove garlic	Parsley for garnish

green sauce

Juice of 1 fresh lemon	1 clove garlic, peeled and mashed
3 egg yolks	
¼ teaspoon salt	½ cup chopped parsley
½ cup olive oil	½ teaspoon dried sweet basil, crumbled
1 slice white bread, soaked in water and squeezed dry	½ teaspoon dried oregano, crumbled
½ teaspoon prepared mustard	

Place the beef, veal, chicken, and marrow bones in a large Dutch oven or stew pot. Cover with water. Add the bay leaves. Peel the onion and stud with cloves.and add to the kettle. Peel the

clove of garlic, sprinkle with the salt and mash with the blade of a knife. Add to the pot with the sugar, peppercorns, and thyme. Bring to a boil. Skim the foam from the surface of the liquid. Reduce the heat to low, cover, and cook for 40 minutes. Remove the chicken, add the carrots and leeks, and cook for 30 more minutes. Meanwhile, make the green sauce. Combine the lemon juice, egg yolks and salt in the jar of an electric blender. Blend on medium speed for 2 minutes. Add the oil a tablespoon at a time, blending well after each addition. Add the bread, mustard and garlic and blend 2 minutes. Pour into a serving bowl and stir in the parsley, sweet basil and oregano. Refrigerate until serving time.
Skin the chicken. Return to the pot along with the tongue and heat through. Remove the meats from the pot and slice. Arrange on a warm platter, garnish with parsley and serve with the green sauce. Reserve the broth for soups.
SERVES 4 GENEROUSLY.

Beef—Parma-style
ITALY

1½ pounds beef round steak
½ cup dry bread crumbs
⅓ cup grated Parmesan cheese
1 egg
2 tablespoons water
¼ cup flour
⅓ cup cooking oil
1 medium onion, minced
1 6-ounce can tomato paste
2 cups hot water
½ teaspoon dried marjoram, crumbled
1 teaspoon salt
¼ teaspoon pepper
½ pound mozzarella cheese, thinly sliced

Place the meat between sheets of waxed paper and pound with a heavy skillet on a hard surface until quite thin. Cut into serving-size pieces.
Combine the bread crumbs and Parmesan cheese. Beat the egg and 2 tablespoons of water together. Dip the meat in the flour, turn to coat and shake off the excess. Dip the meat in the egg

mixture and then in the crumb mixture. Pat the crumbs into the meat to coat well. Heat the oil in a heavy skillet over moderate heat.
Brown the meat on both sides. Remove from the pan. Add the onions and brown lightly. Add the tomato paste, hot water and seasonings. Stir well. Boil for 5 minutes. Place the meat in a shallow baking dish. Cover with the sauce; reserve ¼ cup. Top the meat with the mozzarella cheese and pour the remaining sauce over the cheese. Cover with aluminum foil and bake at 350°F for 2 hours. Serve with pasta and a green salad.
MAKES 4 TO 5 SERVINGS.

Roast leg of lamb w/rosemary
ITALY

1 5-pound whole leg of lamb or sirloin half leg of lamb
1 large clove of garlic
1 teaspoon dried rosemary, crumbled
1 teaspoon grated lemon peel
Salt and freshly ground black pepper
Olive oil

Wipe the meat with a damp cloth. Peel the garlic and rub over the surface of the lamb. Cut the garlic clove into slivers. Make 4 or 5 deep slashes in the meat and insert the garlic slivers. Rub the meat with the rosemary, lemon peel, and salt and pepper. Place in an open roasting pan on a trivet, fat-side-up.
Sprinkle with olive oil. Roast at 325°F for 3 hours or to an internal temperature of 180°-180°, according to whether you like lamb still pink or really brown. Let stand for 20 minutes before carving. Peeled potatoes and carrots can be placed in the pan drippings for the last 1½ hours of cooking time, turning occasionally.
MAKES 6 SERVINGS.

Lamb roast Roman-style
ITALY

1 (3-pound) boned and rolled lamb roast (leg or shoulder)
2 cloves garlic, peeled, cut into slivers
1 teaspoon crumbled dried rosemary

289

½ teaspoon crumbled dried marjoram
Freshly ground pepper
3 slices bacon, cut in half
anchovy sauce
2 anchovy fillets
1½ tablespoons olive oil
1½ tablespoons lemon juice
1 tablespoon fresh bread crumbs
½ cup chopped parsley
1 teaspoon freshly grated lemon rind
½ teaspoon crumbled rosemary

Wipe meat with damp cloth. Cut slits in top; place garlic sliver in each slit. Rub roast with rosemary, marjoram, and pepper. Place in roast pan, fat-side-up. Place bacon slices, slightly overlapping, over top of roast. Roast at 325°F 2¼ hours (internal temperature of 170°F). Roast should still be pink when sliced.

While lamb cooks, prepare sauce. Mash anchovy fillets with oil. Stir in lemon juice and bread crumbs. Add remaining ingredients; stir well. Refrigerate until ready for use.

Serve lamb roast with sauce, steamed broccoli, and tomato salad. Potatoes can also be pan-roasted with lamb.

MAKES 4 TO 5 SERVINGS.

Lamb chops—Venetian-style

ITALY

2 tablespoons butter or margarine
2 tablespoons olive oil
4 lamb shoulder chops (approximately 2 pounds)
Salt and pepper to taste
1 medium onion
1¾ pound eggplant
3 tablespoons tomato paste
½ teaspoon dried sweet basil, crumbled
½ cup boiling water
½ 10-ounce package frozen peas
1 8½-ounce can artichoke bottoms (or substitute 1 can artichoke hearts), drained

Heat the butter and olive oil in a heavy skillet. Wipe the lamb chops with a damp cloth and season with salt and pepper. Sauté in the butter and oil approximately 4 minutes on a side, until well-browned and almost done. Remove from the pan and keep warm.

While the chops cook, peel the onion, quarter it, and separate the layers. Cut the stem from the eggplant, cut in half lengthwise and thinly slice. Add the onions to the skillet and sauté for 5 minutes. Add the eggplant.

Combine the tomato paste, basil, and boiling water. Stir well and add to the skillet. Bring to a boil, reduce the heat to low, cover and cook 15 minutes. Add the peas, artichoke bottoms (quartered) or artichoke hearts, and the lamb chops. Cook covered for 15 more minutes or until the vegetables are done through.

MAKES 4 SERVINGS.

Pork roast in chianti

ITALY

1 4-pound boned, rolled and tied pork roast
1½ cups Chianti wine
1 clove garlic, minced
2 tablespoons lemon juice
1 teaspoon dried rosemary, crumbled
1 teaspoon dried basil, crumbled
3 tablespoons olive oil
1 8-ounce can tomato sauce
Salt and pepper, to taste

Wipe the pork roast with a damp cloth. Place in a glass or porcelain container or a heavy-duty freezer bag. Combine the Chianti, garlic, lemon juice, rosemary, and basil and pour over the meat. Cover and marinate in the refrigerator for 24 hours, turning occasionally (if using a plastic bag, close with a twist-tie).

Bring the roast to room temperature before cooking. Remove the roast from the marinade and pat dry. Reserve the marinade. Heat the oil in a large heavy Dutch oven. Brown the roast well on all sides.

Combine the marinade and the tomato sauce, salt and pepper and pour over the meat. Bring to a boil and then reduce the heat to simmer. Cover and cook for 3 hours (the meat should be fork-tender). Place the roast on a platter and slice. Serve with the pan juices.

MAKES 6 TO 8 SERVINGS.

Roast leg of lamb with rosemary

Pork roast Florentine-style

ITALY

1 (4-pound) pork loin roast
2 tablespoons olive oil
3 cloves garlic, peeled, cut into thirds
1 teaspoon crumbled dried rosemary
Fresh-ground black pepper

Wipe pork with damp cloth. Rub with oil. Cut 9 slits in fat on top; insert 1 garlic sliver in each slit. Rub with rosemary; grind pepper over roast. Place fat-side-up on rack in shallow roasting pan. Roast at 325°F approximately 2 hours or until meat thermometer registers, 175°F. Remove from oven; let rest 15 minutes before carving.

Pizza burgers

Small peeled potatoes and small whole white onions can be added to roasting pan last hour of cooking. Turn vegetables several times during cooking.
MAKES 4 TO 6 SERVINGS.

Breaded pork chops

ITALY

4 loin pork chops, 1-inch thick
Salt and pepper
1 large egg
2 tablespoons water
Bread crumbs
¼ cup clarified butter
½ teaspoon dried sage

Carefully trim the excess fat from the pork chops. Season with salt and pepper. Beat the egg and water. Dip the chops in the egg and then coat with the bread crumbs, pressing the crumbs firmly onto the chops. Let dry 1 hour in refrigerator.
In a heavy skillet, heat the clarified butter over moderate heat. Crumble the sage and add to the butter. Add the chops and cook slowly until well-browned and done through.
MAKES 4 SERVINGS.

Note: 1 pound of well-pounded veal cutlets can be substituted for the pork chops.

291

Pork chops cacciatore

ITALY

Polenta, gnocchi, rice, or mashed potatoes goes well with this dish. It's delicious with the gravy!

2 tablespoons olive oil
4 loin pork chops (1-1½ pounds)
1 small onion, sliced
1 clove garlic, minced
½ cup sliced green pepper
1 4-ounce can sliced mushrooms, drained
1 16-ounce can peeled tomatoes, broken up with a fork
2 tablespoons sherry
½ teaspoon dried oregano, crumbled
½ teaspoon dried basil, crumbled
½ teaspoon sugar
Salt and pepper

Heat the oil in a large skillet. Brown the chops well and remove from the skillet. Add the onion, garlic, and green pepper and sauté lightly over medium heat. Add the mushrooms, tomatoes, sherry, and seasonings. Bring the mixture to a boil.

Return the chops to the skillet. Cover and simmer for 1 hour, or until the chops are tender. Serve with the pan juices.

MAKES 4 SERVINGS.

Pork w/celery

ITALY

2 tablespoons olive oil
1 clove garlic, peeled
1½ pounds lean boneless pork cubes, approximately 1½ inches square
1 medium onion, finely chopped
½ cup dry red wine
1 cup beef broth

Lamb roast Roman-style

Lamb chops—Venetian-style

1 cup plum tomatoes, drained, chopped
1 carrot, peeled, minced
1 teaspoon crumbled marjoram
¾ teaspoon salt
½ teaspoon pepper
2½ cups sliced celery

Heat oil in large heavy saucepan. Add garlic; sauté until golden. Remove from pan; discard. Add pork; brown well on all sides. Push pork to side of pan. Add onion; sauté until tender. Add wine, broth, tomatoes, carrot, and seasonings; bring to boil.

Reduce heat to low. Cover; cook 1½ hours. Add celery; cook 20 minutes. (Pork should be tender and celery crisp-tender.) Serve with plain pasta or gnocchi.

MAKES 4 SERVINGS.

Ham & eggplant sandwiches

ITALY

1 large eggplant
4 slices cooked ham, ¼-inch thick
4 slices (4 inches in diameter) provolone or mozzarella cheese

Flour
1 egg
3 tablespoons water
1 cup Italian-style bread crumbs
3 tablespoons olive oil

Cut 8 slices, each ¼-inch thick, from center of eggplant. Try to get all slices nearly same size. Reserve remaining eggplant for another use. Pare eggplant slices; soak in cold salted water to cover 30 minutes. Drain well; pat dry on paper towels. Make 4 sandwiches by placing ham and cheese slices between eggplant slices.

Dredge eggplant sandwiches lightly in flour, shaking off excess. Beat egg and water together in shallow pan. Place bread crumbs on piece of waxed paper. Dip sandwiches first in egg, then in crumbs, coating well.

Heat oil in heavy skillet. Cook sandwiches over moderate heat until well-browned on both sides. Drain on paper towels. Place on cookie sheet; bake at 350°F 15 minutes. Serve with tomato sauce if desired.

MAKES 4 SERVINGS.

Milanese veal rolls

Sausage & vegetable skillet

ITALY

4 tablespoons olive oil
1 large onion, finely chopped
2 cloves garlic, peeled, minced
1 pound hot Italian sausage, casing removed, cut into
   1-inch chunks
4 medium potatoes, peeled, cut into 1-inch cubes
2 green peppers, cleaned, cut into 1-inch chunks
2 red peppers, cleaned, cut into 1-inch chunks
2 cups tomato sauce
1 bay leaf
¼ teaspoon crumbled oregano
Salt and pepper to taste

Heat oil in Dutch oven. Add onion and garlic; sauté until tender. Add remaining ingredients; mix well. Bring to boil; reduce heat to simmer; cover. Cook over low heat 1 hour, stirring occasionally, until sausage is cooked through and vegetables are tender.
MAKES 4 SERVINGS.

Sausage & vegetable bake

ITALY

1 pound Italian sweet sausage links
4 medium baking potatoes, peeled, quartered and cut in
   ½-inch wedges

1 large green pepper, cleaned and cut in thin strips
1 medium onion, peeled and slivered
Salt and pepper

Pour ½ inch of water into a 13 × 9 × 2-inch baking dish. Prick the sausage links in several places and cut apart. Evenly distribute the sausage links in the baking pan. Surround them with the potatoes, peppers and onions. Salt and pepper lightly. Bake at 350°F for 1 hour, basting occasionally, or until the sausages are browned and the potatoes are cooked through.
MAKES 4 SERVINGS.

Italian sausages & beans

ITALY

1 pound sweet or hot Italian sausage links
Cold water
2 tablespoons olive oil
¼ cup chopped onions
1 8-ounce can tomato sauce
2 16-ounce cans cannelli beans or kidney beans, drained
2 tablespoons chopped parsley

Prick the sausages well on all sides. Place in a large skillet and just barely cover with cold water. Cook over moderate heat, uncovered, until the water evaporates. Then cook, turning occasionally, until the sausages are browned on all

294

sides. Remove from the pan and keep warm. Add the oil and onion to the skillet and sauté until tender. Add the tomato sauce and simmer 5 minutes. Add the beans and sausages to the pan and simmer for 15 minutes, stirring occasionally to prevent sticking. Sprinkle with parsley and serve.
MAKES 4 TO 6 SERVINGS.

Sausage w/lentils

ITALY

This dish is traditionally served in Italy on New Year's Day and is said to bring good luck!

2 cups dried lentils
8 cups water
1 ounce salt pork, diced
2 large tomatoes, peeled, diced
1 garlic clove, peeled
1 bay leaf
2 teaspoons salt
Freshly ground pepper
1 cotechino sausage or 1 zampone (about 2 pounds)

Wash lentils; pick over well to remove foreign matter. Place lentils in large saucepan. Add water, salt pork, tomatoes, garlic, bay leaf, salt, and pepper. Bring to boil over moderate heat. Skim foam from surface of cooking liquid. Reduce heat to low; simmer uncovered, stirring occasionally until lentils are soft and liquid almost evaporated. (Cooking time should be 45 minutes to 1 hour.) If liquid evaporates too quickly, add a little water.
Meanwhile, prick sausage well. Place in large pot; add water to cover. Bring to boil. Reduce heat to low; simmer 1 hour, until tender. Remove from pan; cool slightly. Slice; place on platter. Remove bay leaf and garlic clove from lentils. Spoon lentils around sausage; serve.
MAKES 6 SERVINGS.

Note: Cotechino and zampone are usually available in Italian delicatessens around the New Year. If unavailable, substitute 1½ pounds Italian sausage. Prick well; cook in ½ inch water until water evaporates; brown in own fat.

Veal w/marsala wine

ITALY

1 pound thinly sliced leg of veal or 1 pound tenderized
   unbreaded veal steaks
2 eggs
½ cup flour
½ teaspoon salt
⅛ teaspoon pepper
5 tablespoons butter (divided)
1 cup thinly sliced fresh mushrooms
⅓ cup marsala wine
⅔ cup beef broth

Lightly pound the leg of veal (if used) to an even thickness. Beat the eggs well in a shallow pie plate. Place the meat in the egg mixture and let stand 30 minutes, turning occasionally. Combine the flour, salt, and pepper. Drain the veal and dredge in the flour mixture.
Heat 3 tablespoons of the butter in a heavy skillet over medium heat until hot and foamy. Add the veal and sauté, turning, until golden brown. Remove the veal from the pan and keep warm on a platter. Melt the remaining 2 tablespoons of butter in the skillet and sauté the mushrooms until tender. Add the wine and beef broth and cook 5 minutes. Pour over the veal and serve.
MAKES 4 SERVINGS.

Veal scallopini in lemon sauce

ITALY

1¼ pounds veal for scallopini
2½ tablespoons flour
Salt
White pepper
6 tablespoons clarified butter
¼ cup chicken broth
¼ cup white wine
½ of a fresh lemon, thinly sliced
1 tablespoon finely chopped parsley

Arrange the veal slices close together on a cutting board or waxed paper and lightly sprinkle with the flour, salt, and white pepper. Turn and flour and season the other side of the meat. Heat the clarified butter in a large heavy skillet. Quickly brown the veal a few pieces at a time on both sides.

Remove from the pan and keep warm. Add the chicken broth, wine, and lemon slices. Push the lemon slices down into the liquid. Reduce the heat to simmer, cover the pan and cook over low heat for 5 minutes. Place the veal on a heated platter, pour the sauce over the meat and sprinkle with the parsley.
MAKES 4 SERVINGS.

Veal chops Milanese

ITALY

4 veal sirloin chops, about 6 ounces each (1½ pounds total)
⅓ cup flour
Salt and pepper
2 eggs, beaten
⅔ cup dry bread crumbs
⅓ cup grated Parmesan cheese
¼ cup olive oil
2 tablespoons butter

Wipe veal with damp cloth. Combine flour, salt, and pepper on piece of waxed paper. Dredge chops in flour mixture; shake off excess. Dip in beaten eggs, then in mixture of bread crumbs and cheese, coating well.

Combine oil and butter in large heavy skillet; heat until foam subsides. Add chops; cook over moderate heat, turning occasionally, until golden brown. Drain on paper towels. Serve immediately. Garnish with lemon slices; serve with browned butter or tomato sauce if desired.
MAKES 4 SERVINGS.

Milanese veal rolls

ITALY

1½ pounds rump roast of veal or veal cutlet
Salt and pepper
Ground sage
4 slices prosciutto
8 thin slices mozzarella cheese
3 tablespoons olive oil
1 small onion, chopped
1 clove garlic, minced
1 16-ounce can Italian-style peeled tomatoes

½ cup white wine
Salt and pepper
8 thin strips mozzarella cheese
Parsley sprigs

Pound the meat with a mallet to ⅛ inch thickness. Sprinkle with salt, pepper, and a little sage. Cut into 8 rectangular pieces. Cut the slices of prosciutto in half. Top the veal pieces with a piece of ham and a slice of mozzarella. Roll jelly-roll fashion and tie with string.

In a large skillet, heat the oil and sauté the veal rolls until browned. Remove from the pan. Add the onion and garlic and sauté until tender. Break the tomatoes up with a fork and add to the skillet, with the white wine and salt and pepper. Mix well. Add the veal rolls and cover. Simmer 1½ hours or until tender.

Top with the mozzarella strips, cover, and melt the cheese. Serve on a bed of hot cooked spaghetti, topped with the sauce and garnished with the parsley sprigs.
MAKES 4 SERVINGS.

Veal shanks Milanese

ITALY

3 pounds veal shank, sawed into thick slices with marrow intact	1 clove garlic, peeled, minced
	2 carrots, peeled, diced
	2 stalks celery, chopped
Salt and pepper	½ cup white wine
Flour	¼ cup chicken broth
6 tablespoons butter	1 bay leaf
1 medium onion, peeled, chopped	¼ teaspoon thyme

gremolata

2 tablespoons finely chopped parsley	1 teaspoon finely grated lemon peel
1 clove garlic, peeled, finely minced	

Wipe veal with damp cloth. Season with salt and pepper. Dredge in flour; shake off excess. Heat butter in deep skillet or Dutch oven. Add veal; brown well on all sides. Remove from pan. Add onion and garlic; sauté until tender. Add vegetables, wine, chicken broth, and seasonings. Add veal shanks, standing on their sides to prevent marrow falling from bone during cooking. Bring mixture to boil. Cover pan tightly; reduce heat to simmer. Cook approximately 1 hour, until veal is tender. If mixture looks dry at any time, add a little broth.

Meanwhile, combine gremolata ingredients; mix well. Transfer veal to heated platter. Pour sauce over meat; sprinkle with gremolata. Serve with risotto or plain cooked pasta.

MAKES 4 SERVINGS.

Stuffed breast of veal

ITALY

stuffing

3 tablespoons olive oil	1 egg
1 medium onion, chopped	1/2 cup fresh bread crumbs
1/2 pound fresh spinach, stems removed, shredded	1/4 cup pine nuts
	1/8 teaspoon nutmeg
1/4 pound ground veal	Salt and pepper
1/4 pound ground pork	

veal

1 (4- to 5-pound) veal breast, boned	1 carrot, peeled, sliced
	1 stalk celery, chopped
Salt and pepper	2 bay leaves
2 tablespoons olive oil	Salt and pepper
2 cups beef broth	3 tablespoons cornstarch
1/2 cup white wine	3 tablespoons water

Make the stuffing. Heat oil in heavy skillet. Add onion; sauté until tender. Add spinach; sauté, stirring constantly, until wilted. Remove from heat; cool. Add remaining stuffing ingredients; mix well.

Have butcher cut pocket in veal breast for stuffing. Wipe meat with damp cloth; season with salt and pepper on outside and in pocket. Fill pocket with stuffing; skewer shut. Heat remaining oil in Dutch oven. Brown veal well on all sides. Add broth, wine, carrot, celery, and seasonings. Bring to boil. Cover; roast at 350°F 2½ hours, basting every ½ hour. Remove from oven. Take meat from pan; keep warm.

Combine cornstarch and water; mix well. Add to pan juices; cook over low heat until thickened. Remove skewer; carve veal breast. Serve with gravy.

MAKES 6 SERVINGS.

Savory veal patties w/shells

ITALY

8 ounces seashell macaroni
4 tablespoons butter or margarine
1/4 cup olive oil
1 medium onion, peeled, chopped
1 clove garlic, peeled, minced
4 (3 ounces each) frozen breaded veal patties
1/2 cup finely chopped parsley
grated Parmesan cheese

Cook shells in boiling salted water 9 to 12 minutes, until tender. Drain; keep warm.

Meanwhile, in large skillet heat butter and oil over moderate heat until foam subsides. Add onion and garlic; sauté 1 minute. Remove vegetables with slotted spoon; add to drained macaroni. Pour ½ remaining butter and oil over shells; stir well to combine. Keep warm.

Brown veal patties over moderate heat in remaining butter and oil. Serve shells on platter topped with veal. Pour pan drippings over veal patties. Serve Parmesan cheese in a separate bowl.

MAKES 4 SERVINGS.

Calves liver & onions

ITALY

2 medium onions, thinly sliced
2 tablespoons olive oil
1 tablespoon butter
1/4 teaspoon ground sage
2 tablespoons dry white wine or 1 tablespoon lemon juice
1 pound calves liver, sliced 1/2 inch thick
1/2 cup all-purpose flour
Salt and pepper
1/4 cup cooking oil
1 tablespoon chopped fresh parsley

Sauté the onions in the olive oil and butter until soft and lightly browned. Add the sage and wine. Cover and reduce the heat to low. Simmer while cooking the liver.

Take the calves liver slices and cut into ¾-inch-wide strips, 3 to 4 inches long. Drain well. Combine the flour, salt and pepper on a plate. Heat the oil over moderate heat in a heavy skillet.

Dredge the liver, shaking off the excess, and fry until lightly browned. Drain and keep warm while cooking the remaining liver. Place the liver in a serving dish, top with the onion mixture and sprinkle with the parsley. Serve with risotto or polenta.

MAKES 4 SERVINGS.

Calves liver—Milanese

ITALY

1 pound calves liver, unsliced if possible
¼ cup olive oil
2 tablespoons butter
½ pound sliced fresh mushrooms
½ cup slivered Genoa salami
1 medium onion, peeled and chopped
4 medium tomatoes, peeled and quartered
½ cup dry white wine
¾ teaspoon dried sweet basil, crumbled
Salt and pepper, to taste

Cut the calves liver into ¾-inch cubes (partially freeze the liver for easy slicing) and drain in a colander for 15 to 20 minutes. If a whole piece of calves liver is not available, cut the sliced liver into thin strips and drain.

In a heavy skillet heat 2 tablespoons oil and 1 tablespoon butter over moderate heat. Add the mushrooms, salami, and onions and sauté until the onions are tender. Remove with a slotted spoon and reserve.

Add the remaining butter and oil to the skillet and heat. Add the liver and sauté until lightly browned. Add the tomatoes, wine, seasoning and reserved ingredients. Stir well. Cover and simmer over low heat 10 to 15 minutes. Serve with risotto or cooked macaroni.

MAKES 4 SERVINGS.

Liver Venetian-style

ITALY

2 cups thinly sliced onions
2 tablespoons olive oil
2 tablespoons butter
½ teaspoon crumbled leaf sage

1 bay leaf
2 tablespoons dry white wine
1 pound calves' liver, sliced ½ inch thick
½ cup all-purpose flour
Salt and pepper
¼ cup cooking oil
1 tablespoon chopped fresh parsley

Sauté onions in olive oil and butter in heavy skillet until soft and lightly browned. Add sage, bay leaf, and wine. Cover; reduce heat to low. Simmer while cooking liver.

Cut liver into ¾-inch-wide strips 3 to 4 inches long; drain well. Combine flour, salt, and pepper on plate. Heat cooking oil in heavy skillet over moderate heat. Dredge liver in flour mixture; shake off excess. Fry part of liver until lightly browned. Drain; keep warm while cooking remaining liver.

Place liver in serving dish; top with onion mixture (remove bay leaf). Sprinkle with parsley. Serve with risotto or polenta.

MAKES 4 SERVINGS.

Filet mignon in wine

POLAND

4 2-inch-thick filets mignons
1 teaspoon salt
½ teaspoon black pepper, peppermill-ground
¼ cup butter
4 small onions, peeled and halved
1 cup red wine

Rub filets mignons with salt and pepper. Melt butter in heavy frying pan. Add steaks to melted butter; brown on both sides. Reduce heat to simmer; add onion halves and wine. Cover skillet tightly; simmer steaks for 30 minutes.

MAKES 4 SERVINGS.

Broiled sirloin w/mushrooms

POLAND

4 1-inch-thick sirloin steaks
½ clove garlic
1 teaspoon salt
½ teaspoon black pepper, peppermill-ground

Veal chops Milanese

½ cup butter
2 cups sliced mushrooms

Rub steaks with garlic and sprinkle with half the salt and pepper. Score fatty edges of steak. Place meat on broiling pan 3 inches from heat. Broil on one side to desired degree of doneness. Turn meat; season uncooked side with remaining salt and pepper. Return meat to broiler; cook to desired doneness.

While steak is broiling, melt butter. Add mushrooms; sauté until golden brown and tender. To serve, arrange steaks on serving platter and cover with sautéed mushrooms.

MAKES 4 SERVINGS.

Polish hunter's stew

POLAND

3 pounds stewing-beef cubes	8 whole cloves
1 quart water	2 whole bay leaves
8 peppercorns	2 teaspoons salt

1 teaspoon marjoram	3 leeks
3 pounds chicken, cubed	½ cup butter
2 medium onions	½ teaspoon white pepper
5 large carrots	3 sprigs dill
2 sprigs parsley	½ bunch parsley
4 celery stalks	

Cover beef cubes with 1 quart water; bring to a boil. Tie peppercorns, cloves, and bay leaves in a cloth bag; drop into boiling beef. Sprinkle 1 teaspoon salt and marjoram over beef; continue to simmer 2 hours in covered kettle. Add chicken cubes; continue to simmer, covered.

Peel onions and carrots; cut in rings. Chop 2 sprigs parsley, celery, and leeks. Put butter into a pan; add vegetables, 1 teaspoon salt, and pepper. Sauté vegetables over low heat until wilted.

Chop dill and remaining parsley.

Take cloth bag out of meat; discard. Remove meat from water. Add wilted vegetables to meat stock; simmer until tender. Add meat back to stock and vegetables. To serve, pour into serving

Polish hunter's stew

dish and sprinkle with chopped dill and parsley.
MAKES 8 SERVINGS.

Short ribs & cabbage

POLAND

3 tablespoons shortening
4 pounds short ribs, cut into serving pieces
1 tablespoon salt
½ teaspoon black pepper
½ cup wine vinegar
1 cup water
½ teaspoon oregano
½ teaspoon dried horseradish
2 teaspoons dry mustard
1 bay leaf
½ cup onions, sliced crosswise
1 small head of cabbage, wedged

300 Melt shortening in large Dutch oven. Brown

short ribs on all sides in melted shortening.
Sprinkle with salt and pepper. Add remaining
ingredients (except cabbage wedges). Cover
Dutch oven; simmer 1 to 1½ hours. Add cabbage wedges; cook about 20 minutes, or until
cabbage is tender.
MAKES 4 SERVINGS.

Stuffed lamb chops

POLAND

6 double-rib lamb chops
1 3-ounce can mushroom slices, drained
2 tablespoons mushroom liquid
1 teaspoon salt
¼ cup dry sherry wine
1 egg, beaten
½ cup bread crumbs
¼ teaspoon white pepper

Filet mignon in wine

Using sharp knife, make slit from bone side between rib bones into center of meat on each chop.

Drain mushrooms, reserving 2 tablespoons liquid. Mix together reserved mushroom liquid, ½ teaspoon salt, sherry, beaten egg, mushrooms, and bread crumbs. Stuff chops with mushroom mixture. Sprinkle with remaining ½ teaspoon salt and pepper. Broil lamb chops 4 to 5 inches from flame, 12 minutes on each side. Serve immediately.

MAKES 6 SERVINGS.

Polish sausage cooked in molasses

POLAND

1½ quarts cold water
⅓ cup molasses
1 teaspoon dry mustard
1½ pounds Polish sausage

Combine water, molasses, and dry mustard in large saucepan. Bring mixture to rapid boil. Add Polish sausage. Cover. Reduce heat to simmer. Cook sausage until heated thoroughly, approximately 15 minutes per pound.

While sausage is still in cooking liquid, puncture casing with a fork to reduce pressure inside casing. Remove sausage from water and slice into serving pieces. Serve immediately.

MAKES 4 SERVINGS

Kielbasa pockets

POLAND

¼ cup butter, melted
1 teaspoon prepared mustard
1 package crescent rolls
1 pound Kielbasa (Polish sausage)

Combine melted butter and prepared mustard. Stir until mustard is blended into the butter. Unwrap package of rolls; carefully separate dough into 8 pieces. Brush each piece with some of butter and mustard mixture.

Cut Polish sausage crosswise into 8 equal pieces. Place sausage on dough pieces; roll dough around sausages, being sure to start rolling on wide end of dough. Place rolled sausage on ungreased baking sheet, placing exposed seam on the bottom. Brush tops of dough with remaining butter and mustard mixture. Bake in preheated 350°F oven 15 minutes. Serve Kielbasa immediately.

MAKES 4 SERVINGS.

Polish links in sauerkraut

POLAND

Try this delicious dish for an easy lunch.

2 cups sauerkraut
1 tablespoon caraway seed
¼ cup beer
8 Polish links (hot dogs may be substituted)
8 hot dog buns, warmed
¼ cup finely chopped onions
Mustard

Combine sauerkraut, caraway seed, beer, and Polish links in large saucepan. Bring mixture to a boil, reduce heat to simmer, and cook for 30 minutes.

To serve, place Polish links in buns and top with ¼ cup sauerkraut. Garnish with chopped onions and mustard.

MAKES 4 SERVINGS.

Ham hocks in sauerkraut

POLAND

Delicious served with boiled potatoes and rye bread.

3 large ham hocks
2 cups sauerkraut
1 large onion, sliced into thin rings
1 tablespoon granulated sugar
¼ teaspoon black pepper

Cover ham hocks with water; simmer for 1 hour. Drain. Add sauerkraut, onion, sugar, and pepper to ham hocks. Return to heat; simmer 1½ to 2 hours or until meat falls off the bone.

MAKES 4 SERVINGS.

Broiled sirloin with mushrooms

Lamb in sour-cream sauce

POLAND

3 tablespoons butter
3 pounds lamb shoulder, cut into 1-inch cubes
1 tablespoon salt
½ teaspoon black pepper, peppermill-ground
2 tablespoons paprika
2 onions, sliced thin
1 cup hot water
2 cups sour cream
1 pound egg noodles
1 tablespoon poppy seeds

Melt butter in large Dutch oven. Add lamb cubes; brown evenly. Drain drippings from lamb cubes. Sprinkle cubes with salt, pepper, and paprika. Add onions and water, cover, and simmer 1 hour or until lamb is tender. Add more water during cooking period if needed. Gradually stir in sour cream; heat but do not boil.

While meat is cooking, cook noodles according to package directions; drain. Add poppy seeds to noodles; toss. To serve, arrange noodles on a serving platter. Pour lamb and sauce over noodles.

MAKES 8 SERVINGS.

Noodles & ham

POLAND

3 tablespoons butter
2 tablespoons all-purpose white flour
1 cup half-and-half cream
1 cup shredded cheddar cheese
1 tablespoon prepared horseradish
1 cup cooked peas
2 cups diced cooked ham
1½ cups cooked noodles
¼ cup dry bread crumbs

Melt 2 tablespoons butter in a saucepan. Blend flour into melted butter to form a paste. Add milk, stirring constantly until a smooth, thick sauce forms. Add cheese; stir sauce until cheese melts. Add horseradish, peas, ham, and noodles; blend well.

Pour mixture into a greased 1-quart casserole dish. Top meat and noodle mixture with bread crumbs; dot with remaining 1 tablespoon butter. Bake casserole in 350°F oven 30 minutes or until heated thoroughly.

MAKES 4 SERVINGS.

Pork chops w/cabbage & potatoes

POLAND

4 medium-size potatoes
2 teaspoons salt
1 small head cabbage
¼ cup oil
8 ¼-inch pork chops
¼ teaspoon white pepper

Peel and quarter potatoes. Place potatoes in 3-quart saucepan. Sprinkle with 1 teaspoon salt; cover with cold water. Bring potatoes and water to a boil. Reduce heat; simmer for 10 minutes. Shred cabbage; add to potatoes. Cook for 10 to 15 minutes or until cabbage and potatoes are tender. Drain.

While vegetables are cooking, fry pork chops in oil until brown and well-done. Drain. Reserve ¼ cup of oil and drippings in which pork chops were fried.

Place potatoes and cabbage in center of large serving tray. Pour reserved oil and drippings over vegetables. Sprinkle with ¼ teaspoon white pepper and 1 teaspoon salt. Arrange pork chops around outer rim of serving tray. Serve immediately.

MAKES 4 SERVINGS.

Pork steak in wine sauce

POLAND

2 tablespoons vegetable shortening
4 1-inch-thick pork steaks
½ cup finely chopped onions
1 cup sliced fresh mushrooms
1 cup red wine
1 sprig parsley
2 Dilled Tomato Cups with Peas (see Index)

Heat a brazier or large frying pan, add 2 tablespoons vegetable shortening, and stir until melted. Add pork steaks; brown on both sides. Remove meat from skillet.

Add onions and mushrooms to skillet. Continue cooking until vegetables are wilted but not browned. Re-add steaks to skillet. Pour wine over steaks. Cover tightly; simmer about 1 hour or until steaks are fork-tender. To serve, arrange steaks on serving platter. Garnish with parsley and Dilled Tomato Cups with Peas.
MAKES 4 SERVINGS.

Fried liver patties

POLAND

1 pound calves' liver
4 slices bacon
1 large onion
1 slice white bread
2 tablespoons bacon fat

Grind liver, bacon, and onion alternately in a food grinder. Grind bread after meat and onion have been ground, to clean out grinder. Mix thoroughly. Pour liver mixture into 8x4x4 loaf pan; chill for 24 hours. Unmold liver loaf and slice into ½-inch pieces.

Heat bacon fat in frying pan. Fry liver slices until browned on both sides and cooked through. Serve with Tomato-Horseradish Sauce.
MAKES 8 SERVINGS.

Tomato & horseradish sauce

1 cup tomato catsup
2 tablespoons prepared horseradish

Combine catsup and horseradish. Mix thoroughly. Chill before serving.
MAKES 1 CUP.

Calf's liver in beer

POLAND

¼ cup salad oil
1 large onion, cut into rings
1 pound calf's liver, cut into 1-inch pieces
3 tablespoons flour
1 cup stale beer
½ cup beef broth

1 teaspoon salt
½ teaspoon black pepper, peppermill-ground
1 cup sour cream

Heat oil in large skillet. Sauté onion rings until transparent and tender. Remove onion from oil. Add liver pieces to oil. Cook liver until brown and heated thoroughly, about 15 minutes. Remove liver from oil. Drain.

Measure oil remaining in skillet. If oil does not measure 3 tablespoons, add additional oil. Return oil to skillet; reheat. Add flour. Stir flour and oil to make a paste. Cook paste until golden brown. Add beer and beef broth to paste. Turn heat to high. Stir liquid and paste constantly to form gravy. Add spices. Stir in sour cream. Reheat. Fold liver and onions into gravy. Serve liver with Buttered Noodles (see Index).
MAKES 4 SERVINGS.

Marinated beef roast

SPAIN

1 teaspoon garlic juice or pressed garlic
½ teaspoon freshly ground black pepper
1 bay leaf
2 whole cloves
1½ cups dry red wine
1 4- to 6-pound rolled beef roast
3 tablespoons olive oil
2 tablespoons flour
2 tablespoons water

Combine garlic juice, pepper, bay leaf, cloves, and wine in large roaster. Add roast. Spoon mixture over roast. Cover; marinate overnight in refrigerator, occasionally basting roast with marinade.

Heat oil in large skillet. Remove roast from marinade; pat dry. Brown on all sides. Place roast back into marinade. Cover; bake in 375°F oven 2 hours. Uncover; allow roast to brown about 30 minutes. Remove roast from pan.

Place roasting pan with marinade on burner. Bring to boil. Make paste with flour and water; pour into marinade, stirring constantly. Cook until thickened. Slice roast; serve with gravy.
MAKES 8 TO 10 SERVINGS.

Beef simmered in wine
SPAIN

4 2-inch-thick filets mignons
1 teaspoon salt
½ teaspoon peppermill-ground black pepper
½ cup olive oil
1 large Spanish onion, peeled, sliced into rings
1 cup dry red wine

Rub filets mignons with salt and pepper. Heat oil in heavy frying pan. Add steaks; brown on both sides. Reduce heat to simmer. Add onions and wine. Cover skillet tightly; simmer steaks 30 minutes.

MAKES 4 SERVINGS.

Boiled beef
SPAIN

2 cups navy beans or chick-peas
¼ cup olive oil
4 chicken backs, necks, and wings
3-pound chuck roast
2 to 3 cups water
2 onions
4 carrots
4 parsnips
4 potatoes
1 tablespoon salt
2 to 3 peppercorns
1 bay leaf
Fried Garlic Croutons (see Index)

Cover beans with water. Soak overnight; drain. Heat oil in large Dutch oven. Add chicken and roast; fry until browned. Add beans. Add enough water to cover meat and beans; heat to boiling. Reduce heat to simmer; cook 2½ to 3 hours.

While meat and beans are simmering, clean and slice vegetables. Add vegetables and spices to stew. Simmer 1 to 2 hours or until meat is tender and falls apart when touched.

To serve, ladle broth into soup bowls; serve with croutons. Next serve vegetables. As an extra touch, serve the meat with Garlic Mayonnaise (see Index) or Almond and Hot Pepper Sauce (see Index).

MAKES 6 TO 8 SERVINGS.

Marinated lamb chops
SPAIN

In almost every Spanish fishing port, you will find meat and fish being grilled in the open air.

2 cups dry red wine
2 tablespoons olive oil
2 tablespoons minced garlic
½ cup chopped onion
1 bay leaf
½ teaspoon salt
Dash of pepper
8 lamb chops, 1½ to 2 inches thick

Combine all ingredients except lamb; mix well. Pour marinade over chops. Cover; refrigerate overnight. Turn meat occasionally. Remove chops from marinade; grill over hot coals until desired doneness. Turn once during cooking process.

MAKES 4 SERVINGS.

Fried potatoes w/garlic sausage
SPAIN

A delicious late-evening supper served with wine and hard rolls.

1 pound chorizos or other garlic-flavored sausage
2 tablespoons olive oil
4 large potatoes, peeled, sliced thin
1 tablespoon chopped fresh parsley

Pierce sausage with fork. Place in shallow skillet; cover with water. Bring to boil; reduce heat. Cook 5 minutes; drain. Peel skin from sausage; slice into ½-inch-thick slices.

Heat oil in large skillet until haze forms above oil. Add sausage; brown evenly on both sides. Remove sausage from skillet; reserve. Add potatoes to skillet. Spread evenly over bottom of skillet. Fry over medium heat on one side without stirring, about 12 minutes. When done on one side, use pancake turner and flip potatoes with one turn. Fry other side of potatoes until done.

To serve, garnish with fried sausage and parsley.

MAKES 4 SERVINGS.

Ham hocks in sauerkraut
Pork steak with wine sauce
(pages 308-309)

Marinated beef roast

Tripe stew

SPAIN

1 pound chorizos or garlic-flavored sausage	¼ teaspoon thyme
½ pound Italian or smoked ham	3 peppercorns
	½ teaspoon crushed oregano
½ cup olive oil	1 bay leaf
1 1-pound canned or pickled tripe	1 cup Spanish onions, chopped coarsely
½ cup all-purpose flour	4 carrots
1½ quarts beef broth	4 potatoes
½ teaspoon salt	¼ cup flour
½ teaspoon celery salt	⅓ cup cold water
½ teaspoon onion powder	3 tablespoons tomato paste

Pierce sausage with fork. Place in shallow skillet; cover with water. Bring to boil; reduce heat. Cook 5 minutes; drain. Peel skin from sausage; slice into ½-inch-thick slices.

Chop ham into small cubes. Heat ¼ cup oil in skillet. Fry sausage until brown on each side. Remove sausage from skillet. Add ham; brown. Remove from skillet; reserve meat and remaining frying oil.

Remove gelatin from tripe; reserve. Wash tripe; drain well. Coat with ½ cup flour. If using pickled tripe, bring to a boil in cold water. Drain. Rinse. Drain again before flouring. Add ¼ cup oil to frying skillet. Heat until hot. Add coated tripe; fry until well-browned. Remove tripe from skillet; place in large Dutch oven. Add reserved gelatin, or 2 cups of water, beef broth, salt, celery salt, onion powder, thyme, peppercorns, oregano, bay leaf, and onions. Bring to boil. Cover; simmer 45 minutes.

While tripe is cooking, peel and dice carrots and potatoes. Cover vegetables with water; simmer until tender but not mushy.

Drain broth from tripe. Remove bay leaf and peppercorns. Measure out 2¼ cups broth. If broth is short, add vegetable liquid to obtain 2¼ cups liquid. Reheat. Form paste with ¼ cup flour and cold water. Slowly stir flour paste into heated stock; stir until stock thickens.

Add tomato paste, sausage, ham, and vegetables to tripe. Mix just enough to blend. Pour thickened stock over tripe mixture. Reheat. Serve immediately.

MAKES 6 SERVINGS.

Spanish lamb chops

SPAIN

¼ cup olive oil
3 tablespoons lime juice
1 garlic clove, crushed
2 tablespoons grated onion
½ teaspoon salt
⅛ teaspoon pepper
4 1-inch-thick lamb chops.

Combine oil, lime juice, garlic, onion, salt, and pepper; mix well. Pour mixture over lamb chops; refrigerate. Marinate 24 hours. Grill chops over hot coals, about 4-5 minutes per side. Brush chops with marinade while cooking. Heat remaining marinade; serve with chops.

MAKES 2 TO 3 SERVINGS.

Pork rolls

SPAIN

1 pound lean pork, ground once
¼ teaspoon pepper
1 teaspoon pressed garlic or 1½ teaspoons garlic powder
1 teaspoon salt
1 egg, beaten
1 tablespoon parsley
1 cup soft bread crumbs (about)
1 cup flour
Olive oil

Mix together pork, pepper, garlic powder, salt, egg, and parsley. Add enough bread crumbs to bind mixture together. Form mixture into 6 small rolls. Dredge rolls in flour. Fry in hot olive oil until golden brown and thoroughly cooked; drain.

MAKES 6 SERVINGS.

Homemade chorizo

SPAIN

Use ⅓ cup mixture for each commercial link.

1 pound lean pork shoulder
2 tablespoons vinegar
1 teaspoon crushed oregano
1 garlic clove, mashed

½ teaspoon freshly ground black pepper
1 teaspoon salt
⅛ teaspoon cumin

Coarsely grind pork shoulder or chop in food processor. Add remaining ingredients. Mix thoroughly by hand. (Do not use mixer—meat will toughen.) Pack into crock or glass jar; refrigerate. Use within 1 week.
MAKES 4 SERVINGS.

Pork fillets

SPAIN

2 pounds pork tenderloin
1 large apple
2 tablespoons chopped almonds
1 teaspoon sugar
¼ teaspoon cinnamon
¼ teaspoon garlic powder
1 teaspoon salt
¼ teaspoon freshly ground pepper
¼ cup olive oil
½ cup dry red wine
1 cup stock

Slice tenderloin into 6 pieces. Peel, core, and finely chop apple. Combine apple, almonds, sugar, and cinnamon; mix well. Make slash in center of each tenderloin. Stuff with apple filling. Press meat together; secure with metal clamps if necessary. Combine garlic powder, salt, and pepper. Rub tenderloins with mixture.
Heat oil in deep skillet. Brown tenderloins on all sides. Add wine and stock; bring to boil. Reduce heat; simmer 1 hour, turning meat at 15-minute intervals. These are generally served with a tossed salad and mashed potatoes.
MAKES 4 SERVINGS.

Chick-peas w/garlic sausage

SPAIN

This meal must be planned ahead; you need to soak the chick-peas the day before you prepare the dish.

2 cups dried chick-peas
1 pound chorizos or other garlic-flavored sausage

2 tablespoons olive oil
1 large Spanish onion, chopped
2 garlic cloves, minced
1 large green pepper, seeded, sliced into strips
1½ cups tomato sauce
1 teaspoon salt

Wash chick-peas; place in large Dutch oven. Cover with cold water; soak overnight. Next day bring chick-peas to boil. Reduce heat to simmer; cook 2 hours or until tender, but still retain their shape.
Prick sausage with fork. Place in shallow skillet; cover with cold water. Bring water to boil. Boil sausage 5 minutes; drain. Slice into ¼-inch slices.
Heat oil. Fry sausage until brown. Remove from oil. Add onion and garlic; sauté 8 minutes. Add pepper; sauté until peppers are limp but still crisp. Add chick-peas, sausage, tomato sauce, and salt to skillet; stir. Simmer 15 minutes or until thoroughly heated.
MAKES 8 SERVINGS.

Veal & sour cream w/rice

SPAIN

2 tablespoons olive oil
1¼ pounds veal cubes
1 Spanish onion, chopped
1 green pepper, seeded, chopped
1 teaspoon garlic powder
¼ teaspoon pepper
1 teaspoon paprika
1 teaspoon salt
3 cups beef broth, boiling
1 cup long-grain rice
2 tablespoons snipped fresh parsley
1 cup sour cream

Heat oil until haze forms above pan. Reduce heat; brown veal in oil. Add vegetables and seasonings; sauté until limp. Add broth; cover and simmer 20 minutes. Add rice and parsley; stir; bring to boil; reduce heat. Cover; cook 20 minutes or until rice has absorbed all liquid. Stir in sour cream. Reheat. Serve immediately.
MAKES 4 TO 6 SERVINGS.

Veal kidneys in claret

SPAIN

6 veal kidneys
3 tablespoons butter
1 clove garlic, chopped
2 medium onions, thinly sliced
1 pound fresh mushrooms, cleaned, sliced
3 tablespoons flour
1 cup chicken stock
1 cup claret
1 tablespoon parsley
1 teaspoon salt
Dash of pepper

Split and clean kidneys; remove skin and tissue. Soak in ice-cold water ½ hour. Heat oven to 350°F. Cut kidneys into ½-inch slices. Melt butter in shallow skillet. Add garlic. Sauté kidneys in garlic butter 5 minutes. Remove kidneys; discard garlic. Add onions and mushrooms. Sauté until limp. Remove vegetables.

Add flour to skillet; stir to form paste. Add liquids; bring to boil. Add seasonings. Layer kidneys and vegetables in buttered 2½-quart casserole. Cover with sauce. Cover tightly; bake at 350°F 30 minutes or until tender. Serve over Saffron Rice (see Index).
MAKES 4 SERVINGS.

Dumpling steak

DENMARK

2 pounds chopped beefsteak
3 large onions, chopped fine
5 tomatoes, skinned and chopped
1 teaspoon salt
¼ teaspoon black pepper
Paprika to taste
1 tablespoon butter
Tomato quarters for garnish
Parsley for garnish
Onion rings for garnish

Mix the meat with the onions and tomatoes. Add the salt, pepper, and paprika. Form the ground beef into a large round dumpling and set it in a well-greased casserole. Dot the top of the dumpling with specks of butter. Bake it at 400°F for 1 hour.

Decorate the finished dumpling with tomato quarters, parsley, and onion rings.
MAKES 6 TO 8 SERVINGS.

Beef pie

DENMARK

2 layers pastry dough
1 large onion
1 can mushrooms
4 tablespoons butter
2 tablespoons flour
2 cups beef stock
Salt and pepper to taste
6 to 8 roast-beef slices

Line a deep pie pan or baking dish with pastry. Set it aside.

Peel and slice the onion. Drain the mushrooms, reserving the liquid. In butter, sauté the onions with the drained mushrooms; remove them from the butter. Add the flour to the butter, blend it until it is smooth. Gradually add the beef stock and the liquid from the mushrooms. Season with salt and pepper.

Put a slice of roast beef on the pastry dough in the baking dish. Pour a little sauce over this. Cover it with mushrooms and onions; continue layering in this way until all ingredients are used. Cover it with another layer of pastry dough. Pierce the top with a fork. Bake it in a hot oven (400°F) for about 20 minutes or until the crust is evenly browned. Serve at once.
MAKES 6 SERVINGS.

Beef forcemeat

DENMARK

Forcemeat is really only meat, fish, or poultry ground several times. It is combined with eggs, milk, and bread crumbs or flour, seasoned to taste, and is used as meatballs, croquettes, or in any dish that calls for ground protein as its mainstay.

1 pound ground beef
¼ pound fat or suet
½ cup flour

2 teaspoons salt
½ teaspoon pepper
1 medium onion, grated
1 egg
2 cups milk

Grind the beef and fat together several times. Add the flour, salt, pepper, onion, and egg; mix them thoroughly. Add the milk gradually, being sure it is absorbed after each addition.

For a meatloaf, shape the forcemeat into a greased loaf pan. Bake it at 400°F for 1 hour.
MAKES 6 SERVINGS.

Ham in madeira wine

DENMARK

1 smoked ham (10-12 pounds)
4 bay leaves
8 peppercorns
8 whole cloves
1 bottle Madeira wine

Soak the ham in cold water overnight. In a large pot cover the drained ham with boiling water. Add the bay leaves, peppercorns, and cloves. Cook them slowly for 2½ hours. Drain off the liquid.

Pour the bottle of wine over the ham. Simmer it for at least ½ hour more, basting if necessary. Slice and serve it. If a wine sauce is desired with the sliced ham, slightly thicken 2 cups of the wine liquid.
MAKES 12 OR MORE SERVINGS.

Ham rolls w/horseradish

DENMARK

Ham rolls are attractive served as the main dish for a cold supper and, of course, are a fine addition to any smorgasbord.

½ cup heavy cream
1 teaspoon sugar
2 tablespoons horseradish
½ cup cooked macaroni
6 to 8 slices cooked ham

Whip the cream until thick. Add the sugar and horseradish, and fold in the macaroni. Spread some of the mixture on the ham slices and roll up the ham. Garnish with shredded cheese or parsley.
MAKES 6 TO 8 HAM ROLLS.

Pork chops w/apples

DENMARK

Salt
4 pork chops (1-1¼ pounds)
Black pepper
2 tablespoons butter
2 onions
2 apples
Parsley

Salt the pork chops and spice them with pepper. Heat the butter in a deep skillet and brown the meat. Add enough water so that the meat does not stick to the skillet. Cook the meat over a low heat for at least 60 minutes.

Peel the onions and cut them into rings. Core and peel the apples and cut each into eighths. Add the onions and apples 10 minutes before the end of the cooking period. Cook the ingredients until all are golden brown. Remove the meat and put it on a serving platter. Pour the stock, onions, and apples over the meat; garnish with parsley.
MAKES 4 SERVINGS.

Stuffed pork tenderloin

DENMARK

1 pork tenderloin
12 prunes, pitted
4 tablespoons butter
1 teaspoon salt
Dash of freshly ground black pepper
½ cup water

With a sharp knife cut a slit in the meat deep enough to insert the prunes. After inserting the prunes, close the opening with skewers or wrap it with twine.

Melt the butter in a skillet and brown the meat on all sides. Sprinkle it with salt and pepper. Add the water; cover and cook slowly for 2 hours

Boiled beef

or until the meat is tender. Add water if needed. Slice the meat and serve it. Add flour to the juice in the pan and thicken it slightly if gravy is desired.

MAKES 6 SERVINGS.

Hot ham rolls w/asparagus

DENMARK

18 asparagus spears (white or green)
6 slices cooked ham
1 cup medium white sauce
Parsley for garnish

Put 3 asparagus spears on each ham slice, and roll them up. Arrange the ham rolls in a greased baking dish. Pour your favorite white sauce over the rolls. Bake them in a slow oven (350°F) for 30 minutes. Garnish the ham rolls with parsley, and serve.

MAKES 6 SERVINGS.

Meatballs I

DENMARK

1 pound finely ground veal
½ pound finely ground pork
1 small onion, grated

4 tablespoons flour
1 teaspoon salt
⅛ teaspoon pepper
1 egg, beaten
1¼ cups milk
Butter for browning

Be sure the veal and pork are thoroughly ground. Mix well the meat, onion, flour, salt, and pepper. Add the egg and milk a little at a time. Mix thoroughly until all ingredients are absorbed into the meat.

Melt a little butter in a skillet. Drop the meat mixture by tablespoons into hot fat, forming meatballs. Cook for about 10 minutes, until browned on all sides.

MAKES 6 OR MORE SERVINGS.

Meatballs II

DENMARK

1 pound veal
1 pound pork
1 tablespoon salt
½ teaspoon white pepper
¼ cup flour
4 eggs
½ cup light cream
1 cup milk

315

1 medium onion, chopped
1 tablespoon butter

Grind the veal and pork together several times. Put them in a large bowl. With an electric beater at low speed, add the salt, pepper, and flour. Add the eggs 1 at a time, still at low speed. Add the cream and milk. Brown the onion in butter for just 5 minutes. Add this mixture to the meat. The meat should be mixed enough to be handled easily.

Shape the meat into oval cakes and brown them on both sides. Cook them over slow heat for 15 minutes. Because pork is included, these meatballs must be thoroughly cooked.

MAKES 6 OR MORE SERVINGS.

Meat patties

DENMARK

½ pound boneless veal
½ pound boneless pork
1 medium onion, grated
3 tablespoons flour
1½ cups club soda
1 egg, beaten
1 teaspoon salt
¼ teaspoon pepper
6 tablespoons butter or vegetable oil

Have the butcher grind the meats together twice. Mix the onion with the meat. Add the flour to the ground meat, and mix well—an electric mixer can be used. Gradually add the club soda, beating until the meat is light. Last, add the egg, salt, and pepper. Cover the bowl and refrigerate it for at least 1 hour, so that the meat can be easily handled.

Shape the meat into 4-inch rectangles 1 inch thick. Melt the butter in a large skillet and add the meat patties a few at a time. Cook each batch at least 6 to 8 minutes per side. Since there is pork in the mixture, the meat must be cooked all the way through. The finished patties will be brown on the outside with no tinge of pink in the center.

MAKES 8 TO 10 PATTIES.

Meatloaf in sour-cream pastry

FINLAND

sour-cream pastry dough

2¼ cups flour
1 teaspoon salt
12 tablespoons chilled butter
1 egg
½ cup sour cream

filling

4 tablespoons butter
¼ pound fresh mushrooms, chopped
3 pounds ground meat (beef, veal, or pork)
1 medium onion, chopped
¼ cup chopped parsley
1 cup grated cheddar or Swiss cheese

½ cup milk

1 egg plus 2 tablespoons milk for use on dough

Sift the flour and salt together into a large bowl. With two knives cut in the butter until the mixture is like coarse meal. In a separate bowl mix the egg and sour cream. Add this to the flour mixture until the dough forms a soft, pliable ball. Wrap the dough in wax paper and refrigerate for 1 hour. Next, divide the dough and roll out each half to a rectangle 6 by 14 inches. Save any scraps of dough. Butter flat cookie sheet or jelly-roll pan. Put one sheet of the pastry onto the pan.

Melt butter in a 12-inch skillet. Add the mushrooms and cook them for 6 to 8 minutes, until lightly colored. Add the meat and continue to cook until the meat loses all trace of pink color. Combine the mushrooms, cooked meat, onion, parsley, cheese, and milk in a large mixing bowl. Form the meat mixture into a ball and put it in the center of the dough. With your hands, very gently pat the meat into a loaf shape. Cover this with the second piece of pastry dough and seal the edges with a fork. Moisten the dough with a pastry brush dipped in the egg and milk. Prick holes in the top of the loaf to allow steam to escape.

Roll out the scraps of dough and cut them into strips. Crisscross these over the top of the loaf to

Pork chops with apples

Dumpling steak

form a design. Again brush it with the egg—milk mixture. Bake the loaf at 375°F for 45 minutes, when the pastry will be golden brown. MAKES 6 TO 8 SERVINGS.

Liver pudding

FINLAND

1 cup white rice

3 tablespoons butter

1 medium onion, finely chopped

1½ pounds calf or beef liver

2 cups milk

2 eggs

4 slices cooked, crumbled bacon

½ cup raisins

3 tablespoons dark corn syrup

2 teaspoons salt

¼ teaspoon ground pepper

¼ teaspoon ground marjoram

Cook the rice in 4 quarts of boiling salted water *317*

Stir-fried beef and mushrooms (pg. 327)

for 12 minutes. Drain and set it aside.

In a heavy skillet melt 2 tablespoons of the butter. Add the onion and cook only until transparent. Set aside in the skillet. Put the raw liver through a grinder until it is finely ground.

Combine the rice, milk, and lightly beaten eggs in a large mixing bowl. Add the cooked onions, bacon, raisins, and corn syrup. Season this with salt, pepper, and marjoram. Last, stir in the ground liver.

Generously grease a 2-quart casserole with the remaining butter. Pour in the liver and rice mixture. Bake the pudding in a preheated oven at 350°F for 1½ hours or until a knife comes out clean from the center. Serve the pudding hot with lingonberries or cranberry sauce.
MAKES 6 TO 8 SERVINGS.

Pan-fried lamb slices

ICELAND

1 leg of lamb
2 or 3 medium onions
Butter or vegetable shortening
Salt and pepper

Cut the lamb into ½-inch slices. Peel and slice the onions and brown them in butter. Drain the onions and keep them warm. Fry the meat slices

318

in the same shortening; season with salt and pepper.

To serve, arrange the meat on a platter. Cover the slices with the drained onions and serve them with mashed potatoes and a salad.
MAKES 10 SERVINGS.

Three-meat stew

NORWAY

1½ cups raw beef, diced
½ pound fresh pork, diced
1½ cups cooked corned beef, diced
4 cups raw potatoes, cut in small pieces
1 onion, diced
About 2 cups beef stock
1 teaspoon salt
½ teaspoon freshly ground pepper

Slowly cook the raw beef and pork for ½ hour with enough stock to cover. Add the rest of the ingredients and let them simmer for at least another hour. When the meat is tender, the stew is ready to serve.
MAKES 4 OR MORE SERVINGS.

Skewered lamb

Lamb w/cabbage

NORWAY

2 pounds lamb or mutton
1 tablespoon butter
1 tablespoon flour
¼ cup water
1 head cabbage
1 teaspoon salt
¼ teaspoon ground pepper

Cut the lamb or mutton into bite-size pieces. On the bottom of a 3-quart pot melt the butter. Mix the flour with the water and add this to the melted butter. Mix well to form a paste.

Wash and drain the cabbage and cut it into small pieces. Put a layer of cabbage on top of the paste in the pot. Next add a layer of the lamb. Season each layer with salt and pepper and continue layering the cabbage and meat, with the cabbage on top. Pour in just enough water to cover the meat and cabbage. Cook them over a slow fire until the meat is tender, at least 1 hour. Do not stir this; serve it in the layers.

MAKES 6 SERVINGS.

Ham & vegetable stew

NORWAY

4 or 5 raw carrots, cubed
4 white turnips, cubed
1 pound fresh peas
Salt
1 slice cooked ham or 2 cups diced leftover ham
1 tablespoon flour
1 tablespoon butter
Chopped parsley for garnish

Cook the carrots and turnips with the peas in salted water to cover. Add the diced ham to the vegetables and the water in which they have been cooked, reserving ¼ cup of the vegetable water.

Mix the flour and butter with the reserved vegetable water. Add this mixture to thicken the stew slightly. Before serving, garnish with the chopped parsley.

MAKES 4 TO 6 SERVINGS.

Veal scallops in sour cream

NORWAY

4 veal scallops, no more than ½ inch thick
3 tablespoons butter
3 tablespoons vegetable oil
¼ cup finely chopped onion
1 cup sour cream
½ cup shredded Norwegian goat cheese
Salt to taste
Fresh ground pepper to taste

Pound the scallops to ¼ inch thick. Set them aside.

Melt 1 tablespoon of the butter and 1 tablespoon of the oil in a 12-inch skillet. Add the onion and cook it for 3 to 5 minutes; do not brown it. Take the onion from the skillet and set it aside. Add the remaining butter and oil and fry the veal over moderate heat until golden brown, about 5 minutes per side. Keep the scallops warm in a low oven while you prepare the sauce.

Pour off most of the fat left in the skillet. Add the onions and cook again for 2 to 5 minutes. On a low burner, slowly stir in the sour cream and cheese. Continue stirring until the sauce is smooth. Add seasonings to taste. Return the veal to the sauce. Baste the meat and let it simmer for 2 minutes. Serve immediately.

MAKES 4 SERVINGS.

Beef roll

SWEDEN

Leftover beef roll is just as tasty served cold the next day.

3 pounds top round steak, 1½ inches thick
1 pound ground veal
1 cup chopped onions
½ cup bread crumbs
1 egg
1 cup chili sauce
Flour seasoned with salt and pepper

Pound the steak to ½ inch thick. In a bowl mix the rest of the ingredients in the order given, except the seasoned flour. Spread the veal filling over the round-steak slices and roll up the meat. Tie each roll with a string. Cover the outside of

319

the rolls with seasoned flour.

Brown the rolls at 450°F for 10 to 15 minutes. Reduce the heat to 350°F and roast them for 1½ hours. Slice and serve the rolls.

MAKES 6 OR MORE SERVINGS.

Swedish meatballs

SWEDEN

1 medium onion, finely chopped
3 tablespoons butter
1 cup mashed potatoes
3 tablespoons bread crumbs
1 pound lean ground beef
⅓ cup heavy cream
1 teaspoon salt
1 egg
1 tablespoon chopped parsley (optional)
2 tablespoons vegetable oil

sauce
Fat from the skillet
1 tablespoon flour
¾ cup light or heavy cream

Cook the onion in 1 tablespoon of the butter until the onion is soft but not brown. In a large bowl combine the onion, mashed potatoes, bread crumbs, meat, ⅓ cup heavy cream, salt, egg, and parsley. Mix them with a wooden spoon until well-blended. Shape the mixture into small balls about 1 inch in diameter. Put on a flat tray and chill for at least 1 hour before cooking.

Melt the remaining butter and the oil in a 12-inch skillet. Fry the meatballs on all sides until they are done through, about 8 to 10 minutes. Add more butter and oil if needed. Transfer the finished meatballs to casserole or baking dish and keep them warm.

To make the sauce, remove the fat from the skillet. Stir in the flour and cream. Stir constantly as the sauce comes to a boil and becomes thick and smooth. Pour it over the meatballs. Serve the meatballs and sauce with broad noodles or potatoes.

MAKES ABOUT 48 MEATBALLS.

Dill meat

SWEDEN

2 to 2½ pounds lamb meat (breast or shoulder)	1 bunch dill
	½ bunch parsley
6 cups water	1 piece of lemon rind
1 teaspoon salt	1 onion
½ bay leaf	3 whole cloves
3 peppercorns	2 or 3 carrots, peeled

sauce

1 cup meat stock (from cooked meat)	2 teaspoons sugar
	1 bunch dill
3 tablespoons butter	1 tablespoon lemon juice
3 tablespoons flour	1 egg yolk

Put the meat in a pot with the water, salt, bay leaf, peppercorns, dill, parsley, and lemon rind. Peel the onion and dot it with cloves. Add this to the mixture. Cook it for 2 hours or until the meat is tender.

Forty-five minutes before the end of the cooking, add the carrots. When the meat is tender, remove the meat and carrots from the broth. Cut the meat in strips and the carrots in 2-inch pieces. Serve the meat and carrots together, well-heated, with the accompanying sauce.

To make the sauce, put the meat stock through a sieve. Melt the butter in a small pan. Stir in the flour; mix well. Stirring constantly, cook for 7 minutes. Add the sugar, dill, and lemon juice to the sauce. Remove the pot from the stove. Stir in a beaten egg yolk. Serve this sauce separately from the meat.

MAKES 6 TO 8 SERVINGS.

Turkish meatloaf

MIDDLE EAST

Skin from 3 or 4 large eggplants	2 minced garlic cloves
	2 beaten eggs
4 tablespoons olive oil	½ cup grated Kafaloteri or Parmesan cheese
3 pounds lean lamb or beef, ground twice	
	3 tablespoons olive oil
2 grated onions	½ cup tomato sauce
2 cups seasoned croutons, soaked in milk and squeezed dry	1½ teaspoons salt
	½ teaspoon freshly ground black pepper
½ cup minced parsley	Melted butter to brush over top of mold
½ cup minced green pepper	

Line a buttered bundt pan with the skins of eggplant, which have been tenderized in fat in a skillet for 3 minutes. (Save the scooped out pulp of the eggplants for salad.) Reserve some skins to cover the meat mixture.

Combine and mix the remaining ingredients thoroughly. Press this mixture into the lined mold and cover with remaining skins. Brush generously with melted butter.

Place in a large pan of hot water. Bake for 1 hour at 350°F. Let stand for 5 to 10 minutes and then turn out onto a platter. You may add your favorite white sauce or tomato sauce to cover but it is not really needed. The dish is delicious as is.
MAKES 8 TO 10 SERVINGS.

Stuffed melon

MIDDLE EAST

1 melon (honeydew, Persian, or cantaloupe)
½ pound ground lamb or beef
1 medium-size onion, chopped
2 tablespoons margarine
1 cup cooked rice
⅓ cup currants
⅓ cup pignolias (pine nuts)
⅓ cup sweet white wine or water

Cut off enough of the top of the melon to remove all seeds and some of the flesh. Leave a layer of flesh in the fruit.

Lightly sauté the meat and onion in the margarine. Add rice, currants, and pine nuts, as well as the scooped out melon. Stir until all is well-blended. Fill the melon with the well-blended mixture and put on a baking pan. Pour the white wine into the melon. Bake at 350°F for 50 minutes to 1 hour, adding liquid if needed. Cut into servings by slicing melon from top to bottom.
MAKES 4 SERVINGS.

Okra-lamb casserole

MIDDLE EAST

This can be prepared in the morning and baked before serving.

2 large onions, minced
1 minced garlic clove
1 tablespoon minced parsley
6 tablespoons butter
2 pounds ground lean lamb (or beef)
½ teaspoon salt
Healthy dash of pepper
1 teaspoon oregano (fresh preferred) or
1 tablespoon minced fresh mint
½ teaspoon ground coriander (optional)
3 tablespoons tomato paste
1 16-ounce package frozen okra, defrosted and drained
4 tablespoons butter
½ cup bread crumbs
2 well-beaten eggs
4 tablespoons burnt butter
3 tablespoons lemon juice
Butter to dot the top

Sauté onions, garlic, and parsley in butter. Add and brown the meat with salt, pepper, oregano (or mint), and coriander. Spoon in tomato paste and simmer until the juices are absorbed. Set aside. Sauté okra in butter until vegetable begins to soften. Then set aside.

Add bread crumbs and eggs to the meat. Put in a well-greased casserole and top with burnt butter. Then arrange the okra on top of the meat. Pour lemon juice over all and dot with butter. Cover. Before serving, bake at 350°F for 45 minutes. Serve from the casserole with your favorite pilaf.
MAKES 6 TO 8 SERVINGS.

Lamb w/orange & barley

MIDDLE EAST

This easy entrée can be prepared in the morning and put in the oven 1¾ hours before serving. It takes a minimum of preparation and is delicious.
2 tablespoons oil
2 medium onions, chopped
2 cups diced cooked lamb
1 cup pearl barley
3 unpeeled oranges sliced in thin rounds and seeded
1 tablespoon lemon juice
3 cups beef broth

In oil, lightly brown the onions with the diced, cooked lamb. Place in a casserole dish with barley, oranges, lemon juice, and 1 cup beef broth. Cover and place in 300°F oven for 20 minutes. Add 1 more cup beef broth and cover again. Bake for 30 minutes more. Add last cup of beef broth and bake for 45 minutes more. Remove

from oven and allow to stand covered for 10 minutes and then serve.
MAKES 4 SERVINGS.

Cauliflower w/lamb cubes

MIDDLE EAST

½ pound lamb cut into 1-inch cubes
4 tablespoons margarine
1 4-ounce can tomato purée
1 cup water
2 packages frozen cauliflower, thawed
Salt and pepper to taste

Brown lamb cubes in margarine. Add tomato purée and water and stir well over low heat for 5 minutes. Add the drained, thawed cauliflower, uncooked, to the meat. Salt and pepper to taste and cook for 5 more minutes or until cauliflower is tender. Serve at once.
MAKES 4 SERVINGS.

Lamb w/lemons

MIDDLE EAST

¼ cup olive oil
⅛ teaspoon ground ginger
¼ teaspoon saffron (optional)
½ teaspoon salt
2 pounds boneless lamb, cut into 1½-inch cubes
3 cups water
1½ cups chopped onions
1 finely minced garlic clove
6 crushed coriander seeds
2 quartered and seeded lemons
16 green olives

Use a large skillet and blend oil, ginger, saffron, and salt. When fat is hot, add lamb cubes stirring until meat is browned. Add water, onions, garlic, coriander, and lemons. Meat should be covered so add more water if necessary. Bring all to a boil and then reduce heat and simmer for 1 hour until meat is tender.
Remove meat and continue cooking liquid until it is only 3 cups. Then return meat to skillet. Add olives and heat for 5 minutes. Add extra salt if desired. Serve with Bulgur or rice.
MAKES 4 SERVINGS.

Lamb & spinach stew

MIDDLE EAST

1 chopped onion
1 chopped garlic clove
1 tablespoon butter
2 cups diced lamb
½ teaspoon allspice
Salt and pepper to taste
2 cups water
1 pound fresh spinach, washed and drained
Lemon slices for garnish

In a large skillet, sauté onions and garlic in butter until onions are transparent. Add the diced lamb, seasonings, and water and simmer until lamb is tender, about 45 minutes. Last, add the spinach and simmer for 20 minutes more. Transfer stew to serving platter and garnish with lemon slices.
MAKES 4 SERVINGS.

Lamb kebabs

MIDDLE EAST

1½ pounds chopped lamb
1 finely chopped onion
1 tablespoon chopped parsley
1 teaspoon salt
¼ teaspoon pepper
1 quartered onion
1 quartered tomato
¼ cup oil to brush kebabs

Grind the meat and onion twice. To this, add parsley, salt, and pepper. Form into long, thin fingers and alternate the meat fingers, onion quarters, and tomato quarters on skewers. Brush or drip oil over the kebabs and grill, preferably on an open fire. Remove from skewers and serve on a bed of rice.
MAKES 4 TO 6 SERVINGS.

Skewered lamb

MIDDLE EAST

¼ cup minced onion
1 minced garlic clove
3 tablespoons olive oil

Ginger beef

3 tablespoons lemon juice
1 teaspoon salt
¼ teaspoon pepper
½ teaspoon crumbled dried oregano
1½ pounds leg of lamb or lamb shoulder meat, cut into
  2-inch cubes
16 small boiling onions, peeled
15 mushrooms, cleaned and stems removed
2 red peppers, cut into chunks

Combine the onion, garlic, olive oil, lemon juice, salt, pepper, and oregano in a glass bowl or casserole. Add the lamb cubes and stir well. Cover and marinate for 3 to 4 hours (or longer in the refrigerator), stirring occasionally.

Parboil the onions in salted water for 10 minutes. Drain and cool. Drain the lamb, reserving the marinade. Skewer the vegetables and lamb alternately (lamb cube, onion, mushroom, and then a pepper chunk; repeat). Cook over charcoal or in the broiler about 15 minutes, brushing frequently with the marinade. Serve with rice.
MAKES 4 SERVINGS.

Variation: Substitute cherry tomatoes and green peppers for the red peppers. Skewer the onions and meat alternately. Skewer the vegetables separately, and brush them with marinade. Tomatoes can be grilled only a short time or they will fall off the skewer before the meat is done. Start the meat first and add the skewered vegetables 5 minutes before the meat is finished.

Marinated steak slices

323

Chinese fondue

Lamb stew

MIDDLE EAST

2 pounds cubed boneless lamb
4 tablespoons butter
1 cup minced onions
2 finely minced garlic cloves
½ teaspoon salt
¼ teaspoon pepper
½ teaspoon nutmeg
½ teaspoon allspice
½ teaspoon cumin
½ teaspoon paprika
½ cup white wine
1 8-ounce can tomato sauce
¼ cup minced parsley
1 pound small pearl onions
½ cup white wine

Sauté lamb cubes in butter with onions and garlic cloves until meat is browned on all sides. Add salt, pepper, and other seasonings. Stir wine, tomato sauce, and parsley into the mixture. Add pearl onions and pour the other ½ cup of white wine over all. Cover and simmer for 45 minutes or until lamb is tender. If needed, add extra water during this time.

This stew is good if served over hot rice but is best over Eggplant Base for Stew (see Index).
MAKES 6 TO 8 SERVINGS.

Veal w/kadota figs

MIDDLE EAST

8 4-ounce slices veal
6 tablespoons flour
¼ pound butter
3 cups chicken stock
¼ cup sweet sherry
1 cup chopped mushrooms
¼ cup chopped parsley, fresh preferred
1 tablespoon tomato paste
1 tablespoon lemon juice
½ cup sour cream
1 small can Kadota figs

Prepare veal by dredging each slice on both sides in the flour. Melt butter in a skillet and fry veal slices until golden-brown on both sides. Place the veal slices in a casserole and reserve the juices in the pan.

To those drippings, add chicken stock and remaining flour from the dredging. Stir until smooth and thickened. Add remaining ingredients except for the figs and keep stirring. When all have been added, pour the sauce over the veal and bake at 350°F for 1 hour.

When ready to serve, drain figs and rinse under cold water. Arrange them on top of the casserole.
MAKES 4 TO 6 SERVINGS.

2 cloves garlic, finely chopped
4 green peppers, cut into bite-size pieces
1 cup sliced celery
1½ cups beef bouillon
2 tablespoons cornstarch
¼ cup cold water
1 tablespoon soy sauce
Cooked rice

Cut steak into thin slices and then into 2-inch pieces. To make slicing easier, partially freeze the meat. Heat oil in large skillet. Add salt and pepper. Cook meat over medium to high heat until brown, stirring frequently. Add scallion and garlic. Add green peppers and celery and stir. Add bouillon, cover and cook until vegetables are tender but still crisp. Do not overcook. Meanwhile, combine cornstarch and water. Blend in soy sauce until it makes a smooth paste.

Egyptian veal

MIDDLE EAST

4 tablespoons margarine
½ teaspoon salt
Few grains saffron
2 tablespoons lemon juice
2 pounds boned veal
1 cup water
1 small chili pepper

Cream margarine, salt, and saffron until smooth. Pour lemon juice over the meat slowly and then spread the meat with the creamed mixture. Put the meat in a heavy saucepan or deep skillet. Add water and chili pepper and bring to a boil. Then simmer the meat for 1 hour, basting every 15 minutes or so. When ready to serve, the meat will be fork tender.
MAKES 4 TO 6 SERVINGS.

Oriental pepper steak

CHINA

1 pound round steak
¼ cup oil
½ teaspoon salt
Pepper to taste
½ cup chopped scallion

Beef slices Peking

Slowly add to meat mixture, stirring constantly until liquid is thickened. Serve with rice.
MAKES 4 SERVINGS.

Tomato beef

CHINA

2 tablespoons cornstarch
1 tablespoon soy sauce
1 tablespoon brandy
½ pound flank steak, sliced ⅛ inch thick
2 tablespoons peanut oil
¼ cup chopped onion
¼ cup sliced celery (sliced diagonally)
1 small green pepper, cut into 1-inch squares
2 tomatoes, each cut into 8 sections
¼ cup sliced water chestnuts
1 cup chicken broth, heated
1½ teaspoons catsup
½ (scant) teaspoon salt
1 teaspoon sugar
1 tablespoon cornstarch mixed
   with about 3 tablespoons
   cold water

Mix together cornstarch, soy sauce, and brandy. Place sliced flank steak in mixture and marinate about 15 minutes. Heat oil in wok or pan. Add steak and stir-fry until golden brown. Remove from pan and set aside.

Sauté onion and celery for about 20 seconds, then add green pepper, tomatoes, and water chestnuts. Toss several times. Add broth, cover and let steam for 1 minute. Remove cover, add beef, and mix well. Cover and steam for about 20 seconds. Add catsup, salt, and sugar; mix well.

Thicken with cornstarch mixture. Don't let the sauce get too thick.
MAKES 2 TO 3 SERVINGS.

Szechwan spiced beef

CHINA

2 tablespoons peanut oil
1 pound boneless stewing beef, cut into 1-inch cubes
2 tablespoons dry sherry

Meat platter szechwan

3 tablespoons soy sauce
1 teaspoon sugar
3 scallions, cut into 1-inch pieces
1 cup cold water
¼ teaspoon star anise

Heat oil in skillet over high heat. Add beef; cook, turning constantly, until browned on all sides. Add sherry, soy sauce, and sugar; mix well. Cook 2 minutes. Stir in scallions. Add water; bring to boil. Reduce heat to medium; cover. Cook 15 minutes; stir occasionally.
Stir in star anise. Reduce heat to low; cook 20 minutes.
MAKES 3 SERVINGS.

Stir-fried beef & mushrooms

CHINA

½ pound dried Chinese mushrooms
3 pounds lean steak, cut into thin strips
¼ cup flour
1 tablespoon sugar
½ cup sherry
½ cup soy sauce
¾ cup oil, divided
1 2-inch slice fresh gingerroot, minced
1 cup onions, chopped
2 cups beef bouillon
Salt to taste

Soak the mushrooms in water for 30 minutes. Drain well and set aside. Cut the steak into strips. In a bowl combine flour, sugar, sherry, and soy sauce. Add the beef and marinate for 30 minutes, stirring frequently.
Heat ½ cup of the oil in a wok. Stir-fry the gingerroot for 1 minute. Add the beef with the marinade and stir-fry until the beef changes color. Remove the beef from the wok. Add the remaining oil to wok. Add the onions and stir-fry until almost tender. Add mushrooms and stir-fry until soft. Place the beef in the wok and stir-fry for about 2 minutes. Add the bouillon, bring to a boil and reduce heat. Add salt, cover and cook for 2 minutes.
MAKES 6 TO 8 SERVINGS.

Beef oriental

CHINA

½ pound lean, tender beef, cut into strips
2 tablespoons peanut oil
1 clove garlic, chopped
1 onion, chopped
2 cups frozen green beans, French-style
1 cup celery, sliced
1 tablespoon cornstarch
1 tablespoon soy sauce
¾ cup liquid (1 tablespoon sherry, juice from canned mushrooms and water, or 1 tablespoon sherry and beef bouillon)
1 can sliced mushrooms, or 1 cup fresh mushrooms, sliced
Strips of pimiento for garnish
Cooked rice

Brown beef in oil, to which garlic is added. Add onion, beans, and celery. Cook 4 to 6 minutes, stirring frequently. Combine cornstarch and soy sauce with liquid. Add to meat mixture with mushrooms. Stir, cooking until liquid is glossy. Cover and cook until beans are tender but crisp. Garnish with pimiento and serve with rice.
MAKES 4 SERVINGS.

Beef w/snow peas

CHINA

½ pound beef, thinly sliced

marinade

1 teaspoon cornstarch	¼ teaspoon sugar
1 teaspoon soy sauce	¼ teaspoon oil
2 teaspoons sherry	

½ pound snow peas, with strings removed	½ teaspoon sugar
2 teaspoons cornstarch mixed with 2 teaspoons cold water	2 tablespoons oil, divided
	¼ teaspoon salt
⅛ teaspoon freshly ground black pepper	1 teaspoon grated fresh gingerroot
	½ cup chicken stock

Slice beef and set aside. Mix marinade ingredients and marinate beef while preparing rest of ingredients.
String snow peas. Mix together cornstarch and water. Add pepper and sugar. Heat skillet or wok to medium-high. Add 1 tablespoon oil, salt, and gingerroot. Add snow peas, stir, and add the

chicken stock. Cover for 10 seconds. Uncover, stir, and remove from pan.

Reheat pan and add remaining 1 tablespoon oil. When pan is hot, add beef and stir-fry only about 45 seconds, until beef is almost cooked. Then add snow peas and cornstarch mixture. Stir until sauce is thickened.

MAKES 2 TO 3 SERVINGS.

Ginger beef

CHINA

1 cup onions, minced
2 cloves of garlic, pressed
2 teaspoons turmeric
2 teaspoons ginger
1 teaspoon chili powder
1 teaspoon salt
3 pounds of lean beef, cut into cubes
8 fresh tomatoes, peeled and cut into large pieces
½ cup peanut oil
4 cups beef bouillon
Boiled rice
Strips of red sweet pepper for garnish

Combine onions, garlic, turmeric, ginger, chili powder, and salt in bowl. Mix well. Prepare the beef and place in shallow dish. Sprinkle with the onion-garlic mixture and refrigerate for 3 hours, stirring occasionally.

Prepare tomatoes. In large skillet heat oil. Stir-fry the beef until browned on all sides. Place beef in casserole and add skillet drippings, tomatoes, and bouillon. Bake, covered, in a 325°F oven for about 2 hours or until the beef is tender. Serve with boiled rice and garnish with strips of red sweet pepper.

MAKES 6 TO 8 SERVINGS.

Oriental beef w/vegetables

CHINA

½ pound thinly sliced beef
½ cup thinly sliced carrots, cut at an angle
2 cloves garlic, crushed
2 tablespoons soy sauce
3 tablespoons sherry
2 tablespoons oil

4 scallions, cut into ½-inch pieces
½ cup thinly sliced celery, cut at an angle
½ teaspoon powdered mustard
1 pound fresh spinach, chopped

Marinate beef, carrots, and garlic in a mixture of soy sauce and sherry, for at least 6 hours. Heat oil in wok. Remove meat from marinade and stir-fry for 1 minute. Add remaining ingredients and stir-fry only until vegetables are very bright in color, approximately 2 to 3 minutes. Serve with rice, if desired.

MAKES 3 TO 4 SERVINGS.

Beef w/spinach

CHINA

½ pound beef, thinly sliced

marinade

2 tablespoons rice wine or sherry
½ teaspoon salt
Freshly ground black pepper to taste
1 egg white

1 tablespoon chopped leek (onion may be substituted)
½ teaspoon grated gingerroot
1 teaspoon chili powder
1 teaspoon grated garlic
1 tablespoon cornstarch

Oil for cooking
1 tablespoon soy sauce
1 teaspoon vinegar
1¼ teaspoons sugar, divided

1 package (10 ounces) spinach, washed and torn into bite-size pieces
Salt to taste

Cut beef into bite-size pieces. Mix marinade ingredients and marinate beef for 30 minutes. Heat oil in skillet or wok and sauté beef over medium-high heat for approximately 3 to 4 minutes. Add soy sauce, vinegar, and 1 teaspoon sugar. Stir well and remove meat mixture to serving platter. Heat more oil if necessary and sauté spinach over high heat just until tender, 1 to 2 minutes. Add salt to taste and ¼ teaspoon sugar, and place on serving platter with beef.

MAKES 2 SERVINGS.

Unusual beef

CHINA

marinade

1 tablespoon sherry
2 tablespoons soy sauce

1 teaspoon cornstarch

½ *pound lean beef, sliced and cut into bite-size pieces*
4 *tablespoons oil*
3 *cups potato chips*
1 *cup snow peas, tips broken off*
Sprinkles of sherry

Blend marinade ingredients and marinate beef in mixture for 15 minutes. Heat oil to medium-high heat and stir-fry beef just until color changes. Add potato chips and snow peas and stir just until heated through, about 30 seconds. Sprinkle with sherry to taste and serve immediately.
MAKES 2 SERVINGS.

Marinated flank steak

CHINA

1 *flank steak, approximately 2 pounds*

marinade
4 *tablespoons lemon juice*
¼ *cup soy sauce*
3 *tablespoons honey*
3 *scallions, finely chopped*
2 *tablespoons sesame oil*

Score steak on each side. Combine marinade ingredients and place steak in mixture and refrigerate overnight, turning occasionally. Broil steak on preheated broiler pan about 4 minutes on each side, basting frequently with marinade. Cut steak on angle into very thin slices.
MAKES 4 SERVINGS.

Marinated steak slices

CHINA

1¼ *pounds fillet steak, or sirloin*

marinade
4 *tablespoons sherry*
4 *tablespoons soy sauce*
1½ *heaping tablespoons cornstarch*
Salt to taste
Pinch of sugar
Pinch of white pepper

4 *tablespoons oil*

Cut beef into thin slices. Prepare marinade by blending thoroughly the sherry, soy sauce, and cornstarch. Season with salt, sugar, and white pepper. Pour marinade over meat slices and let marinate for 1 hour.
In large skillet heat oil until very hot. Pour in meat with marinade and cook for 5 minutes. Spoon into preheated bowl and serve with rice.
MAKES 2 TO 3 SERVINGS.

Beef slices Peking

CHINA

marinade
3 *tablespoons soy sauce*
1 *tablespoon sherry*

1 *pound lean beef, sliced paper thin*
1 *cup oil*
2 *tablespoons flour*
2 *leeks, thinly sliced*
2 *garlic cloves, minced*
½ *teaspoon powdered ginger*
2 *tablespoons soy sauce*
⅛ *teaspoon ground anise*
½ *cup beef broth*
1 *teaspoon cornstarch*

In a deep bowl blend soy sauce and sherry. Add beef slices, coat well, cover and let stand for 1 hour. Heat oil in a large skillet. Thoroughly drain beef slices on paper toweling. Sprinkle with flour, add to hot oil, and deep-fry for 3 minutes. Remove meat slices with slotted spoon, drain, set aside, and keep warm.
Take 4 tablespoons of hot oil and pour into another skillet. Throw away rest of frying oil. Reheat oil, add leeks and garlic. Cook for 5 minutes while stirring.
Add meat slices. Season with powdered ginger, soy sauce and anise. Pour in beef broth. Cover and simmer over very low heat for 1 hour. At end of cooking time, bring to a quick boil. Blend cornstarch with small amount of cold water, add to skillet, stirring constantly until sauce is slightly thickened and bubbly. Correct seasoning, if necessary, and serve immediately.
MAKES 3 SERVINGS.

Chinese fondue

CHINA

chicken bouillon

6 cups chicken stock

2 medium carrots, thinly sliced

1 leek, finely sliced

1 stalk celery, thinly sliced

2 tablespoons parsley, coarsely chopped

sauce tartare

5 tablespoons mayonnaise

2 tablespoons capers

2 tablespoons chopped chives

2 dill pickles, finely chopped

2 teaspoons lemon juice

2 tablespoons evaporated milk

Salt

Pinch of sugar

White pepper

catsup sauce

5 tablespoons mayonnaise

2 tablespoons catsup

1 teaspoon Worcestershire sauce

1 teaspoon curry powder

Pinch of sugar

Salt

2 pounds lean beef, cut into paper-thin slices

2 cups boiling water

Pour chicken stock in fondue pot and place on top of stove. Add carrots, leek, celery, and parsley. Let simmer for 20 minutes. Meanwhile prepare sauces.

For Tartare Sauce, blend mayonnaise, capers, chives, dill pickles, lemon juice, and evaporated milk. Season to taste with salt, sugar, and white pepper.

To prepare Catsup Sauce, stir together thoroughly mayonnaise, catsup, Worcestershire sauce, and curry powder. Season to taste with sugar and salt.

Pat meat dry with paper toweling. Cut into thin slices. Place fondue pot with chicken bouillon on burner in middle of table. Make sure that broth continues to simmer. Since broth will evaporate, replenish it from time to time with boiling water. Fondue is eaten in following fashion: Roll up slice of beef, place on fondue fork and let cook in chicken broth to desired doneness. Dunk in sauce—when all the beef slices have been cooked, broth is ladled into bowls and eaten too.

MAKES APPROXIMATELY 4 SERVINGS.

Honan beef pot roast

CHINA

1 teaspoon salt

½ teaspoon freshly ground black pepper

2 teaspoons brown-gravy sauce

¼ cup soy sauce

2 tablespoons margarine

1 5-pound beef pot roast

1 medium onion, sliced

1 cup water

Mix together salt, pepper, brown-gravy sauce, and soy sauce. Rub into meat. Let sit 30 minutes. Brown meat in melted margarine in Dutch oven. Place rack under roast in Dutch oven. Add onion and water. Cover; cook slowly on stove or in 350°F oven approximately 3½ hours or until tender. Add more water if necessary. (There should be about 1 inch water in pot.) Turn meat occasionally during cooking. Serve with gravy.

MAKES ABOUT 8 SERVINGS.

Gravy

6 tablespoons drippings from roast

6 tablespoons flour

2 tablespoons soy sauce

1 teaspoon brown-gravy sauce

½ teaspoon salt

Dash of freshly ground black pepper

½ cup cold water

1½ cups hot water

Melt drippings; blend in flour. Add soy sauce, brown-gravy sauce, salt, pepper, and cold water; mix thoroughly. Stir in hot water. Cook, stirring constantly, until smooth and thickened.

Beef in oyster sauce I

CHINA

1 pound lean beef, cut into bite-size pieces

2 tablespoons soy sauce

1 tablespoon rice wine or sherry

1 teaspoon cornstarch

Oil for cooking

1 teaspoon sugar, more or less, to taste

3 tablespoons oyster sauce

Cooked rice

Lime spareribs

Marinate beef in mixture of soy sauce, wine or sherry, and cornstarch for 30 minutes. Heat oil in skillet or wok to medium-high heat. Add beef and stir-fry until done, approximately 3 to 4 minutes. Add sugar and oyster sauce and mix well. Serve with rice.

MAKES 2 TO 3 SERVINGS.

Beef in oyster sauce II

CHINA

½ teaspoon salt
¾ teaspoon baking soda
4 tablespoons water
3 teaspoons rice wine
½ teaspoon baking powder
¾ tablespoon cornstarch
2 teaspoons soy sauce
8 ounces lean beef, cut into bite-size slices
3½ teaspoons oil
Oil for deep frying
6 scallions, cut into 2-inch slices
2 small slices fresh gingerroot
1½ teaspoons oyster sauce
¼ teaspoon sugar
½ teaspoon sesame oil
½ teaspoon cornstarch

Mix together salt, baking soda, 3 tablespoons water, 1½ teaspoons rice wine, baking powder, ¾ tablespoon cornstarch, and 1 teaspoon soy sauce. Coat beef slices with mixture. Add 1½ teaspoons oil. Let stand 1½ hours.

Deep-fry beef in hot oil until color changes. Remove; drain on paper toweling. Sauté scallions and gingerroot in 2 tablespoons oil. Add beef, 1½ teaspoons rice wine, oyster sauce, 1 teaspoon soy sauce, sugar, sesame oil, and cornstarch mixed with water. Stir-fry quickly until heated through.

MAKES 2 OR 3 SERVINGS.

Wok surprise

CHINA

Oil for cooking
1 cup sliced green pepper
1 cup celery, sliced diagonally
1 cup sliced zucchini
2 cups leftover cooked roast beef, thinly sliced
Beef gravy, beef broth, or chicken broth
½ cup fresh mushrooms, sliced
2 cups fresh bean sprouts
2 cups fresh spinach, torn into bite-size pieces
Freshly ground black pepper to taste

Soy sauce to taste
Cornstarch mixed with cold water

Put small amount of oil in wok and heat to medium-high. Add green pepper and celery. Stir-fry for 1 minute. Add zucchini and stir-fry for 2 more minutes, or until the vegetables are bright in color and still crisp.

Push vegetables up sides of wok (or remove) and place roast beef and a little gravy, beef broth, or chicken broth in wok; toss meat until hot. Push meat up sides of wok and place mushrooms and bean sprouts in wok and stir-fry for 1 minute. Add previously cooked vegetables, beef, spinach, pepper, and soy sauce. If desired, you may add a little cornstarch mixed with cold water to thicken the gravy. Serve with rice, if desired.
MAKES 4 SERVINGS.

Beef & rice oriental

CHINA

1¼ cups cooked rice
1 pound ground beef
2 medium onions, sliced
2 cups fresh bean sprouts
1 package frozen cut green beans
1 cup beef bouillon
⅓ cup soy sauce
½ cup water
½ teaspoon powdered ginger

Preheat oven to 425°F. Mix all ingredients together in casserole dish. Bake covered for about 40 minutes.
MAKES 4 SERVINGS.

Unusual hamburgers

CHINA

1 pound ground beef
1 egg, beaten
¼ cup finely chopped water chestnuts
2 tablespoons minced onions
3 tablespoons minced mushrooms
⅛ teaspoon freshly ground black pepper
1 tablespoon oyster sauce

Mix ground beef with remaining ingredients.

Pork with peas

Shape into two patties, about ¾ inch thick. Broil about 4 inches from heat, for about 5 minutes. Turn and broil other side 4 to 5 minutes.
MAKES 2 SERVINGS.

Meatballs Chinese-style

CHINA

meatballs

2 pounds ground beef	*1 teaspoon salt*
1 egg	*Freshly ground black pepper*
2 tablespoons onion, chopped	*to taste*
1 tablespoon cornstarch	*Peanut oil*

sauce

1 cup pineapple juice	*½ cup sugar*
1 tablespoon oil	*1 green pepper, cut into*
3 tablespoons cornstarch	*small chunks*
1 tablespoon soy sauce	*1 small can pineapple*
3 tablespoons vinegar	*chunks, drained*
6 tablespoons water	

Combine all ingredients for meatballs and shape into 1-inch balls. Brown in small amount of peanut oil. Drain.

In large saucepan combine pineapple juice and oil. Set aside. Mix together cornstarch, soy sauce, vinegar, water, and sugar. Add to pineapple juice and oil. Bring to boil, and simmer 1 minute. Add green pepper and pineapple chunks. Add meatballs.
MAKES APPROXIMATELY 50 MEATBALLS.

Beef balls

CHINA

1 pound lean ground beef
¼ cup dry bread crumbs
1 egg, beaten
2 tablespoons flour
¼ cup cold water
1¼ teaspoons salt
½ cup oil
¼ cup soy sauce
½ cup boiling water
1 pound spinach, washed, stems discarded

Mix together beef, bread crumbs, egg, flour, cold water, and 1 teaspoon salt. Shape into 8 balls. Heat oil in wok or skillet. Brown beef balls in hot oil. Drain off all oil; discard all but 2 tablespoons. Add soy sauce and boiling water. Cover; cook over low heat 35 minutes.
Heat reserved oil in separate skillet. Sauté spinach and ¼ teaspoon salt 2 minutes. Combine with meat balls; cook 3 minutes.
MAKES 3 OR 4 SERVINGS.

Chinese hamburgers

CHINA

2 pounds ground meat, lean
2 tablespoons soy sauce
1 medium onion, finely chopped
1 medium green pepper, finely chopped
4 water chestnuts, finely chopped
Salt to taste
Pepper to taste
2 eggs, lightly beaten

Combine all ingredients and mix thoroughly. Form into patties and broil in oven or cook on hibachi or grill, approximately 5 minutes on each side.
MAKES 8 PATTIES.

Lamb w/garlic

CHINA

2 pounds shoulder lamb chops
Water for boiling
16 cloves garlic
1 leek, cut into 2-inch slices
6 small slices fresh gingerroot
2 cloves star anise
2 teaspoons whole anise pepper
6 tablespoons soy sauce
3 tablespoons sherry
Oil
2 teaspoons cornstarch
1 tablespoon water

Parboil lamb in enough water to cover; discard water. Place lamb, garlic, leek, ginger, star anise, whole anise pepper, soy sauce, and sherry in large pot with water to cover. Cover; bring to boil over high heat. Reduce heat to low; simmer until tender (about 1 hour). Remove lamb; drain liquid. Reserve liquid and garlic.

Vegetables with pork

Chop suey

Heat 1 inch of oil in an electric skillet to 375°F. Fry until lamb is crisp on both sides.

Heat 1 cup reserved liquid. Add cornstarch mixed with water; stir until thickened. Place lamb and garlic on serving platter; pour gravy over lamb.

MAKES 2 SERVINGS.

Lamb w/scallions

CHINA

1 pound boneless lamb, fat trimmed, sliced ⅛ inch thick, cut into strips
½ teaspoon five-spice
1 egg white
3 thin slices fresh gingerroot
3 cloves garlic, minced
3 teaspoons cornstarch
5 teaspoons soy sauce
6 tablespoons sherry
2 tablespoons water
12 whole scallions
2 tablespoons oil

Mix lamb in bowl with five-spice, egg white, ginger, garlic, 1 teaspoon cornstarch, and 1 teaspoon soy sauce. Let stand 20 minutes. Blend rest of cornstarch, soy sauce, sherry, and water; set aside. Cut white part of scallions in half crosswise. Cut green tops into 1-inch pieces; set aside.

Heat oil in wok or skillet to high heat. Add meat mixture; cook, stirring constantly, until meat is slightly browned. Remove from wok. Add cornstarch-soy-sauce mixture and white parts of onion to wok. Cook, stirring constantly, until thickened. Add meat and green tops of onions; stir until simmering.

MAKES 3 OR 4 SERVINGS.

Honan lamb chops

CHINA

2 tablespoons oil
4 shoulder lamb chops, about ¾ inch thick
1 medium onion, diced
½ cup diced green pepper
½ cup diced celery
1 can (approximately 5 ounces) bamboo shoots, sliced
1 pound fresh bean sprouts
½ teaspoon salt
¼ teaspoon freshly ground black pepper
1½ teaspoons soy sauce
1 tablespoon cornstarch
1 tablespoon water
1 medium tomato, cut into wedges

Preheat wok or skillet to 350°F. Pour in oil. Add lamb; cook until browned on both sides. Add onion, green pepper, and celery. Drain bamboo shoots. Add liquid to wok. Cover; simmer on low heat about 30 minutes or until lamb is tender. Add sprouts, bamboo shoots, salt, and pepper.

Mix together soy sauce, cornstarch, and water until smooth. Stir into lamb mixture. Add tomato; cook 2 minutes or until sauce is thickened.
MAKES 4 SERVINGS.

Honan marinated lamb

CHINA

3 pounds boneless lamb, cut into ½-inch cubes
1 cup cider vinegar
½ cup minced onions
3 garlic cloves, minced
2 teaspoons salt
1 teaspoon ground coriander
1 teaspoon ground cumin
½ teaspoon saffron
½ teaspoon dried ground chili peppers
1 teaspoon ground ginger
4 tablespoons oil
½ cup water
Boiled rice

Marinate lamb in vinegar 30 minutes; drain well. Grind together onions, cloves, salt, coriander, cumin, saffron, chili peppers, and ginger to make

paste. Roll lamb in mixture; let stand 30 minutes. Heat oil in pan. Brown lamb. Stir in water. Cover; cook over low heat 45 minutes or until lamb is very tender. Serve with rice.
MAKES 6 SERVINGS.

Stir-fried lamb

CHINA

This is good with boiled rice.

1 tablespoon soy sauce
1 teaspoon light brown sugar
3 tablespoons chicken stock
1 tablespoon gin
¼ teaspoon powdered five-spice
1 pound boned lamb, cut into thin bite-size pieces
2 tablespoons peanut oil
2 teaspoons minced garlic
Salt to taste
3 leeks, white part only, sliced into 1-inch pieces

Mix together soy sauce, sugar, stock, gin, and five-spice. Marinate lamb in mixture 30 minutes. Heat wok to high heat. Add oil, garlic, and salt; stir about 30 seconds or until garlic odor becomes strong. Add lamb and marinade; stir-fry 2 to 3 minutes. Add leeks; stir-fry 1 minute.
MAKES 3 OR 4 SERVINGS.

Meat platter szechwan

CHINA

7 tablespoons oil	Salt
6 ounces fresh mushrooms, sliced	¼ teaspoon ground ginger
½ pound tomatoes, peeled, sliced	½ pound onions, minced
	1 clove garlic, minced
½ pound green peppers, cut in half, seeds removed, cut into julienne strips	2 tablespoons sherry
	1 cup hot beef broth (made from cubes)
1½ pounds lean pork, cut into 2-inch-long julienne strips	1 tablespoon soy sauce
	2 tablespoons cornstarch
	4 tablespoons water

Heat 4 tablespoons oil in skillet. Add mushrooms, tomatoes, and green peppers. Cook 5 minutes; set aside.
Heat 3 tablespoons oil in another skillet. Add meat strips. Season to taste with salt and ginger, stirring constantly. Brown 10 minutes. Add on-

335

ions and garlic; cook 5 minutes. Pour in sherry. After 1 minute pour in broth and soy sauce. Add vegetable mixture. Cover; cook over medium heat 25 minutes.

Blend cornstarch with water; stir in. Cook until thickened and bubbly. Serve immediately on preheated platter.

MAKES 4 SERVINGS.

Sweet-&-sour pork I

CHINA

2½-pound slice pork shoulder, bone removed, meat cut into
   1-inch cubes
2 cups water
½ teaspoon salt
4 tablespoons soy sauce
2 tablespoons sherry

Put meat into large pot. Add water, salt, and soy sauce. Bring to boil on high heat. Turn heat to low; cover pot. Simmer about 1 hour or until tender. Drain off meat broth; reserve. Skim off fat. Add sherry to broth; set aside to use in sauce. Make sauce and pour over pork cubes. Add pineapple chunks; mix carefully.

MAKES 6 SERVINGS.

Sweet-and-sour sauce

⅓ cup sugar
4 tablespoons cornstarch
4 tablespoons cider vinegar
⅓ cup pineapple juice
Broth from meat
⅔ cup pineapple chunks (1 8-ounce can)

Blend sugar, cornstarch, vinegar, and pineapple juice in saucepan; mix until smooth. Slowly stir in meat broth. Stir over medium-high heat until sauce is thick and clear, approximately 8 minutes.

Sweet-&-sour pork II

CHINA

1½ pounds lean pork, cut in 1-inch cubes
3 tablespoons soy sauce
3 tablespoons dry white wine

2 carrots, cut into thin strips
1 red sweet pepper, seeds removed, and cut into thin rings
4 tablespoons olive oil, divided
1 small slice fresh gingerroot, minced
½ cup onions, chopped
¼ pound fresh mushrooms, sliced
½ cup beef broth
1 recipe Chinese Sweet-and-Sour Sauce (see above recipe)
Boiled rice

Place the pork in a shallow dish. Combine soy sauce and wine and pour over the pork. Turn to coat all sides. Marinate for about 20 to 30 minutes, stirring frequently. Cut the carrots and set aside. Cut pepper into rings and set aside.

Heat 2 tablespoons of the oil in a wok and add the gingerroot. Place the pork in the wok and stir-fry for about 5 minutes. Remove the pork and set aside. Add remaining oil to wok. Add carrots, sweet pepper, onions and mushrooms and stir-fry for about 5 minutes or until the carrots and sweet pepper are tender but still on the crisp side.

Add the pork and stir-fry for 5 minutes longer. Add broth and mix well. Stir in the Sweet-and-Sour Sauce and bring to a boil. Reduce heat to low, cover wok and cook for 2 minutes longer. Serve with rice.

MAKES 4 SERVINGS.

Spareribs w/fresh peppers

CHINA

4 pounds spareribs, cut into serving pieces
Salt to taste
⅔ cup brown sugar
3 tablespoons cornstarch
1 teaspoon powdered ginger
1 teaspoon powdered mustard
2 cups fresh orange juice
⅓ cup fresh lemon juice
⅓ cup soy sauce
3 tablespoons butter or margarine
½ pound fresh mushrooms, sliced if large
1 medium onion, chopped
1 green sweet pepper, cut into squares
1 red sweet pepper, cut into squares
1 large can pineapple chunks

Cut the spareribs into serving pieces. Place in roasting pan bone-side-down and sprinkle with salt to taste. Bake in a 350°F oven for 1 hour. Drain off excess fat.

In saucepan combine brown sugar, cornstarch, ginger, and mustard. Stir in orange juice, lemon juice, and soy sauce. Bring to a boil and cook and stir until thickened. Set aside.

Melt the butter or margarine in skillet. Sauté mushrooms for 5 minutes. Pour sauce over spareribs. Add the onion, green and red peppers, pineapple, and mushrooms. Bake for 30 minutes, basting occasionally.

MAKES 4 TO 5 SERVINGS.

Chinese pork w/peas

CHINA

12 ounces lean pork

marinade

2 tablespoons soy sauce	1 teaspoon cornstarch
2 teaspoons sherry	Salt
1 egg white	White pepper

4 ounces frozen peas	1 4-ounce can bamboo
8 tablespoons oil, divided	shoots
½ cup hot beef broth	1 preserved ginger, sliced
Sugar	1 tablespoon sherry
1 leek, cut into julienne	1 tablespoon cornstarch
strips	2 teaspoons soy sauce
1 clove garlic, minced	2 tablespoons oyster sauce
1 4-ounce can sliced	White pepper
mushrooms	Pinch of powdered ginger

Cut meat crosswise into thin strips. Prepare marinade by combining and blending soy sauce, sherry, egg white, and cornstarch. Season to taste with salt and white pepper. Pour over pork strips, cover, and let marinate for 30 minutes. Meanwhile, thaw peas. Heat 2 tablespoons of the oil in a small saucepan. Add peas and pour in beef broth. Season to taste with salt and sugar, and cook for 5 minutes. Drain peas, reserving cooking liquid, and keep warm.

Heat 3 tablespoons of the oil in a large saucepan. Add leek, garlic, mushrooms, bamboo shoots, and ginger. Cook for 5 minutes, stirring constantly. Set aside and keep warm. Heat rest of oil (3 tablespoons) in skillet. Add meat together with marinade and cook for 3 minutes or until meat is browned, stirring occasionally.

Add meat and peas to large saucepan with vegetables. Pour in sherry and reserved cooking liquid and bring to a boil. Blend cornstarch with soy sauce and oyster sauce and stir in until slightly thickened and bubbly. Season to taste with salt, pepper, ginger and sugar. Serve immediately.

MAKES 2 TO 3 SERVINGS.

Lime spareribs

CHINA

4 pounds spareribs, cut into serving pieces
¼ cup olive oil
1 cup onions, chopped
1 cup fresh mushrooms, sliced
1 clove garlic, minced
½ cup chili sauce
2 tablespoons red wine vinegar
¼ cup lime juice
2 tablespoons prepared mustard
¼ cup soy sauce
⅔ cup water
2 tablespoons honey
1 teaspoon salt
Freshly ground pepper to taste

Cut spareribs into serving pieces and place in baking pan. Heat oil in saucepan. Sauté onions, mushrooms and garlic, until tender. Add chili sauce, vinegar, lime juice, mustard, soy sauce, water, honey, salt and pepper, and mix thoroughly. Pour sauce over the spareribs. Bake in a 325°F oven for 1 hour, or until the spareribs are tender. Baste frequently.

MAKES 6 TO 8 SERVINGS.

Vegetables w/pork

CHINA

¼ cup butter
4 cups celery, sliced diagonally
1 green sweet pepper, sliced
1 red sweet pepper, sliced
½ pound fresh mushrooms, sliced

½ cup onions, sliced
2 cups cubed cooked pork
1¼ cups beef bouillon
1 tablespoon cornstarch
3 tablespoons soy sauce
½ teaspoon powdered ginger
¼ teaspoon salt
Freshly ground pepper to taste
Boiled rice

Melt butter in a wok. Add celery and stir-fry for 5 minutes. Stir in the green and red pepper, mushrooms, and onions and stir-fry for another 5 minutes. Stir in the pork and beef bouillon and bring to a boil. Reduce heat and simmer for 5 minutes.

Blend the cornstarch with the soy sauce, ginger, salt, and pepper. Stir into the pork mixture. Cook, stirring constantly, just until heated through and thickened. Serve over rice.

MAKES 6 SERVINGS.

Spicy pork

CHINA

1½ pounds lean pork
3 tablespoons peanut oil
3 cloves garlic, minced
2 small slices fresh gingerroot, minced
½ cup 2-inch pieces leek
½ cup sliced bamboo shoots
½ cup small pieces red or green sweet pepper
¼ teaspoon crushed red pepper
3 tablespoons water
1½ teaspoons sugar
4 tablespoons hoisin sauce
Boiled rice

Boil pork 25 minutes; cool. Slice into bite-size pieces; set aside.

Heat oil in wok or skillet over high heat. Cook garlic and ginger 1 minute. Add leek, bamboo shoots, and sweet pepper; mix well. Stir in red pepper. Add pork slices; mix through. Add water; bring to boil. Add sugar and hoisin sauce; stir quickly 1 minute or until sauce coats ingredients. Serve with rice.

MAKES 4 SERVINGS.

Chop suey

CHINA

1 pound lean pork, cut into thin slices
2 tablespoons sherry
2 tablespoons soy sauce
Salt to taste
Freshly ground pepper to taste
Pinch of powdered ginger
2 ounces transparent noodles, broken into small pieces
1 stalk celery, cut into thin slices
4 tablespoons dried Chinese mushrooms, soaked in water for 30 minutes
8 tablespoons oil
2 medium onions, thinly sliced
¼ cup bamboo shoots, thinly sliced
1 cup fresh bean sprouts
½ pound fresh mushrooms, sliced
3 tablespoons soy sauce
1 teaspoon sugar
1 tablespoon cornstarch
2 jiggers sherry
Cooked rice

Cut pork into thin slices and mix with 2 tablespoons sherry, 2 tablespoons soy sauce, salt, pepper, and ginger. Place in glass or ceramic bowl. Press down meat and cover. Let marinate for 1 hour.

Break noodles into small pieces and boil in salted water for 5 minutes. Drain and set aside. Cut celery in thin slices; blanch for 5 minutes. Drain and set aside. Slice Chinese mushrooms into bite-size pieces.

Heat oil in skillet until very hot. Add marinated pork and fry for 2 minutes. Remove and keep warm. Add onions, bamboo shoots, bean sprouts, and fresh mushrooms. Simmer for 3 minutes. Fold in meat, celery, and noodles. Season with 3 tablespoons soy sauce, and sugar. Stirring carefully, cook for an additional 3 minutes. Blend cornstarch with 2 jiggers sherry and slowly stir into sauce until sauce is thick and bubbly. Correct seasonings if necessary and serve immediately with rice.

MAKES APPROXIMATELY 3 SERVINGS.

Cantonese pork roast

CHINA

2½ to 3 pounds boneless pork roast
1 tablespoon soy sauce
2 tablespoons chicken broth
1 tablespoon honey

Mandarin liver

1 tablespoon sugar
Salt to taste
2 tablespoons sesame-seed oil

Rinse pork and pat dry with paper toweling. Blend next five ingredients and spoon over meat and rub in thoroughly. Place roast in bowl, cover and let stand for 1 hour.

Remove and drain, reserving any marinade. Brush meat with oil and place in ovenproof dish. Brush with reserved marinade. Place in preheated 325°F oven and roast for approximately 1½ hours.
MAKES 4 TO 6 SERVINGS.

Bean curd w/pork

CHINA

½ pound ground pork
3 tablespoons soy sauce
1 tablespoon hoisin sauce
1 teaspoon Tabasco sauce
2 tablespoons cornstarch
¼ teaspoon sesame-seed oil
2 tablespoons chopped scallions
1 tablespoon oil
½ cup diced green peppers
4 pieces bean curd

Mix pork with soy sauce, hoisin sauce, Tabasco sauce, cornstarch, and sesame-seed oil. Quickly fry scallions in 1 tablespoon oil. Add pork mixture, green pepper, and bean curd. Stir-fry 10 to 15 minutes or until pork is done.
MAKES 4 SERVINGS.

Szechwan pork w/vegetables

CHINA

1 cup thinly sliced raw pork
2 cloves garlic, crushed
½ cup slivered carrots
1 tablespoon soy sauce
2 tablespoons sherry
2 tablespoons oil
4 scallions, chopped fine
½ cup thinly sliced celery
½ teaspoon dry mustard
1 pound raw spinach, chopped into bite-size pieces

Place pork, garlic, and carrots into bowl. Mix together soy sauce and sherry. Pour over pork mixture; marinate in refrigerator overnight.

Heat oil in wok or large skillet; stir-fry meat mixture approximately 4 minutes or until pork is cooked. Add scallions, celery, mustard, and spinach; stir-fry 2 minutes.
MAKES 2 OR 3 SERVINGS.

Beef sukiyaki (preceding pages)   Teriyaki steak

Mandarin liver

CHINA

1 pound liver (pork, baby beef, or calves)
2½ tablespoons flour
5 tablespoons safflower oil
Salt to taste
Pepper to taste
3 tablespoons soy sauce
2 tablespoons Chinese rice wine or sherry
2 large onions, sliced thin
1 cup beef bouillon (from cubes)
1 red pepper, cut into strips
1 green pepper, cut into strips
½ pound savoy cabbage, cut into strips
6 ounces fresh bean sprouts
1 small can bamboo shoots (approximately 6 ounces)

Pat liver dry with paper towels; cut into thin slices. Coat with flour. Heat oil in heavy skillet. Add liver; brown on all sides; remove. Season to taste with salt and pepper. Set aside; keep warm. Add soy sauce, wine, and onions to pan drippings; simmer 5 minutes. Pour in beef bouillon. Add red and green peppers and cabbage; simmer 10 minutes. Vegetables should still be crisp. Add bean sprouts, bamboo shoots, and liver; heat through. Serve immediately.
MAKES 4 SERVINGS.

Chinese liver

CHINA

1 pound beef liver
2½ tablespoons flour
5 tablespoons safflower oil
Salt to taste
Pepper to taste
3 tablespoons soy sauce
2 tablespoons sherry
2 large onions, thinly sliced
1 cup beef bouillon
1 red pepper, cut into strips
1 green pepper, cut into strips
½ pound savoy cabbage, cut into strips
½ pound fresh bean sprouts
1 small can bamboo shoots

Pat liver dry with paper toweling and cut into thin slices. Coat with flour. Heat oil in skillet, add liver, and brown on all sides. Remove and season to taste with salt and pepper. Set aside and keep warm.
Add soy sauce and sherry to pan drippings, as well as onion. Simmer for 5 minutes. Pour in beef bouillon. Add green and red peppers and cabbage. Simmer for 10 minutes. Vegetables should still be crunchy. Add bean sprouts, bamboo shoots, and liver. Heat through and serve.
MAKES APPROXIMATELY 3 SERVINGS.

Beef sukiyaki I

JAPAN

1 pound rice	4 leeks
1½ to 2 pounds beef tenderloin	¼ head white cabbage (about ½ pound)
2 tablespoons bacon drippings	½ pound fresh spinach
½ pound transparent or silver noodles	1 pound canned bamboo shoots
8 dried mushrooms	½ pound bean sprouts
4 small onions	

sauce

1 cup soy sauce	2 teaspoons sugar
6 tablespoons rice wine or sherry	4 egg yolks

Cook rice ; keep it warm.

Beef tenderloin must be cut into paper-thin slices. To achieve this, place meat in freezer for about 2 hours, or until partially frozen. You then will be easily able to slice it thin. Or, have the butcher slice it for you. Arrange meat slices on round platter, slightly overlapping. Place 2 tablespoons of bacon drippings (unmelted) into middle, cover with aluminum foil, and refrigerate.

Place noodles and mushrooms into separate bowls. Cover with boiling water; soak for 20 minutes. Repeat procedure two more times. Drain; arrange in separate bowls.

Cut onions and leeks into thin slices. Place in separate bowls. Core cabbage, separate into individual leaves, and tear into bite-size pieces. Clean spinach; remove stems from leaves. Drain bamboo shoots, reserving liquid. Drain bean sprouts, if canned. If fresh, blanch, then rinse with cold water, and drain them.

To prepare sauce, bring soy sauce, rice wine or sherry, and sugar to a boil. Pour into sauce dish. Place wok (or use frying pan on top of burner) in the middle of your table. Spoon rice into 4 individual bowls. Place slightly beaten egg yolks into 4 other small bowls. Now arrange all ingredients around wok.

Prepare meal in portions, i.e. place one-fourth of bacon drippings into wok and heat, add one-fourth of meat slices and brown quickly. Push aside and pour some of the sauce over meat. Add one-fourth of each of the vegetables and noodles and simmer for 3 minutes, while stirring constantly. Each guest is given part of the cooked ingredients and starts eating while the second portion is being prepared. Cooked vegetables are dipped into egg yolk before being placed on plates. Sukiyaki is seasoned with sauce according to each individual's taste.

MAKES 4 SERVINGS.

Beef sukiyaki II

JAPAN

This is an eye-appealing dish, perfect to prepare in front of guests. You must, however, have everything prepared prior to cooking.

2 pounds beef sirloin, cut into strips
1 large Bermuda onion
3 stalks celery
¼ pound fresh mushrooms
12 scallions
5 ounces canned water chestnuts
¼ pound fresh spinach
1 tablespoon oil
¾ cup beef bouillon
½ cup soy sauce
¼ cup vermouth
1 tablespoon sugar

Have the butcher cut the sirloin into thin strips, or, if you are cutting it, partially freeze it to make it easier to slice.

Slice onion; put aside. Slice the celery at an angle into thin slices. Set aside. Thinly slice mushrooms; set aside. Slice scallions into approximately 1½-inch pieces. Drain the water chestnuts; slice in half. Wash the spinach; tear it into pieces. Arrange meat and vegetables on large platter.

Put oil into extra-large skillet or wok. Brown the meat; push to side of pan or wok. Add all vegetables except spinach; stir in bouillon, soy sauce, vermouth, and sugar. Let sizzle for 5 minutes. Add spinach, cover, and cook 2 minutes more. Serve sukiyaki with rice.

MAKES 3 TO 4 SERVINGS.

Teriyaki steak

JAPAN

4 boneless steaks, about ½ pound each

marinade

1 clove garlic, finely minced	Pepper, freshly ground
1 sugared or candied ginger, finely minced	½ cup rice wine or sherry
1 tablespoon brown sugar	6 tablespoons soy sauce
Salt	½ cup white wine
	Juice of half a lemon

stuffed-tomato garnish

4 medium tomatoes	4 tablespoons bean sprouts, canned or fresh
Salt	
White pepper	1 tablespoon tomato catsup

Combine marinade ingredients in shallow dish large enough to hold the steaks. Stir until well blended. Add steaks to marinade; coat well with marinade. Marinate for 12 hours, turning steaks frequently. Drain steaks; arrange on broiler pan. Place under preheated broiler. Broil 4 minutes on each side.

Meanwhile, remove stems from tomatoes; cut off approximately ½-inch slices from bottoms. Scoop out seeds; discard. Sprinkle insides of tomatoes with salt and pepper.

Place bean sprouts and catsup into small skillet. Heat for 5 minutes. Spoon into tomatoes. Arrange steaks on preheated serving platter. Garnish with stuffed tomatoes.

MAKES 4 SERVINGS.

Note: If using fresh bean sprouts, blanch, then rinse them with cold water before using.

Grilled steaks

JAPAN

marinade

½ cup soy sauce
4 tablespoons minced onions
2 cloves garlic, minced
1 tablespoon (or less) sugar
1 tablespoon minced fresh gingerroot
¼ cup rice wine, or dry white wine

4 small steaks of your choice, boneless
Cherry tomatoes for garnish

Mix together marinade ingredients. Pour marinade over steaks. Refrigerate overnight or let sit at room temperature for 3 to 4 hours.

Broil in the oven or on a grill or hibachi. Baste steaks with marinade while they are grilling. When steaks are almost done, grill tomatoes and use for garnish.

MAKES 4 SERVINGS.

Tokyo steak

JAPAN

Delicious with rice and stir-fried bean sprouts.

Salt
Ground ginger to taste
Pepper to taste, freshly ground
2 tablespoons rice wine or sherry
4 filet mignon steaks, about 6 ounces each
1½ tablespoons butter
1 11-ounce can mandarin oranges
1 tablespoon capers
1 tablespoon butter, cut into small pieces

Combine salt, ginger, pepper, and rice wine (or sherry); blend well. Rub mixture onto steaks.

Heat 1½ tablespoons butter in heavy skillet. Add steaks; sauté 2 minutes on each side. Arrange mandarin oranges and capers on top of steaks; dot with remaining 1 tablespoon butter. Place skillet under preheated broiler; broil for 3 minutes. Serve steaks immediately on preheated plates.

MAKES 4 SERVINGS.

Steak Japanese

JAPAN

2 filet mignon steaks, about 12 ounces each
2½ tablespoons soy sauce
1 can bean sprouts, or 8 ounces fresh
3 tablespoons butter
2 tablespoons lemon juice
Sugar
Black pepper
4 ounces mandarin oranges (canned)
4 tablespoons oil

Sprinkle 2 tablespoons of the soy sauce over steaks. Rub in; let steaks marinate for 1 hour.

Meanwhile, drain bean sprouts; or, if using fresh

bean sprouts, blanch them, rinse with cold water, then drain. Heat 2 tablespoons of the butter in a saucepan. Add bean sprouts; season with lemon juice, sugar, pepper, and ½ tablespoon soy sauce. Simmer for 5 minutes, then keep them warm.

In another small saucepan heat remaining 1 tablespoon butter, add drained mandarin oranges, and heat through, about 2 minutes. Keep them warm.

In heavy skillet heat oil over high heat until a light haze forms above it. Add steaks; quickly brown them on each side for about ½ minute. Lower heat; continue cooking steaks for about 10 minutes on each side. Arrange steaks on preheated platter. Garnish with bean sprouts and mandarin oranges. Serve immediately.
MAKES 2 SERVINGS.

Teriyaki meatballs

JAPAN

1 pound lean ground beef	1 egg
2 tablespoons chopped parsley	3 tablespoons bread crumbs
	Salt
2 tablespoons chopped chives	White pepper
Leaves from 2 stalks of celery, finely chopped	Butter or margarine for frying

sauce

½ cup soy sauce	⅛ teaspoon allspice
Salt	Ground ginger
White pepper	1 sugared ginger
Sugar	

Mix ground beef thoroughly with chopped parsley, chives, and celery leaves. Stir in egg and bread crumbs. Season to taste with salt and pepper. Shape into balls about 1½ to 2 inches in diameter. Heat butter or margarine in heavy skillet. Add meatballs; fry for about 5 minutes or until browned on all sides.

While meatballs are frying, prepare sauce. In a small saucepan heat soy sauce over low heat. Season with salt, pepper, sugar, allspice, and ground ginger. Dice sugared ginger; add to sauce. Pour hot sauce over meatballs; let stand for 5 minutes, so flavors can blend. Serve meatballs in preheated bowl.
MAKES 4 SERVINGS.

Japanese beef stew

JAPAN

8 cups beef stock
3 pounds beef stew meat, cut into bite-size pieces
4 turnips, quartered
2 carrots, cut into bite-size pieces
2 cans water chestnuts, sliced if desired
10 small potatoes, peeled and left whole
Salt to taste
Freshly ground black pepper to taste
2 tablespoons soy sauce
4 stalks celery, cut into 1-inch pieces
10 small white onions
4 scallions, cut into ½-inch pieces

Bring beef stock to a boil; add all ingredients except celery, white onions, and scallions. Simmer for 30 minutes, add celery and onions, and simmer until meat is tender. Add scallions; simmer for 2 minutes more. Serve stew with rice, if desired.
MAKES APPROXIMATELY 6 SERVINGS.

Japanese fondue

JAPAN

1 pound beef, cut into cubes
8 ounces hot dogs
4 pimientos
½ pound mushrooms
4 small onions
Oil for deep-frying

sauces
Worcestershire sauce
Lemon juice
Mayonnaise
Catsup

Cut beef into cubes; set aside. Cut hot dogs into bite-size pieces; set aside. Cut pimientos into 2 or 3 pieces. Leave mushrooms whole. Slice onions into wide rings. Arrange all ingredients on platter.

Heat oil in fondue pot or wok set on table. Using fondue forks, pick up one ingredient at a time; deep-fry until done. Eat beef with any of the above sauces.
MAKES 4 SERVINGS.

Sweet-&-sour meatballs

JAPAN

1 pound lean ground beef
1 egg, beaten
1 teaspoon (scant) salt
Pepper to taste, freshly ground
1 tablespoon onion flakes
1 tablespoon cornstarch
Oil for frying
1 13½-ounce can pineapple tidbits, drained (reserve liquid)
1 cup water
1 package sweet-and-sour sauce mix
½ cup thinly sliced green pepper

Combine beef, beaten egg, salt, and pepper to taste. Mix in onion and cornstarch. Shape into small-size meatballs. Brown meatballs in small amount of oil in frying pan or wok. Drain on paper towels. Discard pan drippings.

In same pan combine reserved pineapple liquid, water, and sweet-sour mix. Stir constantly until mixture boils. Add green pepper, meatballs, and pineapple. Bring to a boil; turn heat down; simmer for 5 minutes, stirring occasionally. Serve meatballs on hot rice.
MAKES 4 SERVINGS.

Marinated & broiled lamb chops

JAPAN

4 lamb chops, each about 1½ inches thick

marinade
½ cup soy sauce
½ cup water
2 cloves garlic, minced
1 tablespoon freshly grated gingerroot or 1½ teaspoons ground ginger

Put lamb chops in a dish large enough to hold them and the marinade. Mix together soy sauce, water, garlic, and ginger. Blend well. Pour marinade over chops. Marinate overnight in refrigerator.

Let chops come to room temperature, place on broiler pan, and brush with marinade. Broil about 5 minutes, then turn and brush with additional marinade; broil for about 3 more minutes or until desired brownness is reached. Boil and strain the remainder of the marinade. Serve it with the chops, along with rice, if desired. This can also be cooked on grill or hibachi.
MAKES 4 SERVINGS.

Fried pork

JAPAN

1 medium red pepper
2 tablespoons chopped scallions
2 tablespoons ground sesame seeds
3 tablespoons soy sauce
2 tablespoons rice wine or sherry
1 pound sliced pork, ¼ inch thick
2 tablespoons oil
2 ounces transparent noodles or very thin spaghetti
1 medium cucumber, cut into thin strips
1 medium tomato, cut into thin strips

sauce
2 tablespoons vinegar
1 teaspoon freshly ground black pepper
1 tablespoon sugar

Remove seeds from pepper; dice it fine. Mix with scallions, sesame seeds, soy sauce, and rice wine or sherry. Marinate pork in this mixture for at least 1 hour. Heat oil in frying pan. Drain pork; brown well on both sides in hot oil. Cut into smaller pieces, if desired.

Prepare noodles or thin spaghetti. Combine with cucumber and tomato strips. Place on platter along with the pork.

Prepare sauce by blending the vinegar, black pepper, and sugar. Spoon sauce over the pork.
MAKES 4 SERVINGS.

Skewered pork

JAPAN

1 pound pork, cut into bite-size pieces, ½ inch thick
1 small eggplant cut into bite-size cubes
4 or 5 scallions, cut into 1½-inch lengths
2 green peppers, cut into chunks
Flour for dredging
Oil for frying

Grilled steaks

Skewer pork, eggplant, scallions, and peppers on skewers. Dredge in flour; fry in oil for about 4 minutes, or until browned. Remove from oil and, if desired, brush with soy sauce. Serve pork with rice.

MAKES 2 TO 3 SERVINGS.

Skewered pork & vegetables

JAPAN

8 ounces pork
Salt and pepper to taste
Lima beans
Celery, cut into 1-inch pieces
Small green peppers, cut into cubes
Small onions, quartered
Fresh mushrooms, halved
Flour
Eggs, beaten
Bread crumbs
Oil for frying

sauce
2 tablespoons Worcestershire sauce
1½ tablespoons catsup

Cut meat into 1-inch chunks. Season with salt and pepper. Prepare vegetables, using as much as is needed. Dip meat and vegetables into flour, beaten eggs, and bread crumbs in that order, again using as much as is needed. Put meat and vegetables on skewers; fry pork over medium heat until done. Fry vegetables over high heat until browned.

Serve with sauce made from Worcestershire sauce and catsup.

MAKES 4 SERVINGS.

Pork w/peppers & tomatoes

JAPAN

1½ pounds lean pork
½ pound green peppers
5 ounces fresh mushrooms
½ pound tomatoes, peeled
7 tablespoons oil
Salt
¼ teaspoon ground ginger
½ pound onions
1 clove garlic
2 tablespoons sherry
1 cup hot beef broth
1 tablespoon cornstarch
4 tablespoons cold water

Cut pork and green peppers into long, thin strips. Cut mushrooms and peeled tomatoes into thin slices. Heat 4 tablespoons of the oil in skillet. Add green peppers, mushrooms, and tomatoes; cook for 5 minutes. Set aside.

In second skillet, heat remaining 3 tablespoons oil. Add meat; sprinkle with salt and ginger; brown, stirring constantly, for about 10 minutes.

347

Teriyaki meatballs

1 clove garlic, minced
1½ cups sliced fresh mushrooms
2 cups canned tomatoes
1½ teaspoons chili powder
1 teaspoon sugar
¼ cup red wine
1 tablespoon water
Salt and pepper to taste

Combine 2 tablespoons of the flour, the seasoned salt, and pepper. Dredge steak in flour mixture. Heat oil in electric skillet or large, heavy skillet. Brown steaks well on both sides. Remove from pan. Add onion, garlic, and mushrooms; sauté for 5 minutes, stirring occasionally. Purée tomatoes in blender or food processor with chili powder, sugar, and wine. Add to vegetables in skillet. Return meat to skillet. Coat with sauce. Bring to a boil, reduce heat to low, and cover. Simmer for 2 to 2½ hours or until tender. Combine flour and water to form a paste. Remove steaks from skillet; keep them warm. Slowly add flour and water paste to gravy, stirring well. Cook over low heat until thickened. Serve the steaks and gravy with hot cooked rice.
MAKES 4 SERVINGS.

Chop onions finely; mince garlic. Add to meat; continue cooking for another 5 minutes. Pour in sherry, beef broth, and soy sauce. Add vegetable mixture to meat; cover, and simmer for 25 minutes over medium heat.
Blend cornstarch and water; stir into skillet until smooth and bubbly. Serve pork immediately on preheated platter.
MAKES 4 SERVINGS.

Ranch-style steaks

MEXICO

sauce

2 tablespoons olive oil
1 green pepper, cleaned,
 seeded, and chopped
1 clove garlic, minced
½ cup chopped onion
2 hot peppers, stemmed,
 seeded, and chopped

¼ cup tomato catsup
1 cup beef broth
Salt and pepper to taste
½ teaspoon paprika

steaks

4 filet steaks (3 ounces
 each)
4 tablespoons cooking oil

Salt and pepper to taste
Parsley, pickled hot peppers,
 and tomato wedges

Heat olive oil in small skillet. Add vegetables; sauté for 3 minutes. Add catsup, broth, salt and pepper to taste, and paprika. Reduce heat to low; simmer mixture while cooking steaks.
Slightly flatten steaks. Wipe with a damp cloth; pat dry with a paper towel. Heat cooking oil in heavy skillet over moderately high heat. Sauté

Swiss steak Mexican-style

MEXICO

3 tablespoons flour
½ teaspoon seasoned salt
⅛ teaspoon pepper
1½ pounds bottom round steak
3 tablespoons oil
1 large onion, sliced

348

Tokyo steak

Beef stew Mexican-style

steaks for 3 minutes on each side; transfer to a warm platter. Top steaks with the sauce. Garnish with parsley, tomato wedges, and hot peppers.
MAKES 4 SERVINGS.

Stuffed flank steak w/American sauce

MEXICO

1 2½-pound flank steak	*½ teaspoon thyme*
1 teaspoon salt	*1 clove garlic, minced*
¼ teaspoon freshly ground pepper	*¼ cup wine vinegar*

stuffing

2 tablespoons butter	*⅓ cup chopped parsley*
1 medium onion, chopped	*1 egg, beaten*
½ cup chopped walnuts	*1½ cups bread crumbs*
3 tablespoons olive oil	*1 cup water*
2 cups beef broth	*1 bay leaf*

The day before serving wipe flank steak with a damp cloth and pound with a mallet or the edge of a cleaver to an even thickness. Combine salt, pepper, thyme, garlic, and vinegar. Put steak in a glass or ceramic dish; pour marinade over meat. Cover and refrigerate. Bring steak to room temperature while making the stuffing.
Melt butter in heavy skillet. Sauté onion until limp. Combine walnuts, parsley, egg, and bread crumbs in mixing bowl. Add onion and butter, mix well. Pat steak dry with paper towels; place on flat surface. Spoon stuffing down center of steak; roll steak to completely enclose stuffing. Secure with string tied 1-inch apart the length of the steak. Secure ends of steak with skewers. Heat olive oil in skillet; brown the steak on all sides, and place in casserole. Pour beef broth and water over steak; add bay leaf to liquid. Cover; bake at 375°F for 1¼ hours or until tender. Remove from pan, cut strings, and let stand 10 minutes before slicing. Serve garnished with sautéed peppers and American Sauce.
MAKES 6 SERVINGS.

American sauce

1 tablespoon butter or margarine
1 tablespoon flour
½ teaspoon salt
⅛ teaspoon pepper
1 cup tomato sauce
½ cup heavy cream

Melt butter in small saucepan. Add flour, salt, and pepper; stir well. Cook until bubbly. Add tomato sauce; cook, stirring constantly, over low heat until thickened. Remove from heat. Quickly stir in cream. Serve.

Beef stew Mexican-style

MEXICO

This stew is moderately hot; if you prefer milder food, cut the amount of green chili salsa in half.

1½ pounds lean stewing beef, cut into cubes
1 large onion, sliced

1 clove garlic, minced
4 tablespoons olive oil
3 tablespoons wine vinegar
1/2 cup tomato sauce
1 cup red wine
1 bay leaf
1 teaspoon oregano
1/2 teaspoon salt
1/4 teaspoon pepper
1 7-ounce can green chili salsa

Combine all ingredients in large saucepan. Bring mixture to a boil, stirring occasionally. Reduce heat to simmer; cook for 3 hours or until meat falls apart. Serve with Beer Rice.
MAKES 4 SERVINGS.

Beer rice

2 tablespoons olive oil
1 cup raw long-grain rice
1 10¾-ounce can condensed onion soup
1 10¾-ounce soup can of beer

Heat olive oil in medium saucepan over moderate heat. Add rice; brown lightly, stirring constantly. Add onion soup and beer. Cover tightly; simmer for 20 to 25 minutes or until all liquid is absorbed.

Beef tacos w/Mexican sauce

MEXICO

taco shells
12 to 18 fresh or frozen
 (thawed) tortillas

taco filling

2 pounds lean ground beef	1 teaspoon paprika
2 medium onions, finely chopped	2 teaspoons salt
1 or 2 tablespoons chili powder	1 tablespoon Worcestershire sauce
1 teaspoon oregano	1/3 cup Mexican Sauce

taco garnishes

Shredded lettuce	Chopped onions
Shredded cheese	Mexican Sauce
Chopped tomatoes	

To make folded, crisp-fried tacos, fry 1 corn or flour tortilla at a time in about 1/2 inch hot oil over medium heat, until it becomes soft (just a few seconds). With tongs or two forks fold it in

half and hold slightly, so there is a space between halves for the filling to be added later.
The entire cooking procedure takes only minutes for each shell. To keep fried shells warm until ready to fill, place them on a paper-towel-lined baking sheet in a 200°F oven as long as 10 or 15 minutes.
Brown meat and onions; drain well. Add chili powder, oregano, paprika, salt, Worcestershire sauce, and Mexican Sauce. Serve hot. Season more to taste. This freezes well. Fills 1 to 1½ dozen taco shells.
To assemble tacos, place desired amount of meat filling in center of each fried taco shell; top filling with garnishes such as shredded lettuce, shredded cheese, and Mexican Sauce. Serve tacos hot.

Mexican sauce

2 cups chopped peeled tomatoes or 1 16-ounce can whole
 tomatoes and juice
1 small onion, chopped
1 clove garlic, chopped
1 tablespoon chili powder
1/2 teaspoon oregano
1 teaspoon salt
Few drops of hot sauce

Combine all ingredients in a blender or food processor; spin until smooth. Pour into small saucepan; simmer for 30 minutes. Use on top of taco filling.
MAKES 2½ TO 3 CUPS.

American enchiladas

MEXICO

For those who don't like it hot!
cornmeal crepes

3/4 cup flour	1/4 teaspoon baking soda
1/2 cup cornmeal	3 eggs
1 1/4 cups buttermilk	1 tablespoon butter, melted

sauce

2 tablespoons olive oil	1/2 teaspoon ground cumin
1 pound ground beef	1/2 teaspoon salt
1/4 cup chopped onion	1/4 teaspoon pepper
1 teaspoon chili powder	

1 8-ounce can tomato sauce
Tomato wedges and parsley
   for garnish

Measure flour, cornmeal, buttermilk, baking soda, eggs, and butter into jar of electric blender or food processor. Spin for 30 seconds. Scrape down the sides of blender; blend for 1 minute. Refrigerate for 1 hour.

Meanwhile, make the sauce. Heat oil in large skillet. Brown the meat and onion, stirring frequently. Drain off excess fat. Add chili powder, cumin, salt, pepper, and tomato sauce; simmer for 20 minutes. Keep sauce warm while making crepes.

Heat lightly oiled skillet or small crepe pan over moderate heat until a drop of water sizzles and dances on the hot pan. Stir the batter. Pour a scant ¼ cup batter into pan and tilt pan in all directions to coat the bottom. Cook until bottom is lightly browned and the edges appear dry. Turn; cook a few seconds, until lightly browned. Stack on a towel, with paper towels between each. Keep crepes warm in oven as others are cooked. When all crepes are made, fill each with some meat mixture; roll crepes, and place on warm platter. Garnish enchiladas with fresh tomato wedges and parsley.
MAKES 6 SERVINGS.

Hamburger steaks Mexicano

MEXICO

2 onions, thinly sliced (2 cups)
¼ cup butter or margarine
1 pound lean ground beef
2 tablespoons canned chopped green chilies
¾ teaspoon salt
½ teaspoon garlic powder
¼ teaspoon pepper

Sauté onions in butter or margarine in large skillet until lightly browned. Remove onions from pan with slotted spoon; keep them warm.

In a mixing bowl lightly combine ground beef, green chilies, salt, garlic powder, and pepper with a fork. Form into 4 thick patties. Sauté hamburgers to desired degree of doneness over

medium heat in remaining butter or margarine in skillet. Top hamburgers with the browned onions. Serve.
MAKES 4 SERVINGS.

Chili con carne

MEXICO

1½ pounds stew meat, cubed
2 tablespoons oil
1 medium onion, chopped
1 8-ounce can tomato sauce
1 6-ounce can tomato paste
1 1-pound can kidney beans
1 tablespoon chili powder
½ teaspoon hot-pepper sauce
¾ cup water (more as needed)

Brown stew meat in oil. Add onion; cook until tender. Add tomato sauce, tomato paste, kidney beans, chili powder, and hot-pepper sauce. Mix in ¾ cup water. Cover; simmer for 2½ hours or more, until meat is tender. Add more water as needed.
MAKES 6 TO 8 SERVINGS.

Stuffed chilies

MEXICO

These may be prepared ahead and warmed in the oven or a chafing dish.

2 medium onions, chopped
1 clove garlic, crushed
2 tablespoons oil
½ pound ground beef
½ pound ground pork
1 cup chopped fresh tomatoes
1 teaspoon salt
½ teaspoon pepper
4 tablespoons sliced almonds
4 tablespoons raisins
8 whole canned chilies
4 eggs
½ cup flour
Oil for frying

Sauté onions and garlic in 2 tablespoons oil until onion is transparent. Add ground meats; stir until meat is crumbly. Add chopped tomatoes, seasonings, almonds, and raisins. Simmer.

Remove chili seeds, leaving chili skins whole. Stuff chilies with meat filling; roll them well in flour. Then dip them in the following egg batter. Beat egg whites until stiff; beat egg yolks; combine egg yolks with egg whites. Fry chilies in deep fat at 375°F until golden brown. Remove; drain on toweling.
MAKES 8 SERVINGS.

Meatloaf Mexican-style

MEXICO

1½ pounds meatloaf mix (a mixture of ground beef, veal, and pork) or ground beef
1 cup soft bread crumbs
1 small onion, chopped
1 10-ounce can tomatoes and green chilies
1 egg, lightly beaten
¼ teaspoon garlic powder
½ teaspoon salt
¼ teaspoon pepper
2 hard-cooked eggs, cut in half lengthwise
¼ cup sliced pimiento-stuffed green olives

Combine meat, bread crumbs, onion, ½ can of tomatoes and green chilies, egg, garlic powder, salt, and pepper; mix well. Pack half of mixture into an 8 × 4 × 2-inch loaf pan. Arrange hard-cooked eggs in a single row down center of loaf. Arrange olives in rows on either side of eggs. Press eggs and olives lightly into meat mixture. Top with remaining meat mixture. Pour remaining half can of tomatoes and green chilies over meatloaf. Bake at 350°F for 1 hour.
MAKES 4 TO 5 SERVINGS.

Mexican meat hash

MEXICO

3 tablespoons oil
½ pound lean ground pork
½ pound ground beef
1 small onion, chopped
1 clove garlic, minced
½ cup tomato catsup

1 teaspoon red wine vinegar
1 teaspoon ground cinnamon
½ teaspoon chili powder
⅛ teaspoon cumin
Pinch of ground cloves
½ cup raisins
½ teaspoon salt
¼ teaspoon ground black pepper
½ cup toasted, slivered, blanched almonds

Heat oil in large frying pan. Add meats; cook over moderate heat, stirring occasionally, until meat loses its pink color. Add onion and garlic; cook until browned. Add catsup, vinegar, cinnamon, chili powder, cumin, cloves, raisins, salt, and pepper. Stir to blend. Bring mixture to a boil. Reduce heat to simmer; cook for 15 to 20 minutes. Add almonds; stir. Use this mixture to fill tamales, or serve with rice.
MAKES 4 SERVINGS.

Sandwiches

This mixture also makes delicious sandwiches if served this way:

8 flour tortillas (large ones—about 8 inches in diameter)
1 recipe Mexican Meat Hash
1½ cups shredded cheddar cheese
2 cups shredded lettuce

Warm the flour tortillas in large cast-iron skillet over moderate heat about 30 seconds on each side (just heat them through and make them pliable—do not make them hard and crisp). Fill each with about ½ cup Mexican Meat Hash; top each with 3 tablespoons cheese and ¼ cup lettuce. Fold up tortillas like packages by folding bottoms and top edges in 1 inch; then pull the 2 sides to the center, overlapping each other.

Meatballs in almond sauce

MEXICO

1 egg, beaten
½ cup water
3 slices dry bread, cubed
½ teaspoon salt
⅛ teaspoon black pepper

½ teaspoon dried oregano
½ teaspoon chili powder
½ cup raisins
¾ pound ground beef
¾ pound ground pork

almond sauce

½ cup slivered almonds	3 tablespoons meat drippings
1 slice dry bread, cubed	1½ cups chicken broth
1 clove garlic, minced	¼ cup tomato sauce
2 tablespoons chopped onions	Salt and pepper to taste

For the meatballs: Mix egg, water, bread cubes, salt, pepper, oregano, chili powder, and raisins. Mix into beef and pork mixture. Shape into about 36 meatballs. Brown the meatballs. Drain, saving 3 tablespoons fat.

For the almond sauce: Cook almonds, bread cubes, garlic, and onions in meat drippings until browned. Remove from fat, cool, and blend to consistency of a paste by diluting with broth. Add this paste to tomato sauce, remaining broth, salt, and pepper. Simmer for 5 to 10 minutes. Combine almond sauce and meatballs. Simmer for 10 more minutes. Serve meatballs hot. Meatballs and sauce may be served over rice.
MAKES 6 TO 8 SERVINGS.

Tamales

MEXICO

Tamales are of Aztec origin and provide an easy and filling dish to use up small quantities of leftover meat and poultry.

24 corn husks (dried) or 24 6-inch squares of cooking
  parchment

tamale dough

1 cup lard
2½ cups instant Masa Harina
½ teaspoon salt
1¾ cups chicken broth

tamale filling

1½ cups Pork in Red Chili Sauce (see Index) or Mexican
  Meat Hash (see Index) or any Mexican meat and sauce
  dish or 1½ cups cooked shredded meat mixed with Red
  Chili Sauce to moisten or 24 small cheese slices (1 × 3
  inches)
24 small strips of green chili

Soak corn husks in hot water to cover, if used. Next make the dough. Beat lard with electric mixer until light. Add masa, salt, and chicken broth; beat until light and fluffy. Divide into 24 equal parts.

Drain corn husks; pat dry. Place each portion masa dough on parchment square or corn husk; spread to form a 4-inch square, keeping one side even with one edge of the paper or husk. Top with 1 tablespoon of filling or 1 slice of cheese plus one strip of chili pepper. Roll up as for a jelly roll, starting with the side of the dough that is even with the side of the paper or husk. Fold the ends over, sealing well.

The tamales are cooked by steaming. A steamer pot is ideal (the kind used for crabs or corn), but one can be easily improvised. Select a large, deep pot. Place a vegetable steaming basket or metal colander in bottom of pan. Line steamer or colander with any leftover corn husks. Bring 1 to 2 inches of water to boil in bottom of kettle or steamer pot.

Meanwhile, place tamales upright in steamer, packing tightly. Place basket in steamer kettle; cover tightly. Steam for 1 hour or until dough no longer sticks to paper. Serve tamales hot with chili sauce (for example: Red Chili Sauce).
MAKES 24 TAMALES.

Tamale pie

MEXICO

½ pound ground beef
½ pound bulk pork sausage
1 large onion, sliced
⅛ teaspoon minced garlic
1 16-ounce can tomatoes with juice
1 12-ounce can whole-kernel corn, drained
1 tablespoon chili powder
1 teaspoon salt
¼ teaspoon pepper

cornmeal pastry

1 cup cornmeal
2 medium eggs
1 cup milk
18 green olives, chopped

Olive slices for garnish

Cook meats with onion and garlic until browned. Stir in tomatoes with juice, corn, and seasonings. Simmer for 10 minutes. Pour into greased oblong baking dish.

American enchiladas

Prepare cornmeal crust by mixing cornmeal, eggs, milk, and chopped olives. Spread over hot mixture. Decorate top with a few olive slices. Bake at 350°F for 30 to 35 minutes. Serve tamale pie warm.

MAKES 4 TO 6 SERVINGS.

Leg of lamb Mexican-style

MEXICO

2 cloves garlic
1 tablespoon dried oregano
⅛ teaspoon ground cumin
1 teaspoons chili powder
1 4- to 5-pound leg of lamb
Salt and pepper
2 tablespoons wine vinegar
3 tablespoons olive oil
1 onion, chopped

Peel garlic; mash with oregano and cumin. Add a few drops of water, so that mixture forms a stiff paste. Stir in chili powder. Wipe leg of lamb with damp cloth. With sharp knife make incisions all over surface of lamb. Put some spice mixture in each incision. Rub roast with salt and pepper.

Combine vinegar, olive oil, and onion. Put roast in large plastic bag; pour oil and vinegar mixture over roast. Tie bag shut; marinate roast overnight.

Bring roast to room temperature. Remove lamb from bag. Roast lamb in open pan at 325°F for 30 minutes per pound. Serve lamb with pan-roasted potatoes.

MAKES 8 TO 10 SERVINGS.

Lamb chops Mexican-style

MEXICO

4 large shoulder lamb chops (about 1½ pounds total)
4 tablespoons olive oil
2 tablespoons lime juice
1 clove garlic, crushed
2 tablespoons grated onion
¼ cup flour
Salt and pepper
¼ cup lard
½ cup sherry

Wipe chops with a damp cloth; pat dry. Combine olive oil, lime juice, garlic, and onion; rub into chops. Refrigerate for several hours. Drain chops.

Combine flour and salt and pepper to taste. Dredge chops, shaking off excess flour. Heat lard in heavy skillet. Brown chops well on all sides over moderate heat. Reduce heat to very low; cook for 20 minutes. Remove to warm platter. Slowly pour sherry into pan, scraping browned bits from bottom and sides of pan. Cook, stirring, several minutes. Pour sauce over the chops, and serve.

MAKES 4 SERVINGS.

Pork chops w/rice

MEXICO

4 loin pork chops, about 1½ pounds total
3 tablespoons olive oil
1 medium onion, chopped
1 clove garlic, minced
1 green pepper, seeded and chopped
1 cup raw long-grain rice
2 cups boiling water
2 tablespoons dry sherry
2 teaspoons chicken-broth granules
2 packs cilantro and achiote seasoning mix (5 grams each)
½ cup sliced black olives

Sauté pork chops in olive oil in large, heavy skillet until well-browned. Remove from skillet. Add onion, garlic, and pepper, sauté over medium heat until limp. Add rice; sauté until lightly browned.

Combine boiling water, chicken-broth granules, cilantro and achiote seasoning mix, and sherry. Pour over rice. Top with pork chops; cover. Reduce heat to low; cook for 20 to 25 minutes or until all liquid is absorbed. Top the chops with the sliced olives, and serve.

MAKES 4 SERVINGS.

Note: Cilantro and achiote seasoning mix is sold in Latin American and Caribbean markets and is sometimes referred to as Creole seasoning. If you cannot obtain it, substitute 2 tablespoons tomato paste and ½ teaspoon ground cumin for the seasoning mix.

Mexican lamb w/fruit

MEXICO

4 cups milk
1 onion, chopped
2 bay leaves
½ teaspoon dried thyme
1 teaspoon salt
¼ teaspoon pepper
¼ cup butter
2 pounds lamb, trimmed well and cut into cubes
4 cups rice cooked with ½ cup raisins
½ cup sliced canned peaches
½ cup sliced canned pears
½ cup toasted sliced almonds
2 tablespoons fresh parsley

Combine milk, onion, bay leaves, thyme, salt, and pepper. Heat mixture, but do not boil. Heat butter in a skillet; sauté lamb until golden. Add lamb to hot milk. Simmer uncovered over low heat until lamb is tender and milk has cooked away (about 1 hour or more).

Place lamb in center of serving dish that has been covered with the hot rice and raisin mixture. Arrange sliced peaches and pears around the lamb. Sprinkle the lamb with almonds and parsley.

MAKES 4 TO 6 SERVINGS.

Pork roast cooked in beer w/green sauce

MEXICO

2 medium onions, chopped
2 carrots, peeled and sliced
1 4- to 5-pound loin or shoulder pork roast
2 teaspoons salt
½ teaspoon oregano
½ teaspoon ground coriander
½ to ¾ cup beer

Place onions and carrots in roasting pan. Rub pork with salt, oregano, and coriander. Place pork on top of vegetables; add beer. Cover; roast at 350°F for 2¾ hours. Add more beer, if necessary. Slice and serve pork with Hot Dip (see Index) or Green Sauce and rice and Refried Beans (see Index).

Note: This may be cooked in a slow cooker on a low setting with 2 cups of beer for 8 to 12 hours.

Green sauce

2 tablespoons olive oil
1 medium onion, chopped
1 clove garlic, peeled and chopped
1 10-ounce can Mexican green tomatoes (tomatillos)
½ teaspoon crumbled dried oregano
½ teaspoon dried cilantro
2 tablespoons wine vinegar
Salt and pepper

Heat olive oil in small skillet. Sauté onion and garlic until limp. Drain tomatillos; reserve liquid. In jar of electric blender or food processor combine tomatillos, ½ cup reserved liquid, onion, garlic, and olive oil, oregano, and cilantro; purée.

Heat skillet once again over moderate heat. Pour in sauce; cook for 10 minutes. Remove from heat; add wine vinegar and salt and pepper to taste. Chill sauce and serve with meat dishes.
MAKES 6 TO 8 SERVINGS.

Pork spareribs in Mexican barbecue sauce

MEXICO

mexican barbecue sauce
1 tablespoon olive oil
1 medium onion, chopped
1 clove garlic, peeled and minced
1 fresh chili pepper, stemmed, seeded, and chopped
½ tablespoon salt
2 large tomatoes, peeled and cut up
2 tablespoons chili powder
2 tablespoons sugar
¼ cup vinegar
⅓ cup olive oil
¼ cup beer

4 pounds pork spareribs (country-style)

First make the sauce. Heat the tablespoon of olive oil in saucepan. Sauté onion in oil until lightly browned. Add garlic, chopped chili, salt, and tomatoes; simmer until mixture thickens. Add remaining sauce ingredients; cook for 8 minutes, stirring constantly.

Pork kebabs Yucatan

Marinate spareribs in sauce for several hours before grilling (if possible). Grill over hot charcoal, basting periodically with sauce, until tender, well-browned, and crusty. Pour extra sauce on the ribs before serving.
MAKES 6 TO 8 SERVINGS.

Pork kebabs Yucatan

MEXICO

This dish is especially good charcoal-grilled.

Juice of 1 lime
¼ cup salad oil
¼ teaspoon crushed whole coriander
¼ cup chopped onion
1 clove garlic, mashed
¼ teaspoon pepper
1¼ pounds lean pork, cut in 1½-inch cubes
1 medium zucchini, sliced
2 red peppers, stemmed, seeded, and cut in chunks
½ pound mushrooms, cleaned and stems cut off

357

The day before cooking combine lime juice, oil, coriander, onion, garlic, and pepper in a glass or pottery bowl or casserole. Add meat; stir to coat with marinade. Cover; refrigerate 24 hours, stirring once or twice.

To cook, drain meat, reserving marinade. Skewer meat alternately with zucchini, red peppers, and mushrooms. Broil until done through (20 to 25 minutes), basting occasionally with marinade. Serve kebabs with cooked rice.
MAKES 4 SERVINGS.

Pork in red chili sauce

MEXICO

2 tablespoons lard (optional)
1 medium onion, chopped
1 clove garlic, minced
1½ to 2 tablespoons chili powder
1½ pounds lean pork, cut into 1½-inch cubes (reserve the fat)
1½ cups canned tomatoes, broken up with a fork
½ teaspoon salt
½ teaspoon crumbled oregano
½ teaspoon ground cumin
⅛ teaspoon ground cloves
1 small cinnamon stick

Render strips of pork fat or heat lard in Dutch oven over moderate heat. Remove strips of fat, if used; add onion and garlic, and brown lightly. Add chili powder; stir well.

Push vegetables to sides of pan; brown meat on all sides. Add tomatoes, salt, oregano, cumin, cloves, and cinnamon stick. Stir well; bring to a boil. Reduce heat to low, cover, and cook for 2 hours or until meat is very tender. Stir mixture occasionally while it is cooking. If sauce is quite thin, cook uncovered the last 15 to 20 minutes of cooking. Serve pork with rice and tortillas.
MAKES 4 SERVINGS.

Veal w/Mexican sauce

MEXICO

mexican sauce
2 cups chopped peeled tomatoes or 1 16-ounce can whole tomatoes and juice
1 small onion, chopped
1 clove garlic, chopped
1 green pepper, chopped
1 tablespoon chili powder
½ teaspoon oregano
1 teaspoon salt
Few drops of hot sauce

4 cubed veal steaks
2 eggs, beaten
1 cup dry bread crumbs
Salt and pepper
½ cup butter
½ cup shredded Jack cheese

Combine all sauce ingredients in blender or food processor; spin until smooth. Pour into small saucepan; simmer for 30 minutes. Makes 2½ to 3 cups sauce.

Dip veal in beaten eggs. Coat with bread crumbs, salt, and pepper. Fry in butter until browned; drain. Put veal in pan, cover with sauce, and top with shredded cheese. Bake at 350°F for 20 minutes.
MAKES 4 SERVINGS.

Rice w/veal & sour cream

MEXICO

1½ pounds veal, cut into small pieces
2 tablespoons oil
1 medium onion, chopped
1 clove garlic, minced
1 medium green pepper, chopped
2 tablespoons minced parsley
1 teaspoon paprika
3 cups beef broth
1 cup uncooked rice
1 cup sour cream
Salt and pepper to taste

Brown the veal in oil. Add onion, garlic, and green pepper. Cook for a few minutes. Add parsley, paprika, and broth.

Simmer, covered, for 15 minutes. Add rice, stir, cover, and cook an additional 15 minutes. Slowly stir in sour cream, season to taste, cover, and cook 15 minutes longer. Serve rice hot.
MAKES 4 TO 6 SERVINGS.

❧ Seafood ❧

Sole w/mushrooms

FRANCE

1 cup fresh mushrooms
2 tablespoons minced shallots
2 tablespoons chopped parsley
½ teaspoon salt
Dash pepper
1½ pounds sole fillets
½ cup dry white wine (more, if needed)
2 tablespoons flour
2 tablespoons butter
2 to 4 tablespoons heavy cream

Mix mushrooms, shallots, parsley, salt, and pepper. Place in greased flat baking dish. Place fish over mushrooms. Add enough wine to cover bottom of dish. Bring to a simmer. Cover with foil. Place in preheated 350°F oven 15 to 20 minutes, until fish is opaque. Remove fish; keep it warm. Mix flour and butter. Boil the juices remaining from fish until they are reduced by one-half. Beat in flour-butter mixture; cook until thickened. Add juices that have drained from fish and enough cream to make a medium sauce. Pour sauce over fish. Serve.
MAKES 4 SERVINGS.

Sole w/tomatoes

FRANCE

1 pound tomatoes, peeled, seeded, and chopped (about 1½ cups)
2 tablespoons minced shallots
2 tablespoons minced parsley
½ teaspoon salt
Dash pepper
1½ pounds sole fillets
¾ cup dry white wine
¼ cup water or clam juice
2 tablespoons butter or margarine
2 tablespoons flour
½ teaspoon sugar
3 to 4 tablespoons heavy cream

Mix tomatoes, shallots, parsley, salt, and pepper; place in bottom of greased flat baking dish. Place fillets over tomatoes. Add wine and water; bring to simmer on the range. Cover with aluminum foil. Place in preheated 325°F oven 13 to 15 minutes, until fish is opaque. Remove fish to serving dish; keep it warm.
Boil juices until mixture is reduced to about one-half. Mix butter and flour. Stir into juices; cook until thickened. Add sugar, cream, and juices drained from fish on platter. Pour sauce over fish. Serve.
MAKES 4 SERVINGS.

Fried trout Grenoble

FRANCE

4 freshwater trout, fresh or frozen, thawed, (each about ½ pound)
Juice of 1 lemon
Salt
5 tablespoons flour
½ cup vegetable oil
¼ cup butter
1 slice dry bread, crumbled
2 tablespoons capers
1 lemon, sliced
Parsley sprigs for garnish

Thoroughly wash fish; pat dry with paper towels. Sprinkle with half the lemon juice; let stand 5 minutes. Salt trout inside and out; roll it in flour.
Heat oil in frypan. Add trout; fry for 5 minutes on each side or until golden. Remove fish carefully with slotted spoon; discard oil. Melt butter in same frypan. Return trout to pan; fry for 5 minutes on each side. Remove; arrange on preheated platter.
Add bread crumbs to butter; cook until browned. Pour over trout. Sprinkle rest of lemon juice over trout. Top with drained capers. Garnish with lemon slices and parsley sprigs.
MAKES 4 SERVINGS.

Stuffed fillets of sole

FRANCE

shrimp stuffing
2 tablespoons minced shallots or green onions
2 tablespoons butter or margarine

½ pound mushrooms, sliced
2 tablespoons chopped parsley
½ pound tiny shrimp, cooked and cleaned
6 fillets of sole
2 tablespoons butter
2 tablespoons flour
1 cup dry white wine
½ cup heavy cream or half-and-half cream
¼ teaspoon salt
2 tablespoons brandy
½ cup grated Swiss chesse

Cook shallots in 2 tablespoons melted butter until transparent. Add mushrooms; cook until all liquid has evaporated. Add parsley and shrimp.
Place about 2 tablespoons stuffing on large end of each fillet. Roll up fillets; place in greased flat baking dish (12 X 8 X 2 inches). Melt 2 tablespoons butter; mix with flour. Add white wine; cook until thick. Stir in cream, salt, and brandy. Add any remainng stuffing to sauce. Pour sauce overfillets.
Bake in preheated 400°F oven about 20 to 25 minutes, until fish is done. Sprinkle with Swiss cheese the last 5 minutes of baking. The top should be golden brown.
MAKES 6 SERVINGS.

Poached fish

FRANCE

5 cups boiling water
2 medium onions, sliced
1 carrot, chopped
1 stalk celery
4 sprigs parsley
1 bay leaf
2 tablespoons salt
1 lemon, sliced
2 cups dry white wine
8 fish fillets or 1 3- to-4-pound whole dressed fish
2 tablespoons butter
2 tablespoons flour
½ cup heavy cream
1 egg yolk
1 tablespoon lemon juice

In 3-quart saucepan combine water, onions, carrot, celery, parsley, bay leaf, salt, and lemon.

Bring to a boil. Reduce heat; simmer for 15 minutes. Add wine; simmer 15 minutes longer. Strain liquid. Cool to lukewarm.
Place fresh fillets in bottom of greased casserole. Cover with above stock. Bring just to simmer on the range. Cover tightly; place in preheated 325°F oven. Cook fish 10 to 15 minutes, until done, or simmer on top of stove. If poaching a whole fish, first wrap in cheesecloth. Then place fish in large shallow pan, such as a French fish-poacher; cover with liquid. Cook fish at simmer about 10 minutes per inch of thickness. Remove from heat; leave fish in broth while preparing sauce.
To prepare sauce for fish, melt butter in small pan. Add flour; stir to blend. Add 1 cup of the poaching liquid. Cook, stirring constantly, until thickened.
Mix cream and egg yolk. Stirring rapidly, add cream and lemon juice to sauce. Keep sauce warm. Serve over fish.
MAKES 8 SERVINGS.

Baked salmon loaf

FRANCE

2 tablespoons butter
¼ cup finely chopped celery
2 tablespoons chopped shallots or green onions
½ cup chopped mushrooms
2 cups cooked or canned salmon (2 1-pound cans)
1½ cups soft bread crumbs
½ teaspoon dried chervil
2 tablespoons lemon juice
3 eggs, beaten
2 tablespoons chopped parsley
1 cup evaporated milk or heavy cream
2 tablespoons brandy
Mushroom Sauce (see Index)

Melt butter in small frying pan. Cook celery and shallots several minutes. Add mushrooms; cook until liquid has evaporated. Place mushroom mixture in 2-quart bowl with remaining ingredients; mix thoroughly. Pour into well-greased 9 X 5 X 3-inch loaf pan or 2-quart fish mold. Bake salmon in preheated 350°F oven 40 to 45 minutes, until done in the center.

Unmold salmon. Serve with Mushroom Sauce (see Index).
MAKES 6 SERVINGS.

Salmon mousse

FRANCE

The mousse may also be served as an hors d'oeuvre, since it is very rich.

2 tablespoons gelatin
1½ cups fish stock, from poaching fish (or 1½ cups bottled clam juice)
½ cup mayonnaise
1 tablespoon lemon juice
1 1-pound salmon steak, cooked, boned, and mashed, or 2 cups canned salmon
1 tablespoon Madeira
¼ teaspoon salt
⅛ teaspoon white pepper
½ cup heavy cream, whipped
Lemon or cucumber slices for garnish

Sprinkle gelatin over ½ cup cold stock, then heat stock to dissolve gelatin completely. With wire whisk, beat in mayonnaise and lemon juice. Cool until slightly thickened. Fold in salmon and Madeira. Add salt and pepper to taste. Gently fold in whipped cream. Pour into oiled 2-quart fish mold. Chill until set.
Unmold mousse to serve. Garnish with lemon or cucumber slices. Makes a 2-quart mold.
MAKES 8 TO 12 SERVINGS.

Salmon steaks w/hollandaise sauce

FRANCE

¼ pound fresh small mushrooms
1 tablespoon butter
½ cup white wine
6 tablespoons water
½ teaspoon salt
⅛ teaspoon white pepper
4 salmon steaks, each about 6 to 8 ounces
Juice of ½ lemon
1 recipe Hollandaise Sauce (see Index)
8 ounces fresh oysters

1 4½-ounce can deveined shrimp
1 ounce truffles, sliced (optional, found in specialty stores)

Clean mushrooms; cut into thin slices. Heat butter in frypan. Add mushrooms; sauté for 3 minutes. Add ¼ cup wine and the water. Season with salt and pepper; simmer for 10 minutes. Meanwhile, rinse salmon steaks under cold running water; pat dry. Sprinkle with lemon juice. Let stand 5 minutes. Strain mushrooms, reserving juice. Set mushrooms aside.
Add mushroom juice to frypan. Add rest of wine. Bring to a boil; add salmon steaks. Cover; simmer over low heat 20 minutes. While salmon is cooking, prepare Hollandaise Sauce. Keep it warm. Remove salmon steaks with slotted spoon to preheated platter. Keep them warm.
Add oysters to simmering stock. Heat about 5 minutes or until edges begin to curl. Add shrimp; just heat through. Remove; drain. Spoon around salmon steaks. Pour Hollandaise Sauce over salmon. Garnish with reserved reheated mushrooms and truffle slices if desired.
MAKES 4 SERVINGS.

Bouillabaisse

FRANCE

2 tablespoons vegetable oil
2 onions, chopped, or 3 leeks, sliced
4 cloves garlic, crushed
2 fresh tomatoes, peeled and diced
3 tablespoons tomato paste
2 cups bottled clam juice

4 cups chicken bouillon
1 tablespoon salt
⅛ teaspoon pepper
¼ teaspoon saffron
½ teaspoon thyme
1 bay leaf
6 sprigs parsley
Grated rind of 1 orange

seafoods
1 2-pound lobster and/or other shellfish, such as clams, mussels (with shells), scallops, crab, or shrimp

2 pounds assorted white fish fillets, such as sea bass, perch, cod, sole, flounder, or red snapper

Chopped parsley for garnish

Heat vegetable oil in large saucepan or Dutch oven. Sauté onions or leeks several minutes, until translucent. Add remaining sauce ingredients; simmer 45 minutes.
Prepare seafoods by cooking lobster. (Place in

361

large kettle of boiling salted water 10 minutes.) Break claws and tail from body; crack claws; cut tail into 1-inch chunks. Remove black vein from tail pieces; leave shell on meat. Wash and cut fish fillets into 2-inch pieces.

Add lobster and firm-fleshed fish (sea bass, perch, etc.) to boiling sauce. Boil 5 minutes, then add tender-fleshed fish, such as clams, scallops, sole, or cod. Simmer another 5 minutes. Lift seafoods out as soon as cooked; keep them warm in soup tureen or platter. Boil liquid 10 minutes to reduce. Strain liquid through coarse sieve into tureen, mashing through some of the vegetables. Garnish with parsley. Serve.
MAKES 6 SERVINGS.

Scallops

FRANCE

1 pound scallops
2 tablespoons chopped shallots or green onions
6 tablespoons butter
1 teaspoon lemon juice
⅓ cup fine bread crumbs
2 tablespoons chopped parsley

Wash scallops to remove sand; dry on paper towels. Place scallops in 4 buttered shells or in a buttered casserole. Sauté shallots in 2 tablespoons butter until soft. Distribute evenly over scallops.

Melt remaining butter. Add lemon juice. Pour over scallops; sprinkle with crumbs. Bake in preheated 375°F oven 12 to 15 minutes, until scallops are tender when pierced with a knife. Serve scallops very hot, garnished with chopped parsley.
MAKES 4 SERVINGS.

Scallops w/mushrooms

FRANCE

1½ pounds scallops
10 tablespoons butter
1 cup dry white wine
½ teaspoon salt
⅛ teaspoon pepper

1 green onion, minced
4 tablespoons flour
1 cup heavy cream
1 cup milk
½ pound fresh mushrooms, sliced
1 teaspoon lemon juice
Salt and pepper to taste
1 tablespoon cognac
6 scallop shells or pyrex dishes
Parsley for garnish

Wash scallops well in slightly salted water to remove all grit. Drain and dry on paper towels. Cut scallops in half or in fourths to make them bite-size. In medium saucepan bring ½ cup butter, wine, ½ teaspoon salt, ⅛ teaspoon pepper, and onion to simmer. Add scallops; return to simmer. Cover; simmer slowly 5 minutes. Remove scallops with slotted spoon; set aside.

Boil pan liquids; reduce to just the butter. Add flour; cook, stirring, for 3 minutes. Stir in cream, milk, mushrooms, lemon juice, and salt and pepper to taste. Over medium heat, cook until thickened, stirring frequently. Add cognac. Blend two-thirds of sauce with scallops.

Grease shells or dishes. Divide scallop mixture between them. Cover with rest of sauce. Dot with 2 tablespoons butter. Just before serving, place in preheated 400°F oven; heat about 10 minutes or until sauce is bubbling. Garnish with parsley.
MAKES 6 SERVINGS.

Blue trout

GERMANY

4 ¾-pound freshwater trout (eviscerated only)
2 teaspoons salt
1 cup vinegar, heated
4 cups water
¼ cup white wine
1 sprig parsley for garnish
1 lemon for garnish
1 tomato for garnish

Rinse fish thoroughly with cold water. Sprinkle ¼ teaspoon salt inside each fish. To make the

Fried trout Grenoble

Bouillabaisse

trout look attractive, tie a thread through the tail and the underside of the mouth to form a ring (see picture). Arrange fish on a large platter and pour hot vinegar over them. This process will turn them blue in color.

In a 4-quart saucepot bring water, remaining salt, and wine to a simmer. Carefully place the trout in the water and simmer (be sure not to boil) about 15 minutes. Remove trout with a slotted spoon, drain on paper towels, and arrange on a preheated platter. Garnish with parsley, lemon, and tomato slices.

MAKES 4 SERVINGS.

Note: In Germany, freshwater trout is served with small boiled potatoes that have been tossed in melted butter and sprinkled with chopped parsley. A cold sauce accompanies the dish. This is made from 1 cup whipped heavy cream, 1/4 teaspoon sugar, 2 tablespoons prepared horseradish, 1 teaspoon lemon juice, and salt and pepper to taste.

Fish kabobs

GREECE

1/4 cup olive oil
1/4 cup dry white wine
1/4 cup lemon juice
2 cloves garlic, minced
3 bay leaves
1/2 teaspoon dried oregano
1/2 teaspoon salt
1/4 teaspoon pepper
1 1/4 to 1 1/2 pounds swordfish or halibut steak
2 red peppers, cut in chunks
2 green peppers, cut in chunks
1 onion, cut in wedges
Paprika

The day before serving: Combine the oil, wine, lemon juice, garlic, bay leaves, oregano, salt, and pepper. Cut the fish into 1 1/2-inch squares and add to the marinade. Cover and marinate in the refrigerator overnight.

To cook: Alternate the fish, peppers, and onions on thin skewers. Dust with paprika and broil for approximately 10 minutes. (May also be charcoal-grilled.)

Serve the kabobs on a bed of rice and pass the Cocktail Sauce.

MAKES 4 SERVINGS.

Cocktail sauce

1 cup tomato catsup
2 tablespoons horseradish
1/2 teaspoon dry mustard

Combine the catsup, dry mustard, and horseradish. Mix to combine well and let stand a few minutes before serving.

Baked fish

GREECE

1 pound fish fillets (sole, flounder, or red snapper)
1 tablespoon chopped parsley
1 tablespoon lemon juice
¾ teaspoon seasoned salt
3 tablespoons olive oil
1 medium onion, thinly silced
1 clove garlic, minced
1 large tomato, thinly sliced
3 slices lemon
2 tablespoon white wine

Arrange the fish in an 8- or 9-inch-square baking dish. Sprinkle with the parsley, lemon juice, and seasoned salt.

Heat the oil in a small skillet and fry the onion and garlic until limp. Top the fish with the onion mixture, including the oil from the skillet. Arrange the tomatoes on top of the onion mixture, then place the lemon slices between the tomato slices. Pour the wine over all and bake at 350°F for 30 to 35 minutes or until the fish flakes with a fork. Serve with Braised Potatoes (see Index).

MAKES 3 SERVINGS.

Fish & rice casserole

GREECE

¼ cup olive oil
½ cup chopped celery
½ cup chopped onion
¼ cup chopped green pepper
1 cup raw long-grain rice
¼ cup chopped parsley
2 tablespoons chopped pimiento
1 bay leaf
½ pound cooked medium shrimp, peeled and deveined
½ pound fillet of sole, cut in 1-inch chunks
2 cups chicken stock
2 tablespoons white wine

Blue trout

½ teaspoon salt
¼ teaspoon pepper

Heat the olive oil in a skillet and sauté the celery, onion, and green pepper until limp. Remove with a slotted spoon. Add the rice to the oil left in the pan and sauté the rice over medium heat until lightly colored.

Pour the rice and oil into a 2-quart casserole. Add the sautéed vegetables, parsley, pimiento, bay leaf, shrimp, and sole and mix gently. Add the chicken stock, wine, salt, and pepper. Cover and bake at 375°F for 35 to 45 minutes or until all the liquid is absorbed. Fluff with a fork and serve.

MAKES 4 SERVINGS.

Marinated fish

GREECE

1¼ pounds rockfish, red snapper, or sole fillets
½ cup all-purpose flour
½ teaspoon salt
¼ teaspoon pepper
4 tablespoons olive oil
2 cloves garlic, finely chopped
4 tablespoons wine vinegar
½ teaspoon rosemary

Thaw the fish, if frozen. Combine the flour, salt, and pepper and dredge the fish fillets, coating well. Shake off the excess flour. Heat the oil in a large skillet. Fry the fish fillets, a few at a time,

until golden brown. Drain on paper towels and keep them warm.

When all the fish has been cooked, add the garlic, vinegar, and rosemary. Stir, scraping up the browned bits in the pan. Cook for a few minutes and then pour over the fish on a platter. Serve the fish warm or cold.

MAKES 4 SERVINGS.

Fish w/vegetables & yoghurt

GREECE

1 onion, sliced
1 green pepper, sliced
1 tomato, peeled and chopped
1¼ pounds fish fillets
1 clove garlic, minced
½ teaspoon oregano
½ teaspoon salt
¼ teaspoon pepper
3 tablespoons butter
1 cup plain yoghurt or sour cream

Place half of the vegetables on the bottom of a greased baking dish. Top with the fish fillets.

Baked fish

Sprinkle with the oregano, salt, and pepper. Top with the remaining vegetables and dot with the butter. Bake at 350°F for 30 minutes. Top the dish with the yoghurt, and cook 10 minutes more.

MAKES 4 SERVINGS.

Shrimp w/feta cheese

GREECE

1 tablespoon lemon juice
1¼ pounds medium shrimp, peeled and deveined
2 tablespoons olive oil
¼ cup chopped onion
½ bunch green onions, finely chopped (use only part of the green stems)
1 clove garlic, minced
1 cup tomato purée
¼ cup dry white wine
1 tablespoon butter
1 tablespoon brandy or ouzo
¼ teaspoon oregano
1 tablespoon chopped parsley
¼ pound feta cheese, cut in ½-inch squares

Pour the lemon juice over the shrimp and let stand while making the sauce.

Heat the oil in a heavy skillet. Add the onions (green and white) and the garlic, and sauté until limp. Add the tomato purée and wine and let simmer 15 minutes.

Melt the butter and sauté the shrimp until pink (3 to 4 minutes). Gently warm the brandy. Ignite and pour it over the shrimp. When the flame extinguishes, add the oregano and parsley. Transfer the shrimp to a small casserole (1½ quart).

Take the remaining juice from the pan in which the shrimp were cooked and mix with the tomato-purée sauce. Pour this over the shrimp. Top with the feta cheese and press the cheese into the sauce. Bake at 375°F for 15 minutes or until hot and bubbly.

MAKES 4 SERVINGS.

Broiled shrimp

GREECE

½ cup olive oil
½ cup white wine
¼ cup lemon juice
2 tablespoons chopped parsley
½ teaspoon crumbled oregano
Lemon wedges for garnish
1½ pounds extra-large shrimp, shelled and deveined
1 bunch green onions, trimmed and cut in 2-inch lengths

Combine the oil, wine, lemon juice, parsley, and oregano. Skewer the shrimp alternately with the onions and marinate in the oil mixture in a shallow pan, turning frequently, for ½ hour. Broil the shrimp for 2½ to 3 minutes on each side, basting with marinade. Garnish with lemon wedges.

MAKES 4 SERVINGS.

Squid Athenian-style

GREECE

3 pounds frozen squid
1 cup chopped onions
1 clove garlic, chopped
3 tablespoons olive oil
2½ cups canned tomatoes, chopped
½ cup chopped fresh parsley
½ teaspoon salt
¼ teaspoon pepper
¾ teaspoon crumbled dried oregano
¼ cup white wine

Thaw the squid. Remove the tentacles; chop and reserve. Remove and discard the head, chitinous pen and viscera. Wash the mantle well and cut into pieces.

Sauté the onion and garlic in the olive oil until lightly browned. Add the tomatoes, parsley, salt, pepper, oregano, wine, and squid. Cover and simmer for 1 hour or until the squid is tender. Serve with rice.

MAKES 4 OR 5 SERVINGS.

Pan-fried fish fillets

HUNGARY

1 pound fresh or frozen firm whitefish fillets (such as flounder, haddock, or sole)
2 eggs
2 tablespoons milk
¾ cup fine dry bread crumbs
½ teaspoon Hungarian sweet paprika
1 teaspoon dried parsley flakes
Salt and pepper
4 tablespoons butter or margarine
2 tablespoons lemon juice
1 tablespoon chopped parsley

Defrost fish if frozen. Drain well; pat dry. Beat eggs and milk together in shallow bowl; set aside. Combine bread crumbs and seasonings on waxed paper; mix well.

Heat 2 tablespoons butter in heavy skillet. Dip fish in egg mixture, then in crumbs, coating well; shake off excess. Fry in hot butter over moderate heat until golden; turn once. Drain on absorbent paper. Add more butter as needed; continue until all fillets are cooked. Keep warm. Add lemon juice and parsley to skillet; stir well. Pour over fish.

MAKES 4 SERVINGS.

Fish fillets w/walnuts

HUNGARY

3½ cups water
½ cup dry white wine
¼ cup coarsely chopped celery
2 sprigs parsley
2 cloves
1 bay leaf
1 slice lemon
¾ teaspoon salt
1 pound whitefish fillets, defrosted if frozen

sauce
1½ tablespoons butter or margarine
1½ tablespoons flour
Salt and pepper
¾ cup reserved fish stock
¼ cup sour cream
¼ cup toasted walnuts
Chopped parsley

Combine water, wine, vegetables, and seasonings in large saucepan; bring to boil. Reduce heat to low; cook 25 minutes. Strain liquid into large shallow skillet; bring to boil. Add fish pieces; cover. Simmer 5 to 6 minutes or until fish flakes easily. Carefully transfer to platter; keep warm while making sauce.

Melt butter in small saucepan. Add flour, salt, and pepper; cook over low heat until bubbly. Add reserved fish stock slowly, stirring constantly; cook over low heat until thickened. Remove from heat; add sour cream, stirring well. Pour sauce over fish; sprinkle with toasted walnuts and a little chopped parsley. Serve with steamed potatoes or rice.

MAKES 4 SERVINGS.

Sautéed brook trout

HUNGARY

4 whole trout, cleaned (5 to 7 ounces each)
¼ cup flour
Salt and pepper
6 tablespoons butter
3 tablespoons cooking oil
¼ cup coarsely chopped walnuts
Juice of ½ lemon
2 tablespoons finely chopped parsley

Wash trout well; pat dry. Combine flour, salt, and pepper; dredge fish in mixture. Heat 3 tablespoons butter and oil in large heavy skillet until foam subsides. Add trout; cook 4 minutes over medium-high heat. Fish should be well-browned. Turn; cook until fish flakes easily. Carefully transfer to warm platter.

Pour off any fat remaining in pan; wipe out pan with paper towel. Add remaining butter; cook over low heat until melted. Add walnuts; sauté 3 minutes. Add lemon juice and parsley; pour over fish. Serve trout with boiled or steamed potatoes.

MAKES 4 SERVINGS.

Fish fillets baked w/sour cream

HUNGARY

1 pound firm white fish fillets
Salt and pepper
½ cup sour cream
1½ tablespoons Parmesan cheese
¾ teaspoon Hungarian sweet paprika
¼ teaspoon crumbled tarragon

2 tablespoons seasoned bread crumbs
2 tablespoons butter or margarine
Finely chopped parsley
Lemon wedges

Arrange fish in single layer in lightly greased shallow baking dish. Season with salt and pepper.

Combine sour cream, cheese, paprika, and tarragon; mix well. Spread evenly over fillets. Sprinkle with bread crumbs; dot with butter. Bake in preheated 350°F oven 20 to 25 minutes or until fish flakes easily. Sprinkle fish with parsley; serve with lemon wedges.
MAKES 4 SERVINGS.

Fishermen's soup

HUNGARY

2 tablespoons lard
2 medium onions, peeled, chopped
2½ to 3 pounds freshwater fish (trout, pike, and bass); use one or more kind of fish, as desired
1 quart water
1 teaspoon salt
1 tablespoon Hungarian sweet paprika

Melt lard in Dutch oven. Add onions; cook until tender and lightly browned.

Clean and bone fish, reserving heads and bones. Cut fish into 2-inch pieces. Add fish trimmings, water, and salt to Dutch oven. Stir well; bring to boil. Reduce heat to low; cover pan. Simmer 20 minutes.

Strain broth; return to Dutch oven. Add paprika; stir well. Add fish. Simmer, uncovered, 20 minutes, shaking pan occasionally. Do not stir; fish pieces will break. Serve soup hot in individual bowls with crusty bread.
MAKES 4 SERVINGS.

Hungarian-style fish fillet

HUNGARY

1 pound firm whitefish fillets, defrosted if frozen
Juice of 1 lemon
3 slices bacon, diced
2 tablespoons lard

2 tablespoons flour
Salt and pepper
2 small peppers (1 green and 1 red), cleaned, cut into ½-inch strips
1 large onion, peeled, sliced
1 medium cucumber (unpeeled), thinly sliced
White pepper
½ teaspoon Hungarian sweet paprika
¼ cup finely chopped parsley
4 lemon wedges

Rinse fish; pat dry. Place in shallow bowl; sprinkle with lemon juice. Let stand 10 minutes.

Place bacon in large heavy skillet; cook over moderate heat until crisp. Remove bacon with slotted spoon. Add lard to skillet; melt.

Combine flour and salt and pepper to taste. Drain fish; dredge in flour mixture. Brown fish in hot fat, turning once. Remove to hot platter. Add peppers, onion, and cucumber to skillet; sauté until tender, stirring frequently. Add salt, white pepper, and paprika; stir well. Spoon over fish. Sprinkle fish with reserved bacon and parsley; garnish with lemon wedges.
MAKES 4 SERVINGS.

Halibut w/tomato sauce

HUNGARY

2 tablespoons lard
1 cup chopped onion
1 clove garlic, peeled, minced
Salt and white pepper
1 16-ounce can tomatoes, drained, chopped
Dash of Tabasco
2 tablespoons dry sherry
2 tablespoons finely chopped parsley
4 halibut steaks, approximately 6 ounces each
4 tablespoons lemon juice
2 tablespoons butter or margarine

First make sauce. Melt lard in small skillet over moderate heat. Add onion; cook 3 minutes. Add garlic; cook until onion is lightly browned. Add salt, pepper, tomatoes, and Tabasco. Cover; simmer 15 minutes. Keep warm while cooking fish. Stir in sherry and parsley just before pouring over fish.

Rub fish steaks with 2 tablespoons lemon juice;

369

let stand 10 minutes. Place on preheated, lightly greased broiler pan; brush with remaining lemon juice and butter. Broil 6 inches from heat source 5 to 6 minutes per side; baste once. Turn; cook 5 minutes. Transfer fish to warm platter. Pour sauce over fish. Serve with boiled potatoes.
MAKES 4 SERVINGS.

Fish goulash esterházy

HUNGARY

1 pound firm white fish fillets (pike, perch, or carp, if available, are good)	Juice of 1 lemon

broth

2 tablespoons lard	1/8 teaspoon crumbled dried marjoram
1 medium onion, peeled, sliced	3 slices lemon
2 carrots, peeled, sliced	Salt and pepper
2 tablespoons chopped parsley	4 cups water
1 bay leaf	

vegetables

1 cup chicken broth	1 stalk celery, cut into matchstick strips
3 medium carrots, peeled, cut into matchstick strips	

sauce

2 tablespoons lard	Salt and white pepper
2 tablespoons flour	1 1/2 cups reserved fish broth
2 teaspoons Hungarian sweet paprika	1/2 cup sour cream
	1 tablespoon chopped capers

Wash fish; pat dry. Cut into serving-size pieces; place in shallow bowl. Sprinkle with lemon juice; refrigerate until needed.
Heat 2 tablespoons lard in large shallow skillet. Add onion and sliced carrots; cook until limp. Add remaining broth ingredients; bring to boil. Reduce heat to low; cook 20 minutes. Strain broth; return to skillet. Bring to boil.
Drain fish; add to skillet. Cover; reduce heat to low; cook 20 minutes or until fish flakes easily. Reserve broth; strain. Place broth in small saucepan; bring to boil. Add matchstick vegetables. Reduce heat to low; cook 10 minutes. Drain; keep warm.
Make sauce. Melt lard in medium saucepan. Add flour; cook until bubbly. Remove from heat; stir in paprika, salt, and pepper. Add fish broth. Re-

turn to heat; cook, stirring constantly, until thickened. Stir in sour cream and capers; cook over very low heat until heated through.
Arrange fish in serving dish. Pour sauce over fish; garnish with matchstick vegetables. Serve immediately with crusty bread.
MAKES 4 SERVINGS.

Creamed fresh haddock

IRELAND

1 pound fresh haddock fillets (or other firm white-fish fillets)
1/2 cup melted butter or margarine
Flour
1/2 cup slivered onion
Salt and pepper
1 cup light cream
1/2 teaspoon dry mustard

Wash fillets; pat dry. Dip fillets in melted butter; dredge in flour. Arrange in shallow baking dish in single layer. Arrange onion on top of fish. Sprinkle with salt and pepper. Add cream; top with any remaining butter. Bake in preheated 350°F oven 20 to 25 minutes or until fish flakes easily with fork. Baste with pan juices several times during cooking. Remove fish from baking dish; keep warm.
Stir dry mustard into cream mixture in baking dish. Taste sauce; add salt and pepper if necessary. Pour sauce over fish. Serve fish garnished with chopped parsley and sprinkled lightly with paprika.
MAKES 4 SERVINGS.

Poached cod w/lemon sauce

IRELAND

1 pound cod fillets
Seasoned salt and pepper
1 tablespoon lemon juice
2 shallots, peeled, chopped
1/4 cup white wine
1 tablespoon butter or margarine

lemon sauce

1 tablespoon butter or margarine
3/4 cup mayonnaise

Juice of ½ lemon
½ teaspoon dry mustard
½ teaspoon salt
½ tablespoon capers, drained, chopped

Wash fish; pat dry. Sprinkle with salt, pepper, and 1 tablespoon lemon juice. Place in small, greased casserole dish. Sprinkle with shallots; pour wine over all. Dot with 1 tablespoon butter; cover. Bake at 350°F 20 to 25 minutes or until fish flakes easily with fork.

Meanwhile, melt 1 tablespoon butter in top of double boiler. Add remaining sauce ingredients, except capers. Cook, stirring constantly, over simmering water until heated through. Stir in capers. Place fish on a heated platter and top with the sauce. Serve immediately, garnished with lemon slices.

MAKES 4 SERVINGS.

Shrimp with feta cheese

Poached salmon w/egg sauce

IREDNAL
IRELAND

1 quart water	4 peppercorns
½ lemon, sliced	1 teaspoon salt
½ cup white wine	4 small salmon steaks
¼ cup sliced onion	(approximately 4 ounces
1 bay leaf	each)

egg sauce

3 tablespoons butter or margarine	⅓ cup broth in which fish was cooked
1 tablespoon finely chopped onion	¾ cup milk
	½ teaspoon dry mustard
1 tablespoon finely chopped green pepper	Salt and pepper
	2 hard-cooked eggs, chopped
1½ tablespoons flour	

Combine water, lemon, wine, ¼ cup onion, bay leaf, peppercorns, and 1 teaspoon salt in heavy skillet; bring to boil. Wrap salmon steaks in cheesecloth; secure. Place in boiling stock; cover. Reduce heat to low; cook 10 minutes. Drain; keep warm while making sauce.

Melt 3 tablespoons butter in small saucepan. Add 1 tablespoon onion and green pepper; sauté 3 minutes. Add flour; cook, stirring constantly, until bubbly. Stir in fish stock, milk, mustard, salt, and pepper; cook, stirring constantly, until thickened. Stir in eggs. Serve.

MAKES 4 SERVINGS.

Grilled salmon w/lemon butter

IRELAND

lemon butter
¼ cup butter (½ stick), room temperature
1 tablespoon chopped fresh parsley
1 small shallot, finely chopped
½ tablespoon lemon juice

grilled salmon
4 salmon steaks, 1 inch thick
2 tablespoons melted butter
1 tablespoon lemon juice
1 tablespoon chopped fresh dill or ½ teaspoon dried dillweed

Make Lemon Butter at least 8 hours in advance of serving. (It can be prepared and refrigerated at least 1 month before use.) Combine all ingredients for flavored butter; beat with electric mixer until well-blended. Place on piece of plastic wrap; form into 3 X 3-inch square, using spatula. Wrap with plastic wrap; refrigerate.

Light standard charcoal barbecue fire. When fire has burned down and coals are glowing, place salmon steaks on grill. Combine melted butter, lemon juice, and dill; brush steaks well with mixture. Grill approximately 12 minutes (6 to 7 minutes per side), turning once and basting with butter mixture. Remove from grill.

Divide Lemon Butter into 4 pats; place 1 pat on each salmon steak. Serve immediately.

MAKES 4 SERVINGS.

Squid Athenian-style

Dressed crab

IRELAND

1 pound cooked crab meat
2 tablespoons butter
1 cup fresh bread crumbs
½ cup whipping cream, lightly whipped
1 tablespoon lemon juice
1 tablespoon finely minced green onion
1 teaspoon Worcestershire sauce
½ teaspoon dry mustard
Few drops of Tabasco
Salt and pepper
2 tablespoons melted butter
Parsley flakes and paprika

Lightly grease 4 natural crab shells, if available, or use 4 small ovenproof ramekins. Pick over crab meat, discarding any bits of shell and cartilage.

Melt 2 tablespoons butter in heavy skillet; heat until lightly browned. Add crab meat; toss well. Combine crab and remaining ingredients, except 2 tablespoons melted butter, parsley flakes, and paprika. Mix lightly but thoroughly. Place in shells or ramekins.

Drizzle with melted butter; sprinkle with parsley flakes and paprika. Place on baking sheet; bake at 375°F 15 minutes or until lightly browned. Serve hot.

MAKES 4 SERVINGS.

Cocklety pie

IRELAND

pastry crust

1 cup all-purpose flour
½ teaspoon salt
3 tablespoons cold butter
2 to 3 tablespoons cold water

scallop and mushroom filling

1 pound sea scallops
½ cup white wine
1 cup water
3 chopped shallots (green onions can be substituted)
1 bay leaf
2 peppercorns
1 cup peeled, diced potatoes
1 6½-ounce can button mushrooms

2 tablespoons chopped parsley
3 tablespoons butter
3 tablespoons flour
¼ teaspoon dry mustard
Salt and pepper
1 cup light cream
¾ cup reserved fish stock

1 egg yolk
1 tablespoon milk

First make pastry for crust. Combine flour and salt, mixing well. Cut butter into flour until mixture resembles coarse cornmeal. Blend water into flour mixture a tablespoon at a time while mixing with fork, just until moistened. Gather into ball; wrap in plastic wrap. Refrigerate while making Scallop and Mushroom Filling.

Wash scallops under cold running water to remove sand and grit. Halve or quarter scallops if large. Combine wine, water, shallots, bay leaf, and peppercorns in medium saucepan. Bring to boil over moderate heat. Add scallops; cover. Reduce heat to low; cook 10 minutes.

Meanwhile, cook potatoes in small saucepan of salted water until tender. Drain; reserve. Drain scallops; reserve cooking liquid. Combine scallops, potatoes, mushrooms, and parsley in lightly greased 1½-quart casserole. Mix well; set aside.

Melt butter in heavy saucepan. Add flour, mustard, salt, and pepper; cook, stirring constantly, until bubbly. Add cream and ¾ cup reserved fish broth (strained); cook over low heat, stirring constantly, until mixture thickens. Pour over fish and mushrooms in casserole; mix well.

Roll pastry crust on lightly floured board to fit top of casserole. Place crust over fish mixture; turn edges under; flute. Reroll any scraps; use to make leaves or other decorations. Beat egg yolk and milk together; brush crust well. Bake in preheated 425°F oven 20 to 30 minutes or until crust is golden brown. Serve hot.
MAKES 4 SERVINGS.

Haddock & potato bake

IRELAND

1 pound potatoes (approximately 3 medium potatoes)
Water
½ teaspoon salt
1 pound haddock fillets, thawed if frozen
4 tablespoons butter or margarine
2 medium onions, peeled, sliced
Salt and pepper
1 egg yolk
⅔ cup sour cream
¼ teaspoon ground mace
⅓ cup dry bread crumbs
1 tablespoon melted butter or margarine
Paprika
Dried parsley flakes

Hungarian-style fish fillet

Peel potatoes; cover with cold water. Add salt; cover; bring to boil. Reduce heat to low; cook 15 to 20 minutes or until fork-tender. Drain. Place tea towel over pan; steam over very low heat 5 minutes. Cool slightly.

Cut haddock into 1-inch squares; pat dry with paper towels. Slice potatoes. Melt butter in heavy saucepan; sauté onions until lightly browned. Lightly grease 1½-quart casserole. Place ⅓ of potatoes in casserole; sprinkle with salt and pepper. Top with ½ of haddock and ½ of onion and butter mixture. Top with ⅓ of potatoes, salt, pepper, and remaining haddock and onion mixture. Top with remaining potatoes.

Combine egg yolk, sour cream, and mace; spread over top layer of potatoes. Combine bread crumbs and melted butter; sprinkle over casserole. Dust lightly with paprika and parsley flakes. Bake at 350°F 30 to 40 minutes or until top is golden brown.
MAKES 4 SERVINGS.

Halibut with tomato sauce

Fillet of fish baked in tomato sauce

ITALY

Olive oil
1 pound haddock, cod or other white fish fillets, fresh or
  thawed and separated
1 8-ounce can tomato sauce
¼ teaspoon dried sweet basil, crumbled
Salt and pepper

Lightly grease a baking dish with olive oil. Arrange the fish fillets in the baking dish. Combine the tomato sauce, sweet basil, and salt and pepper and pour evenly over the fillets. Cover the dish with foil. Bake at 350°F for 15 minutes. Remove the foil and bake 15 more minutes or until the fish is tender and flakes with a fork.

374   MAKES 4 SERVINGS.

Rolled fish fillets

ITALY

1¼ pounds flounder or haddock fillets (4 to 5 fillets)
4½ tablespoons butter
2 tablespoons chopped onion
2 tablespoons chopped celery
1 cup dry bread crumbs
1 tablespoon chopped parsley
2 tablespoons grated Parmesan cheese
½ teaspoon dried tarragon, crumbled
Salt and pepper
1 egg, beaten
2 tablespoons milk
½ of a lemon, thinly sliced

Wash the fish fillets, and pat dry. Heat 1½ tablespoons of butter in a small skillet. Sauté the onion and celery in the butter until tender. Remove from the heat.

In a bowl, combine the bread crumbs, parsley, Parmesan cheese, tarragon, and salt and pepper and mix well. Add the celery, onion, and butter and mix. Beat the egg and milk; add to the crumb mixture and thoroughly combine. Pat about ⅓ cup of the crumb mixture on top of each fillet and roll up like a jelly roll. Fasten with toothpicks.

Melt 1½ tablespoons of butter in an 8-inch baking dish. Place the fish rolls on end in the baking dish. Dot with the remaining butter and top with the lemon slices. Bake at 350°F for 30 minutes or until the fish is tender and flakes easily with a fork.

MAKES 4 SERVINGS.

Fish soup

ITALY

Although this dish is called a soup, it is really more of a stew. Serve with lots of crisp-crusted Italian bread or bread sticks.

3 quarts water
1 tablespoon salt
1 large onion, sliced
1 bay leaf
3 stalks celery (with tops), chopped
1 1¼-pound lobster
½ pound shrimp
3 pounds fish heads, bones and trimmings
1 dozen clams
½ cup olive oil
2 cloves garlic, peeled and minced
2 pounds fish fillets (any firm white fish can be used; select one or more kinds from this list of possibilities: red snapper, bass, rockfish, cod, haddock, flounder, or perch), cut into chunks
2 cups drained Italian-style tomatoes, broken up
1 cup dry white wine
¼ cup chopped parsley
¼ teaspoon thyme
1 teaspoon dried sweet basil, crumbled
Freshly ground pepper
A scant ¼ teaspoon of saffron

In a large stockpot (5 to 6 quarts), combine the water, salt, onion, bay leaf, and celery and bring to a boil. Add the lobster and return to a boil. Reduce the heat to low and cook 10 minutes. Add the shrimp and cook 5 minutes more. Remove the shrimp and lobster. Add the fish heads and trimmings and cook, uncovered, 1 hour. When the shrimp and lobster are cool enough to handle, remove the shrimp from the shells and add the shells to the stock. Remove the sand veins and discard.

Clean the lobster and remove the shell. Add the shell to the stock and cut the meat into large chunks. Scrub the clams and wash well to remove the grit. Add to the stock and cook 15 minutes. Remove from the pot and reserve.

In a Dutch oven, heat the olive oil. Add the garlic and sauté until lightly browned. Add the fish and brown in the oil. Add the tomatoes, wine, parsley, thyme, basil, and pepper and stir well.

Strain the fish stock through a fine sieve. You should have 2 quarts. Dissolve the saffron in the broth. Add to the fish and tomato mixture. Bring to a boil. Reduce the heat to low and cook 15 minutes. Add the lobster, shrimp and clams and cook 10 minutes more. Serve in large soup bowls.

Fish in sour sauce

ITALY

1 pound sole fillets, defrosted if frozen
⅓ cup flour

sauce
2 tablespoons olive oil
1 medium onion, peeled, diced
1 carrot, peeled, diced
1 stalk celery, diced
½ cup white wine

1½ tablespoons pine nuts
1½ tablespoons dark raisins, soaked in warm water to plump

Salt and white pepper
6 tablespoons olive oil

½ cup white wine vinegar
1 bay leaf
1 teaspoon sugar
Salt
White pepper

Wash fish; pat dry. Cut into serving-size pieces. Combine flour, salt, and pepper on piece of waxed paper. Dredge fish in flour mixture. Heat olive oil in heavy skillet. Over moderate heat brown fish few pieces at a time, without crowding. Drain on paper towels. Place in 9- X 9-inch glass baking dish.

In another skillet heat oil for sauce. Add onion, carrot, and celery. Cook, stirring constantly, until tender but not browned. Add wine, vinegar, and seasonings; mix well.

Pour sauce over fish. Sprinkle with pine nuts and raisins. Cover tightly; refrigerate at least 4 hours before serving. Remove bay leaf; serve at room temperature with crisp bread as luncheon dish or antipasto.

MAKES 4 SERVINGS.

Salt cod Bacalao

ITALY

1½ pounds salt cod
¾ cup olive oil
2 medium onions, peeled, sliced
1 clove garlic, peeled, minced
Flour
1½ cups milk
Fresh-ground pepper
2 tablespoons chopped parsley
2 tablespoons grated Parmesan cheese

Place cod in cold water to cover; soak 24 hours, changing water several times. Drain well. Skin and bone cod. Cut into serving-size pieces.

Heat oil in heavy skillet. Add onions and garlic; sauté until tender. Lightly dredge cod in flour. Tightly pack into shallow casserole dish. Pour onion mixture over cod. Add milk to casserole; sprinkle with fresh ground pepper, parsley, and cheese. Cover tightly with foil; bake at 250°F 4½ hours, stirring occasionally. Serve with polenta.

MAKES 4 TO 5 SERVINGS.

Fried salt cod

ITALY

1 pound salt cod
1 cup all-purpose flour
1 teaspoon baking powder
1 egg, well beaten
¾ cup water
1 tablespoon olive oil
Flour for dredging

Soak cod in cold water to cover at least 12 hours. Change water several times. Drain fish well. Remove any skin and bones; dry well with paper towels.

Combine flour and baking powder in mixing bowl. Add egg, water, and oil; beat until smooth. Dredge fish lightly in flour; dip in batter, coating well. Fry in 1½ inches hot oil (375°F), turning once. Fish should be golden brown and crisp. Drain fish on paper towels; keep warm in oven until all fish is cooked. Serve immediately with Green Sauce (see Index).

MAKES 4 SERVINGS.

Cod w/olive & caper sauce

ITALY

sauce
2 tablespoons olive oil
¼ cup chopped onion
1 clove garlic, minced
1½ cups tomato puree
½ teaspoon sugar
¼ cup chopped pitted black olives
1 tablespoon drained chopped capers
½ teaspoon crumbled oregano
Pepper
1½ pounds boneless salt cod fillets, freshened and poached in water 15 minutes

Heat oil in saucepan. Add onion and garlic; sauté until tender. Add remaining sauce ingredients; simmer 15 minutes.

Rinse fish under cold running water; pat dry. Place in lightly greased shallow baking dish in single layer. Pour sauce over fish. Bake at 350°F 25 minutes, until fish flakes easily with fork.

MAKES 4 SERVINGS.

Shrimp broiled with garlic

ITALY

2 pounds large or jumbo shrimp, raw, in shells
¾ cup olive oil
2 cloves garlic, crushed
1 teaspoon salt
½ teaspoon freshly ground pepper
¼ cup chopped parsley
Lemon wedges

Wash shrimp well. Slit down back almost to tail with very sharp knife. Devein shrimp; leave shell intact. Place in single layer in shallow pan.

Combine oil, garlic, salt, and pepper; pour over shrimp. Cover; refrigerate 2 hours.

Thread 4 to 5 shrimp (depending on size) on each skewer. Grill over hot charcoal fire or in broiler (4 inches from heat source) 4 to 5 minutes on each side. Baste with oil in which shrimp were marinated. Serve immediately; sprinkled with parsley, topped with lemon wedges.

MAKES 6 SERVINGS.

Shrimp w/marinara sauce

ITALY

1 pound large shrimp (18 to 22)	Salt
1 quart water	1 bay leaf
	1 slice lemon

sauce

2 tablespoons olive oil	¼ cup tomato purée
½ cup chopped onion	½ teaspoon sugar
1 clove garlic, minced	½ teaspoon dried sweet basil, crumbled
1½ cups Italian-style peeled plum tomatoes	Salt and pepper

garnish

2 tablespoons dry bread crumbs	1 tablespoon parsley, finely chopped
2 tablespoons grated Parmesan cheese	

Peel and devein the shrimp. Combine the water, salt to taste, bay leaf, and lemon in a large saucepan. Bring to a boil. Add the shrimp; bring the water to a boil and simmer 3-5 minutes. Drain.

Heat the oil in a heavy skillet. Add the onion and garlic and sauté until tender. Break up the tomatoes, and add to the onion and garlic along with the tomato purée and seasonings. Reduce the heat to low and cook uncovered 20 minutes. Place the shrimp in a lightly greased au gratin dish. Top with the sauce. Combine the bread crumbs, cheese and parsley and sprinkle over the top of the shrimp and sauce. Preheat the oven to 450°F and bake for 10 minutes.

MAKES 3 SERVINGS.

Shrimp, lobster, & crab diavolo

ITALY

1 1¼-pound live lobster
1 pound king crab legs
2 pounds medium shrimp, raw
½ cup butter
2 tablespoons olive oil
2 cloves garlic, peeled and minced
⅛ teaspoon crushed red pepper
Juice of 1 lemon
2 tablespoons chopped parsley

Steam the lobster and crab legs and cool. Peel the shrimp, leaving the tails intact. Butterfly and remove the sand vein. Drain well. Remove the lobster and crab from the shell and slice.

In a large heavy skillet, heat the butter and oil over moderate heat. Add the garlic and sauté for 2 minutes. Add the shrimp and pepper and satué until the shrimp turns pink. Add the crab and lobster and heat through. Sprinkle with the lemon juice and parsley and serve with garlic bread.

MAKES 4 TO 5 SERVINGS.

Note: You may substitute any combination of shellfish that you prefer in this dish. Count on a 50 percent loss for shells (meaning: use 2 pounds raw shellfish, shells removed).

Mixed fish fry

ITALY

batter

3 large eggs	¼ teaspoon dried sweet basil, crumbled
¼ cup olive oil	Salt and pepper
¼ cup all-purpose flour	
¼ teaspoon dried rosemary, crumbled	

for the fish fry

1½ pounds fish fillets, shrimp, cleaned squid, clams, mussels or eel (if the fish is frozen, defrost and drain well)	Salt and pepper
	Oil for frying (half olive oil if possible)
½ cup flour	Parsley, lemon wedges and quartered tomatoes

Beat the eggs with a wire whip until well-mixed. Add the olive oil and beat to mix well. Add the 377 flour and seasonings and beat until a smooth batter is formed. Let stand 30 minutes and beat again before dipping the fish.

Rinse the fish and pat dry. Heat 3 inches of oil in a deep-fat fryer or 1 inch of oil in an electric skillet to 360°F. Dredge the fish in the flour, seasoned with salt and pepper. Coat well and shake off the excess. Dip the fish in the batter a few pieces at a time, and deep-fat fry until golden. Drain on absorbent paper. Keep warm until all the fish is cooked.

Garnish with parsley and lemon wedges. Vegetables are also delicious cooked in this manner. Trim and slice 1 medium zucchini and ¼ pound of mushrooms and cut the amount of fish to be cooked to ¾ of a pound. Cook as above. Serve with your favorite sauce or with Green Sauce.
MAKES 4 TO 6 SERVINGS.

Green sauce

½ cup mayonnaise
2 tablespoons chopped onion
1 teaspoon chopped capers
2 tablespoons lemon juice
2 teaspoons chopped chives
2 tablespoons chopped parsley

Combine all of the ingredients and mix well. Refrigerate 1 hour before serving.

Fried squid

ITALY

3 pounds frozen squid
2 cups Italian-style bread crumbs
3 eggs, well-beaten
1 teaspoon salt
½ teaspoon pepper

Thaw the squid. Remove the tentacles by cutting them from the head and reserve. Remove and discard the head, chitinous pen and viscera. Wash thoroughly and drain. Cut the mantle into rings. Combine the bread crumbs, salt, and pepper. Dip the tentacles and mantle rings first in the egg and then in the crumbs, coating well. Deep-fat fry at 350°F until golden brown. Serve immediately with lemon wedges.
MAKES 4 TO 5 SERVINGS.

Rice w/squid

ITALY

2 pounds squid
¼ cup olive oil
1 medium onion, peeled, chopped
2 cloves garlic, peeled, minced
½ cup white wine
Salt and pepper
1 cup raw long-grain rice
1½ cups fish stock or chicken broth
Several strands saffron
1 teaspoon hot water
2 teaspoons chopped parsley
2 tablespoons butter

Thaw squid if frozen. Remove tentacles by cutting from head; reserve. Remove and discard head, chitinous pen, and viscera. Wash thoroughly; drain. Cut mantle into thin rings.

Heat oil in large skillet. Add onion and garlic; sauté until tender. Add squid rings, tentacles, and wine. Season with salt and pepper. Cover; simmer 20 minutes. Add rice and stock; mix well. Bring mixture to boil over moderate heat. Cover; reduce heat to low. Cook 20 minutes. Dissolve saffron in hot water; stir into fish and rice. Add parsley and butter, cut into small chunks. Season with salt and pepper to taste; serve.
MAKES 4 SERVINGS.

Poached fillet of fish in shrimp sauce

POLAND

shrimp sauce
1 pound shrimp, cooked
⅓ cup butter
⅓ cup all-purpose white flour
1½ quarts half-and-half cream
1½ teaspoons paprika
3 teaspoons salt
½ teaspoon white pepper
1 cup canned mushroom caps
8 large white fish fillets
½ cup milk
½ cup water
2 sprigs parsley

Gilled salmon with lemon butter

Peel and devein shrimp. Melt butter in top of double boiler. Stir in flour; gradually add half-and-half cream. Cook over hot water, stirring frequently, until sauce is thickened. Add paprika, 2 teaspoons salt, ¼ teaspoon white pepper, mushrooms, and shrimp. Let simmer in top of double boiler while preparing fish.

Split fillets down centers. Begin at larger end of fillet and roll it up. Fasten each with a toothpick. Place in large skillet. Add milk, water, 1 teaspoon salt, and ¼ teaspoon white pepper. Cover fish tightly; simmer gently 10 minutes. Remove fish to hot platter; remove toothpicks and cover fish with Shrimp Sauce. Garnish with parsley before serving.

MAKES 8 SERVINGS.

Sweet-sour carp

POLAND

1 4-pound dressed carp
¼ cup carp blood
2 tablespoons vinegar
2 tablespoons butter
6 green spring onions, chopped
1 bay leaf
3 peppercorns
1 teaspoon salt
¼ teaspoon white pepper
1 teaspoon sugar
6 ounces malt liquor (beer)
⅓ cup crushed gingersnaps
2 tablespoons raisins
1 sprig parsley
2 medium tomatoes, cut into wedges

Drain blood from carp; reserve. Wash fish well under running water; dry with paper towels. Cut into serving pieces. Mix fish blood and vinegar well; reserve.

Melt butter in skillet. Add chopped onions;

Fish goulash esterhazy

379

Shrimp with marinara sauce

sauté for 3 minutes. Mix bay leaf, peppercorns, salt, white pepper, sugar, and beer. Cook for 20 minutes. Strain. Add blood and vinegar to strained liquid. Stir to mix. Add gingersnaps and raisins; bring to boil. Lay carp pieces in sauce; boil gently 30 minutes.

Arrange carp on serving platter. Cover with sauce; garnish with parsley and tomato wedges. MAKES 4 SERVINGS.

Broiled salmon steaks w/herbs

POLAND

4 fresh salmon steaks, ¾ inch thick
2 tablespoons grated onion
⅓ cup butter, melted
1 teaspoon salt
¼ teaspoon black pepper, peppermill-ground
½ teaspoon marjoram
1 tablespoon chopped fresh dill
2 tablespoons chopped parsley

Place salmon steaks on broiler pan. Mix remaining ingredients; pour half of mixture over steaks. Broil 2 inches from source of heat about 4 minutes. Turn steaks. Pour remaining sauce over steaks. Return steaks to broiler; broil an additional 6 to 7 minutes or until fish flakes easily with a fork.

380　MAKES 4 SERVINGS.

Baked fish w/mushroom stuffing

POLAND

4-pound whole fish or your choice, dressed
1 teaspoon salt

mushroom stuffing
3 tablespoons butter
1 small onion, chopped
½ cup chopped fresh mushrooms
2 cups dry bread crumbs
¾ cup chicken stock
1 egg, beaten
½ teaspoon salt
¼ teaspoon pepper
4 strips bacon

Clean and rub inside of fish with 1 teaspoon salt. Prepare Mushroom Stuffing. Put butter in saucepan. Add onion; sauté until onion is golden but not brown. Add chopped mushrooms; cook until water from mushrooms cooks away. Remove from heat. Add bread crumbs, chicken stock, egg, ½ teaspoon salt, and pepper. Mix well with your hands.

Stuff fish. Fasten with toothpicks. Place fish, underside down, in greased baking dish. Layer bacon over top of fish. Bake in moderate (350°F) oven 1 hour or until fish flakes easily with a fork. Remove fish to a hot platter to serve. MAKES 8 SERVINGS.

Lobster & rice

POLAND

¼ cup butter
1 medium onion, chopped
2 cups rice
1 quart fish stock (chicken stock may be substituted)
1 bay leaf
2 tablespoons grated Parmesan cheese
2 cups cooked lobster
¼ cup sour cream
½ teaspoon salt
¼ teaspoon white pepper
¼ teaspoon paprika

Melt butter in frying pan. Add onion; cook over low heat until soft. Add rice; cook about 5 minutes, stirring constantly. Cover with stock, bring to a boil, and add bay leaf. Reduce heat, cover tightly, and steam until rice is tender. Add cheese, lobster meat, sour cream, salt, white pepper, and paprika.
MAKES 6 SERVINGS.

Oyster soufflé

POLAND

1 pint standard oysters
3 tablespoons butter
3 tablespoons flour
1 cup half-and-half cream
1 teaspoon salt
¼ teaspoon white pepper
3 egg yolks, beaten
3 egg whites, beaten stiff

Drain and chop oysters. Melt butter; blend in flour until a paste forms. Add half-and-half cream; cook, stirring constantly, until thick. Remove from heat. Add oysters, seasonings, and beaten egg yolks.
Beat egg whites until stiff. Fold into oyster mixture. Pour mixture into greased casserole. Bake in 350°F oven 30 minutes or until brown.
MAKES 6 SERVINGS.

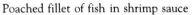

Poached fillet of fish in shrimp sauce

Galician steamed fish in tomato sauce

Galician steamed fish in tomato sauce

SPAIN

2 pounds white fish fillets
1 small onion, peeled, quartered
1 bay leaf
2 tablespoons olive oil
1 garlic clove, minced
½ cup chopped onion
6 medium tomatoes, peeled, seeded, chopped
1 teaspoon paprika
Dash of cayenne
1 teaspoon chopped chives
⅓ cup white wine
Vinegar

Place fish, quartered onion, and bay leaf on large piece of aluminum foil. Securely close foil. Place fish in steamer; steam 25 minutes or until fish flakes easily.

Heat oil in deep skillet. Add garlic and chopped onion; sauté until tender. Add tomatoes, paprika, cayenne, chives, and wine. Simmer 30 minutes. Place fish on serving platter; top with tomato sauce. Serve with vinegar.
MAKES 4 TO 6 SERVINGS.

Cod bake

SPAIN

2 tablespoons olive oil
1 Spanish onion, chopped
1 green pepper, peeled, seeded, chopped
1 cup sliced fresh mushroom
1 garlic clove, minced
1 bay leaf
1 16-ounce can stewed tomatoes
1½ pounds cod fillets

Heat oil until haze forms above skillet. Add onion, pepper, mushroom, and garlic; sauté until limp. Add bay leaf and tomatoes; simmer 30 minutes. Remove bay leaf. Arrange cod in greased baking dish. Pour sauce over cod. Bake in 350°F oven 40 minutes or until fish flakes easily.
MAKES 4 SERVINGS.

382

Fried fish w/sour sauce

SPAIN

1 pound firm whitefish fillets
¾ teaspoon salt
1 Spanish onion, sliced
½ cup olive oil
1 clove garlic, minced
½ cup water
1 bay leaf
6 whole peppercorns
½ teaspoon toasted coriander seeds
1 egg, well-beaten
2 tablespoons water
¾ cup flour
½ cup vinegar
3 tablespoons olive oil
⅓ cup sliced pimiento-stuffed Spanish olives
¼ cup chopped onion

Sprinkle fish with salt; let stand ½ hour.
Slowly fry sliced onion in ½ cup oil in a heavy frying pan. Add garlic; fry 3 minutes. (Do not brown.) Remove onion and garlic from oil with slotted spoon; place in saucepan. Add ½ cup water, bay leaf, peppercorns, and coriander; simmer while frying fish.
Beat egg and 2 tablespoons water together. Dip fish in egg wash, then in flour. Fry in seasoned oil until golden brown. Drain on brown paper bag. Add vinegar and 3 tablespoons oil to onion and spice mixture. Remove bay leaf, peppercorns, and coriander seeds. Pour sauce over fish; garnish with olives and chopped onion.
MAKES 4 SERVINGS.

Andalusia daily soup

SPAIN

This fish soup gets its name from the fact that Andalusian housewives make soup from their husbands' daily catch at sea.

3 pounds assorted fish
¼ cup olive oil
2 garlic cloves, peeled, chopped
1 onion, peeled, chopped
1½ quarts water
2 peppercorns

1 bay leaf
Dash of cayenne
Lemon slices

Clean and dress fish. Cut into bite-size pieces. Scrub mussels, if used, and soak in cold water 20 minutes to remove excess salt.
Heat oil in large Dutch oven; sauté garlic and onion 10 minutes. Add all fish but shellfish, water, peppercorns, bay leaf, and cayenne. Cover; simmer 15 minutes or until fish flakes easily. Remove fish from stock; remove skin and bones. Add fish meat back to stock, along with any shellfish used. Cook 7 to 10 minutes or until shellfish are done. Remove peppercorns and bay leaf. Serve with lemon slices.
MAKES 6 SERVINGS.

Broiled fish

SPAIN

6 dressed whole fish
2 teaspoons salt
Dash of cayenne (optional)
3 tablespoons olive oil
3 tablespoons freshly squeezed lemon juice
Fresh parsley sprigs, snipped
1 recipe Almond and Pepper Sauce (see Index)
1 recipe Garlic Mayonnaise (see Index)

Wash and drain fish. Scrape scales. Combine salt, cayenne, oil, and lemon juice; mix well. Baste fish with sauce. Let marinate 2 hours in refrigerator or on crushed ice.
Place fish over hot coals; grill 10 minutes. Turn fish; grill 10 minutes or until fish flakes easily. Remove to serving platter; sprinkle with parsley. Prepare sauces as directed; serve with fish.
MAKES 6 SERVINGS.

Baked fish

SPAIN

Spanish cooking uses only olive oil. If you find the olive oil taste too strong, butter can be substituted to prepare the bread crumbs.

3 pounds hake, haddock, or cod fillets
1 teaspoon salt

½ teaspoon pepper
Dash of cayenne pepper
1 tablespoon olive oil
2 Spanish onions, peeled, sliced thin
2 large tomatoes, peeled, sliced
2 tablespoons chopped pimiento
1 Valencia orange, sliced
12 fresh mushrooms, cleaned, sliced
3 tablespoons chopped chives
⅓ cup white wine
½ cup olive oil or butter, melted
1¼ cups fresh bread crumbs

Pat fish dry with paper towel. Combine salt, pepper, and cayenne. Sprinkle mixture over fish. Grease large baking dish with 1 tablespoon oil. Arrange onions in layers on bottom of dish. Layer fish over onions. Cover fish with tomato slices, pimiento, and orange slices. Layer mushrooms around fish. Sprinkle with chives. Pour wine over fish and vegetables. Cover with foil; marinate in refrigerator 6 to 8 hours. Bake, covered, in 375°F oven 25 to 30 minutes or until fish flakes easily. Uncover.
Combine ½ cup oil and bread crumbs. Sprinkle fish with bread crumbs. Bake 5 to 10 minutes or until browned.
MAKES 6 SERVINGS.

Baked fresh sardines

SPAIN

3 pounds fresh sardines, dressed
1 teaspoon salt
½ teaspoon pepper
2 tablespoons olive oil
2 Spanish onions, peeled, sliced thin
2 large tomatoes, peeled, sliced
1 green pepper, seeds removed, sliced into rings
3 tablespoons chopped chives
⅓ cup dry white wine
6 large lettuce leaves (Use the outer leaves that you generally throw away.)

Pat fish dry. Sprinkle with salt and pepper. Grease large casserole with oil. Arrange onions in layers on bottom of casserole. Layer fish over onions. Cover fish with tomato slices and pepper rings. Sprinkle with chives. Pour wine over fish

and vegetables. Cover dish with lettuce leaves. Marinate in refrigerator 6 hours.
Bake, covered, in 375°F oven 30 minutes or until fish flakes easily. Remove lettuce leaves; discard. Bake 10 minutes.
MAKES 6 SERVINGS.

Tuna fish w/rice salad

SPAIN

2 7-ounce cans tuna fish, drained
2 cups cooked rice
2 green peppers, seeds removed, chopped
2 tomatoes, peeled, seeded, chopped
1 small onion, peeled, chopped
¾ cup Garlic Mayonnaise (see Index)
1 tablespoon dry mustard
4 large lettuce leaves
2 hard-cooked eggs, sliced
½ cup pitted black olives

Combine tuna, rice, peppers, tomatoes, and onion. Combine mayonnaise and mustard; mix well. Add to tuna mixture; toss. Chill salad thoroughly. Place lettuce leaves in bottom of serving bowl. Lightly spoon salad over lettuce. Garnish with egg slices and olives.
MAKES 4 TO 6 SERVINGS.

Tuna stew

SPAIN

2 tablespoons olive oil
1 medium onion, chopped
1 large clove garlic, pressed, or 1 teaspoon garlic powder
2 tablespoons parsley flakes
1 1-pound can stewed tomatoes
2 large potatoes, diced
1 beef bouillon cube
1 cup frozen peas
½ cup diced red pepper
1 bay leaf
1 teaspoon salt
½ teaspoon pepper
2 6½-ounce cans tuna

Heat oil in large skillet. Add onion; sauté until transparent. Add remaining ingredients, except tuna; stir to mix. Cover; simmer ½ hour or until

potatoes are tender. Add tuna; mix well. Simmer 10 minutes to heat tuna thoroughly. Serve tuna with rice or toast.
MAKES 4 SERVINGS.

Boiled shrimp w/sauces

SPAIN

2 quarts water
Dash of hot sauce
5 peppercorns
1 lemon, sliced
2 teaspoons salt
1 garlic clove, peeled
2 bay leaves
1 onion, quartered
1 celery heart
3 pounds fresh medium shrimp
Garlic Mayonnaise (see Index)
Almond and Pepper Sauce (see Index)

Bring water to boil. Add hot sauce, peppercorns, lemon, salt, garlic, bay leaves, onion, and celery. Boil 10 minutes. Add shrimp. Bring water to simmer. Cook shrimp just until pink. Cover; remove from heat. Let stand 15 minutes; drain. Peel and devein shrimp; chill. Prepare sauces as directed in recipes. Place shrimp on serving platter. Serve with sauces, large salad, and Continental Bread (see Index).
MAKES 6 SERVINGS.

Note: This dish can also be used as an appetizer, serving 12.

Shrimp w/vegetables

SPAIN

2 15-ounce cans artichoke hearts	Dash of cayenne
1 small head cauliflower	½ teaspoon dry mustard
1½ cups olive oil	1½ quarts water
½ cup vinegar	5 peppercorns
¼ cup dry white wine	½ lemon, sliced
1 tablespoon sugar	1 bay leaf
1 teaspoon garlic juice	1 onion, peeled, quartered
4 teaspoons salt	1½ pounds fresh medium shrimp

Drain artichoke hearts.
Select saucepan large enough to accommodate head of cauliflower. Cover bottom of pan with 1 to 2 inches water. Add salt to water; bring to rapid boil. Add cauliflower to saucepan; cover. Cook 25 minutes or until forktender. Drain immediately; cool. Break into florets.
Combine oil, vinegar, wine, sugar, garlic juice, 2 teaspoons salt, cayenne, and mustard in jar. Cover; shake vigorously. Pour vinegar and oil mixture over vegetables. Cover; marinate in refrigerator overnight.
Bring water to boil. Add peppercorns, lemon, 2 teaspoons salt, bay leaf, and onion; boil 10 minutes. Add shrimp; bring water back to boil. Cook shrimp just until pink. Cover; remove from heat. Let stand 15 minutes; drain. Peel and devein shrimp; chill.
Add shrimp to marinating vegetables first thing in morning. Re-cover. Return mixture to refrigerator; marinate at least 6 hours prior to serving. Drain before serving.
MAKES 6 TO 8 SERVINGS.

Shrimp & lobster salad

SPAIN

1½ cups cooked lobster meat
1½ cups cooked shrimp
½ cup chopped Spanish onion
2 tablespoons olive oil
2 tablespoons lemon juice
4 tomatoes
2 hard-cooked eggs
Lettuce leaves
Lemon wedges
1 recipe Garlic Mayonnaise (see Index)

Combine lobster, shrimp, onion, oil, and lemon juice; mix well. Refrigerate until ready to use.
Slice tomatoes and eggs. Arrange lettuce leaves on 4 plates. Place 1 sliced tomato on each lettuce leaf. Top tomatoes with seafood salad. Garnish with hard-cooked egg slices and lemon wedges. Serve with Garlic Mayonnaise.
MAKES 4 SERVINGS.

Flounder w/shrimp

DENMARK

Salt
4 fillets of flounder
Flour
2 eggs
2 tablespoons water
Dried bread crumbs
8 tablespoons butter
½ pound small cooked shrimps
Lemon wedges

Salt the fillets lightly and dip them in flour, being sure to shake off the excess. Beat the eggs together with the water. Put the bread crumbs on wax paper. Batter the fish by dipping each fillet first in the egg mixture and then in bread crumbs, coating each side thoroughly. Set aside the battered fish for at least 10 minutes.

Heat about 4 tablespoons of butter in a skillet. Sauté the fillets for 3 to 4 minutes. Keep them warm while you prepare the shrimps and sauce.

Melt 2 tablespoons of butter in a separate pan. Toss the shrimps in the butter so that each shrimp becomes coated with butter. Place shrimps down the center of each fillet. Brown the remaining butter, pour it over the fillets, and serve garnished with lemon wedges.

MAKES 4 SERVINGS.

Minced fish

DENMARK

1½ pounds fish (cod, haddock, or salmon)
2 tablespoons salt
¼ pound butter
2 tablespoons flour
¼ teaspoon pepper
Milk or cream

Remove all skin and bones from the fish. With a spoon or an electric blender mince the fish until it is a fine, smooth mixture. Add the salt, and mince a little longer.

In a separate bowl cream the butter and add the flour and pepper. Add the butter mixture to the fish. Add 1 teaspoon of milk and work the mixture again. Add milk by teaspoons only until the mixture is soft, not mushy. Put the minced fish into a greased baking dish. Set the baking dish in a pan of hot water and bake it at 350°F for about 1 hour.

MAKES 6 OR MORE SERVINGS.

Boiled codfish

DENMARK

1 whole, cleaned cod
Salt
Melted butter
Chopped raw onion
Chopped pickled beets
Chopped hard-cooked eggs
Chopped parsley

Rub the fish, inside and out, with salt and let it stand for an hour. Place the whole fish in cold water to cover and bring to a boil. Slowly cook the fish uncovered until it is tender. Remove and drain the fish.

Put the fish on a serving platter and pour melted butter over it. The other chopped vegetables may be arranged around the platter as a garnish that will complement the flavor of the fish.

MAKES 4 SERVINGS.

Baked salmon

DENMARK

1 large can red or pink salmon
½ teaspoon salt
⅛ teaspoon pepper
½ cup bread crumbs
2 tablespoons butter
2 cups milk

Remove the bones and skin from the salmon. Place one layer of the salmon in a well-greased baking dish. Sprinkle this with salt and pepper. Add a layer of bread crumbs and dot with butter. Repeat this until the fish is used up and has crumbs on top. Heat the milk and pour it into the baking dish at the sides without disturbing the crumbs on top. Bake the salmon at 375°F for 40 minutes.

MAKES 6 SERVINGS.

Boiled shrimp with sauces

Baked fish (Spain) next pages

Fish dumplings w/crab sauce

DENMARK

1 pound pike or perch
1 onion
1 tablespoon butter
2 egg whites
⅛ teaspoon cream
½ cup bread crumbs
1 teaspoon salt
Dash of pepper
1 cup meat broth

Fillet the fish. Peel and dice the onion. Cook the onion in butter until transparent. Put the fish through a food grinder or food processor. Add the onion, egg whites, cream, and bread crumbs. Put the mixture through the food grinder or processor again. Add the salt and pepper and form the mixture into dumplings.

Place the fish dumplings in a greased casserole and add the hot meat broth. Cover the dish and

bake it at 350°F for 20 minutes. Serve the dumplings warm with Crab Sauce.

MAKES 6 TO 8 SERVINGS.

Crab sauce

3 tablespoons butter
3 tablespoons flour
Fish broth from dumplings
1 egg yolk
2 tablespoons cream
Salt and pepper to taste
¼ pound crab meat
1 can green or white asparagus tips

Heat the butter and add the flour, stirring constantly. Add the fish broth from the already baked dumplings and let this simmer for a few minutes. Add the egg yolk, cream, and salt and pepper to taste. Last, put in the crab meat and asparagus tips. Pour the sauce over the fish dumplings and enjoy.

Fish dumplings with crab sauce

Fishballs

Fishballs

FINLAND

2 pounds cod fillets	½ bunch fresh dill
4 teaspoons lemon juice	2 eggs, beaten
1 can sardines in oil	2 rolls, crumbed
3 tablespoons butter	4 teaspoons aquavit
Dash of pepper	Parsley for garnish
1 large onion, finely chopped	Lemon slices for garnish
½ bunch parsley	

batter
2 eggs, beaten
4 tablespoons bread crumbs
Oil for frying

Rinse the cod fillets under cold water and dry them on paper towels. Cover fillets with lemon juice and let them sit for 5 minutes. Next, put the cod and the sardines through a food chopper. Reserve the sardine oil for future use.

Cream the butter in a large bowl. Add the fish and pepper. Add the onion, parsley, and dill. Last, put in 2 beaten eggs, the sardine oil, rolls, and the aquavit. Mix well and season to taste.

With wet hands form the mixture into balls that are pressed somewhat flat. Dip the balls into the 2 beaten eggs, then dust them with bread crumbs. Heat a generous amount of oil in a frypan. Fry the fishballs for about 15 minutes or until they are golden brown. Serve the fishballs garnished with parsley and slices of lemon.
MAKES 6 SERVINGS.

Herring salad

FINLAND

1 young white cabbage head
6 cups water
6 to 8 strips bacon
4 matjes herring
2 tablespoons wine vinegar
1 teaspoon sugar
Freshly ground pepper

Clean and wash the cab age. Drain and slice it fine. In a large pot bring the water to a boil and add the cabbage. Let the water come to a boil again, then remove and drain the cabbage and allow it to cool.
Brown the bacon lightly and break it into small pieces. Skin and fillet the herring. Wash and rinse the fish well. Cut it into fine strips. Mix the cabbage, bacon, and herring in a dish and season with vinegar, sugar, and pepper. Cover the dish for 30 minutes, then serve.
MAKES 6 SERVINGS.

Baked halibut

ICELAND

1 slice halibut, about 2 inches thick
3 tablespoons butter
1 teaspoon salt
Dash of freshly ground pepper
1 cup canned tomatoes
1/2 teaspoon sugar
1 medium-size onion
1/2 cup heavy cream

Pat the halibut dry on paper towels. Remove the skin. Put the fish in a buttered baking dish and sprinkle it with salt and pepper. Brush the re-maining butter over the fish. Add the tomatoes crushed with sugar. Cover with thinly sliced onion.
Bake the fish for 20 minutes at 400°F, then pour the cream over it and bake it for 10 minutes more.
MAKES 4 OR MORE SERVINGS.

Haddock & dill

NORWAY

1 package frozen haddock
1/2 bunch fresh dill
2 or 3 sliced tomatoes
1/4 cup water
1/2 teaspoon salt
2 tablespoons butter

Put the frozen haddock into a pot. (Do not thaw it.) Cover the fish with the dill and tomato slices. Add the water and salt, and dot with butter. Cover the pot tightly. Simmer the fish for about 1/2 hour. Serve the fish with boiled potatoes.
MAKES 3 SERVINGS.

Fish cutlets

NORWAY

1 pound fish fillets
1 tablespoon lemon juice
4 leeks or 2 onions
2 eggs
Salt and pepper to taste
1 onion, finely chopped
4 tablespoons butter
2 tablespoons oil

Rinse and dry the fish fillets. Coat them with lemon juice and let them sit for 10 minutes. Clean, wash, and cut the 4 leeks or 2 onions into rings. Drain them well. Put the fish fillets through a food chopper. Mix the finely ground fish with the eggs, salt, pepper, and 1 onion. Form the mixture into balls and press the balls flat.
Fry the fish balls in butter until browned on all sides. Keep them warm. Lightly brown the leeks

391

in oil for 10 minutes and serve them around the fish.

MAKES 4 TO 6 SERVINGS.

Oysters & macaroni

NORWAY

½ pound uncooked macaroni
3 dozen shucked oysters
½ teaspoon salt
Paprika
¼ pound butter
¼ pound grated cheese
½ cup bread crumbs

Cook the macaroni according to directions on the box. Drain it. Grease a baking dish and put in a layer of macaroni. Next, add a layer of oysters, salt, and paprika, and dot with butter. Top this with grated cheese. Continue in this way, with the layers ending with oysters on top. Sprinkle the top with salt and paprika.

Melt the rest of the butter and add the bread crumbs to it; sprinkle this over the oysters. Bake the oysters and macaroni at 400 °F for 15 minutes.

MAKES 6 OR MORE SERVINGS.

Baked fish fillets

SWEDEN

4 fresh or thawed frozen fish fillets
3 tablespoons butter
3 egg yolks
1 teaspoon salt
½ teaspoon paprika
1 small onion (3 tablespoons when grated)
3 tablespoons chopped parsley
3 tablespoons chopped capers (optional)
3 tablespoons lemon juice

Place the fillets in a buttered baking dish. Dot them with butter and bake them at 400°F for 12 to 15 minutes.

While the fillets are baking, cream the butter and beat in the egg yolks until they are light and fluffy. Add the salt, paprika, grated onion, parsley, capers, and lemon juice. Put the well-mixed

sauce in a double boiler to keep it from hardening.

When the fillets are cooked, spread the sauce over them and return them to the oven for 3 to 5 minutes. Serve at once.

MAKES 4 SERVINGS.

Jellied fish in tomato juice

SWEDEN

1 pound fresh salmon or trout
1 teaspoon salt
6 allspices
2 bay leaves
1½ cups tomato juice
2 cups water
1 bouillon cube
1 package unflavored gelatin

Simmer the fish, salt, and spices in 2 cups of water until well-done. Cool the fish and pick out the bones and skin. Flake the fish and place it in a greased fish mold.

Strain the broth and return it to the stove. Add the tomato juice and bouillon and bring the broth to a boil. Dissolve the gelatin in 2 tablespoons of cold water and add it to the hot broth and pour it over the fish in the mold. Chill it until firm and set. Unmold the jellied fish onto a platter and garnish with parsley.

MAKES 6 SERVINGS.

Salmon soufflé

SWEDEN

1 can salmon, red or pink
2 tablespoons butter
1 tablespoon flour
1 cup milk
½ teaspoon salt
Dash of freshly ground black pepper
1 teaspoon chopped chives (optional)
3 eggs, separated
2 teaspoons lemon juice

Remove the dark skin and all bones from the salmon. Mash it with a fork. Melt the butter on top of the stove; add the flour, and blend. Gradually add the milk, stirring until the sauce is slightly thickened. Add the salmon to the white sauce, and add the salt, pepper, and chives. Remove it from the heat.

Beat the egg whites until stiff. Add beaten egg yolks and lemon juice to the salmon mixture. Last, fold in the stiffly beaten egg whites. Bake the mixture in a greased mold at 350°F for 45 minutes. The salmon is done when a knife comes out of the center clean.

MAKES 4 TO 6 SERVINGS.

Herring balls

SWEDEN

1 medium salt herring or 4 hearring fillets
1 small onion
1 tablespoon butter
1 cup cooked meat
4 medium cold cooked potatoes
1 tablespoon cornstarch
⅛ teaspoon white pepper
¼ cup milk or cream
Bread crumbs
Shortening for frying

If salt herring is used, clean the fish and soak it in cold water overnight. Fillet the herring. Brown the onion lightly in butter. Grind the herring, onion, meat, and potatoes and mix them together in a large bowl. Add the cornstarch and pepper, mixing again. Add the milk or cream gradually—just enough to be able to shape the mixture into small balls. Shape the balls and roll them in bread crumbs.

Heat the shortening in a large skillet and fry the herring balls until they are brown on both sides. Serve the herring balls with currant jelly or a hot currant sauce.

MAKES 4 TO 6 SERVINGS.

Crusted herring

SWEDEN

8 green herring
2 tablespoons lemon juice
1 teaspoon salt

3 tablespoons fine herbs
2 tablespoons bread crumbs
Parmesan cheese
4 tablespoons butter

Fillet the herring carefully; wash and let them dry. Cover them with lemon juice and set them aside for 10 minutes. Put the herring in a greased baking dish and sprinkle them with salt and fine herbs. Spread the bread crumbs and Parmesan cheese over that. Melt the butter and pour it over the fish.

Bake the fish for 20 minutes at 425°F. Serve it hot.

MAKES 4 TO 6 SERVINGS.

Baked shrimp & crab

SWEDEN

1 cup boiled, clean shrimps
1 cup crab meat
½ cup pimiento
½ green pepper
1 small onion
6 eggs, well-beaten
½ teaspoon salt
Heavy dash of freshly ground pepper
1 cup bread crumbs

Cut up the shrimps finely and break up the crab meat. Chop the pimiento, green pepper, and onion. Mix them together well. Add the eggs, salt, pepper, and bread crumbs.

Grease a loaf pan or mold. Shape the mixture to fit the loaf pan. Set the loaf pan in a pan of water. Bake it in the water at 350°F for 30 minutes. This loaf can be served as is or with a seasoned white sauce poured over it. Garnish with chopped pimiento.

MAKES 6 SERVINGS.

Herring & potato casserole

SWEDEN

3 large potatoes
1 large onion
2½ tablespoons butter
2 matjes herring fillets cut in ½-inch diagonal slices
Freshly ground black pepper

1 tablespoon bread crumbs
⅓ cup light or heavy cream

Peel and cut the potatoes into ⅛-inch slices. Put them in cold water to keep them from discoloring. Peel and slice the onion. Cook the onion lightly in 2 tablespoons of butter until soft and transparent.

Butter a 2-quart baking dish. Drain the potatoes and dry off any excess moisture with a paper towel. Put a layer each of potatoes, herring, and onion in the baking dish. Continue with alternate layers, ending with potatoes on top, and seasoning each layer with pepper. Sprinkle the top layer with bread crumbs and dot it with butter.

Bring the cream to a boil on top of the stove. Then pour the hot cream over the casserole. Bake the casserole at 400°F for 1 hour or until the potatoes are tender.
MAKES 4 SERVINGS.

Stuffed bass

MIDDLE EAST

1 3-pound bass
Salt and pepper
1 tablespoon butter
2 large onions, grated
½ cup finely-ground almonds
1 teaspoon sugar
½ teaspoon cinnamon
¼ teaspoon cumin
2 tablespoons sweet butter
2 tablespoons almond paste
3 tablespoons quince preserves
½ cup water
Lemon wedges and parsley for garnish

Sprinkle fish inside and out with salt and pepper. In a skillet, sauté the onions in butter until onions are transparent. Layer this on the bottom of a baking dish.

Make a paste of the almonds, sugar, cinnamon, cumin, sweet butter, almond paste, and preserves. Spread this onto the fish with a spatula until all fish is covered with a smooth paste. Then put the fish on top of the onions and pour water around but not over the fish. Bake at

350°F for 45 minutes or until fish is fork tender. Garnish with lemon wedges and parsley.
MAKES 4 TO 6 SERVINGS.

Deep-fried fish balls

MIDDLE EAST

1 pound fresh fish fillets
2 large potatoes, sliced
Salt water
1 beaten egg
1 teaspoon minced onion
½ teaspoon salt
¼ teaspoon black pepper
½ teaspoon dry mustard
1 teaspoon lemon juice
2 tablespoons parsley
Oil for deep frying

Place fish and potatoes in salt water to cover and cook for 20 minutes until both are tender. Drain well. Place drained fish and potatoes in a large bowl and stir gently to mix them. Add the egg, onion, salt, pepper, mustard, lemon juice, and parsley.

When all are mixed well, form into balls about 2 inches in diameter. Heat oil to 370°F for deep frying and drop balls, frying until golden-brown. Remove cooked balls to a heated platter. When all are finished, serve at once.
MAKES 4 SERVINGS.

Deep-fried cod

MIDDLE EAST

2½ pounds salt cod
3 cups flour
2 cups lukewarm water
½ teaspoon baking soda
½ teaspoon salt
Oil for deep frying
Lemon wedges for garnish

A day ahead, put cod in a glass pan or bowl, cover with cold water, and soak for at least 12 hours, changing the water 3 times. When ready to cook, drain and rinse cod under water and cut into pieces 2 inches × 1 inch.

Fish cutlets

With a wooden spoon, combine 2 cups flour, water, baking soda, and salt, mixing until creamy. Let batter mixture stand for 1 hour at room temperature.

Heat fat to 370°F in deep fryer. Dip fish, one piece at a time, into remaining cup of flour. Drop into liquid batter and when coated on all sides, deep fry for 5 minutes or until golden-brown. Keep finished pieces warm in the oven. When all are done, transfer to serving platter and garnish with lemon wedges.

MAKES 4 SERVINGS.

Baked fish

MIDDLE EAST

4 fish fillets
Lemon juice
Salt and freshly ground black pepper
⅓ cup olive oil
3 large onions, chopped (about 3 cups)
2 cups canned tomato sauce
⅓ cup chopped parsley
1 teaspoon oregano
⅛ teaspoon cinnamon
⅓ cup sweet red wine
⅓ cup grated bread crumbs
2 tablespoons butter

Rub fish slices with lemon juice and wash. Then season well with salt and pepper and let stand for 10 minutes.

Sauté onions in olive oil in a skillet for 5 minutes or until transparent. Add tomato sauce, parsley, oregano, cinnamon, and wine. Cover and cook for 10 minutes.

In a greased baking dish, arrange the fish and pour sauce over it. Sprinkle the surface with the bread crumbs and dot with butter. Bake at 350°F

Crusted herring

for 30 minutes or until a nice crust has formed over the fish. Serve at once.
MAKES 4 SERVINGS.

Fish in ginger sauce

MIDDLE EAST

4 fillets of fish, preferably sole
3 chopped scallions
1 tablespoon oil
2 tablespoons tahina (sesame sauce)
2 tablespoons soy sauce
½ teaspoon freshly grated ginger
2 cups water
2 tablespoons cornstarch
¼ cup water
Salt to taste

Place fillets in baking dish and bake for 20 minutes at 350°F. While they are baking, sauté scallions in oil for 5 minutes. Add tahina paste, soy sauce, ginger, and 2 cups of water. While this is heating, make a paste of the cornstarch in ¼ cup of water. Add to the sauce stirring until thickened. Taste and add salt. Simmer together for about 10 minutes or until fish is done. Pour the sauce over the fish and serve at once.
MAKES 4 SERVINGS.

Fish in curry sauce

MIDDLE EAST

2 pounds of your favorite fish
Salt
½ cup pine nuts
4 tablespoons oil
1 cup water

2 tablespoons lemon juice
1 tablespoon chopped parsley
1 teaspoon curry powder
Dash of cayenne
Dash of freshly ground black pepper

After washing the fish and drying on paper towels, sprinkle with salt and allow to stand for ½ hour. Just before you are ready to cook the fish, wash it again and dry as before.

Put the pine nuts in heated fat and let brown lightly. Brown the fish quickly on both sides. Place fish in a greased oven dish. Combine remaining ingredients and pour over the fish. Bake at 350°F until the sauce is absorbed, about 30 minutes.
MAKES 4 TO 6 SERVINGS.

Deep-fried cod

Fish in ginger sauce

Persian sturgeon

MIDDLE EAST

2 pounds sturgeon cut into 1½-inch chunks
3 tablespoons olive oil
2 tablespoons lemon juice
2 tablespoons minced fresh dill weed
Paprika to taste

Marinate the sturgeon chunks in olive oil, lemon juice, and dill weed for at least 20 minutes. Drain and reserve the marinade.

Place the fish chunks on skewers and sprinkle liberally with paprika. Broil quickly, basting often with reserved marinade for at least 10 minutes per side. When fish is tender, but not overcooked, remove from skewers and serve. This is particularly good served with a pilaf.
MAKES 4 SERVINGS.

Skewered swordfish

MIDDLE EAST

1 small onion, thinly sliced and separated into rings
4 tablespoons fresh lemon juice
4 teaspoons olive oil
2 teaspoons salt
½ teaspoon freshly ground black pepper
1½ pounds swordfish, skinned, boned and cut into 1-inch cubes

2 cups boiling water
20 large bay leaves

Prepare a marinade of onions, 2 tablespoons lemon juice, 2 teaspoons olive oil, salt, and pepper. To this, add the fish, coating each cube well. Marinate for 4 hours in the refrigerator stirring occasionally. Soak the bay leaves in boiling water for 1 hour.

When ready to cook, drain bay leaves and layer cubes of fish and bay leaves alternately on skewers. Combine remaining lemon juice and oil and brush onto the fish. Place skewers in a roasting pan and broil for 8 to 10 minutes, turning once, until fish is lightly browned. Remove from skewers and serve at once. MAKES 4 SERVINGS.

Steamed whole fish

CHINA

1½ pounds whole fish (flounder, pike, trout, or sea bass)
1 teaspoon salt
½ teaspoon freshly ground pepper
¼ teaspoon powdered ginger
3 cups water
2 teaspoons mixed pickling spices (or more if you prefer it spicier)
2 bay leaves
2 cloves garlic, cut in half
2 tablespoons chopped scallion

397

garnish
Lemon slices
Tomato
Parsley

Have fish scaled and cleaned and head removed, if you prefer. Lightly score the skin so seasonings will flavor the fish. Combine salt, pepper, and ginger and rub on fish thoroughly.

Pour water into large frying pan or wok and add pickling spices, bay leaves, garlic, and scallion. Place rack in pan or wok so that the fish will sit above the liquid, in order to allow the steam to circulate. Place the fish on the rack, cover and let simmer for approximately 30 minutes, or until fish is tender. Garnish with lemon slices, tomato, and parsley.
MAKES 3 SERVINGS.

Poached fish mandarin-style

CHINA

½ teaspoon shredded fresh gingerroot
2 scallions, cut into 1-inch pieces
1 tablespoon soy sauce
1 tablespoon peanut oil
1 tablespoon sherry
1 whole fresh fish (bass, flounder, sole, butterfish, whitefish), cleaned, washed, dried inside and out (about 1½ to 2 pounds)

Mix together ginger, scallions, soy sauce, oil, and sherry. Rub mixture all over fish, inside and out. Place water in bottom of wok; put fish on rack in wok, making sure water does not touch fish. Steam over high heat about 20 minutes or until fish is done.
MAKES 3 OR 4 SERVINGS.

Fish roll

CHINA

3 eggs, beaten
1 tablespoon water
2 tablespoons oil
¾ cup chopped flounder
2 tablespoons water chestnuts, chopped
2 tablespoons scallions, chopped

Salt to taste
1 tablespoon soy sauce
Flour
sauce
1½ tablespoons soy sauce
1 tablespoon cornstarch
¾ cup water
½ teaspoon sugar

Beat the eggs with the water. Heat a little of the oil in a large skillet and fry half of the egg mixture until it's set. Turn it over and cook the other side. Repeat this with the rest of the egg mixture. Mix together the fish, water chestnuts, scallions, salt, and soy sauce. Put half of it on one of the egg pieces, covering the whole thing. Roll it up jelly-roll style, put some flour on the edges and press together. Repeat with the other piece of egg. With a sharp knife, cut the rolls into ¼-inch slices. Heat oil in skillet and fry the slices until golden brown.

To make the sauce, mix together the soy sauce and cornstarch until smooth. Blend in water and sugar and place in small saucepan. Boil slowly for about 3 minutes. Serve the sauce separately.
MAKES 5 TO 6 SERVINGS.

Baked fish w/cabbage leaves

CHINA

1 whole trout, about 1 pound	1 pound fresh mushrooms
1 whole carp, about 3 pounds	2 pieces sugared ginger
Juice of 1 lemon	3 tablespoons soy sauce
Salt	Pinch of ground anise
White pepper	1 cup hot water
2 slices lean bacon	2 teaspoons cornstarch
Margarine to grease pan	2 tablespoons bacon drippings
4 large leaves savoy cabbage (if unavailable, use regular cabbage)	Juice of half a lemon

garnish

2 tablespoons chopped parsley	Lemon slices

Have fishmonger scale and clean out the insides of the fish, but leave whole. At home wash fish thoroughly under running water, pat dry and rub with lemon juice. With sharp knife make shallow incisions in backs of both fish and rub with salt and pepper. Cut bacon into small strips and insert one strip in each incision.

Grease ovenproof baking dish with margarine and line with cabbage leaves. Place fish on top. Slice mushrooms and sugared ginger. Mix together and spoon over fish. Sprinkle with soy sauce and ground anise. Pour in small amount of hot water. Cover with lid or aluminum foil and place in preheated oven at 350°F. Bake for 30 minutes. While baking, gradually add rest of hot water and baste fish with pan drippings.

Remove fish and cabbage leaves from pan. Arrange on a preheated platter. Bring pan drippings to a boil, scraping all brown particles from bottom of pan and adding some more water, if necessary. Blend cornstarch with small amount of cold water, add to pan drippings and stir until sauce is smooth and bubbly. Correct seasoning if necessary, and serve separately. Melt and heat bacon drippings. Pour over fish and sprinkle with lemon juice. Garnish fish with chopped parsley and lemon slices.
MAKES APPROXIMATELY 4 SERVINGS.

Halibut cantonese

CHINA

1½ pounds halibut, cut into small chunks
1 tablespoon oil
1 medium onion, chopped

sauce
1½ cups water
1 tablespoon oil
Pinch salt
3 teaspoons soy sauce
Pinch of freshly ground pepper
2 tablespoons cornstarch dissolved in 3 tablespoons water

2 cloves garlic, minced
1 scallion, sliced
1 tablespoon celery, chopped
1 egg, beaten

Boil the halibut in a pot of water for 2 minutes. Heat the oil in a skillet and brown the onions. Transfer the fish to the skillet. Mix together the sauce ingredients, except for the cornstarch and water. Pour the sauce on the fish, and add the garlic, scallion, and celery.

Cover the skillet and simmer for 2 minutes. Pour the beaten egg slowly into the sauce, mixing constantly. Mix cornstarch with water and stir into sauce. Cook until thickened.
MAKES 2 SERVINGS.

Sweet-and-sour fish

CHINA

3 to 3½ pounds fish fillets (carp, bass, or fish of your choice)
4 tablespoons finely chopped onions
2 teaspoons chopped fresh gingerroot
Pinch of salt
¼ teaspoon freshly ground black pepper
1 teaspoon soy sauce
1 teaspoon sherry
½ cup cornstarch (more if needed)
Fat for deep frying

Sprinkle fish with onions, gingerroot, salt, pepper, soy sauce, and sherry. Let stand 30 minutes. Roll in cornstarch; let stand 10 minutes.

Heat fat in deep-fryer or deep skillet over medium-high heat. Fry fish 10 to 15 minutes or until done. Drain fish. Serve with sauce.
MAKES 4 SERVINGS.

Sweet-and-sour sauce

¾ cup cider vinegar
1 tablespoon cornstarch
1 green pepper, cut into julienne strips
1 carrot, peeled, cut into julienne strips
2 teaspoons chopped fresh gingerroot
4 scallions, sliced into ½-inch pieces
2 tablespoons sweet pickle relish
Salt to taste
¼ cup sugar

Mix together all ingredients. Cook over low heat, stirring constantly, until thickened.

Sesame salmon

CHINA

3 salmon steaks, cut into thirds
1 green pepper, cut into thin strips

1 leek, cut into thin strips
2 cloves garlic, minced
½ red chili pepper, minced
1 tablespoon sesame seeds
2 teaspoon vinegar
1 tablespoon sesame-seed oil
2 tablespoons soy sauce
2 teaspoons sugar
3 tablespoons water

Combine all ingredients; let stand 45 minutes. Preheat oven to 400°F. Wrap each piece of fish in foil; bake until tender, about 20 to 25 minutes.
MAKES 3 SERVINGS.

Oriental-style tuna casserole

CHINA

1 small can tuna
½ cup diced onion
½ cup diced celery
2 cups fresh bean sprouts or 1 can bean sprouts
¼ cup diced green pepper
Soy sauce to taste

Drain tuna and mix with onion, celery, bean sprouts, green pepper, and soy sauce to taste. If fresh bean sprouts are used, blanch in colander and rinse with cold water. Drain well. If canned bean sprouts are used, drain, rinse with cold water and drain well. Place in casserole and bake at 350°F for 30 minutes. Add additional soy sauce, if desired.
MAKES 2 TO 3 SERVINGS.

Shrimp w/mandarin oranges

CHINA

2 teaspoons sherry
1 teaspoon cornstarch
½ pound shrimp, cleaned
Oil for cooking
½ cup drained canned mandarin orange segments
¼ teaspoon sugar
¼ teaspoon salt

Mix together sherry and cornstarch and marinate shrimp in mixture for 5 minutes. Heat oil in skil-

let or wok, enough to cover bottom of pan, and stir-fry shrimp just until color changes. Add mandarin orange segments, sugar, and salt and stir-fry just until heated through, no more than 1 minute.
MAKES 2 SERVINGS.

Shrimp w/cucumber

CHINA

1 pound uncooked shrimp
1 tablespoon sherry
2 teaspoons salt, divided
1 teaspoon sugar
2 teaspoons cornstarch
2 cucumbers, peeled and cut into 1-inch pieces with seeds removed
Oil for cooking

Shell and devein the shrimp. Wash and drain. Cut in half lengthwise and then cut each half into 2 pieces crosswise. Combine shrimp with sherry, 1 teaspoon salt, sugar, and cornstarch. Prepare the cucumbers and set aside.
Heat oil in saucepan over high heat and sauté the cucumber. Add the rest of the salt and stir until cucumber is slightly transparent, about 4 minutes. In another saucepan heat oil over high heat and sauté the shrimp until they turn pink. Add cucumber, mix well and cook for another 2 minutes.
MAKES 2 TO 3 SERVINGS.

Shrimp & bean sprouts

CHINA

1 cup celery, sliced diagonally
1 cup fresh mushrooms, sliced
½ cup scallions, sliced
Oil for cooking
½ pound fresh bean sprouts
½ pound cooked shrimp
Soy sauce to taste

Prepare celery, mushrooms, and scallions. Heat oil in skillet or wok and stir-fry celery until it turns bright green. Add mushrooms and scallions and stir-fry for 1 minute. Add bean sprouts and

shrimp and toss lightly until heated through, approximately 2 minutes. Sprinkle with soy sauce.
MAKES 2 SERVINGS.

Hot-mustard shrimp

CHINA

3 tablespoons powdered mustard
¼ teaspoon salt
1 teaspoon sugar
1 teaspoon horseradish
¾ cup flat beer
1 pound shrimp, cleaned
4 tablespoons melted butter
Duck sauce

Mix mustard, salt, sugar, and horseradish together. Add enough beer to make a smooth paste. Gradually add rest of beer to make it thin. Let mixture stand for 1 hour. If it becomes too thick, add more beer or cold water.
Dip shrimp in mustard sauce, skewer, and brush with melted butter. Grill on hibachi or grill for approximately 8 minutes. Turn frequently for even browning. Serve with duck sauce.
MAKES 2 TO 3 SERVINGS.

Shrimp & asparagus

CHINA

1 pound cooked shrimp, shelled and deveined
1 can water chestnuts, drained and sliced
1 medium onion, sliced
1 cup fresh mushrooms, sliced
1 cup celery, sliced diagonally
1 small can mandarin oranges, drained
1½ pounds fresh asparagus, steamed
2 tablespoons oil
¼ teaspoon salt
½ teaspoon freshly ground black pepper
2 tablespoons sugar
2 tablespoons soy sauce
Cooked rice

Prepare the shrimp and set aside. Drain and slice the water chestnuts. On a large tray arrange the shrimp, chestnuts, onion, mushrooms, celery, mandarin oranges, and asparagus.

Heat the oil in a wok. Add onion, celery, salt, pepper, and sugar. Stir-fry until the vegetables are tender, but still on the crisp side. Add asparagus and shrimp. Place the water chestnuts and mushrooms over the shrimp. Sprinkle with the soy sauce and place the orange sections on top. Cover and cook until mixture steams. Reduce heat and simmer about 10 minutes. Serve with rice.
MAKES 6 SERVINGS.

Sesame shrimp

CHINA

½ cup sesame seeds, toasted
1 pound shrimp, cleaned
Salt
Freshly ground black pepper
6 tablespoons melted butter

Place sesame seeds in ungreased skillet over low heat and stir until browned. Set aside. Sprinkle shrimp lightly with salt and pepper. Dip in melted butter. Roll in toasted sesame seeds. Skewer shrimp and grill approximately 8 minutes over a grill or hibachi, turning frequently to brown evenly.
MAKES 2 TO 3 SERVINGS.

Grilled oriental shrimp

CHINA

1 pound shrimp, cleaned
⅓ cup soy sauce
¼ cup sesame oil
1 tablespoon brown sugar
1 tablespoon finely chopped fresh gingerroot or ¾ teaspoon powdered ginger
3 scallions, finely chopped

Combine all ingredients and marinate in refrigerator 6 hours. Drain the shrimp, reserving the marinade. Skewer the shrimp and grill over a grill or hibachi approximately 5 minutes, turning frequently and basting with marinade.
MAKES 2 TO 3 SERVINGS.

Crab rangoon

CHINA

¼ pound crab meat, chopped
¼ pound cream cheese
¼ teaspoon A-1 sauce
⅛ teaspoon garlic powder
Won ton squares
1 egg yolk, beaten
Oil for deep frying

Blend chopped crab meat with cream cheese, A-1 sauce, and garlic powder. Put ½ teaspoon of mixture in center of each won ton square. Fold square over cornerwise, moisten edges with beaten egg yolk and twist together. Fry in oil until lightly browned. Drain, and serve hot.
MAKES ABOUT 95 FILLED WON TON SQUARES.

Shrimp w/peas

CHINA

2 quarts water
2 cups frozen peas
1 tablespoon vegetable oil
1 small slice fresh gingerroot
¼ cup diagonally sliced green onions
1 cup uncooked shrimp, deveined, cut in half
Salt to taste
Freshly ground black pepper to taste
1 teaspoon cornstarch
1 tablespoon cold water
½ teaspoon sesame-seed oil

Bring water to boil. Add peas; bring to boil again. Drain peas; set aside.
Preheat wok (or skillet); coat bottom and sides with oil. Rub gingerroot on bottom and sides of wok, then discard. Stir-fry onions quickly. Add shrimp; stir-fry until just cooked. Shrimp will turn pink when done. Add salt and pepper.
Blend cornstarch with cold water. Stir this and peas into shrimp mixture. Add sesame oil; stir. Serve immediately.
MAKES 4 SERVINGS.

Shrimp Peking

CHINA

1 pound shrimp, cleaned, shelled
½ teaspoon salt
1 egg, beaten
2 tablespoons cornstarch
3 tablespoons peanut oil
2 tablespoons finely chopped scallions
1 small slice gingerroot, chopped
2 cloves garlic, minced
2 tablespoons soy sauce
2 tablespoons chicken broth
1 tablespoon dry sherry
2 teaspoons chopped red pepper
1 tablespoon vinegar
2 teaspoons sugar
4 water chestnuts, sliced

Sprinkle shrimp with salt. If shrimp are very large, cut in half. Mix together egg and cornstarch to make batter. Coat shrimp evenly with batter. Heat oil in wok (or frying pan) over medium-high heat. Stir-fry shrimp 3 minutes, separating them. Remove shrimp from wok. Drain; keep warm.
Place scallions and ginger in wok; stir-fry 1 minute. Add garlic, soy sauce, broth, sherry, red pepper, vinegar, and sugar. Cook, stirring constantly, until mixture comes to boil. Return shrimp to wok. Add water chestnuts; stir-fry 2 minutes. Serve immediately.
MAKES 2 SERVINGS.

Fried shrimp w/pineapple

CHINA

1 cup sifted all-purpose flour
1 teaspoon baking powder
1 teaspoon salt
1 egg, beaten
½ cup beer
Fat for deep frying
1 pound raw shrimp, shelled, deveined
1 tablespoon cornstarch
1 tablespoon sugar
4 tablespoons vinegar
½ cup pineapple juice
1 cup pineapple chunks

Steamed whole fish

Sift flour, baking powder, and ½ teaspoon salt into bowl. Beat in egg and beer. Heat fat in deep-fryer or deep skillet to medium high. Dip shrimp in batter, coating well on all sides. Fry in hot fat until nicely browned. Drain; keep warm. Mix cornstarch with sugar, ½ teaspoon salt, and vinegar. Add pineapple juice; cook over low heat, stirring constantly, until thickened.

Arrange shrimp on serving platter. Place pineapple chunks around shrimp; pour sauce over all.
MAKES 4 SERVINGS.

Curried shrimp

CHINA

1 pound fresh shrimp, shelled, cleaned
Juice of 1 lemon
1 egg white
1 tablespoon cornstarch
2 cups sesame-seed or vegetable oil
1 tablespoon dried Chinese mushrooms
1 can (approximately 6 ounces) bamboo shoots
1 medium onion, chopped
½ teaspoon ground ginger
1 green pepper, sliced thin
2 teaspoons curry powder
1 teaspoon sugar
2 tablespoons soy sauce
8-ounce can tiny peas, drained
2 tablespoons rice wine or sherry

Sprinkle shrimp with lemon juice. Blend egg white and cornstarch; coat shrimp with mixture. Heat oil in heavy, deep skillet or deep-fryer. Fry

shrimp 2 to 3 minutes; remove with slotted spoon. Set aside; keep warm.

Break mushrooms into small pieces; cover with boiling water. Let soak 15 minutes. Drain bamboo shoots; reserve liquid. Cut shoots into thin strips. Pour 2 tablespoons oil used for frying into skillet. Add bamboo shoots and onion; cook until transparent. Pour in ½ cup reserved liquid from bamboo shoots. Season with ground ginger. Add green pepper; cook 5 minutes. Pepper should be crisp. Add curry powder, sugar, and soy sauce.

Drain soaked mushrooms. Add mushrooms, peas, and shrimp to skillet. Fold in carefully; heat through. Heat wine in small saucepan; pour over dish just before serving.
MAKES 4 SERVINGS.

Oysters in ginger sauce

CHINA

1 pint oysters, preferably small ones
⅛ teaspoon five-spice powder
1½ teaspoons cornstarch
4 teaspoons soy sauce
3 tablespoons sherry
10 whole scallions
2 tablespoons oil
4 thin slices fresh gingerroot

Mix oysters with five-spice powder, 1 teaspoon cornstarch, and 1 teaspoon soy sauce; set aside. Blend ½ teaspoon cornstarch, 3 teaspoons soy sauce, and sherry; set aside. Cut white part from 403

Baked fish with cabbage leaves

1 cup sliced fresh mushrooms
3 tablespoons flour
2 cups fresh bean sprouts
2 tablespoons soy sauce
Salt to taste
Freshly ground black pepper to taste
Chow-mein noodles

Melt ¼ cup butter in skillet. Cook oysters over medium heat until edges curl.

Melt 3 tablespoons butter in another skillet. Sauté onion, green pepper, celery, and mushrooms until tender. Stir in flour. Add oysters and liquid, adding enough water to make ¾ cup. Cook, stirring constantly, until thickened. Add bean sprouts, soy sauce, salt, and pepper. Heat through, stirring gently. Serve over chow-mein noodles.

MAKES 3 OR 4 SERVINGS.

Fried fish

CHINA

2 eggs, beaten
2 tablespoons water
4 fish fillets
Bread or cracker crumbs

Curried shrimp

scallions; cut each in half crosswise. Cut green parts into 1-inch sections.

Heat oil in wok or large frypan over high heat. Add ginger and white parts of onions; cook and stir about 1 minute. Remove onion from pan; set aside. Spread out oysters in pan. Lower heat to medium; cook until oysters are just firm, turning once. Remove oysters from pan.

Cook drippings until browned. Blend in cornstarch-sherry mixture; cook and stir until thickened. Blend in whites and greens of onions and oysters; heat through until mixture simmers.
MAKES 2 SERVINGS.

Oyster chow mein

CHINA

¼ cup butter
1 pint oysters, drained, liquid reserved
3 tablespoons butter
1 medium onion, chopped
½ cup chopped green pepper
¾ cup diagonally sliced celery

Cod fillets in shrimp sauce

Oil for frying
Soy sauce

Beat eggs, add water, and mix together. Dip fish in egg mixture, then into bread or cracker crumbs. Fry fish in heated oil until done. Sprinkle with soy sauce to taste, and serve with rice, if desired.

MAKES 4 SERVINGS.

Fish in sweet-and-sour sauce

JAPAN

1 to 1½ pounds fish fillet (cod, haddock, or turbot)
Juice of half a lemon
2 tablespoons soy sauce
Salt
3 tablespoons cornstarch

sweet-and-sour sauce
5 tablespoons vinegar
½ cup water
6 teaspoons sugar
3 tablespoons soy sauce
3 slices lemon
3 tablespoons cornstarch
Cold water
4 cups oil for frying

Wash fish thoroughly; pat dry. Sprinkle with lemon juice and soy sauce. Cut into 1½-inch-wide strips. Set aside for 15 minutes and let marinate. Season to taste with salt and roll in cornstarch.

To prepare sauce, bring vinegar, water, sugar, soy sauce, and lemon slices to a boil over high heat. Reduce heat to lowest point; simmer sauce for 20 minutes. Blend cornstarch with small amount of cold water; add to sauce. Stir until smooth and bubbly.

About 5 minutes before sauce is done, place fish in hot oil, and fry for about 8 minutes. Fish is done when it floats to the surface. Remove fish pieces with slotted spoon; drain on paper towels. Arrange on serving platter and spoon sauce over fish. Serve immediately. Sauce can also be served separately.

MAKES APPROXIMATELY 3 TO 4 SERVINGS.

Raw fish

JAPAN

1 pound very fresh salmon, tuna, or other fish of your choice
Handful of fresh dill, parsley, watercress, or other type of greens
2 teaspoons horseradish
4 tablespoons soy sauce

Slice fish; arrange on platter along with greens. Mix horseradish and soy sauce; dip the fish into sauce before eating. If desired, freshly grated ginger may be substituted for the horseradish. Capers may be used for garnish.

MAKES APPROXIMATELY 4 SERVINGS.

Eel Kababs

Fish teriyaki

JAPAN

This is a tasty, easy to prepare "something different" dish.

marinade

1 cup soy sauce

¼ cup sugar (a little more, if you prefer it sweeter)

¼ cup salad oil

2 teaspoons grated fresh gingerroot or ground ginger

1 large clove of garlic, chopped fine

1½ to 2 pounds fish fillets (rock, red snapper, ocean perch, or haddock)

1 tablespoon sesame seeds

Combine soy sauce, sugar, oil, ginger, and garlic in a bowl. Let fish fillets marinate in marinade for 3 to 4 hours. After arranging fish on broiling pan, pour on a little of the marinade. Broil 6 inches from heat for about 4 minutes. Turn, add a little more marinade, and sprinkle fish with sesame seeds. Broil about 4 minutes longer, or until fish flakes.

MAKES 4 SERVINGS.

Easy fish teriyaki

JAPAN

4 fish fillets

Soy sauce

Oil

Place fish on broiler, brush with soy sauce and oil. Broil fish, turning frequently and basting with soy sauce, until fish flakes.

MAKES 4 SERVINGS.

Fish & vegetables in foil

JAPAN

4 fillets of white fish meat, about 4 ounces each

1 teaspoon salt

1 tablespoon rice wine or sherry

12 shrimp, with shells

Pepper to taste

4 fresh mushrooms

Aluminum foil, heavy duty

Salad oil

20 gingko nuts, canned (optional)

Wash fish, pat dry, and sprinkle with ½ teaspoon of the salt and the rice wine or sherry. Set aside while preparing shrimp. Keeping the shrimp in their shells, slit the shells in the backs, and remove veins. Sprinkle with ½ teaspoon salt and pepper.

Wash mushrooms; set aside. Brush a piece of foil (large enough to wrap the fish, shrimp, mushrooms, and gingko nuts in) with oil. Lay the fish, shrimp, mushrooms, and nuts on foil; pinch ends together to seal it. Heat frying pan over medium heat; place foil package in pan. Cover; bake for approximately 15 minutes.

MAKES 4 SERVINGS.

Eel kababs

JAPAN

2 eels, about 1 pound each

marinade

¾ cup rice wine or sherry

3 teaspoons honey

5 tablespoons soy sauce

Skin eels, cut off heads, and, with a very sharp knife, remove eel fillets from bone. Cut into 1½-inch pieces; place in deep bowl. Combine rice wine (or sherry), honey, and soy sauce. Heat. Pour marinade over eel pieces. Let marinate for 30 minutes.

Light coals in your barbecue grill; wait until white hot. Thread eel pieces on metal skewers; place on grill. Turn skewers occasionally; baste with marinade. Grill for 15 minutes. This can also be done under the oven broiler or on a hibachi.

MAKES APPROXIMATELY 2 TO 3 SERVINGS.

Note: To skin and fillet an eel, tie a string around the "neck" of the eel. Attach it to a board (or the barn door). Slit the skin around the neck and pull off the skin with a pair of pliers. Remove the fins with scissors. Clean the eel and remove the fillets by cutting the flesh on each side of the backbone.

Cod fillets in shrimp sauce

JAPAN

4 cod fillets, about 6 ounces each	2 tablespoons butter
Juice of 1 lemon	1 medium onion, sliced
Salt	2 tablespoons chopped parsley
White pepper	½ cup dry white wine

shrimp sauce

2 tablespoons butter	4 ounces fresh shrimp
1½ tablespoons flour	2 teaspoons lemon juice
1 cup hot beef broth	Salt
½ cup dry white wine	2 egg yolks
6 ounces fresh mushrooms	

garnish

Lemon slices	Parsley

Sprinkle cod fillets with lemon juice. Let stand for 10 minutes. Season to taste with salt and pepper. Heat butter in large skillet. Add fish; brown well for about 10 minutes on each side. Add sliced onion; cook until golden. Stir in chopped parsley. Pour in white wine; simmer for another 5 minutes. Remove cod fillets to preheated platter; keep them warm. Reserve pan drippings.

To prepare sauce, melt butter in a saucepan. Stir in flour; pour in hot beef broth, as well as reserved pan drippings. Add white wine. Let simmer over low heat. Cut mushrooms into thin slices and add, together with shrimp, to sauce; simmer for 15 minutes. Season to taste with lemon juice and sa . Remove small amount of sauce; blend with egg yolks. Return to sauce; stir thoroughly; heat through, but do not boil, since yolks will curdle. Pour sauce over cod fillets. Garnish with lemon slices and parsley.

MAKES 4 SERVINGS.

Skewered shrimp

JAPAN

4 large shelled shrimp

sauce

1 tablespoon (or less) salt
4 tablespoons soy sauce
¾ tablespoon rice wine or sherry
¼ teaspoon freshly grated ginger
Asparagus tips

Cut shrimp into bite-size pieces. Make a sauce by blending together the salt, soy sauce, rice wine (sake) or sherry, and ginger. Dip shrimp into sauce; place on skewers. Dip the asparagus tips into the sauce, then place on skewers. Broil in oven, basting with sauce; or grill, or use hibachi.

MAKES 2 SERVINGS.

Boiled shrimp

JAPAN

2 ounces cabbage, thinly sliced
8 ounces cucumbers, peeled and cut into ¼-inch cubes
8 ounces shrimp

sauce

2 teaspoons horseradish
¼ cup soy sauce

Dip cabbage quickly into boiling water; let dry. Peel and slice cucumbers. Boil the shrimp in salted water for about 5 minutes.

Serve the cabbage, cucumber, and shrimp in small bowls. The shrimp is dipped into a sauce made from the horseradish and soy sauce.

MAKES 2 SERVINGS.

Boiled shrimp w/bamboo shoots

JAPAN

2 cups boiling water
2 tablespoons mirin (sweet rice wine)
3 tablespoons soy sauce
12 shrimp, shelled and cleaned
1 pound bamboo shoots

Bring water to a boil; add mirin and soy sauce to it. If substituting sherry for the mirin, add 1 tablespoon sugar. Cook the shrimp in the mixture until done. Cut the bamboo shoots into small pieces; cook them in the same liquid used for the shrimp. Serve shrimp and bamboo shoots with rice.
MAKES 3 TO 4 SERVINGS.

Golden shrimp

JAPAN

12 large fresh shrimp

marinade
3 tablespoons soy sauce
1 tablespoon rice wine or sherry
Ginger to taste, either ground or grated gingerroot
Cornstarch

Oil for frying

Rinse shrimp. Mix together soy sauce, rice wine or sherry, and ginger. Marinate shrimp in the marinade for 30 minutes. Drain well. Sprinkle shrimp with cornstarch; set aside for 3 minutes. Heat oil in deep fryer or frying pan; fry shrimp. The shrimp may be left whole for a main course or cut into approximately 3 pieces each for an appetizer.
MAKES 2 TO 4 SERVINGS.

Japanese crab cakes

JAPAN

12 ounces fresh crab meat, or canned, if fresh is unavailable
1 cup frozen peas
3 eggs
1 cup chopped fresh mushrooms
1 teaspoon freshly grated ginger or ½ teaspoon ground ginger

Oil
Soy sauce for dipping

Combine crab meat, peas, eggs, mushrooms, and ginger. Mix well. Heat oil in large frying pan; fry all the batter at once, like a pancake. Fry well on one side, then turn carefully and fry well on the other side. Cut into slices and dip into soy sauce.
MAKES 3 SERVINGS.

Crab-meat dumplings

JAPAN

12 ounces fresh crab meat, or frozen, if fresh is unavailable
3 tablespoons bread or cracker crumbs
1 egg, beaten
Flour for hands

batter
1 cup flour
1 egg
1 cup water

Oil for frying

Mix together thoroughly the crab meat, bread or cracker crumbs, and egg. Make small balls with floured hands; refrigerate for about 30 minutes. Meanwhile make batter of flour, egg, and water; blend until well-mixed. If it remains lumpy, it's all right. Heat oil; dip balls into batter, then fry in hot oil. Drain on paper toweling. Serve with soy sauce, if desired.
MAKES 2 TO 3 SERVINGS.

Onion & seafood in miso sauce

JAPAN

1 pound small onions
1 cup small clams or scallops
Vinegar for soaking clams

miso sauce
2 tablespoons sugar
2 tablespoons dashi
4 tablespoons miso
2 tablespoons vinegar

Slice the onions; boil until just tender. Soak the clams in a small amount of vinegar while onions are boiling. If using scallops, lightly salt them before soaking in the vinegar. Add sugar and dashi to the miso; blend very well. Stir in the vinegar. Drain the clams or scallops; add, along with the onions, to the sauce. Serve seafood immediately.
MAKES 2 SERVINGS.

Broiled scallops

JAPAN

1 pound fresh scallops
Melted butter
Lemon juice
Freshly ground pepper (optional)
Soy sauce
Rice

Place scallops on broiler; brush with melted butter mixed with lemon juice. Sprinkle with pepper; broil just until done. Sprinkle with soy sauce and serve with rice.
MAKES 2 TO 3 SERVINGS.

Fried fish w/Mexican sauce

MEXICO

1 pound firm fish fillets, defrosted if frozen (flounder or sole)	½ teaspoon salt
	¼ teaspoon pepper
	½ cup flour
2 tablespoons lemon juice	¼ cup cooking oil

mexican sauce

2 tablespoons olive oil	2 tablespoons dry sherry
1 small onion, chopped	Salt and pepper
½ cup chopped green pepper	1 large pinch saffron
¼ cup chopped celery	2 tablespoons chopped parsley (for garnish)
1 clove garlic, minced	
1 cup drained and chopped canned peeled tomatoes	

Sprinkle fish fillets with lemon juice, salt, and pepper; set aside while making the sauce.
Heat olive oil in saucepan or small skillet. Add onion, green pepper, celery, and garlic; sauté until limp. Add tomatoes, sherry, salt and pepper to taste, and saffron. Stir well; simmer while frying fish.

Drain fish well. Heat cooking oil over moderate heat in large frying pan. Dip fish in flour, coating well; fry until golden, turning once. Drain fish and serve hot, topped with the sauce. Garnish with chopped parsley.
MAKES 4 SERVINGS.

Red snapper a la Veracruz

MEXICO

1 to 1¼ pounds red-snapper fillets (4 fillets)
2 tablespoons lemon juice
Salt and pepper
2 tablespoons chopped capers
¼ cup sliced pimiento-stuffed green olives
2 tablespoons olive oil
½ cup chopped onion
1 clove garlic, minced
2 cups chopped canned tomatoes
¼ teaspoon crumbled thyme
¼ teaspoon crumbled marjoram
½ teaspoon crumbled oregano

Lightly oil small ovenproof baking dish, big enough to hold fish fillets in a single layer. Arrange fish in baking dish. Sprinkle with lemon juice; salt and pepper lightly. Sprinkle with capers and sliced olives.
Heat oil in small skillet. Add onion and garlic; cook until limp. Add tomatoes, thyme, marjoram, and oregano; simmer for 10 minutes. Pour over fish. Cover baking dish; bake at 350°F for 25 to 30 minutes or until fish flakes easily with a fork. Serve fish with small, boiled new potatoes.
MAKES 4 SERVINGS.

Fillet of sole Acapulco-style

MEXICO

Acapulco, due to the international character of its many visitors, provides some of the best continental-style cuisine to be found anywhere!

1 pound fresh spinach
1 tablespoon butter
1 tablespoon olive oil
1 clove garlic, minced
Salt and pepper

1 pound sole fillets
¼ cup butter or margarine
½ cup flour
Juice of ½ lemon
5 large slices fresh tomato
1 cup grated Edam cheese

Clean and wash spinach well. Remove all coarse stems; shake as much water as possible from leaves. Heat 1 tablespoon each butter and oil in large skillet. Add garlic; sauté 2 minutes. Add spinach; immediately cover pan. Cook over high heat until steam appears. Reduce heat to low; simmer 5 minutes. Season with salt and pepper; turn into an 11 × 7 × 1¾-inch casserole dish. Melt ¼ cup butter in skillet. Dredge fish in flour; sauté in butter until browned. Drain; lay on top of spinach. Squeeze lemon juice over fish. Arrange tomato slices, overlapping on top of fish. Sprinkle with cheese; bake at 350°F for 20 to 25 minutes or until cheese is melted.
MAKES 4 SERVINGS.

Poached fish w/avocado sauce

MEXICO

1½ to 2 pounds fresh or frozen fish fillets, thawed
2 onions, thinly sliced
2 lemons, thinly sliced
2 tablespoons butter, melted
2 teaspoons salt
1 bay leaf
½ teaspoon black pepper
3 cups water
1 lemon (cut in half—squeeze 1 half, slice other half)

avocado sauce
2 mashed avocados
½ cup sour cream
2 tablespoons lemon juice
½ small onion, finely chopped

Cut fillets into serving portions. Combine onions and lemon slices with butter, salt, bay leaf, and black pepper in an ovenproof baking dish. Place fillets on top of onion and lemon slices; add the water. Cover; cook at 350°F for 45 minutes.

Before serving, carefully remove fish fillets with slotted spoon or spatula. Place on heated platter. Sprinkle with juice from ½ lemon. Garnish with additional lemon slices.
Prepare Avocado Sauce by mixing all sauce ingredients well. Serve the hot fish with the sauce, or chill the fish and serve it cold.
MAKES 6 SERVINGS.

Shrimp fritters

MEXICO

tomato sauce
2 tablespoons olive oil
1 medium onion, chopped
1 clove garlic, minced
1 10-ounce can tomatoes and green chilies
½ teaspoon salt
¼ teaspoon pepper

fritters
4 eggs, separated
½ teaspoon salt
¼ teaspoon celery salt
2 teaspoons dried parsley flakes
2 tablespoons flour
1 cup well-drained chopped cooked shrimp (fresh, frozen, or canned)
Oil for frying

First make the sauce; keep it warm while making fritters. Heat oil in medium saucepan. Add onion and garlic; sauté until limp. Add tomatoes and green chilies and seasonings. Bring to a boil. Reduce heat to simmer. Cover; cook for 20 minutes.
Meanwhile, beat egg whites until stiff. Beat egg yolks, salt, celery salt, parsley flakes, and flour. Fold into egg whites. Fold shrimp into egg-white batter.
In heavy skillet or deep fryer heat at least 1 inch of oil to 365°F. Fry fritters a few at a time (using ¼ cup batter for each fritter) until golden. Drain well. Serve fritters immediately with the Tomato Sauce.
MAKES 4 SERVINGS.

ᴥTempuraᴥ

Tempura cornstarch batter

JAPAN

1½ cups cornstarch
¾ teaspoon salt
¾ cup cold water
1 egg
Peanut or vegetable oil for frying

Blend ingredients together, but do not overmix.
Dip fresh vegetables or seafood into batter, then
fry in hot peanut or vegetable oil. The foods you
are frying should be cut into bite-size pieces. You
may use a frying pan or a wok.
MAKES APPROXIMATELY 2 SERVINGS.

Tempura flour batter

JAPAN

2 eggs, beaten
1 cup cold water
¾ cup flour
Pinch of salt

Combine 2 beaten eggs with cold water until
frothy. Blend in flour. Add salt. Blend well.

Fish tempura

Keep batter cool while using it; i.e. set it in a
bowl of ice.
Use a variety of vegetables, or seafood, cut into
bite-size pieces. Dip into batter and fry in hot
peanut or vegetable oil in wok or frying pan.
MAKES APPROXIMATELY 2 SERVINGS.

Extra-light tempura batter

JAPAN

1 egg, separated
½ cup sifted flour
2 tablespoons cornstarch
¼ teaspoon salt
½ teaspoon pepper
½ cup cold water

In small bowl beat egg white until stiff peaks
form. In another bowl sift together flour, cornstarch, salt, and pepper. In a separate bowl beat
egg yolk and water until frothy. Gradually add
flour mixture to egg yolk and water, mixing constantly. Blend until smooth. Fold egg white into
yolk mixture. Blend thoroughly.
MAKES APPROXIMATELY 2 SERVINGS.

Tempura / Japan

Tempura dipping sauce

JAPAN

2 teaspoons soy sauce
¼ teaspoon salt
½ teaspoon sugar
½ cup grated white radish
2 cups dashi (broth made from dried bonito and seaweed)
1 tablespoon chopped scallions

Mix together soy sauce, salt, sugar, and grated radish. Blend in dashi, then add scallions. This sauce can be used with any food that has been fried in a tempura batter.

MAKES APPROXIMATELY 3 TO 4 SERVINGS.

More tempura sauces

JAPAN

Any of the following may be used for dipping the tempura-fried foods:

Grated white radish
Hot (or mild) mustard
Catsup

Soy sauce
Sweet-and-sour sauce

sweet-and-sour sauce

1 tablespoon butter
1 cup water
½ cup cider vinegar
3 tablespoons soy sauce

¼ cup sugar
1 tablespoon cornstarch
3 tablespoons sherry

Melt butter in saucepan over medium heat. Blend in water, vinegar, soy sauce, and sugar. Bring to boil. Lower heat; simmer for 10 minutes. Make a paste of the cornstarch and sherry; slowly blend it into rest of ingredients, stirring constantly until thickened.

MAKES APPROXIMATELY 2 CUPS.

Vegetable tempura

JAPAN

vegetables
Use a variety of the following, or whatever is available to you:

Eggplant
Green pepper
String beans

Mushrooms
Onion
Potato

tempura batter

1 egg
½ cup ice water

1 cup sifted flour
Oil for deep-frying

Slice vegetables into thin strips, keeping them separate, and set aside.

To mix batter, beat egg: add cold water and sifted flour all at once. Blend thoroughly, but do not overmix. Heat oil in deep pan (or wok) until a drop of water dropped into oil sizzles. Dip vegetables, a few at a time, in batter, then fry them until crisp, using tongs to turn them. Take out of pan or wok with slotted spoon. Drain on paper towels. Dip vegetables in soy sauce before enjoying.

MAKES APPROXIMATELY 2 SERVINGS.

Fish tempura

JAPAN

2 pounds fresh fish fillets
Salt to taste
Lemon juice
½ recipe Basic Tempura Batter
Oil
Chili-Horseradish Sauce
Soy sauce

basic tempura batter

2 cups all-purpose flour, sifted
3 egg yolks
2 cups ice water

Cut the fish fillets into bite-size pieces and drain well on paper toweling. Prepare other ingredients. Season the fish with salt and squeeze desired amount of lemon juice over fish. Make up the batter.

Sift flour 3 times. Combine the yolks and water in a large bowl over ice and beat with a whisk until well-blended. Gradually add the flour, stirring and turning the mixture with a spoon. Don't overmix. Keep the batter over ice while frying. Makes approximately 4½ cups.

Place all the fish in the batter. When ready to fry, remove the fish from the batter with a fork and drain slightly. Heat the oil in a wok, an electric skillet or deep-fat fryer to between 350 and 375°F. Fry the fish, a few pieces at a time, for about 5 minutes, turning to brown evenly. Remove the fish from the oil with a slotted spoon and drain well on paper toweling. Keep fish warm until all is cooked.

Shrimp tempura

Serve with Chili-Horseradish Sauce (recipe follows) or just dipped into soy sauce. Use this batter for vegetables also, or meat, or seafood. Skim off loose particles of food as they appear, to keep the oil clean. Keep the batter cold.

Chili-horseradish sauce

1 cup mayonnaise
⅓ cup chili sauce
3 tablespoons horseradish

Combine all ingredients in small bowl and mix thoroughly. Chill well before serving.
MAKES APPROXIMATELY 1½ CUPS.

Shrimp tempura

JAPAN

1 pound fresh large shrimp
8 ounces bamboo shoots
4 peppers, green, red, and yellow
4 small onions
2 sugared or candied ginger

tempura batter
2 ounces rice flour
6 ounces flour
1 cup water
4 jiggers rice wine or sherry
8 egg whites

4 cups oil for frying

Rinse shrimp. Drain bamboo shoots; cut into ½-inch pieces. Cut green peppers into ½-inch strips. Cut onions into thick slices; separate into rings. Slice sugared ginger. Arrange these ingredients in separate small bowls.

To prepare batter, place flour in a bowl. In a separate bowl combine water and rice wine or sherry and egg whites until well-blended. Gradually stir into flour to form loose batter.

Heat oil in fondue pot or wok. Each person places a shrimp or piece of vegetable on a fondue fork, dips it in batter, and deep-fries it in hot oil.
MAKES 4 SERVINGS.

413

Dessert tempura

JAPAN

This is a fun dessert to do at the table in a fondue pot or wok.

Fruit for 4 (apples, bananas, pears)
Tempura batter
Powdered sugar

Peel fruit; cut it into chunks. Dip it into tempura batter; fry it in oil. Drain on paper towels. Sprinkle with powdered sugar. Delicious with hot tea.
MAKES 4 SERVINGS.

Tempura ice-cream balls

JAPAN

Oil for frying
4 ice-cream balls frozen very, very hard (vanilla, or another
flavor of your choice)
Tempura batter
Sugar and cinnamon or powdered sugar

Heat oil to medium high. Remove balls from freezer; immediately dip into tempura batter, and fry until golden brown. Serve immediately, sprinkled with cinnamon and sugar or powdered sugar.
MAKES 4 SERVINGS.

Pasta, rice,
❦ and other grain dishes ❦

Cooked potato dumplings

GERMANY

6 medium potatoes, cooked in skins
½ to 1 cup flour
2 eggs, beaten
1 teaspoon salt
1 cup day-old white bread crumbs, sautéed in ½ cup melted
   butter or margarine
6 to 8 cups hot beef or chicken broth
½ cup melted butter

Peel and grate potatoes while warm. Blend in flour, eggs, and salt to form a dough stiff enough to shape with fingers. Shape into balls 2 or 3 inches in diameter. There will be 8 to 12 dumplings, depending on size. If dumplings do not shape well, add more flour to dough. Force a few fried bread crumbs into the center of each ball; seal over. Reserve rest of crumbs.

Cook dumplings in boiling broth until they rise to the top, about 10 minutes. Spoon melted butter over tops; sprinkle with remaining fried bread crumbs.

MAKES 4 to 6 SERVINGS.

Spaetzle noodles

GERMANY

3 cups flour
1 teaspoon salt
¼ teaspoon nutmeg
4 eggs, beaten
½ cup water (or more)
¼ cup butter

Sift flour, salt, and nutmeg together in a bowl. Pour eggs and ¼ cup water into middle of flour mixture; beat with a wooden spoon. Add enough water to make the dough slightly sticky, yet keeping it elastic and stiff.

Using a spaetzle machine or a colander with medium holes, press the noodles into a large pot full of boiling salted water. Cook noodles in the water about 5 minutes or until they rise to the surface. Lift noodles out and drain on paper towels. Brown noodles in melted butter over low heat.

MAKES 4 TO 5 SERVINGS.

Homemade noodles

Spaetzle cheese noodles

GERMANY

3 tablespoons butter or margarine
3 onions, sliced in small rings
3 ounces Emmenthaler cheese, grated
1 teaspoon dry mustard
2 cups cooked spaetzle noodles or thin noodles (see recipe for
   spaetzle)
2 tablespoons chopped chives

Heat butter in a frypan, add onions, and brown lightly.

Toss cheese with dry mustard. Add cooked noodles to cooked onions and cheese: mix well. Place mixture in an ovenproof casserole. Bake at 300°F for 20 to 30 minutes or until hot and bubbly. Sprinkle top with chopped chives before serving.

MAKES 4 SERVINGS.

Rice w/fides

GREECE

1 cup long-grain rice
½ cup crushed fides or vermicelli
3 tablespoons butter or margarine
2 cups chicken broth
1 teaspoon freeze-dried chives

Combine the rice and fides and sauté in the butter or margarine in a 2-quart saucepan until golden brown. Add the chicken broth and chives.

Cover tightly and cook 20 to 25 minutes over very low heat, until all the liquid is absorbed. Fluff with a fork and serve.

MAKES 4 SERVINGS.

Rice pilaf

GREECE

2 cups chicken broth, or 2 cups boiling water and 2
   teaspoons instant chicken-broth granules
1 cup long-grain raw rice

Heat the chicken broth to boiling and add the rice. Reduce the heat to simmer and cook for 20 minutes or until all the liquid is absorbed. Fluff

with a fork and serve.
MAKES 4 TO 5 SERVINGS.

Variations: The stock used to make the pilaf should complement the dish with which it is served. For example, if you are serving a dish made with beef, substitute beef broth for the chicken broth in the recipe above. If you are serving the rice with fish, substitute clam juice diluted with water (1 cup clam juice + 1 cup water) for the chicken broth and cook the recipe in the same manner. Garnish with chopped parsley before serving.

Rice pilaf w/raisins & nuts

GREECE

6 tablespoons butter or margarine
1 cup chopped onion
1 clove garlic, minced
1 cup raw long-grain rice
2½ cups chicken broth
2 tablespoons chopped parsley
¼ cup golden raisins
½ teaspoon salt
¼ teaspoon pepper
¼ cup pine nuts

Melt 4 tablespoons of butter in a small skillet. Add the onion and garlic and sauté until golden. Pour into a 2-quart casserole. Add the rice, chicken broth, parsley, raisins, salt, and pepper. Stir well. Cover the casserole and bake at 375° for 30 minutes or until the liquid is absorbed. Brown the pine nuts in the remaining 2 tablespoons of butter. Fluff the rice and stir in the pine nuts before serving.
MAKES 4 SERVINGS.

Rice pilaf w/onion

GREECE

2 tablespoons olive oil
1 cup raw long-grain or converted rice
2 cups chicken broth, or 2 cups hot water and 2 teaspoons
    chicken-broth granules
2 tablespoons green-onion tops, thinly sliced
⅛ teaspoon garlic powder

Heat the oil in a medium-size saucepan over medium-low heat. Add the rice and cook until golden in color, stirring occasionally.
Meanwhile, heat the chicken broth to boiling. Add the chicken broth to the rice. Add the green-onion tops and garlic powder. Cover and simmer for 25 minutes or until all the liquid is absorbed. Fluff the rice with a fork, and serve.
MAKES 4 TO 5 SERVINGS.

Bulgur-wheat pilaf

GREECE

¼ cup butter or margarine
1 cup bulgur (cracked wheat)
2 cups chicken broth
1 teaspoon salt
¼ teaspoon pepper
Yoghurt
Chopped parsley

Melt the butter or margarine in a heavy saucepan. Add the bulgur and sauté, stirring constantly, until the butter is lightly browned. Add the broth, salt, and pepper. Cover, and reduce the heat to simmer. Cook for 25 to 30 minutes or until the liquid is absorbed and the wheat is tender. Let stand, covered, for 15 minutes before serving.
Top with yoghurt and chopped parsley for garnish when served.
MAKES 4 SERVINGS.

Macaroni Athenian-style

GREECE

6 ounces macaroni (either whole and unbroken or elbow
    macaroni)
¼ cup butter
1 cup grated Kasseri cheese

Cook the macaroni in 3 quarts of boiling salted water, according to the package directions, and drain. Meanwhile, melt the butter in a small skillet and cook until golden brown.
In a large bowl place a layer of ⅓ of the cheese; add ½ of the macaroni. Top with ⅓ of the cheese, the remaining macaroni, and the rest of

the cheese. Pour the browned butter over all and serve.
MAKES 4 SERVINGS.

Homemade noodles

HUNGARY

Noodles and dumplings hold a unique place in Hungarian cuisine. They are prepared as sweet and savory dishes and are often served for dessert.

1⅓ cups all-purpose flour
¾ teaspoon salt
2 eggs
2 teaspoons cooking oil
2 teaspoons water

Combine flour and salt in mixing bowl. Make well in center. Beat eggs, oil, and water together; pour into well. Stir with fork from outside of mixture to center. Add small amount of water if necessary, so that very stiff dough is formed. Turn out onto lightly floured surface; knead until smooth and elastic (about 15 minutes). Let rest, covered, 30 minutes.

Divide dough into 4 equal parts; roll 1 piece at a time, as thin as possible. It should be 1/16th inch thick. Roll up; cut into ½-inch strips. Unroll strips; allow to dry several hours on lightly floured towel.

Bring several quarts salted water to boil in Dutch oven. Add noodles; stir to keep from sticking to bottom of pot. Cook approximately 10 minutes. Test frequently for doneness; noodles should still be firm, not mushy. Drain well. Top with melted butter and serve, or use in other recipes.
MAKES 4 TO 5 SERVINGS.

Pinched noodles

HUNGARY

½ cup flour
⅛ teaspoon salt
1 egg, well-beaten
Flour for kneading

Combine flour and salt in small bowl. Make well in center; add egg. Mix to form stiff dough. Turn out onto lightly floured surface; knead 5 minutes. Divide into 3 parts; roll each part with your hands to form long cylinder about as big around as your little finger. Pinch off small pieces; add directly to boiling soup, or cook in boiling salted water until tender (about 5 minutes). When done, noodle should cut easily and not be floury in center. Generally, half of this recipe is sufficient for 1½ quarts soup.

Pinch remaining noodles; allow to stand on lightly floured board until dry. Store airtight for future use.
MAKES APPROXIMATELY 8 SERVINGS.

Variations: Above dough can be rolled to form thin sheet and allowed to dry 2 hours. It is then broken into irregularly shaped pieces and added to soup. Dough may also be rolled and cut into standard soup noodles.

To make *galuska,* or Soup Dumplings, decrease flour in preceding recipe to 3 tablespoons. Mix flour, egg, and salt well; drop resulting soft dough by ¼ teaspoons directly into soup. Cook as above.

Poppy-seed noodles

HUNGARY

4 tablespoons butter
1 recipe Homemade Noodles (see Index)
1 tablespoon poppy seeds

Lightly brown butter in heavy skillet. Toss noodles with butter and poppy seeds.
MAKES 4 TO 5 SERVINGS.

Noodles w/walnuts

HUNGARY

1 cup finely chopped walnuts
⅓ cup confectioners' sugar
1 teaspoon grated lemon rind
1 recipe Homemade Noodles (see Index)
3 tablespoons melted butter

Combine walnuts, sugar, and lemon rind; mix well. Toss noodles with butter. Sprinkle individual servings with nut mixture.
MAKES 4 TO 5 SERVINGS.

Noodles and cabbage

HUNGARY

3 tablespoons butter
3 cups finely shredded cabbage
1 teaspoon sugar
Salt and pepper
1 recipe Homemade Noodles (see Index)

Melt butter in heavy skillet. Add cabbage, sugar, salt, and pepper; cook, stirring constantly, over moderate heat until lightly browned. Combine with drained noodles.

MAKES 4 TO 5 SERVINGS.

Noodles w/cheese & bacon

HUNGARY

6 ounces broad egg noodles
Boiling salted water
3 slices bacon, diced
2 tablespoons finely minced onion
½ cup creamed cottage cheese or farmer cheese
¼ cup sour cream
Salt and pepper

Cook noodles in boiling salted water in large saucepan according to package directions; drain well.

Meanwhile cook bacon until lightly browned. Add onion; cook until bacon is crisp. Remove bacon and onion with slotted spoon; reserve. Add noodles to bacon fat; mix well. Pour back into saucepan.

Combine cheese, sour cream, salt, and pepper; mix well. Add cheese mixture, bacon, and onion to noodles. Toss to combine thoroughly.

MAKES 4 SERVINGS.

Chicken-flavored rice

HUNGARY

2 tablespoons butter or margarine
2 tablespoons finely chopped onion
1 cup converted rice
2 tablespoons chopped carrot
2 tablespoons chopped parsley
½ teaspoon crumbled dried marjoram
Salt and pepper
2½ cups reserved chicken stock

Melt butter in heavy saucepan. Add onion; cook until lightly browned. Add rice; cook, stirring occasionally, 3 minutes. Add remaining ingredients; bring to boil. Reduce heat to low; cook, covered, 20 to 25 minutes. All liquid should be absorbed.

Fluff rice with fork; stir in minced giblets. Cover; let stand 10 minutes. Turn rice into serving dish. Serve with any poultry dish.

MAKES 4 SERVINGS.

Chicken stock

3 cups water
1 giblet pack containing chicken gizzards, heart, and liver
1 chicken neck
1 chicken back
1 carrot, peeled, sliced
1 stalk celery, sliced
2 sprigs parsley
1 small onion, studded with 2 cloves
1 teaspoon seasoned salt and pepper mixture
¼ teaspoon poultry seasoning

Combine all stock ingredients (except liver) in large saucepan; bring to boil. Skim foam from surface; cover. Reduce heat to low; cook 40 minutes. Add liver; cook 20 minutes. Remove liver and giblets; mince; reserve. Strain stock; reserve.

Dunmurry rice

IRELAND

2 tablespoons butter
1 small onion, finely minced
1 cup rice
1 cup sliced mushrooms
2½ cups chicken stock or broth
2 tablespoons chopped parsley
Salt and pepper
3 medium tomatoes
2 tablespoons butter or margarine, melted
½ cup fine dry bread crumbs
1 tablespoon grated Parmesan cheese
Paprika

Melt butter in heavy saucepan. Add onion, rice, and mushrooms; sauté until rice starts to brown. Add stock, parsley, salt, and pepper; bring to boil. Reduce heat to low; cook, covered, 25 minutes or until all liquid is absorbed. Grease 1-quart

Egg noodles—charcoal makers style

mixing bowl. Pack rice into bowl tightly. Keep warm while preparing tomatoes.

Split tomatoes in half. Combine melted butter, bread crumbs, cheese, salt, pepper, and paprika; mix well. Sprinkle crumb mixture over tomatoes; broil in preheated broiler 4 inches from heat until golden.

Unmold rice onto warm serving dish; surround with tomatoes. Serve.

MAKES 6 SERVINGS.

Egg noodles

ITALY

1⅓ *cups flour*
½ *teaspoon salt*
2 *eggs*
2 *teaspoons olive oil*
2 *teaspoons water*

Combine the flour and salt in a mixing bowl. Make a well in the center. Beat the eggs, oil and water together and pour into the well. Mix thoroughly, adding a little more water if necessary to form a stiff dough. Turn out on a lightly floured surface and knead to form a smooth, elastic dough (about 15 minutes). Let rest, covered, for 30 minutes.

To roll by hand: Divide the dough into 4 equal parts. Lightly flour a smooth surface and roll the dough ¼ at a time until it is as thin as you can roll it. Ideally it should be 1/16th of an inch thick. Select a ball-bearing rolling pin if possible, since it is very easy to get blisters. Cut according to the recipe of your choice or use the following 419

Macaroni with sauce amatrice

to substitute for package noodles:

Tagliatelle: Roll up like a scroll and cut into ⅜ inch strips. Unroll and dry on a towel.

Lasagne: Cut into strips 2 inches wide and as long as your baking dish. Dry on towels.

Manicotti: Cut into squares 5 X 5 inches and dry on towels.

To roll by pasta machine: If you enjoy home-made noodles and pasta and make them frequently, a pasta machine might be a good investment for you. It consists of two rollers that can be moved close together or far apart and turned by a crank. Several cutting blades are also provided. The machine can also be used to roll wonton wrappers or certain specialty breads such as poppadums. It is not necessary to knead the dough by hand if you are rolling the dough by machine as both operations can be accomplished at the same time.

Let the dough rest without kneading and then divide into quarters. Take the dough, one-quarter at a time, and pass the dough through the machine with the rollers set as far apart as possible (usually number 10 or the highest numerical setting on the machine). Fold the dough into thirds and pass through again. After passing the dough through the machine 10 times, turn the setting down one notch and roll through. Continue to roll the dough, reducing the setting one notch each time, until the desired thickness is achieved. The dough strip will become long. Do not fold it. If it becomes unwieldy, get someone to hold it or cut it in half and roll the pieces separately. Roll to slightly less than 1/16th of an inch thick. Cut as directed above, and dry by hanging them on a line or something similar.

Noodles can be prepared ahead. Simply roll them, cut, and dry for ½ hour and then freeze. It is best to quick-freeze the noodles on a tray and then carefully transfer them to a bag or box and seal. Remove from the freezer when ready to use and cook the same as you would freshly made pasta.

To cook: Bring 4 to 5 quarts of salted water to a boil. Float 1 tablespoon of oil on the surface of the water. Add the pasta a few pieces at a time and stir. Cook until the pasta floats to the surface of the water. Test for doneness. It should be firm, and not mushy. Drain well.

MAKES ABOUT ¾ OF A POUND.

Variation: To make green noodles, omit the water and add ¼ cup of well-drained, cooked and pureed spinach and proceed as above.

Note: The yield for the pasta recipes given is based on machine-rolled pasta. If you are rolling the dough by hand, make twice the amount of dough, since the product will not be as thin. If you have extra, make noodles and freeze them for future use.

420

Egg noodles—charcoal makers style

ITALY

2 tablespoons olive oil
¼ pound lean, thick sliced bacon
A pinch crushed, dried red pepper flakes
2 tablespoons butter
3 quarts water
3 teaspoons salt
1 tablespoon cooking oil
12 ounces tagliatelle or broad egg noodles
3 medium eggs, well beaten
½ cup freshly grated Parmesan cheese

In a heavy skillet heat the olive oil. Chop the bacon and fry in the oil until crisp. Add the pepper flakes and butter and heat just until the butter melts. Remove from the heat.

Meanwhile, bring the 3 quarts of water to a boil. Add the salt and oil. Add the noodles and cook until they are al dente (tender, but still firm in texture). Drain. Add immediately to the bacon mixture. Pour the eggs over the noodles and toss the eggs, bacon and noodles together. The mixture should be hot enough to "cook" the eggs. If the eggs do not appear cooked, continue to toss the noodles over very low heat for 1 or 2 minutes.

MAKES 3 TO 4 SERVINGS.

Fettuccine w/butter & cheese

ITALY

1 recipe Egg Noodles (see Index)
½ cup butter, cut in small pieces
1 cup freshly grated Parmesan cheese
Freshly ground black pepper

Prepare the noodle dough according to the recipe directions. Divide the dough into quarters. Roll one part at a time on a lightly floured surface until paper-thin.

Roll the dough up like a jelly roll and slice ¼-inch-thick slices. Unroll the noodles and dry on a towel for 30 minutes or longer. Heat 6 quarts of salted water to boiling in a large kettle. Float 1 tablespoon of cooking oil on the surface of the

water. Carefully add the noodles and boil gently for 5 minutes or until done to your taste. Drain well.

Place the noodles in a heated bowl or platter. Add the butter and some freshly ground black pepper and toss with a fork and spoon until the butter melts. Sprinkle with the cheese and toss to coat. Serve immediately. Serve this dish as a first course, pasta course or as an accompaniment to a main dish.

MAKES 3 OR 4 SERVINGS.

Fettuccine w/zucchini & mushrooms

ITALY

sauce
½ pound mushrooms
1¼ pounds young zucchini squash
¾ cup (1½ sticks) butter
1 cup heavy cream

fettuccine
1 pound fettuccine noodles
Boiling salted water
1 tablespoon olive oil
¾ cup freshly grated Parmesan cheese
½ cup chopped parsley (preferably Italian flat-leaf parsley)

Ravioli

Salt and white pepper
Freshly grated Parmesan cheese

Wipe mushrooms with damp cloth, or wash if much dirt is adhering to them; pat dry with paper towels. Trim as necessary; slice. Scrub zucchini; slice into julienne strips.

Melt ¼ cup (½ stick) butter in large heavy skillet over moderate heat. Add mushrooms; sauté 4 minutes. Add zucchini; sauté 3 minutes. Add cream and remaining butter, cut into small pieces. Reduce heat to low. Heat through, stirring gently.

Meanwhile, cook noodles in large amount of boiling salted water with oil floating on surface. Consult package directions for cooking times but test frequently so noodles are al dente. Drain well. Place noodles in warm bowl. Add Parmesan and parsley; toss lightly. Add sauce, salt, and pepper; lightly toss with 2 forks. Place on warm platter; serve with freshly grated Parmesan.
MAKES 4 TO 6 SERVINGS.

Macaroni w/sauce amatrice

ITALY

sauce
2 tablespoons olive oil
2 cloves garlic, peeled and minced
¼ pound salt pork, diced
1 small onion, chopped
¼ cup dry white wine
1 28-ounce can Italian plum tomatoes, drained and minced

1 teaspoon sugar
1 teaspoon chili powder
½ teaspoon paprika
½ teaspoon dried sweet basil, crumbled
½ teaspoon dried oregano, crumbled
Salt and pepper

pasta
3 quarts water
1 tablespoon salt
1 tablespoon cooking oil

12 ounces penne or other macaroni

Grated Parmesan cheese

Heat the olive oil in a large saucepan. Add the garlic, salt pork, and onion and sauté until the onion is tender. Add the white wine and cook until it has evaporated. Add the tomatoes and spices and simmer 20 minutes, uncovered.

Meanwhile, heat the water to boiling. Add the salt and float the oil on the surface of the water.

Add the penne and cook until al dente. Drain. Place in a serving bowl, top with the sauce and serve with Parmesan cheese.
MAKES 4 SERVINGS.

Spaghetti w/white clam sauce

ITALY

18 fresh cherrystone clams
1 tablespoon butter
1 tablespoon olive oil
1 tablespoon flour
¾ cup water or clam juice
¼ teaspoon dried oregano, crumbled
¼ teaspoon dried sweet basil, crumbled
¼ teaspoon garlic powder
Salt and pepper to taste
1 tablespoon chopped parsley

Scrub the clams well under running water. Place on a baking sheet and bake at 450°F until the clams open. Remove the clams from the shells and chop. Reserve the juice for the sauce or for another use. Heat the butter and oil in a medium saucepan. Stir in the flour and cook, stirring constantly, for 2 minutes. Gradually stir the water or clam juice into the flour mixture.

Mix well and continue to cook until thickened. Add the clams and seasonings and simmer 2 minutes. Add the parsley and serve over hot cooked spaghetti.
MAKES 3 TO 4 SERVINGS.

Spaghetti pancake

ITALY

This recipe is a good way to use up leftover cooked spaghetti. Delicious served with fried Italian sausage, peppers, and onions!

2 eggs
2 tablespoons finely minced onion
½ teaspoon dried oregano, crumbled
½ teaspoon salt
⅛ teaspoon pepper
3½ cups cold cooked spaghetti
3 tablespoons butter or margarine
2 tablespoons grated Parmesan cheese

In a medium-size mixing bowl, beat together the eggs, onion, oregano, salt, and pepper. Add the spaghetti and toss well to coat.

In a medium-size skillet, heat 2 tablespoons of the butter over moderate heat until the foam subsides. Add the spaghetti mixture and sprinkle with the cheese. Cook until the bottom is lightly browned. Turn out onto a plate.

Heat the remaining tablespoon of butter in the pan. Slide the spaghetti pancake back into the pan, uncooked side down. Cook until lightly browned. Cut into 4 pieces and serve.

Spaghetti w/sauce & Italian-style meatballs

ITALY

meatballs
1 pound lean ground beef
½ cup Italian-style bread crumbs
1 egg, slightly beaten
1 tablespoon dried onion flakes
Salt and pepper
3 tablespoons cooking oil

tomato sauce
2 tablespoons olive oil
1 medium onion, chopped
1 clove garlic, minced
1 can (28 ounces) Italian-style peeled tomatoes
1 can (6 ounces) tomato paste
¾ cup water (or refill tomato-paste can)
1½ teaspoons mixed Italian herbs
1 teaspoon sugar
½ cup dry red wine

plus one of the following:
½ pound Italian sausage, cut in 1-inch pieces and browned; or ½ pound stewing beef, cut in 1½-inch cubes and browned in oil; or 1½ cups leftover cooked pork roast, cut in 1½-inch cubes; or 1 (4-ounce) can sliced mushrooms, drained

spaghetti
12 ounces thin spaghetti
4½ quarts boiling salted water
1 tablespoon cooking oil

First make the meatballs. Combine the ground beef, bread crumbs, eggs, onion flakes, and salt and pepper. Mix well and form into meatballs the size of a walnut. Brown in a medium-size skillet in the cooking oil. Drain.

Next make the tomato sauce. Heat the olive oil in a large saucepan. Add the onion and garlic and sauté 5 minutes. Purée the tomatoes in a blender or force through a sieve. Add to the onion mixture with the tomato paste, water, seasonings, and wine. Bring to a boil and reduce the heat to low. Add the meatballs and/or one or more of the items from the *plus section.* Simmer covered for 1 to 1½ hours or until thick.

Bring the salted water to a boil. Float the cooking oil on the surface of the water. Add the spaghetti and stir with a fork to prevent sticking. Cook according to the package directions and drain. To serve in the Italian manner, separate the meats from the sauce. Toss the sauce and the spaghetti together to coat lightly.

Serve the meats on a platter so that guests can serve themselves. Pass the grated Parmesan cheese.

MAKES 4 SERVINGS.

Ravioli

ITALY

pasta
1 double recipe Egg Noodles (see Index)

filling
¾ pound meat-loaf mix
¼ cup dry bread crumbs
2 tablespoons grated Parmesan cheese
1 egg
1 tablespoon dehydrated parsley flakes
½ teaspoon garlic salt
¼ teaspoon pepper

Prepare the pasta according to the recipe and let rest covered 15 minutes. Combine the filling ingredients in a bowl and mix well. Refrigerate until ready to use.

Divide the dough into 8 pieces. Roll one piece at a time on a lightly floured surface, keeping the remainder of the dough tightly covered. Roll the dough as thin as possible. If using a pasta machine to roll the dough, roll it to slightly less than 1/16th of an inch thick. Cut the dough into 2-inch squares. Place 1 teaspoon of filling in the center of ½ of the squares. Top with the remainder of the squares. Press the edges together tightly to seal. Moisten the edges with a little water if necessary to ensure a tight seal. Dust a cookie sheet lightly with cornmeal. Place the ravioli on the sheet and refrigerate, covered, or freeze until ready to cook. Makes about 96 ravioli.

To cook, heat 4 quarts of water to boiling. Add 1 tablespoon of salt, and float 1 tablespoon of cooking oil on the surface of the water. Drop the ravioli into the water a few at a time and stir to prevent them from sticking to the bottom of the pan. Reduce the heat so that the water boils gently and cook for approximately 12 minutes or until tender. Drain. Serve hot with your favorite tomato or meat sauce and grated cheese or toss with melted butter and freshly grated Parmesan cheese.

MAKES 6 TO 8 SERVINGS.

Note: Any leftover filling can be fried and added to the meat sauce for the ravioli. Any of the fillings used for manicotti or tortellini can be used instead of the meat filling given here.

Ziti with sausage and cream sauce

ITALY

2 tablespoons olive oil
3 tablespoons butter or margarine
¼ cup chopped onion
1 pound Italian sweet sausage (casing removed)
1 cup heavy cream
½ teaspoon salt
¼ teaspoon pepper
1 package (1 pound) ziti
¼ cup grated Parmesan cheese

Heat the butter and oil in a large skillet. Add the onion and sauté over moderate heat 2 minutes. Add the sausage and cook, crumbling with a fork, until lightly browned (about 10 minutes). Reduce the heat to low and add the cream, salt, and pepper and continue to cook, stirring until thickened. Do not boil.

Meanwhile, cook the ziti in boiling salted water until tender. Drain well. Transfer to a serving bowl and toss with the sauce and sprinkle with cheese. Serve hot.

MAKES 4 SERVINGS.

Stuffed rigatoni

ITALY

Cook a pound of rigatoni to be sure you have enough, since they break very easily. Eat any leftover unstuffed rigatoni with marinara sauce.

sauce

4 tablespoons olive oil	*1 6-ounce can tomato paste*
2 pounds meat-loaf mixture (ground beef, veal, and pork)	*¾ cup water*
	1 28-ounce can peeled Italian tomatoes
4 cloves garlic, peeled and chopped	*2 teaspoons sugar*
½ cup finely chopped celery	*1 teaspoon salt*
½ cup finely chopped carrots	*½ teaspoon pepper*
½ cup finely chopped green pepper	*½ teaspoon dried sweet basil, crumbled*
¼ cup finely chopped parsley	*½ teaspoon dried oregano, crumbled*
1 medium onion, finely chopped	

pasta and filling

1 pound rigatoni No. 28	*2 eggs*
2 10-ounce packages frozen chopped spinach, thawed	*Salt and pepper*
¼ cup grated Parmesan cheese	*1 clove garlic, peeled and minced*
½ cup plain dry bread crumbs	

topping
½ cup grated Parmesan cheese

First make the sauce. Heat 2 tablespoons of oil in a heavy skillet and add the meat and 3 cloves of garlic. Sauté slowly, without browning, until the meat loses its pink color. Drain and reserve ½ of the meat mixture for the pasta stuffing. In a Dutch oven, heat the rest of the oil and sauté the celery, carrot, green pepper, parsley and onion and 1 clove of garlic over medium heat until limp. Add the tomato paste and water. Sieve the tomatoes or puree in the blender and add to the sauce. Add ½ of the cooked meat and the seasonings. Bring to a boil. Reduce the heat to low and simmer 1½ to 2 hours.

Meanwhile, prepare the pasta and stuff it. In a large kettle, bring 4½ quarts of salted water to a boil over high heat. Float 1 tablespoon of cooking oil on the surface of the water. Add the rigatoni and stir well. Reduce the heat to medium-high and cook, stirring occasionally, for approximately 12 minutes or until almost done. Drain well and rinse with cold water.

Squeeze the spinach in a sieve until dry. Combine the spinach, remaining meat, bread crumbs, eggs, salt, pepper and garlic and mix well. Stuff the rigatoni with the mixture, using a pastry tube or your fingers. Lightly grease a 13 X 9 X 2-inch baking dish. Layer the rigatoni and sauce in the baking dish. Sprinkle with the Parmesan cheese. Bake at 350°F for 30 to 45 minutes or until hot and bubbly.

MAKES 8 SERVINGS.

Note: This casserole can be prepared in advance and refrigerated until baking time. Make it a day ahead, if you are serving it for a party.

Cannelloni

ITALY

pasta

½ recipe Egg Noodles (see Index)	4 quarts boiling salted water
	1 tablespoon oil

filling

1 large onion, chopped	2 eggs, beaten
1 clove garlic, minced	¾ teaspoon dried oregano, crumbled
2 tablespoons olive oil	½ teaspoon salt
1 10-ounce package frozen chopped spinach, thawed	¼ teaspoon pepper
2½ cups ground cooked ham	

sauce

⅓ cup butter or margarine	1 cup chicken broth
⅓ cup all-purpose flour	1 cup light cream
½ teaspoon salt	½ cup grated Parmesan or Romano cheese
Dash of nutmeg	1 cup grated white cheddar or Swiss cheese
Dash of white pepper	

Prepare the pasta according to the recipe. Allow to rest, covered, and roll on a lightly floured surface into sheets 1/16th of an inch thick and cut into 4 × 4-inch pieces. Allow to dry on lightly floured cookie sheets for 30 minutes. Float the oil on the surface of the water. Cook the pasta in the boiling water for 5 to 7 minutes or until al dente. Drain well and pat dry with paper towels. Next make the filling. Sauté the onions and garlic in the oil until tender. Press the thawed spinach firmly in a strainer to remove all the water. Combine the onion mixture, spinach, ham,

eggs, and seasonings in a large bowl and mix well. Fill the noodles with 3 tablespoons of the filling and roll jelly-roll fashion to form a cylinder. Place a single layer in a shallow baking dish. Next make the sauce. In a medium-size saucepan, melt the butter. Blend in the flour and seasonings. Cook, stirring constantly, until bubbly. Add the chicken broth and cream, all at one time, stirring well. Cook over moderate heat, stirring constantly, until thickened and smooth. Remove from the heat and add the cheese. Stir until the cheese has melted.

Pour the sauce evenly over the cannelloni. Bake in a 350°F oven for 30 minutes. Garnish with finely chopped parsley and paprika. Makes 15 stuffed noodles.

SERVES 4 TO 5.

Cannelloni w/tomato sauce

ITALY

pasta

15 (4½ × 5-inch) paper-thin pieces fresh pasta dough or 15 entrée crepes

sauce

1 large onion, peeled	¼ pound mushrooms, sliced
2 cloves garlic, peeled, minced	3 tablespoons tomato paste
2 ounces slab bacon	3 tablespoons red wine
2 cups Italian-style plum tomatoes (undrained)	Salt and pepper

filling

2 tablespoons olive oil	2 eggs, beaten
1 large onion, peeled, chopped	½ cup freshly grated Parmesan cheese
1 clove garlic, peeled, finely minced	½ teaspoon crumbled oregano
1 pound lean ground beef	Salt and pepper
2 chicken livers	
1 (10-ounce) package frozen chopped spinach, defrosted	

garnish

¼ cup grated Parmesan cheese	2 tablespoons melted butter

Cook pasta, if used, in large amount of boiling salted water 5 minutes, until just tender. Drain well; place on paper towels to dry.

While noodles cook, begin sauce. Finely mince

425

onion, garlic, and bacon together. Transfer mixture to heavy skillet; sauté over moderate heat until mixture begins to brown. Add tomatoes; break up with fork. Add remaining sauce ingredients; stir well. Cover; simmer 20 minutes.

To make filling, heat oil in a large skillet. Add onion and garlic; sauté until tender. Add ground beef; sauté, breaking up into small pieces, 5 minutes. Add livers; cook until meat is browned. Remove livers; finely chop. Drain meat mixture. Combine meat and livers in large mixing bowl. Place spinach in sieve; press dry with back of spoon. Add to meat mixture along with remaining filling ingredients; mix well.

Place 3 tablespoons filling on each pasta rectangle or crepe; roll up jelly-roll fashion. Pour thin layer of sauce in bottom of shallow casserole dish. Place pasta rolls close together in a dish. Cover with remaining sauce. Garnish with cheese; drizzle with butter. Bake at 350°F 30 minutes.
MAKES 4 TO 5 SERVINGS.

Baked lasagna

ITALY

pasta
3 quarts water	1 tablespoon vegetable oil
2 teaspoons salt	8 ounces lasagna noodles

sauce
1 pound ground beef	1 6-ounce can tomato paste
2 mild Italian sausage links (with casing removed)	½ teaspoon dried oregano, crumbled
1 tablespoon olive oil	½ teaspoon dried sweet basil, crumbled
1 medium onion, finely diced	1 teaspoon sugar
1 clove garlic, minced	
1 28-ounce can peeled Italian tomatoes	

filling
8 ounces ricotta or pot cheese	½ cup freshly grated Parmesan cheese
8 ounces mozzarella cheese, thinly sliced	

In a large kettle combine the water and salt. Float the 1 tablespoon of oil on the surface of the water. Bring to a boil. Slowly add the lasagna noodles, a few at a time, and cook 15 minutes. Drain and rinse with cold water.

Meanwhile, brown the ground beef and sausages

in a large skillet. Remove from the pan and pour the drippings away. Add the olive oil to the skillet and sauté the onion and garlic over low heat for 5 minutes. Add the tomatoes, broken up with a fork, the tomato paste and seasonings. Stir well and add the meat to the sauce. Cook over low heat for 40 minutes or until thick.

Lightly grease a 13 × 9 × 2-inch baking dish. Ladle approximately ¾ cup of the sauce into the pan. Top with ⅓ of the noodles. Dot with ½ of the ricotta and ½ of the mozzarella. Add a layer of sauce and ⅓ of the noodles and the remaining ricotta and mozzarella. Top with more sauce and then the remaining noodles. Top with remaining sauce and sprinkle with the Parmesan cheese. Bake at 350°F for 30 minutes or until heated through. Serve with garlic bread and green salad.
MAKES 6 SERVINGS.

Lasagna w/meat and Bechamal sauces

ITALY

pasta
3 quarts water	8 ounces green or white lasagna noodles
2 teaspoons salt	
1 tablespoon vegetable oil	

meat sauce
4 tablespoons butter	1(16-ounce) can Italian style tomatoes, puréed
2 tablespoons olive oil	6 tablespoons tomato paste
1 medium onion, finely chopped	½ cup water
½ cup finely chopped carrot	1 teaspoon sugar
½ cup finely chopped celery	½ teaspoon salt
¼ cup finely chopped parsley	¼ teaspoon pepper
1 pound meat-loaf mix (ground beef, pork, and veal)	½ teaspoon crumbled sweet basil
¼ cup red wine	½ teaspoon crumbled oregano

bechamal sauce
6 tablespoons butter	Pepper
6 tablespoons flour	¼ teaspoon freshly grated nutmeg
2½ cups milk	
½ teaspoon salt	
1 cup freshly grated Parmesan cheese for topping	

Cook the pasta. Bring water and salt to boil in

Cut pasta dough into 4 ½ x 5-inch rectangles.   Prepare filling.   Fill pasta; roll firmly and seal.

Boil cannelloni 5 minutes.   Prepare sauce.   Cover boiled cannelloni with sauce and Parmesan cheese.

Preparation of cannelloni with tomato sauce

large kettle. Float oil on surface of water. Add noodles; cook according to package directions until al dente. Add cold water to pan to stop pasta from cooking further. Drain well; spread on paper towels.

Make meat sauce. Heat butter and oil in large saucepan. Add onion, carrot, celery, and parsley; sauté until tender. Add meat; sauté until lightly browned, breaking into small pieces with spoon while it cooks. Add remaining meat-sauce ingredients; mix well. Bring to boil; cover. Reduce heat to low; simmer 1 to 1½ hours or until thick.

Prepare Bechamal Sauce. Melt butter in heavy saucepan. Add flour; cook, stirring constantly, 2 minutes. Add milk all at once; cook, stirring constantly, until mixture thickens. Add salt, pepper, and nutmeg; stir well. Cool.

Lightly grease 13 × 9 × 2-inch casserole. Place thin layer of meat sauce in bottom of casserole. Top with ¼ noodles, spread with ¼ meat mixture, then with ¼ bechamal; sprinkle with ¼ cup Parmesan. Continue in this manner until all ingredients are used. Bake at 350°F 30 to 40 minutes, until heated through.

MAKES 6 SERVINGS.

Baked lasagna

Manicotti

ITALY

These noodles can be prepared ahead and baked just before serving. In using this recipe, select the noodle or substitute of your choice and select *one* of the fillings. Top with the sauce and bake.

pasta
12 packaged manicotti shells
Boiling water

or 12 prepared entrée crêpes

or 12 cooked homemade manicotti noodles, 6 inches square (see Index for Egg Noodles)

filling I	**filling II**
1 pound ricotta cheese or pot cheese	*1 pound ricotta cheese or pot cheese*
1 cup grated mozzarella cheese (¼ pound)	*¼ cup grated Parmesan cheese*
¼ cup grated Parmesan cheese	*1 tablespoon dehydrated parsley flakes*
1 tablespoon dehydrated parsley flakes	*3 links Italian sweet sausage, removed from the casing, cooked and chopped*
1 egg, lightly beaten	*1 egg, lightly beaten*
½ teaspoon salt	*¼ teaspoon salt*
¼ teaspoon white pepper	*⅛ teaspoon pepper*
¼ teaspoon garlic powder	

filling III
1 medium onion, minced
1 clove garlic, peeled and chopped
2 tablespoons butter or margarine
1 10-ounce package frozen chopped spinach, thawed and pressed dry in a sieve
½ cup finely chopped chicken
1 teaspoon lemon juice
½ teaspoon salt
¼ teaspoon ground nutmeg
1 pound ricotta cheese
1 egg, lightly beaten

sauce
3 cups marinara sauce
½ cup water (omit the water if using crêpes or homemade noodles)
3 tablespoons grated Parmesan cheese

filling IV
2 tablespoons olive oil
1 small onion, chopped
½ pound ground beef
¼ pound Italian sweet sausage
¼ cup marinara sauce
¼ cup Italian style bread crumbs
1 cup grated mozzarella cheese (¼ pound)
½ tablespoon dehydrated chopped parsley flakes
Salt and pepper

If using the manicotti shells, cover with boiling water and let stand 5 minutes (of course you may cook the manicotti noodles in boiling salted water before stuffing, but it really isn't necessary and they break very easily when cooked and stuffed). Drain and rinse in cold water. Set aside while making the filling of your choice.

For fillings I and II, combine all of the ingredients and mix well. For filling III, sauté the onion and garlic in the butter or margarine until transparent. Add the rest of the ingredients and mix well. For filling IV, heat the oil in a medium skillet. Add the onion, ground beef and sausage and cook over moderate heat until the meat is lightly browned. Stir frequently and break up the meat into small pieces. Drain well and remove from the heat. Allow to cool 5 minutes. Add the remaining ingredients and mix well.

Combine the marinara sauce and water (omit the water if using crêpes or homemade noodles) in a medium saucepan and heat on low while stuffing the noodles. Stuff each shell or pancake with ⅓ to ½ cup of filling. Pour ¾ cup of the heated sauce into a 13 × 9 × 2-inch baking dish and tilt to coat lightly. Place the stuffed noodles in the dish. Top with remaining sauce.

If using the manicotti noodles, cover with foil and bake 45 minutes at 375°F. Uncover and sprinkle with the Parmesan cheese and bake 5 more minutes. If using crêpes or homemade noodles, bake at 350°F for 30 minutes, uncovered. Sprinkle with the grated Parmesan and bake 5 more minutes. Serve with a green salad and garlic bread.

MAKES 6 SERVINGS.

Manicotti Venetian-style

ITALY

1 (8-ounce) package manicotti noodles	Boiling salted water
	1 tablespoon cooking oil

meat filling

1 pound meat-loaf mixture (ground pork, beef, and veal)	1 cup fresh bread crumbs
	1/4 cup finely chopped parsley
1 large onion, peeled, diced	1 teaspoon crumbled sweet basil
1 clove garlic, peeled, minced	Salt and pepper
1 egg, well beaten	

sauce

6 tablespoons butter	1 1/2 cups chicken broth
6 tablespoons flour	1 cup light cream
1/2 teaspoon salt	3/4 cup freshly grated Parmesan cheese
White pepper	
1/4 teaspoon ground nutmeg	Nutmeg
	Chopped parsley

Cook manicotti shells in large pan boiling salted water, with oil floating on surface, 15 minutes, until al dente. Drain well; rinse with cold water. Set aside.

For filling, in heavy skillet cook meat-loaf mixture, onion, and garlic over low heat until meat loses all red color. Break meat into small chunks as it cooks. Drain well. Combine meat mixture, egg, bread crumbs, parsley, and seasonings; mix well. Stuff manicotti shells with filling. Place in lightly greased baking dish.

Make sauce in large saucepan. Melt butter; add flour; cook, stirring constantly, until bubbly. Add seasonings; stir well. Add broth and cream all at one time. Cook, stirring constantly, until thickened. Remove from heat; stir in cheese.

Pour sauce evenly over stuffed manicotti noodles. Sprinkle lightly with nutmeg and chopped parsley. Bake at 350°F 30 minutes. Serve immediately.

MAKES 6 TO 8 SERVINGS.

Agnolotti w/cream sauce

ITALY

pasta dough

2 cups all-purpose flour	2 teaspoons olive oil
1 teaspoon salt	1 tablespoon water
3 eggs	

filling

2 tablespoons olive oil	1 egg
1/4 cup finely chopped onion	1 cup cooked finely chopped chicken breast
1/4 pound ground veal	

429

Venetian rice and peas

¹/₈ pound finely chopped prosciutto

¹/₄ teaspoon crushed rosemary

¹/₈ teaspoon nutmeg

Salt and pepper

cream sauce

3 tablespoons butter

6 tablespoons flour

Salt and pepper

1¹/₂ cups chicken broth

1¹/₂ cups light cream

¹/₂ cup freshly grated Parmesan cheese

¹/₈ teaspoon ground nutmeg

Prepare pasta dough. Combine flour and salt in mixing bowl. Combine eggs, oil, and water; mix well. Add to flour; mix to form stiff dough. Turn out onto board; knead 5 minutes. Cover with plastic wrap; let rest 30 minutes.

While dough rests, prepare filling. Heat oil in small, heavy skillet. Add onion; sauté until tender. Add veal; cook, sitrring, until meat is crumbly and lightly browned. Transfer mixture to mixing bowl; cool slightly. Add remaining filling ingredients; mix well.

Divide pasta dough into 4 parts. Cover any dough not being used, to prevent drying. Roll dough, one part at a time, on lightly floured surface to ¹/₁₆ inch thick. Cut into 3-inch circles with round cutter or glass. Reroll scraps. Place heaping ¹/₂ teaspoon filling on each round. Dampen edge of circle with a little water. Fold into half-moon shape; seal. With folded edge to-

ward you, bring two ends together; pinch. (Finished pasta looks like small circular hats with cuffs.) Place pasta on tray; cover with towel until ready to cook, or freeze for future use.

Prepare sauce. Melt butter in medium saucepan. Add flour, salt, and pepper; mix well. Cook 1 minute. Gradually stir in broth. Cook, stirring constantly, until thickened. Remove from heat; stir in cream. Return to heat; cook, stirring constantly, until thickened. Add cheese and nutmeg. Keep sauce warm while cooking pasta.

Cook pasta 10 minutes in large amount boiling salted water, with small amount oil added. Drain well. Serve immediately, topped with cream sauce. Sprinkle with additional Parmesan cheese, if desired. Agnolotti can also be served with marinara sauce. Makes about 80 agnolotti. MAKES 6 SERVINGS.

Note: If available, use pasta machine for rolling dough.

Green noodles

ITALY

1¹/₃ cups flour

¹/₂ teaspoon salt

4 egg yolks or 2 whole eggs

2 teaspoons olive oil

¹/₃ cup frozen chopped spinach, cooked, pressed dry in sieve

1 tablespoon oil

Melted butter

Freshly grated Parmesan cheese

Combine flour and salt in mixing bowl. Mix well. Make a well in center of flour mixture. In blender or food processor combine eggs, olive oil, and spinach; blend until smooth. Add to dry ingredients; stir to form very stiff dough. Add small amount water, if necessary. Knead dough until smooth and elastic. Cover; let rest 30 minutes. Divide into 4 parts; roll out until paper-thin on floured surface. Cut into required shapes. Let dry on lightly floured surface 1 hour.

Cook in boiling salted water (float 1 tablespoon oil on surface of water) 5 to 7 minutes until al dente. Drain well. Serve dressed with melted but-

ter and fresh-grated Parmesan cheese or use according to recipe directions.
MAKES ¼ POUND OR 4 SERVINGS.

Stuffed jumbo shells
ITALY

16 jumbo shells (6 ounces)

tomato sauce
2 tablespoons olive oil
½ cup finely chopped onion
1 clove garlic, peeled, minced
1 (16-ounce) can peeled Italian tomatoes, pureed

3 tablespoons tomato paste
½ teaspoon sugar
½ teaspoon mixed Italian seasoning
Salt and pepper

filling
1 (10½-ounce) package frozen spinach
1 (16-ounce) package ricotta
½ cup freshly grated Parmesan cheese

1 egg, slightly beaten
¼ teaspoon ground nutmeg
Salt and pepper

Cook shells, according to package directions, in large amount boiling salted water until al dente. Drain; rinse with cold water. Set aside.
Meanwhile, make sauce. Heat oil in medium saucepan. Add onion and garlic; sauté until tender. Add remaining sauce ingredients; mix well. Bring to boil. Reduce heat to low; simmer ½ hour.
Prepare filling. Place spinach in sieve; press dry. In mixing bowl combine ricotta, egg, spinach, and seasonings; mix well. Stuff mixture into cooked shells. Place side by side in lightly greased 9 × 9-inch pan. Pour sauce over shells. Sprinkle with cheese. Bake in preheated 350°F oven 30 minutes. Serve with garlic bread and green salad.
MAKES 4 SERVINGS.

Gnocchi
ITALY

These can be served as a pasta course or an accompaniment to a meat dish.

4 medium potatoes
1½ to 1¾ cups all-purpose flour
1 teaspoon salt
¼ teaspoon white pepper

Wash, peel, and dice potatoes. (You should have approximately 3½ cups diced potatoes.) Cook potatoes in boiling salted water until tender. Drain well. Mash potatoes; immediately add enough flour to make thick dough. Add salt and pepper. Divide dough into 4 equal parts. Using ¼ of dough, on floured surface roll into cylinder ½ inch in diameter. Cut into pieces ½ inch long.
Flour tines of fork; slightly flatten each gnocchi. Place on lightly floured towel until ready to cook. Handle remaining dough in same manner; add more flour if dough becomes sticky.
Cook gnocchi in large kettle of gently boiling salted water. Drop gnocchi into kettle one by one until bottom of pot is covered; cook approximately 5 minutes, until they float to surface. Remove with slotted spoon; drain well. Serve immediately topped with marinara or meat sauce.
MAKES 4 SERVINGS.

Baked gnocchi
1 recipe cooked gnocchi
¼ cup butter or margarine
¼ cup grated Parmesan cheese

Place gnocchi in casserole. Lightly brown butter in small, heavy skillet over moderate heat. Pour butter over gnocchi; sprinkle with cheese. Bake at 375°F 10 minutes; broil until lightly browned.
Note: Gnocchi can be prepared and frozen in single layer on cookie sheet before cooking. Store in plastic bag. Boil as usual before serving. Cooking time will be slightly increased.

Spinach gnocchi
ITALY

1 (10-ounce) package frozen spinach, thawed
1 pound ricotta cheese
1 egg
½ cup grated Parmesan cheese
½ teaspoon salt
¼ teaspoon pepper
¼ teaspoon freshly grated nutmeg
½ cup all-purpose flour
¼ cup flour for coating gnocchi
Melted butter

Freshly grated Parmesan cheese for topping

Place spinach in sieve; press with back of spoon until dry. In mixing bowl combine ricotta, spinach, and egg; mix well. Stir in Parmesan and seasonings. Add all-purpose flour; mix well.

Place ¼ cup flour on plate. Form rounded teaspoons of spinach-and-cheese mixture into gnocchi dumplings by coating lightly with flour and rolling between palms of hands to form round balls. Place on waxed paper in single layer until ready to cook.

Bring 4 quarts salted water to boil in large kettle. Drop gnocchi one by one into boiling water until bottom of pot is filled with gnocchi in single layer. When gnocchi are done, they will rise to surface of water. Remove with slotted spoon; drain well. Place in warm serving bowl. Continue until all gnocchi are cooked.

Drizzle with melted butter, sprinkle with Parmesan cheese; serve.

MAKES 6 SERVINGS.

Semolina dumplings

ITALY

2 cups milk
1 tablespoon butter
½ teaspoon salt
A pinch of freshly grated nutmeg
Ground white pepper, to taste
½ cup farina (or semolina)
2 eggs, beaten
½ cup grated Parmesan cheese

for garnish
2 tablespoons melted butter
1 tablespoon grated Parmesan cheese

Butter a cookie sheet and set aside. In a heavy saucepan, combine the milk, butter, salt, nutmeg, and pepper and bring to a boil over moderate heat. Slowly add the farina, stirring constantly. Reduce the heat to low and cook until very thick and a spoon will stand unsupported in the center of the pan. Remove from the heat. Add the eggs and Parmesan cheese and mix well. Spread on the cookie sheet in a rectangle ½ inch thick. Refrigerate until firm.

Cut into rounds about 1½ inches in diameter (or cut into squares or triangles, if you prefer). Arrange in a greased casserole or baking dish, slightly overlapping. Drizzle with the melted butter and sprinkle with the Parmesan cheese. Bake in a preheated 350°F oven for 20 minutes. Serve hot.

MAKES 3 TO 4 SERVINGS.

Cornmeal savory pudding

ITALY

½ cup coarse yellow cornmeal
2 cups water (divided)
¾ teaspoon salt
2 tablespoons butter or margarine
¼ cup freshly grated Parmesan cheese

topping
3 tablespoons butter
2 tablespoons freshly grated Parmesan cheese

Combine the cornmeal with ½ cup of cold water, stirring well. In a medium saucepan, combine 1½ cups cold water and the salt and bring to a boil. Slowly stir the cornmeal mixture into the boiling water, stirring constantly to prevent lumps. Cook over medium heat, stirring occasionally until very thick (approximately 25 to 30 minutes). Remove from the heat and stir in the 2 tablespoons of butter and ¼ cup of cheese.

Pour the mixture into a 4 × 8-inch or other small loaf pan and chill one hour. Turn out on a wooden board and slice ¾ inch thick. Place the slices, overlapping, in a small casserole. In a small skillet, heat the remaining 3 tablespoons of butter until lightly browned. Pour over the polenta and sprinkle with the remaining cheese. Bake in a 350°F preheated oven for 20 minutes. Broil 1 to 2 minutes, until the cheese is bubbly and the top lightly browned.

Alternately, the polenta may be served freshly cooked from the saucepan topped with gravy, marinara sauce, or your favorite tomato sauce and cheese.

MAKES 4 SERVINGS.

Venetian rice and peas

ITALY

3 tablespoons butter or margarine
1/4 cup chopped onion
2 cups chicken broth
1 cup raw long-grain rice
1 10-ounce package frozen green peas
1/2 cup cooked ham, diced
Salt and pepper
Grated Parmesan cheese

In a large saucepan melt the butter and sauté the onion until transparent.

Meanwhile, heat the chicken broth to boiling. Add the rice to the onions and stir to coat with the butter. Add the peas, ham, and chicken broth and stir well. Cover and cook over low heat approximately 20 minutes or until all of the liquid is absorbed. Sprinkle with Parmesan cheese and serve.

MAKES 4 TO 6 SERVINGS.

Rice pilaf—risotto

ITALY

4 tablespoons butter
1 cup medium-grain or short-grain rice (preferably Italian)
4 tablespoons finely minced onion
2 tablespoons dry white wine
Pinch of saffron
4 cups hot chicken broth
2 tablespoons grated Parmesan cheese

Melt 3 tablespoons butter in heavy saucepan. Add rice and onion; sauté until lightly browned, stirring constantly. Add wine; cook until absorbed.

Dissolve saffron in chicken broth. Add broth to rice alittle at a time; continue cooking, stirring constantly, until all liquid is absorbed and rice is tender and creamy in consistency. (This should take 18 to 20 minutes.) Add remaining butter and cheese; mix well. Let cheese melt; serve immediately.

MAKES 4 SERVINGS.

Risotto Milanese

ITALY

1/2 small onion, finely minced
1/2 cup long-grain white rice
1 tablespoon butter
1 tablespoon olive oil
2 teaspoons beef marrow
2 tablespoons dry white wine
Pinch of saffron
2 cups hot beef broth
1 tablespoon butter
2 tablespoons grated Parmesan cheese

Sauté the onions and rice in the butter and olive oil over moderate heat until very lightly browned. Add the beef marrow and cook gently until it melts. Add the wine and cook until it is absorbed. Dissolve the saffron in the hot beef broth.

Add the beef broth a little at a time and continue to cook, stirring constantly, until all of the liquid is absorbed and the rice is tender and creamy in consistency. This process should take 18 to 20 minutes. Stir in the remaining butter and the Parmesan cheese and allow the cheese to melt. Serve immediately. Risotto does not reheat well.

MAKES 4 SERVINGS.

Saucepan stuffing

ITALY

3 cups water
1/2 teaspoon salt
2 3/4 cups dry bread crumbs (plain or Italian-style)
1 egg, lightly beaten
Salt and pepper
2 tablespoons butter
Grated Parmesan cheese

In a medium saucepan combine the water and salt and bring to a boil. Slowly add the bread crumbs while stirring constantly. Stir well so that there are no lumps. Reduce the heat to low. Cover the pan and cook for 1 hour, stirring occasionally.

Remove from the heat and cool slightly. Add the egg and stir well. Add salt and pepper to taste and the butter and return to the heat for 10 minutes, stirring constantly to keep the mixture from sticking. Turn into a serving dish, sprinkle with Parmesan cheese and serve.

MAKES 4 SERVINGS.

Note: Italian-style (seasoned) bread crumbs used for all the bread crumbs in this dish are too strong for many people's taste. You may use half Italian-style bread crumbs and half plain bread crumbs for a milder flavor.

Stuffed rice fritters

ITALY

4 cups water	2 whole eggs, well beaten
1 tablespoon instant chicken-broth granules	½ cup grated Parmesan cheese
2 cups raw long-grain rice	

filling

3 tablespoons olive oil	⅓ cup water
⅓ cup finely minced onion	1 teaspoon crumbled basil
¼ cup chopped celery	⅓ cup cooked peas
½ pound lean ground beef	(1 pound ricotta cheese can be used in place of above filling)
⅓ cup tomato paste	

coating

2 eggs, well beaten	Oil for frying
1 cup dry bread crumbs	

Combine water and broth granules in large saucepan. Bring to a boil. Add rice; stir well. Cover; reduce heat to low. Cook 20 minutes, until all liquid is absorbed. Cool rice mixture. Stir in eggs and cheese. Refrigerate 1 hour. Meanwhile, make filling. Heat oil in heavy skillet. Add onion and celery; sauté until tender. Remove from skillet with slotted spoon. Add ground beef; sauté until lightly browned. Drain well. Add tomato paste, water, basil, and sautéed vegetables. Bring to boil; reduce heat to low. Simmer until thick. Stir in peas. Cool.

To form fritters, place heaping tablespoon rice in palm of hand. Top with ¾ tablespoon filling and another ½ tablespoon rice. Form into ball. If using ricotta, follow same method.

Beat eggs well. Dip rice fritters in egg; roll in crumbs. Refrigerate at least 1 hour. Heat 3 inches oil to 365°F in medium saucepan. Fry few at a time until golden. Drain on paper towels; serve with tomato or marinara sauce if desired.

MAKES ABOUT 30 FRITTERS OR 6 SERVINGS.

Homemade noodles

POLAND

Delicious with homemade chicken soup.

2¾ cups all-purpose white flour
2 eggs, lightly beaten
¼ cup cold water*
½ cup butter, melted

Combine 2½ cups flour and eggs; mix well. Add cold water 1 tablespoon at a time until a stiff dough forms. Work dough until bubbles begin to form. Roll dough out to about ⅛ inch thick; sprinkle with remaining flour.

Let dough stand until dry. Cut into strips; drop into boiling salted water. Cook for 20 minutes. Stir while cooking to prevent sticking. Drain noodles and serve with melted butter.

MAKES 6 SERVINGS.

*The amount of water needed will vary with the brand of flour used and the humidity in the air.

Stew dumplings

POLAND

1 cup mashed potatoes
2 teaspoons shortening
¼ cup bread crumbs
2 tablespoons flour
¼ teaspoon paprika
¼ teaspoon celery seed
¼ teaspoon dried minced parsley
1 egg yolk
½ bunch fresh parsley

Mix ingredients thoroughly.

Dust your hands generously with flour. Shape potato dough into 2-inch balls by rolling dough between the palms of your hands. Ten minutes before serving time, place dumplings on top of cooking stew. Cover and steam for 10 minutes. Remove dumplings from stew and arrange on serving platter. Garnish with parsley.

MAKES 4 SERVINGS.

Dumplings

POLAND

1½ cups all-purpose white flour
2 egg yolks
¾ cup beef broth
1 teaspoon salt
¼ teaspoon white pepper
1 quart beef bouillon

Mix flour, egg yolks, beef broth, salt and white pepper. Beat vigorously. If batter is too thin, add additional flour. Using a teaspoon, drop batter into boiling bouillon. When dumplings float to top, soup is ready to serve.
MAKES 4 SERVINGS.

Spanish rice

SPAIN

3 tablespoons olive oil
1 garlic clove, crushed
1 small onion, chopped
½ cup chopped red pepper
1 cup long-grain rice
1 teaspoon salt
2 cups boiling chicken stock
2 tomatoes
1 cup frozen peas

Heat oil in large skillet until haze begins to form. Add garlic, onion, and pepper; sauté until vegetables are limp. Add rice; be sure it is well-coated with oil and turns opaque. Add salt and chicken stock. Bring to boil; cover. Reduce heat; simmer 30 minutes or until liquid is absorbed by rice.
Peel, seed, and dice tomatoes. Add tomatoes and peas to rice; stir. Cook just long enough to heat peas and tomatoes.
MAKES 6 SERVINGS.

Saffron rice

SPAIN

3 tablespoons olive oil
1 green pepper, chopped
1 red pepper, chopped
½ cup chopped Spanish onion

Saffron rice

1 cup long-grain rice
1 clove garlic, pressed
⅛ teaspoon saffron
2 cups chicken broth

Heat oil in skillet. Add peppers and onion; sauté until wilted. Add rice; cook until opaque. Add remaining ingredients. Bring mixture to boil; cover. Reduce heat; simmer 30 minutes or until liquid is absorbed by rice.
MAKES 4 TO 6 SERVINGS.

Bulgur

MIDDLE EAST

This side dish is a substitute for the starch of your meal. In the Middle East, it is often used in place of rice.

1 cup bulgur (cracked wheat)
4 tablespoons oil

435

2 cups soup stock
Salt and pepper to taste

Sauté the bulgur in oil until well-covered. Add the soup stock and seasonings and lower the flame to a simmer. Allow to cook until the liquid is all absorbed, about 2 hours. Add extra salt and pepper if needed. Serve at once.
MAKES 4 SERVINGS.

Falafel

MIDDLE EAST

Falafel, although a staple food in Israel, is also used as a filler for pita bread and many times as an hors d'oeuvre. Prepared according to this recipe, it can be a starchy vegetable as well.

½ pound fresh chickpeas
Water
3 tablespoons bulgur (cracked wheat)
2 tablespoons flour
2 crushed garlic cloves
1 teaspoon salt
Dash chili pepper
1 teaspoon ground cumin
Pinch of ground coriander
Oil for deep frying

Cover the chickpeas in water and soak overnight. Soak bulgur in water for 1 hour. Put both chickpeas and bulgur through the meat grinder. Add flour and seasonings and then mix thoroughly. Form the mixture into small balls about 1½ inches in diameter.
Deep-fry the balls in oil until lightly browned.

Fried rice I

Drain on paper towels and keep warm until all balls are fried. Serve at once.
MAKES ABOUT 30 BALLS.

Sweet noodle kugel

MIDDLE EAST

8 ounces cooked and drained broad noodles
1 cup cottage cheese
1 cup sour cream
4 beaten eggs
1 cup sugar
1½ teaspoons cinnamon
¼ cup raisins or currants, optional
½ cup chopped nuts, optional

Place cooked and drained noodles in a large bowl. Using a wooden spoon to mix, stir in the rest of the ingredients as given.
Place this mixture in a greased 9- by 13-inch baking dish. Bake at 350°F for 30 to 45 minutes until noodles on top are lightly-browned. Serve hot.
MAKES 6 TO 8 SERVINGS.

Pharaoh's wheel

MIDDLE EAST

This recipe is a holiday dish in Israel. Each ingredient is symbolic of the events in Exodus. The sauce is the Red Sea, the raisins are the Egyptians, and the white pine nuts are their horses.

½ pound narrow egg noodles
2½ cups meat gravy
6 ounces thinly sliced salami
½ cup raisins
½ cup pine nuts

Cook noodles in boiling water for 9 minutes and drain. Grease a 2-quart casserole dish. Alternate layers of noodles, gravy, salami slices, raisins, and nuts. Top the casserole with noodles and decorate with last slices of salami. Bake at 400°F for 15 to 20 minutes.
MAKES 4 TO 6 SERVINGS.

Cauliflower with noodles

Fried rice I

CHINA

½ pound long-grain rice
½ pound cooked ham, cut into strips
1 6-ounce can shrimp, drained
3 tablespoons oil
2 tablespoons soy sauce
1 leek, sliced
4 eggs
Freshly ground black pepper

Cook rice according to package directions.
Cut ham into strips. Drain shrimp. Heat oil in large skillet, add ham and shrimp and cook until lightly browned, approximately 5 minutes. Add rice and soy sauce. Cook another 5 minutes. Add leek and cook for an additional 5 minutes, stirring occasionally.
Lightly beat eggs with pepper. Pour over rice and cook until eggs are set. Serve on preheated platter.
MAKES 4 SERVINGS.

Deep-fried crispy noodles and soft-fried noodles with mushrooms

Fried rice II

CHINA

This is an excellent recipe for using leftover rice.

3 tablespoons oil, salad or peanut
3-4 cups rice, cooked and chilled
¼ pound fresh, or 1 small can, mushrooms
2 tablespoons scallions, chopped
2 tablespoons soy sauce
2 beaten eggs

Heat oil in skillet. Add rice, mushrooms, drained if canned, or sliced if fresh, scallions and soy sauce. Cook over low heat about 10 to 15 minutes, stirring occasionally. Add beaten egg; cook and stir another 2 to 3 minutes. Serve with additional soy sauce.

Note: You may add leftover chicken and vary the seasonings according to taste.

Fried rice III

CHINA

2 tablespoons oil
1 green pepper, chopped
½ cup fresh mushrooms, sliced
3 cups cooked cold rice
½ cup cooked chicken or beef (leftover)
Soy sauce to taste

Heat oil in skillet to medium-high heat. Sauté pepper and mushrooms until pepper just begins to get soft. Add rice and chicken or beef and sauté until hot, approximately 5 minutes, stirring frequently. Sprinkle with soy sauce to taste.
MAKES 4 SERVINGS.

Fried rice w/mushrooms

CHINA

½ cup sliced dried mushrooms
¼ cup olive oil
¼ cup sliced green onions
2 cups long-grain rice
4 cups chicken stock
⅛ teaspoon dry mustard
1 tablespoon soy sauce
½ cup white bean curd, cut into cubes
¼ cup safflower oil
¾ cup cooked fresh green peas
Radish flowers for garnish

Soak mushrooms in cold water 5 minutes; drain well.
Heat olive oil in wok or deep skillet over medium heat. Add onions; stir-fry until onions are limp and transparent. Add rice; stir-fry until rice is golden. Add 1 cup stock and mustard; stir-fry

2 to 3 minutes or until liquid is absorbed. Add 1 cup stock and soy sauce; stir-fry until liquid is absorbed. Add 1 cup stock; reduce heat to low. Stir in bean curd; cook, stirring occasionally, until liquid is absorbed.

Add remaining stock, safflower oil, peas, and mushrooms. Cover; cook, stirring occasionally, about 20 to 25 minutes or until rice is tender. Spoon into serving dish; garnish with radish flowers.
MAKES 10 SERVINGS.

Almond fried rice

CHINA

1 large onion, chopped
1 green pepper, chopped
¼ cup butter
4 cups cooked rice
1 teaspoon garlic salt
¼ teaspoon freshly ground black pepper
¼ cup soy sauce
1 cup slivered toasted almonds

Cook onion and green pepper in butter until tender. Add remaining ingredients. Cook, stirring occasionally, 10 minutes.
MAKES 4 TO 6 SERVINGS.

Egg noodles w/mushrooms

CHINA

8 ounces fine egg noodles
2 tablespoons oil
1 cup bamboo shoots
1 cup sliced almonds
1 cup fresh mushrooms, sliced
½ cup chicken broth
3 tablespoons soy sauce
Salt to taste

Cook noodles according to package directions for 8 minutes. Drain. Heat oil in a wok. Stir-fry noodles for 3 minutes. Stir in the bamboo shoots, almonds, and mushrooms and mix thoroughly. Stir in the broth, soy sauce, and salt. Simmer, covered, until the liquid is almost gone.
MAKES APPROXIMATELY 8 SERVINGS.

Ginger rice

CHINA

3 tablespoons oil
½ cup chopped scallions
2 tablespoons diced candied ginger
4 cups hot cooked rice

Heat oil in large skillet. Sauté scallions 1 minute. Add ginger and rice; stir lightly. Heat through.
MAKES 6 TO 8 SERVINGS.

"Sizzling" rice

CHINA

To get the "sizzling" effect, food, rice, and containers must be hot.

1 cup long-grain rice
4 cups water
2 teaspoons salt
Oil for deep frying

At least a day in advance combine rice, water, and salt in 2-quart saucepan. Let stand 30 minutes. Bring to boil; cover. Simmer 30 minutes; drain. Spread evenly on heavily greased cookie sheet. Bake in 250°F oven 8 hours, turning occasionally with spatula. Break crusty rice into bite-size pieces. Can be stored in airtight containers in refrigerator several weeks.

Just before serving time, heat oven to 250°F; warm serving platter. Pour oil about 2 inches deep in 6-quart saucepan (or deep-fryer). Heat to 425°F. Fry rice, stirring with slotted spoon, until golden brown, approximately 5 minutes. Drain quickly; place in warmed serving platter.
MAKES 5 OR 6 SERVINGS.

Chinese rice

CHINA

1 cup medium or long-grain rice
Cold water

Put rice in heavy pan that has a tight-fitting lid. Add cold water until it is about 1 inch above the rice. Place pan over high heat and boil, uncovered, until most of the water has been absorbed, stirring often to prevent sticking. Turn heat to

lowest setting, place lid on pan, and let rice steam for approximately 20 minutes, depending upon how soft you like rice. (Do not lift the lid while rice is steaming.)
MAKES APPROXIMATELY 4 SERVINGS.

Cauliflower w/noodles

CHINA

1 small head of cauliflower
2 tablespoons oil, divided
1/2 pound thinly sliced beef
Salt to taste
1 small onion, chopped
2 tablespoons soy sauce
1 cup beef bouillon
1 teaspoon cornstarch
1/2 teaspoon cold water
1/2 pound egg noodles

Clean cauliflower and divide into small florets. Heat 1 tablespoon oil in heavy skillet. Add cauliflower and beef slices and cook until lightly browned. Season with salt. Add chopped onion and soy sauce and cook for 5 minutes. Pour in beef bouillon and simmer for 35 minutes. Blend cornstarch with cold water. Stir into cauliflower mixture until slightly thick and bubbly.
Cook egg noodles in 3 quarts of salted water for 10 minutes. Drain. Heat other tablespoon of oil in skillet, add noodles and fry until golden. Mix noodles with cauliflower. Heat through and serve.
MAKES 4 SERVINGS.

Deep-fried crispy noodles

CHINA

1 5-ounce package fine egg noodles
Vegetable oil

Place noodles in large saucepan in enough water to cover; bring to boil. Cook, stirring occasionally, 5 minutes; drain well.
Fill deep-fat fryer half full with oil; heat to 350°F. Drop noodles into basket in oil; cook 2 minutes. Remove from oil; drain well on paper toweling. Heat oil to 375°F. Return noodles to fryer; cook until golden brown and crisp. Drain well on paper toweling; separate noodles if necessary.
MAKES 4 TO 5 CUPS NOODLES.

Soft-fried noodles w/mushrooms

CHINA

1 5-ounce package fine egg noodles
2 tablespoons safflower oil
1 cup bamboo shoots
1 cup sliced fresh mushrooms
1 cup sliced almonds
1/2 cup chicken broth
3 tablespoons soy sauce
Salt to taste

Cook noodles in large pot in boiling, lightly salted water 8 minutes; drain well.
Heat oil in wok or skillet over low heat. Add noodles; stir-fry 4 minutes. Stir in bamboo shoots, mushrooms, and almonds; mix thoroughly. Stir in broth, soy sauce, and salt. Reduce heat to low; simmer, covered, 20 minutes or until liquid is almost absorbed.
MAKES 8 SERVINGS.

Chicken rice

JAPAN

6 ounces (1 heaping cup) chicken meat
3 1/2 tablespoons soy sauce
2 tablespoons mirin (sweet rice wine)
4 cups chicken stock
4 cups hot cooked rice

Thinly slice chicken; marinate it for 30 minutes in a sauce made from the soy sauce and mirin. If substituting sherry for the mirin, add 1 tablespoon sugar to the sauce.
Remove the chicken with a slotted spoon. Mix the sauce with the chicken stock. Use this mixture, instead of water, to boil the rice in, adding a little water if necessary. Allow 1 1/3 cups rice and 3 cups of liquid. Serve the rice in 4 individual bowls, with the chicken slices on top.
MAKES 4 SERVINGS.

Breads and Pancakes

French bread

FRANCE

7 cups all-purpose flour
1 cup cake flour
2 packages active dry yeast
2½ cups water
1 tablespoon sugar
1 tablespoon salt
1 tablespoon butter
1 to 2 tablespoons cornmeal
1 egg white
1 tablespoon water

In large bowl combine 2½ cups all-purpose flour, cake flour, and yeast. Heat 2½ cups water, sugar, salt, and butter until just warm (115 to 120°F). Butter may not be completely melted. Add to flour-yeast mixture; beat for 3 minutes with an electric mixer, scraping bowl often. By hand, stir in enough remaining flour to make a soft dough. Place dough on floured surface; let rest for 10 minutes.

Knead dough until smooth and elastic (about 12 to 15 minutes). Add small amounts of flour to kneading surface to prevent sticking, but do not add too much; dough must remain soft. After kneading, shape dough into a ball. Place in greased bowl; turn to grease all sides. Cover; let rise until double (1 to 1½ hours).

Punch down dough. Divide in half for 2 loaves or fourths for 4 loaves. Roll each piece into a rectangle about ½ inch thick. Roll up tightly from the long side; pinch to seal edges and ends. Grease 2 baking sheets; coat with cornmeal. Place loaves diagonally on baking sheets. Cut ¼-inch diagonal gashes across tops every 2 inches. Beat egg white with a fork; add 1 tablespoon water. Brush tops and sides of loaves with egg white. Cover; let rise until double (about 1 hour).

Preheat oven to 400°F. Place flat pan of boiling water on lowest rack of oven. Bake bread until light brown, about 20 minutes. Brush again with glaze. Lower heat to 375°F. Bake for 10 to 20 minutes, depending on size of loaves. Remove from baking sheets; cool.

MAKES 2 LARGE OR 4 SMALL LOAVES.

Brioche

FRANCE

1 package dry yeast
¼ cup warm water
½ cup butter
¼ cup sugar
1 teaspoon salt
3¼ cups all-purpose flour
½ cup milk
¾ cup cake flour
4 eggs
Water
1 egg yolk
1 tablespoon water

Soften yeast in ¼ cup warm water (110°F). Cream butter, sugar, and salt with electric beater. Beat 1 cup all-purpose flour and the milk into creamed mixture. Add cake flour, eggs, and softened yeast; beat well. Beat in remaining flour. Beat by hand 6 to 10 minutes. Cover; let rise in warm place until double in bulk (about 2 hours).

Stir down dough. Beat well. Turn out dough onto floured board. Form a long roll. Cut off ¼ of dough; set aside. Cut remaining dough into 6 pieces; form each piece into 4 balls. Tuck under cut edges; place in greased individual brioche pans or greased muffin pans. Cut reserved dough into 6 pieces; cut each of 6 pieces into 4 pieces. Shape 24 balls. Make small indentations in middles of large balls; brush holes with water. Press small balls into indentations.

Beat egg yolk and 1 tablespoon water. Brush tops of balls. Cover; let rise until double (about 30 minutes). Bake at 375°F about 15 minutes or until golden. Brush again with yolk mixture. Bake for 5 more minutes. Remove from pans immediately. Brioches may be frozen and reheated in a 350°F oven.

MAKES 24 ROLLS.

Basic crêpes

FRANCE

3 eggs
⅛ teaspoon salt

1½ cups flour
1½ cups milk
2 tablespoons vegetable oil or melted butter
1 teaspoon sugar (Dessert Crêpes only)

Blender method: Combine ingredients in blender jar; blend about 1 minute. Scrape down sides with rubber spatula; blend for another 15 seconds or until smooth.

Mixer or whisk method: In medium mixing bowl, combine eggs and salt. Gradually add flour, alternating with milk. Beat until smooth. Beat in oil or melted butter and sugar if desired. Let crêpe batter rest for at least 1 hour.

MAKES APPROXIMATELY 24 CREPES.

Technique for making crepes: You can use your pan to make crepes either upside down or right side up. To use it upside down, preheat pan and dip bottom into batter in a 9-inch pie pan. Hold hot pan bottom in batter only a moment. Gently lift pan up; turn it over. Immediately return upside-down pan to heat, so that the flame or hot element is beneath inside of pan. Cook until batter loses its wet look and—with most batters—a very slight browning begins to show on edge of crepe. Remove from heat. Turn pan over; gently loosen outer edge of crepe with a thin plastic, wooden, or Teflon™-coated pancake turner or spatula. The crepe should fall onto the stack already cooked. If not, loosen center of crepe with a spatula.

To use pan right side up, put about 1 tablespoon oil in pan; heat until oil is hot. Tip out oil. A little will cling to pan surface; this will be enough to cook the crepes. A well-seasoned pan needs no additional oil. Return pan to medium-high heat. With one hand pour in 2 to 3 tablespoons batter. At same time lift pan above heat source with your other hand. Immediately tilt pan in all directions, swirling batter so it covers bottom of pan in a very thin layer. Work quickly, before batter cooks too much to swirl. Return to heating unit; cook over medium-high heat. Cook crepe until bottom is browned. Slide knife or spatula under edge of crepe to loosen it. Then carefully turn with a spatula. Brown other side a few seconds. Remove from heat; shake pan to loosen crepe; slide crepe from pan with spatula or knife. Add to stack of already cooked crepes.

The batter should be about the consistency of light cream. If it gets too thick while it is standing, thin batter by adding more liquid. If batter becomes too thin, put it into a blender and add more flour. If batter forms a clump in the middle of pan, pan is too hot. Wave pan about in the air to cool it down; lower heat.

Crepes have an inside and an outside. The side that cooks first is the outside because it looks more attractive. The inside of crepe is rolled or folded into direct contact with the filling.

Croissants

FRANCE

1½ cups butter
¼ cup all-purpose flour
2 packages dry yeast
½ cup warm water
¾ cup milk
3 tablespoons sugar
1 teaspoon salt
1 egg
3½ to 4¼ cups all-purpose flour
1 egg yolk
1 tablespoon milk

Soften butter to room temperature. Cream butter with ¼ cup all-purpose flour. Roll mixture between waxed paper to a 12 × 6-inch rectangle. Chill at least 1 hour.

Soften yeast in warm water (110°F). Heat ¾ cup milk, sugar, and salt in small pan. Stir to dissolve sugar. Cool to lukewarm. Beat in softened yeast and 1 egg. Beat in 2 cups flour. Add enough remaining flour to make a soft but not sticky dough.

Knead dough on floured board until smooth and elastic (10 to 20 minutes). Roll out to a 15-inch square. Place chilled butter on one half; fold over other half; moisten edges with cold water to seal edges. Roll to a 21 × 12-inch rectangle; seal edges. Fold in thirds. It is necessary to chill dough between rollings for 20 minutes. Repeat rolling and folding dough 2 more times, turning the dough by 45° to roll the dough in the oppo-

Place oiled crepe or omelet pan over medium-low heat; heat until oil is hot. Tip out oil. Oil that clings to pan will be enough to cook crepes. Or, brush heated pan with oil.

Return pan to medium-high heat. Then lift pan from heat and pour the batter on the side in a very thin layer.

Immediately swirl pan so batter completely covers the bottom in a very thin layer. Return to heat. Cook crepe until it is browned.

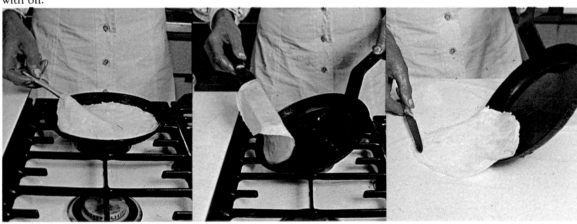

Slide a knife or spatula under edge of crepe to loosen.

Preparation of crepes

Lift carefully with a spatula and turn over gently. Brown other side for several seconds.

Remove from heat. Shake pan to loosen crepe; slide crepe from pan. Continue cooking crepes until all batter is used.

site directions. Seal edges; chill dough 45 minutes. Cut dough crosswise in fourths. Cut out a cardboard triangle with a 4-inch base and 4½-inch sides. Roll out each piece in a long strip about 6 inches wide and ¼ inch thick. Lay cardboard triangle on dough; cut out a triangle with sharp knife. Reverse cardboard triangle on dough every other time. Roll loosely from base of triangle toward point, stretching slightly to make dough thinner. Place on ungreased baking sheets, point down, with ends curled. Press ends to cookie sheet. Roll small pieces also. Cover; let rise at 85°F until double (about 1½ hours). Beat egg yolk with 1 tablespoon milk; *gently* brush on rolls. Bake in preheated 375°F oven about 15 minutes. Remove from sheets to cool. Serve part of this recipe as Dessert Croissants (see Index). Freeze cooled croissants in plastic bags. Reheat on baking sheet at 375°F about 10 minutes.

MAKES ABOUT 24 ROLLS.

Rye bread

GERMANY

2 packages dry yeast
½ cup warm water
1½ cups lukewarm milk
2 tablespoons sugar
1 teaspoon salt
½ cup molasses
2 tablespoons butter
3¼ cups unsifted rye flour
2½ cups unsifted all-purpose white flour

Dissolve yeast in warm water. In a large bowl combine milk, sugar, and salt. Use a mixer to beat in molasses, butter, yeast mixture, and 1 cup rye flour. Use a wooden spoon to mix in remaining rye flour. Add white flour by stirring until the dough is stiff enough to knead. Knead 5 to 10 minutes, adding flour as needed. If the dough sticks to your hands and the board, add more flour. Cover dough and let rise 1 to 1½ hours or until double.

Punch down dough and divide to form 2 round loaves. Let loaves rise on a greased baking sheet until double, about 1½ hours. Preheat oven to 375°F. Bake 30 to 35 minutes.
MAKES 2 LOAVES.

Old-country rye bread

GERMANY

2 cups rye flour
¼ cup cocoa
2 yeast cakes
1½ cups warm water
½ cup light molasses
2 tablespoons caraway seeds
2 teaspoons salt
2½ tablespoons butter
2½ cups whole-wheat flour (more may be needed)
2 tablespoons cornmeal

Combine rye flour and cocoa. Do not sift. Dissolve yeast in ½ cup warm water. In a large bowl combine remaining water, molasses, caraway seeds, and salt. Stir well. Add the rye flour and cocoa mixture, dissolved yeast, butter, and 1 cup whole-wheat flour. Beat until dough is smooth. Spread remaining flour on breadboard. Turn out dough; knead flour into dough. If necessary, add more flour and knead until dough is elastic and smooth. Place in greased bowl, cover, and let rise until doubled.

Punch down dough, shape into a round or oval loaf, and place on greased cookie sheet that has been dusted with cornmeal. Let rise about 45 to 50 minutes. Bake at 375°F for 35 to 40 minutes.
MAKES 1 LARGE LOAF.

Croissants

Molasses brown bread

GERMANY

2½ cups whole-wheat flour
1½ cups wheat germ
⅓ cup brown sugar
½ teaspoon salt
1 cup raisins (mixed, light and dark)
2 teaspoons baking soda
1⅞ cups buttermilk
⅓ cup molasses

Preheat oven to 325°F. Grease a 9 × 5 × 3 inch pan. Combine the flour, wheat germ, brown sugar, salt, and raisins in a mixing bowl. Mix well.

In a second mixing bowl mix baking soda, buttermilk, and molasses, using a wooden spoon. This mixture will start to bubble. Immediately stir it into the dry ingredients. Spoon the batter into the greased pan. Bake at once. The bread is done when a toothpick comes out clean, about 1 hour. Turn out of the pan and cool on a wire rack.

MAKES 1 LOAF.

Dill bread

GERMANY

1 package dry yeast
¼ cup warm water
1 cup creamed cottage cheese, heated to lukewarm
2 tablespoons sugar
1 tablespoon minced onion
1 tablespoon melted butter
1 egg
1 teaspoon salt
2 teaspoons dillseed
2¼ to 2½ cups flour

Dissolve yeast in warm water. Combine all ingredients in mixing bowl, except add flour a little at a time. Beat until well-mixed and mixture becomes a stiff dough. Cover and let rise in a warm place until doubled.

Punch down and put dough in a bread pan, or arrange in a round shape on a greased cookie sheet. Let rise again. Bake for 30 to 45 minutes at 350°F. While warm, brush loaf with soft butter; sprinkle well with salt.

MAKES 1 LOAF.

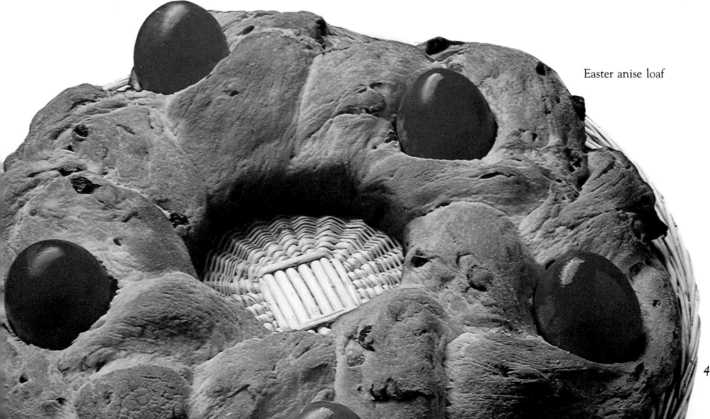

Easter anise loaf

Pretzels

GERMANY

1 package active dry yeast or 1 cake compressed yeast
1½ cups warm water
1 teaspoon salt
1 tablespoon sugar
4 cups flour
1 large egg, beaten
Coarse salt

Dissolve yeast in warm water. Add salt and sugar to yeast mixture. Blend in flour and knead dough until smooth, about 7 or 8 minutes. Cover and let the dough rise until double in bulk.

Punch down. Cut dough into small pieces and roll into ropes. Twist the ropes into pretzel shapes and place on a greased cookie sheet. Using a pastry brush, brush pretzels with egg and sprinkle with coarse salt. Allow pretzels to rise until almost double in bulk.

Bake at 425°F for 10 to 15 minutes or until browned. Best if eaten immediately. If not, store in airtight container.

MAKES 12 6-INCH PRETZELS.

New year's pretzels

GERMANY

A traditional good-luck bread served by German families at New Year's.

2 cups milk
½ cup butter or margarine
2 packages active dry yeast
2 teaspoons salt
½ cup sugar
7 to 7½ cups flour
2 eggs
1 cup confectioners' sugar
1 to 2 tablespoons water
1 teaspoon vanilla
¼ cup almonds, chopped

Heat milk and butter until very warm (120 to 130°F). Mix yeast, salt, sugar, and 1 cup flour. Slowly beat into warm milk. Beat for 2 minutes. Add eggs and 1 cup flour. Beat for an additional 2 minutes. Add enough flour to form a soft dough. Knead until smooth and elastic, about 5 minutes. Place dough in a greased bowl. Let rise in a warm place until doubled in bulk, about 1 hour.

Punch dough down and let rise again until doubled (1 hour more). Divide dough in half. Shape pretzel as follows: Roll dough into a rope about 30 inches long and 1½ inch in diameter. Cross the ends, leaving a large loop in the center. Flip loop back onto crossed ends to form a pretzel. Repeat with remaining dough.

Place pretzels on greased baking sheets. Let rise 15 minutes more. Bake at 375°F for 25 to 30 minutes, until golden brown. Cool on wire racks. Mix confectioners' sugar, water, and vanilla to form a thin icing. Spread icing on pretzels and sprinkle with chopped almonds.

MAKES 2 LARGE PRETZELS.

Chocolate pretzels

GERMANY

½ cup butter or margarine
¼ cup sugar
1 egg, beaten
1 teaspoon vanilla
¼ cup milk
¼ cup cocoa
2 cups unsifted flour

cocoa frosting
2 tablespoons cocoa
1¼ cups confectioners' sugar
2 tablespoons butter or margarine, melted
½ teaspoon vanilla

Cream ½ cup butter and the sugar until light and fluffy. Beat in the egg, vanilla, and milk. Sift cocoa and flour. Mix into butter mixture until thoroughly blended. Chill dough until firm enough to handle (about 30 minutes).

Using 2 tablespoons dough, roll a rope about 12 inches long between your hands. Shape into a pretzel as follows: Make a loop about 1½ inches in diameter by crossing the ends, leaving 1-inch tails. Flip the loop down over the crossed ends. Press firmly into place. Place pretzels on greased baking sheets. Bake at 350°F for about 10 minutes.

Make frosting in a small bowl. Mix cocoa and confectioners' sugar. Gradually stir in butter and vanilla. If frosting is too thick, thin with milk. When pretzels are cool, spread with Cocoa Frosting.
MAKES 2 DOZEN.

Dresden stollen

GERMANY

A traditional Christmas bread, often given as a gift. This bread is moist and heavy and full of fruits. It keeps well.

½ cup raisins	1 cup milk
½ cup currants	½ cup butter or margarine
1 cup mixed candied fruit	2 eggs
½ cup candied cherries, cut in half	1 teaspoon vanilla
½ cup rum	½ cup chopped hazelnuts, if desired
1 package active dry yeast	½ cup chopped almonds
5 cups flour	¼ cup butter or margarine, melted
½ teaspoon salt	1 cup confectioners' sugar
1 cup sugar	

Place fruits in a small bowl. Pour on rum and let stand 1 hour. Drain fruits and reserve rum. Pat fruits dry and toss with 2 tablespoons of the flour.

Mix yeast, 1 cup flour, salt, and ¾ cup sugar. Heat milk and margarine until milk is 120 to 130°F (very warm). Beat milk and reserved rum into flour mixture. Beat for 2 minutes. Add eggs, vanilla, and an additional 1 cup flour. Beat for 2 minutes more. Add enough flour to make a soft dough. Knead for 5 to 10 minutes, until dough is smooth and elastic. Place dough in a lightly greased bowl. Cover and let dough rise until double in bulk, about 2 hours.

Punch dough down. Gently knead in candied fruits and nuts. Shape stollen. Divide dough in half. Roll one half into a rectangle 8 × 12 inches, about ½-inch thick. Brush with melted butter and sprinkle with 2 tablespoons sugar. Fold ⅓ of the dough to the center. Repeat with other side, overlapping about 1 inch. Place on greased baking sheet. Mold the loaf by tapering the ends to form an oval. Repeat with other half

of dough. Brush top of loaves with melted butter. Let rise until doubled in bulk, about 1 hour. Bake in preheated 375°F oven about 25 minutes, until golden brown and crusty. When cool, sprinkle with confectioners' sugar, or make a glaze with 2 tablespoons water and the sugar.
MAKES 2 LOAVES.

Christmas bread

GERMANY

2 cups milk, scalded and cooled	1 pound golden raisins
1 teaspoon sugar	1 pound assorted candied fruits and peels
2 teaspoons salt	1 pound chopped walnuts or slivered blanched almonds
11 cups white flour (may require more)	½ teaspoon mace
2 packages of active dry yeast or 2 cakes compressed yeast dissolved in ¼ cup warm water	½ teaspoon nutmeg
	Grated rind of 1 lemon
1 pound butter	¼ cup melted butter for tops of loaves
1½ cups sugar	⅓ cup rum or brandy for tops of loaves
6 large eggs, beaten	¼ cup powdered sugar for tops of loaves
⅓ cup rum or brandy	

In medium-size saucepan combine milk, 1 teaspoon sugar, salt, 1 cup flour, and dissolved yeast. Blend, cover, and let stand until bubbly in texture. Cream 1 pound of butter and 1½ cups sugar until fluffy. Add eggs and liquor; blend well. Stir in 5 cups of flour. Add yeast mixture. Blend 1 cup flour with fruits and nuts. Add remaining flour and rest of dough ingredients, using enough flour for a firm dough. Mix well. Turn dough onto a floured breadboard and knead thoroughly. Place in a large greased bowl, cover, brush with melted butter, and let rise until double in size.

Punch dough down and turn onto floured board again. Separate dough into 3 or 4 sections and shape each part into a thick oval shape. Fold one long side of loaf about ¾ of the way over the other and gently press edges together for traditional stollen shape. Place on greased cookie sheets and let loaves rise until doubled.

Brush loaves with melted butter. Bake at 350°F about 1 hour to 1 hour and 20 minutes, depend-

447

ing on size of loaves. If loaves brown too fast, cover tops with aluminum foil. When loaves are done, brush with melted butter and spoon over a little more rum or brandy and let soak in. Sprinkle thickly with powdered sugar.

Allow bread to mellow for 2 or 3 days before cutting. Slice thinly and serve with whipped butter. Keep well-wrapped.

MAKES 3 TO 4 LOAVES.

Sesame bread

GREECE

½ cup water
2 tablespoons oil
5 tablespoons milk
1 ¼-ounce package active dry yeast
2¼ cups all-purpose flour
½ teaspoon salt
1 egg
2 tablespoons milk
1 tablespoon sesame seeds

Combine the water, oil, and milk in a small saucepan and heat to lukewarm (105 to 115°F). Pour into a small mixing bowl and dissolve the yeast in the liquids.

Combine the flour and salt. Add 1 cup of the flour mixture and beat with an electric mixer for 2 minutes. Add the rest of the flour mixture and stir to form a stiff dough. Turn out the dough onto a floured board and knead until smooth and elastic.

Lightly grease a mixing bowl with cooking oil and place the dough in it, rotating to oil the entire surface. Cover and remove to a warm place to rise until light and airy (1 to 2 hours).

Punch the dough down. Form it into a round loaf and place on a lightly floured cookie sheet. Beat the egg with the milk and brush the loaf with this mixture. Sprinkle with sesame seeds. With a very sharp knife cut a cross on the top. Cover and allow to rise until double in bulk and light (1 to 2 hours).

Preheat the oven to 400°F. Put the bread on the middle shelf of the oven and place a small cake pan with 1 inch of hot water in it on the shelf

beneath it. Bake for 15 minutes, then reduce the heat to 350°F and bake for an additional 15 minutes. Remove from the oven and cool on a rack.

MAKES 1 ROUND LOAF.

For rolls: Let the dough rise once. Punch it down. Place on a floured board and divide into 6 equal pieces. Shape and place on a cookie sheet. Brush with egg mixture and sprinkle with seeds. Cover and let rise for 45 minutes or until doubled in bulk.

Preheat the oven to 450°F. Place the cookie sheet on the center shelf in the oven and place a cake pan with 1 inch of hot water in it on the shelf just below it. Bake for 10 minutes. Remove to a rack and cool.

MAKES 6 ROLLS.

Easter anise loaf

GREECE

2 envelopes active dry yeast
¼ cup lukewarm milk
1 teaspoon sugar
½ cup (1 stick) butter
⅔ cup sugar
1 tablespoon grated lemon rind
¾ teaspoon anise seed
1 teaspoon salt
¾ cup scalded milk
4 eggs, beaten
6 cups all-purpose flour
¾ cup currants
5 hard-boiled eggs, dyed red with food coloring

In a small bowl proof the yeast with the ¼ cup warm milk and 1 teaspoon sugar. In a large bowl combine the butter (softened and cut into bits), sugar, lemon rind, anise seed, and salt. Add the scalded milk (while still hot) and stir well. Cool the mixture to lukewarm.

Add the yeast mixture to the milk mixture. Add the eggs and 2 cups of the flour and beat with an electric mixer on medium speed for 2 minutes. By hand, mix in 2½ cups more flour and the currants. The dough should be soft and slightly sticky.

Turn out the dough onto a well-floured board

and knead in 1½ cups flour. Knead for 10 minutes or until the dough is smooth and satiny. Form the dough into a ball and place in a greased bowl. Turn the dough in the bowl to grease the top. Cover and let rise in a warm place for 1½ hours or until double in bulk.

Punch down the dough. Divide into 3 equal pieces. Shape each piece into a 20-inch rope. Braid the 3 dough ropes and form into a circle. Press the ends together. Place on a greased cookie sheet. Press the dyed eggs into the braid at intervals. Brush with melted butter, cover, and let rise in a warm place until double in bulk. Bake in a preheated 325°F oven for 45 to 50 minutes or until golden brown. Cool the loaf on a cake rack.

MAKES 1 LOAF.

New year's bread

GREECE

This cake is traditionally served at midnight on New Year's Eve. The head of the household cuts the cake and the lucky family member getting the coin is said to have good fortune in the coming year.

⅓ cup sugar
4 tablespoons butter
½ teaspoon salt
½ cup milk
1 package active dry yeast
¼ cup warm water (105 to 115°F)
1 teaspoon ground cardamom
2 eggs, beaten
3 to 3¼ cups all-purpose flour
Silver coin wrapped in foil
1 egg, beaten with 1 tablespoon water
Sesame seeds
Blanched almonds

Combine the sugar, butter, salt, and milk in a small saucepan. Heat just until the butter melts. Cool to lukewarm. In a large mixing bowl dissolve the yeast in the warm water. Add the milk mixture, cardamom, and eggs and beat until combined. Add 1½ cups of the flour and beat for 5 minutes. Stir in enough of the remaining flour to form a soft dough.

Knead on a floured surface for 10 minutes or until smooth and satiny. Form into a ball. Place in an oiled bowl. Rotate the dough to grease the surface. Cover with a towel and let rise in a warm place until double in bulk.

Punch down the dough. Let rise again until almost doubled in bulk. Punch down the dough again. Form into a 9-inch-round cake, placing the foil-wrapped silver coin in the loaf. Place on a greased cookie sheet. Cover and let rise until double in bulk.

Brush with the egg and water mixture, sprinkle with sesame seeds, and decorate with blanched almonds. Bake at 375°F for 25 minutes or until golden brown.

MAKES 1 9-INCH-ROUND LOAF.

Sweet pancakes

HUNGARY

pancake batter

2 large eggs, separated
1 cup milk
½ cup flour
1 tablespoon sugar
1 tablespoon rum (optional)
⅛ teaspoon salt
2 tablespoons melted butter

Butter or margarine for greasing
¾ to 1 cup apricot jam or preserves
½ cup ground hazelnuts
2 tablespoons powdered sugar

Beat egg yolks in medium-size mixing bowl until well-mixed. Add milk, flour, sugar, rum, and salt; beat with wire whisk until smooth. Blend in melted butter. Refrigerate batter 1 hour. Beat egg whites until stiff but not dry; fold into batter, combine well.

Lightly grease 8-inch heavy skillet or omelet pan with butter. Place over moderate heat until few drops of water sprinkled in skillet dance.

Stir batter. Remove pan from heat; pour in 3 tablespoons batter. Quickly tilt pan in all directions to coat bottom with batter. Return to heat; cook until lightly browned. Turn; cook few seconds on other side. Transfer to warm plate. Continue in same manner, stirring batter before making each pancake. Stack with waxed paper between; keep warm until all pancakes are cooked.

Place 1½ tablespoons jam in center of each pancake; roll. Place side by side on ovenproof platter. Combine hazelnuts and sugar; sprinkle over pancakes. Heat in 325°F oven 10 minutes. Serve pancakes with coffee.

MAKES 10 TO 12 PANCAKES.

Savory pancakes

HUNGARY

2 large eggs
½ cup milk
½ cup club soda
½ cup flour
⅛ teaspoon salt
2 tablespoons melted butter or margarine
Butter or margarine for greasing skillet

Beat eggs well in mixing bowl. Add milk, club soda, flour, and salt alternately, mixing well after each addition. Stir in butter. Refrigerate batter at least 1 hour.

Lightly grease 8-inch heavy skillet; heat until few drops of water sprinkled in pan dance.

Stir batter. Remove pan from heat. Pour 3 tablespoons batter into pan; tilt pan back and forth to coat bottom of pan completely with batter. Return to heat; cook until pancake is lightly browned. Cook on one side only. Continue in same manner, greasing pan occasionally, until all batter is used. Stack pancakes on plate with waxed paper between each. Pancakes can be tightly wrapped and frozen at this point, but must be defrosted before use. Stuff with either of the 2 following fillings.

MAKES 10 TO 12 PANCAKES.

Savory pancakes w/cabbage filling

HUNGARY

1 recipe Savory Pancakes

cabbage filling
1 small head cabbage, finely shredded
1 teaspoon salt
4 tablespoons lard
1 teaspoon sugar
1 red pepper, cleaned, cut into thin strips

½ cup hot water
3 slices bacon, diced
1 medium onion, peeled, diced
1 teaspoon caraway seeds
½ cup sour cream
1 tablespoon flour
2 tablespoons melted butter
3 tablespoons grated Parmesan cheese

Prepare pancakes first; keep warm in slow oven while preparing filling.

Combine cabbage and salt; let stand 20 minutes. Drain well. Heat lard in large heavy saucepan. Add sugar; cook, stirring constantly, until golden. Add cabbage and pepper; sauté 10 minutes, stirring constantly. Add water; cover. Simmer 20 minutes.

Meanwhile fry bacon in small skillet until crisp. Drain; reserve. Add onion to skillet; sauté until tender. Stir bacon, onion, and caraway seeds into cabbage mixture.

Mix sour cream and flour together; stir into cabbage mixture. Cook over very low heat until slightly thickened. Place some cabbage filling in center of each pancake; roll up. Place on warm platter. Drizzle with melted butter; sprinkle with cheese. Serve as a side dish with a plain roast or chops.

MAKES 5 TO 6 SERVINGS.

Savory pancakes w/ham filling

HUNGARY

1 recipe Savory Pancakes

ham filling
1½ cups finely minced baked or canned ham
½ cup sour cream
1 egg yolk

for rolled pancakes:
2 egg whites, lightly beaten
¾ cup fine dry bread crumbs
3 tablespoons melted butter or margarine

for layered pancakes:
⅓ cup sour cream
1½ tablespoons light cream
Paprika
Finely minced parsley

Combine ham, ½ cup sour cream, and egg yolk in mixing bowl; mix well. Serve in either rolled or layered pancakes.

To make rolled pancakes: Place 1 heaping tablespoon filling on each pancake. Fold in sides; roll pancake to form small rectangular package. Lightly beat egg whites. Dip rolled pancakes in egg whites, then in bread crumbs, coating well. Place on baking sheet. Drizzle with melted butter; bake at 350°F 20 to 25 minutes. Serve pancakes hot.

MAKES 10 TO 12 STUFFED PANCAKES.

To make layered pancakes: Lightly grease 9- or 10-inch pie plate. Place 1 pancake in bottom of dish. Top with 1 heaping tablespoon filling; spread evenly over pancake. Top with another pancake; continue in same manner until all pancakes are used. Substitute cabbage filling, if desired. Combine sour cream and light cream; pour over pancake stack. Sprinkle lightly with paprika; bake at 400°F 8 to 10 minutes or until heated through. Cut pancake in wedges with very sharp knife.

MAKES 4 SERVINGS.

Potato bread w/caraway seeds

HUNGARY

1 medium potato, peeled, diced
1½ cups water
1 package active dry yeast
2 tablespoons sugar
2 tablespoons shortening
2 eggs
1½ teaspoons salt
2 teaspoons caraway seeds
4 to 4½ cups all-purpose flour

Place potato in small saucepan with water; cover. Bring to boil; reduce heat to low. Cook 10 to 12 minutes or until potato is tender. Drain potato; reserve 1 cup water in which potato was cooked. Steam diced potato a few minutes in saucepan so that it is quite dry; mash without added ingredients.

When potato water has cooled to lukewarm, pour into mixing bowl. Add yeast; stir until dissolved. Add mashed potato, sugar, shortening, eggs, salt, caraway, and 2 cups flour. Beat with electric mixer on low speed 1 minute, scraping bowl frequently. Increase speed to medium; beat 2 minutes. Mix in enough remaining flour to form dough that can be easily handled. Turn out onto floured board; knead until smooth and elastic. Place in greased bowl; cover. Let rise in warm place until double in bulk (1 to 1½ hours).

Punch down dough. Turn out onto floured board; form into round loaf. Place in lightly greased 2-quart round casserole; cover. Let rise until double in bulk.

Bake in 375°F oven 30 to 35 minutes or until loaf is golden and sounds hollow when tapped. Remove from casserole; cool on wire rack.

MAKES 1 LARGE LOAF.

Crackling biscuits

HUNGARY

½ package active dry yeast
2 tablespoons warm water (100 to 105°F)
1¾ cups all-purpose flour
1 teaspoon sugar
½ teaspoon salt
¼ teaspoon pepper
1 egg, well-beaten
½ cup sour cream, room temperature
½ cup crumbled crisply fried bacon (approximately 8 slices)
1 egg yolk
1 teaspoon warm water

Dissolve yeast in 2 tablespoons warm water. Stir well; set aside. Combine flour, sugar, salt, and pepper in warm mixing bowl, stirring well. Combine egg and sour cream. Add to flour mixture along with dissolved yeast; stir to combine. Turn out onto floured board; knead until smooth and satiny. Place in greased bowl; cover. Let rise in warm place 1 to 2 hours or until double in bulk. Punch down dough; knead in crumbled bacon. Roll on lightly floured surface to rectangle ½ inch thick. Cut into 2-inch rounds. Place on lightly greased cookie sheet; cover. Let rise in warm place 30 minutes.

With sharp knife place several diagonal slits in

each biscuit. Beat egg yolk and 1 teaspoon water together; brush biscuits with mixture. Bake in preheated 350°F oven 20 to 25 minutes or until golden.

MAKES 12 2-INCH BISCUITS.

Irish brown bread

IRELAND

1 cup unsifted all-purpose flour
2 tablespoons sugar
1 teaspoon baking powder
1 teaspoon baking soda
½ teaspoon salt
1½ tablespoons butter or margarine
2 cups whole-wheat flour (stone-ground if possible)
¼ cup rolled oats
1½ cups buttermilk

Combine all-purpose flour, sugar, baking powder, soda, and salt. Cut in butter until in very small particles. Stir in whole-wheat flour and rolled oats well. Make well in center; add buttermilk. Stir lightly but thoroughly until all flour is moistened. Turn out onto lightly floured board; knead 5 times. Gather into ball; place on lightly greased cookie sheet. Pat into 7-inch circle. Using sharp knife, make large cross on top of loaf to allow for expansion.

Bake at 375°F 40 minutes, until loaf is browned and sounds hollow when tapped. Remove from oven; place on rack. Brush with melted butter. Allow to cool before serving.

MAKES 1 LOAF, 7 INCHES IN DIAMETER.

Sweet pancakes

Variation: To make yellow-meal bread, use 1½ cups all-purpose flour and 1½ cups finely ground cornmeal in place of flour and whole-wheat flour in recipe. Omit rolled oats. Mix as listed in above recipe.

Oatmeal bread

IRELAND

2 cups boiling water
1 cup dry rolled oatmeal (old fashioned)
2 packages active dry yeast
⅓ cup warm water (105 to 115°F)
2 teaspoons salt
½ cup honey
2 tablespoons melted butter
4 to 5 cups unsifted all-purpose flour

1 egg yolk
1 teaspoon water

Combine boiling water and oatmeal; let stand 30 minutes (oatmeal should be quite soft). Combine yeast and warm water; stir until dissolved. Set aside.

Stir salt, honey, and butter into oatmeal, mixing well. Add yeast mixture; stir well. Gradually add enough flour to make dough that is not sticky and can be easily kneaded. Knead on lightly floured board 5 to 10 minutes, adding more flour as necessary, to form smooth, elastic dough. Place in oiled bowl, rotating to grease surface of dough. Cover; allow to rise in warm place, without drafts, until double in bulk (approximately 1½ hours).

Punch down dough; form into 2 loaves. Place in 453

Barmbrack

2 greased 9 × 5-inch loaf pans. Cover; allow to rise until double in bulk (approximately 45 minutes).

Preheat oven to 350°F. Meanwhile, beat egg yolk and water together. Brush loaves with mixture. Bake 50 to 60 minutes or until loaves are brown and sound hollow when tapped.

MAKES 2 9 × 5-INCH LOAVES.

Soda bread

IRELAND

4 cups unsifted all-purpose flour
2 tablespoons sugar
1 teaspoon baking soda
1 teaspoon salt
1 cup seedless raisins
1 to 1¼ cups buttermilk
2 tablespoons soft butter

Combine flour, sugar, soda, salt, and raisins in mixing bowl; stir well. Make well in center of mixture. Add buttermilk; stir until lightly but thoroughly blended. Use only enough buttermilk to make stiff dough. Turn out onto lightly floured board; knead 5 times. Form into ball;

place on lightly greased cookie sheet. Pat to 8-inch circle, approximately 1½ inches thick. With floured knife make large cross on top of loaf to keep it from cracking during baking. Spread top of loaf with softened butter. Bake in preheated 375°F oven 40 to 50 minutes or until golden and loaf sounds hollow when tapped. Serve bread hot, with plenty of butter.

MAKES 1 LOAF, 8 INCHES IN DIAMETER.

Boxty

IRELAND

1 cup peeled grated potato
1 cup cold mashed potatoes
2 cups all-purpose flour
2 tablespoons melted butter
¾ teaspoon salt
Pepper

Squeeze grated potato dry in tea towel. Combine grated potato in mixing bowl with mashed potatoes. Add flour, butter, salt, and pepper; mix well. Turn out onto floured board; knead 1 minute. Roll out to ½-inch-thick circle; cut into wedges.

Bake on ungreased griddle over gentle heat 30 to 40 minutes; turn once. Bread should be well-browned. Serve bread split and buttered.

MAKES 4 SERVINGS.

Currant buns

IRELAND

1 13¾-ounce package hot-roll mix
¾ cup warm water
2 tablespoons soft butter
2 tablespoons currants
2 tablespoons seedless raisins
1 egg, lightly beaten
⅓ cup sugar
1 teaspoon ground cinnamon
½ teaspoon nutmeg
1 egg yolk
1 tablespoon milk

In large mixing bowl dissolve yeast from hot-roll mix in warm water. Add butter, currants, and

454

raisins; mix well. Add egg; stir to combine. Add flour mixture from hot-roll mix, sugar, and spices; stir well to incorporate flour. Cover with towel; let stand in warm place 45 minutes or until double in bulk.

Punch down dough. Flour smooth surface; turn out dough. Knead until no longer sticky. Divide into 12 buns of equal size. Place in greased 9 × 9-inch-square pan. Cover with towel; let rise in warm place until double in bulk.

Beat together egg yolk and milk. Brush buns with mixture. Preheat oven to 375°F; bake buns 15 minutes. Cool; ice with Confectioners' Sugar Icing.

MAKES 12 BUNS.

Confectioners' sugar icing

1 cup sifted confectioners' sugar
½ teaspoon vanilla
Dash of salt
2 tablespoons milk

Combine sugar, vanilla, and salt. Add enough milk to make firm icing; drizzle over buns.

Barmbrack

IRELAND

A golden ring is kneaded into the dough, and the lucky recipient is said to be married within the year.

4 cups all-purpose flour
¾ cup sugar
½ teaspoon ground cinnamon
¼ teaspoon ground allspice
⅛ teaspoon ground nutmeg
½ teaspoon salt
1 package active dry yeast
1 cup milk
3 tablespoons butter or margarine
1 egg, lightly beaten
1¼ cups golden raisins
½ cup currants
½ cup mixed chopped candied peel
1 tablespoon confectioners' sugar
2 tablespoons boiling water

Combine 1½ cups flour, sugar, spices, salt, and yeast; mix well. Combine milk and butter in small saucepan; heat on low until very warm. Gradually add to dry ingredients; beat 2 minutes. Add egg and ½ cup flour; beat 2 minutes. Stir in enough of remaining flour to form stiff, elastic dough. Turn out onto lightly floured board; knead until smooth. Knead in fruit and peel. Place in greased bowl; cover. Set in warm place to rise until double in bulk (approximately 1½ hours).

Punch down dough; form into loaf or round ball. Place in greased 8-inch-round cake pan or casserole or greased 9 × 5 × 3-inch loaf pan. Cover; let rise until double in bulk (45 minutes).

Bake in preheated 400°F oven 50 to 60 minutes. Loaf should be well-browned and sound hollow when tapped. Combine sugar and water; brush hot loaf. Return to oven 3 minutes. Remove loaf from pan; cool on wire rack.

MAKES 1 LOAF.

Potato rolls

IRELAND

1 medium potato, peeled, diced
1½ cups water
1 package active dry yeast
4 tablespoons sugar
½ cup hydrogenated vegetable shortening
2 eggs
1½ teaspoons salt
4 to 4½ cups all-purpose flour

Place potato and water in small saucepan; cover. Bring to boil. Reduce heat to low; cook approximately 10 minutes or until potato is tender. Drain; reserve potato water. (There should be 1 cup.) Steam potato in saucepan until dry. Mash without added ingredients. (There should be ½ cup.)

When potato water is lukewarm, pour into mixing bowl; add yeast. Stir until dissolved. Add mashed potato, sugar, shortening, eggs, salt, and 2 cups flour. Beat on low 1 minute, scraping bowl frequently. Increase speed to medium; beat 2 minutes. Mix in enough of remaining flour to make dough that can be easily handled. Turn out onto floured board; knead until dough is smooth and elastic. Place in greased bowl; rotate dough to grease surface. Cover; let rise in warm place until double in bulk.

Punch down dough; place on floured board. Flour surface of dough; divide into 16 rolls. Place in greased 10 × 10-inch-square pan. Cover; let stand in warm place until double in bulk.

Bake in 375°F oven 20 to 25 minutes, until golden and sounds hollow when tapped. Remove from pan. Serve rolls hot with plenty of butter. MAKES 16 LARGE OR 20 SMALLER ROLLS.

Variation: 1 tablespoon caraway seed can be added to dough with last addition of flour.

Note: Alternately, dough can be cut into 20 rolls and placed in 11 × 7-inch baking dish, following above directions.

Italian bread

ITALY

1 package active dry yeast
⅓ cup warm water
3½ to 4 cups all-purpose flour
2 teaspoons salt
1¼ cups water
1 tablespoon coarse cornmeal
1 egg white
1 tablespoon cold water

Dissolve the yeast in the ⅓ cup of warm water (105 to 115°F). Mix well and let stand 5 minutes. Mix the flour and salt together. In a large bowl, combine the dissolved yeast and add the 1¼ cups water. Slowly add the flour mixture, stirring well after each addition, to form a stiff dough. Turn out on a floured board and knead for 10 to 15 minutes, adding flour as necessary, until smooth and elastic. Place in a greased bowl and rotate to coat the surface of the dough. Cover and let rise in a warm place 1 to 2 hours or until double in bulk.

Punch down. Lightly flour a smooth surface. Toss the dough with the flour until no longer sticky. Divide into two parts. Roll the dough with a rolling pin to a 12 × 8-inch rectangle. Roll up jelly-roll fashion, beginning with a 12-inch side to form a long loaf. Pinch the edges to seal. Taper the ends of the loaf by rolling between the palms of the hands. Sprinkle a large baking sheet with cornmeal. Place the two loaves on the baking sheet and cover with a towel. Let rise in a warm place until double in bulk (1 to 2 hours).

With a razor blade, make 3 diagonal slits in the surface of the loaf. Beat the egg white and water together until well-mixed. Brush the loaves with the mixture.

Preheat the oven to 400°F. Put the bread on the middle shelf of the oven and place a small cake pan with 1 inch of hot water on the shelf beneath it. Bake for 15 minutes, then reduce the heat to 350°F and bake for an additional 15 minutes. The loaves should sound hollow when tapped and be well-browned. Cool on a rack. MAKES 2 12-INCH LOAVES.

Bread sticks

ITALY

1 recipe Italian Bread (see Index)
1 egg white
1 tablespoon cold water
3 tablespoons sesame seeds

Prepare the Italian bread dough and allow to rise once as directed in the recipe. Punch the dough down. Lightly flour a smooth surface. Toss the dough on the floured surface until no longer sticky. Divide the dough into 24 equal parts. Roll the pieces of dough into 10-inch-long sticks. Place on baking sheets 1 inch apart. Cover with towels and allow to rise in a warm place until double in bulk (about 45 minutes).

Preheat the oven to 425°F. Meanwhile, beat the egg white and water together. Brush the bread sticks well with the egg white mixture and sprinkle with the sesame seeds. Place the baking sheet or sheets (you will have to bake only one or two sheets at a time, keeping the remainder covered) on the middle shelf in the oven. Place a cake pan with 1 inch of hot water in it on the shelf below the bread sticks. Bake for 10 minutes at 425°F and then reduce the heat to 350°F for 15 to 20 minutes or until browned and dry throughout. Cool on a rack.

MAKES 24.

Note: The process of rolling each piece of dough to form a 10-inch stick is very time-consuming, so it is wise to have help or allow a leisurely afternoon for this project. As each baking sheet is filled with bread sticks, cover it and put in a warm place to rise. In this way, all the bread sticks will not be ready to bake at the same time.

Batter bread w/pepperoni

ITALY

This loaf is delicious served with soup and salad or try it buttered and grilled with mozzarella cheese!

1 package active dry yeast
1¼ cups warm water (105 to 115°F)
2 tablespoons vegetable oil
1 tablespoon sugar
1 teaspoon salt
¼ teaspoon garlic powder
½ teaspoon dried oregano, crumbled
3 cups all-purpose flour (divided)
¼ cup finely diced pepperoni

In a large mixing bowl, dissolve the yeast in the warm water. Add the oil, sugar, salt, garlic powder and oregano and 2 cups of flour. Using an electric mixer, combine the ingredients on low speed. Then, increase the speed to medium and beat for 3 minutes, scraping the bowl occasionally. Stir in the remaining flour and the pepperoni. Scrape the batter down from the sides of the bowl. Cover and let rise in a warm place (80°F) until double in bulk (45 to 60 minutes).

Stir the batter down and spread evenly in a greased 9 × 5 × 3-inch loaf pan. Cover and let rise until double (30 to 40 minutes).

Preheat the oven to 375°F and bake for 35 to 40 minutes or until the loaf sounds hollow when tapped. Cool on a rack before slicing.

MAKES 1 9 × 5-INCH LOAF.

Pizza

ITALY

Feel free to use the toppings of your choice on this delicious crust.

crust
1½ cups all-purpose flour
½ teaspoon salt
1 package active dry yeast

½ cup warm water (105 to 115°F)
1 tablespoon vegetable oil

sauce
1 tablespoon olive oil
¼ cup onion, finely chopped
1 clove garlic, minced
1 16-ounce can Italian style peeled tomatoes

2 tablespoons tomato paste
½ teaspoon dried oregano, crumbled
½ teaspoon sugar
½ teaspoon salt

topping
½ pound bulk sausage
1 cup shredded mozzarella cheese
¼ cup grated Parmesan cheese

1 4-ounce can sliced mushrooms, drained

To make the crust, combine the flour and salt and set aside. Dissolve the yeast in the warm water. Add the oil. Stir in the flour and salt. Turn out on a lightly floured board and knead until smooth and elastic. Lightly grease a medium bowl. Place the dough in the bowl and rotate to grease the whole surface. Cover the bowl and place in a warm place until double in bulk (1 to 1½ hours).

Meanwhile, make the sauce. In a medium saucepan, heat the oil. Add the onion and garlic and sauté over medium heat for 5 minutes, stirring constantly. Do not brown. Purée the tomatoes and their juice in an electric blender or break up with a fork. Add the tomatoes, tomato paste, and seasonings to the saucepan. Bring the mixture to a boil, then reduce the heat to low. Cook, uncovered, stirring occasionally for 50 minutes, or until thick. Set aside to cool.

When the dough has doubled in bulk, punch down. Place the dough on a lightly floured surface and let rest 10 minutes. Roll to a 12-inch circle and place in a 12-inch-round pizza pan. Preheat the oven to 400°F and bake the crust for 13 to 15 minutes.

Meanwhile, lightly fry the sausage. Remove the crust from the oven and top with the sauce. 457

Sprinkle with the mozzarella and Parmesan cheese. Top with the sausage and mushrooms. Return to the oven and bake for 10 more minutes. Remove from the pan and cut.
MAKES 1 12-INCH PIZZA.

Note: The sauce recipe can be easily doubled and frozen for later use.

Pizza Naples-style

ITALY

pizza dough

1½ cups all-purpose flour
½ teaspoon salt
1 package active dry yeast

½ cup warm water (105 to 115°F)
1 tablespoon olive oil

tomato sauce

1 tablespoon olive oil
¼ cup finely chopped onion
1 clove garlic, minced
1 (16-ounce) can Italian-style plum tomatoes, broken up with fork

2 tablespoons tomato paste
½ teaspoon crumbled oregano
½ teaspoon sugar
½ teaspoon salt

topping

Olive oil
8 anchovy fillets, halved
½ cup canned mushrooms, drained

1 cup shredded mozzarella cheese
¼ cup grated Parmesan cheese

First make crust. Combine flour and salt in mixing bowl. Dissolve yeast in warm water; add oil; mix well. Add to flour mixture. Stir to form stiff dough. Turn out on lightly floured surface; knead until smooth and elastic. Place dough in greased bowl; rotate to grease surface. Cover with towel; place in warm place to rise until double in bulk (1 to 1½ hours).

Meanwhile, make sauce. Heat oil in medium saucepan. Add onion and garlic; sauté until tender. Add remaining ingredients; stir well. Simmer sauce until thick (approximately 50 minutes).

When dough has doubled in bulk, punch down. Place on floured surface; roll to 12-inch circle of even thickness. Place on 12-inch-round pizza pan. Bake in 400°F oven 12 to 14 minutes. Remove from oven. Brush crust with oil; top with sauce. Arrange anchovy fillets and mush-

rooms on top. Sprinkle with cheese. Return to oven; bake 10 minutes. Remove from pan; cut.
MAKES 1 (12-INCH) PIZZA.

Note: It is easy to have pizza ready in your freezer. Simply double above recipe. Make 2 shells. Bake second shell first for 13 minutes; cool completely. Package and freeze shell. Freeze remaining sauce. When ready to eat, defrost pizza shell and sauce; continue as above.

Calzone

ITALY

Literally translated, this means trouser legs.

crust

2½ cups all-purpose flour
1 teaspoon salt
1 package active dry yeast
1 cup warm water

2 tablespoons cooking oil
or
Substitute 1 package hot roll mix prepared according to the package directions

filling

2 tablespoons olive oil
1 medium onion, chopped
1 clove garlic, peeled and minced
½ cup fresh mushrooms, chopped
½ cup chopped prosciutto
½ cup chopped salami

¾ cup shredded mozzarella cheese
2 tablespoons chopped parsley
½ teaspoon dried sweet basil, crumbled
Salt and pepper
1 egg yolk

glaze

1 egg

1 tablespoon water

Stir the flour and salt together and set aside. Dissolve the yeast in the warm water. Add the oil. Stir in the flour mixture. Turn out on a lightly floured board and knead until smooth and elastic. Lightly grease a medium bowl. Place the dough in the bowl and rotate to grease the surface. Cover and let rise in a warm place until double in bulk (approximately 2 hours).

Meanwhile, make the filling. Heat the oil in a medium skillet. Add the onion, garlic and mushrooms and sauté 5 minutes. Remove from the heat and allow to cool. Add the remaining filling ingredients and mix well. Set aside.

Lightly flour a smooth surface. Punch the dough down, and toss the dough on the floured surface until it is no longer sticky. Divide the dough into 12 equal parts. Roll each part to a 5-inch circle. Spoon about 2 tablespoons of the filling on ½ of the round. Fold over and moisten the edge lightly with water. Seal by pressing with the fingers. Place on lightly greased cookie sheets. Beat the egg and water together and brush the turnovers thoroughly with the mixture. Bake in a preheated 375°F oven for 20 minutes or until golden and serve hot.

Calzone may also be deep fried at 360°F (_do not brush with the egg and water mixture_) until golden.

MAKES 12 TURNOVERS (ABOUT 6 SERVINGS).

Variation: For another tasty filling, combine 8 ounces shredded mozzarella cheese, ½ cup drained and chopped canned tomatoes, and ½ teaspoon dried sweet basil, crumbled.

Herb & cheese bread ring

ITALY

This bread makes a delicious accompaniment to any antipasto.

1 13¾-ounce package hot-roll mix
¾ cup warm water (105 to 115°F)
1 egg, lightly beaten
1 teaspoon dried oregano, crumbled
1 teaspoon dried sweet basil, crumbled
Flour
1 cup coarsely shredded sharp cheddar cheese
1 tablespoon dried parsley flakes
1 egg yolk
1 tablespoon milk
3 tablespoons grated Parmesan cheese
Paprika

In a large mixing bowl, dissolve the yeast from the hot-roll mix. Add the egg and mix. Stir in the flour from the roll mix and the oregano and sweet basil. Stir well to incorporate all the flour. Cover with a towel and let stand in a warm place until double in bulk (about 45 minutes).

Punch down. Flour a smooth surface and turn out the dough. Knead lightly until no longer sticky. Roll the dough with a rolling pin to a rectangle 8 × 18 inches. Sprinkle evenly with the cheddar cheese and sprinkle with the parsley flakes. Roll like a jelly roll, beginning on an 18-inch edge. Pinch the edges to seal. Form into a ring and pinch to seal. Place on a slightly greased cookie sheet. With a very sharp knife, slit the outside edge of the ring at 2-inch intervals. Cover with a towel and let rise in a warm place until double in bulk.

Beat the egg yolk and milk together. Brush the ring well with the egg-yolk mixture. Sprinkle with the Parmesan cheese and dust with paprika. Bake in a preheated 350°F oven for 30 to 35 minutes or until golden and the loaf sounds hol-

Cheese pizza

low when tapped. Remove from the cookie sheet and cool on a rack.

MAKES 1 LARGE LOAF (SERVES ABOUT 6).

Honey balls

ITALY

2½ cups all-purpose flour	**honey syrup**
½ teaspoon baking powder	¾ cup honey
4 eggs	⅓ cup sugar
1 tablespoon cooking oil	⅓ cup water
Vegetable oil for frying	1 tablespoon lemon juice
	Multicolored candy decorettes

Sift the flour and baking powder together. Make a well in the center of the flour mixture. Beat the eggs and oil together and pour into the well. Stir with a fork to form a soft dough that can be handled. Turn out on a lightly floured board and knead until smooth and elastic. Divide the dough into 10 equal pieces and cover with a towel. Roll the pieces, one at a time, into an 18-inch-long string and cut into 36 small pieces. Place on a lightly floured cookie sheet.

Heat 3 inches of vegetable oil in a heavy saucepan to 375°F on a deep-fry thermometer. Fry a few at a time until golden brown and remove with a slotted spoon. Drain on paper towels.

Next make the syrup. In a heavy saucepan, combine the honey, sugar, water, and lemon juice. Cook, stirring constantly, over moderate heat until the sugar dissolves. Continue cooking over low heat, uncovered, 15 minutes without stirring until thickened. Add the fried pastry and stir to coat. Pile the honey-coated pastry on a platter in a cone shape. Sprinkle with decorettes.

MAKES ABOUT 4 CUPS.

Raised doughnuts

ITALY

4 cups all-purpose flour
¼ teaspoon salt
1 cup warm water (105 to 115°F)
1 package active dry yeast

Calzone   Poppy-seed egg roll

Poppy-seed kuchen

5 tablespoons granulated sugar
1 egg, lightly beaten (room temperature)
Vegetable oil for frying
Confectioners' sugar

Sift together the flour and salt and place in a medium-size mixing bowl and set aside. Dissolve the yeast in the warm water. Let stand 5 minutes. Stir in the sugar and egg, mixing well. Make a well in the center of the flour mixture and add the yeast mixture. Mix thoroughly with a fork to moisten all the flour mixture. Turn the dough out on a lightly floured board and knead for 20 minutes or until the dough is smooth and elastic. Place the dough in a greased bowl, cover with a towel, and leave in a warm place to rise until double in bulk (1 to 2 hours).

Place 4 inches of oil in a deep-fat fryer or 2 inches of oil in a heavy skillet and begin heating. Lightly oil your hands. Take a golf-ball-size

piece of the dough between the palms and form into a square (2 × 2½ inches). Punch several holes in the dough with your finger. Drop the dough immediately into 365°F fat and fry until golden. Drain on absorbent paper. Sprinkle with confectioners' sugar and serve. Keep any leftovers in a plastic bag and reheat on a cookie sheet in a warm oven.
MAKES ABOUT 30.

Holiday coffee bread

ITALY

2 packages active dry yeast
½ cup lukewarm water (105 to 115°F)
½ cup sugar
3 eggs
½ teaspoon anise extract
½ teaspoon salt
½ cup butter, softened
3 cups flour (approximately)
½ cup citron, diced
½ cup dark or golden raisins
1 tablespoon flour
2 tablespoons butter or margarine, melted

Mix the yeast, water, and 2 teaspoons of the sugar in a small bowl, stirring well. Cover and let stand 3 to 5 minutes or until bubbly and double in volume. In a large bowl, combine the eggs, remaining sugar, anise, and salt and add the yeast mixture. Beat by hand or with an electric mixer for 2 minutes. Add the butter and 1½ cups of the flour and beat to combine. Add ½ cup more flour and beat in by hand. Turn out on a lightly floured board and knead in enough flour to make a soft dough that is no longer sticky. Form into a ball, place in a greased bowl, cover and let rise in a warm place until double in bulk. Lightly coat the citron and raisins with the tablespoon of flour. Punch the dough down, turn out on a floured surface and gently knead the fruit into the dough. Lightly grease a 1½-quart soufflé dish and place the dough in the dish or form into a ball and place on a greased baking sheet. Cover and let rise until double in bulk. Brush with melted butter or margarine. Preheat the oven to 400°F and bake for 10 minutes. Re-

duce the heat to 350°F and bake for 30 to 40 minutes more, brushing once with butter, until crisp and golden. Turn out on a rack and cool. Let stand 24 hours before slicing.
MAKES 1 LOAF THAT SERVES 8.

Holiday fruit bread

ITALY

½ cup milk, scalded, cooled to lukewarm
½ cup sugar
¼ cup soft butter or margarine
¾ teaspoon salt
2 packages active dry yeast
½ cup lukewarm water (105 to 115°F)
2 eggs, beaten
4¾ to 5½ cups sifted all-purpose flour
½ cup diced candied citron
½ cup dark or golden raisins
½ cup chopped walnuts
¾ teaspoon anise extract
3 tablespoons melted butter

Combine milk, sugar, ¼ cup butter, and salt in large mixing bowl. Dissolve yeast in water. Add yeast mixture, eggs, and 1 cup flour to milk mixture. Beat with electric mixer 2 minutes on medium speed. Add 2 cups flour; mix well. Cover; let rise in warm place, free of drafts, until double in bulk (1½ to 2 hours). Stir down batter.
Combine citron, raisins, and nuts. Alternately add fruit mixture and remaining flour, stirring well, to make soft dough. Stir in anise extract. Turn out onto lightly floured board; knead until smooth and elastic. Place in greased bowl. Cover; let rise in warm place until double in bulk (45 minutes to 1 hour).
Meanwhile, grease 2 (7-inch) cake pans. Attach a 2-inch greased brown-paper collar to pans. Greased coffee cans can also be used or bread can be shaped into round loaves and placed on cookie sheet. Punch dough down; divide into 2 balls. Place in prepared pans or far apart on greased cookie sheet. Cover; let rise until double in bulk. Brush with melted butter; bake 20 to 25 minutes, until loaves sound hollow when tapped. Remove from pan; cool on rack. Serve plain or toasted on Christmas morning with butter.
MAKES 2 LOAVES.

Onion biscuits

POLAND

2 cups all-purpose white flour
2½ teaspoons baking powder
1 teaspoon salt
⅓ cup shortening
¾ cup milk
¼ cup grated onions
2 tablespoons butter, melted
1 tablespoon poppy seeds

Heat oven to 450°F.
Combine dry ingredients; cut in shortening to resemble cornmeal. Add milk and grated onions; stir just enough to mix. Turn dough out onto a floured surface; knead lightly. Roll dough out to ½ inch thick. Cut close together with floured biscuit cutter. Place biscuits on ungreased cookie sheet.
Brush biscuit tops with melted butter; sprinkle with poppy seeds. Bake in 450°F oven 10 to 12 minutes or until golden brown.
MAKES 20 BISCUITS.

Nut rolls

POLAND

1 package active dry yeast
¼ cup lukewarm water
¾ cup milk
½ cup butter
1 cup granulated sugar
1 teaspoon salt
2 eggs, beaten
4 to 5 cups all-purpose white flour
½ cup brown sugar
1 tablespoon cinnamon
¼ cup butter, melted
1 cup chopped English walnuts

Dissolve yeast in warm water. Scald milk. Add ½ cup butter, ½ cup sugar, and salt; stir until shortening dissolves. Cool milk mixture to lukewarm; pour into dissolved yeast mixture. Mix well. Add beaten eggs and flour. Stir until flour is worked in and a dough has formed.
Turn dough out onto floured surface; knead for 10 minutes or until a smooth dough has formed.

463

Place dough in greased bowl. Cover; let rise until doubled in bulk, about 1 hour. Punch down. Combine ½ cup granulated sugar, brown sugar, and cinnamon. Divide dough into 2 equal parts. On floured surface roll dough into 2 oblongs measuring 8 × 16 inches. Spread each oblong with equal parts of ¼ cup melted butter. Over the butter, sprinkle the sugar and cinnamon mixture evenly between the 2 dough oblongs. Finally, sprinkle ½ cup English walnuts on top of dough oblongs. Roll dough jelly-roll fashion, being sure to seal edges to prevent leakage. Cut each oblong into 16 equal pieces. Place in greased muffin tins. Cover; let rise until double in bulk, about 45 minutes.

Bake in preheated 350°F oven 25 minutes or until golden brown. Remove from muffin tins; cool. Nut rolls may be glazed while still warm (see Glaze for Sweet Breads in Index).
MAKES 32 ROLLS.

Poppy-seed egg roll

POLAND

2 packages active dry yeast
1 cup lukewarm water
1 teaspoon granulated sugar
½ cup milk
½ cup half-and-half cream
2½ teaspoons salt
⅓ cup sugar
2 eggs, beaten
6½ to 7 cups all-purpose white flour
⅓ cup butter, melted
4 12-ounce cans poppy-seed filling
½ cup butter, melted

Soften yeast in lukewarm water with 1 teaspoon sugar. Combine milk and half-and-half cream; scald. Stir in salt and ⅓ cup sugar; cool to lukewarm. Stir in yeast mixture. Add beaten eggs; mix well. Stir in 4 cups flour; beat until smooth. Add ⅓ cup melted butter; beat until mixed. Knead in enough remaining dough to form a medium-soft dough. Knead dough 10 minutes or until smooth and elastic. Place in lightly greased bowl; grease top. Cover; let rise in warm place until doubled in bulk.

Punch down and divide dough in half. Roll each dough half into a 12 × 18-inch rectangle. Spread 2 cans poppy-seed filling over each piece of dough. Starting at one end, roll dough jelly-roll fashion halfway. Repeat process, starting at other end. Prepare remaining dough in same manner. Place rolls on greased cookie sheets. Cover; let rise until doubled in bulk.

Brush tops with melted butter; bake in 400°F oven 30 minutes or until golden brown. Cover with Glaze for Sweet Breads (see Index) while still warm.
MAKES 2 ROLLS.

Poppy-seed kuchen

POLAND

½ cup milk
½ cup half-and-half cream
¾ cup butter
1 cup granulated sugar
1 teaspoon salt
1 package active dry yeast
2 eggs, beaten
4 to 5 cups all-purpose white flour
1 cup raisins
½ cup water
¼ cup vodka
1 can poppy-seed filling
1 cup chopped English walnuts
⅔ cup all-purpose flour

Combine milk and half-and-half cream; scald them. Add ½ cup butter, ½ cup sugar, and salt to scalded-milk mixture; stir until butter dissolves. Cool to lukewarm. Add yeast; mix well. Add eggs and 4 cups flour. Stir until flour is worked in and a dough forms.

Turn dough onto floured surface; work in enough remaining flour to form medium-stiff dough. Knead dough for 10 minutes or until a smooth dough forms. Place dough in greased bowl; cover and let rise until doubled in bulk, about 1 hour. While dough is rising, combine raisins, water, and vodka in small saucepan. Simmer until raisins absorb all liquid. Combine poppy-seed filling, nuts, and raisins. Mix well. Punch down dough; divide it into 2 equal parts. Roll each dough ball into a 12 × 10-inch rectangle. Place on greased baking sheet. Spread filling evenly over rectangles.

Combine ¼ cup butter, ¼ cup sugar, and flour; mix well. Spread over poppy-seed filling. Cover; let kuchen rise until doubled in bulk. Bake in 350°F oven 30 minutes or until dough is golden brown.

MAKES 2 KUCHEN.

Kielbasa & cheese loaf

POLAND

¾ cup warm water
1 package hot-roll mix
1 egg, beaten
½ cup grated Swiss cheese
½ cup cooked, finely chopped Kielbasa
¼ cup butter, melted

Pour ¾ cup warm water into a medium-size bowl. Sprinkle yeast from roll mix over the water; stir until dissolved. Add beaten egg; mix well. Blend in flour from roll mix, Swiss cheese, and Kielbasa. Continue blending until all ingredients are combined to form a sticky dough ball. Cover; let dough rise in a warm place until doubled in bulk, about 45 minutes. Punch down.

Work dough on floured surface to form an oblong roll. Place loaf on greased baking sheet. Cover loosely. Let bread rise again in warm place until light and doubled in size, about 30 minutes.

Brush top of loaf with melted butter. Bake in preheated 400°F oven 30 minutes or until bread is golden brown. Remove loaf from oven; cool it on a rack.

MAKES 1 LOAF.

Round potato bread

POLAND

1 cup milk
¼ cup margarine
⅓ cup granulated sugar
1 cup mashed potatoes, unseasoned

6 cups all-purpose white flour
2 eggs, beaten
2 packages active dry yeast
½ cup lukewarm water
1 teaspoon salt
2 tablespoons all-purpose white flour

Scald milk; add margarine, sugar, and mashed potatoes. Cool to lukewarm. Add 1 cup flour; stir in. Add eggs; mix well. Dissolve yeast in lukewarm water. Add to above mixture; mix well. Cover; let rest until mixture bubbles, about 1½ hours. Stir down. Add enough remaining flour to form a stiff dough.

Turn dough out onto floured surface; knead until dough is smooth and elastic, about 10 minutes. Place in greased bowl. Cover; let rise until doubled in bulk. Punch down; form into 2 round loaves. Cover; let rise until loaves double in size. With a sharp knife make an "X" design on the top of each loaf. Dust the top of each loaf with 1 tablespoon flour. Bake in 375°F oven 40 minutes or until loaves are evenly browned.

MAKES 2 LOAVES.

Brown-&-serve dinner rolls

POLAND

1 cup milk
½ cup all-vegetable shortening
⅓ cup granulated sugar
1 teaspoon salt
1 package active dry yeast
2 eggs, beaten
4 to 5 cups unbleached white flour

Scald milk; add shortening, sugar, and salt. Stir until shortening dissolves. Cool to lukewarm. Add yeast; mix well. Add eggs and flour. Stir until flour is worked in and a dough forms.

Turn dough out onto floured surface; knead for 10 minutes or until a smooth dough forms. Place dough in a greased bowl. Cover bowl; let dough rise until doubled in bulk, about 1 hour. Punch down. Shape into rolls. Cover; let rise until doubled in bulk.

Bake rolls at 257°F until slightly brown, about 12 to 15 minutes. Remove from baking tray; seal in

freezing bags. Freeze immediately. To serve rolls, remove from freezing bags and bake at 450°F for 10 minutes. Serve immediately.
MAKES 2 DOZEN.

Cottage-cheese pierogis

POLAND

1 cup dry cottage cheese
1 egg, beaten
½ teaspoon salt
¼ teaspoon black pepper, peppermill-ground
1 tablespoon chopped chives

Mix all ingredients together thoroughly. Fill and cook Pierogis as instructed in directions given with Pierogi Dough recipe. Serve Pierogis with melted butter.
MAKES 4 SERVINGS.

Dessert pierogis

POLAND

Prepare Pierogi Dough as directed. Fill dough circles with one of the following fillings:

1 cup puréed peach preserves
2 cups pitted fresh cherries
1 can apricot filling

To cook, drop into boiling salted water and cook for 3 to 5 minutes; or deep-fat fry in oil heated to 360°F until golden brown. Serve Pierogis with sour cream.
MAKES 4 SERVINGS.

French-fried pierogis

POLAND

1 cup mashed potatoes
½ cup grated cheddar cheese
1 egg, beaten
½ teaspoon salt
¼ teaspoon black pepper, peppermill-ground
Mustard

Combine all ingredients except mustard; mix well. Prepare dough and fill Pierogis as instructed in directions given with Pierogi Dough recipe.

Drop into frying oil preheated to 360°F. Fry until dough turns a golden brown. To serve, garnish with mustard.
MAKES 4 SERVINGS.

Hamburger & sauerkraut pierogis

POLAND

½ pound hamburger
¼ cup minced onions
½ cup sauerkraut
Melted butter

Brown hamburger in skillet. Add onion; cook for 5 minutes. Drain fat; add sauerkraut. Mix well. Fill and cook Pierogis as instructed in directions given in Pierogi Dough recipe. Serve Pierogis with melted butter.
MAKES 4 SERVINGS.

Pierogi dough

POLAND

Pierogis are a favorite dish of Poland. They are served as a main dish with butter, as a dessert with sour cream, or are French-fried and garnished with mustard. The dough used for all three types of Pierogis is the same. The fillings and garnishes vary the Pierogi dishes.

2 cups all-purpose white flour
1 large egg or 2 small eggs
½ teaspoon salt
⅓ to ½ cup water

Mix flour, eggs, and salt. Stir in water until a stiff dough forms. Divide dough in half; roll paper-thin. Cut circles in dough with biscuit cutter. Place a teaspoon of filling on half the biscuit circle. Moisten edges. Fold over the unfilled side; seal edges.
Drop into boiling salted water; cook for 3 to 5 minutes. Using a slotted spoon, lift gently out of water and place in single layer on serving dish. Do not stack. Serve immediately.
MAKES DOUGH FOR 4 TO 6 SERVINGS.

Kielbasa and cheese loaf

Orange bread sticks

POLAND

¼ cup milk
¼ cup granulated sugar
½ teaspoon salt
2¼ cups all-purpose flour
¼ cup butter
1 package active dry yeast
¼ cup warm water
1 egg, beaten
½ cup chopped English walnuts
1 tablespoon grated orange peel
½ cup candied fruit
¼ cup white raisins
¼ cup granulated sugar

Scald milk. Cool to lukewarm. Combine sugar, salt, and flour, Cut in butter. Dissolve yeast in warm water. Stir in lukewarm milk. Add beaten egg and flour mixture; mix well. Place in greased bowl; grease top. Cover; let rise in warm place until doubled in bulk, about 1½ hours.

While dough is rising, combine remaining ingredients. When dough has doubled in bulk, punch down and turn out on lightly floured board. Divide in half. Roll out each half into an oblong about 16 × 12 inches. Place one oblong on large greased baking sheet. Spread with nut and fruit mixture. Cover with remaining oblong of dough. Cover. Let rise in warm place until doubled in bulk, about 1 hour.

Bake sticks in 350°F oven 20 minutes or until golden brown. Cool. Frost sticks with Orange Glaze. Cut into bars.

MAKES 20 BARS.

Orange glaze

1 cup confectioners' sugar
1 tablespoon orange juice
¼ teaspoon vanilla

Combine all ingredients. Mix well.

467

King's bread ring

Glaze for sweet breads

POLAND

2 cups confectioners' sugar
2 to 3 tablespoons sour cream
1 teaspoon vanilla

Combine confectioners' sugar and liquid. Beat vigorously until glaze forms.
MAKES 2 CUPS.

Caraway-seed-cheese rolls

POLAND

¾ cup warm water
1 package hot-roll mix
1 egg, beaten
½ cup shredded caraway-seed cheese
¼ cup butter, melted

Pour ¾ cup warm water into medium-size bowl. Sprinkle yeast from roll mix over water; stir until dissolved. Add beaten egg; mix well. Blend in flour from roll mix and caraway-seed cheese. Continue blending until all ingredients are combined to form a sticky dough. Let dough rise in warm place until doubled in bulk, about 45 minutes. Punch down.

Divide dough into 16 equal parts; shape into balls. Place in greased 13 × 9-inch pan. Cover. Let rise until doubled in bulk, about 45 minutes. Brush ball tops with melted butter. Bake in preheated 400°F oven 15 minutes or until golden brown.
MAKES 16 ROLLS.

King's bread ring

SPAIN

2 packages active dry yeast
1 cup warm milk
⅓ cup sugar
⅓ cup margarine
2 teaspoons salt

1½ teaspoons freshly grated orange peel
3 eggs, well beaten
4 to 4½ cups all-purpose flour
¼ cup margarine, melted

rum icing
1⅓ cups powdered sugar
1 to 2 tablespoons milk
1 teaspoon rum flavoring

candied-fruit topping
5 candied cherries, chopped
10 candied orange peel strips

Sprinkle yeast on milk; stir to dissolve. Cream sugar and ⅓ cup margarine. Blend in salt and orange peel. Add 1 egg, yeast mixture, and enough flour to make stiff dough. Turn out on lightly floured surface; knead until smooth and elastic, about 10 minutes. Place in greased bowl; grease top. Cover; let rise until double in bulk. Punch down.

Knead until smooth, about 2 minutes. Roll dough into long rope; place on greased cookie sheet. Shape into ring, sealing ends together. Push a coin into dough so it is completely covered. Brush with ¼ cup margarine. Cover; let rise until double in bulk, about 1½ hours. Bake at 375°F 30 minutes or until golden brown; cool. Combine powdered sugar, milk, and rum flavoring. Beat until smooth. Frost bread with icing; decorate with candied fruit as illustrated.
MAKES 12 SERVINGS.

Traditional fried crullers

Cinnamon muffins

SPAIN

1½ cups all-purpose flour
1½ teaspoons baking powder
¼ teaspoon salt
½ teaspoon cinnamon
5 tablespoons butter, room temperature
½ cup sugar
1 egg
½ cup milk

Sift together flour, baking powder, salt, and cinnamon.

Cream butter until fluffy. Beat in sugar; beat until creamy. Add egg; beat well. Stir in dry ingredients alternately with milk; stir just enough to mix. Spoon batter into greased muffin tins. Bake in preheated 400°F oven 30 minutes. Serve muffins warm.
MAKES 1 DOZEN.

Continental rolls

SPAIN

1 cake compressed yeast or 1 package dry yeast
2 cups warm water
1 tablespoon sugar
2 teaspoons salt
5 to 6 cups flour
1 egg white, unbeaten

Crumble yeast over water. Stir until dissolved. Add sugar, salt, and 3 cups of flour. Stir to mix; beat until smooth. Work in 2¼ cups more flour with your hands. Sprinkle some of remaining flour over flat surface. Turn dough onto floured surface; knead until smooth, about 10 minutes. If dough sticks to surface, add more flour. Shape dough into smooth ball. Place ball in greased bowl; grease top. Cover; let rise until doubled in bulk. Punch down.

Form rolls by pinching off pieces of dough the size of an egg. Shape into smooth roll. Place on greased cookie sheet. With scissors make cross-shaped gash ½ inch deep in top of each roll. Cover; let rise until double in bulk.

Bake in 425°F oven in which shallow pan of boiling water has been placed on floor of oven. 469

Bake 20 minutes. Remove from oven; brush with egg white. Return to oven 2 minutes.
MAKES 2 DOZEN ROLLS.

Traditional fried crullers

SPAIN

Oil for deep frying
½ lime
1 cup water
1 10-ounce package pie-crust mix
3 eggs
Powdered sugar

Heat oil to 370°F in large, heavy skillet. Oil should be 3 inches deep and pan no more than half full. Add lime.

Bring water to boil. Quickly stir in pie-crust mix; stir until mixture forms ball and leaves sides of pan. Remove pan from heat. Add eggs, one by one, beating hard after each addition. Transfer dough to pastry bag fitted with star tip.

Remove lime from fat. Squeeze dough into hot fat in continuous spiral to fill pan. Do not crowd. Cook until golden brown, turning once during cooking process; drain. Dust with powdered sugar. Serve immediately.
MAKES 6 SERVINGS.

Continental bread

SPAIN

1 package active dry yeast
2 cups warm water
1 tablespoon sugar
1½ teaspoons salt
5 to 6 cups flour
Cornmeal
1 egg white, unbeaten

Stir yeast in water until dissolved. Add sugar, salt, and 3 cups flour. Stir to mix; beat until smooth. Work in 2¼ cups more flour with your hands. Sprinkle some of remaining flour over flat surface. Turn dough onto floured surface; knead until smooth, about 10 minutes. If dough sticks to surface, add more flour. Shape dough into smooth ball. Place ball in greased bowl; grease top. Cover; let rise until double in bulk. Punch down.

Turn the dough onto lightly floured board. Divide into 2 equal portions. Roll each portion into 15 × 10-inch oblong. Beginning at widest side, roll dough up tightly. Pinch edges together. Taper ends by gently rolling dough back and forth. Place loaves on greased baking sheets sprinkled with cornmeal. Cover; let rise in a warm place about 1 hour or until doubled in bulk.

With sharp razor make diagonal cuts on top of each loaf. Brush with unbeaten egg white. Place loaves in cold oven in which pan of boiling water has been placed. Set oven at 450°F; bake loaves about 35 minutes or until golden crust has formed. Remove from oven; cool on wire rack.
MAKES 2 LOAVES.

Lefser

470

Holiday fruit bread

SPAIN

3 teaspoons baking powder
½ teaspoon salt
¾ cup granulated sugar
¾ cup butter
1½ cups chopped candied fruit
1½ cups all-purpose flour
½ cup raisins
2 eggs, beaten
1 tablespoon light rum

Sift flour, baking powder, salt, and sugar together into mixing bowl. Cut in butter until mixture resembles fine bread crumbs. Stir in fruit. Add eggs and rum; mix well. Spread batter into greased loaf pan. Bake in 325°F oven 60 minutes or until done. Cool slightly; remove from pan.
MAKES 1 9-INCH LOAF.

Rum glaze
1¼ cups powdered sugar
3½ tablespoons rum

Combine sugar and rum; stir to form smooth icing. Drizzle over warm cake. Cool before cutting.

Saffron almond braid

SPAIN

1 package active dry yeast
¾ cup warm water
1 cup all-purpose flour
¼ cup sugar
¼ cup olive oil or melted butter
1 teaspoon salt
⅛ teaspoon saffron
1 egg, beaten
3 to 4 cups all-purpose flour
1½ cups blanched whole almonds
¾ cup white raisins
Melted butter
Coarse sugar crystals

Dissolve yeast in water. Stir in flour and sugar. Let stand covered in warm place 1 hour to allow yeast to work.

Add oil, salt, saffron, and egg to yeast mixture; mix. Add 1 cup flour to sponge; mix well. Pour 1 cup flour on top of kneading surface. Pour sponge mixture on top of flour. Cover sponge with ½ cup flour. Knead until flour is worked into dough. Add almonds and raisins; work in. Continue adding flour until soft dough is formed. Knead dough 10 minutes or until folds form in dough. Place in greased bowl; grease top. Cover; let rise until double in bulk. Punch down.
Divide dough into 3 pieces. Roll each piece into 15-inch-long rope. Lay each rope 1 inch apart on greased cookie sheet. Braid by starting in center and working toward each end. Cover; let rise until doubled in bulk.
Bake at 375°F 30 minutes or until done. Brush with butter; sprinkle with sugar.
MAKES 1 BRAID.

Spanish french toast (torrijas)

SPAIN

Oil for frying
1 loaf Continental Bread (see Index)
2 eggs
1 teaspoon cinnamon
2 tablespoons water
1 cup sifted powdered sugar

Heat oil to 370°F in large, heavy saucepan.
Slice bread into 8 thick slices; discard ends. Cut 2 circles from each slice, using biscuit cutter. Beat eggs until fluffy. Add cinnamon and water; mix well. Dip both sides of each bread circle into egg mixture. Do not soak, or bread will fall apart. Fry in oil until light brown on each side. Remove from oil; drain on brown paper bag. Sift powdered sugar over each side. Serve immediately.
MAKES 16 TORRIJAS.

Oat cakes

DENMARK

¼ pound unsalted butter
¼ cup sugar
2 cups instant oatmeal

¼ cup white corn syrup

Melt the butter in a 12-inch skillet. Add the sugar and stir with a wooden spoon until they are mixed. Do not let the butter mixture burn. Add the oatmeal and stir occasionally while it is cooking, 5 to 10 minutes. Remove it from the heat and stir in the corn syrup.

Rinse the cups of a muffin tin with cold water. Shake out the excess. Pack the bottom and sides of the muffin cups with the mixture. Refrigerate them for at least 3 hours. Loosen the cakes from the muffin tin by running a knife around the edges. Slide out the cakes and serve.

MAKES 12 CAKES.

Butter rolls

DENMARK

1 cup hot water
4 tablespoons butter
¼ cup sugar
1 teaspoon salt
1 package dry yeast
¼ cup lukewarm water
1 egg, well-beaten
4 cups flour
Melted butter

Pour the hot water over the butter, sugar, and salt. Let it stand until lukewarm. Dissolve the yeast in the lukewarm water. Add the dissolved yeast and well-beaten egg to the butter mixture. Add the flour and beat thoroughly. Refrigerate the dough for several hours or overnight.

Roll out the chilled dough on a floured board to ⅛ inch thick. Brush the top with melted butter. Fold the dough in half and again brush the top with melted butter. Fold the dough in half again. It will now be ½ inch thick. Cut it with a small round cutter. Place the rolls in greased muffin pans; cover and let them rise for at least 1 hour. Bake at 400°F for about 20 minutes.

MAKES 2-DOZEN ROLLS.

Coffee bread I

FINLAND

¼ pound butter
1 package dry yeast
¼ cup warm water
¾ cup warm milk
½ cup sugar
½ teaspoon salt
3 eggs
1 teaspoon ground cardamom
4½ cups flour
Almonds (or other nuts), coarsely chopped
1 tablespoon coarsely crushed sugar lumps

Melt the butter and set it aside to cool. In a large mixing bowl dissolve the yeast in warm water. Blend in the milk, sugar, salt, 2 eggs, cardamom, and 2 cups of the flour. Be sure the mixture is smooth. Add the butter and then 2¼ more cups of the flour. Beat until all flour is absorbed.

Use the last ¼ cup of flour on the pastry board. Put the dough in the center of the board and knead it for about 10 minutes or until the dough is smooth and elastic. Put the dough in a greased bowl, turning it once, then cover it. Allow it to rise for about 2 hours or until doubled in size.

Divide the dough into 6 portions. Roll each into a 12-inch strand between your hands. Place 3 strands on the center of a greased baking sheet. Braid from the center to each end and seal the edges. Repeat for the second loaf. Cover them lightly and set them aside to rise slightly—about 30 minutes.

Beat the remaining egg and brush the loaves with it. Sprinkle the loaves with almonds (or other nuts) and coarsely crushed sugar lumps. Bake the loaves at 350°F 25 minutes. Cool them on wire racks.

MAKES 2 LOAVES.

Coffee bread II

FINLAND

2 packages active dry yeast
2 cups warm water
1 egg

6 to 7 cups flour
½ teaspoon ground cardamom
⅓ cup sugar
2 teaspoons salt
¼ cup soft butter or margarine
Confectioners' Sugar Icing

Dissolve the yeast in the warm water. Add the egg, 3 cups of flour, the cardamom, sugar, and salt to the yeast mixture. Beat with an electric mixer at medium speed for 2 minutes. The batter should be smooth. Add the butter and enough of the remaining flour to make a fairly soft dough. Use a wooden spoon or, better still, your hands to mix so that dough leaves the sides of the bowl. On a lightly floured board knead the dough until it is smooth and elastic. Place it in a greased bowl, cover, and let it rise for 1 hour. Punch down the dough. Turn it over and let it rest 10 minutes more, then divide it in half. Cut each half into 3 equal parts. Make each part a strip about 12 inches long. Braid the strips and pinch the ends to seal. Place the braid in a greased 9 × 5 × 2-inch loaf pan. Repeat this process with the second half of the dough. Cover the loaves and let them rise for about 1 hour. Bake the loaves at 400°F for 40 to 50 minutes. To prevent dark loaves, cover them with a piece of foil during the last 15 minutes of cooking. Cool the loaves on a wire rack. When cool, brush the loaves with icing.
MAKES 2 LOAVES.

Confectioners' sugar icing

1 tablespoon plus 2 teaspoons light cream
1 cup confectioners' sugar

Briskly stir the cream and sugar together until the icing is smooth.

Round loaf Finnish bread

FINLAND

Recipe for Coffee Bread II

Using the recipe for Coffee Bread II, shape the dough into 2 round loaves. Place them in a greased round form. Slash the top of the loaves 3 or 4 times with a sharp knife. Cover and let them rise until doubled in size.

Bake and cool them as for the coffee bread. Omit the icing.
MAKES 2 LOAVES.

Salt horns

ICELAND

2 cups flour
3 teaspoons baking powder
1 teaspoon salt
⅓ cup butter
½ cup milk
1 egg

Sift the flour with the baking powder and salt. Cut in the butter with 2 knives, then add the milk. Knead the dough thoroughly on a floured board. When completely blended, divide the dough in half. Roll out half of the dough into a round. Cut the round into 8 wedges. Starting at the round edge, roll each wedge to make a horn shape. Put the horns on a greased baking sheet. Repeat this with the second half of the dough. Brush each horn with slightly beaten egg.
Bake the horns at 425°F for 15 minutes or until golden brown.
MAKES 16 HORNS.

Rye crackers

ICELAND

½ teaspoon salt
4 cups rye flour
1 cup butter
1 cup milk

Blend the salt with the flour. Cut in the butter with two knives, as for pastry. Add the milk and mix it in well. Knead it with your hands until it is well-blended. On a floured board roll out the dough very thin. Cut it into squares or rounds. Put the crackers on a greased baking sheet and prick the center of each with a fork.
Bake the crackers at 450°F until lightly browned, about 10 minutes.
MAKES 6-DOZEN CRACKERS.

Lefser

NORWAY

3 or 4 potatoes
¾ cup cold water
1 teaspoon salt
3 cups rye flour
1 cup wheat flour
Extra flour for kneading

Peel, wash, and dry the potatoes. Grate them into a large bowl. Add the water, salt, and the flours, and mix well. Let the dough stand covered overnight.

The next day, on a flour-covered board, roll out the dough very thin. Cut it into circles about 6 inches round. Place the rounds at least 1 inch apart on a greased baking pan. (This amount of dough will cover 3 pans.)

Bake at 400°F for 6 minutes. Then turn the lefser and bake it for 6 more minutes. Serve the lefser fresh with plenty of butter.
MAKES 12 PIECES.

Easy Christmas bread

NORWAY

5 tablespoons butter
3 eggs
1 cup sugar
1½ cups milk
1 cup raisins
½ cup chopped citron
5 cups flour
2 tablespoons baking powder
½ teaspoon salt
½ teaspoon ground cardamom

Melt the butter in a small pan; set it aside. In a mixing bowl beat the eggs well with the sugar. Add the milk, melted butter, raisins, and citron. Sift the dry ingredients together. Add them to the liquid mixture, stirring vigorously. Divide the dough and put it into 2 well-greased loaf pans. Bake the bread at 350°F for 1 hour.
MAKES 2 LOAVES.

Hartshorns

NORWAY

¼ pound butter
4 eggs
1 cup sugar
½ lemon rind, grated
½ teaspoon ground cardamom
2 teaspoons baking soda
4½ cups flour

Melt the butter and allow it to cool. Beat the eggs and sugar together. Add the butter, lemon rind, cardamom, baking soda, and flour. Mix them well and set them in the refrigerator to chill overnight.

Roll small lumps of the dough into strips, 6 inches long and as thick as your little finger. Form each strip into a ring. Cook them in deep fat until they are golden brown. Drain them well on paper towels and store them in a sealed tin.
MAKES 36 HARTSHORNS.

Rye bread

NORWAY

1 cup water
1½ cups milk
1 teaspoon sugar
2 packages dry yeast
2 teaspoons salt
6 cups rye flour plus 1 cup extra for kneading

Add the water to the milk and scald it. Allow the liquid to cool to lukewarm. In a large bowl add the sugar to the yeast; add 3 tablespoons of the liquid mixture and 1 tablespoon of flour. Mix thoroughly and let it rest for 15 minutes.

After 15 minutes add the rest of the milk-water liquid. Next add the salt and flour and knead the mixture thoroughly. A little flour on your hands will make the kneading easier. When all the flour is worked in and the dough is smooth and elastic, set it aside to rise in a warm place. Allow at least 1 hour.

After the dough has risen, beat it down and knead it again. Divide it in half and shape it into loaves in well-greased loaf pans. Set them aside

Sweet or salty pretzels

to rise again for at least 1 hour. Bake the loaves at 350°F for about 45 minutes.
MAKES 2 LOAVES.

Saffron bread

NORWAY

2 cups milk
2 packages dry yeast
About 7 cups flour
½ cup butter
½ cup sugar
½ teaspoon saffron
2 eggs
¼ cup almonds, blanched and ground or chopped
½ cup raisins
¼ cup candied lemon peel, cut fine
Extra sugar for decorating the top

Heat the milk to lukewarm. Dissolve the yeast in the milk. Add the flour and let the mixture rise until doubled in size.

In a small bowl cream the butter and sugar together. Add the saffron and 1 beaten egg, mixing well. Blend these ingredients into the milk dough. Add the almonds, reserving some for the top; add the raisins and candied peel. Knead again, adding more flour if required. Shape the dough into 3 loaves. Set them aside in a warm place to rise again.

Place them in greased loaf pans. Just before baking, brush each loaf with beaten egg; sprinkle with almonds and sugar. Bake the bread at 375°F for 45 minutes.
MAKES 3 LOAVES.

Sweet or salty pretzels

SWEDEN

1 package dry yeast
½ cup lukewarm milk
4 or more cups of flour
1 teaspoon sugar
½ teaspoon salt
2 egg yolks
½ pound butter
2 tablespoons kosher salt or 4 tablespoons fine sugar

Dissolve the yeast in the lukewarm milk. Put the flour in a large bowl, making a depression in the center. Add the dissolved yeast and milk, the sugar, and the salt. Add 1 egg yolk and mix well. Liberally dot the mixture with ¼ pound of the butter; knead it quickly and lightly. Roll out the dough on a floured board to a large square. Dot this with the other ¼ pound of butter. Cover the dough and set it in the refrigerator for 15 minutes.

Put the dough on the flour-covered work surface and roll it out again to a square. The butter should now be worked into the batter. Knead the dough 4 times and let it rest in the refrigerator. Repeat this process again. Then let the 475

Lucia bread

dough rest for 30 minutes at room temperature. Roll out the dough for the final time to about 1 inch thick and 10 inches long, so that you can cut sticks about 1 inch wide. Cut and form these sticks into pretzel shapes. Put them onto a greased cookie sheet. Brush the pretzels with egg yolk. Then sprinkle them with coarse salt or sugar, according to your taste. Bake the pretzels at 425°F for 20 minutes. Allow them to cool before serving.

MAKES 18 OR 19 PRETZELS.

Lucia bread

SWEDEN

St. Lucia of Syrakus was a young Christian murdered in the Middle Ages. The young maiden is traditionally remembered in Sweden by the baking of this bread for her holiday on December 13th.

1 package dry yeast
½ cup lukewarm milk
¼ cup sugar
3 to 4 cups flour
1 egg
½ teaspoon saffron
½ teaspoon salt
4 tablespoons butter
Extra flour for kneading

476

1 egg yolk for glazing
Dried currants for garnishing

Dissolve the yeast in 2 tablespoons of milk which has been heated to lukewarm. Mix this with the sugar, flour, egg, and 2 more tablespoons of milk to make a dough. Cover the dough and place it in a warm spot to rise for 15 minutes.

Put the saffron into a bowl with 4 tablespoons of milk. Add the salt. Melt but do not heat the butter. Pour this over the saffron mixture. Add this mixture to the risen dough and knead thoroughly until the dough does not stick to the bowl. Cover the dough and again place it in a warm spot to rest for 30 minutes. If necessary or desired, knead and let it rise again.

On a floured board roll out the dough to ½ inch thick. Shape it into rolls about 8 inches long. These can then be worked into shapes of spirals, pretzels, or crosses. Place them on a greased baking sheet. Glaze them with the beaten egg yolk and dot them with dried currants. Bake them at 425°F for about 15 minutes. Serve the Lucia bread warm with plenty of butter and hot coffee.

MAKES ABOUT 24 PIECES.

Orange bread

SWEDEN

3 cups flour
3 tablespoons baking powder
⅔ cup sugar
1 teaspoon salt
1¼ cups milk
2 tablespoons melted butter
1 egg
Peel of 1 orange, finely chopped

Measure the dry ingredients into a 4-cup measure. Sift them into a mixing bowl. Add the milk, butter, and beaten egg and mix with a wooden spoon. Last, add the chopped orange peel. Place the mixture in a greased loaf pan, 9 × 5 × 2 inches, and let it rise for about 15 minutes.

Bake the bread in a moderate 350°F oven for 50 minutes.

MAKES 1 LOAF.

Picnic bread

SWEDEN

2 packages dry yeast
2 cups lukewarm milk
1 egg
½ pound butter
½ teaspoon salt
1 cup sugar
2 teaspoons cinnamon
6 to 8 cups flour

topping
1 egg
2 tablespoons water
½ teaspoon salt
2 tablespoons sugar
2 tablespoons chopped almonds

Mix the yeast with 2 tablespoons of the warm milk. Add the egg. Warm the rest of the milk with the butter, salt, sugar, and cinnamon and add this to the yeast mixture. Add the flour gradually. Knead the dough until it no longer sticks to your fingers. Put the well-kneaded dough into a greased bowl and cover it. Set it in a warm place until it has doubled in size, about 30 minutes.

Shape the dough into 2 8-inch-long loaves. Put the loaves on a greased baking sheet and make crossed slices on the tops of them. Make the topping by mixing the egg, water, and salt. Spread this over the loaves of bread with a pastry brush. Sprinkle the bread with sugar and then with almonds. Wait at least 20 minutes for the bread to rise again before placing it in the oven.

Bake the bread at 400°F for 20 minutes.
MAKES 2 LOAVES.

Syrian sesame biscuits

MIDDLE EAST

These hard biscuits should be crisp and golden when served and make a delightful change from your normal bread.

3 cups flour
1 teaspoon baking powder
½ cup water
1 beaten egg

2 tablespoons cooking oil
1 tablespoon salt
½ cup sesame seeds

In a large bowl, mix all ingredients in the order given. Roll out the dough, using extra flour if needed, and cut into rounds. Bake in a slow oven at 375°F for 15 minutes to a half hour. Biscuits are done when they are crisp and gold.
MAKES 12 TO 24 BISCUITS.

Yoghurt pancakes

MIDDLE EAST

4 egg yolks
¼ cup sugar
2 cups unflavored yoghurt
4 tablespoons melted butter
1½ cups flour
2 teaspoons baking powder
1 teaspoon baking soda
1 teaspoon salt
3 stiffly beaten egg whites

Add all of the ingredients in the order given, lastly gently folding in the beaten egg whites. Drop by tablespoons onto a hot griddle. Turn once to brown both sides of the pancake. Remove finished ones to a heated platter and keep warm until all are finished. Serve at once.
MAKES 4 TO 6 SERVINGS.

Lovash bread

MIDDLE EAST

¼ cup warm water
1 package dry yeast
¼ cup warm water
5 cups flour
2 teaspoons salt
2 cups warm milk
1 tablespoon sugar
¼ pound melted butter

Dissolve yeast in warm water and set aside. Combine flour and salt in a large mixing bowl and make a well in the center. Into this well, pour the yeast mixture and the remaining ingredients and stir with a wooden spoon. You may want to finish the mixing process with your own

477

well-floured hands. Transfer dough to a floured board and knead, adding more flour if needed, until smooth and elastic. Place dough in a greased bowl, turning it to grease the whole ball. Cover and set aside to rise for at least 3 hours. Divide the dough into 4 parts. Work with 1 part at a time leaving remaining dough covered in bowl. Roll each part out into thin ovals or rounds and place on an ungreased baking sheet. Bake at 350°F for about 25 minutes or until lightly-browned and crisp. Break off pieces to eat with your favorite stew or the dip of your choice.
MAKES 4 LARGE ROUNDS.

Pita I

MIDDLE EAST

2 packages active dry yeast
2 teaspoons sugar
1¼ cups lukewarm water
4 cups flour
1 teaspoon salt

Place dry yeast and sugar in the water and stir until well-dissolved. Add the flour and salt. When all is well-mixed, knead the dough generously for 5 minutes. Then divide the dough into equal parts to make 18 or 20 balls. Roll out each ball on a floured board to about 5 inches in di-

ameter and ¼ inch thick. (If you prefer thinner pita, roll some more.) Let the pitas rise in a warm place for ½ hour or until puffy.
Bake a few at a time in a 500°F oven for no more than 5 minutes or until they get puffy. Pitas are particularly good served with a dip—but this useful bread has any number of other uses—all good.
MAKES 18 TO 20 PITAS.

Pita II

MIDDLE EAST

1 ¼-ounce package active dry yeast
1¼ cups lukewarm (105 to 115°F) water
3 cups all-purpose flour
1¼ teaspoons salt
2 teaspoons sugar

Dissolve the yeast in the warm water in a medium-size bowl. Combine the flour, salt, and sugar. Add the flour mixture to the yeast-and-water mixture, stirring to form a sticky dough. Knead well (15 to 20 minutes) on a floured board, adding more flour if necessary to prevent sticking. The dough should be smooth and satiny. Place in a medium-size bowl and cover with plastic wrap and then a towel. Put in a warm place to rise until double in bulk (1 to 1½ hours).
Punch the dough down. Divide the dough into 6 equal pieces, forming each piece into a ball. With a rolling pin, roll each ball into a 5-inch circle on a floured board. Place the circles on lightly oiled pieces of waxed paper. Place on cookie sheets and cover with lightly floured towels. Allow to rise 45 minutes, or until puffed. Preheat the oven to 450°F. Place the bread on baking sheets or in a preheated cast-iron skillet, by inverting the waxed paper onto the cookie sheet and gently peeling the paper away. Bake for 15 minutes, until browned and puffed. If the rounds are not brown enough after 15 minutes, turn on the broiler unit for 2 minutes to brown. Remove from cookie sheets and wrap in towels to cool. Bread will be hard but will soften as it cools.

Challah

478

Store in a plastic bag. These freeze very well.
MAKES 6 ROUNDS.

Challah

MIDDLE EAST

The Challah is the traditional Sabbath bread in Jewish homes.

¾ cup milk
¼ pound butter
⅓ cup sugar
½ teaspoon salt
1 package dry yeast
¼ cup warm water
4½ cups sifted flour
2 beaten eggs
1½ tablespoons lemon juice
1 beaten egg for topping

Warm milk, butter, sugar, and salt in a saucepan until butter has melted. Set aside to cool. Mix the yeast in warm water until dissolved. Place flour in large bowl. Add milk mixture, yeast, eggs, and lemon and mix thoroughly with a wooden spoon. Knead the dough on a floured board until smooth. Let dough rise at least 2 hours in a greased, covered bowl.

Punch down dough on floured surface. For 1 large loaf, divide dough into 3 equal parts. Roll each part into a long strip. When there are 3 strips, join them at one end and braid, being sure to seal the edges at each end. Place twist on a greased sheet or in a 9- by 13-inch pan. Brush over the entire top with reserved egg and set aside to rise for at least 1 hour more.

Bake 10 minutes at 325°F and then 30 to 35 minutes more at 350°F. Cool on a rack.
MAKES 2 SMALL LOAVES OR 1 LARGE TWIST.

Yoghurt bread

MIDDLE EAST

1½ cups warm water
2 packages active dry yeast
1 cup unflavored yoghurt at room temperature
1 tablespoon salt
About 5 cups flour

Pour water into large mixing bowl and sprinkle yeast on top. Allow to rest for 5 minutes. Stir to dissolve yeast. Add yoghurt and salt. Stir in 3 cups of flour, beating with a wooden spoon until smooth. Add remaining flour a little at a time and knead the dough in the bowl until it is no longer sticky. Then remove to a floured surface and knead until dough is stiff. Place ball in a lightly greased bowl turning once and cover. Let rise in a warm place until doubled in bulk—at least 1½ hours.

Punch down dough and divide into 2 parts. Shape each into a long or round loaf. Place shaped bread in baking dish. Cover and allow to rise again for another hour or until doubled in size.

Make an X mark on top of each loaf about ½ inch deep. Brush loaves with water. Bake at 400°F for 45 minutes or until crusts are golden-brown. Brush with water twice during baking period.
MAKES 2 LOAVES.

Yemenite bread

MIDDLE EAST

6 cups flour
1 teaspoon salt
1 package dry yeast
3 cups water

Mix flour and salt. Dissolve the yeast in ¼ cup of the water. Add the yeast mixture and remaining water. Set aside to rise for 2 hours or more. Roll out the dough on a floured board. The thinner the dough is rolled, the more cracker-like the finished product will be. You may prefer to divide the dough out into 3 or 4 balls before rolling to make large ovals or rounds. When dough is rolled thin, place on a greased baking sheet and bake at 450°F for about 5 minutes if very thin, longer as needed. The amount made depends on how thin the dough is rolled.

Mandarin pancakes

CHINA

These are traditionally served with Peking Duck (see Index). As a shortcut use leftover duck that has a crisp skin. These are really very easy to make!

2 cups sifted all-purpose flour
¾ cup boiling water
1 to 2 tablespoons sesame-seed oil

Make well in sifted flour in bowl; pour water into it. Mix with wooden spoon until soft dough. Knead dough gently on lightly floured surface 10 minutes. It should be smooth. Let rest under damp kitchen towel 15 minutes.

On lightly floured surface roll dough to about ¼ inch thick. With 2½-inch glass cut as many circles as you can. Use scraps of dough, kneading them again and cutting out more circles. Brush half of circles lightly with sesame-seed oil. Place unoiled circle on top of oiled one. Flatten each pair with rolling pin to diameter of about 6 inches. Turn once to roll both sides, trying to keep circular shape. Cover pancakes with dry towel.

Heat 8-inch ungreased skillet to high heat. Reduce heat to moderate. Cook pancakes one at a time, turning them as little bubbles and brown specks appear. Cook about 1 minute on each side. As each pancake is cooked, gently separate halves; stack on plate.
MAKES ABOUT 24.

Corn tortillas

MEXICO

2 cups instant Masa Harina
1 teaspoon salt
1¼ cups water

Combine Masa and salt in mixing bowl. Make a well in center; stir in water. Dough must be stiff enough to hold together, and not sticky. Add a little more water if necessary. Knead dough until pliable. Form into a 12-inch log; cut into 1-inch pieces. Roll pieces into balls; cover with a damp cloth while shaping tortillas.

To shape with a tortilla press: Place dough between 2 polyethylene bags, center on the press, and flatten. Carefully peel off plastic bags; stack tortillas between sheets of waxed paper until all are ready to cook.

To shape without a tortilla press: Place dough ball between sheets of waxed paper; flatten with heavy skillet or large pie plate (and a lot of energy), or use a rolling pin. Turn tortilla to keep it round as you roll. Tortillas should be 6 inches in diameter and quite thin.

To cook tortillas: Heat a griddle or cast-iron skillet (ungreased) until quite hot. Peel waxed paper off top of tortilla; place it on griddle. Wait several seconds, then gently peel waxed paper off other side of tortilla as the first side cooks on the griddle. Bake until lightly flecked with brown (about 2 minutes). Turn; cook 1 minute more. Stack, wrap in foil, and keep tortillas warm in oven.
MAKES 12 6-INCH TORTILLAS.

Flour tortillas

MEXICO

2 cups unsifted all-purpose flour
1 teaspoon salt
¼ cup lard
½ cup water

Combine flour and salt in mixing bowl. Work lard into flour mixture with your fingers until mixture resembles coarse cornmeal. Make a well in center of flour mixture. Add water; stir to combine. Form into a ball. If mixture is dry, add a little more water. Knead for 3 minutes on a floured board. Divide into 6 balls. Cover; let rest 20 minutes.

Roll each ball on a floured pastry cloth to a 7- to 8-inch circle; trim, if necessary, using a dinner plate as a guide. Stack tortillas between sheets of waxed paper until all are rolled. Bake on an ungreased, moderately hot griddle until edges dry and brown flecks appear (2 minutes). Turn; bake 1 minute more. Wrap tortillas in foil and keep them warm until all are cooked.
MAKES 6 7- TO 8-INCH TORTILLAS.

Cinnamon tea cakes

MEXICO

1 cup butter
1½ cups sugar
2 eggs
2¾ cups flour
1 teaspoon cream of tartar
¼ teaspoon salt
1 teaspoon baking powder
2 tablespoons sugar
2 teaspoons cinnamon

Cream butter and 1½ cups sugar. Add eggs. Sift dry ingredients; add to egg mixture. Shape dough into small balls, using approximately 1 teaspoon dough for each cookie.

Roll balls in mixture of 2 tablespoons sugar and 2 teaspoons cinnamon. Flatten slightly. Place on greased cookie sheet. Bake for 8 to 10 minutes at 400°F. Remove from cookie sheet and cool on a rack.

MAKES 4 DOZEN.

King's bread ring

MEXICO

King's Bread is served on Twelfth Night. The lucky (?) one who gets the coin in the bread must give a party on February 2, which is El Dia de la Candelaria (The Day of the Candle Mass).

1 teaspoon dried orange peel
2 tablespoons rum
2 packages active dry yeast
½ cup warm water
½ cup milk, scalded
⅓ cup sugar
⅓ cup shortening
2 teaspoons salt
4 cups all-purpose flour
3 eggs, well-beaten
Melted butter or margarine

topping
Candied cherries, cut into small pieces
Candied orange peel, in strips

Soak dried orange peel in rum. To make bread, soften yeast in warm water. Pour hot milk over sugar, shortening, and salt in large bowl, stirring until sugar is dissolved and shortening is melted. Cool to lukewarm. Beat in 1 cup flour, then the eggs and softened yeast, and the rum-soaked orange peel. Add enough flour to make a stiff dough.

Turn dough onto a floured surface; knead until smooth and satiny. Roll dough into a long rope; shape into a ring, sealing the ends together. Transfer to greased cookie sheet. Push a coin into the dough so it is completely covered. Brush with melted butter. Cover with a towel; let rise until double in bulk (about 1½ hours).

Bake at 375°F for 25 to 30 minutes or until golden brown. Cool on wire rack. When cool, frost bread ring with Confectioners' Sugar Icing, and decorate with candied cherries and orange-peel strips.

MAKES 1 LARGE RING OF BREAD.

Confectioners' sugar icing

1⅓ cups confectioners' sugar
4 teaspoons water
½ teaspoon vanilla

In a small bowl combine confectioners' sugar, water, and vanilla until smooth.

Puffed bread

MEXICO

4 cups flour
4 teaspoons baking powder
2 teaspoons salt
¼ cup shortening
1 to 1½ cups water, as needed
Oil for frying

Sift dry ingredients into mixing bowl. Cut in shortening. Add water, a little at a time, stirring to form a stiff dough. Knead until smooth. Roll thin; cut into 2-inch squares or triangles.

Heat oil in deep, heavy pan to 365°F; deep fry dough pieces a few at a time until golden brown. They will puff up as they fry. Serve Puffed Bread hot with butter and jelly or honey or serve with soup or guacamole.

MAKES ABOUT 40.

❧ Vegetables ❧

Ratatouille

FRANCE

1 medium eggplant
1 tablespoon salt
¼ cup olive or vegetable oil
2 large onions, sliced
3 cloves garlic, crushed
1 medium red pepper (optional), cored and cut into cubes
1 medium green pepper, cored and cut into cubes
4 medium zucchini, sliced ¾ inch thick

3 medium tomatoes, peeled, seeded, and cut into coarse cubes
¼ teaspoon salt
Freshly ground pepper to taste
¼ teaspoon thyme
¼ teaspoon oregano
1 bay leaf
2 tablespoons chopped parsley

Cut eggplant into ½-inch-thick slices, then into chunks. Sprinkle with 1 tablespoon salt; let stand 30 minutes. Dry thoroughly after standing. Heat oil in large frying pan. Sauté onions and garlic 2 minutes. Add red and green peppers; cook for 2 minutes more. Add eggplant; brown lightly on both sides (about 3 minutes). Add zucchini, tomatoes, and seasonings, except parsley. Simmer gently, uncovered, 30 to 40 minutes, until all vegetables are just tender. Baste vegetables often; do not scorch. Cover and reduce heat if necessary. Remove bay leaf; chill. Garnish casserole with parsley. Serve. May be served hot or cold.
MAKES 8 TO 10 SERVINGS.

Green peas w/lettuce

FRANCE

¼ pound Canadian bacon, cut into 1-inch pieces
1 tablespoon vegetable oil
3 cups fresh green peas
6 small white onions, peeled
Inner leaves of lettuce head
½ cup water
½ teaspoon salt
¼ teaspoon pepper
½ teaspoon sugar
1 tablespoon finely chopped parsley

Fry bacon in vegetable oil until lightly browned. Add peas, onions, lettuce, water, salt, pepper, and sugar. Cover; cook for 10 to 15 minutes or until peas are tender. When peas are done, drain

remaining liquid. Sprinkle with parsley before serving.
MAKES 6 SERVINGS.

Zucchini & tomato casserole

FRANCE

2 tablespoons vegetable oil
1 small onion, chopped
½ clove garlic, minced
2 zucchini squash, sliced
2 tomatoes, peeled, or 1 cup canned tomatoes
½ teaspoon salt
½ teaspoon basil
¼ teaspoon black pepper
2 tablespoons grated Parmesan cheese

Heat oil in heavy frypan. Sauté onion and garlic. Stir in zucchini; cover; cook until vegetables are tender. Add tomatoes, salt, basil, and pepper. Continue cooking, uncovered, until mixture is well-blended, about 10 minutes. Sprinkle with grated cheese. Place under broiler a few minutes to brown the top.
MAKES 4 SERVINGS.

Niçoise spinach

FRANCE

2 pounds spinach
1 tablespoon olive oil
1 clove garlic, minced
½ teaspoon salt
⅛ teaspoon pepper
⅛ teaspoon ground nutmeg
4 eggs
¼ cup heavy cream
Butter to grease dish
2 tablespoons dried bread crumbs (packaged)
1 tablespoon butter

Thoroughly wash spinach; drain. Heat oil in large Dutch oven or saucepan. Add garlic; cook for 1 minute. Add spinach; cover; steam for 3 minutes. Season with salt, pepper, and nutmeg. In small bowl beat eggs and cream until well-blended. Stir in spinach. Grease ovenproof dish with butter; spoon in spinach mixture. Sprinkle with bread crumbs; dot with butter. Place in pre-

Ratatouille

heated 425°F oven. Bake spinach about 15 minutes or until lightly browned.
MAKES 6 TO 8 SERVINGS.

Baked tomatoes

FRANCE

8 small tomatoes
Butter to grease casserole
½ teaspoon salt
⅛ teaspoon pepper
2 green onions, minced
2 anchovy fillets (flat), rinsed and chopped
2 hard-cooked eggs, peeled and chopped
2 tablespoons chopped fresh parsley (or 2 teaspoons dried)
2 tablespoons chopped fresh chervil (or 2 teaspoons dried)
2 slices dry white bread, broken into pieces
3 tablespoons olive oil

Peel tomatoes; core; cut into halves. Grease flat ovenproof dish with butter. Set tomato halves in dish. Season with salt and pepper.
Blend green onions, anchovy fillets, and eggs with herbs and bread pieces; spoon over tomatoes. Sprinkle olive oil over top. Bake in preheated 400°F oven 20 minutes.
MAKES 6 TO 8 SERVINGS.

Baked stuffed tomatoes

FRANCE

4 firm, red tomatoes
½ teaspoon salt
⅛ teaspoon pepper
1 clove garlic, mashed
3 tablespoons minced green onions
1 teaspoon dried basil
2 teaspoons dried parsley
⅛ teaspoon thyme
½ cup fine, dry bread crumbs
2 tablespoons oil

Preheat oven to 400°F. Core tomatoes; cut slice off each top. With a knife, gently press out juice and seeds. Sprinkle with salt and pepper. Mix together remaining ingredients. Fill each tomato with spoonful or two of mixture.
Arrange in small greased pan. Bake about 15 minutes. Tomatoes should be tender but holding their shape.
MAKES 4 SERVINGS.

Potato-garlic scallop

FRANCE

1 clove garlic
4 tablespoons butter
4 cups thinly sliced potatoes (¼ inch thick)
1 cup grated Swiss cheese

483

Green peas with lettuce

1½ cups hot milk
1 teaspoon salt
⅛ teaspoon pepper

Cut garlic in half; rub over inside of 2-quart baking dish. Using 1 tablespoon butter, thoroughly grease casserole. Spread half of potatoes in dish. Cover with half of cheese. Add remaining potatoes; top with cheese.

Mix milk, salt, and pepper. Pour over potatoes. Dot with remaining 3 tablespoons butter. Bake in preheated 375°F oven 45 to 60 minutes. Reduce heat or add more milk if potatoes become

dry before they are tender. When done, the top should be nicely browned.
MAKES 4 TO 6 SERVINGS.

Dauphine potatoes

FRANCE

3 medium potatoes
½ teaspoon salt
5 tablespoons butter
2 egg yolks, slightly beaten
1 cup water
Pinch of salt
1½ cups flour
4 eggs
Grated nutmeg
Salt to taste
1½ cups vegetable oil

Peel potatoes; boil them in salted water until done. Drain; put through potato ricer or food mill. Let potatoes cool. Beat in 2½ tablespoons butter and egg yolks. Set aside.

In heavy saucepan bring water, 2½ tablespoons butter, and pinch of salt to a boil. Remove from heat. Pour flour into pan all at once; stir quickly with wooden spoon until dough is smooth. Return saucepan to heat. Over low heat, stir constantly until dough forms one big dumpling. Stir in 1 egg. Remove from heat; let cool about 5 to 10 minutes. Add other 3 eggs, beating dough well after each addition. Stir in potatoes. Season to taste with grated nutmeg and salt.

Heat oil for deep frying. Put dough into pastry bag. Using a large round opening, press out dough, cutting off 1½-inch-long pieces. Fry dough in oil until golden. Drain on paper towels. Serve immediately.
MAKES 6 SERVINGS.

Skillet cabbage

GERMANY

2 tablespoons vegetable oil
3 cups finely shredded cabbage
1 cup chopped celery
1 small green pepper, chopped

1 small onion, chopped
½ teaspoon salt
¼ teaspoon pepper

Heat the oil in a large frypan about 20 minutes before serving time. Add ingredients and cook over medium to low heat about 15 minutes. Stir often. Cover pan during last 5 minutes of cooking time. Stir once or twice. Serve immediately. (Vegetables will be crisp.)
MAKES 4 SERVINGS.

Stuffed cabbage rolls

GERMANY

1½ cups brown rice	¼ cup bread crumbs
3 cups water	¼ cup minced fresh parsley
2 teaspoons salt	2½ pounds cabbage
1 teaspoon dillseed	Cheesecloth (about 6 feet)
½ teaspoon marjoram	2½ cups chopped canned
¾ teaspoon pepper	tomatoes
2½ cups chopped onion	½ cup dry vermouth
5 tablespoons vegetable oil	½ cup beef broth
½ teaspoon paprika	2 tablespoons tomato paste
2 cloves garlic, minced	½ teaspoon sugar
2 eggs, lightly beaten	

In a medium bowl cover brown rice with hot water and soak for 3 hours. Drain. In a 2-quart saucepan combine rice, 3 cups water, and 1½ teaspoons salt. Simmer covered for 40 minutes or until the liquid is absorbed. Add the dillseed, marjoram, and ½ teaspoon pepper.

In a large skillet sauté 1½ cups chopped onion in 3 tablespoons hot vegetable oil until soft, about 6 to 8 minutes. Add paprika and garlic; continue cooking and stirring for 2 minutes. Stir in the rice mixture, eggs, bread crumbs, and

parsley. Adjust seasonings to taste.

Core the cabbage and, in a large pot, blanch the cabbage core-side-down in boiling salted water for 5 minutes or until it is softened. Drain. Remove 12 leaves and cut off one-fourth of each leaf from the base. Arrange 1 leaf curved-side-down on a square of dampened cheesecloth and place 3 tablespoons of the rice mixture in the center. Wrap the leaf around the filling and twist the corners of the cheesecloth to form the leaf into a roll. Continue making rolls with remaining filling.

Chop remaining cabbage to make 3 cups and, in a large frypan, sauté with 1 cup chopped onions and 2 tablespoons vegetable oil until soft. Add tomatoes, vermouth, broth, tomato paste, sugar, ½ teaspoon salt and ¼ teaspoon pepper. Simmer the mixture for 5 minutes, stirring occasionally. Adjust seasonings.

Transfer cabbage-tomato sauce mixture to a large baking dish. Arrange the cabbage rolls close together in one layer on the sauce. Spoon some of the mixture over the rolls. Bake at 325°F for 1½ hours. Baste rolls 4 to 5 times during cooking. Let the dish cool. Cover and refrigerate overnight. Remove cheesecloth. Heat in a preheated 350°F oven for 30 minutes before serving.
MAKES 6 SERVINGS.

Sweet-and-sour red cabbage

GERMANY

¼ cup butter
4 medium apples, peeled and sliced
½ red onion, chopped

Niçoise spinach

Westphalian cabbage

1 head red cabbage, finely shredded
1 cup red wine
4 whole cloves
⅓ cup brown sugar
2 bay leaves
¼ cup vinegar
¼ cup butter
Juice of ½ lemon

Melt butter in 4-quart Dutch oven. Add apples and onions; sauté slightly. Add cabbage, red wine, cloves, sugar, and bay leaves. Simmer, covered, for 1 hour, then add the remaining ingredients. Heat to melt the butter and serve immediately.
MAKES 6 SERVINGS.

Westphalian cabbage

GERMANY

1 head cabbage, approximately 2 pounds
3 tablespoons vegetable oil
1 teaspoon salt
1 teaspoon caraway seeds
1 cup hot beef broth
2 to 3 small tart apples
1 tablespoon cornstarch
2 tablespoons cold water
3 tablespoons red wine vinegar
¼ teaspoon sugar

Shred cabbage. Heat vegetable oil in Dutch oven, add cabbage, and sauté for 5 minutes. Season with salt and caraway seeds. Pour in beef broth, cover, and simmer over low heat about 15 minutes.

Meanwhile, peel, quarter, core, and cut apples into thin wedges. Add to cabbage and simmer for another 30 minutes.

Blend cornstarch with cold water, add to cabbage, and stir until thickened and bubbly. Season with vinegar and sugar just before serving.
MAKES 4 TO 6 SERVINGS.

Fresh asparagus

GERMANY

2 pounds fresh asparagus (green or white)
Boiling salted water
¼ cup butter
3 tablespoons grated Parmesan cheese
1 large hard-cooked egg

Wash asparagus spears and trim off tough ends. Place asparagus in boiling salted water and cook until tender, 7 to 9 minutes. Drain off liquid.

In a small saucepan, melt the butter; cook over low heat until lightly browned. Sprinkle cheese over butter, mix, and spoon over asparagus. Garnish with sliced hard-cooked egg.
MAKES 6 SERVINGS.

White asparagus in white sauce
GERMANY

2 14½-ounce cans white asparagus
2 tablespoons margarine
2 tablespoons flour
½ cup reserved liquid (from asparagus)
½ cup milk
4 ounces cooked lean ham, cut into julienne strips
⅛ teaspoon nutmeg (freshly ground if possible)
¼ teaspoon salt

Drain asparagus spears, reserving ½ cup of liquid. Heat margarine in a saucepan. Add flour; blend. Gradually pour in asparagus liquid and milk. Stir constantly over low heat until sauce thickens and bubbles. Add ham and seasonings. Gently stir in asparagus spears; heat through, but do not boil. Serve in a preheated serving dish.
MAKES 4 SERVINGS.

Brussels sprouts in beer
GERMANY

1 pound fresh Brussels sprouts
Beer (enough to cover sprouts)
½ teaspoon salt
2 tablespoons butter

Trim and wash sprouts. Place in medium-size saucepan and pour over enough beer to cover. Bring to boil, reduce heat, and simmer for 20 minutes or until tender. Add more beer if needed, as liquid evaporates. Drain; add salt and butter. Serve hot.
MAKES 3 TO 4 SERVINGS.

Carrots in beer
GERMANY

4 large carrots
1 tablespoon butter
1 cup dark beer
¼ teaspoon salt
1 teaspoon sugar

Peel and slice carrots into long, thin slices. Melt butter in medium-size frypan; add beer and carrots. Cook slowly until tender, stirring fre-

quently. Stir in salt and sugar. Cook for another 2 minutes and serve hot.
MAKES 4 SERVINGS.

Mushrooms in cream sauce
GERMANY

1½ to 2 pounds fresh mushrooms
¼ pound bacon, diced
¼ cup butter or margarine
2 large onions, diced
1 cup white wine
½ teaspoon salt
¼ teaspoon pepper
¼ teaspoon paprika
Pinch of nutmeg
Pinch of mace
1 cup heavy cream
Juice from ½ lemon
2 sprigs parsley

Clean mushrooms and slice in half if large. Pat dry. Fry the bacon in a large pan until lightly browned. Remove from pan and reserve. Add the butter to the pan drippings. Add onions; sauté until lightly browned. Add mushrooms; cook until tender, stirring often. Stir in wine, salt, pepper, paprika, nutmeg, and mace. Cover frypan and cook over low heat 15 minutes.
Off the heat, add the cooked bacon, cream, and lemon juice. Reheat until just warm. Do not let the mixture boil! Garnish with parsley and serve with noodles or dumplings.
MAKES 4 TO 6 SERVINGS.

Onion pie
GERMANY

This is traditionally served in restaurants and wine stubes in the autumn when new wine is opened. May be served with salad for lunch.

1 package active dry yeast
1 teaspoon sugar
1½ teaspoons salt
3 to 3¼ cups unsifted flour
1 tablespoon shortening
1 cup water, 120 to 130°F (very warm)

6 slices bacon, cut-up
2 medium onions, sliced
¼ teaspoon cumin
½ teaspoon salt
Pepper, as desired
1 egg yolk
1 cup sour cream

Mix yeast, sugar, 1 teaspoon salt, and ½ cup flour. Blend in shortening and warm water. Beat for 2 minutes. Add enough flour to make a soft dough. Knead dough until smooth and elastic, about 5 minutes. Place dough in a lightly greased bowl. Cover and let dough rise in a warm place ½ hour. Pat dough into a lightly greased 12-inch pizza pan or onto a lightly greased baking sheet. Press up edges to make a slight rim.

Fry bacon until crisp. Remove from grease and drain on absorbent paper. Add onions to bacon grease; cook slowly until tender but not brown. Sprinkle onion, bacon, cumin, ½ teaspoon salt, and pepper over dough. Bake at 400°F for 20 minutes.

Blend egg yolk and sour cream. Pour over onions. Bake for 10 to 15 minutes longer or until golden brown and sour cream is set. Serve warm or at room temperature.
MAKES 8 SERVINGS.

Yellow split-pea purée
GERMANY

1 pound (2 cups) dried yellow split peas
6 cups water or stock broth
1 large onion, whole
1 large carrot
1 large turnip or parsnip
⅛ teaspoon dried marjoram
⅛ teaspoon dried thyme
1 teaspoon salt
1 small onion, minced
2 tablespoons butter, melted
2 tablespoons flour

Presoak peas, if necessary, according to package directions. Drain well, if presoaked. In a large pot, add peas, water or stock, whole onion, carrot, turnip or parsnip, marjoram, thyme, and salt. Cook until peas and vegetables are tender,

about 1½ to 2 hours. Drain well.
Mash peas and vegetables in blender or press through a sieve.
In a small frying pan, sauté the minced onion in butter until lightly browned; blend in flour and cook about 2 minutes. Add to blended peas and vegetables. Beat until fluffy.
MAKES 6 TO 8 SERVINGS.

Marinated tomatoes
GERMANY

4 large tomatoes, peeled and sliced
1 cup vegetable oil
¼ cup wine vinegar
¼ teaspoon dry mustard
1 teaspoon salt
¼ teaspoon black pepper
1 large clove garlic, minced
1 tablespoon chopped fresh basil
2 sprigs fresh thyme, chopped
1 sprig fresh marjoram, chopped
1 tablespoon minced scallion

Place tomato slices in serving bowl. Combine remaining ingredients and pour over tomatoes. Toss lightly. Chill for 1 hour or longer before serving.
MAKES 4 SERVINGS.

Sweet-and-sour potatoes
GERMANY

6 to 8 new potatoes, boiled in skins
1 medium onion, diced
¼ teaspoon salt
¼ teaspoon pepper
¾ cup sugar
4 slices bacon, cut up
¾ cup vinegar

Peel and cube potatoes. Add diced onion, salt, pepper, and sugar. Reserve in a covered bowl.
In a small frypan fry the bacon until crisp. Add the vinegar to the hot bacon and bring to a boil. Pour immediately over potato mixture; mix well. If too tart, add a little more sugar before serving. Cut endive or leaf lettuce added to this is very good.
MAKES 4 TO 6 SERVINGS.

Mashed potatoes w/horseradish cream

GERMANY

4 to 6 potatoes
Boiling water
½ teaspoon salt
2 tablespoons butter
Freshly ground pepper
½ cup sour cream
1 tablespoon horseradish
2 teaspoons minced parsley

Peel and quarter potatoes. Cook in boiling salted water in medium-size saucepan until tender; drain. Mash, adding 1 tablespoon butter and the pepper. Add sour cream, horseradish, and minced parsley. Whip as for mashed potatoes. Place in serving bowl; top with 1 tablespoon melted butter.
MAKES 3 TO 4 SERVINGS.

Potato pancakes

GERMANY

2 large potatoes (grated on medium grater, makes about
  2½ cups)
3 cups water
1 teaspoon lemon juice
1 boiled potato, mashed
1 egg, beaten
2 tablespoons milk
½ teaspoon salt
6 to 8 tablespoons vegetable oil

Grate raw potatoes into water to which lemon juice has been added. Place potatoes in a strainer or cheesecloth and drain off liquid well. Beat raw and cooked potatoes with egg, milk, and salt to form a batter.
Using 3 tablespoons oil for each batch, drop batter for 3 or 4 pancakes at a time into hot oil in large frypan. When firm on bottom side, loosen edges and turn. Brown other side. Remove, drain on paper towels, and keep warm. Continue until all batter is used; makes 8 to 10 pancakes. Serve immediately.
If potato cakes are served with meat, sprinkle with salt. Sprinkle with sugar if served with applesauce.
MAKES 3 TO 4 SERVINGS.

Fried artichokes

GREECE

Fried vegetables are delicious served with Garlic Sauce (see Index).

8 small artichokes
Juice of 1 lemon
4 tablespoons flour
Bowl of cold water
2 eggs
1 tablespoon warm water
¾ cup bread crumbs
2 tablespoons grated Kafaloteri or Parmesan cheese
Fat for deep-frying

Peel the tough outer leaves from the artichokes. Slice 1 inch off the tips and a small portion of the stem. Cut the artichokes in half lengthwise and remove the purple choke. Scrape the upper portion and stem to remove any dark green.
Add the lemon juice and flour to the bowl of cold water. Drop the artichoke hearts into the bowl as you work. Drain just before cooking. Parboil the artichoke hearts in boiling salted water 30 to 45 minutes or until tender. Drain well. Dip the artichoke hearts in the eggs and then in the bread crumbs and then dip them in the eggs and crumbs again. Fry in the hot fat (365°F) until brown. Drain on paper towels and serve.
MAKES 4 SERVINGS.

Variations: Any of the following vegetables can be breaded and fried in the above manner.
Eggplant (1 pound): Cut into slices ½ inch thick. Soak in salted water before breading. Drain, dip in egg and water mixture and then in crumbs. Dip again. Shallow-fry in hot oil until golden.
Squash (1 pound): Cut into slices ½ inch thick. Do not parboil. Bread and deep-fry, using the same method as for the artichoke hearts.
Cauliflower (1 medium head): Clean the cauliflower head, separate into florets, and parboil in salted water until crisp-tender. Drain well. Bread

489

and deep-fry, using the same method as for the artichoke hearts.

Baked artichoke hearts

GREECE

2 8½-ounce cans artichoke hearts, drained
4 tablespoons olive oil
¾ cup fresh bread crumbs
Salt and pepper
½ teaspoon paprika

Cut the artichoke hearts in half. Place in a small casserole and sprinkle with 2 tablespoons of the olive oil. Top with the bread crumbs, salt and pepper to taste, and paprika. Sprinkle with the remaining olive oil. Bake at 350°F for 30 minutes. Serve with Egg and Lemon Sauce (see Index).

MAKES 4 SERVINGS.

Variation: 2 packages (10½ ounces) frozen artichoke hearts (thawed) can be substituted for the canned artichoke hearts.

Stuffed eggplant

GREECE

2 small eggplants (about ¾ pound each)
3 tablespoons olive oil
2 tablespoons butter
2 medium onions, thinly sliced
1 pound tomatoes, peeled, seeded, and chopped
2 cloves garlic
½ teaspoon salt
1 bay leaf
1 2-inch stick of cinnamon
¼ teaspoon pepper
½ cup finely chopped parsley
8 black olives
8 anchovy fillets

Remove stems and caps from the eggplants. Heat the olive oil in a large skillet, add the eggplants, and cook over medium-high heat for 5 minutes. Remove from the pan. Cut in half lengthwise and carefully scoop out the pulp, leaving a thin shell. Chop the eggplant pulp coarsely.
Heat the butter in the same skillet. Add the on-

ions and cook until golden. Add the tomatoes and eggplant pulp and cook for 10 minutes. Crush the garlic cloves with the salt. Add to the tomato mixture. Add the bay leaf, cinnamon stick, pepper, and parsley and cook for 10 more minutes.
Fill the eggplant shells with this mixture. Garnish each shell with 2 olives and 2 anchovy fillets. Bake at 375°F for 10 minutes and serve.

MAKES 4 SERVINGS.

Eggplants stuffed w/rice & meat

GREECE

2 eggplants (1 pound each)
Salt
3 tablespoons olive oil
1 onion, chopped
1 clove garlic, minced
½ cup long-grain raw rice
1 cup chicken broth
1 tablespoon chopped parsley
½ cup finely chopped cooked beef, ham, or pork
2 medium tomatoes, peeled and quartered
4 slices processed cheese

Wash the eggplants and cut in half lengthwise. Cut several deep slits in the flesh. Sprinkle with salt and let stand 15 minutes. Scoop the pulp from the eggplants, leaving a ¾-inch-thick shell. Chop the pulp.
Heat the oil in a medium skillet. Fry the onion and garlic for 3 minutes. Add the rice and sauté for several minutes. Add the chicken broth. Cover, and reduce the heat to simmer. Cook for 20 minutes or until the rice is tender. Remove from the heat. Add the eggplant pulp, parsley, meat, and tomatoes. Mix well and stuff the eggplant shells with the mixture.
Place the shells in an open baking dish. Bake at 375°F for 20 minutes. Top with the cheese slices and bake 10 minutes more. Serve with a crisp green salad.

MAKES 4 SERVINGS.

Stuffed eggplant

Zucchini fritters

GREECE

2 medium zucchini, grated (2 cups)
½ teaspoon salt
2 eggs
¼ cup grated Kasseri cheese
½ teaspoon oregano
2 tablespoons all-purpose flour
¼ teaspoon pepper
2 tablespoons olive oil
2 tablespoons butter

Mix the zucchini and salt and let stand for 1 hour. Drain well and pat dry with paper towels. Beat the eggs. Add the zucchini, cheese, oregano, flour, and pepper, and mix well.

Heat the olive oil and butter over medium heat until the foam subsides. Cook the batter a tablespoon at a time, turning to brown both sides. Serve with tomato sauce.

MAKES 4 SERVINGS (12 PANCAKES).

Carrots plaki

GREECE

1 pound carrots, peeled and sliced
2 tablespoons olive oil
1 clove garlic, minced
4 large green onions, sliced
½ teaspoon crumbled oregano
½ teaspoon salt
1 tablespoon lemon juice

Parboil the carrots in boiling, salted water for 5 minutes. Drain.

Heat the oil in a medium-size saucepan. Add the garlic and fry for 2 minutes. Add the green onions, carrots, oregano, and salt. Cook over low heat for 15 minutes. Sprinkle with lemon juice and serve.

MAKES 4 SERVINGS.

Variation: Add ½ cup finely chopped nuts (walnuts, almonds, pine nuts, or pistachios) before serving, and thin with stock.

Cauliflower oregano

GREECE

1 large head cauliflower or 2 9-ounce packages frozen
   cauliflower
¼ cup lemon juice
¼ cup olive oil
1 tablespoon chopped parsley
½ teaspoon dried oregano
½ teaspoon salt

Clean the fresh cauliflower and break into florets. Cook in boiling salted water for 10 minutes or until just tender. (Cook frozen cauliflower according to the package directions.)

Meanwhile, combine the lemon juice, olive oil, parsley, oregano, and salt. Drain the cauliflower and place in a serving dish and top with the dressing. Serve hot.

MAKES 4 SERVINGS.

Green beans plaki

Variation: Substitute 1 large bunch of broccoli or 2 9-ounce packages of frozen broccoli for the cauliflower.

Celeriac plaki

GREECE

1½ pounds celeriac or celery roots
1 cup hot beef broth
5 tablespoons olive oil
½ teaspoon salt
¼ teaspoon white pepper
2 tablespoons lemon juice
1 bunch parsley, chopped
1 bunch fresh dill, chopped, or 2 teaspoons dried dillweed
4 tablespoons fresh bread crumbs

Clean and peel the celeriac and slice ¼ inch thick. Put into a small bowl. Add the beef broth and let stand covered for 10 minutes.
Heat the oil in a large saucepan. Drain the celeriac, reserving the broth. Place half of the drained celeriac in the saucepan. Season with salt, pepper, and 1 tablespoon of the lemon juice. Sprinkle with half of the herbs and bread crumbs. Repeat the process. Pour 1 cup of the beef broth over the layers. Cover and simmer over low heat for 40 minutes.
MAKES 4 TO 5 SERVINGS.

Braised green beans

GREECE

3 tablespoons olive oil
½ cup chopped onion
1 clove garlic, minced
1 pound fresh green beans, washed and the tips removed
1 cup canned tomatoes
1 tablespoon tomato paste
½ teaspoon salt
¼ teaspoon pepper
½ teaspoon oregano
½ cup water (approximately)

Heat the olive oil in a heavy saucepan. Add the onion and garlic and cook until golden. Add the remaining ingredients. The juices should just cover the beans in the pan. If not, add a little more water. Cover and cook over low heat for 45 minutes or until fork-tender. Serve the beans with the pan juices.
MAKES 4 SERVINGS.

Mixed-vegetable casserole

GREECE

3 medium zucchini, sliced
2 medium potatoes, peeled and sliced
1 small eggplant, peeled and sliced ¼ inch thick
2 large carrots, peeled and sliced

Green beans with ham

Hungarian sauerkraut

2 medium onions, peeled and sliced
2 cups peeled and chopped tomatoes
2 cloves garlic, minced
½ teaspoon sugar
½ cup olive oil
¼ cup chopped parsley
¾ teaspoon salt
¼ teaspoon pepper

Oil a large casserole and layer ¼ of the zucchini, potatoes, eggplant, carrots, and onions in it. Combine the tomatoes, garlic, and sugar. Put ¼ of the tomato mixture, 2 tablespoons of oil, 1 tablespoon of parsley, and some of the salt and pepper over the vegetables. Continue in this manner until all the vegetables have been used. Cover and bake at 350°F for 1 hour or until the vegetables are tender.

494   MAKES 4 SERVINGS.

Braised green beans & potatoes

GREECE

2 tablespoons butter
½ cup chopped onions
1 pound green beans, ends nipped, and cut into 1-inch pieces
4 medium potatoes, pared and cut in ¼-inch slices
1 cup chicken broth
½ teaspoon salt
¼ teaspoon oregano

Melt the butter in a large saucepan and sauté the onions until limp. Add the beans and stir to combine with the onions. Arrange the potatoes on top of the beans. Pour on the chicken broth and sprinkle with salt and oregano. Heat to boiling. Cover and lower the heat to simmer. Cook for 15 minutes or until the vegetables are tender. MAKES 4 SERVINGS.

Tomatoes plaki

GREECE

1½ pounds tomatoes
4 medium onions
2 bunches parsley
1 bunch fresh dill or 1 tablespoon dried dillweed
½ cup olive oil
¾ teaspoon dried thyme
¾ teaspoon salt
¼ teaspoon pepper
¾ teaspoon sugar
Juice of ½ lemon

Scald, peel, and slice the tomatoes. Peel the onions; slice very thin. Wash and dry the parsley and dill; chop fine. Reserve ⅓ of the parsley and dill for garnish.

Place 1 tablespoon of oil in the bottom of a 2-quart casserole. Layer ¼ of the tomatoes in the casserole. Top with ⅓ of the onions and ⅓ of the parsley and dill. Sprinkle with some of the thyme, salt, pepper, sugar and 1 tablespoon of oil. Continue layering, ending with tomatoes. Pour on the lemon juice and remaining oil. Cover and bake for 25 minutes at 400°F. Cool and garnish with the remaining parsley and dill. Serve cold.

Green beans plaki

GREECE

1½ pounds green beans
¼ cup olive oil
2 medium onions, chopped
Juice of 1 lemon
¾ teaspoon salt
¼ teaspoon pepper
⅓ cup bread crumbs
¾ teaspoon dried savory
1 bunch parsley, chopped
2 cups hot water

Clean the beans, wash, and cut in half. Heat the oil in a large saucepan. Then layer the beans, onions, lemon juice, salt, pepper, bread crumbs, and herbs, reserving ½ cup parsley for garnish. The last layer should be beans. Add the water. Cook over low heat for 30 to 35 minutes or until the beans are tender. Garnish with parsley and cool. Serve cold as an accompaniment to a main dish.
MAKES 6 SERVINGS.

Spinach & rice

GREECE

1 pound fresh spinach
½ cup chopped green onions
¼ cup olive oil
1 cup long-grain raw rice
¼ cup tomato sauce
2 cups water
2 teaspoons instant beef-broth granules (or 2 bouillon cubes)
½ teaspoon salt
¼ teaspoon pepper

Rinse the spinach well. Discard the stems and yellow or damaged leaves. Tear the spinach into bite-size pieces.
Sauté the onions in the olive oil in a large saucepan for 2 minutes. Add the rice and sauté until golden. Add the spinach, tomato sauce, water, beef-broth granules, salt, and pepper. Bring the mixture to a boil. Cover, reduce the heat to simmer, and cook for 20 minutes or until the rice is tender. Serve as a side dish with meat or fowl.
MAKES 4 SERVINGS.

Tomatoes w/feta cheese

GREECE

This recipe makes a delicious first course or an attractive accompaniment for chicken or fish.

4 medium ripe tomatoes
1 cup crumbled feta cheese
1 teaspoon crumbled oregano
Salt and pepper

Slice the tomatoes in half. Use a decorative zig-zag pattern if you wish. Sprinkle each tomato half with 2 tablespoons of cheese and some of the oregano, salt, and pepper. Broil and serve immediately.
MAKES 4 SERVINGS.

Braised potatoes

GREECE

8 small new potatoes
2 tablespoons butter
2 tablespoons olive oil
½ teaspoon salt
¼ teaspoon pepper
¼ teaspoon oregano, crumbled

Scrub the potatoes and peel away a wide band of skin around the center of the potato, leaving the skin on the remainder of the potato intact. Parboil the potatoes in boiling salted water to cover for approximately 20 minutes or until barely fork-tender. Drain.
Heat the butter and oil in a large saucepan or skillet until the foam from the butter subsides. Add the potatoes and brown on all sides. Add the salt, pepper, and oregano, and lower the heat to simmer. Cook, covered, until the potatoes are tender.
MAKES 4 SERVINGS.

Gourmet braised potatoes

GREECE

8 small new potatoes
1½ cups chicken stock
1 tablespoon white wine
¼ teaspoon oregano

½ *teaspoon salt*
¼ *teaspoon pepper*
2 tablespoons butter

Scrub the potatoes and peel a wide band of skin around the middle of the potato, leaving the remainder of the skin intact.

In a large saucepan combine the chicken stock, wine, oregano, salt, pepper, and butter. Heat to boiling. Add the potatoes and reduce the heat to low. Cook for 45 minutes or until tender.
MAKES 4 SERVINGS.

Variation: These potatoes can also be baked in the oven—with a roast, for example. Place the potatoes in a 2-quart casserole and pour on the chicken broth, wine, and seasonings. Dot with butter. Cover and cook at 350°F for 1 hour and 15 minutes, or slightly longer, if your roast is cooked at 325°F.

Spicy braised potatoes

GREECE

1 cup finely chopped onion
¼ *cup olive oil*
4 medium potatoes, peeled and sliced
2 tablespoons tomato paste
½ *teaspoon salt*
¼ *teaspoon pepper*
Water to cover

In a medium-size skillet sauté the onion in olive oil until browned. Add the potatoes, tomato paste, salt, pepper, and enough water barely to cover the potatoes. Bring to a boil. Reduce the heat to simmer and cook for 30 minutes or until the potatoes are tender.
MAKES 4 SERVINGS.

Lecsó

HUNGARY

This delightful combination of peppers, onions, and tomatoes may be served with any plain meat dish or used as a sauce for meat or egg dishes.

2 tablespoons lard
1 medium onion, peeled, sliced, separated into rings
1 pound green peppers, cleaned, sliced

¾ *pound tomatoes, peeled, quartered*
½ *teaspoon sugar*
2 teaspoons Hungarian sweet paprika
Dash of cayenne pepper
Salt and pepper

Melt lard in heavy skillet. Add onion; cook over moderate heat until onion is wilted. Add green peppers; cook until crisp-tender. Add remaining ingredients; cook, covered, over low heat 10 minutes, stirring occasionally. Taste for seasoning.
MAKES 4 TO 6 SERVINGS.

Variations: 1 pound smoked sausage, sliced, can be cooked in lecsó for an interesting lunch dish. For a delicious brunch, try adding 4 eggs to lecsó; cook until set. Serve on buttered toast.

Red cabbage and apples

HUNGARY

1 small head red cabbage (1 to 1¼ pounds)
3 slices bacon, chopped
½ *cup slivered onion*
1 tart apple, peeled, cored, sliced
2 tablespoons apple-cider vinegar
1 tablespoon brown sugar
1 bay leaf
Salt and pepper

Wash, core, and shred cabbage. Sauté bacon in large saucepan until lightly browned. Add onion; sauté until tender. Add cabbage, apple, vinegar, brown sugar, bay leaf, salt, and pepper; stir well. Cover; bring to boil over moderate heat. Reduce heat to low; cook 45 minutes. Remove bay leaf.
MAKES 4 SERVINGS.

Mushrooms & sour cream

HUNGARY

4 tablespoons butter or margarine
1 small onion, peeled, minced
1 pound fresh mushrooms, washed, trimmed, sliced ¼ inch thick
½ *teaspoon garlic salt*
⅛ *teaspoon pepper*
½ *teaspoon paprika*
½ *cup thick dairy sour cream*

Melt butter in large heavy skillet. Add onion; cook over moderate heat 3 minutes. Add mushrooms; cook quickly over moderate heat, stirring occasionally, until tender. Stir in garlic salt, pepper, and paprika; mix well. Remove from heat.

Slowly stir in sour cream. Return to heat; very gently heat through.

MAKES 4 SERVINGS.

Zucchini w/dill sauce

HUNGARY

4 cups sliced zucchini squash
Boiling salted water
1 teaspoon dried dillweed
1 1.25-ounce package sour-cream-sauce mix
½ cup cold milk
2 teaspoons lemon juice

Cook zucchini in medium saucepan with ½ teaspoon dillweed in boiling salted water just to cover. Cook only until crisp-tender; drain well. Return to saucepan; keep warm.

Combine sour-cream-sauce mix and milk in small mixing bowl; beat 1 to 1½ minutes or until well-blended. Let stand 10 minutes. Stir in lemon juice and ½ teaspoon dillweed; pour over zucchini. Heat very gently 3 to 4 minutes or until heated through.

MAKES 4 SERVINGS.

Crisp-fried cauliflower w/sour-cream sauce

HUNGARY

1 medium head cauliflower (approximately 1½ pounds)
Boiling salted water
2 eggs
2 tablespoons milk
¾ cup dry bread crumbs
2 tablespoons grated Parmesan cheese
Oil for deep frying

Clean cauliflower; wash well. Separate into florets. Cook in large saucepan of boiling salted water until crisp-tender (12 to 15 minutes). Drain well; pat dry on paper towels.

Beat eggs and milk together in shallow bowl. Combine bread crumbs and cheese on sheet of waxed paper; mix well. Dip cauliflower in egg mixture, then in crumbs, coating well.

Heat several inches oil in deep-fat fryer or heavy kettle to 365°F. Cook cauliflower, few pieces at a time, in hot fat until golden. Remove with slotted spoon; drain on absorbent paper. Keep hot while cooking remaining cauliflower.

MAKES 4 SERVINGS.

Sour-cream sauce

1 1.25-ounce package sour-cream-sauce mix
½ cup milk
1 tablespoon chopped parsley
½ teaspoon lemon juice
½ teaspoon Hungarian sweet paprika
¼ teaspoon Worcestershire sauce
Salt and pepper

Combine sauce ingredients in small saucepan; mix well. Cook over very low heat, stirring constantly, until heated through. Serve over cauliflower.

Green beans w/ham

HUNGARY

1 pound fresh green beans
2 cups boiling chicken broth
2 tablespoons butter
2 ounces baked or boiled ham, cut into thin strips
1 small onion, peeled, chopped fine
1 clove garlic, peeled, minced
¾ cup sour cream
2 egg yolks
Salt and pepper
¼ cup chopped parsley

Wash beans; snap off ends. Cut into 1-inch lengths. Add to boiling chicken broth in large saucepan. Cook over low heat approximately 20 to 25 minutes or until tender; drain well.

Meanwhile melt butter in skillet; sauté ham until lightly browned. Remove with slotted spoon; reserve. Add onion and garlic to skillet; cook until onion is transparent. Add onion and garlic to beans; mix lightly.

Beat sour cream and egg yolks together well.

497

Add yolks, salt, and pepper to beans; cook over very low heat 5 minutes. Transfer beans to warm serving dish; sprinkle with ham and parsley.
MAKES 4 TO 5 SERVINGS.

Hungarian sauerkraut

HUNGARY

1 16-ounce can sauerkraut
¾ teaspoon caraway seeds
3 slices diced bacon
1 small onion, peeled, diced
1 cup sliced smoked sausage (preferably Debrecziner sausage)
2 teaspoons Hungarian sweet paprika
2 sweet gherkin pickles, sliced thin
4 tablespoons sour cream

Combine sauerkraut and caraway in small saucepan. Bring to boil; cover. Reduce heat to low; cook 15 minutes.

Meanwhile sauté bacon in heavy skillet until crisp. Remove with slotted spoon. Add onion and sausage to skillet; cook until lightly browned. Remove from heat; stir in paprika.

Drain sauerkraut; add to skillet. Add bacon and pickles; stir well. Cook over low heat 10 minutes. Serve sauerkraut topped with sour cream.
MAKES 4 SERVINGS.

Potato dumplings

HUNGARY

This dough must be handled very quickly, so do not prepare until ready to cook the dumplings.

2 tablespoons butter or margarine
1 tablespoon finely minced onion
2 slices stale white bread
3 pounds potatoes, washed, or 1 6½-ounce package instant mashed-potato flakes (5 ½-cup servings size)
¾ cup water
¼ cup milk
½ teaspoon salt
¼ cup flour
2 eggs, well-beaten
Boiling salted water
1 tablespoon melted butter
2½ tablespoons dry bread crumbs

Melt 2 tablespoons butter in small skillet. Add onion; cook until lightly browned. Remove with slotted spoon; reserve. Cut crusts from bread; cut bread into small cubes. Add to skillet; brown on all sides. Remove from skillet; set aside.

Place potato flakes in medium mixing bowl. Peel, boil, and mash potatoes with salt and milk or, if using instant potatoes, place potato flakes in medium mixing bowl. Bring ¾ cup water to boil. Pour over potato flakes. Add milk and salt; let stand 3 minutes. Mix well. Add onion, flour, and eggs; mix well. Form mixture into small balls 2 to 3 inches in diameter. Force 2 to 3 bread cubes into center of each ball.

Drop into large saucepan of boiling salted water; cook 5 minutes. Remove with slotted spoon; place in warm serving dish. Combine melted butter and dry bread crumbs; sprinkle over dumplings.
MAKES 10 TO 12 DUMPLINGS.

Snowy potatoes w/ham

HUNGARY

5 medium potatoes, peeled, diced
Water
1 teaspoon salt
1 3-ounce package cream cheese
½ cup sour cream
¼ teaspoon garlic salt
White pepper
2 tablespoons chopped chives
2 tablespoons butter or margarine
½ cup diced baked ham
Paprika

Place potatoes in large saucepan; cover with cold water. Add salt; bring to boil. Cover; reduce heat to low. Cook 20 to 25 minutes or until tender; drain well.

Combine potatoes, cream cheese, sour cream, garlic salt, and pepper in mixing bowl; beat with electric mixer until smooth and fluffy. Stir in chives. Place in 1½-quart lightly greased casserole.

Melt butter in small saucepan. Add ham; sauté until lightly browned. Scatter ham over potato

casserole; drizzle with butter from saucepan. Sprinkle lightly with paprika. Bake at 350°F 30 minutes or until lightly browned and heated through.
MAKES 4 SERVINGS.

Paprika potatoes

HUNGARY

1½ tablespoons lard
¾ cup sliced onion
¾ cup chopped green pepper
1 clove garlic, peeled, minced
4 medium potatoes, peeled, diced
½ cup chopped, peeled, canned tomatoes
¾ teaspoon Hungarian sweet paprika
Salt and pepper

Heat lard in heavy saucepan. Add onion; cook 3 minutes. Add green pepper and garlic; cook, stirring occasionally, until onion is tender. Add potatoes; stir well. Cover; cook over low heat 25 minutes or until potatoes are fork-tender, shaking pan occasionally.
Add tomatoes, paprika, salt, and pepper; stir gently. Cook 5 minutes, uncovered. Serve potatoes hot.
MAKES 4 SERVINGS.

Creamed cauliflower

IRELAND

1 10½-ounce package frozen cauliflower
Boiling salted water
1 cup milk
1½ tablespoons butter or margarine
1½ tablespoons flour
2 tablespoons water
Salt and pepper
½ teaspoon dry mustard
2 tablespoons chopped parsley

Cook cauliflower in boiling salted water to cover until fork-tender. Drain. Add milk and butter; heat over moderate heat 2 to 3 minutes.
Combine flour and water; mix well. Add to cauliflower; cook, stirring constantly, over low heat until thickened. Season with salt, pepper, and

Potato dumplings

mustard. Transfer cauliflower to heated serving dish; garnish with parsley. Serve.
MAKES 4 SERVINGS.

Carrots cooked in milk

IRELAND

¾ pound baby carrots
1 tablespoon butter
⅔ cup milk
½ teaspoon sugar
¼ cup cream
2 egg yolks
Salt and pepper
Dash of mace
1 tablespoon chopped parsley

Trim carrots; scrub well with stiff brush. Split in half lengthwise any carrots longer than 2½ inches. Melt butter in heavy saucepan. Add 499

Snowy potatoes with ham

milk, sugar, and carrots; stir well. Cover; bring just to boil over medium heat. Reduce heat to low; cook approximately 10 minutes, until fork-tender.

Beat cream and egg yolks well. Stir slowly into carrot mixture. Cook over low heat, stirring frequently, until thickened. (Do *not* let mixture boil, as it will curdle.) Season to taste with salt and pepper; add dash of mace. Place carrots in warm serving dish; top with chopped parsley. MAKES 4 SERVINGS.

Glazed carrots & onions

IRELAND

1 pound carrots, peeled, sliced ½ inch thick
1½ cups peeled, sliced white onions
Water
1 teaspoon salt
3 tablespoons butter
1 tablespoon brown sugar

1½ tablespoons lemon juice
2 teaspoons cornstarch
3 tablespoons water

Combine carrots and onions in medium saucepan. Add enough cold water just to cover vegetables; add salt. Cover saucepan; bring to boil. Reduce heat to low; cook 10 to 12 minutes or until crisp-tender. Drain well; keep warm.

Melt butter in small saucepan over low heat. Add brown sugar; stir to dissolve. Add lemon juice; stir well. Combine cornstarch and 3 tablespoons water. Add to sugar mixture; stir to combine. Cook over low heat, stirring constantly, until thickened.

Combine carrots, onions, and sauce; stir well. Serve this immediately in warm serving dish. MAKES 4 TO 6 SERVINGS.

Turnip bake

IRELAND

1 pound rutabagas
½ pound white turnips
4 slices bacon, diced
¼ cup chopped onion
1 cup water
Salt and pepper
Chopped parsley

Peel rutabagas and turnips; cut into small cubes. Cook bacon in heavy skillet until crisp; remove from pan. Crumble; reserve. Add onion to bacon fat in skillet; cook until tender. Add water, salt, and pepper; bring to boil.

Combine rutabagas, turnips, and reserved bacon in 2-quart casserole. Add boiling water and onion. Cover; bake at 350°F 45 minutes or until fork-tender. Sprinkle casserole with chopped parsley. Serve.

MAKES 6 SERVINGS.

Brussels sprouts au gratin

IRELAND

1 10-ounce package frozen Brussels sprouts
Boiling salted water
2½ tablespoons butter or margarine
1½ tablespoons flour
Salt and pepper
1 cup milk
¾ cup grated sharp cheddar cheese
2 tablespoons bread crumbs
Parsley flakes
Paprika

Cook Brussels sprouts in boiling salted water to cover until tender. Drain; reserve.

Melt 1½ tablespoons butter in medium saucepan. Add flour, salt, and pepper; cook until bubbly. Add milk; cook, stirring constantly, until thickened. Add cheese; stir well. Place Brussels sprouts in 1-quart lightly greased casserole. Top with sauce.

Melt 1 tablespoon butter. Add bread crumbs; mix well. Sprinkle over casserole. Sprinkle with parsley flakes; dust with paprika. Bake at 350°F 20 minutes. Serve.

MAKES 3 TO 4 SERVINGS.

Summer mixed vegetables

IRELAND

2 medium carrots, peeled, sliced
1 medium turnip, peeled, diced into ½-inch cubes
1 cup frozen peas
2 tablespoons butter or margarine
½ teaspoon sugar
1 tablespoon water
Salt and pepper

Cook each vegetable in separate, small saucepan in boiling salted water until crisp-tender. Drain well.

Melt butter in medium saucepan. Add sugar, water, salt, and pepper; mix well. Add vegetables; cook, stirring, 3 minutes, until glazed and water has evaporated. Serve immediately.

MAKES 4 SERVINGS.

Cabbage w/bacon

IRELAND

1 medium head cabbage (about 2 pounds)
1 quart meat stock (preferably water in which ham, corned beef, or sausage was cooked)
4 slices crisply fried bacon, crumbled
2 tablespoons melted butter
Salt

Cabbage with bacon

Oakhill potatoes

Freshly ground black pepper
Ground mace

Quarter cabbage head. Remove any coarse outside leaves; cut out core. Tie with kitchen cord as you would a package. Bring stock to boil in large saucepan. Add cabbage wedges; cook, covered, over low heat 15 to 20 minutes or until tender. Remove from saucepan, draining well. Place cabbage in warm serving dish. Drizzle with melted butter; sprinkle lightly with salt, pepper, and mace. Garnish with crumbled bacon. Serve. MAKES 4 TO 6 SERVINGS.

Minted peas

IRELAND

1 10-ounce package frozen green peas
1 teaspoon dried mint
1 teaspoon sugar
Boiling salted water
1 tablespoon butter or margarine
Salt and pepper to taste

Cook peas, mint, and sugar in boiling salted water to cover 5 to 7 minutes or until peas are tender. Drain; stir in butter, salt, and pepper. Serve immediately. MAKES 4 SERVINGS.

Creamed peas & potatoes

IRELAND

Delicious served with fish dishes.

3 medium potatoes, peeled, diced
Cold water
1 teaspoon salt
1 10-ounce package frozen green peas
2 cups milk
2 tablespoons butter or margarine
1 tablespoon flour
1 tablespoon water
Salt and pepper

Place potatoes in medium saucepan. Add cold water to barely cover potatoes; add 1 teaspoon salt. Bring to boil over moderate heat; cook 10 to 15 minutes or until tender. Drain. Meanwhile, cook peas according to package directions. Drain; keep warm until needed. Add milk and butter to potatoes; heat until bubbling. Combine flour and 1 tablespoon water; mix well. Add to potatoes; cook, stirring, until thickened. Add peas; mix well. Season with salt and pepper to taste. MAKES 4 SERVINGS.

Oakhill potatoes

IRELAND

Delicious served with broiled lamb chops and green peas.

1½ pounds (4 to 5 medium) potatoes, peeled, diced
½ teaspoon salt
3 tablespoons butter or margarine
2 tablespoons flour
Salt and pepper
2 cups milk
2 hard-boiled eggs, peeled, sliced
2 tablespoons chopped onion
3 tablespoons dry bread crumbs

Place potatoes in large saucepan. Cover with cold water; add ½ teaspoon salt. Bring to boil. Reduce heat to low; cook 20 to 25 minutes or until potatoes are tender. Drain; reserve. Melt 2 tablespoons butter in medium saucepan. Add flour, salt, and pepper; cook until bubbly.

Add milk; stir well. Cook, stirring constantly, until thickened.

Combine potatoes, hard-boiled eggs, onion, salt, and pepper in lightly greased 1½-quart casserole. Add white sauce; blend lightly with spatula. Melt remaining 1 tablespoon butter. Add bread crumbs; mix well. Sprinkle buttered crumbs over casserole. Bake at 350°F 30 minutes. Serve. MAKES 4 SERVINGS.

Potato collops

IRELAND

¼ pound bacon, diced
1½ pounds potatoes, peeled, sliced
1½ tablespoons flour
3 tablespoons chopped onion
1½ teaspoons parsley flakes
Salt and pepper
1½ cups hot milk

Place bacon in heavy skillet; fry 4 to 5 minutes or until lightly browned but not crisp.

Grease 1½-quart casserole. Place ¼ of potatoes in bottom. Sprinkle with ½ tablespoon flour, 1 tablespoon onion, ½ teaspoon parsley flakes, ⅓ of cooked bacon, and 1 teaspoon bacon fat. Sprinkle lightly with salt and pepper. Top with ¼ of potatoes. Continue layering until all ingredients are used, ending with potatoes. Pour milk down side of casserole. Cover; bake 30 minutes at 350°F. Uncover; cook 60 minutes. Serve hot. MAKES 4 SERVINGS.

Potatoes stuffed w/corned beef

IRELAND

4 medium baking potatoes
4 tablespoons butter or margarine
¼ cup finely minced onion
¼ cup finely minced green pepper
2 to 3 tablespoons milk
1 teaspoon Worcestershire sauce
1 cup chopped corned beef
Salt and pepper
3 cups water
1 teaspoon salt

2 teaspoons vinegar
4 eggs
Minced parsley

Scrub potatoes well; prick with fork in several places. Bake at 375°F 1 to 1¼ hours or until easily pierced with fork. Meanwhile, melt 2 tablespoons butter in small saucepan. Sauté onion and green pepper until tender.

When potatoes are cool enough to handle, remove thin slice from top of each potato. Scoop out inside of potato, leaving ¼-inch-thick shell. Place potato pulp in mixing bowl with remaining 2 tablespoons butter. Beat, adding enough milk to make stiff mashed-potato mixture. Add Worcestershire sauce, corned beef, onion, green pepper, and butter in which they were cooked; mix well. Add salt and pepper to taste. Fill potato shells with mixture, making a well in top of each potato. Bake at 350°F 30 minutes.

Meanwhile, combine water and 1 teaspoon salt in medium saucepan; bring to boil. Add vinegar to boiling water. Break eggs, 1 at a time, into saucer; slide into boiling water. Poach eggs to to desired degree of doneness.

Place 1 poached egg in well on top of each potato. Garnish with parsley. Serve. MAKES 4 SERVINGS.

Note: The stuffed potatoes can be prepared a day in advance and refrigerated until baking time. Allow a few extra minutes to heat.

Parsley-buttered new potatoes

IRELAND

8 to 12 small new potatoes (number depends on size)
2 cups water
1½ teaspoons salt
¼ cup melted butter
2 tablespoons finely chopped parsley
Salt and pepper

Scrub potatoes well.

Bring water and 1½ teaspoons salt to boil in large saucepan over high heat. Add potatoes; cover. Bring to boil; reduce heat to low. Cook 10 to 15 minutes or until just tender. Drain; place folded tea towel over pan. Place cover on 503

pan; return to burner. Allow to steam on very low heat a few minutes (the residual heat in an electric burner is sufficient). Remove towel. Add butter, parsley, and salt and pepper to taste. Serve immediately.
MAKES 4 SERVINGS.

Champ

IRELAND

4 large or 6 medium potatoes
Cold water
1 teaspoon salt
½ cup milk
½ cup sliced green onions or leeks
Salt and pepper
4 tablespoons melted butter

Peel potatoes; remove eyes. Quarter large potatoes; halve medium potatoes. Place in large saucepan. Cover with cold water; add salt. Bring to boil. Reduce heat to low; cook approximately 20 minutes or until tender. Drain well; return to saucepan. Place tea towel between pan and lid; steam over very low heat 10 minutes.
While potatoes are cooking, combine milk and onions in small saucepan; bring to gentle boil. Reduce heat; cook 2 minutes. Reserve.
Place hot potatoes in mixing bowl. Strain onions from milk mixture. Reserve onions. Beat potatoes with just enough hot milk to make stiff mashed potatoes. Fold in onions. Season with salt and pepper. Place in warm serving dish. Make well in center; pour in melted butter.
Serve champ immediately. Each diner serves himself some potatoes and butter.
MAKES 4 SERVINGS.

Bubble & squeak

IRELAND

This dish is named for the noise it makes in the skillet as it cooks.

3 tablespoons butter or bacon fat
1 small onion, peeled, diced

2 cups shredded cooked cabbage
2 cups leftover mashed potatoes

Heat butter over moderate heat until melted. Add onion; sauté until tender.
Combine cabbage and mashed potatoes. Add to skillet; press with fork to form large cake. Cook over moderate heat until well-browned. Loosen potato cake with spatula; slide onto plate. Flip back into skillet, uncooked-side-down. Cook until well-browned. Serve this cut into wedges.
MAKES 4 SERVINGS.

Colcannon

IRELAND

This dish is traditionally served on Halloween night.

4 large or 6 medium potatoes
Cold water
1 teaspoon salt
4 cups finely shredded cabbage
2 cups boiling salted water
½ cup warm milk
Salt and pepper
4 tablespoons butter, melted

Peel potatoes; remove eyes. Cut large potatoes in quarters; cut medium potatoes in half. Place in large saucepan; cover with cold water. Add salt; bring to boil. Reduce heat to low; cook approximately 20 minutes or until fork-tender. Drain well; return to saucepan. Place tea towel between pan and lid; steam over very low heat 10 minutes.
Meanwhile, cook cabbage in boiling salted water 5 minutes. Drain well; reserve.
Mash potatoes with warm milk. Season with salt and pepper. Beat in cooked cabbage to form pale-green fluff. Place in warm serving dish. Make well in center; pour in melted butter. Serve immediately.
MAKES 4 TO 5 SERVINGS.

Variation: An equal amount of shredded kale may be substituted for cabbage in this recipe.

Asparagus—Milanese style

ITALY

1 10-ounce package frozen asparagus spears, partially thawed
1 tablespoon melted butter or margarine (divided)
2 tablespoons dry sherry
½ teaspoon seasoned salt and pepper mixture
⅓ cup Italian-style bread crumbs
2 tablespoons grated Romano cheese

Preheat the oven to 350°F. Separate the asparagus spears and place in a 9-inch pie plate. Mix the melted butter or margarine, sherry, and salt and pepper mixture and pour over the asparagus. Tightly cover with foil and bake for 30 minutes or until crisp-tender. Uncover and drain the liquid from the asparagus.

Melt the remaining butter and combine with the crumbs. Sprinkle over the asparagus. Sprinkle with the cheese. Broil until the crumbs are lightly browned and the cheese is melted.

MAKES 3 SERVINGS.

Mixed vegetables in the Italian manner

ITALY

2 tablespoons olive oil
1 medium onion, peeled and chopped
1 clove garlic, peeled and minced
1 green pepper, cleaned and cut into chunks
1 red pepper, cleaned and cut into chunks
½ pound eggplant (1 small or ½ of a large eggplant), unpeeled and cut into chunks
1 medium zucchini, cut into ½-inch slices
3 medium tomatoes, peeled and quartered
¼ teaspoon dried rosemary, crumbled
¼ teaspoon dried basil, crumbled
Salt and pepper

Heat the olive oil in a large skillet. Add the onion and garlic and sauté until the onion and garlic are transparent. Add the peppers, eggplant, zucchini, tomatoes, and seasonings and bring to a boil. Reduce the heat to low and cook until the vegetables are tender.

MAKES 3 TO 4 SERVINGS.

Romano beans in tomato sauce

ITALY

2 tablespoons olive oil
1 small garlic clove, minced
2 tablespoons chopped onion
¼ cup minced prosciutto or baked ham
½ cup tomato sauce
Salt and pepper
2 tablespoons water
1 9-ounce package frozen Italian (or Romano) green beans

Heat the oil in a medium saucepan. Add the garlic, onion, and prosciutto and sauté for 5 minutes. Add the tomato sauce, salt and pepper, and water and mix well. Add the frozen green beans and bring to a boil, stirring to break up the beans. Cover, reduce the heat to low and cook 15 minutes.

MAKES 3 TO 4 SERVINGS.

Roman-style green beans

ITALY

1 9-ounce package frozen French-cut green beans
1 tablespoon fresh lemon juice
2 tablespoons olive oil
¼ teaspoon dried oregano, crumbled
⅛ teaspoon garlic powder
Salt and pepper
¼ cup sliced black olives

Cook the beans in boiling salted water according to the package directions. Drain well.

Meanwhile, combine the lemon juice, olive oil, seasonings and olives in a small saucepan and heat through. Pour over the cooked beans and toss well. Serve immediately.

MAKES 4 SERVINGS.

Mixed vegetables Milanese-style

ITALY

3 slices bacon, diced
1 medium onion, peeled, sliced
1 red pepper, cleaned and cut into strips
3 carrots, peeled, sliced
2 medium potatoes, peeled, diced
½ cup chicken broth

1 (10-ounce) package frozen tiny peas
Salt and pepper

Cook bacon in large saucepan until crisp. Remove with slotted spoon; reserve. Add onion; sauté 2 minutes. Add pepper, carrots, potatoes, and chicken broth; bring to boil. Reduce heat to low; cook, covered, 15 minutes, until vegetables are crisp-tender. Add peas; simmer 5 minutes. Season with salt and pepper. Sprinkle with bacon; serve. MAKES 4 TO 5 SERVINGS.

Carrots piedmontese

ITALY

3 cups peeled carrots, thinly sliced
2 tablespoons butter or margarine
¼ cup onion, finely chopped
1 small clove garlic, peeled
½ teaspoon salt
2 teaspoons red wine vinegar
2 teaspoons freeze-dried chopped chives

Cook the carrots in boiling salted water in a medium, covered saucepan for 5 minutes. Drain in a colander.

Melt the butter in the saucepan. Add the onion, garlic, salt and drained carrots. Stir well. Cover and cook over low heat 10 minutes or until the carrots are crisp but tender. Remove and discard the garlic clove. Stir in the vinegar and chives and let stand several minutes, then serve. MAKES 4 SERVINGS.

Sautéed broccoli

ITALY

1 pound fresh young broccoli
Boiling salted water
3 tablespoons olive oil
1 clove garlic, peeled and chopped
Salt and pepper, to taste

Cut off any dry woody stems and trim the broccoli of all discolored parts and dead leaves. Separate into small spears and peel the stalks with a vegetable peeler. Cook in 1 inch of boiling salted water until crisp but tender. Drain well.

In a large skillet, heat the oil over moderate heat. Sauté the garlic until lightly browned. Add the broccoli and sauté, stirring constantly for 5 minutes. Add salt and pepper to taste and serve topped with the oil from the pan.
MAKES 4 SERVINGS.

Zucchini & potatoes

ITALY

4 medium potatoes
Boiling salted water
2 medium zucchini squash
¼ cup olive oil
1 clove garlic, minced
¼ teaspoon pepper

Peel the potatoes and dice. Cook in boiling salted water until tender. Drain well and keep warm.

Meanwhile, cut the ends from the zucchini, wash well and slice ½ inch thick. Pat dry on paper towels. In a large skillet, heat the oil over moderate heat. Cook the zucchini and garlic, stirring occasionally until crisp but tender. Add the zucchini, oil, and seasonings to the potatoes and continue to cook over low heat for 5 to 10 minutes, crushing the potatoes slightly until the mixture becomes thick. Serve hot.
MAKES 4 SERVINGS.

Zucchini w/tomato sauce

ITALY

2 medium zucchini squash
3 tablespoons olive oil
1 8-ounce can tomato sauce
½ teaspoon dried oregano, crumbled
Salt and pepper

Trim the blossom end from the zucchini and scrub well under running water. Leave the skin intact (do not peel), and slice in ½-inch thick slices. Dry on paper towels.

Heat the oil in a large saucepan over medium heat. Sauté the zucchini in the oil, stirring, for approximately 10 minutes or until crisp but tender. Add the tomato sauce and seasonings and reduce the heat to simmer. Cook 10 more minutes. Serve hot.
MAKES 4 SERVINGS.

Mixed vegetables Milanese-style

Honeyed carrot nuggets (next pages)

Fried mushrooms

ITALY

Excellent on a hot antipasto tray or with steak.

3 dozen mushrooms, about 1 inch in diameter
2 eggs
1 tablespoon water
½ teaspoon salt
¼ teaspoon pepper
½ cup flour
1 cup Italian-style bread crumbs
Oil for frying

Wash, trim the stems, and drain the mushrooms. Beat the egg, water, salt, and pepper together. Impale on a fork and dip in flour, then dip in the egg mixture and coat with bread crumbs. Allow to dry while heating 3 inches of vegetable oil to 360°F in a deep-fat fryer or deep saucepan. Fry a few at a time for 4 minutes or until golden brown. Drain and serve hot.

MAKES 6 SERVINGS.

Mushrooms w/garlic & oil

ITALY

1 pound fresh mushrooms
2 tablespoons olive oil
2 cloves garlic
¼ teaspoon salt

Clean the mushrooms with a damp cloth or, if necessary, wash in cold water. Remove the stems and reserve for another use. Pat dry; cut large mushrooms in quarters. Cut medium-size mushrooms in half and leave the small ones whole.

Heat the oil over moderate heat in a heavy skillet. Peel the garlic cloves and slice. Sauté the garlic in the oil until lightly browned. Remove the garlic from the pan with a slotted spoon. Sprinkle the oil with the salt.

Add the mushrooms and sauté over moderately high heat until the liquid coming from the mushrooms has evaporated. Stir constantly to prevent sticking. Reduce the heat to low and cook uncovered for 40 minutes, stirring occasionally, until the mushrooms are golden. Serve with steak or other meat dishes.

MAKES 4 SERVINGS.

Macaroni w/cauliflower

ITALY

1 (10-ounce) package frozen cauliflower
3 cups dry uncooked penne, rigatoni or ziti (or the macaroni of your choice)
2 tablespoons butter
2 tablespoons olive oil
1 clove garlic, peeled and minced
¼ teaspoon dried oregano, crumbled
½ tablespoon dehydrated parsley flakes
Salt and pepper
Grated Parmesan cheese

Cook the cauliflower in boiling salted water until crisp but tender. Drain well. Meanwhile, cook the macaroni in boiling salted water, according to the package directions. Drain and rinse briefly with cool water.

In a large skillet, heat the butter and oil over moderate heat. Add the garlic and sauté 2 minutes. Add the cauliflower and sauté for 5 minutes or until lightly browned. Add the macaroni, oregano, parsley and salt and pepper and heat through. Serve sprinkled with the Parmesan cheese.

MAKES 4 SERVINGS.

507

Braised fennel and tomatoes

Cauliflower w/tomato sauce

ITALY

1 medium-size head of cauliflower, trimmed of the outer
   green leaves
6 cups water
2 teaspoons salt

sauce
3 tablespoons olive oil
2 chopped shallots or ¼ cup chopped onion
¼ cup ham, finely chopped
¼ cup canned sliced mushrooms
1½ tablespoons flour
2 tablespoons tomato paste
¾ cup hot chicken broth
¼ cup white wine
¼ cup chopped parsley
Salt and pepper, to taste

Make a deep x-shaped cut in the base of the cauliflower, then place on a vegetable steamer rack.
Combine the water and salt in a large heavy kettle and bring to a boil. Lower the rack into the
kettle, cover the pot tightly and cook 20 minutes. The cauliflower should be crisp but tender.
Drain.

Meanwhile, heat the oil in a saucepan. Sauté the
shallots or onion in oil until lightly browned.
Add the ham and mushrooms and sauté 2 min-

utes. Remove the onion, ham, and mushrooms
with a slotted spoon.

Add the flour to the oil in the saucepan and
cook until bubbly. Combine the chicken broth
and tomato paste and add to the saucepan, stirring well. Add the wine, reserved ingredients,
parsley, salt and pepper and serve hot over the
cauliflower.

MAKES 6 SERVINGS.

Fried eggplant

ITALY

1 medium eggplant (about 1 pound)
1 egg
2 tablespoons water
⅓ cup flour
¾ cup dry bread crumbs
2 tablespoons grated Parmesan cheese
Cooking oil

Peel the eggplant and cut into ½-inch-thick
slices. Soak in cold salted water to cover for 15
minutes. Meanwhile, beat the egg with the water
in a shallow pan. Place the flour on a sheet of
waxed paper. On a separate sheet of waxed paper, combine the bread crumbs and Parmesan
cheese.

Drain the eggplant well and pat dry with paper
towels. Dip in the flour, then in the egg mixture, and finally coat well with bread crumbs,
shaking off the excess. Place on a baking sheet
until all the slices are coated.

Heat ½ inch of vegetable oil in a large heavy
skillet over moderate heat. Cook a few slices of
eggplant at a time until golden, turning once.
Drain on paper towels and serve immediately.

MAKES 4 SERVINGS.

Variation: 2 medium zucchini squash can be
substituted for the eggplant. Trim the ends from
the zucchini and cut in half crosswise. Then cut
the unpeeled zucchini into sticks. Do not soak in
cold water. Bread in the same manner as the eggplant and fry until golden. Drain on paper towels
and serve.

Stuffed zucchini

ITALY

8 medium zucchini (7 to 8 inches long)

filling
½ pound lean ground beef
½ pound sausage meat
2 tablespoons Parmesan cheese
2 tablespoons chopped parsley
⅛ teaspoon garlic powder
Salt and pepper

tomato sauce
3 tablespoons olive oil
1 medium onion, finely chopped
2 cloves garlic, minced
1 (12-ounce) can tomato sauce
1 teaspoon crumbled oregano
Salt and pepper

Cut ends from zucchini. Using apple corer, hollow out center of squash, removing all seeds. Leave ¾-inch-thick shell. In mixing bowl combine filling ingredients; mix well. Stuff zucchini shells with mixture.

Prepare sauce. Heat oil in Dutch oven. Add onion and garlic; sauté until tender. Add remaining sauce ingredients; mix well. Bring to boil over moderate heat. Add stuffed zucchini shells to sauce. Cover; simmer 1 hour. Serve zucchini topped with tomato sauce.
MAKES 4 SERVINGS.

Stuffed eggplant

ITALY

2 firm medium eggplants
Boiling salted water
2 small green peppers
2 small fresh tomatoes
1 (12-ounce) can artichoke hearts
½ cup olive oil
2 cloves garlic, peeled, minced
1 small onion, peeled, chopped
3 cups thickly sliced fresh mushrooms
1½ teaspoons crumbled oregano
1 teaspoon crumbled sweet basil
1 teaspoon salt
1 cup freshly grated Parmesan cheese

Cut eggplants in half lengthwise. Cut ½ inch from edges all around halves. Scoop pulp from center to form shells. Be careful not to pierce eggplant skin. Dice pulp. Parboil eggplant shells in 1 inch boiling salted water until barely tender. Drain carefully; set aside.

Clean green peppers; cut into 1-inch chunks. Peel tomatoes; cut into wedges. Drain artichoke hearts; halve.

Heat oil in heavy skillet. Sauté garlic, onion, and mushrooms until mushroom liquid evaporates. Add eggplant pulp; sauté until lightly browned. Stir in seasonings. Gently stir in peppers, tomatoes, and artichoke hearts; heat through. Stir in ½ cup Parmesan cheese.

Place reserved eggplant shells cut-side-up in lightly greased baking dish. Mound vegetable mixture in shells. Sprinkle with remaining cheese. Bake at 350°F 20 minutes.
MAKES 4 SERVINGS.

Eggplant parmigiana

ITALY

sauce
¼ cup olive oil
1 pound ground round steak (or lean ground beef)
1 medium onion, chopped
1 clove garlic, peeled, chopped
½ cup chopped celery
½ cup chopped green pepper
1 (15-ounce) can tomato sauce
1 (6-ounce) can tomato paste
1 (16-ounce) can Italian plum tomatoes, broken up with fork
¾ teaspoon crumbled mixed Italian seasoning

eggplant and filling
1 medium eggplant
1 egg
2 tablespoons water
Fine dry bread crumbs
½ cup cooking oil
1 cup ricotta cheese
1 (8-ounce) ball mozzarella cheese, thinly sliced
½ cup freshly grated Parmesan cheese

Heat oil in heavy skillet. Add ground round, onion, garlic, celery, and green pepper. Cook, stirring until lightly browned. Drain well. Add remaining sauce ingredients; mix well. Bring to boil over moderate heat. Reduce heat to low. Cover; simmer 1 hour.

511

Peel eggplant; cut into ¼- to ½-inch slices. Soak in cold salted water 30 minutes. Drain well; pat dry with paper towels. Beat egg and water together in shallow plate. Place bread crumbs on sheet of waxed paper. Dip eggplant in egg mixture, then bread crumbs, coating well.

Heat cooking oil in heavy skillet. Brown eggplant slices, few at a time, over moderate heat. Drain on paper towels.

In 13 × 9 × 2-inch casserole dish place layer of half of eggplant slices. Dot with half of the ricotta; top with half of the mozzarella. Spoon half of sauce mixture evenly over cheese. Repeat layers, ending with tomato sauce. Sprinkle with Parmesan. Bake at 350°F 60 minutes.
MAKES 8 SERVINGS.

Sautéed sweet peppers

ITALY

3 tablespoons olive oil
1 clove garlic, peeled
2 large green peppers, cleaned, cut into strips
2 large red peppers, cleaned, cut into strips
1 pound tomatoes, peeled, cut into chunks
Salt and pepper
Chopped parsley

Heat oil in heavy skillet. Add garlic; cook over moderate heat until browned; discard. Add peppers; sauté, stirring constantly, 5 minutes. Add tomatoes and salt and pepper to taste. Simmer, uncovered, until mixture is thick. Serve hot or cold garnished with parsley.
MAKES 4 SERVINGS.

Stuffed artichokes Roman-style

ITALY

4 large artichokes
1 lemon
¾ cup dry bread crumbs
¾ cup fresh-grated Romano or Parmesan cheese
2 cloves garlic, peeled, finely minced
3 tablespoons minced parsley
1 tablespoon crumbled dried mint
Salt and pepper
1½ sticks (12 tablespoons) butter, melted

Wash artichokes. Break off stems; discard. Discard discolored outer leaves. With sharp knife cut off top of artichoke 1 inch below tip. Snip off sharp tips of leaves. Trim artichoke base with knife so it sits flat and level. Rub cut surfaces with lemon.

In stainless steel or enamel pot bring 2½ inches water to rolling boil. Add juice of ½ lemon. Add artichokes. Cover; cook 15 minutes. Drain upside down in bowl. Pull out centers of artichokes; with small spoon scrape out the choke.

Combine bread crumbs, cheese, garlic, parsley, mint, salt, and pepper; mix well. Stuff mixture between leaves and into center of each artichoke.

Place artichokes upright in large saucepan, tightly packed in pan. Drizzle each with 3 tablespoons melted butter; be sure to get butter between leaves. Add ½ inch hot water to pan. Bring to boil over moderate heat. Cover; bake at 400°F 1 hour, until artichokes are tender.
MAKES 4 SERVINGS.

Broccoli Roman-style

ITALY

1 pound fresh young broccoli
3 tablespoons olive oil
1 clove garlic
Salt and pepper

Cut off dry ends of broccoli stalks. Incise bottoms of stalks with 4 gashes. Parboil in boiling salted water until crisp-tender. Drain well.

Heat oil in large heavy saucepan. Add garlic; sauté until golden. Discard garlic. Add broccoli; sauté, stirring constantly, 5 minutes. Season with salt and pepper to taste. Serve topped with oil from pan.
MAKES 4 SERVINGS.

Peas w/ham

ITALY

2 tablespoons butter
1 small onion, minced
⅛ pound prosciutto, diced

1 (10½-ounce) package frozen peas
1 tablespoon water

Melt butter in heavy saucepan. Add onion; sauté until tender. Add remaining ingredients; stir well. Cover pan tightly; simmer over low heat approximately 10 minutes. Check to be sure peas are tender. Cooking time can vary, depending on age and size of peas.
MAKES 4 SERVINGS.

Stirred beans

ITALY

1 tablespoon olive oil
2 tablespoons chopped onion
¼ cup chopped green pepper
1 (10-ounce) package Romano beans
½ cup chicken broth
⅓ cup sliced black olives
1 teaspoon cornstarch
2 teaspoons water

Heat olive oil in large saucepan. Add onion and pepper; sauté until tender. Add beans and broth. Separate beans with fork. Bring to boil. Reduce heat to simmer; cover. Cook 10 minutes, until tender. Add olives; stir.
Combine cornstarch and water; stir into vegetable mixture. Simmer 3 minutes, until sauce thickens slightly. Serve immediately.
MAKES 4 SERVINGS.

Braised fennel & tomatoes

ITALY

2 small fennel bulbs
3 tablespoons butter
¼ cup water
2 tablespoons white wine
4 ripe tomatoes, peeled, quartered
Salt and pepper
Parsley, chopped

Cut off stalks of fennel; peel away stringy, pulpy outside layers of bulb. Cut in quarters; core. Slice into thin wedges.
Heat butter in heavy saucepan until melted. Add fennel, water, and wine. Cover; simmer approxi-

mately 10 minutes, until fennel is crisp-tender. Add tomatoes; season with salt and pepper; stir gently. Simmer 10 minutes. Place in serving dish; garnish with chopped parsley.
MAKES 4 SERVINGS.

Honeyed carrot nuggets

POLAND

2 10-ounce packages frozen carrot nuggets
honey butter
¼ cup butter
¼ cup honey

Cook carrot nuggets according to package directions. Drain. Melt butter in shallow saucepan. Add honey to melted butter. Heat Honey Butter until bubbles start to form on surface. Arrange carrots on serving platter; pour Honey Butter over carrots. Serve immediately.
MAKES 4 SERVINGS.

Green beans in mushroom sauce

POLAND

1 1-pound can cut green beans
1 can cream of mushroom soup
½ cup Dilled Croutons (see Index)

Combine green beans and soup. Mix well. Pour green-bean and soup mixture into greased 1-quart casserole dish. Top mixture with Dilled Croutons. Bake in preheated 350°F oven 20 minutes or until soup begins to bubble.
MAKES 4 SERVINGS.

Spiced green beans

POLAND

The secret to using commercially canned vegetables is to remember the vegetables have been cooked in the canning process. Therefore, when serving canned vegetables, only reheat them.

2 1-pound cans whole green beans
¼ cup butter

lemon butter
2 tablespoons lemon juice
½ teaspoon salt
½ teaspoon dried basil
2 teaspoons dried parsley flakes

Drain green beans. Bring drained liquid to a boil in saucepan large enough to hold green beans horizontally when re-added to liquid. When liquid comes to a boil, reduce heat to simmer; add beans. Simmer beans just 4 minutes or until heated. Do not boil. Drain beans. Reserve liquid for soup stock.

Prepare Lemon Butter. Melt butter. Stir in lemon juice, spices, and parsley flakes. Arrange green beans on serving platter; coat with Lemon Butter. Serve immediately.
MAKES 6 SERVINGS.

Steamed white asparagus

POLAND

2 pounds white asparagus
⅓ cup butter
⅔ cup water
1 teaspoon salt

Break off each asparagus stalk as far as it will snap off easily. Peel off scales with a potato peeler. Rinse several times to remove sand.

Heat butter and water to a boil in a pan large enough to accommodate asparagus stalks. Add asparagus and salt to boiling water; cover pan. Cook over high heat 12 minutes or until asparagus is fork-tender. Drain; serve immediately.
MAKES 6 SERVINGS.

Cauliflower w/buttered bread crumbs

POLAND

1 head cauliflower
1 teaspoon salt

buttered bread crumbs
¼ cup butter
3 tablespoons bread crumbs
¼ teaspoon white pepper

Wash cauliflower head; remove large outside leaves. Select a saucepan large enough to accommodate the head of cauliflower. Cover bottom of pan with 1 to 2 inches of water. Add salt to water; bring water to rapid boil. Add cauliflower head to saucepan; cover. Boil cauliflower 25 minutes or until fork-tender. Drain immediately. Brown butter in small skillet. Add bread crumbs and white pepper; stir until all butter is absorbed into the bread crumbs. Place cooked cauliflower head on serving platter. Garnish with Buttered Bread Crumbs. Serve immediately.
MAKES 8 SERVINGS.

Sautéed red cabbage

POLAND

A traditional holiday meal in Warsaw.

2 tablespoons bacon fat
1 head red cabbage, shredded
1 large onion, sliced thin
1 tart cooking apple, cored and shredded
¼ cup cider vinegar
1 tablespoon granulated sugar
½ teaspoon salt
¼ teaspoon black pepper
Water as needed

Melt bacon fat in large skillet. Add remaining ingredients to skillet. Stir to mix. Cover skillet; simmer vegetables 1 hour or until tender. Add water as needed to prevent sticking.
MAKES 8 SERVINGS.

Paprika-buttered broccoli

POLAND

1 cup water
1 teaspoon salt
2 10-ounce packages frozen whole broccoli

paprika butter
¼ cup butter
½ teaspoon salt
¼ teaspoon white pepper
¼ teaspoon paprika

Bring water to rapid boil in saucepan. Add 1 teaspoon salt and broccoli; continue to boil for 15 minutes or until broccoli is fork-tender but not mushy. Drain immediately.

Make Paprika Butter by melting butter; stir in ½ teaspoon salt, white pepper, and paprika. Arrange broccoli on serving platter. Pour Paprika Butter over broccoli. Serve immediately.
MAKES 6 SERVINGS.

Cauliflower Polonaise
POLAND

2 hard-cooked egg yolks
1 teaspoon dried parsley flakes
2 tablespoons sour cream
¼ teaspoon white pepper
1 head cauliflower
1 teaspoon salt
¼ cup butter
3 tablespoons bread crumbs

Mash egg yolks in a small bowl. Add parsley flakes, sour cream, and white pepper to egg yolks. Blend. Reserve for later.

Wash cauliflower head; remove outside leaves. Select a saucepan large enough to accommodate the head of cauliflower. Cover bottom of pan with 1 to 2 inches of water. Add salt to water; bring water to rapid boil. Add cauliflower to saucepan; cover. Boil cauliflower 25 minutes or until fork-tender. Drain immediately.

Melt butter; stir in bread crumbs. Pour buttered bread crumbs over cauliflower; garnish with reserved egg-yolk mixture.
MAKES 8 SERVINGS.

Brussels sprouts w/Parmesan cheese
POLAND

1½ pounds Brussels sprouts
1 cup water
1 teaspoon salt
¼ teaspoon white pepper
¼ cup butter, melted
¼ cup Parmesan cheese

Clean Brussels sprouts, being sure to remove all tough and bruised outer leaves. Cover Brussels

Cauliflower Polonaise

sprouts with cold water; soak for 30 minutes. Drain.

In saucepan large enough to accommodate Brussels sprouts, bring 1 cup water to a rapid boil. Add salt and Brussels sprouts to boiling water; cover. Continue to cook Brussels sprouts 15 minutes or until fork-tender. Drain.

Combine pepper and butter; pour over Brussels sprouts. Garnish with Parmesan cheese.
MAKES 4 SERVINGS.

Mushroom-stuffed onions
POLAND

4 large Spanish onions
Boiling water
2 hard rolls
¾ cup whole milk
2 tablespoons butter, melted
1 cup sliced fresh mushrooms
2 tablespoons water
½ teaspoon salt
¼ teaspoon black pepper
¼ cup butter
½ cup boiling water

Skin onions; place in large saucepan. Cover with boiling water. Boil for 15 minutes or until onion meat becomes wilted. While onions are boiling, soak hard rolls in ¾ cup milk.

Melt butter in small skillet. Add mushrooms and 2 tablespoons water to butter. Stir to mix. Cover skillet; steam until mushrooms are limp. Stir oc- 515

Stuffed baked tomatoes

casionally to prevent mushrooms from sticking. Form a stuffing base by squeezing soaked hard rolls until a bread and milk sponge develops. Add cooked mushrooms, salt, and pepper to bread sponge to form stuffing. Mix well. Press out centers of onions; fill with stuffing mixture. Bake in 400°F oven 20 minutes or until tender. Melt ¼ cup butter in ½ cup boiling water. Use this butter and water mixture to baste onions while they are baking.
MAKES 4 SERVINGS.

French-fried eggplant

POLAND

1 medium eggplant
1 cup all-purpose white flour
½ teaspoon salt
¼ teaspoon black pepper
1 egg, beaten
½ cup milk
1 cup bread crumbs

Peel eggplant; cut into ¾-inch strips. Combine flour and spices in a shallow bowl. Combine egg and milk in another shallow bowl. Pour bread crumbs into a third shallow bowl.
Dip eggplant strips in seasoned flour, then in egg mixture; shake, then dip into crumbs and shake again. Fry breaded strips in oil heated to 375°F for 4 minutes, turning them once during cooking period. Drain on a brown paper bag.
MAKES 4 SERVINGS.

Marinated mushroom caps

POLAND

2 cups canned mushroom caps

marinade
½ cup finely chopped onions
½ cup salad vinegar
½ teaspoon black pepper, peppermill-ground
1 small clove garlic or ½ teaspoon garlic powder
½ cup salad oil

Drain mushrooms; pour into quart jar. Combine marinade ingredients. Add marinade to jar and marinate mushrooms for 24 hours, mixing 3 to 4 times during marinating period.
To serve, drain mushrooms and arrange on serving platter.
MAKES 6 SERVINGS.

Seasoned peas

POLAND

2 pounds fresh peas, shelled
2 cups water
1 teaspoon salt

dilled butter
¼ cup butter
½ teaspoon white pepper
2 tablespoons chopped fresh dill

Wash peas thoroughly in cold water. Drain. Bring water to rapid boil in large saucepan. Add peas and salt. Cover pan; continue to cook for 15 minutes or until peas are tender. Drain.

Melt butter in a small saucepan. Stir in pepper and chopped dill. Pour peas in serving dish and cover with Dilled Butter.

MAKES 6 SERVINGS.

Seasoned parsnips

POLAND

1½ pounds parsnips
Small piece salt pork
¼ cup butter, melted

Wash, peel, and core parsnips. Cut into strips; add to boiling salted water, along with salt pork. Boil parsnips 25 minutes or until fork-tender. Drain. Remove salt pork. Serve coated with melted butter.

MAKES 4 SERVINGS.

Creamed peas & corn

POLAND

1 10-ounce package frozen peas
1 10-ounce package frozen corn

white sauce
2 tablespoons butter
2 tablespoons all-purpose white flour
1 cup milk
½ teaspoon salt
¼ teaspoon white pepper

Cook peas and corn as directed on packages. While vegetables are cooking, make White Sauce. Melt butter in saucepan; add flour. Cook for 2 minutes, stirring constantly. Add milk, salt, and pepper; stir and continue to cook until White Sauce forms. Remove from heat.

Drain cooked vegetables. Add White Sauce to vegetables. Mix well. Serve immediately.

MAKES 6 SERVINGS.

Creamed corn

POLAND

A great use for leftover corn on the cob.

4 large ears corn

cream sauce
1 tablespoon butter
1 tablespoon all-purpose white flour
1 cup half-and-half cream
½ teaspoon salt
¼ teaspoon white pepper

Place corn in large saucepan; cover with cold water. Bring water to a boil. Reduce heat to simmer; continue cooking corn 10 minutes. Drain. When corn ears are cool enough to handle, remove kernels from husks, being careful not to cut into husks.

Prepare Cream Sauce. Make a roux by melting the butter in a 2-quart saucepan. Stir in flour, making sure flour and butter are well-blended. Gradually add half-and-half cream to the roux, stirring constantly to prevent lumping. Continue cooking sauce until it has thickened. Add salt and pepper. Mix well.

Stir corn kernels into Cream Sauce. Serve immediately.

MAKES 4 SERVINGS.

Creamed peas and corn

Polish chicory

Polish chicory

POLAND

1-2 chicory heads
1½ cups water
1 teaspoon salt
1 teaspoon white vinegar
¼ teaspoon white pepper
8 tablespoons butter
2 hard-cooked eggs
1 bunch parsley

Clean and wash chicory; cut out the bitter center and divide into 6 large bunches, binding each
one with kitchen twine. Bring water, salt, white
vinegar, white pepper, and 2 tablespoons butter
to a boil. Reduce liquid to simmer; add chicory.
Simmer for 15 minutes. Drain.
Brown remaining 6 tablespoons butter; pour over
cooked chicory. Chop eggs and parsley. Chop
and garnish chicory.

518   MAKES 6 SERVINGS.

Stuffed baked tomatoes

POLAND

4 large tomatoes
¼ cup butter
½ cup finely chopped onions
½ cup tomato centers (from above tomatoes)
½ teaspoon salt
¼ teaspoon black pepper
¼ teaspoon oregano
2 cups bread crumbs
1 bunch parsley

Thoroughly wash tomatoes. Dry on a paper
towel. With a sharp knife, remove tops from tomatoes. Save tomato tops for later use. Scoop
centers from tomatoes; reserve ½ cup for later
use. Heat butter in medium-size skillet. Add onions; cook until tender. Add ½ cup tomato centers to onions; cook until tomato pieces are
mushy.
Combine spices and bread crumbs. Add cooked

vegetables and butter. Work bread and vegetables with your hands until well-combined and stuffing mix has formed. If stuffing mix is too dry, add more melted butter.

Fill tomato cavities with stuffing mixture. Place tomatoes close together in a slightly greased baking pan. If tomatoes are small enough, they can be baked in a greased muffin tin. Replace tomato tops. Bake tomatoes in 350°F oven 30 minutes or until fork-tender. Carefully arrange tomatoes on serving platter. Garnish with fresh parsley.
MAKES 4 SERVINGS.

Broiled tomatoes

POLAND

4 medium tomatoes

seasoned butter

¼ cup butter
1 clove garlic, pressed, or 1 teaspoon garlic salt
¼ teaspoon white pepper
¼ teaspoon dry mustard

Wash tomatoes. Place upside down on broiler pan. With a sharp knife, slash skins of tomatoes in an "X" design.

Make Seasoned Butter. Melt butter; stir in garlic salt, white pepper, and dry mustard. Brush tomatoes with Seasoned Butter.

Place broiling pan in farthest slot from flame. Broil tomatoes 2 minutes. Remove tomatoes from broiler; baste tomatoes again with Seasoned Butter. Return tomatoes to broiler; continue to broil for an additional 3 minutes.
MAKES 4 SERVINGS.

Dilled tomato cups w/peas

POLAND

4 medium tomatoes

seasoned butter

2 tablespoons butter, melted
½ teaspoon salt
¼ teaspoon white pepper
½ teaspoon dried dillweed
½ cup water
1 cup peas, frozen

Slice tops from tomatoes; spoon out centers, being sure not to damage the structure of the tomato walls. Melt butter. Add salt, white pepper, and dillweed. Brush insides of tomatoes with Seasoned Butter. Bake tomatoes in 400°F oven 15 minutes or until tender.

While tomatoes are baking, bring ½ cup water to rapid boil. Add peas; cook for 8 to 10 minutes or until tender. To serve, fill tomato halves with hot peas. Serve immediately.
MAKES 4 SERVINGS.

Parsley buttered potatoes

POLAND

1 to 1½ pounds new potatoes
1 cup water
1 teaspoon salt
⅓ cup butter, melted
1 tablespoon dried parsley flakes

With a paring knife, scrape skins from new potatoes*. Bring water and salt to a rolling boil. Add potatoes, cover, and simmer for 20 minutes or until fork-tender. Drain.

Pour potatoes into serving bowl, coat with melted butter, and sprinkle with parsley flakes.
MAKES 4 SERVINGS.

Do not use a potato peeler. The skins of new potatoes are too thin to remove them with a potato peeler.

Potatoes with bacon

POLAND

2 pounds small round potatoes
1 teaspoon salt
4 strips bacon

Peel potatoes, wash well, and cover with water. Add salt to water; bring to boil. Reduce heat to simmer; cook, covered, for 25 minutes or until done. Drain; cut into bite-size pieces.

Cut bacon into small pieces; fry until brown and crisp. To serve, pour bacon and bacon drippings over cooked potatoes.
MAKES 4 SERVINGS.

Fried potatoes w/sausage

POLAND

1 pound Kielbasa
4 large white potatoes, peeled and sliced
1 tablespoon chopped fresh parsley

Slice Kielbasa; fry in large skillet. Remove Kielbasa from skillet. Add potatoes to skillet. Fry on one side without stirring. When done on one side, use a pancake turner and flip potatoes with one turn. Fry remaining side of potatoes until done. To serve, garnish with fried Kielbasa and parsley. Serve with beer and rye bread.
MAKES 4 SERVINGS.

Green beans w/ham

SPAIN

2 tablespoons olive oil
1 Spanish onion, chopped
2 10-ounce packages frozen green beans
½ teaspoon pressed garlic
½ teaspoon salt
1 cup diced Italian or other smoked ham
Pimiento

Heat oil until light haze forms above pan. Reduce heat; sauté onion and beans until tender. Add garlic, salt, and ham; cook 5 minutes or until ham is heated. Serve beans and ham warm, garnish with pimiento.
MAKES 6 SERVINGS.

Green beans in tomato sauce

SPAIN

3 tablespoons olive oil
½ cup chopped Spanish onion
1 clove garlic, minced
1 pound fresh green beans, washed, tips removed
1 16-ounce can stewed tomatoes
1 tablespoon tomato paste
½ teaspoon salt
Dash of pepper
1 teaspoon sugar
1 tablespoon parsley

Heat oil in deep cast-iron skillet. Sauté onion and garlic until golden brown. Add remaining ingredients. Cover; cook 30 minutes or until beans are fork-tender. Remove beans.
Cook tomato sauce until almost all liquid evaporates. Re-add beans to sauce; reheat.
MAKES 6 SERVINGS.

Steamed white asparagus w/garlic mayonnaise

SPAIN

White asparagus are grown under mounds of dirt to prevent the chlorophyll in the spears from turning green.

2 pounds white asparagus
⅓ cup olive oil or butter
⅔ cup water
1 teaspoon salt
Garlic Mayonnaise (see Index)

Break off each asparagus spear as far as it will snap easily; peel off scales with potato peeler. Rinse several times to remove sand.
Heat oil and water to boiling in pan large enough to accommodate asparagus stalks. Add asparagus and salt to boiling water; cover pan. Cook over high heat 12 minutes or until asparagus is fork-tender; drain. Serve asparagus immediately with Garlic Mayonnaise.
MAKES 6 SERVINGS.

Lima beans & peppers

SPAIN

¾ cup water
1 10-ounce package frozen lima beans
3 tablespoons olive oil
½ cup thin strips green pepper
½ cup thin strips red pepper
¼ cup chopped onion

Bring water to boil. Add beans; cook 10 minutes or until tender. Drain; keep warm.
Heat oil in skillet. Add remaining vegetables; sauté 5 minutes. Combine beans with vegetables. Serve immediately.
MAKES 4 SERVINGS.

Onions & green peppers

SPAIN

¼ cup olive oil
6 medium onions, peeled, sliced thin
3 green peppers, seeded, sliced into thin rings
½ teaspoon salt
¼ teaspoon pepper

Heat oil in skillet; sauté onions 10 minutes. Add peppers; sauté 10 minutes or until tender. Sprinkle with salt and pepper.
MAKES 4 SERVINGS.

Cabbage w/apples

SPAIN

1 small head cabbage
1 cooking apple
2 tablespoons olive oil or bacon drippings
1 teaspoon caraway seed
1 cup dry white wine
½ teaspoon salt
¼ teaspoon pepper
Lemon wedges

Core and shred cabbage. Peel, core, and coarsely grate apple.
Pour oil into large skillet. Add cabbage; sauté 10 minutes. Add apple, caraway seed, and wine. Cover; simmer 10 minutes or until cabbage is tender. Season with salt and pepper. Serve with lemon wedges.
MAKES 4 TO 6 SERVINGS.

Summer garden casserole

SPAIN

3 summer squash, sliced
2 potatoes, peeled, sliced
2 carrots, peeled, sliced
2 medium onions, peeled, sliced
2 cups chopped peeled tomatoes
2 garlic cloves, minced
½ cup olive oil
¼ cup snipped parsley
¾ teaspoon salt
¼ teaspoon pepper

Oil large casserole; layer ¼ of squash, potatoes, carrots, and onions. Combine tomatoes and garlic. Put ¼ of tomato mixture, 2 tablespoons oil, 1 tablespoon parsley, and some of salt and pepper over vegetables. Repeat until all vegetables are layered. Cover; bake at 350°F 1 hour or until tender.
MAKES 4 TO 6 SERVINGS.

Pepper pot

SPAIN

2 red sweet peppers
2 green peppers
1 large Spanish onion
3 large tomatoes
¼ cup olive oil
1 teaspoon salt
½ teaspoon garlic powder
¼ teaspoon pepper

Remove tops, seeds, and white membranes from peppers. Slice into rings. Peel onion; slice into rings. Peel tomatoes. Remove cores; slice into wedges.
Heat oil in large skillet; reduce heat. Add peppers and onion; sauté 10 minutes. Add tomatoes and seasonings. Sauté 10 minutes or until vegetables are tender but still retain their shape.
MAKES 4 SERVINGS.

Boiled potatoes w/garlic mayonnaise

SPAIN

2 pounds new potatoes
1 teaspoon salt
1 recipe Garlic Mayonnaise (see Index)
1 tablespoon snipped fresh parsley

Scrape skin from potatoes.* Cut large potatoes in two. Cover with water. Add salt; bring to boil. Boil 20 minutes or until tender; drain.
Prepare mayonnaise as directed. Toss potatoes in mayonnaise; garnish with parsley. Serve hot.
MAKES 6 TO 8 SERVINGS.

* Use paring knife, not potato peeler. Skins of new potatoes are too thin to remove with peeler.

521

Asparagus w/creamed shrimp

DENMARK

4 tablespoons butter
4 tablespoons flour
2 cups liquid drained from shrimps and asparagus
½ teaspoon salt
⅛ teaspoon pepper
2 cans shrimp
1 can asparagus, green or white

Melt the butter; add the flour, and blend. Slowly add the liquid, stirring constantly until the mixture thickens. Add the seasonings to the liquid; last, add the shrimps, reserving a few for garnish. Lay 3 or 4 stalks of heated asparagus on buttered toast. Pour the hot shrimp sauce over this. Garnish with 1 or 2 shrimps on top. Serve.
MAKES 6 SERVINGS.

Red cabbage I

DENMARK

1 large head red cabbage
2 tablespoons bacon fat or oil
½ cup red wine
3 tablespoons red currant jelly
1 teaspoon salt
Dash of white pepper
Pinch of powdered cloves
1 tablespoon sugar

Wash, shred, and drain the red cabbage. Heat the bacon fat or oil in a large pot. Add the cabbage and heat it for 5 minutes. Then add the red wine, currant jelly, salt, pepper, cloves, and sugar. Mix very well and continue to stir for a few minutes until all flavors are absorbed. Cover and cook the cabbage over low heat for 25 minutes. Serve the cabbage hot.
MAKES 6 TO 8 SERVINGS.

Red cabbage II

DENMARK

1 large head red cabbage
4 tablespoons butter
2 tablespoons sugar
¼ cup water

¼ cup wine vinegar
1 teaspoon salt
½ teaspoon pepper
3 apples

Wash the cabbage and drain it well, then shred it. Melt the butter in a large pot and add the shredded cabbage. Add sugar, and stir well. Cook gently for a few minutes. Add the water, vinegar, salt, and pepper; cover and cook the cabbage very slowly for 1½ hours.
Core and chop the apples. (Peel them if you prefer, but the apple skin adds flavor.) Add the apples to the cabbage; cover this and cook it for another ½ hour. Add more sugar and salt if needed, and serve.
MAKES 8 TO 10 SERVINGS.

Sour cabbage

DENMARK

1 head cabbage
2 tablespoons butter
2 tablespoons flour
1 teaspoon salt
1 teaspoon caraway seeds
2 cups water
2 tablespoons vinegar
2 tablespoons sugar
¼ cup wine (optional)

Shred the cabbage into a large pot. Add all the ingredients as listed. Cook over very low heat for at least 2 hours. Add more water if needed. Just before serving, add the wine and mix thoroughly.
MAKES 4 TO 6 SERVINGS.

Mashed potatoes w/apples

DENMARK

2 medium apples
3 large potatoes
½ cup water
2 cups milk, heated
3 tablespoons butter
2 tablespoons sugar
Salt and pepper to taste

Peel, core, and slice the apples; peel the potatoes. Cook these together in ½ cup of water until they are soft. Mash them together thoroughly. Add the milk a little at a time; be sure it is absorbed before each addition. Last, whip in the butter, sugar, salt, and pepper. The mixture will be a little softer than mashed potatoes but just as fluffy.

MAKES 4 TO 6 SERVINGS.

Hot diced pumpkin

DENMARK

1 medium-size pumpkin
3 tablespoons butter
3 tablespoons flour
2 cups liquid from cooked pumpkin
2 tablespoons lemon juice
2 egg yolks, beaten
2 tablespoons cold butter
1 tablespoon chopped parsley

Remove the seeds from the pumpkin; peel and cut it into cubes. Cook the pumpkin in a small amount of salted water until it is tender. Drain it, reserving the liquid from the sauce.

Melt the 3 tablespoons of butter; stir in the flour until well-blended. Add 2 cups of liquid from the pumpkin (add water to make this amount, if needed). Stir the mixture until it is slightly thickened. Add the lemon juice and egg yolks, beating vigorously. Add the cold butter and stir until it is melted in. Last, add the chopped parsley. Pour the mixture over the hot pumpkin and serve.

MAKES 6 OR MORE SERVINGS.

Carrot pudding

FINLAND

½ cup pearl barley
2 cups water
2 cups boiling milk
1 pound carrots
1 egg, beaten
½ teaspoon salt
2 teaspoons sugar

Potatoes with bacon

Cook the barley in 2 cups of water. Gradually add the boiling milk and cook the barley for 1 hour.

Peel and grate the carrots. Add the carrots, egg, salt, and sugar to the barley. Pour the mixture into a buttered baking dish. Cover it with bread crumbs and dot the top with butter. Bake the pudding at 400°F for 1 hour.

MAKES 4 OR MORE SERVINGS.

Cabbage w/bacon & dill

NORWAY

1 small head cabbage
6 slices bacon
1 small onion
½ teaspoon salt
¼ teaspoon pepper
1 teaspoon dillweed or 3 dill leaves chopped fine

Wash, core, and slice the cabbage. Set it aside to drain. Fry the bacon slices crisp and set them aside.

Slice the onion fine and brown it in the bacon fat. Add the salt, pepper, and dill. Last, add the drained cabbage. Cover, and simmer over a low heat until the cabbage is tender, about 1 hour. Add water if needed during the cooking.

523

Fried potatoes with sausage

When the cabbage is tender, remove it from the pan to a serving dish. Garnish with the bacon slices.

MAKES 4 OR MORE SERVINGS.

Stuffed onions

NORWAY

6 large onions
2 tablespoons butter
1 pound ground beef or veal
1 teaspoon salt
¼ teaspoon pepper
1 cup beef stock

Peel the onions and cut a ½-inch slice from the top of each. Put these aside to use for topping.

Hollow out the centers of the onions to form holes for the stuffing. Save the center of the onions, and chop them fine. Melt the butter and brown the chopped onions. Add the ground meat, salt, and pepper. Mix them well.

When the meat is browned, stuff the centers of the onions with the meat mixture. Put the top slices of the onions back on and secure them in place with toothpicks. Put the onions in a baking dish and pour the beef stock over them. Bake them at 375°F for 1 hour or until the onions are soft.

MAKES 6 SERVINGS.

Steamed asparagus with garlic mayonnaise

Lima beans & peppers (pg. 520)

Roast potatoes

SWEDEN

6 baking potatoes small enough to fit in a deep spoon
3 tablespoons melted butter
1 teaspoon salt
2 tablespoons bread crumbs
2 tablespoons Parmesan cheese (optional)

Preheat the oven to 425°F.

Peel the potatoes and put them in cold water to prevent discoloring. Put 1 potato in the deep spoon and slice it down to the edge of the spoon, making the slices about ⅛ inch apart. The spoon will prevent you from cutting through the potato. Return the sliced potato to the cold water and slice the others in the same manner. Drain the potatoes and pat dry. Put the potatoes, cut-side-up, in a large buttered baking dish. Baste them with some of the melted butter. Sprinkle them with salt and cook them for 30 minutes in the preheated oven.

Now sprinkle the bread crumbs over each potato and baste them with the remaining melted butter. Continue to cook the potatoes for another 15 minutes or until they are golden brown and tender. Parmesan cheese may be added 5 minutes before the potatoes are done.

526 MAKES 6 PORTIONS.

Potato pancakes w/chives

SWEDEN

2 tablespoons chives
4 medium baking potatoes
2 teaspoons salt
Several twists of freshly ground black pepper
2 tablespoons butter
2 tablespoons vegetable oil

First chop the chives and set them aside. Peel and grate the potatoes coarsely into a large mixing bowl. The potatoes will accumulate potato water. Do not drain it. Mix in the chopped chives, salt, and ground pepper. Work as quickly as you can, so that the potatoes do not turn brown.

Melt the butter and oil in a 12-inch skillet. Drop the potato mixture by spoonfuls (2 tablespoons per pancake) into hot fat. The 3-inch pancakes will take about 3 minutes a side to become crisp and golden. Serve them piping hot.

MAKES 4 SERVINGS.

Stuffed cabbage

MIDDLE EAST

1 large head cabbage, with center core removed
Boiling water to cover
1 cup uncooked long-grain rice
½ cup minced onions
1 well-beaten egg
2 tablespoons parsley
2 tablespoons olive oil
2 tablespoons tomato sauce
1 minced garlic clove
1 teaspoon salt
1 teaspoon minced mint leaves
½ teaspoon allspice
½ teaspoon black pepper
¼ cup or more olive oil
4 to 6 cups chicken broth

Place cabbage in large pot with the core on the bottom of the pot. Cover with boiling water and allow to boil for 5 minutes. Remove, drain, and allow to cool until able to handle. Separate the leaves of the cabbage and set aside.

In a bowl, combine rice, onions, egg, parsley,

olive oil, tomato sauce, garlic, and seasonings. Mix well. This is the stuffing mixture.

At the core end of the cabbage leaves, place about 1 tablespoon of the stuffing. Roll the leaf once and then fold in the ends, envelope-style. Roll the rest of the leaf until stuffing is well-covered. Continue to do this with the leaves until all stuffing is used.

In a heavy saucepan, layer the remaining cabbage leaves. Cover with the cabbage rolls placed seam-side down. Sprinkle the first layer of rolls with olive oil and some chicken broth. Proceed in this way with the layering until all of the stuffed rolls are in the pan. When all rolls are used, cover with chicken broth. Cook on a low flame for 1 hour or until leaves are tender and the rice done. Remove to a heated platter, pour some of the liquid over all and serve.

MAKES 6 SERVINGS.

Eggplant base for stew

MIDDLE EAST

2 large eggplants
1 cup white sauce (cream of celery soup can be used)
Salt and pepper to taste
2 tablespoons butter
1/4 cup pine nuts
Minced parsley
Green pepper rings for garnish
Lemon wedges for garnish

Broil eggplants until skins are blackened and pulp is fork tender. Peel and drain pulp thoroughly. Then place pulp in a deep bowl and mash to a fine consistency. Add a cup of white sauce and salt and pepper, continuing to whip. Mound on a heated platter and make a well in the center with a spoon.

Heat butter and pine nuts until nuts are golden-brown. Then put nuts in the well of the eggplant. Sprinkle with parsley and garnish the platter with pepper rings and lemon wedges. This dish is good with any entrée but particularly tasty with lamb stew.

MAKES 6 TO 8 SERVINGS.

Cabbage & sour cream

MIDDLE EAST

6 cups finely shredded cabbage, (1 medium head)
4 tablespoons butter
1 1/2 teaspoons salt
1 1/2 teaspoons lemon juice
2 tablespoons sugar
1 egg
1 cup sour cream

Over a low heat, sauté cabbage in butter for 45 minutes. Stir frequently so it doesn't stick to the pan. Add salt, lemon juice, and sugar and cook 5 minutes longer. Combine the egg and sour cream in a bowl, beating until the egg disappears. Gradually add to the cabbage while stirring until all begins to thicken. Serve at once topped with additional sour cream, if desired.

MAKES 4 TO 6 SERVINGS.

Turkish eggplant

MIDDLE EAST

4 small eggplants
3 tablespoons vegetable oil
2 medium onions, sliced
3 peeled and sliced tomatoes
2 minced garlic cloves
1/2 teaspoon salt
1 tablespoon chopped parsley
1 bay leaf
1 cinnamon stick
1/8 teaspoon white pepper
8 black olives
8 rolled anchovy fillets

Remove stems and approximately 1/2-inch slice from top of eggplants (see picture). Heat 2 tablespoons of the oil in a frypan and fry eggplants on all sides for 5 minutes. Remove eggplants from pan, cool slightly, and scoop out pulp, leaving a shell approximately 1-inch thick.

Heat 1 tablespoon oil in same pan, add onions, and sauté lightly. Stir in tomatoes and simmer for 5 minutes. Return diced pulp to frypan. Add garlic, salt, parsley, bay leaf, cinnamon stick, and white pepper. Cook for another 5 minutes; remove bay leaf and cinnamon.

Arrange eggplant shells in a greased baking dish and fill with vegetable mixture. Bake in a preheated oven, 350 °F for 15 minutes. Garnish with olives and anchovies.
MAKES 4 SERVINGS.

Spinach pie

MIDDLE EAST

½ package prepared filo leaves (about 16, 12 by 15 inches)
4 tablespoons butter
½ cup finely chopped onions
3 10-ounce packages chopped spinach, thawed and drained
3 eggs
½ pound crumbled Feta cheese
¼ cup chopped parsley
2 tablespoons chopped fresh dill
1 teaspoon salt
Hearty dash of freshly ground pepper
¼ cup melted butter

Allow filo leaves to come to room temperature. In medium skillet, melt butter and sauté onions until golden, about 5 minutes. Add spinach and stir well. When blended, remove from the heat. Beat the eggs with a rotary beater. Then use a wooden spoon to stir in cheese, parsley, dill, salt, pepper, and spinach mixture. Mix well.

With some of the melted butter, grease a 13- by 9- by 2-inch baking pan. Layer 8 of the filo leaves in the bottom of the dish, brushing the top of each with melted butter before adding the next leaf. When 8 leaves have been brushed with butter, spread the spinach mixture evenly. Then cover with 8 more leaves, again brushing each leaf with butter. If any butter remains, pour over the top of all.

Trim off any rough edges using a scissors. Then take a sharp knife and cut into squares before baking. Bake at 350°F for 30 minutes or until top crust is puffy and golden. Serve warm.
MAKES 8 TO 10 SERVINGS.

Tip for the cook: cover filo leaves not being used with damp paper towels to prevent drying out and to make them easier to handle.

Lentil & spinach pilaf

MIDDLE EAST

This dish is filling enough to be served by itself as a meatless dinner or can accompany the meat of your choice as a vegetable.

3 tablespoons butter
1 pound spinach, washed, dried and chopped
1 minced garlic clove
1½ cups cooked lentils
1 tablespoon chopped parsley
½ teaspoon salt
¼ teaspoon pepper
¼ teaspoon cumin
1 recipe basic Pilaf (see Index)
3 tablespoons melted butter

Melt butter in skillet and sauté the spinach and minced garlic until it is wilted. Add the lentils, parsley, and seasonings and sauté together for about 5 minutes or until all are blended and heated through. Taste to add extra seasonings if needed. Put onto a heated platter and top with the pilaf. Cover with melted butter and serve.
MAKES 4 TO 6 SERVINGS.

Stuffed grape leaves

MIDDLE EAST

1 medium-size jar of grape leaves
1 cup of rice
¼ cup of boiling water
1 grated onion
1 bunch chopped green onions
1 teaspoon salt
1 teaspoon pepper
1 teaspoon dill
1 tablespoon dry mint
½ cup oil
¼ cup chopped parsley

Wash the grape leaves with water and set aside. Soak the rice in boiling water until it absorbs the liquid. Add onions, seasonings, and ¼ cup of the oil and stir well.

Take a grape leaf and place 1 teaspoon of the mixture in the center. Wrap well. When all are wrapped, place the grape leaves in a saucepan. Pour remaining ¼ cup of oil and 1½ cups water over them. Bring to a boil, then cover, reduce heat, and simmer for 40 minutes. Serve with lemon sauce with egg.

MAKES 4 TO 6 SERVINGS.

Lemon sauce with egg

2 eggs
Juice of 1 lemon
½ cup broth from grape leaves
½ cup water

Beat eggs with whisk until frothy and add lemon juice. Add ½ cup broth from the grape leaves and ½ cup water. Stir this mixture over low heat until it thickens. Pour over the stuffed grape leaves.

Potato latkes

MIDDLE EAST

Potato pancakes are particularly popular in Israel during the Jewish festival of Hannukah, but they are enjoyed whenever they are served.

6 medium potatoes, peeled and grated
½ teaspoon baking soda
2 grated onions
2 eggs
Dash of ginger or nutmeg (optional)
½ cup flour
1 teaspoon salt
Dash of black pepper
Fat for deep frying

Sprinkle the grated potatoes with the baking soda. Spoon out most of the excess liquid. Add the remaining ingredients in the order given. Heat the fat in a large skillet and drop batter by spoonfuls to form potato cakes about 4 inches in diameter. When crisp on both sides, remove and drain on paper towels. Keep warm until all are cooked and then watch them disappear at the table as everyone enjoys them.

MAKES 6 TO 8 SERVINGS.

Mixed Chinese vegetables

CHINA

5 large dried Chinese mushrooms
1 cup lukewarm water
5 ounces green cabbage
4 ounces carrots
4 ounces cucumber
5 ounces canned bamboo shoots
4 tablespoons sesame-seed oil
2 ounces frozen peas
½ cup hot chicken broth
2 tablespoons soy sauce
Salt
Pinch of sugar

Soak mushrooms in water for 30 minutes. Shred cabbage, cut carrots, cucumber, and bamboo shoots into julienne strips. Cube mushrooms. Heat oil in skillet, add cabbage, and cook for 2 minutes. Add mushrooms, cucumbers, carrots, bamboo shoots, and peas. Pour in chicken broth. Season with soy sauce, salt, and sugar. Simmer over low heat for 15 minutes. Serve immediately.

MAKES 2 SERVINGS.

Grow-your-own bean sprouts

CHINA

There is nothing like growing your own bean sprouts to have them available when you desire and to know that they are fresh. It's a very simple procedure and takes very little time. All you need is a package of mung beans (bean sprouts), a quart jar, water, and a strainer.

¼ cup mung beans
Water

Soak ¼ cup mung beans in a quart jar overnight. Pour off the water, use a strainer if desired, and place the jar in a dark place for 3 days, rinsing the beans 3 times a day and draining them thoroughly after each rinsing. At the end of 3 days you will have ready-to-eat, home-grown bean sprouts. Refrigerate and use as needed.

Stir-fried celery & bean sprouts

CHINA

2 cups celery, sliced diagonally
Oil
4 cups fresh bean sprouts
Sprinkles of soy sauce

Slice celery and set aside. Heat oil in skillet and stir-fry celery for about 2 minutes, until bright green and tender but still crisp. Add bean sprouts and stir-fry for 1 minute, or until bean sprouts are heated through. Sprinkle with soy sauce to taste and serve immediately.
MAKES 2 SERVINGS.

Chinese fried vegetables

CHINA

Oil for cooking
½ cup celery, sliced diagonally
4 ounces bamboo shoots
4 ounces water chestnuts, sliced
3 scallions, sliced into 1-inch pieces
½ cup fresh mushrooms
1 cup bean sprouts, fresh or canned
Soy sauce to taste

Heat oil in skillet or wok. Add celery, bamboo shoots, and water chestnuts. Stir-fry for 2 minutes. Add scallions, mushrooms, and bean sprouts and stir-fry for 1 minute or until heated through. Sprinkle with soy sauce to taste and serve immediately.
MAKES 2 SERVINGS.

Frying-pan bean sprouts

CHINA

2 cups fresh bean sprouts
Oil for frying—enough to cover bottom of pan
Sprinkles of soy sauce
Chopped scallion (optional)

Place bean sprouts in colander and rinse well with cold water. Drain well. Heat oil in frying pan until hot. Place bean sprouts in pan and toss until heated through. Cook quickly on high heat. Remove to serving plate and sprinkle with soy sauce to taste. If desired, chopped scallion may be added when cooking.
MAKES 2 SERVINGS.

Bean sprouts w/celery & mushrooms

CHINA

2 tablespoons oil
3 stalks celery, sliced diagonally
1 onion, chopped
¼ pound fresh mushrooms, sliced
½ cup chicken stock
1 tablespoon soy sauce
1 pound fresh bean sprouts
1 tablespoon cornstarch mixed with ¼ cup cold water

Add oil to preheated pan. Sauté celery, onion, and mushrooms until onion is soft. Add chicken stock and soy sauce. Bring to a boil and add bean sprouts. Stir-fry only for about 30 seconds. Cover and simmer 3 seconds. Thicken with cornstarch mixture, adding it a little at a time. Serve immediately.
MAKES 4 SERVINGS.

Pea-pod casserole

CHINA

1 package frozen pea pods, boiled
1 can water chestnuts, sliced
2 cups fresh bean sprouts, or 1 can bean sprouts
1 can cream of mushroom soup
1 can onion rings (optional)

Boil pea pods for 2 minutes. Drain and place in casserole dish. Place sliced water chestnuts on top of pea pods. Next, place a layer of bean sprouts. If fresh sprouts are used, first blanch, then rise with cold water and drain well. If canned bean sprouts are used, drain, rinse with cold water and drain well.
Cover with cream of mushroom soup. Bake for 15 minutes at 350°F. Place onion rings on top and heat again for about 2 or 3 minutes.
MAKES 4 SERVINGS.

Red cabbage I (pg. 522)

Grilled green peppers

CHINA

2 green peppers, cut into 1-inch squares
Melted butter or meat marinade

Parboil peppers gently for 2 minutes. Drain and dry. Brush with melted butter or marinade. Skewer and cook on a hibachi or grill for 4 minutes.
MAKES 2 SERVINGS.

Red & green pepper pot

CHINA

¼ cup butter
3 red peppers, cut into rings
3 green peppers, cut into rings
6 yellow onions, peeled, cut into wedges
12 tomatoes, stem ends cut off, cut into wedges
Salt to taste
Freshly ground black pepper to taste

Melt butter in skillet. Add peppers and onions; sauté over low heat 10 minutes, stirring frequently. Add tomato wedges. Season with salt and pepper. Cook 10 minutes, stirring frequently.
MAKES 6 SERVINGS.

Bean sprouts & vinegar

CHINA

1 teaspoon Szechwan peppercorns
3 tablespoons oil
1½ pounds fresh bean sprouts
¼ cup thin strips green pepper
1 teaspoon salt
½ teaspoon sugar
2 teaspoons vinegar

Fry peppercorns in oil until fragrant. Remove peppercorns; discard. Add remaining ingredients to same pan; stir-fry until heated through. Serve immediately.
MAKES 4 OR 5 SERVINGS.

531

Roast potatoes (pg. 526)

Red and green pepper pot

String beans Chinese-style

CHINA

2 cloves garlic, minced
1 medium onion, chopped
1 tablespoon oil
2 tablespoons soy sauce
1 pound fresh string beans
1 cup chicken broth

Mince garlic, chop onion and set aside. Heat oil in skillet to medium-high. Sauté garlic and onion until golden. Add soy sauce and string beans. Pour in the chicken broth, turn temperature down, and let mixture simmer for approximately 7 to 8 minutes, until beans are tender, but still crisp.

532   MAKES 4 SERVINGS.

Stuffed cabbage (pg. 526)

Wok broccoli

CHINA

1 pound fresh broccoli
2 tablespoons peanut oil
1 teaspoon sugar
½ teaspoon salt
½ cup water

Wash broccoli; break away small upper branches. Cut more-tender parts of stem into small crosswise slices.

Preheat oil in wok to 350°F. Add broccoli; stir-fry 1 minute. Add sugar, salt, and water; cover. Let broccoli steam 3 minutes. Cook another 5 minutes, stirring frequently.

MAKES 4 SERVINGS.

Delicious Chinese cabbage

CHINA

1 Chinese cabbage
½ cup water
1 tablespoon salt
1 tablespoon sesame oil
½ cup shredded carrot
2 tablespoons shredded gingerroot
1 tablespoon sugar
½ teaspoon salt
2 tablespoons vinegar
Few drops Tabasco

Slice cabbage, sprinkle with water and salt, and let stand overnight. Squeeze water from cabbage and arrange on serving platter.

Heat oil in skillet or wok to medium-high heat and sauté carrot and ginger for approximately 3 minutes. Add sugar, salt, vinegar, and a few drops of Tabasco. Bring to a boil. Pour over cabbage. Let stand at least 15 minutes before serving.

MAKES 4 SERVINGS.

Cabbage & mushrooms

CHINA

1 pound cabbage
2 tablespoons oil
2 cloves garlic, crushed
½ cup fresh mushrooms, sliced
½ teaspoon sugar
½ teaspoon soy sauce

Cut cabbage into bite-size pieces and set aside. Heat oil in skillet to medium-high heat and sauté garlic approximately 3 minutes. Discard garlic. Add cabbage and sauté for 2 minutes. Add mushrooms, sugar and soy sauce and mix well to heat through. Serve immediately.

MAKES 4 SERVINGS.

Chow choy

CHINA

This is a very unusual and tasty vegetable dish.

¼ cup olive oil
1 teaspoon cayenne pepper
1 clove garlic, minced
Salt to taste
4 cups chopped Chinese cabbage
2 tablespoons soy sauce
2 tablespoons red-wine vinegar
1 teaspoon sugar
3 scallions, chopped
1 tablespoon cornstarch
2 tablespoons cold water

Heat oil in wok or large skillet over medium heat. Stir in pepper, garlic, and salt. Add cabbage and soy sauce; stir-fry 2 minutes. Add vinegar, sugar, and scallions; stir-fry 1 minute.
Mix cornstarch with cold water until smooth; stir into cabbage mixture. Stir-fry about 2 minutes or until mixture is lightly browned.
MAKES 4 SERVINGS.

Mixed Chinese vegetables

Stuffed grape leaves (pg. 528)

Baked Chinese cabbage

CHINA

2 heads Chinese cabbage
4 cups beef bouillon
1 small onion, coarsely chopped
Margarine to grease ovenproof baking dish
6 tablespoons grated cheese, Emmenthal or Gruyère
2 tablespoons butter or margarine

sauce
½ cup sour cream
2 tablespoons chopped parsley
1 small onion, chopped
Salt to taste
White pepper to taste
1½ tablespoons grated cheese, Emmenthal or Gruyère

Remove outer wilted leaves from cabbage and cut cabbage in half lengthwise. Cut each half into 3 or 4 pieces. Wash thoroughly and pat dry. Bring beef bouillon to boil, add onion and cabbage, and simmer for 20 minutes. Remove cabbage with slotted spoon and drain.
Grease ovenproof baking dish with margarine. Place ⅓ of cabbage in dish, sprinkle with ⅓ of cheese, and dot with ⅓ of butter or margarine. Repeat this until cabbage, cheese, and butter are used.
Prepare sauce by combining and stirring thoroughly sour cream, parsley, onion, salt, and pepper. Pour over cabbage. Sprinkle with 1½ table-

spoons grated cheese. Bake in preheated 375°F oven until cheese melts completely, approximately 10 to 15 minutes.
MAKES APPROXIMATELY 4 SERVINGS.

Cauliflower and mushrooms

CHINA

1 small cauliflower
2 tablespoons oil
¼ pound fresh mushrooms, sliced
1 cup chicken broth, warmed
2 tablespoons soy sauce
1 tablespoon cornstarch mixed with ¼ cup cold water

Trim cauliflower, wash, and separate into florets. Slice large florets. Pour oil into preheated pan. Add cauliflower and sauté lightly. Add mushrooms and sauté a few seconds longer. Add chicken broth, and soy sauce. Bring to a boil, cover and simmer until cauliflower is done, but still crisp. Thicken with cornstarch mixture, adding it slowly.
MAKES APPROXIMATELY 4 SERVINGS.

Fried bean curd Peking-style

CHINA

1 cup peanut oil
2 bean curds, each cut into 8 pieces
¼ cup soy sauce
2 tablespoons red-wine vinegar
1 tablespoon white vinegar
4 tablespoons chopped scallions
1½ teaspoons hot oil

Heat peanut oil to 350°F. Cook bean curds until golden brown. Mix together soy sauce, red-wine vinegar, white vinegar, scallions, and hot oil in bowl. Serve sauce with bean curds.
MAKES ABOUT 4 SERVINGS.

Mushrooms in chicken broth

CHINA

1½ cups dried mushrooms, sliced
2 cups chicken broth
1 scallion

1 ½-inch slice of fresh gingerroot
¼ cup soy sauce
1 teaspoon sugar
1 teaspoon salt
1 tablespoon cornstarch blended with small amount chicken broth
Cooked rice

Soak the mushrooms in the chicken broth for 30 minutes. Place broth and mushrooms in wok. Add scallion and ginger. Bring to boil. Cover and reduce heat. Simmer for 1 hour.
Remove scallion and ginger. Stir in soy sauce, sugar and salt. Blend cornstarch with small amount of broth and stir into mixture in wok slowly. Cook, stirring constantly, until slightly thickened. Serve this over cooked rice.
MAKES APPROXIMATELY 2 CUPS.

Delicious spinach

CHINA

1 pound fresh spinach, washed and cut into 2-inch pieces
2 tablespoons oil
Salt to taste
1 small can bamboo shoots
8 fresh mushrooms, sliced
¼ cup chicken broth

Wash and cut the spinach into pieces. Heat oil in wok or skillet. Add salt and spinach and stir-fry for 2 minutes. Add bamboo shoots, mushrooms, and chicken broth. Mix, cover and simmer for about 2 minutes, or until heated through.
MAKES 2 SERVINGS.

Stir-fry spinach

CHINA

½ pound spinach
1 tablespoon oil
1 clove garlic, crushed
½ cup chicken stock, warmed
Salt to taste
Sugar to taste
1 teaspoon soy sauce
½ teaspoon cornstarch
2 teaspoons water

535

Wash spinach and tear into bite-size pieces. Drain well and set aside.

Heat oil in skillet or wok and fry garlic until lightly browned. Discard garlic. Add spinach and stir-fry for 1 minute. Add chicken stock, salt, sugar, and soy sauce. Simmer for 2 minutes. Mix together cornstarch and water and slowly stir into spinach mixture. Simmer for 1 minute. Serve immediately.

MAKES 2 SERVINGS.

Chestnuts w/mushrooms

CHINA

2 tablespoons butter

1 pound small fresh mushrooms

18 chestnuts, scalded, skinned, simmered in water until tender

1/4 cup sherry

Salt to taste

Heat butter in skillet. Sauté mushrooms over low heat until soft. Add chestnuts; heat over high heat. Add sherry and salt; cook 1 minute.

MAKES APPROXIMATELY 4 SERVINGS.

Zucchini Chinese-style

CHINA

2 pounds zucchini, sliced in 1/4-inch slices

1/2 pound fresh mushrooms, sliced

1/4 cup oil

1 tablespoon soy sauce

1/2 cup chicken broth

2 teaspoons cornstarch mixed with 4 teaspoons cold water

Wash and slice zucchini, and set aside. Wash and slice mushrooms. Heat oil in skillet and sauté mushrooms for a few seconds. Add zucchini and stir-fry until zucchini is coated with oil. Add soy sauce and chicken broth. Bring to a boil, cover and simmer until zucchini is bright green and just tender and still crisp. Thicken with cornstarch mixture and serve immediately.

MAKES APPROXIMATELY 6 SERVINGS.

Steamed eggplant

CHINA

1 large eggplant, stem end sliced off, eggplant cut into 6 wedges

Vegetable oil

1 large scallion, cut into 2-inch pieces

2 tablespoons soy sauce

1/4 teaspoon sugar

Dash of freshly ground black pepper

Steam eggplant, covered, 30 minutes over boiling water. Remove from heat.

Coat bottom and sides of preheated wok with oil. When hot, add scallion; quick-fry few seconds. Add eggplant, soy sauce, sugar, and pepper. Cook about 3 minutes, stirring constantly.

MAKES 4 SERVINGS.

Sweet-and-sour yams & pineapple

CHINA

1 20-ounce can sliced pineapple; drain and reserve syrup

1 tablespoon cornstarch

1/4 teaspoon salt

3 tablespoons fresh lemon juice

2 1-pound cans of yams, drained

Oil

4 scallions, sliced

1 small green pepper, cut into small chunks

1/2 cup celery, sliced diagonally

Drain pineapple; reserve syrup. In saucepan, combine reserved syrup, cornstarch, and salt. Blend well. Bring to a boil over medium heat. Cook until thickened, stirring constantly. Stir in the lemon juice. Arrange pineapple and yams in casserole and pour the sauce over mixture. Bake, covered, in a 350°F oven for about 30 minutes or until hot.

In small amount of oil in skillet, sauté scallions, green pepper chunks and celery until just tender, but still crisp. Stir carefully into yam mixture. Serve immediately.

MAKES APPROXIMATELY 8 SERVINGS.

Eggplant Szechwan

CHINA

1 large eggplant, peeled, cut in half lengthwise, cut into
   2½-inch sections
Oil for deep frying
4 ounces ground pork
3 tablespoons oil
2 teaspoons hot soybean paste
2 tablespoons chopped scallions
1 tablespoon chopped fresh gingerroot
2 tablespoons chopped garlic
1 teaspoon soy sauce
1 teaspoon rice wine
1 teaspoon sugar
1 teaspoon dark vinegar
1 teaspoon cornstarch
1 teaspoon water

Deep-fry eggplant until tender. Remove; drain on paper toweling. Stir-fry pork in 3 tablespoons oil. Add soybean paste, scallions, ginger, and garlic; stir-fry 1 minute. Add eggplant, soy sauce, rice wine, sugar, and vinegar.

Mix cornstarch with water; stir into eggplant mixture until thickened.

MAKES 4 OR 5 SERVINGS.

Sweet-potato balls

CHINA

1½ pounds sweet potatoes
½ cup flour
5 tablespoons sugar
¼ teaspoon salt
1 beaten egg
Oil for deep-frying
Powdered sugar

Peel sweet potatoes and boil until very soft. Mash and remove any stringy fibers. Mix with flour, sugar, salt, and egg and form small balls. Deep-fry in oil over medium heat until lightly browned. Drain on paper toweling and sprinkle with powdered sugar.

MAKES 2½ DOZEN BALLS.

Stir-fried bok choy

CHINA

2 tablespoons peanut oil
2 cloves garlic, minced fine
1 pound bok choy, sliced diagonally
Salt to taste
Freshly ground black pepper to taste

Heat oil in wok or skillet. Add garlic. Add bok choy; stir-fry until coated with oil and heated through. Sprinkle with salt and pepper; mix thoroughly. Serve immediately.

MAKES 4 SERVINGS.

Spicy seaweed

CHINA

4 ounces seaweed strips
3 cups boiling water
1 tablespoon salt
1½ teaspoons finely chopped scallions
1 tablespoon finely chopped fresh gingerroot
1½ teaspoons finely chopped hot red pepper
½ teaspoon salt
⅓ teaspoon dark vinegar
½ teaspoon sesame oil

Place seaweed in boiling water. Add 1 tablespoon salt. When water comes to boil, remove seaweed. Rinse in cold water; drain well. Mix together remaining ingredients. Add seaweed; toss.

MAKES ABOUT 6 SERVINGS.

Grilled Brussels sprouts

JAPAN

1 pint fresh Brussels sprouts
Melted butter
Lemon juice
Paprika
Freshly ground pepper (optional)

Cook Brussels sprouts as usual. Dip them in a mixture of melted butter and lemon juice; skewer them. Sprinkle with paprika and pepper; grill or put on a hibachi for only 2 or 3 minutes, or until browned.

MAKES 4 SERVINGS.

Sweet-potato & banana casserole

CHINA

4 medium sweet potatoes
4 tablespoons butter
1½ teaspoons salt
4 bananas, sliced
¾ cup brown sugar
¾ cup orange juice

Cook the sweet potatoes in boiling water until tender but still firm. Cool. Peel and slice ¼ inch thick. Place in buttered casserole in alternate layers, dotted with butter and sprinkled with salt, with bananas sprinkled with brown sugar. End the top layer with bananas, dotted with butter. Add orange juice. Bake in a 350°F oven for about 30 minutes, or until the top is browned.
MAKES 6 SERVINGS.

Japanese pickles

JAPAN

2 large cucumbers
⅛ cup soy sauce
¼ cup vinegar
¼ cup sugar

Peel cucumbers; slice them very thin. Mix together soy sauce, vinegar, and sugar. Pour this over the cucumber slices; mix well, gently. Refrigerate for at least 2 hours before serving.
MAKES APPROXIMATELY 4 SERVINGS.

Boiled pumpkin w/soy sauce

JAPAN

2-pound pumpkin
Pinch sugar
Soy sauce
Sherry

Cut pumpkin in half; take out seeds and fibers. Cut pumpkin meat into bite-size pieces; boil until tender. When cooked, mash until smooth; add pinch of sugar and soy sauce and sherry to taste.
MAKES 4 SERVINGS.

Cabbage w/sesame seeds

JAPAN

1 head cabbage
1 tablespoon sesame seeds, toasted
Soy sauce
Sugar
Pepper

Shred cabbage. Place in pot with small amount of water; cook until just tender. Drain well. Toss with sesame seeds, soy sauce to taste, pinch of sugar, and pepper to taste.
MAKES APPROXIMATELY 4 SERVINGS.

Fried eggplant

JAPAN

1 medium eggplant
2 eggs, beaten
Bread or cracker crumbs
Oil for frying
Soy sauce

Peel eggplant; cut it into "french-fry" size pieces. Dip pieces of eggplant in beaten egg, then into bread or cracker crumbs. Fry in oil over medium heat, in single layer, until brown. Drain on paper towels.
Serve eggplant hot with soy sauce for dipping. This can be served as an appetizer (serves 4) or as a side dish (serves 2).
MAKES 2 TO 4 SERVINGS.

Grilled eggplant

JAPAN

1 eggplant
Salt
Butter, melted, or olive oil

Peel and cube eggplant. Sprinkle thoroughly with salt; let stand about 45 minutes. Rinse, drain, and pat dry. Put eggplant cubes on skewer; brush with either melted butter or olive oil. Grill, or cook on hibachi, for about 5 minutes.
MAKES APPROXIMATELY 4 SERVINGS.

Baked Chinese cabbage

Pickled eggplant

JAPAN

1 large eggplant
Salt
4 tablespoons oil
4 tablespoons soy sauce
4 tablespoons sugar
4 tablespoons vinegar

Peel eggplant; slice it thin. Salt it lightly; let stand 20 minutes. Drain thoroughly. Combine oil, soy sauce, sugar, and vinegar in a saucepan; heat to boiling. Pour over eggplant; refrigerate for at least 3 hours before serving.

This can be served as an appetizer (serves 8) or as a side dish (serves 4). Serve it cold.

MAKES 4 TO 8 SERVINGS.

Stuffed eggplant

JAPAN

6 eggplants, small size

stuffing
½ onion, chopped
Oil, butter, or margarine
8 ounces ground chicken (approximately 2 cups)
½ to ¾ cup bread crumbs
½ teaspoon salt
1 tablespoon water (a little more, if necessary)
4 tablespoons grated cheese

Cornstarch
Oil for frying
Grated gingerroot
Soy sauce for dipping

Remove stem part of eggplants. Make a cut lengthwise in half, but not all the way through. Soak eggplants in salted water.

Sauté onion in a small amount of oil, butter, or margarine just until soft. Combine with chicken, bread crumbs, salt, and water. Gently mix in cheese. Divide into 6 parts.

Wipe eggplants dry. Sprinkle cut surfaces with cornstarch. Place a layer of meat mixture inside eggplant. Sprinkle a small amount of cornstarch on meat. Heat oil in deep-frying pan; cook over medium heat until meat is well-done. Serve with grated ginger and soy sauce.

MAKES 4 TO 6 SERVINGS.

Cauliflower w/water chestnuts & mushrooms

JAPAN

1 small cauliflower
2 tablespoons oil
8 mushrooms, sliced
1 cup hot chicken broth
¼ cup sliced water chestnuts
2 tablespoons soy sauce
Salt to taste
1 tablespoon cornstarch mixed with cold water

Trim and wash cauliflower. Break into florets. If florets are large, slice them. Heat oil in pan; gently sauté cauliflower. Add sliced mushrooms; sauté for about 30 seconds. Add chicken broth, sliced water chestnuts, soy sauce, and seasonings.

539

Bring mixture to a boil, cover, and simmer until cauliflower is just tender, i.e. still crunchy.

Mix cornstarch with enough cold water to make a smooth paste; slowly add to cauliflower mixture, stirring constantly until thickened.

MAKES 4 SERVINGS.

Vinegar turnips

JAPAN

Turnips, about 2 pounds
1 cup sugar
1/3 cup of vinegar
1 cup water
3 tablespoons salt

Peel turnips; slice them very thin. Put into a bowl or, preferably, a crock. Combine sugar, vinegar, water, and salt in saucepan; bring to a boil. Pour the mixture over the sliced turnips; mix gently, but thoroughly. Cover; refrigerate for 5 days.

Refried beans

MEXICO

1 pound pinto beans
1/2 pound lean bacon (plus bacon grease)
1 medium onion, chopped
1 clove garlic, chopped (or 1 teaspoon garlic salt)
Shredded cheese for topping (optional)

Soak beans overnight. Next day simmer beans 2 to 3 hours, until beans are soft, adding water as

Sweet-and-sour yams and pineapple

necessary to keep beans from boiling dry. Drain, saving liquid. Mash beans with potato masher or mixer.

Dice and fry bacon, onion, and garlic. Add mashed beans; fry until everything is well-mixed. If additional liquid is necessary, add some of liquid drained from beans. Serve beans hot. Top with shredded cheese if desired.

MAKES 3 TO 4 CUPS BEANS.

Beans in savory sauce

MEXICO

1 pound black beans (frijoles negroes)
Water
2 teaspoons salt

savory sauce
2 tablespoons lard or olive oil
1/2 cup chopped onion
1 clove garlic, minced
2 pickled jalapeño peppers, seeded and finely chopped
   (Jalapeños en Escabeche)
1 large tomato, peeled, seeded, and chopped
1 teaspoon crushed marjoram
1 teaspoon crushed oregano
Salt and pepper to taste

Chopped onions for topping

Wash and pick over beans. Place in large saucepan; cover with water. Add salt; cook over low heat, replenishing water so that beans are always just covered. Cook at least 4 hours or until beans are very tender and mixture is thick.

Heat lard or oil in small skillet over moderate

heat. Add onion and garlic; sauté until limp. Add peppers, tomato, herbs, and seasonings; reduce heat to simmer. Cook for 20 minutes. Add 1 cup beans and liquid to sauce. Mash well. Add this mixture to pot of beans; cook 20 minutes more.

Serve beans hot in bowls; top with chopped onions.

MAKES 6 SERVINGS.

Note: If you have a slow cooker, the beans can be cooked in it all day. Be sure to add water occasionally so that they don't boil dry.

Refried black beans

MEXICO

¼ pound bulk chorizo sausage
¼ pound lard
1 recipe Beans in Savory Sauce (see Index)
½ cup Queso Blanco (or Jack cheese)
½ cup chopped onion

Fry chorizo in large, heavy skillet until lightly browned. Add lard; melt it. Add beans slowly (a cup at a time) while mashing with potato masher to form a thick paste. Fry over low heat, stirring and mashing occasionally, until thick and crusty. Top with cheese; melt cheese.

Roll beans onto a platter and top with onion. Serve with tortillas or tostadas.

MAKES 6 SERVINGS.

Beans & corn

MEXICO

½ pound black beans
4 cups cold water
1 onion, peeled and chopped
¼ pound salt pork, diced
1 teaspoon salt
1 16½-ounce can whole-kernel corn, drained
1 sprig fresh mint (optional)
Several dashes Tabasco

Wash beans; pick over well. Soak beans overnight in 4 cups cold water.

The following day add water to cover beans, if necessary. Add onion, salt pork, and salt to beans. Bring to a boil, reduce heat to low, and cook until beans are tender. Add corn and mint. Add Tabasco to taste; heat through.

MAKES 6 SERVINGS.

Green beans w/lime juice

MEXICO

2½ cups fresh or frozen green beans, cut into ¾-inch lengths
2 tablespoons butter
2 tablespoons parsley
½ teaspoon salt
¼ teaspoon pepper
1 tablespoon lime juice

Cook beans in boiling salted water until tender. Drain well. Melt butter in heavy skillet. Add beans, parsley, salt, and pepper. Cook, stirring constantly, for 5 minutes. Add lime juice. Mix well; serve immediately.

MAKES 4 SERVINGS.

Banana squash w/brown sugar

MEXICO

3 pounds banana squash or pumpkin
¼ cup brown sugar
3 tablespoons butter
½ teaspoon cinnamon

Pare squash or pumpkin; cut into 2-inch cubes. Cook in boiling salted water until tender. Drain well. Add brown sugar, butter, and cinnamon. Cook over low heat until butter melts and sugar softens. Stir to combine well. Serve squash hot.

MAKES 4 SERVINGS.

Baked summer squash w/cheese

MEXICO

1 pound (2 medium) summer squash
2 California green chilies, seeded and chopped
1½ cups grated Jack cheese
2 eggs, beaten
1 small can evaporated milk (5⅓ ounces)
Salt and pepper to taste
Paprika

1 tablespoon butter or margarine
2 tablespoons chopped onion

Slice summer squash in ½-inch slices. Parboil in boiling salted water until just tender. Drain. Grease a 2-quart casserole. Place squash, chilies, and grated Jack cheese into casserole; toss gently to combine well. Beat eggs, milk, salt, and pepper together. Pour over squash. Sprinkle with paprika.

Melt butter in small skillet; sauté onion until limp. Sprinkle onion and butter on top of casserole. Bake at 350°F for 40 minutes or until set. MAKES 4 SERVINGS.

Mexican corn

MEXICO

2 tablespoons vegetable oil
½ cup chopped green pepper
¼ cup chopped red pepper
½ fresh hot pepper, finely minced
1 16½-ounce can whole-kernel corn, drained
½ cup chopped well-drained canned tomatoes
½ teaspoon salt
¼ teaspoon pepper

Heat oil in medium saucepan. Sauté the peppers over medium heat 5 minutes. Add corn, tomatoes, salt, and pepper; heat through. Serve corn hot. MAKES 4 SERVINGS.

Fried spinach & onions

MEXICO

4 tablespoons bacon drippings or lard
1 large onion, sliced (1 cup)
1½ pounds fresh spinach leaves, washed, trimmed, and
  stems removed
Salt and pepper to taste
⅛ teaspoon finely crushed dried red chilies (optional)

Melt lard or bacon drippings in large, heavy kettle over medium-high heat. Add onion; fry, stirring frequently, until lightly browned. Add spinach; cook, tossing constantly, 3 to 5 minutes, until wilted and coated with drippings. Season with salt, pepper, and powdered chilies to taste. MAKES 4 SERVINGS.

Zucchini w/corn & peppers

MEXICO

2½ pounds zucchini
3 ears corn on the cob
1 medium green or red pepper, chopped
1 medium onion, chopped
2 cloves garlic, minced or pressed
3 tablespoons bacon drippings or melted butter
Salt and pepper to taste

Scrub zucchini and dice into bite-size pieces. Cut corn off cob. Combine zucchini, corn, pepper, onion, and garlic in frypan with butter. Cook, stirring often, until vegetables are tender-crisp, about 5 minutes. Add salt and pepper to taste. Serve hot. MAKES 8 TO 10 SERVINGS.

Zucchini fritters

MEXICO

¾ cup all-purpose flour, sifted
¾ teaspoon baking powder
½ teaspoon salt
1 cup grated zucchini squash
1 egg, slightly beaten
2 tablespoons milk

Sift together flour, baking powder, and salt. In mixing bowl toss together flour mixture and grated zucchini. Beat together egg and milk. Stir egg mixture into flour mixture.

Meanwhile, in deep fryer heat oil at least 1-inch deep to 360°F. Fry heaping tablespoons of batter until golden brown, turning occasionally. Drain on paper towels. Serve fritters hot. MAKES 3 TO 4 SERVINGS (9 FRITTERS).

❧ Sauces and Stocks ❧

Sauce vinaigrette

FRANCE

Excellent on salads or for marinades. With capers added, this sauce is particularly good on boiled chicken, fish, or vegetables.

½ cup fresh chopped herbs (chervil, tarragon, parsley, chives)
1 teaspoon capers (optional)
6 tablespoons vegetable oil
2 tablespoons white wine vinegar
½ teaspoon salt
⅛ teaspoon white pepper
Pinch of sugar

Mince herbs and capers until very fine. Blend oil with vinegar, salt, pepper, and sugar. Stir in herbs and capers. Store for several hours to age.
MAKES ABOUT ¼ CUP.

Basic beef stock

FRANCE

3 pounds beef bones
2 pounds lean beef
4 quarts water
4 green onions with tops
1 large onion, studded with 10 cloves
1 celery stalk and leaves
2 carrots

Place bones and beef in large baking pan. Bake at 400°F about an hour. Remove from pan; place in large pot.
Pour off fat from baking pan. Add ½ cup water to pan; scrape up brown particles from pan bottom. Pour into pot. Add remaining ingredients. Slowly bring to a boil. Skim off the impurities which collect on the top of the liquid. Partially cover; simmer for 3 to 4 hours.
Remove meat and vegetables. Strain stock through wet cheesecloth. Chill. Remove fat before using.
MAKES ABOUT 2 QUARTS.
Note: To make chicken stock, substitute 2 medium fryers for bones and meat.

Basic brown sauce

FRANCE

2 onions, diced
2 carrots, diced
4 tablespoons butter
¼ cup flour
2 cups beef bouillon or basic beef stock
2 cups water
1 clove garlic, minced
2 sprigs parsley
1 bay leaf
⅛ teaspoon thyme
1 tablespoon tomato paste
¼ teaspoon salt
⅛ teaspoon pepper
1 tablespoon Madeira
2 tablespoons cognac

Sauté onions and carrots in butter for 20 minutes. Add sugar; increase heat to brown vegetables. Cook about 10 minutes, stirring very often. Do not let vegetables burn. Stir in flour; cook about 3 minutes. Add bouillon, water, garlic, parsley, bay leaf, thyme, tomato paste, salt, and pepper. Bring to a boil while stirring. Reduce heat; partially cover; simmer about 1¼ hours.
Strain sauce into clean pan; discard vegetables. After cooling, sauce may be frozen at this point. Just before serving, add Madeira and cognac.
MAKES 2 CUPS.

Bearnaise sauce

FRANCE

¼ cup white vinegar
¼ cup dry white wine
1 tablespoon minced green onion
1 teaspoon dried tarragon
3 peppercorns
3 egg yolks
1 tablespoon warm water
½ cup butter
¼ teaspoon salt

Boil vinegar, wine, onion, tarragon, and peppercorns in small saucepan until liquid has reduced to 2 tablespoons. Pour liquid through fine sieve. In top of double boiler, over just simmering water, blend egg yolks and warm water until creamy. Bottom of double boiler should not touch water.

Melt butter over low heat; add by ½ teaspoons to yolk mixture, beating well with a wire whip after each addition. (Set bottom of pan in a cold-water bath if eggs start to look like scrambled eggs.) After some butter has been added, up to 1 teaspoon of butter can be added at one time. Leave the white residue in bottom of butter pan. After butter is added, stir in vinegar mixture and salt.

MAKES ABOUT ¼ CUP.

Hollandaise sauce (blender method)

FRANCE

3 egg yolks
2 tablespoons lemon juice
¼ teaspoon salt
⅛ teaspoon white pepper
½ cup butter

Place egg yolks, lemon juice, salt, and pepper in blender. Carefully melt butter in small pan; heat to foaming. Blend yolk mixture at top speed 3 seconds. Remove center of cover. Pour in hot butter *by droplets* at first, then in a thin stream. Omit the milky residue at bottom of pan. Adjust seasonings, if desired.

Set jar in lukewarm water until ready to use. Reheating usually causes curdling, so prepare close to serving time.

MAKES ¼ CUP.

Basic aspic

FRANCE

1 envelope unflavored gelatin
1¼ cups cold water
1 cup canned beef bouillon
1 tablespoon lemon juice
1 tablespoon port
1 tablespoon cognac

Soften gelatin in ¼ cup cold water. Combine bouillon and 1 cup cold water in small saucepan; bring to a boil. Add softened gelatin; stir until

dissolved. Remove from heat. Stir in lemon juice, port, and cognac. Use aspic for congealed molds or glazes.

MAKES 2 CUPS.

Bearnaise sauce—blender method

FRANCE

¼ cup white vinegar
¼ cup dry white wine or vermouth
1 tablespoon minced green onion
1 teaspoon dried tarragon
¼ teaspoon salt
⅛ teaspoon white pepper
½ cup butter
3 egg yolks

Boil vinegar, wine, herbs, and seasonings in small saucepan until liquid has reduced to about 2 tablespoons. Let cool. In another pan melt butter over low heat.

Strain vinegar mixture. Place vinegar liquid and egg yolks in blender jar. Cover; blend at high speed about 5 seconds. Remove center of cover; pour in butter *by droplets*. When ⅔ of butter has been blended, butter can be added more quickly. Set jar in lukewarm water until ready to use. Do not reheat, as sauce will curdle.

This sauce is also very good served cold. It may be prepared ahead and refrigerated.

MAKES ABOUT 1 CUP.

Basic white sauce (Béchamel Sauce)

FRANCE

3 tablespoons butter
3 tablespoons flour
2 cups milk
¾ teaspoon salt
¼ teaspoon white pepper

Melt the butter in top of a double boiler over boiling water; stir in the flour with a wooden spoon until smooth. Add the milk gradually, stirring constantly; cook until sauce is thick. Stir in salt and pepper. Remove top of double boiler from water.

Strain sauce through a fine sieve; use as desired. Pour any remaining sauce into a small bowl. Cover top of sauce with a circle of wet waxed paper; refrigerate for future use.

MAKES 2 CUPS.

Basic velouté sauce

FRANCE

¼ cup butter
½ cup flour
6 cups clarified Basic Chicken Stock
¼ cup sauterne

Melt the butter in medium saucepan; blend in the flour gradually. Cook and stir for several minutes until smooth. Add stock gradually, stirring until smooth. Simmer over medium heat for about 1 hour, stirring frequently until reduced by ⅓. Sauce should be consistency of heavy cream. Add sauterne. Strain through a fine sieve.

Basic chicken stock

FRANCE

1 4-pound hen
1 pound chicken wings
2 tablespoons salt
4 peppercorns
5 quarts water
½ bay leaf
Pinch of thyme
6 green onions with tops
4 large carrots, quartered
2 stalks celery with leaves, cut in 2-in pieces
1 large onion, studded with 3 cloves

Place the chicken, salt, peppercorns and water in a stock pot. Bring to a boil over medium heat, removing scum from the surface. Cover the pot and reduce the heat. Simmer for 1 hour, skimming frequently.

Add remaining ingredients; cover and cook for about 2 hours and 30 minutes. Skim off fat; season to taste with additional salt and pepper.

Remove chicken and vegetables from stock.

Strain stock through wet muslin. Chill and remove fat before using.

Basic mornay sauce

FRANCE

1 recipe Basic White Sauce (see Index)
2 tablespoons butter
1 cup grated Parmesan cheese

Prepare Basic White Sauce and remove from heat. Cut the butter into small pieces. Stir the Parmesan cheese and butter into white sauce, beating with wooden spoon until butter is melted. The amount of salt in white sauce may be decreased if desired, because Parmesan cheese sometimes imparts a salty flavor.

Sauce thickener (beurre manié)

FRANCE

For 10 tablespoons:
8 tablespoons butter, softened
8 tablespoons flour

For 1 tablespoon:
1 tablespoon butter, softened
1 tablespoon flour

Cream butter and flour. Add 1 tablespoon of mixture to thicken about ¾ cup liquid. Stir in beurre manié; bring sauce to boiling point.

This mixture freezes well and is most convenient if placed in an ice-cube tray by tablespoons. Freeze, then transfer to a plastic bag. Add frozen paste directly to sauce.

Basic mayonnaise

FRANCE

4 medium egg yolks
1 teaspoon salt
⅛ teaspoon white pepper
2 cups vegetable oil
1 tablespoon wine vinegar

Place the egg yolks, salt, and pepper in a medium bowl. Beat with electric hand-mixer at medium speed until thick, pale, and fluffy. Add 5 ounces oil in very thin stream, beating constantly, until thickened and oil is absorbed. Beat in the vinegar. Add the remaining oil slowly, beating constantly, until all the oil is blended into the mixture. Mayonnaise will be very thick. Place in refrigerator container. Cut waxed paper to fit over top; rinse in cold water. Place over mayonnaise; cover and refrigerate until ready to use.
MAKES 1¼ CUPS.

Mushroom sauce

FRANCE

¼ cup butter
1½ cups chopped mushrooms
¼ cup flour
1¼ cups milk
½ cup white wine
¼ teaspoon salt
3 tablespoons lemon juice
2 egg yolks
1 can shrimp, rinsed and drained (optional)

Melt butter. Cook mushrooms until liquid has evaporated. Stir in flour. Add milk and wine. Cook over medium heat, stirring constantly, until thickened. Add salt and lemon juice.
Add small amount of hot sauce to egg yolks, then add egg yolks to sauce, stirring constantly. Heat gently. Stir in shrimp, if desired. Use sauce with salmon loaf, poached fish, or soufflés.
MAKES 2 CUPS.

Tuna sauce for spaghetti

ITALY

6 tablespoons butter
6 tablespoons olive oil
2 (7-ounce) cans tuna packed in olive oil
⅓ cup chopped parsley
2 tablespoons chopped capers
2 tablespoons lemon juice
¼ cup chicken broth
Salt and pepper

Heat butter and oil over moderate heat in heavy skillet. Meanwhile, drain tuna; finely chop. When butter has melted, add tuna, parsley, and capers to skillet. Heat through, stirring occasionally. Stir in lemon juice, broth, salt, and pepper. Cook 1 pound spaghetti or your favorite pasta al dente. Drain well. Place in large heated bowl. Add sauce; toss gently. Serve immediately.
MAKES 4 SERVINGS.

Green sauce

ITALY

1 (1½-inch) cube Italian bread
1½ tablespoons white wine vinegar
2 anchovy fillets
1½ tablespoons olive oil
2 hard-boiled egg yolks
½ cup finely minced parsley
¼ cup chopped scallions
Salt and pepper

Soak bread cube in vinegar in small bowl. Mash anchovy fillets with olive oil. Add to bread; mash together thoroughly. Mash in egg yolks. Add parsley and scallions; stir to combine. Season with salt and pepper.
MAKES ⅔ CUP.

Meat sauce for spaghetti

ITALY

¼ cup olive oil
1 medium onion, finely chopped
2 cloves garlic, peeled, minced
¾ pound lean ground beef
½ pound bulk Italian sausage (sweet or hot)
1 (28-ounce) can Italian-style plum tomatoes (sieved or
    blenderized)
1 (6-ounce) can tomato paste
1 (6-ounce) can water
½ cup dry red wine
1 teaspoon crumbled mixed Italian herbs
1 teaspoon sugar
⅛ teaspoon crushed red pepper
Salt and pepper

Heat oil in large heavy saucepan. Add onion and garlic; sauté until tender. Add beef and sausage.

546

Sauce vinaigrette

Cook, breaking into small chunks, until lightly browned. Drain well.

Add remaining ingredients; mix well. Bring to boil, reduce heat to simmer. Cook partially covered 2 hours, until thick. Serve over hot cooked spaghetti or macaroni.

MAKES 4 SERVINGS.

Garlic sauce

GREECE

2 medium potatoes
4 cloves of garlic, chopped
½ teaspoon salt
1 egg yolk
Juice of 1 lemon
2 tablespoons white wine vinegar
½ cup olive oil

Boil the potatoes in their jackets. Cool, peel, and mash them. Place the potatoes, garlic, salt, egg yolk, lemon juice, and vinegar in the blender. Blend until smooth. Very slowly add the oil while blending. Chill until ready to serve and thin, if desired, with stock.

MAKES 1½ CUPS

Egg & lemon sauce

GREECE

1 cup broth
1 tablespoon cornstarch
1 tablespoon water
3 eggs, separated
¼ cup lemon juice

Use the stock in which the meat, poultry, or vegetables was cooked, or use canned chicken broth. Heat the broth to boiling and thicken with a mixture of the cornstarch and water.

Beat the egg whites until stiff. Add the egg yolks and continue beating. Add the lemon juice slowly while beating. Slowly beat in ½ cup of the chicken broth.

Return the egg mixture to the pot with the rest of the broth, mixing thoroughly. Cook over very low heat until the mixture thickens. Do not boil. Be sure to stir constantly (a wire whisk would be ideal for this purpose) or the mixture will curdle. Serve with meat, fish, vegetables, or poultry or use to thicken fish or vegetable dishes.

MAKES 2 CUPS.

Garlic mayonnaise

SPAIN

1 egg
½ teaspoon salt
¼ teaspoon pressed garlic
Dash of cayenne pepper
1 cup olive oil
3 tablespoons fresh-squeezed lemon juice

Combine egg, salt, garlic, and ¼ cup oil in blender container. Blend thoroughly. With the blender running, very slowly add ½ cup oil. Gradually add lemon juice and remaining ¼ cup oil. Blend until thick. Occasionally scrape sides of bowl.

MAKES ABOUT 1 CUP.

Chilindron sauce

SPAIN

¼ cup olive oil
1 garlic clove, chopped
1 onion, sliced into rings
1 green pepper, seeded, cut into strips
1 red pepper, seeded, cut into strips
Pinch of saffron
1 teaspoon salt
1 teaspoon paprika
Dash of cayenne*
1 cup diced Italian or other smoked ham
1 tablespoon tomato paste
1½ cups tomato sauce

Heat oil in skillet. Add garlic; fry 10 minutes. Add onion and peppers; sauté until tender. Add remaining ingredients; bring to boil. Reduce heat; simmer 15 minutes. Use as sauce for chicken, rabbit, or lamb.

MAKES ABOUT 2 CUPS.

* If hotter sauce is desired, use more cayenne.

Mild almond & pepper sauce

SPAIN

1 cup Garlic Mayonnaise (see Index)
1 tablespoon lemon juice
2 tablespoons ground almonds
1 small tomato, peeled, seeded, chopped fine
Dash of cayenne*
¾ teaspoon anchovy paste

Combine ingredients in mixing bowl; mix well.
Store in small covered jar in refrigerator.
MAKES 1¼ CUPS.

*For hot sauce, add 1 to 2 teaspoons cayenne.

Chinese sweet-and-sour sauce

CHINA

Serve this with chicken, beef, pork, or seafood.

4 tablespoons catsup
¼ cup brown sugar
2 tablespoons soy sauce
3 tablespoons wine vinegar
2 tablespoons dry white wine
2 tablespoons cornstarch dissolved in ½ cup cold water

Combine catsup, sugar, soy sauce, vinegar, and
wine in saucepan. Bring to a boil. Add the cornstarch dissolved in water to the sauce. Cook over
low heat, stirring constantly, until sauce has
thickened.
MAKES ABOUT 1¼ CUPS SAUCE.

Sweet-and-sour plum sauce

CHINA

½ cup water
1 cup plum jelly
2 tablespoons catsup
2 tablespoons vinegar

Place ingredients in saucepan and stir. Bring to
boil. Serve warm.
MAKES APPROXIMATELY 1½ CUPS SAUCE.

Meat sauce for spaghetti

Red chili sauce

MEXICO

5 dried Ancho chilies
1 cup boiling water
1 teaspoon crushed red chili peppers
1 cup cut-up drained canned Italian plum tomatoes
½ cup chopped onion
1 clove garlic, minced
¼ cup olive oil
1 teaspoon sugar
½ teaspoon salt
⅛ teaspoon pepper
1 tablespoon red wine vinegar

Under cold running water, remove the stems
from the Ancho chilies. Tear each in half; remove seeds and thick veins. Tear into pieces;
place into small mixing bowl. Pour boiling water
over chilies; let stand 30 minutes. Drain chilies,
reserving ¼ cup liquid.
Combine chilies, reserved liquid, crushed chili,
tomatoes, onion, and garlic in blender jar. Puree
until smooth.
Heat oil in small skillet. Add puree; cook uncovered 5 minutes. Add sugar, salt, and pepper. Remove from heat; add vinegar. Serve sauce warm.
MAKES 2 CUPS.

549

Desserts

Floating island

FRANCE

3 eggs, separated
Dash salt
¾ cup sugar
2 cups milk
1 tablespoon cornstarch
1 teaspoon vanilla

Beat egg whites with salt in small (1½-quart) bowl until foamy. Gradually add ½ cup sugar, 1 tablespoon at a time. Continue beating until sugar is dissolved and whites form very stiff peaks.

Pour milk into large frying pan; heat to very warm. Make snowballs (or egg shapes) from meringue, using 2 spoons. Drop each snowball into hot milk. Poach for 2 minutes on one side, turn gently, and poach for 2 minutes more. It's important that milk not boil, or an off-flavor will develop. When snowballs are done, remove from milk; drain on paper towels.

Beat egg yolks until lemon-colored. Beat in remaining ¼ cup sugar and cornstarch. Beat until well-blended. Add hot milk to egg yolks, beating constantly. Pour mixture into 1-quart saucepan; cook over medium heat until custard thickens. Add vanilla; strain, if desired. Cool.

Spoon custard into large serving dish or individual dishes. Float snowballs on top. Serve chilled.
MAKES 4 SERVINGS.

Pears in chocolate sauce

FRANCE

1 large can pear halves (29-ounce)

chocolate sauce
8 ounces semisweet chocolate
2 tablespoons hot water
1 tablespoon butter
1 egg yolk
½ cup heavy cream
1 egg white

Pears in chocolate sauce

Drain pear halves; arrange in 6 individual serving dishes.

Place chocolate in top of double boiler. Stir in hot water; melt chocolate over boiling water. Remove from heat. Stir in butter until melted. Add egg yolk and heavy cream. Beat egg white until stiff peaks form; fold into Chocolate Sauce. Spoon Chocolate Sauce over pears. Serve immediately.

MAKES 6 SERVINGS.

Pastry cream

FRANCE

⅔ cup sugar
3 egg yolks
⅓ cup flour
1½ cups boiling milk
1 tablespoon butter
⅓ cup ground almonds (optional)
¼ teaspoon almond extract (optional)
1 teaspoon vanilla

In small bowl beat sugar and egg yolks until mixture forms a ribbon on the surface. Gradually beat in flour; beat until smooth. Slowly add hot milk, beating constantly. Pour mixture into 1-quart saucepan; cook over low heat until mixture thickens, stirring constantly. Add butter, almonds, and extracts.

Cool Pastry Cream. Use for tarts or other desserts. Keeps several days, but must be refrigerated.

MAKES 2 CUPS.

Sweet pastry dough

FRANCE

2 cups flour
2 tablespoons sugar
¼ teaspoon salt
¾ cup unsalted butter
1 egg yolk
4 tablespoons cold water

Mix flour, sugar, and salt. Cut in butter until coarse crumbs form. Add egg yolk and water; gently mix to form a dough. Wrap in waxed paper; chill dough 1 hour. Divide dough in half. Roll out each half ¼ inch thick and 2 inches larger than the pie or tart pan. Gently ease the dough into pan, pressing the dough to the sides. Prick the bottom well with a fork.

Trim off excess dough with a sharp knife. Chill 1 hour before baking. Bake in preheated 425°F oven 10 to 15 minutes, until golden brown.

MAKES CRUST FOR 2 9-INCH SHELLS.

Note: For savory tarts, do not put in sugar.

Puff pastry

FRANCE

4 sticks (1 pound) unsweetened butter
4 cups all-purpose flour
2 tablespoons cornstarch
1 teaspoon salt
1 tablespoon lemon juice
1¼ cups cold water

Cut each stick of butter into 3 lengthwise strips. Place all 12 strips on waxed paper, side by side, to form a rectangle. With rolling pin, shape into 6 × 12-inch rectangle. Refrigerate butter until ready to use.

Mix flour, cornstarch, and salt in mixing bowl. Add lemon juice to water. Add liquid to flour. Knead gently several minutes to form a dough. Wrap dough in plastic wrap and refrigerate. Let rest ½ hour.

Pat or roll dough, on lightly floured board, into 18 × 6-inch rectangle. Place chilled butter over upper ⅔ of dough, spreading it to within ½ inch of edges. Dough will be rough-looking. The lower third is unbuttered. Fold bottom ⅓ up to middle; fold top ⅓ down to cover it. Turn dough so top flap is at the right. Roll dough to a 16 × 6-inch rectangle. Fold top and bottom to the middle, then fold all dough in half. This completes the second turn. The dough will look smooth. Traditionally, the dough is marked with 2 depressions made with the fingertips. Refrigerate dough 30 to 60 minutes.

Repeat above procedure, making 2 more turns. Mark dough with 4 fingers. You may use dough now or repeat, making 6 or 8 turns. However, before shaping, chill dough 2 hours.

The dough may be used for Napoleons, Cream Horns, or patty shells. It can also be used for appetizers. The dough can be stored in refrigerator several days, or frozen up to 1 year.
MAKES 2½ POUNDS DOUGH.

Note: After chilling dough, it may be necessary to beat dough with rolling pin to soften the butter and aid rolling.

Molded ice cream

FRANCE

1 quart coffee ice cream, softened
¾ cup chopped nuts
1 quart chocolate ice cream, softened
1 pint vanilla ice cream, softened
2 tablespoons brandy
2 ounces unsweetened chocolate, melted and cooled
¼ cup light corn syrup
1 egg

Line 2-2½ quart bowl or mold with heavy-duty aluminum foil. Blend coffee ice cream with ½ cup nuts. Line mold with coffee ice cream. Freeze until firm (about 1 hour).

Use softened chocolate ice cream to form second layer, leaving a deep hole in center. Freeze until firm. Blend vanilla ice cream and brandy. Fill hole; smooth bottom of mold. Freeze several hours. Turn out ice cream onto cold tray. Carefully remove foil; return to freezer.

Combine chocolate, corn syrup, and egg; beat for 4 minutes. Working quickly, spread frosting over molded ice cream. Garnish with remaining ¼ cup nuts. Slice to serve.
MAKES 8 to 12 SERVINGS.

Baked caramel custard

FRANCE

1 cup sugar
¼ cup water
1 4- to-6-cup metal mold

4 eggs
2 egg yolks
2½ cups milk, hot
Dash of salt
1 teaspoon vanilla

Put ½ cup sugar and ¼ cup water into mold. Heat until sugar caramelizes and turns dark brown. Immediately dip mold into pan of cold water for 2 to 3 seconds to cool. Tilt pan so that mixture films bottom and sides of mold with caramel.

Combine eggs, yolks, and ½ cup sugar in medium-size bowl. Beat until well-mixed and foamy. Stir in 1¼ cups hot milk; mix well. Add remaining milk, salt, and vanilla; stir well. Strain sauce through sieve to remove any coagulated egg. Pour into mold. Skim off foam on top. Preheat oven to 325°F.

Set mold in larger pan. Pour boiling water around mold to come halfway up its sides. Place on lowest rack of oven. Bake custard 45 minutes or until center is firm. Cool, then refrigerate custard.

When ready to unmold, run a knife around edge; set in lukewarm water 1 to 2 minutes. Place serving plate upside down over mold; quickly invert.
MAKES 4 SERVINGS.

Pear tart w/almond cream

FRANCE

½ recipe Sweet Pastry Dough (see Index)
½ recipe Pastry Cream (see Index)
½ cup sugar
1 cup water
4 ripe pears, peeled and sliced
¼ cup apricot preserves

Roll pastry ¼ inch thick; fit into tart shell with removable bottom or into 9-inch pie pan. Bake in preheated 425°F oven 5 minutes. Cool. When cool, spread with Pastry Cream.

Dissolve sugar and water in 1-quart saucepan. Gently poach pears 3 to 4 minutes, until tender. Remove pears from syrup. Arrange in rows over Pastry Cream.

Heat preserves; press through sieve. Spread glaze

thinly over pears. Bake tart 5 to 8 minutes more at 425°F. Serve at room temperature or chilled. MAKES 8 SERVINGS.

Strawberry tarts

FRANCE

1 recipe Sweet Pastry Dough (see Index)
6 egg yolks
½ cup sugar
½ cup flour
2 cups whole milk
2 tablespoons butter
1 tablespoon vanilla
1 cup apricot jam or jelly
2 tablespoons sugar
1 pint strawberries

Make pastry; chill 1 hour and roll out. Cut in circles 1 inch larger than the tart pans. Line the pans with the dough. Cover with waxpaper and fill with uncooked beans or rice. Bake 6 minutes at 400°F. Remove the paper and beans or rice. Continue baking for 6 minutes or until lightly browned. Reserve the beans and rice for future use. To make cream, place yolks in heavy-bottomed saucepan; beat in ½ cup sugar with wire whip. Continue beating about 2 minutes. Beat in flour, then hot milk in a thin stream. Place pan over moderate heat; stir slowly and continuously with whip until mixture thickens. As it becomes lumpy, beat vigorously to smooth it out. Lower heat; continue cooking for several minutes to thicken the cream. Prevent scorching cream in bottom of pan by stirring and not using high heat. Remove from heat; beat in butter and vanilla. Cover; chill.

Prepare glaze by boiling jam or jelly with 2 table-spoons sugar several minutes, until drops falling from spoon are thick and sticky (228°F). Place pan in hot water until ready to use.

Spread a layer of cream about ½ inch deep in shells. Arrange fresh, hulled strawberries, stem-ends-down, in shell over cream. Spoon warm glaze over strawberries. Chill until ready to serve. Best if served within an hour.

MAKES 8 TO 10, DEPENDING ON SIZE OF TART MOLDS.

Cream horns

FRANCE

½ recipe Puff Pastry (see Index), chilled
1 egg white
1 tablespoon water
Granulated sugar
1 recipe Pastry Cream (see Index)
½ cup heavy cream, whipped (optional)
Ground pistachio nuts and powdered sugar for garnish
  (optional)

Roll pastry into a 12 × 18-inch rectangle ⅛ inch thick. Cut 12 strips 1 inch wide and 10 inches long. This fits a cornet tube (available at gourmet and specialty shops) that is 4½ inches long. Starting at narrow end, wrap pastry around tube, overlapping rows by ¼ to ½ inch. Do not stretch dough. Press to seal ends. Place tubes 2 inches apart on baking sheets lined with brown paper of 3 to 4 layers of paper towels. Refrigerate dough ½ hour.

Bake dough in preheated 400°F oven 20 minutes. Beat egg white and water. Remove horns from oven and brush egg white on tops of horns. Sprinkle with granulated sugar. Return to oven. Bake an additional 5 minutes or until golden and glazed. Place on wire racks; cool slightly. Remove from tubes; cool completely.

Fold whipped cream into pastry cream; fill the horns. Garnish with nuts and powdered sugar if desired.

MAKES 12 HORNS.

Note: To make a cornet tube, use 2 layers of heavy-duty aluminum foil cut into a 9-inch square. Fold in half to make a triangle. Roll triangle into horn or cone shape 4½ inches long and 1½ inches wide at top. Fold foil edges to secure it.

Dessert croissants

FRANCE

4 tablespoons apricot jam or red currant jelly
3 tablespoons water
6 hot Croissants (see Index), freshly made or reheated
1 tablespoon corn syrup
1 teaspoon cognac

1 teaspoon lemon juice
About ¼ cup powdered sugar

Boil jam or jelly with 2 tablespoons water 1 minute. With pastry brush, coat hot croissants with mixture.

Boil corn syrup and 1 tablespoon water 1 minute. Off heat, add cognac and lemon juice. Stir in enough powdered sugar to make a thin paste. Spread over jam coating. Serve croissants while warm.
MAKES 6 SERVINGS.

Cream-cheese tart w/prunes
FRANCE

1 cup red wine	1 cup heavy cream
1½ cups water	4 tablespoons sugar
1 piece cinnamon stick (about ¾ inch long)	3 egg whites
4 whole cloves	1 teaspoon vanilla
¾ pound pitted prunes	Grated rind of ½ lemon
1½ pounds cream cheese, softened	⅛ to ¼ cup powdered sugar
3 egg yolks	1 unbaked pie shell (see Index for Sweet Pastry Dough; place into 10-inch springform pan
6 tablespoons cornstarch	

In medium saucepan combine red wine, water, cinnamon stick, cloves, and prunes. Bring to a boil; boil for 1 minute; simmer for 10 minutes. Set aside until ready to use.

In large bowl beat cream cheese, egg yolks, and cornstarch until light and fluffy. In separate bowl beat heavy cream until stiff; gradually add 3 tablespoons sugar. In another bowl beat egg whites until stiff; beat in rest of sugar. Fold whipped cream, beaten egg whites, vanilla, and lemon rind carefully but thoroughly into cream-cheese mixture.

Drain prunes; discard cinnamon stick and cloves. Distribute over pie shell. Spread cream-cheese mixture over prunes. Smooth top with spatula. Bake in preheated 375°F oven 55 minutes. Remove tart from springform pan immediately after removing from oven. Let cool on cake rack. Sift a light coating of powdered sugar over top of tart.
MAKES 10 TO 12 SERVINGS.

Chocolate mousse
FRANCE

8 ounces semisweet chocolate pieces
2 tablespoons water
¼ cup powdered sugar
½ cup unsalted butter, softened
6 eggs, separated
1 tablespoon dark rum
½ teaspoon vanilla
2 tablespoons sugar

Melt chocolate and 2 tablespoons water in double boiler. When melted, stir in powdered sugar; add butter bit by bit. Set aside. Beat egg yolks until thick and lemon-colored, about 5 minutes. Gently fold in chocolate. Reheat slightly to melt chocolate, if necessary. Stir in rum and vanilla. Beat egg whites until foamy. Beat in 2 tablespoons sugar; beat until stiff peaks form. Gently fold whites into chocolate-yolk mixture. Pour into individual serving dishes. Chill at least 4 hours. Serve with whipped cream, if desired.
MAKES 6 TO 8 SERVINGS.

Lomousin cherry pudding cake
FRANCE

2 cups pitted black cherries, fresh, or 1 1-pound can Bing cherries, drained
2 tablespoons cognac or brandy
2 tablespoons sugar
1 cup milk
⅓ cup sugar
3 eggs
2 teaspoons vanilla
½ teaspoon almond extract
⅛ teaspoon salt
1 cup flour
Powdered sugar

Place cherries in small bowl; pour brandy over them. Stir in 2 tablespoons sugar; set aside.
In blender container place remaining ingredients, except powdered sugar, in order listed. Blend on high 1 minute, or beat all ingredients to form a smooth batter. Pour ¼ of batter into

Cream horns

9-inch pie pan (2 inches deep). Place in 350°F oven about 2 minutes, until batter is set. Place cherries on top of batter; add any cherry juice and remaining batter. Return to oven; continue to bake for 45 minutes, until a knife inserted in center can be withdrawn clean. Sprinkle cake generously with powdered sugar. Serve cake warm.

MAKES 6 TO 8 SERVINGS.

Crepes suzette

FRANCE

6 sugar cubes
2 oranges
1 lemon
1 stick soft unsalted butter
¼ cup Grand Marnier curacao, Benedictine, or Cointreau
12 Dessert Crepes (see Index, Basic Crepes)
¼ cup brandy

Rub sugar cubes over rinds of oranges and lemon; combine with butter. Place flavored butter in chafing dish; add juice of 1 orange and 1 lemon and ¼ cup of one of above liqueurs. When contents of pan are hot and bubbling, add crepes, one at a time. Coat each crepe with sauce, fold it in half and then fold it again into a triangle, and push it to side of dish. When all crepes are coated with sauce, arrange them over surface of dish; allow them to heat through.

Add the brandy and when heated touch it with a flame. Spoon the sauce over the crepes until the flame starts to subside. Serve immediately.

MAKES 6 SERVINGS.

Cherries jubilee

FRANCE

3 tablespoons red currant jelly
1 tablespoon butter
2 cups canned tart cherries, well-drained
½ cup kirsch
1 pint vanilla ice cream

Melt jelly in frypan or chafing dish. Add butter; stir until melted and hot. Add cherries; heat through.

Heat kirsch in small saucepan. Pour over cherries, ignite with long match, and let burn until flames die. Spoon hot cherries over ice cream. Serve.

MAKES 4 SERVINGS.

Brown-sugar cookies

GERMANY

1½ cups brown sugar, firmly packed
⅔ cup shortening
2 eggs
2 tablespoons milk
1 tablespoon grated orange rind
2 teaspoons baking powder
1 teaspoon cinnamon
½ teaspoon cloves
¼ teaspoon salt
2 cups flour
1 cup raisins
½ cup chopped nuts, if desired

Cream sugar and shortening until light and fluffy. Beat in eggs, milk, and orange rind. Sift

555

Cream-cheese tart with prunes

together baking powder, spices, salt, and flour. Mix into sugar mixture. Stir in raisins and nuts. Drop dough by teaspoonfuls onto greased cookie sheets. Bake at 350°F about 10 to 12 minutes, until done. Remove from baking sheets and cool cookies on rack. Store in airtight tins.
MAKES 4 TO 5 DOZEN.

Spice cookies

GERMANY

½ cup butter or margarine
¼ cup shortening
1 cup brown sugar, firmly packed
1 egg
¼ cup molasses
2½ cups unsifted flour
¼ teaspoon salt
2 teaspoons baking soda
1 teaspoon cinnamon
½ teaspoon ginger
½ teaspoon ground cloves
½ teaspoon ground allspice

Cream butter, shortening, and brown sugar thoroughly. Blend in egg and molasses. Sift together remaining ingredients. Stir into sugar mixture. Shape dough into ¾-inch balls. Place 2 inches apart on greased baking sheet. Flatten each ball with bottom of glass that has been greased and dipped in sugar.

Bake in preheated 350°F oven for 12 to 15 minutes. Cool cookies on racks. Store in airtight tins.
MAKES 4 DOZEN.

Spritz cookies

GERMANY

1 cup butter
⅔ cup confectioners' sugar
1 egg
1 egg yolk
1 teaspoon almond or lemon extract
2¼ cups unsifted flour
¼ teaspoon salt ·
½ teaspoon baking powder

Beat butter and sugar until light. Beat in egg, egg yolk, and extract. Sift flour, salt, and baking powder. Gradually add flour mixture to eggs. Chill dough ½ hour.
Shape ¼ of dough into cookie press. Keep remaining dough chilled. Shape cookies into greased baking sheet. Bake in 400°F oven 7 to 10 minutes, until done. Cool on wire racks. Repeat process 3 times. Store in airtight tins.
MAKES 4 TO 6 DOZEN.

Crepes suzette

Almond crescents

GERMANY

1 cup butter or margarine
¾ cup sugar
1 teaspoon vanilla extract
1½ teaspoons almond extract
2½ cups flour
1 cup ground almonds
Confectioners' sugar

Beat together butter and sugar until very light and fluffy. Blend in extracts. Mix in flour and almonds. Using about 1 tablespoon of dough for each, shape into logs and bend into crescents. Place on greased cookie sheet. Bake 12 to 15 minutes at 350°F, until light brown.

While warm, roll crescents in confectioners' sugar. Cool on racks. Store in a tightly sealed container.

MAKES 3 DOZEN.

Nut crescents

GERMANY

1 package active dry yeast
4 cups unsifted flour
1 cup butter or margarine, softened
1 cup sour cream
3 egg yolks

filling

3 egg whites, beaten
1 cup ground nuts
1 cup sugar (or more, to taste)
1 teaspoon vanilla

Mix yeast, flour, butter, sour cream, and egg yolks thoroughly until dough is formed. Cover and let dough rest 1 hour in refrigerator.

For filling, beat egg whites until soft peaks form. Fold in nuts, sugar, and vanilla.

Roll dough ⅛ inch thick. Cut out rectangles about 2 × 3 inches. Spread with 1 teaspoon filling. Roll up jelly-roll fashion. Place on greased baking sheet and curve to form crescents. Bake at 350°F for 15 to 20 minutes, until lightly

557

browned. Cool on wire racks. Store in airtight tins.
MAKES 4 TO 5 DOZEN.

Anise drops

GERMANY

3 eggs
1 egg white
1 cup plus 2 tablespoons sugar
1¾ cups unsifted flour
½ teaspoon baking powder
⅛ teaspoon salt
1 to 1½ teaspoons anise extract

Beat eggs and egg white until very light and fluffy, about 5 minutes. Add sugar gradually; continue to beat for 20 minutes. Sift flour, baking powder, and salt. Fold flour mixture and anise extract into beaten eggs. Make sure it is well-blended.
Drop by teaspoonfuls onto well-greased and floured baking sheet. Round cookies by using bowl of spoon. Let stand overnight. Cover with paper towel.
Bake at 325°F for 10 minutes, no longer. Cookies should not brown. Store in covered tin. Cookies keep several weeks.
MAKES 4 TO 5 DOZEN.

Hazelnut macaroons

GERMANY

3 egg whites
¾ cup sugar
1 teaspoon almond extract
Pinch of salt
1 cup ground hazelnuts*
4 tablespoons cocoa
½ cup shredded coconut, if desired

Beat the egg whites until soft peaks form. Gradually beat in the sugar, 1 tablespoon at a time. Beat until stiff peaks form, about 5 minutes. Fold in almond extract and salt. Mix the nuts, cocoa, and coconut. Fold into the egg whites.

Cherries jubilee

Drop cookies by the tablespoon onto well-greased cookie sheets. Bake at 325°F for 15 minutes or until cookies are firm. Remove from baking sheet and cool on wire rack. Store cookies in an airtight container.
MAKES 4 DOZEN.

*Hazelnuts (filberts) are available at gourmet or specialty stores. Remove skins by blanching for 10 minutes in boiling water and peeling. To grind, place about ¼ cup at a time in a blender, or chop very finely.

Sand tarts

GERMANY

2½ cups sugar
2 cups butter or margarine
2 eggs
4 cups unsifted flour
1 egg white, beaten
Sugar
Cinnamon
Pecan halves

Cream sugar and butter. Beat in 2 eggs. Gradually blend in flour. Chill dough overnight.
Roll as thin as possible on well-floured board. Work with ¼ of dough at a time. Keep remaining dough chilled. Cut into diamonds with a knife. Place on greased cookie sheets. Brush each cookie with beaten egg white. Sprinkle with sugar and a pinch of cinnamon. Place a pecan half in center of each cookie. Bake in preheated 350°F oven 8 to 10 minutes, until edges are lightly browned. Cool on cookie sheets 1 minute, then remove to wire racks. Store in airtight tins.
MAKES 9 DOZEN.

Spice bars

GERMANY

1 teaspoon cinnamon
1 teaspoon ground allspice
¼ teaspoon ground cloves
½ teaspoon salt
2¼ cups unsifted flour

½ teaspoon baking powder
½ cup ground almonds
1 teaspoon grated lemon rind
2 eggs
¾ cup sugar
¾ cup honey
½ cup milk

almond glaze
1 cup confectioners' sugar
½ teaspoon almond extract
1 teaspoon rum
1 to 2 tablespoons water

Sift together the spices, salt, flour, and baking powder. Stir in the almonds and lemon rind. In a separate bowl beat the eggs and sugar until a ribbon is formed when the beater is removed. Stir in the honey and milk. Gradually stir in the flour mixture; beat until smooth.

Spread the batter in an 11 × 17-inch jelly-roll pan that is well-greased and floured. Bake at 400°F for 12 to 15 minutes, until the cake is done. While still warm, turn the cake out onto a rack.

To make the almond glaze, mix the confectioners' sugar, almond extract, rum, and 1 to 2 tablespoons water. Beat until glaze is smooth and of the right consistency. Add more water, if necessary, to thin. Spread the warm cake with almond glaze. Cut cake into 1 × 2½-inch bars while still warm.

Spice bars keep 6 to 8 weeks in a sealed container if not glazed.
MAKES 4 DOZEN.

Pepper balls

GERMANY

4 cups unsifted flour
1 teaspoon baking powder
1 teaspoon cinnamon
1 teaspoon ground cloves
½ teaspoon mace
1 teaspoon ground allspice
Dash to ¼ teaspoon black pepper, if desired
1¼ cups honey
2 tablespoons butter
2 eggs

1 cup confectioners' sugar
1 teaspoon vanilla
1 to 2 tablespoons water

Sift flour, baking powder, and spices. Heat honey and butter until butter melts. Cook to lukewarm and beat in eggs. Add flour mixture. Chill dough ½ hour.

Shape dough into 1-inch balls. Place on greased cookie sheet. Bake at 350°F for 15 minutes. Cool cookies on wire racks. Mix confectioners' sugar, vanilla, and water to form a thin glaze. Dip cookies in glaze and place on wire rack to dry. Store cookies in airtight tins.
MAKES 4 DOZEN.

Apple & rum custard cake

GERMANY

crust
1½ cups unsifted flour
5 tablespoons sugar
1 tablespoon grated lemon rind

⅔ cup butter or margarine
1 egg yolk
1 tablespoon milk

filling
½ cup soft bread crumbs
2 tablespoons melted butter or margarine
4 cups tart sliced apples
1 tablespoon lemon juice

¼ cup sugar
¼ cup raisins, soaked ½ hour in ¼ cup rum
3 eggs, beaten
⅓ cup sugar
1¾ cups milk

To make crust, mix flour, sugar, and lemon rind. Cut in butter or margarine until mixture resembles coarse crumbs. Add egg yolk and 1 tablespoon milk; mix gently to form a dough. Pat into bottom of 10-inch springform pan that has sides only greased. Press dough up sides of pan 1 inch. Toss together bread crumbs and melted butter. Spread evenly over pastry crust. Toss apple slices, lemon juice, and ¼ cup sugar. Spread apples over crumbs. Drain raisins, reserving rum, and sprinkle raisins over apples. Bake in preheated 350°F oven for 15 minutes.

Beat eggs and sugar until thick and lemon-colored. Stir in milk and reserved rum. Pour custard over apples and bake for 45 to 60 minutes at 350°F until custard is set. Cool completely before

serving. Do not remove springform pan until cool.
MAKES 8 SERVINGS.

Apple pancakes
GERMANY

⅔ cup unsifted flour
2 teaspoons sugar
¼ teaspoon salt
4 eggs, beaten
½ cup milk
2 cups apple slices
¾ cup butter or margarine
2 tablespoons sugar
¼ teaspoon cinnamon

Sift together flour, 2 teaspoons sugar, and salt. Beat eggs and milk together. Gradually add flour mixture; beat until smooth.
Sauté apples in ¼ cup butter until tender. Mix 2 tablespoons sugar and the cinnamon together; toss with apples.
Melt 2 tablespoons butter in 6-inch frypan. Pour in batter to a depth of about ¼ inch. When set, place ¼ of apples on top; cover with more batter. Fry pancake until lightly browned on both sides. Repeat procedure 3 times, until all batter and apples are used. Serve immediately.
MAKES 4 PANCAKES.

Apple strudel
GERMANY

6 cups sliced tart apples
¾ cup raisins
1 tablespoon grated lemon rind
¾ cup sugar
2 teaspoons cinnamon
¾ cup ground almonds
½ box (16-ounce size) frozen phyllo leaves, thawed*
1¾ cups butter or margarine, melted
1 cup fine bread crumbs

Mix apples with raisins, lemon rind, sugar, cinnamon, and almonds. Set aside.
Place 1 phyllo leaf on a kitchen towel and brush with melted butter. Place a second leaf on top and brush with butter again. Repeat until 5 leaves have been used, using about ½ cup of butter. Cook and stir the bread crumbs with ¼ cup butter until lightly browned. Sprinkle ⅜ cup crumbs on the layered phyllo leaves.
Mound ½ of the filling in a 3-inch strip along the narrow edge of the phyllo, leaving a 2-inch border. Lift towel, using it to roll leaves over apples, jelly-roll fashion. Brush strudel with butter after each turn. Using towel, place strudel on greased baking sheet. Brush top of the strudel with butter and sprinkle with 2 tablespoons crumbs. Repeat the entire procedure for the second strudel. Bake the strudels at 400°F for 20 to 25 minutes, until browned. Serve warm.
MAKES 2 STRUDELS, 6 TO 8 SERVINGS EACH.
*Frozen phyllo leaves for strudel can be found at many supermarkets.

Apple & cream kuchen
GERMANY

1 package active dry yeast
½ teaspoon salt
4 tablespoons sugar
2 to 2½ cups unsifted flour
¼ cup butter or margarine
½ cup milk
1 egg

filling

3 cups sliced tart apples
1 tablespoon lemon juice
1 teaspoon cinnamon
¾ cup sugar
2 tablespoons flour
8 ounces cream cheese, softened
1 egg

Mix yeast, salt, 4 tablespoons sugar, and ¾ cup flour. Add butter to milk. Heat until very warm, 120 to 130°F. Gradually add milk to flour mixture. Beat for 2 minutes. Add egg and ½ cup flour. Beat with electric beater on high speed for 2 minutes. Mix in enough flour to form a soft dough. Knead for 5 to 10 minutes, until dough is smooth and elastic. Place in greased bowl and let rise 1 hour, until doubled in bulk.
Pat dough into well-greased 10-inch springform

561

pan, pressing 1½ inches up the sides of the pan. Toss apples with lemon juice, cinnamon, ¼ cup sugar, and 2 tablespoons flour. Arrange in rows on top of dough. Beat together cream cheese, ½ cup sugar, and egg. Spread over apples. Let rise in warm place 1 hour.

Bake at 350°F for 30 minutes. Best when served warm.

MAKES 1 9-INCH CAKE.

Vanilla Bavarian cream

GERMANY

2 packages unflavored gelatin
½ cup cold water
9 tablespoons sugar
1 tablespoon cornstarch
2 eggs, beaten
1½ cups milk, scalded
1 cup vanilla ice cream
1 teaspoon vanilla
1 cup heavy cream, whipped

Sprinkle gelatin over cold water to soften. Heat to dissolve gelatin completely.

Mix together sugar and cornstarch. Add eggs; beat for 2 minutes. Slowly add warm milk, beating constantly. Pour into a 1-quart saucepan. Cook over medium heat until custard coats a spoon. Add gelatin and ice cream while custard is hot. Cool until slightly thickened.

Add vanilla. Fold in whipped cream. Pour into 1-quart mold. Chill until set. Unmold carefully and serve garnished with fresh fruit.

MAKES 6 TO 8 SERVINGS.

Strawberry Bavarian

GERMANY

1 quart fresh strawberries
¾ cup sugar
1 tablespoon gelatin (1 envelope)
½ cup cold water
2 teaspoons lemon juice
1 cup heavy cream, whipped

Slice strawberries and mix with sugar. Let stand until sugar dissolves. Sprinkle gelatin over cold

water. Let stand 5 minutes, then heat gently until gelatin dissolves completely. Add gelatin and lemon juice to sliced berries. Fold in whipped cream.

Pour into 1-quart mold or serving dish. Chill until set. Unmold to serve.

MAKES 6 SERVINGS.

Apple cake

GERMANY

4 to 6 tart apples (medium size)	1 teaspoon baking powder
2 lemons, juiced	1½ cups flour
3 tablespoons sugar	¾ cup milk
3 tablespoons butter	1 tablespoon rum
¾ cup sugar	2 egg whites
2 egg yolks (do not put 2 yolks together, as they will be used individually)	1 teaspoon butter (to grease cake pan)
½ lemon, juiced and peel grated	1 teaspoon vegetable oil
	3 tablespoons powdered sugar

Peel apples, cut in half, and core. Cut decorative lengthwise slits in apples, about ½ inch deep. Sprinkle with lemon juice and sugar. Set aside. Cream butter and sugar together. One at a time, beat in egg yolks. Gradually beat in lemon juice and grated peel. Sift baking powder and flour together. Gradually add to batter. Blend in milk and rum. In a small bowl beat egg whites until stiff. Fold into batter.

Generously grease a springform pan. Pour in batter and top with apple halves. Brush apples with oil. Bake in preheated 350°F oven 35 to 40 minutes. Remove from pan and sprinkle with powdered sugar.

MAKES 6 SERVINGS.

Drop donuts

GERMANY

¼ cup soft butter
1 cup sugar
2 egg yolks, beaten
1 whole egg, beaten
4 cups flour

2 teaspoons baking powder
¼ teaspoon nutmeg
½ teaspoon soda
¾ cup buttermilk
Powdered sugar

Cream the butter and sugar. Stir in egg yolks and whole egg; blend. In a separate bowl sift all dry ingredients except powdered sugar; add to creamed mixture, alternating with buttermilk. Stir to mix all ingredients.

Cook by dropping spoonfuls of dough into 375°F deep fat. Fry a few at a time, to keep fat temperature constant. Turn to brown on all sides. Drain on paper towels; sprinkle with powdered sugar.
MAKES 3 DOZEN.

Jelly doughnuts

GERMANY

3 to 4 cups unsifted flour
¼ cup sugar
1½ teaspoons salt
1¼ cups warm water (105 to 115°F)
1 package active dry yeast
2 egg yolks, beaten
¼ cup butter or margarine
Grated rind of 1 lemon
¼ cup plum or apricot jam

Mix 2 cups flour with sugar and salt. Make a well in the center and add ¼ cup warm water and the yeast. Allow to rise 20 minutes. Add egg yolks, remaining water, and butter. Beat until well-blended. Add lemon rind and remaining flour until a soft dough is formed.

Knead for 5 to 10 minutes, until dough is smooth and elastic. Place dough in a lightly greased bowl. Cover and let rise in a warm place until doubled in bulk, about 1½ hours.

Punch dough down. On lightly floured board roll dough ¼-inch thick. Cut dough into 2-inch rounds. On half of the rounds place about 1 teaspoon of jam or jelly. Moisten edges with water; place a second round on top. Press firmly to seal edges. Let rise 15 minutes.

Fry in deep fat heated to 375°F for 4 minutes on each side or until browned. Cut into first dough-

nut to be sure it's done in the center. Drain on absorbent paper and sprinkle with lots of sugar, as the doughnuts are not sweet.
MAKES 24 DOUGHNUTS.

Old German muffins

GERMANY

¾ cup butter or margarine
½ cup sugar
2 eggs
1 tablespoon rum
1 teaspoon vanilla
3 tablespoons milk
½ teaspoon cinnamon
2 teaspoons baking powder
2¼ cups flour
¼ cup ground almonds
1 tablespoon grated orange rind
¼ cup raisins, if desired

Cream butter and sugar. Beat in eggs, rum, vanilla, and milk.

Mix cinnamon, baking powder, and flour. Add flour mixture to butter mixture. Gently mix in almonds, orange rind, and raisins. Pour batter into greased muffin tins, filling half full. Bake at 375°F for 25 to 30 minutes, until browned.
MAKES 18 MUFFINS.

Red-wine jelly w/fruit

GERMANY

Served as a dessert in Germany.
2 tablespoons (2 envelopes) unflavored gelatin
½ cup water
½ cup sugar
2 tablespoons lemon juice
3 cups dry red wine
2 cups fresh fruit, such as peaches, plums, strawberries, raspberries

Sprinkle the gelatin over the water. When gelatin is softened, heat gently to dissolve completely. Add sugar and lemon juice to wine. Stir to dissolve sugar. While still warm, stir in the gelatin mixture. Chill until slightly thickened. Add fruit; mix gently to distribute fruit throughout.

Pour into 1- to 1½-quart mold; chill until set. Unmold to serve.
MAKES 10 TO 12 SERVINGS.

Meeresburg cherry dessert

GERMANY

1 pound fresh tart cherries
3 tablespoons kirsch
6 tablespoons sugar
2 tablespoons water
12 ladyfingers
8 ounces cream cheese, softened to room temperature
½ teaspoon vanilla extract
2 ounces ground almonds (grind whole almonds in blender)
1 cup heavy cream
Chopped pistachio nuts for garnish

Stem, wash, and drain cherries. Remove stones but reserve 8 whole cherries for garnish. Place cherries in a bowl; add kirsch. In a small pan boil 3 tablespoons sugar and the water for a minute to make a thin sugar syrup. Add syrup to cherries; stir to blend. Cover and let soak for 20 minutes.

Cut the ladyfingers in half, divide in 4 portions, and place in individual glass dishes. Arrange cherries on top. Thoroughly blend cream cheese, 3 tablespoons sugar, vanilla extract, and ground almonds. Whip the cream and carefully fold it into the cream-cheese mixture. Spoon over the cherries. Garnish with the chopped pistachio nuts and whole cherries.
MAKES 4 SERVINGS.

Swabian pancakes

GERMANY

This dish is generally a dessert, but, if preceded by a light soup, it may be served as a main dish for lunch.

1¼ cups flour
3 eggs
½ teaspoon salt
2 cups milk
1 teaspoon vegetable oil
1 16-ounce can applesauce
4 ounces raisins
1 teaspoon oil or butter (to grease dish)
2 tablespoons sugar
3 tablespoons sliced blanched almonds
1 tablespoon butter

Prepare pancake batter by blending flour, 2 eggs, ¼ teaspoon salt, and 1 cup milk. Lightly oil a large frypan and cook 6 to 8 pancakes (2 or 3 at a time). Heat the applesauce and stir in the raisins. Divide the sauce between the pancakes and spread over each top. Roll up the pancakes like jelly rolls and cut each in half with a sharp knife. Grease an ovenproof dish with oil or butter; place pancakes in the dish, setting them up on the cut edges. Blend 1 egg with sugar, ¼ teaspoon salt, 1 cup milk, and sliced almonds. Pour over the pancakes. Dot with butter. Place in a preheated 375°F oven; bake for 40 minutes. Serve immediately.
MAKES 6 SERVINGS.

Black Forest cherry cake

GERMANY

6 eggs
1 cup sugar
1 teaspoon vanilla
4 squares unsweetened baking chocolate, melted
1 cup sifted flour

filling
1½ cups confectioners' sugar
⅓ cup unsalted butter
1 egg yolk
2 tablespoons kirsch liqueur

syrup
¼ cup sugar
⅓ cup water
2 tablespoons kirsch

topping
2 cups drained, canned sour cherries
2 tablespoons confectioners' sugar
1 cup heavy cream, whipped
8-ounce semisweet chocolate bar

Beat eggs, sugar, and vanilla together until thick and fluffy, about 10 minutes. Alternately fold chocolate and flour into the egg mixture, ending with flour. Pour the batter into 3 8-inch round cake pans that have been well-greased and floured. Bake in a preheated 350°F oven 10 to 15 minutes, until a cake tester inserted in center comes out clean. Cook cakes in pans 5 minutes; turn out on racks to cool completely.

Make syrup by mixing together sugar and water and boiling for 5 minutes. When syrup has cooled, stir in kirsch. Prick the cake layers and pour syrup over all 3 layers.

To make the butter-cream filling, beat together sugar and butter until well-blended. Add egg yolk; beat until light and fluffy, about 3 to 5 minutes. Fold in kirsch.

To assemble cake, place 1 layer on cake plate. Spread with the butter-cream filling. Using ¾ cup cherries, which have been patted dry, drop cherries evenly over cream. Place second layer on cake. Repeat. Place third layer on top. Fold 2 tablespoons confectioners' sugar into whipped cream. Cover sides and top of cake with whipped cream. Decorate top of cake with remaining ½ cup cherries.

To make chocolate curls from chocolate bar, shave bar (at room temperature) with vegetable peeler. Refrigerate curls until ready to use. Press chocolate curls on sides of cake and sprinkle a few on top. Chill until serving time.

MAKES 8 TO 10 SERVINGS.

Frankfurt crown cake

GERMANY

1 cup butter	1½ teaspoons grated lemon rind
1½ cups sugar	8 tablespoons rum
6 eggs, separated (egg yolks will be used one at a time, so keep them separated from each other)	4 teaspoons baking powder
	3½ cups sifted flour

butter-cream filling

praline topping

1 cup sugar	2 tablespoons butter
¾ cup water	1 cup sugar
6 egg yolks	½ cup water
1 tablespoon rum	1 cup blanched sliced almonds
1 cup unsalted butter	

apricot glaze
½ cup apricot jam
1 tablespoon sugar

To prepare cake, cream butter and sugar until very light and fluffy, about 5 minutes. Beat in egg yolks, one at a time. Mix in lemon rind and 2 tablespoons rum. Sift baking powder and flour together. Gently mix into butter mixture.

Beat egg whites until stiff but not dry. Gently fold the beaten egg whites into the batter. Pour into a well-greased 10-inch tube pan. Bake in a preheated 325°F oven about 60 minutes, until cake tests done. Cool cake in the pan 10 minutes, then turn out on wire rack to cool completely. Slice cake crosswise into 3 layers. Pour about 2 tablespoons rum over each layer.

For butter-cream filling, boil sugar and water to 238°F (soft-ball stage). Beat egg yolks until very light and fluffy, 5 to 10 minutes. While still beating the egg yolks, add the sugar syrup in a thin stream. Beat 5 minutes more, until very thick and doubled in bulk. Slowly beat in rum. Beat the butter in a small bowl until soft and light. Beat butter into the egg mixture a little at a time. Continue beating until thick. Chill until mixture can be spread. If mixture is too soft, beat in additional butter.

While butter-cream is cooling, spread 2 tablespoons butter thickly in a 9 × 13-inch baking pan for praline topping. Then, in a 1-quart saucepan boil sugar and water to 238°F (soft ball stage). Stir in almonds; cook until mixture reaches 310°F or until syrup caramelizes. Pour syrup into prepared baking pan. When cool, break up praline and grind it in a blender for a few seconds.

Finally, heat jam with sugar and press through a strainer or sieve to make apricot glaze.

To assemble cake, place bottom layer of cake on cake plate and spread with half of the butter cream. Repeat with second layer. Place third layer on top. Spread tops and sides of cake with apricot glaze. Press praline powder onto glaze. Any remaining butter cream can be used to decorate top of cake.

MAKES 10 TO 12 SERVINGS.

Crumb cake

GERMANY

topping	cake
¼ cup sugar	2¼ to 2½ cups unsifted flour
¼ cup brown sugar	¼ cup sugar
2 teaspoons cinnamon	¼ teaspoon salt
1 cup unsifted flour	1 package active dry yeast
½ cup butter or margarine	¾ cup milk
	½ cup butter or margarine
	1 egg

Baklava

For topping, mix sugars, cinnamon, and flour. Cut in butter until mixture is crumbly.

To make cake, mix 1 cup flour, sugar, salt, and yeast in a large bowl. Place milk and butter in a saucepan and heat until very warm (120 to 130°F). Gradually add to dry ingredients; beat for 2 minutes. Beat in egg and 1 cup flour. Beat on high speed 2 minutes. Stir in remaining flour to make a stiff batter. Spread batter into well-greased 9-inch-square cake pan. Sprinkle with topping. Let rise in a warm place until double in bulk, about 1½ hours. Bake at 350°F about 45 minutes or until done.

MAKES 1 9-INCH CAKE.

Golden bundt cake

GERMANY

This rich, moist cake needs no frosting and keeps well.

3 cups sugar
1 cup butter or margarine
½ cup shortening
5 eggs
3 cups unsifted flour
¼ teaspoon salt
5-ounce can evaporated milk plus water to make 1 cup
2 tablespoons vanilla butter and nut flavoring

Beat sugar, butter, and shortening until light and fluffy, about 5 minutes. Beat in eggs, one at a time, beating well after each addition. Mix flour and salt. Alternately add flour and milk, ending with flour. Fold in flavoring.

Bake in greased tube pan at 325°F for 1 hour and 45 minutes, until done. Start in cold oven. Do not open door. Remove from pan and cool on wire rack.

MAKES 10 TO 12 SERVINGS.

Gugelhopf

GERMANY

1 package active dry yeast
1 cup milk, scalded and cooled
1 cup sugar
1 cup butter or margarine
5 eggs
1 teaspoon vanilla
Rind of 1 lemon, grated
¾ cup raisins
⅓ cup ground almonds (2-ounce package)
½ teaspoon salt
4 cups unsifted flour

Sprinkle yeast in milk to dissolve. In a large bowl beat sugar and butter until light and fluffy. Beat in eggs, one at a time. Stir in vanilla, lemon rind, raisins, and almonds. Mix salt and flour. Add milk and flour mixture alternately, ending with flour.

Grease a gugelhopf mold*, bundt pan, or tube pan. Pour batter into pan. Cover and let rise until doubled in bulk, about 2 hours. Bake in preheated 375°F oven for 40 minutes, until browned and done. Serve warm with butter.

MAKES 8 TO 10 SERVINGS.

This bread is traditionally baked in a gugelhopf pan or turban-head pan. If these are unavailable, a bundt pan or tube pan works just as well.

566

Hazelnut torte

GERMANY

5 eggs, separated
¾ cup sugar
6 tablespoons water
1¾ cups sifted cake flour
1 teaspoon baking powder
1½ cups ground hazelnuts (filberts)*
1 teaspoon vanilla
2 tablespoons confectioners' sugar
1 cup heavy cream, whipped
Fresh strawberries, if desired

Beat the egg yolks and sugar until very light, about 5 minutes. Slowly add the water. Sift the flour and baking powder together. Mix with 1 cup of the nuts. Fold the flour mixture into the egg yolks.

Beat the egg whites until soft peaks form. Gently fold the beaten whites into the batter. Pour into a greased and floured 10-inch springform pan. Bake at 375°F for 30 minutes or until cake tests done. Cool the cake on a rack. When completely cooled, split the cake into 2 layers.

Fold the vanilla, confectioners' sugar, and remaining ½ cup nuts into the whipped cream. Spread whipped cream between the 2 cake layers and on top of the cake. Chill until serving time. Garnish with fresh strawberries, if desired.

MAKES 8 SERVINGS.

*Hazelnuts are available at specialty or gourmet stores. They should be blanched. To blanch, boil the nuts 5 minutes and, when cool enough to handle, remove the skins. To grind, place about ¼ cup at a time in a blender, or chop finely.

Fruit torte

GERMANY

pastry	**filling**
2 cups flour	3 to 4 cups fresh, canned, or frozen fruit
¼ cup sugar	
1 cup unsalted butter	½ cup sugar if fresh fruit is used
2 egg yolks	
	¼ cup water, if needed
	2 tablespoons cornstarch

almond coating	**topping**
1 egg white	2 tablespoons sugar
1 tablespoon sugar	1 teaspoon vanilla
½ cup sliced toasted almonds	1 cup heavy cream, whipped

Mix flour and sugar. Cut in butter until mixture resembles coarse crumbs. Add egg yolks; mix to form dough. Press dough into bottom and sides of a 10-inch springform pan. Dough should come 1½ inches up sides. Bake in preheated 375°F oven 20 to 25 minutes, until pastry is firm and light brown.

Drain canned or frozen fruit, reserving juice. Crush 1 cup fresh fruit to make juice. Add sugar to fresh fruit and let stand ½ hour. Drain juice. Add water to make 1 cup. Mix cornstarch and fruit juice. Cook over medium heat until thickened. Place whole fruit in baked pastry shell. Pour thickened fruit juice over top. Chill thoroughly. Carefully remove torte from springform pan.

Beat egg white until foamy. Gradually beat in the sugar. Beat until stiff peaks are formed. Spread the meringue around the outside of the pastry shell. Press in the almonds so they completely cover the sides. Gently fold sugar and vanilla into whipped cream. Spread over fruit. Garnish with sliced toasted almonds, if desired.

RECIPE MAKES 8 TO 10 SERVINGS.

Grape torte

GERMANY

dough	**topping**
2 cups unsifted flour	1 pound grapes
⅔ cup sugar	3 egg whites
¼ cup butter or margarine	6 tablespoons sugar
1 whole egg	Juice of ½ lemon
1 egg yolk	4 ounces ground almonds
Grated rind of 1 lemon	
⅛ teaspoon salt	

Sift flour and sugar into a medium-size bowl. Cut in butter or margarine until mixture resembles coarse crumbs. Add egg, egg yolk, lemon rind, and salt; mix with a fork to form dough. Cover dough and let rest in refrigerator 20 minutes.

Roll out dough into a circle; place in an ungreased 10-inch springform pan. Form a 1-inch-high rim. Bake in preheated 350°F oven for 10 minutes.

Meanwhile, clean and halve the grapes, and remove seeds if necessary. Beat egg whites until stiff; blend in sugar, lemon juice, and ground almonds. Carefully fold in the grapes. Remove cake from the oven. Fill baked cake shell with grape mixture, return to the oven, and bake for another 30 minutes at 350°F. Remove cake from pan and cool on wire rack.
MAKES 8 SERVINGS.

Fugger lemon torte
GERMANY

"Fuggers," a family of businessmen in the Middle Ages, lived in the town of Augsburg. They were so famous and rich that even the German emperor borrowed money from them. This is one of their family recipes.

dough	filling
1½ cups flour	6 ounces ground almonds
⅛ teaspoon salt	⅔ cup sugar
¼ cup butter or margarine	Grated rind of 1 lemon
1 whole egg	Juice of 2 large lemons
1 egg yolk	

topping
2 tablespoons milk
2 ounces slivered almonds

Sift flour and salt into a medium-size bowl. Cut in butter or margarine until mixture resembles coarse crumbs. Add egg and egg yolk; mix with a fork to form dough. Cover and refrigerate for 15 minutes.

To prepare the filling, mix thoroughly almonds, sugar, lemon rind, and lemon juice. Roll out half of dough into a circle and place in a 10-inch springform pan, forming a ¾-inch-high rim. Prick dough with a fork in several places. Spoon in filling. Roll out rest of dough, place on filling, and pinch edges together. Prick dough with fork in a decorative spiral pattern. Brush cake with milk and sprinkle with slivered almonds, pressing almonds lightly into the dough. Place cake into a preheated 350°F oven and bake for 40 minutes. Remove cake from pan and cool on a wire rack. The lemon flavor will intensify if cake is held 2 days before serving. (Wrapped in aluminum foil, cake keeps up to a week.)
MAKES 8 SERVINGS.

Ouzo cake
GREECE

1 cup chopped walnuts
1 18½-ounce lemon cake mix
1 3¾-ounce instant lemon pudding mix
4 eggs
¾ cup water
½ cup cooking oil
¼ cup ouzo

Preheat the oven to 325°F.

Grease and flour a 10-inch tube pan. Sprinkle the walnuts evenly over the bottom of the pan. Combine the cake mix, pudding mix, eggs, water, oil, and ouzo. Beat for 3 minutes. Pour the batter over the nuts in the tube pan. Bake for 1 hour.

Place on a rack to cool for 30 minutes. Invert onto a serving plate. Prick with a skewer or meat fork (carefully!) and pour on the honey syrup. Let stand at least ½ hour, and serve.
MAKES 12 SERVINGS.

Honey syrup
1 cup sugar
1 cup water
1 2-inch piece cinnamon stick
2 whole cloves
1 cup honey
2 tablespoons ouzo

Combine the sugar, water, cinnamon, and cloves. Bring the mixture to boiling, and reduce the heat. Cook for 25 minutes, without stirring, or until the mixture is syrupy (230°F on a candy thermometer). Stir in the honey and strain. Stir in the ouzo.

Mock baklava

GREECE

This recipe is great for emergencies! Try this when the phyllo sticks together and won't unroll or is too dry to work with.

honey syrup

2 cups sugar

1½ cups water

2 teaspoons lemon juice

½ cup honey

dough

1 pound rolled phyllo dough

2 sticks sweet butter, melted and cooled slightly

filling

1½ cups walnuts, finely chopped

¾ cup blanched almonds, finely chopped

¼ cup sugar

1 teaspoon cinnamon

In a saucepan combine the sugar, water, and lemon juice. Bring the mixture to a boil over low heat. Wash down the sides of the pan with a wet pastry brush and cook for 10 minutes. Remove from the heat, add the honey, and allow to cool. With a sharp knife cut across the rolled phyllo dough, cutting it into thin shreds. In a bowl toss the pastry shreds with the melted butter. Spread ½ of the shreds in a 13 × 9 × 2-inch baking dish.

Combine the filling ingredients and sprinkle evenly over the dough in the pan. Top with the remaining dough and butter mixture. Press lightly. Cover with foil and bake at 350°F for 30 minutes. Uncover and bake 15 minutes more or until golden. Remove from the oven and immediately pour on the syrup. Cover and let cool. Cut into squares and serve.

MAKES 16 TO 20 SERVINGS.

Yoghurt pie

GREECE

crust

1¼ cups graham-cracker crumbs

¼ cup sugar

¼ cup softened butter or margarine

1 teaspoon ground cinnamon

filling

12 ounces ricotta or farmer cheese

1½ cups plain yoghurt

3 tablespoons honey

1 teaspoon vanilla extract

Combine the graham-cracker crumbs, sugar, butter, and cinnamon and press evenly into a 9-inch pie pan. Bake at 375°F for 5 minutes, then cool.

Beat the ricotta or farmer cheese well, then add the yoghurt a little at a time, mixing well. Stir in the honey and vanilla. Pour into the pie shell and refrigerate for at least 24 hours before serving.

MAKES 8 SERVINGS.

Note: This pie is delicious with fresh fruit (blueberries, strawberries, or bananas with lemon juice) on top.

Baklava

GREECE

½ pound sweet butter, melted

1 pound phyllo sheets

1 cup finely chopped pecans

1 cup finely chopped walnuts

1 cup finely chopped almonds

½ cup sugar

1½ teaspoons ground cinnamon

Brush a 13 × 9 × 2-inch baking dish with some of the melted butter. Fold a phyllo sheet in half and place in the dish. Brush with butter and top with another folded sheet of phyllo and brush with butter.

In a small bowl, combine the pecans, walnuts, almonds, sugar, and cinnamon and mix well. Top phyllo with ½ cup of the nut mixture. Top with 2 more folded sheets of phyllo, brushing each with butter. Top with ½ cup of nuts. Continue layering 2 folded sheets of phyllo (buttering each) and nut mixture until 2 sheets of phyllo remain. Fold, butter, and layer them to form the top crust.

With a razor blade cut through the top layers into 24 small rectangles. Bake at 325°F for 50 minutes. Remove from the oven and with a sharp knife cut through all the layers of pastry, using the top layers as a guide, to form individual rectangles.

Pour cooled honey syrup over the pastry and cool. Cover and let stand overnight.

MAKES 24 PIECES OF PASTRY.

Honey syrup

1 small lemon
1 cup sugar
1 cup water
1 2-inch piece stick cinnamon
4 whole cloves
1 cup honey

Remove the zest from the lemon (the thin yellow skin only, not the white pith). Squeeze 1½ teaspoons of lemon juice from the lemon and set aside. Combine the lemon zest, sugar, water, cinnamon stick, and cloves in a heavy saucepan. Bring to a boil. Lower the heat and continue cooking without stirring for 25 minutes. The mixture should be syrupy (230°F on a candy thermometer). Stir in the honey and pour through a strainer into a pitcher or measuring cup. Add the lemon juice. Stir and allow to cool.

Yoghurt cake

GREECE

1 18-ounce yellow cake mix
4 eggs
½ cup vegetable oil (not olive)
1 cup plain or lemon-flavored yoghurt
½ teaspoon lemon extract
1 teaspoon grated lemon peel
1 teaspoon ground cinnamon
1 cup chopped walnuts

Grease and flour a 10-inch tube or fluted pan.

In a large mixing bowl combine the cake mix, eggs, oil, yoghurt, lemon flavoring, lemon peel, and cinnamon. Blend until moistened. Beat for 2 minutes. Add the nuts and mix just until combined. Pour into the prepared pan. Bake at 350°F for 60 minutes or until done. Cool 10 minutes and then turn out on a rack to finish cooling. Slice and serve.

MAKES 16 SERVINGS.

Walnut torte

GREECE

½ pound shelled walnut meats
9 eggs, separated
1 cup sugar
½ cup zwieback crumbs
1 tablespoon grated orange peel
½ teaspoon salt
1 teaspoon ground cinnamon
½ teaspoon ground cloves
2 teaspoons baking powder
¼ cup brandy
3 tablespoons water
½ pint heavy cream
2 tablespoons confectioners' sugar
1 teaspoon vanilla extract
Whole hazelnuts or almonds, or walnut halves, for garnish

Grind the walnuts through the medium blade of a food chopper. You should have 3 cups. Beat the egg yolks and sugar until thick and lemon-colored. Mix the ground nuts, zwieback crumbs, orange peel, salt, cinnamon, cloves, and baking powder. Stir into the egg-yolk mixture. Add the brandy and water. Beat the egg whites until stiff but not dry. Fold into the nut mixture.

Pour into a greased 9-inch springform pan (or 2 9-inch layer-cake pans). Bake at 350°F for 30 to 35 minutes or until the cake tests done in the center. (Bake the 9-inch layers 20 to 25 minutes.) Cool in the pan. When cold, remove from the pan.

Cut horizontally into 2 layers. Whip the cream and add to sugar and vanilla. Cover the lower layer with the cream. Place the outer layer on top and "frost" the top and sides. Garnish with whole hazelnuts, almonds, or walnut halves.

MAKES 12 SERVINGS.

Shortbread cookies

GREECE

These cookies are traditionally served at Christmas. The clove in each cookie symbolizes the spices brought to the Christ Child by the Three Wise Men.

2 sticks (½ pound) sweet butter
½ cup sifted confectioners' sugar
1 egg yolk
½ teaspoon vanilla extract
1 tablespoon brandy
2½ cups flour, sifted and then measured
½ teaspoon baking powder
½ cup walnuts, chopped fine (almonds may be substituted)
48 cloves
Additional confectioners' sugar

Let the butter soften at room temperature, then beat with an electric mixer until very light and fluffy. Sift the sugar into the butter, and cream them. Add the egg yolk, vanilla, and brandy. Sift the flour and baking powder together. Add the nuts and then the flour mixture and stir to form a soft dough. Knead lightly and chill for several hours.

Form the dough into balls, using a rounded teaspoon of dough for each cookie, and place on an ungreased cookie sheet 2 inches apart. Place a whole clove in each cookie. Bake at 350°F for 15 to 20 minutes or until light brown.

Roll the cookies in powdered sugar while still hot. Cool and store in an airtight container. Be very careful in handling these cookies, as they are very delicate.
MAKES 4 DOZEN COOKIES.

Sesame-seed cookies

GREECE

1 cup sweet butter
1½ cups sugar
1 teaspoon vanilla extract
3 eggs
5 cups self-rising flour
½ teaspoon ground cinnamon
½ cup sesame seeds
1 egg beaten with 2 tablespoons milk

Cream the butter until light. Add the sugar and vanilla and beat well. Add the eggs one at a time and beat well after each addition. Sift the flour and add to the creamed mixture to form a soft 571

Sesame-seed cookies

dough. Chill the dough several hours or overnight.

To form the cookies, take a scant tablespoon of the dough and roll into a 3½-inch-long rope. Pinch the 2 ends together to form a doughnut shape. Dip in the sesame seeds and place several inches apart on a greased baking sheet. Brush with the egg beaten with milk. Bake at 375°F for 15 minutes or until lightly browned. Cool on a rack and store in an airtight container.
MAKES 6 DOZEN COOKIES.

Blitz torte

HUNGARY

4 eggs, separated
½ cup confectioners' sugar
1 cup granulated sugar
½ cup butter
4 egg yolks
1 teaspoon vanilla extract
1 cup sifted cake flour
1½ teaspoons baking powder
⅛ teaspoon salt

4 tablespoons milk
½ cup chopped pecans
1 tablespoon granulated sugar
1 cup prepared vanilla instant pudding

Grease and flour 2 8-inch-round cake pans.
Place egg whites in mixing bowl; beat until foamy. Gradually beat in confectioners' sugar and ½ cup granulated sugar, forming stiff, glossy meringue; set aside. Cream butter and ½ cup sugar in mixing bowl until light. Add egg yolks and vanilla; beat well.

Stir flour, baking powder, and salt together. Add alternately with milk to creamed mixture; beat well, scraping bowl occasionally. Spread in prepared cake pans. Spread meringue evenly over batter. Sprinkle with nuts and 1 tablespoon sugar. Bake at 350°F 30 to 35 minutes or until meringue is set. Cool in pan.

Before serving, carefully remove cakes from pans. Place 1 layer, meringue-side-up, on serving plate. Spread with pudding. Top with remaining layer, meringue-side-up. Chill 1 hour.
MAKES 8 SERVINGS.

Gypsy John

Gypsy John

HUNGARY

chocolate cake

1 cup cake flour	3 large eggs
¼ cup unsweetened cocoa	1 cup sugar
1 teaspoon baking powder	⅓ cup water
¼ teaspoon salt	1 teaspoon vanilla

chocolate filling

10 squares semisweet chocolate	2 cups heavy cream
	2 tablespoons rum

chocolate icing

¼ cup light corn syrup	1 6-ounce package semisweet chocolate bits
2 tablespoons hot water	
2 tablespoons butter	

Sift together flour, cocoa, baking powder, and salt twice; set aside. Line jelly-roll pan with waxed paper; grease. Place eggs in small mixing bowl. Beat with electric mixer 5 minutes or until thick and lemon-colored. Slowly beat in sugar, tablespoon at a time. Mixture will become very thick. Transfer to large mixing bowl. Beat in water and vanilla. Slowly add flour mixture; beat until smooth. Pour into prepared pan, spreading evenly to corners. Bake in preheated 375°F oven 12 to 15 minutes or until cake tests done.

Loosen from pan. Turn out on rack; remove waxed paper. Invert; cool completely.

Combine chocolate, broken into pieces, and cream in heavy saucepan. Heat slowly, stirring constantly, until chocolate melts. Transfer to medium-sized mixing bowl. Stir in rum; chill 1 to 2 hours. Beat with electric mixer until stiff and thick.

Cut cake in half crosswise. Place 1 piece of cake on small cookie sheet. Top with Chocolate Filling; spread to form even layer 1½ inches thick. Top with remaining cake layer. Chill at least 1 hour.

Prepare frosting. Combine corn syrup, water, and butter in small saucepan. Bring to boil; cook until butter melts. Remove from heat. Add chocolate bits; stir until chocolate melts. Cool to room temperature. Spread over top of cake. Chill until frosting sets. Cut cake into 12 squares; arrange on decorative plate.

MAKES 12 SERVINGS.

Strudel

HUNGARY

Choose 1 filling recipe:

apple filling

1½ cups peeled, sliced tart apples	¼ cup sugar
¼ cup golden raisins	¼ teaspoon ground cinnamon
¼ cup chopped walnuts	¾ teaspoon grated lemon peel

cherry filling

1¼ cups well-drained pitted sour cherries, fresh or canned	½ cup fine dry crumbs
	¼ cup ground almonds
¾ cup sugar	Dash of ground mace

nut filling

1½ cups ground nuts (walnuts, almonds, pecans, and hazelnuts in any combination you prefer)	½ cup condensed milk
	¼ cup golden raisins

Shortbread cookies

strudel

4 strudel leaves
  (approximately 16½ ×
  12)
4 tablespoons melted sweet
  butter
2 tablespoons fine dry bread
  crumbs
1 egg yolk, well-beaten

First make filling. Combine all ingredients for filling of your choice in small bowl; mix well. Set aside.

You will need 2 linen tea towels. Spread 1 on table or counter. Lightly dampen other towel. Unwrap strudel leaves. Unroll on dampened towel; cover with plastic wrap. Place 1 strudel leaf on dry tea towel. Brush with butter or sprinkle with ½ tablespoon bread crumbs. Top with another strudel leaf. Continue in this manner until 4 leaves have been used. With long side of rectangular strudel leaves facing you, arrange filling in 3-inch-wide band, 1 inch from edge of dough, leaving 1½ inches free on both ends. Roll up like jelly roll, using towel to support dough.

Carefully transfer to lightly greased cookie sheet. Turn ends under to seal. Cut several slits in top of roll. Brush with egg yolk. Bake in preheated 375°F oven 25 minutes or until golden. Carefully remove strudel from cookie sheet; place on platter.

MAKES 6 SERVINGS.

Decker pastry

HUNGARY

4 cups flour, unsifted
4 teaspoons baking powder
2 cups sugar
1 cup butter or margarine
4 egg yolks, lightly beaten
1 cup sour cream
1 26-ounce jar cherry pie filling
4 egg whites
1 cup ground walnuts

Thoroughly combine flour, baking powder, and 1 cup sugar in mixing bowl. Cut in butter until mixture resembles coarse crumbs. Add egg yolks and sour cream; mix well to form thick dough. Press evenly in lightly greased 10½ × 15½-

Raspberries with tokay cream

inch baking sheet. Be sure to make ½-inch-high rim around edge of crust. Spread with pie filling. Bake at 350°F 25 minutes.

Meanwhile, beat egg whites until stiff but not dry. Fold in 1 cup sugar. Spread over pie filling. Sprinkle with walnuts. Return to oven; bake 15 minutes or until lightly browned. Allow to cool; cut into squares.
MAKES 12 SERVINGS.

Raspberries w/tokay cream
HUNGARY

1 pint fresh raspberries (or 1 package frozen raspberries, defrosted)
5 medium egg yolks
6 tablespoons sugar
1 pinch salt
1 tablespoon lemon juice
1 teaspoon grated lemon rind
¾ cup Tokay wine

Wash raspberries (if fresh); drain well. Divide evenly among 4 crystal goblets or sherbet dishes. Beat egg yolks in top of double boiler until well-mixed. Beat in sugar and salt. Slowly add lemon juice, lemon rind, and wine; beat until foamy. Place over simmering water; beat constantly with wire whip until mixture becomes thick and hot. Pour over raspberries.
MAKES 4 SERVINGS.

Kiffels
HUNGARY

8 ounces cream cheese
⅔ cup butter
2½ cups sifted flour

nut filling
1 egg white
12 ounces shelled English walnuts, ground
½ cup granulated sugar

Confectioners' sugar

Make sure cream cheese and butter are at room temperature before starting this recipe. Combine cream cheese, butter, and flour in mixing bowl;

work mixture well with your hands until stiff dough is formed. Divide into 60 small pieces; roll into balls. Refrigerate, covered, overnight.

The following day prepare filling before rolling dough. Beat egg white in small mixing bowl until stiff but not dry. Add walnuts and granulated sugar; mix well.

Roll dough to small thin ovals on board dusted with confectioners' sugar. Place rounded ½ teaspoons filling on each oval; roll up. Pinch ends shut; form into crescent shapes. Place on ungreased cookie sheet. Bake in preheated 375°F oven on middle rack approximately 10 minutes or until lightly browned. Remove from oven; cool on rack. Store in airtight container.
MAKES 5 DOZEN COOKIES.

Hussar's kisses
HUNGARY

½ cup butter or margarine
¼ cup sugar
2 egg yolks
2 teaspoons lemon juice
½ teaspoon grated lemon rind
1½ cups all-purpose flour (do not sift)
2 egg whites, lightly beaten
1¼ cups ground or grated blanched almonds (walnuts or other nuts may be substituted)
Apricot or plum jam or canned leckvar (poppy-seed) filling

Cream butter and sugar until light. Add egg yolks, lemon juice, and lemon rind; mix well. Thoroughly blend in flour. Refrigerate dough 2 hours.

Using teaspoon of dough for each cookie, form into 1-inch balls. Dip in egg white; roll in nuts. Place 1 inch apart on ungreased cookie sheets. Indent top of each cookie with your thumb to form small hollow. If using leckvar, fill hollows with ½ teaspoon filling before baking. Bake in preheated 375°F oven 10 minutes or until lightly browned. Remove from cookie sheet; if using jam, fill hollows now. Allow to cool on rack.
MAKES 2½ TO 3 DOZEN COOKIES.

Tea scones

IRELAND

2 cups all-purpose flour
1 tablespoon baking powder
½ teaspoon salt
1 tablespoon sugar
4 tablespoons butter or margarine
2 medium eggs
⅓ cup milk
1 egg, lightly beaten
1 tablespoon milk

Combine flour, baking powder, salt, and sugar in mixing bowl; mix well. Cut in butter. Make well in flour mixture. Beat 2 eggs and ⅓ cup milk together. Add to flour mixture; mix lightly but thoroughly. Turn out onto floured board; knead 5 times. Roll dough to 9-inch circle approximately ¾ inch thick. Cut into 8 pie-shaped wedges. Place on lightly greased baking sheet. Beat remaining egg and tablespoon of milk together. Brush tops of scones with mixture. Bake in preheated 400°F oven 7 to 10 minutes or until lightly browned. Split scones. Serve with butter and jam or honey.
MAKES 8 SCONES.

Variations:

Orange scones: Add 1 tablespoon grated orange rind to dry ingredients in basic recipe.
Currant scones: Add ½ cup currants to dry ingredients in basic recipe.
Oatmeal scones: Use 1 cup rolled oats and 1¼ cups flour in place of 2 cups flour in basic recipe.

Jam cake

IRELAND

1¾ cups sifted cake flour
¾ teaspoon baking powder
⅛ teaspoon salt
4 eggs (room temperature)
¾ cup granulated sugar
1 teaspoon grated lemon rind
½ teaspoon lemon extract
1 cup strawberry, raspberry, or blueberry jam
Confectioners' sugar

Preheat oven to 350°F. Sift together flour, bak-

ing powder, and salt; set aside. Grease and flour 2 8-inch cake pans; line with waxed paper.
In large mixing bowl beat eggs until thick and lemon-colored. Gradually beat in sugar; mixture should be thick and light. Using spatula, fold in flour mixture, lemon rind, and lemon extract. Spread in prepared cake pans. Bake 20 to 25 minutes or until toothpick inserted in center comes out clean. Cool slightly. Turn out onto rack; remove paper immediately. Cool completely.
Center one layer on serving plate. Spread with jam; top with second layer. Top with sifted confectioners' sugar.
MAKES 6 SERVINGS.

Simnel cake

IRELAND

1 cup butter	1 teaspoon ground ginger
1 cup sugar	½ teaspoon ground allspice
4 eggs	2 cups light (golden) raisins
2 tablespoons whiskey	1 cup dark seedless raisins
2 cups flour	1 cup currants
1 teaspoon baking powder	½ cup finely chopped citron
½ teaspoon salt	

marzipan mixture

2 7-ounce cans almond paste	6 tablespoons light corn syrup
2 cups confectioners' sugar	
	1 egg white, lightly beaten

Place several thicknesses of greased waxed paper in bottom of 9-inch springform pan; set aside.
Cream butter until light. Add sugar; continue creaming until well-mixed. Beat together eggs and whiskey; add to butter and sugar, beating well. Sift together flour, baking powder, salt, and spices. Wash raisins and currants in hot water; pat dry with paper towel. Combine with chopped citron. Add ½ of flour mixture to creamed mixture; stir well. Add fruits and remaining flour; mix thoroughly.
Next, prepare the Marzipan Mixture. In mixing bowl break almond paste into small pieces. Add confectioners' sugar and corn syrup; mix well. Divide into 3 equal parts.
Place ½ of cake batter in prepared pan. On

board dusted with confectioners' sugar roll ⅓ of marzipan to 9-inch circle. Place in cake pan on top of batter. Cover with remaining batter; spread evenly on top of marzipan. Bake cake in preheated 325°F oven 90 minutes. Turn oven off; let cake stand undisturbed in oven 30 minutes. Remove from oven. Cool; remove from pan.

Roll ⅓ of marzipan to 9-inch circle on confectioners'-sugar-dusted board. Place cake on cookie sheet; brush top with beaten egg white. Place marzipan on top of cake; press down firmly so it adheres to cake.

Make 12 small balls with remaining marzipan. Place 1 ball in center of cake and others around edge in a circle. Preheat broiler; lightly brown marzipan 3 to 4 inches from heat. Watch carefully. This cake freezes well or can be kept in an airtight cake tin.

MAKES 10 TO 12 SERVINGS.

Ginger cake

IRELAND

1 cup firmly packed brown sugar
½ cup butter or margarine
¼ cup unsulfured molasses
2 cups all-purpose flour
2 teaspoons ground ginger
1½ teaspoons baking powder
½ teaspoon baking soda
⅛ teaspoon salt
1 egg, lightly beaten
½ cup milk, warmed

lemon butter icing
3 tablespoons soft butter or margarine
1½ cups confectioners' sugar, sifted
1 tablespoon lemon juice (approximately)

Combine brown sugar, butter, and molasses in small saucepan; cook over low heat until sugar is dissolved. Cool. Grease and flour 8-inch-square cake pan; set aside.

Sift together flour, ginger, baking powder, soda, and salt into mixing bowl. Make well in center. Add cooled sugar mixture; mix well. Add egg and milk; continue beating 3 minutes. Pour mix-

ture into prepared cake pan. Bake in preheated 325°F oven 45 minutes or until toothpick inserted in center of cake comes out clean. Let cake stand 5 minutes. Loosen from pan; turn out onto wire rack to cool completely. Place cake on serving dish.

Beat together soft butter, sugar, and enough lemon juice to make spreadable icing. Spread on sides and top of cake.

MAKES 6 SERVINGS.

Shrove Tuesday pancakes

IRELAND

2 cups sifted all-purpose flour
2 teaspoons baking soda
2 teaspoons sugar
½ teaspoon salt
2 eggs, lightly beaten
3 tablespoons melted butter or margarine
2 cups buttermilk

Sift dry ingredients together into mixing bowl. Beat eggs, butter, and buttermilk together well. Add to dry ingredients; combine thoroughly without overmixing (small lumps may remain). Bake on a hot, lightly greased griddle or heavy frying pan until golden. Turn; continue cooking. Serve pancakes hot, spread with butter and sprinkled with sugar.

MAKES 12 PANCAKES.

Oatmeal porridge

IRELAND

2 cups water
2 cups milk
1 teaspoon salt
1 cup Irish oatmeal
½ cup seedless raisins (optional)

Combine water, milk, and salt in heavy saucepan; bring to boil. Add oatmeal and raisins; cook, stirring constantly, until mixture is smooth and starting to thicken. Reduce heat to simmer; cook 30 minutes, stirring frequently.

MAKES 4 SERVINGS.

Carrageen milk pudding

IRELAND

Carrageen is an edible form of dry seaweed, rich in vitamins, and noted for its gelling properties. It is available in health food or import stores.

½ cup tightly packed carrageen (½ ounce)
Boiling water
2 cups milk
¼ cup sugar
1 teaspoon vanilla extract
Food coloring (optional)

Pick over carrageen, discarding any foreign matter. Place in small bowl. Add boiling water to cover; stir. Drain. Combine carrageen and milk in small saucepan; cook over moderate heat, stirring frequently, approximately 15 minutes or until mixture is thick and creamy. Add sugar and vanilla; stir until sugar is dissolved. Add food coloring, if desired.

Strain mixture to remove carrageen; pour into individual molds, rinsed in cold water. Refrigerate several hours, until set. Unmold; serve with whipped cream or chocolate sauce.

MAKES 4 SERVINGS.

Variations:

Lemon milk pudding: Add grated rind of 1 lemon to milk before cooking. Omit vanilla extract; substitute ½ teaspoon lemon extract. Tint with few drops yellow food coloring, if desired.

Peppermint milk pudding: Omit vanilla extract; substitute ¼ teaspoon peppermint extract and few drops of green food coloring.

Chocolate milk pudding: Combine 1 tablespoon unsweetened cocoa with sugar; add to milk mixture.

Stuffed baked apples

IRELAND

4 baking apples (for example, Rome Beauties or Greening apples)
½ cup prepared mincemeat
1 cup apple cider
2 tablespoons butter or margarine

Wash and core apples. Pare upper half of each apple to prevent splitting. Place apples upright in small baking dish. Fill cavities in apples with mincemeat. Pour apple cider around apples; dot tops of apples with butter. Bake at 375°F 30 to 40 minutes, basting with pan juices several times during cooking.

MAKES 4 SERVINGS.

Plum pudding

IRELAND

A traditional Christmas treat.

½ cup golden raisins	*¼ teaspoon salt*
½ cup chopped citron	*½ teaspoon ground allspice*
½ cup currants	*¼ teaspoon ground nutmeg*
½ cup seedless raisins	*½ teaspoon ground ginger*
¾ cup Irish whiskey	*1¼ cups milk*
1 cup brown sugar	*1 teaspoon grated orange rind*
½ cup chopped beef suet or butter	*1 teaspoon grated lemon rind*
2 eggs	*½ cup chopped almonds*
1½ cups bread crumbs	*Boiling water*
½ cup flour	*3 tablespoons Irish whiskey*
½ teaspoon baking soda	

Combine dried fruits in small bowl. Add whiskey; mix well. Allow to stand 12 hours, stirring occasionally.

Cream sugar and suet until soft. Add eggs; mix well. Combine with bread crumbs, flour, soda, salt, and spices; add alternately with milk, mixing well after each addition. Add grated peels, soaked fruits, and nuts; stir well. Place in well-greased mold. Place mold on trivet in deep kettle. Cover top of mold with lid or 2 layers of cheesecloth tied to cover mold, topped with aluminum foil. Add boiling water ⅔ up side of mold; bring rapidly to boil. Reduce heat to low; boil 5 hours, adding more water as necessary. Cool; recover. Store in refrigerator until ready to serve.

Steam for an hour before serving to heat through. Unmold. To serve, warm 3 tablespoons whiskey; ignite. Pour over pudding. Garnish with sprig of holly; serve immediately. Serve with Hard Sauce.

MAKES 12 SERVINGS.

Hussar's kisses

Hard sauce

½ cup butter
1 cup powdered sugar
⅛ teaspoon salt
1 teaspoon vanilla extract
2 tablespoons cream
2 tablespoons Irish whiskey

Cream butter until light. Beat in sugar, salt, vanilla, and cream, mixing well. Refrigerate until needed. Just before serving, beat in whiskey. Hard sauce is best prepared several days in advance and refrigerated until needed.

Tipsy parson

IRELAND

This dessert was named for its expected effect on the parson at tea time.

1 cup blackberries, raspberries, or strawberries, thawed if frozen
6 tablespoons sugar
½ stale sponge cake, cut into 1-inch cubes (4 to 5 cake cubes).
3 tablespoons sweet sherry
1 tablespoon cornstarch
¼ teaspoon salt
2 cups milk
2 eggs, slightly beaten

1 teaspoon vanilla extract
½ cup whipping cream, whipped
Additional whipped cream for garnish
Toasted almonds

If you have a decorative cut-glass or crystal bowl, it is the ideal container for this dessert. If not, assemble dessert in individual sherbet glasses.

Pick over fruit; wash well, cutting away stems and defects. Drain well. Combine fruit and 2 tablespoons sugar in bowl; set aside. Toss cake cubes and sherry in separate bowl; set aside.

Combine 4 tablespoons sugar, cornstarch, and salt in heavy saucepan; stir to combine. Add milk; stir until well-blended. Cook over moderate heat, stirring constantly until mixture boils. Add small amount of hot mixture to beaten eggs; beat well. Slowly add egg mixture to saucepan, stirring constantly. Reduce heat to low; cook, stirring constantly, until mixture begins to bubble. Stir in vanilla; cool 15 minutes. Fold in whipped cream.

Layer cake squares, fruit, and custard in serving bowl or individual dishes. Refrigerate at least 4 hours before serving. Decorate with whipped cream and toasted almonds.

MAKES 6 SERVINGS.

Note: Any fruit can be substituted for berries. Drain canned fruit; sweeten fresh fruits to taste.

579

Tea scones

Irish fry

IRELAND

2 cups peeled, diced apples, pears, peaches, or plums or a
  mixture of these
3 tablespoons Irish whiskey
2 egg yolks
⅔ cup flat beer
1 tablespoon melted butter or margarine
1 cup all-purpose flour
¼ teaspoon salt
1 tablespoon sugar
2 egg whites
Oil for deep frying
Confectioners' sugar

Combine diced fruit and whiskey; mix well. Let
stand while preparing batter. Beat egg yolks,
beer, and butter together. Add dry ingredients;
beat until no lumps remain. Cover; refrigerate 2
hours.

Drain fruit well; mix with batter. Whip egg
whites until stiff but not dry. Fold into fritter
batter lightly but thoroughly.

Meanwhile, heat 3 inches oil in deep fryer to
375°F. Drop batter by tablespoons into hot oil;
cook until golden (3 to 4 minutes). Drain on absorbent paper. Dust with confectioners' sugar.
Serve immediately.

MAKES 6 SERVINGS.

Sweet sesame sticks

ITALY

1 cup butter or margarine
1½ cups sugar
1 teaspoon vanilla
3 eggs
5 cups self-rising flour
Milk
About 2 cups white sesame seeds

Cream the butter with an electric mixer until
light. Gradually add the sugar, beating well. Add
the vanilla and the eggs, one at a time, and beat
well after each addition. Sift the self-rising flour
and add to the creamed mixture, mixing just until smooth. Cover the dough and refrigerate for
several hours or overnight.

Pour 1 inch of milk into a shallow pie pan.
Sprinkle the sesame seed on a large sheet of
waxed paper. Using a scant tablespoon of the
dough roll on a board or between the palms of
the hands to a 3½-inch-long log. Dip in the
milk and then roll in the sesame seeds to coat
well. Place on a greased cookie sheet 1 inch
apart. Bake in a preheated 375°F oven for 15
minutes. Cool on a rack.

MAKES 6 DOZEN.

*Note: Any leftover seeds can be dried and toasted in
the oven and sprinkled on breads or salads.*

Madigan's velvet trousers

IRELAND

1 package (¼ ounce) unflavored gelatin
¼ cup cold water
½ cup heavy cream
½ cup light cream
1½ tablespoons clear honey
2 tablespoons Irish whiskey

Soak gelatin in cold water in small measuring cup. Set measuring cup in saucepan of gently boiling water; stir until gelatin dissolves (approximately 3 minutes). Remove from pan of water; set aside.

Combine creams in small well-chilled bowl; whip until light and thick. Slowly add honey and whiskey, mixing well. Place bowl in pan of ice water; fold in dissolved gelatin. Continue to mix and gently fold mixture until it begins to set. Spoon into 4 small glass serving dishes; cover. Refrigerate several hours before serving. Serve this with lady fingers or small fancy cookies.

MAKES 4 SERVINGS.

Chocolate potato cake

IRELAND

1 medium potato	*1 teaspoon baking powder*
1½ ounces semisweet chocolate	*½ teaspoon ground cinnamon*
⅔ cup butter	*¼ teaspoon ground nutmeg*
6 tablespoons sugar	*⅛ teaspoon salt*
2 eggs	*½ cup milk*
1 teaspoon vanilla	*½ cup finely chopped hazelnuts*
1½ cups flour	

chocolate-rum icing

1 tablespoon egg white	*1 tablespoon cocoa*
1 cup confectioners' sugar	*1½ tablespoons rum*

Grease and flour 9 × 5 × 3-inch loaf pan; set aside. Peel potato; coarsely grate. Place in tea towel; squeeze dry. There should be ¾ cup potato. Set aside. Grate chocolate; set aside.
Cream butter and sugar until light. Add eggs and vanilla; beat well. Sift together flour, baking powder, spices, and salt. Add alternately with milk to creamed mixture. Add potato, choco-

late, and nuts; mix well. Turn into prepared loaf pan. Bake in preheated 350°F oven 55 minutes or until cake tests done. Cook cake in pan 30 minutes; turn out onto wire rack. Ice cake while still warm.
Beat egg white in small bowl with fork until foamy. Add confectioners' sugar, cocoa, and rum; stir until smooth. Spread over cake.
MAKES 6 SERVINGS.

Irish coffee mold

IRELAND

1¼ cups coffee
¼ cup sugar
2 cloves

Jam cake

Chocolate potato cake

1 strip lemon peel
1 strip orange peel
1 small piece cinnamon stick
1 envelope unflavored gelatin
¼ cup Irish Mist or whiskey
Lightly whipped cream, flavored with sugar and vanilla
    extract

Combine coffee, sugar, cloves, lemon peel, orange peel, and cinnamon in small saucepan. Bring to boil; boil 2 minutes. Strain. Soften gelatin in Irish Mist. Add hot-coffee mixture to gelatin; stir until gelatin is dissolved.

Rinse 3 or 4 small molds with cold water. Pour in gelatin mixture; chill overnight. Unmold at serving time by dipping molds briefly in hot water. Top with whipped cream.

MAKES 3 TO 4 SERVINGS.

Sicilian cheese-filled pastries

ITALY

pastry	filling
2 cups flour	⅔ cup sugar
1 teaspoon salt	½ cup flour
2 tablespoons sugar	⅛ teaspoon salt
2 tablespoons soft butter, cut into small pieces	2 cups scalded milk
1 egg, beaten	2 eggs, lightly beaten
10 tablespoons white wine	½ teaspoon vanilla extract
Oil for frying	¼ teaspoon almond extract
5-inch long × 1-inch in diameter cannoli forms or pieces of dowel	1 pound ricotta cheese
	½ cup powdered sugar
	½ cup finely chopped candied fruit
	1 1-ounce block semisweet chocolate, grated

Combine the flour and salt in a mixing bowl. Make a well in the center and add the sugar, butter, and egg. Add the wine and stir with a fork until the liquid is absorbed. Turn out on a floured board and knead until smooth. Divide the dough into four equal parts. Roll out on a floured surface until ¹⁄₁₆th of an inch thick. Cut into 3½ inch squares. Roll the squares diagonally onto the forms, overlapping the corners. Seal with a little water. Heat ¾ of an inch of oil in a heavy skillet to 375°F. Fry the cannolis, 3 at a time, in the hot oil. When light golden, remove from the oil and slip off the forms as soon as they are cool enough to handle. Allow to cool completely.

Next make the cream filling. Combine the sugar, flour, and salt in the top of a double boiler. Slowly stir in the scalded milk. Cook the mixture over boiling water until the mixture thickens. Combine 1 cup of the custard mixture with the eggs and beat well. Pour the mixture back into the double boiler and continue to cook, stirring, 3 minutes. Cool, then stir in the flavoring (filling must be cold before adding the ricotta). Beat the ricotta and powdered sugar until the ricotta is smooth. Fold in the custard, mixed fruit, and chocolate.

Fill the cannoli with a small spatula, carefully packing the filling. Refrigerate until serving time.

MAKES 30 TO 35.

Note: Shells can be made ahead and frozen and filled as needed.

582

Almond dessert
ITALY

1 cup milk
2 eggs, separated
½ cup sugar
½ tablespoon unflavored gelatin
2 tablespoons milk
1 cup heavy cream
8 crushed almond macaroons
½ teaspoon almond extract
Almond macaroon crumbs
Candied cherries

In a medium saucepan, scald the milk. Cool slightly. Beat the egg yolks and sugar together until well-blended. Pour a little of the milk into the egg-yolk mixture. Beat well and add to the scalded milk in the saucepan. Cook over moderate heat, stirring constantly, until the mixture coats a spoon. Soften the gelatin in the 2 tablespoons of milk. Dissolve the gelatin in the hot custard. Stir well. Strain and cool the mixture covered with waxed paper.

Beat the egg whites until stiff and fold into the custard. Whip the cream until stiff and fold the cream, macaroons, and flavoring into the custard. Place in 8 individual serving dishes and garnish with macaroon crumbs and candied cherries. Refrigerate until ready to serve.
MAKES 8 SERVINGS.

Neapolitan torte
ITALY

dough
¾ cup butter
1 cup sugar
2 eggs
½ cup ground almonds
1½ teaspoons grated lemon rind
3½ cups flour

filling
1⅓ cups raspberry jam (very thick, with lots of fruit)

glaze and garnish
2 cups sifted confectioners' sugar
2 tablespoons hot water
2 tablespoons maraschino cherry liqueur
A few drops red food coloring
½ cup whipping cream
6 candied cherries, halved

Cream the butter and sugar well. Beat in the eggs one at a time. Add the almonds and lemon rind and mix. Slowly add the flour, mixing in well by hand. Form into a large ball, cover, and refrigerate 1 hour.

Divide the dough into 5 equal parts. Grease the bottom of a 10-inch springform pan. Roll out the dough 1 part at a time and cut to fit the springform pan. Place one layer of dough on the bottom section of the springform pan. Spread with ⅓ cup of the jam. Top with another layer of dough, spread with jam, and proceed as above until all the dough is used. Place the ring around the springform pan. Bake at 400°F on the bottom oven rack for 45 minutes. Cool and place on a platter.

Mix the confectioners' sugar, hot water, and maraschino liqueur and red food coloring to form a smooth glaze. Smooth over the top of the cake. Whip the cream until stiff. Place in a pastry bag fitted with a rose tip and pipe 12 rosettes around the edge of the cake. Top each rosette with ½ of a candied cherry.
MAKES 12 SERVINGS.

Neapolitan cream cake
ITALY

1 (8 × 4-inch) pound cake
3 tablespoons amaretto or brandy

chocolate cheese filling
1 pound ricotta cheese
3 tablespoons amaretto or brandy
¼ cup sugar
3 tablespoons chopped candied fruit
3 tablespoons chopped semisweet chocolate

whipped topping
1½ cups heavy cream
1 teaspoon vanilla extract
¼ cup confectioners' sugar
Additional candied fruit for garnish
Chocolate curls

With serrated knife, slice pound cake into 4 equal horizontal slices. Brush layers with 3 tablespoons liqueur; set aside. In small mixing bowl, combine ricotta, 3 tablespoons liqueur, and 583 sugar; beat until smooth. Fold in candied fruit and chocolate.

Place 1 cake layer on serving platter. Spread evenly with ⅓ cheese mixture. Top with another cake layer; continue layering until all ingredients are used. Press cake gently together. Cover; refrigerate 2 hours.

One hour before serving, chill small mixing bowl and beaters. Pour (cold) cream into chilled bowl. Add vanilla; whip until foamy. Slowly add sugar; continue beating until cream is stiff. Spread sides and top of cake lightly and evenly with whipped cream. Place remaining whipped cream in pastry bag fitted with star tip; decorate cake. Garnish with candied fruit and chocolate curls.

MAKES 8 SERVINGS.

Casrata

ITALY

1½ quarts vanilla ice cream, softened
1 quart raspberry sherbet, softened
¾ quart pistachio ice cream, softened
½ cup diced candied fruit
2 tablespoons rum
3 large egg whites
½ cup sugar
½ cup whipping cream

For garnish
1 cup whipping cream
Candied fruit

Line a 2-quart mold evenly with the vanilla ice cream. Freeze until firm, preferably in a 0°F freezer. Cover the vanilla ice cream evenly with a layer of raspberry sherbet and freeze again. Then cover with a layer of pistachio ice cream and freeze solid.

Cover the chopped candied fruit with the rum and set aside. Beat the egg whites until foamy. Slowly beat in the sugar. Whip the ½ cup of whipping cream until stiff. Fold the cream and rum-soaked fruit into the egg-white meringue, until thoroughly combined. Spoon the egg-white mixture into the center of the molded ice cream. Spread to make a smooth bottom layer. Cover

and freeze until firm (5 hours or will keep up to 2 weeks).

To unmold, dip the outside of the mold in hot water for 6 seconds and invert onto a cold platter. Whip the remaining cup of whipping cream until stiff and place in a pastry bag fitted with a decorative tip. Decorate with the cream and candied fruit and serve sliced.

SERVES 12 TO 16.

Sweetmeat

ITALY

1 cup shelled filberts
¾ cup blanched almonds
½ cup sifted flour
1 cup mixed glacéd fruit
1 tablespoon cinnamon
2 tablespoons chopped mixed candied peels
½ cup sugar
½ cup honey
Confectioners' sugar

Toast filberts in moderate oven; rub in kitchen towel to remove skins. Lightly toast almonds. Combine nuts, flour, glacéd fruit, cinnamon, and candied peels; set aside.

Combine sugar and honey in heavy saucepan. Bring to boil over moderate heat. Reduce heat to low; cook mixture undisturbed to soft-ball stage (238°F on candy thermometer). Pour into large bowl; add fruit and nut mixture; mix well. Place in 2 greased 7-inch-round cake pans (or substitute greased 10-inch pie plate). Bake at 325°F 35 minutes, until firm. Cool; dust with confectioners' sugar. Serve cut in wedges.

MAKES 12 SERVINGS.

Soft Italian nougat

ITALY

1 cup honey
2⅓ cups whole hazelnuts
2 cups whole blanched almonds
1 cup sugar
2 tablespoons water

2 egg whites
2 teaspoons vanilla extract

Thoroughly grease cookie sheet with no sides; reserve.

Place honey in top of double boiler over boiling water; cook, stirring occasionally, 1 hour or to hard-ball stage (255°F) on candy thermometer. Meanwhile place hazelnuts on cookie sheet; toast at 375°F 15 minutes. Place on tea towel; rub off skins; reserve. Place almonds on cookie sheet; toast 10 minutes; set aside. Combine sugar and water in heavy pan; cook, stirring occasionally, until caramelized. Keep warm.

Beat egg whites until stiff but not dry. When honey has reached desired temperature, beat egg whites into honey, tablespoon at a time with wooden spoon while continuing to cook. Mixture will become white and fluffy. Beat in caramelized sugar, then vanilla. Fold in nuts. Spread on prepared cookie sheet in rectangle 1½ inches thick. Cool completely; cut into 1 × 2-inch pieces. Wrap in waxed paper or cellophane.
MAKES ABOUT 32 (1 × 2-INCH) PIECES.

Bow knots

ITALY

1¼ cups flour
1 tablespoon sugar
Pinch of salt
1 tablespoon butter
1 egg
½ teaspoon lemon rind
2 tablespoons white wine
Vegetable oil for frying
Confectioners' sugar

Combine flour, sugar, and salt in mixing bowl. Cut in butter. Make well in center of flour mixture. Add egg, lemon rind, and wine. Mix to form stiff dough, adding more wine if necessary. Turn out on lightly floured surface; knead until smooth and elastic. Cover; let rest 1 hour.

Roll dough ¹⁄₁₆th inch thick; cut into rectangles 3 × 4½ inches. Make 3 lengthwise cuts in each piece of dough. The strips formed can be intertwined to form knots.

Heat at least 1 inch cooking oil to 365°F; fry 2 at a time until puffed and golden. Drain on paper towels; sprinkle with confectioners' sugar.
MAKES 15 PASTRIES.

Wine custard

ITALY

6 medium egg yolks
3 tablespoons sugar
1 pinch salt
¼ teaspoon vanilla extract
½ cup Marsala wine

In top of double boiler beat all ingredients together until foamy. Place top of double boiler over simmering (not boiling) water. Beat constantly with wire whip or eggbeater until mixture becomes thick and hot. Pour into sherbet glass; serve immediately.
MAKES 4 SERVINGS.

Variation: Omit vanilla; add juice and grated rind of 1 lemon.

Italian trifle

ITALY

pastry cream
1 cup milk
½ cup sugar
2 tablespoons cornstarch
Pinch of salt
3 egg yolks
1 teaspoon vanilla extract

cake
1 recipe Sponge Cake (see Index), baked, completely cooled cooled
3 tablespoons rum
¼ cup apricot jam

meringue
5 egg whites
¼ teaspoon cream of tartar
1 cup powdered sugar

In medium saucepan heat milk to boiling point over moderate heat. Combine sugar, cornstarch, and salt; mix well. Stir into hot milk. Cook, stirring constantly, until thickened. Remove from heat.

In small bowl beat egg yolks well. Pour small amount of hot mixture into eggs; beat well. Slowly add remaining hot mixture, beating well. Return to heat. Cook, stirring constantly, until mixture bubbles. Stir in vanilla; cool completely. Cut sponge cake into 3 equal layers. Place 1 layer on cookie sheet. Sprinkle with 1 tablespoon rum; spread with 2 tablespoons jam. Spread with ½ pastry cream. Top with another cake layer. Sprinkle with 1 tablespoon rum; spread with 2 tablespoons jam. Spread with remaining pastry cream. Top with last cake layer; sprinkle with remaining rum.

Combine egg whites and cream of tartar in large mixing bowl. Beat until foamy. Slowly add sugar, tablespoon at a time. Continue beating until stiff and glossy. Spread layer of meringue over top and sides of cake. Put remaining meringue in pastry bag; decorate cake.

Bake in preheated 350°F oven about 15 minutes, until golden. Cool. Carefully transfer to serving dish. Chill.

MAKES 8 TO 10 SERVINGS.

Coffee ice

ITALY

2 cups water

1 cup sugar

4 cups espresso coffee (fresh or made from instant according to package directions)

½ cup whipping cream

½ teaspoon vanilla

2 tablespoons sugar

Chopped pistachio nuts (optional)

Combine water and sugar in small heavy saucepan. Bring to boil over moderate heat, stirring until sugar is dissolved. Reduce heat to low. Cook, stirring occasionally, 3 to 4 minutes, until mixture is syrupy. Combine with espresso, mixing well; cool. Place in freezer trays in zero-degree freezer. Freeze 3 hours; stir several times the first hour, until firm ice is formed.

Whip cream, vanilla, and sugar until stiff. Empty coffee ice into blender; whirl briefly to break up ice crystals. Place in chilled sherbet glasses; top with whipped cream. Sprinkle with chopped pistachio nuts.

MAKES 6 SERVINGS.

St. Joseph's fig cookies

ITALY

fig filling

1 cup dried figs

½ cup light raisins

¼ cup candied cherries

¼ cup almonds

¼ cup hot water

2 tablespoons honey

dough

2½ cups flour

⅓ cup sugar

¼ teaspoon baking powder

½ teaspoon salt

½ cup butter

½ cup milk

1 egg, beaten

3 tablespoons butter or margarine

2 tablespoons sugar

First make filling. Put figs, raisins, cherries, and almonds through food grinder or processor, or finely mince. Add water and honey; mix well. Set aside.

Make dough. In mixing bowl combine flour, sugar, baking powder, and salt. Cut in butter. Beat milk and egg together. Add to flour mixture; mix to form stiff dough. Turn out on lightly floured surface; knead 5 times. Roll to rectangle measuring 18 × 15 inches. Cut into 16 rectangular pieces.

Place 1 heaping tablespoon filling in center of each rectangle dough. Fold corners of each rectangle toward center. Place on lightly greased cookie sheet. Brush with melted butter; sprinkle with sugar. Bake at 350°F 20 to 25 minutes, until lightly browned.

Almond macaroons

ITALY

1 (8-ounce) package almond paste
4 egg whites
¾ cup sugerfine granulated sugar
2 tablespoons cake flour
¼ teaspoon salt

Cut almond paste into small pieces. Work 2 egg whites into almond paste. Slowly add sugar, flour, and salt. Mix well after each addition. Work in remaining egg whites; mix until free of lumps.

Grease and flour cookie sheets. Drop almond paste mixture by 1-inch balls 2 inches apart on cookie sheets. Bake at 300°F 20 to 30 minutes, until lightly browned. Remove from cookie sheet while still warm; cool completely.

MAKES ABOUT 2½ DOZEN COOKIES.

Note: Cookies can be decorated with halves of blanched almonds or pieces of candied cherry before baking.

Sponge cake

ITALY

3 large eggs
1 cup granulated sugar
⅓ cup water
1 cup cake flour
1 teaspoon baking powder
¼ teaspoon salt
1 teaspoon grated lemon peel

Line 15 × 10½ × 1-inch baking pan with waxed paper. Grease paper well. Preheat oven to 375°F.

Beat eggs in mixing bowl until thick and lemon-colored. Slowly add sugar to eggs; beat until mixture is pale in color and double in volume. Add water; blend on low speed.

Combine flour, baking powder, and salt. Gradually add egg mixture and lemon peel; beat until batter is smooth. Spread evenly in prepared pan. Bake at 375°F 12 to 15 minutes, until pick inserted in cake comes out clean. Turn out on tea towel; remove paper. Cool completely.

MAKES 1 (15 × 10½ × 1-INCH) LAYER.

Cannelloni alla Siciliana

Pears poached in red wine

ITALY

4 firm ripe pears with stems (about 2 pounds)
1 tablespoon lemon juice
1½ cups rosé wine
¾ cup sugar
1 cinnamon stick
4 cloves
3 strips lemon peel
Lemon slices

Skin, halve, and core pears, leaving stems intact. Place in water with lemon juice to prevent darkening. Combine wine, sugar, cinnamon, cloves, and lemon peel in large skillet. Heat to boiling, stirring to dissolve sugar.

Drain pear halves; add to skillet. Poach over low heat 10 to 15 minutes, until fork-tender (not mushy). Chill (in syrup); serve garnished with lemon slices.

MAKES 4 SERVINGS.

Neopolitan torte

Crisp wafer cookies (Pizelle)

ITALY

Although a special iron is required to make these cookies, they are delicious and addictive! Pizzelle plates are also available for many electric waffle irons.

½ cup margarine, room temperature
⅔ cup sugar
4 eggs, well beaten
1 teaspoon vanilla extract or anise extract
1½ cups flour
1 teaspoon baking powder
Pinch of salt
½ cup finely chopped nuts (optional)

Cream margarine well. Add sugar; beat until light and fluffy. Add eggs and flavoring; beat well. Sift together flour, baking powder, and salt. Slowly add dry ingredients to creamed mixture; mix well after each addition. Fold in nuts. Batter should be soft and sticky.
Lightly grease pizzelle iron; follow manufacturer's directions for baking. Use approximately 1 rounded teaspoon batter for each pizzelle. Discard first one or two cookies; they absorb excess oil from iron. These cookies keep very well in airtight container or can be frozen.
MAKES ABOUT 3 DOZEN COOKIES.

Anise cookies

ITALY

These cookies are very crisp and are often used for dunking in coffee or in wine.

1 cup butter
2 cups sugar
6 eggs
4 tablespoons aniseed
1 teaspoon vanilla
3 tablespoons anisette
5½ cups flour
1 tablespoon baking powder
2 cups chopped blanched almonds

Cream butter until soft. Slowly add sugar; mix well. Beat in eggs, 1 at a time. Add aniseed, vanilla, and anisette; mix well. Sift flour and baking powder together; stir into egg mixture. Stir in almonds; chill dough 2 to 3 hours.
Lightly grease several cookie sheets. On lightly floured board form dough into flat loaves ½ inch thick, 2 inches wide, and almost as long as cookie sheets. Place several inches apart on cookie sheets. (You should have 6 loaves.) Bake at 375°F 20 minutes. Remove from oven; cool. Slice loaves diagonally into ½ - to ¾-inch-thick slices. Lay slices, cut-side-down, close together on cookie sheet. Bake at 375°F 15 minutes, until lightly browned. Cool; store airtight.
MAKES APPROXIMATELY 100 COOKIES.

Florentines

ITALY

½ cup butter
¾ cup sugar
3 eggs
¾ teaspoon almond extract
1 teaspoon grated orange peel
2½ cups all-purpose flour
1½ teaspoons baking powder
¼ teaspoon salt
1 cup ground almonds
1 cup semisweet chocolate chips
2 tablespoons hot water

Cream the butter and sugar. Add the eggs one at a time, beating well after each addition. Beat in the almond extract and the orange peel. Sift together the flour, baking powder, and salt and add to the creamed mixture and stir well to combine. Add the almonds and stir well. Refrigerate the dough for several hours.

Lightly grease a cookie sheet. Form the dough into long loaves 1½ inches wide and ½ inch thick. Make sure the loaves are several inches apart as the cookies spread in baking. Make the loaves as long as your cookie sheet allows, but leave at least an inch space between the end of the loaf and the edge of the cookie sheet to prevent burning. Bake at 375°F for 12 to 15 minutes or until lightly browned and a toothpick inserted in the center of the loaf comes out clean. While still warm, cut the loaves into ¾-inch strips and cool on a cake rack.

Melt the chocolate chips over hot water, stirring occasionally. When completely melted, stir in just enough boiling water to make a thick mixture with consistency of layer-cake icing. Dip both ends of the cookie strips in the chocolate and allow to dry on a rack until the chocolate has hardened.

MAKES 3½ TO 4 DOZEN COOKIES.

Casrata

Italian trifle

Chocolate cookies

ITALY

dough

4 cups all-purpose flour	¾ cup raisins
1 teaspoon baking powder	¾ cup chopped walnuts
¼ cup cocoa	1¼ cups hydrogenated
¾ teaspoon ground	shortening
cinnamon	1 cup plus 2 tablespoons
¾ teaspoon ground allspice	sugar
¾ teaspoon ground cloves	2 eggs, slightly beaten
¾ teaspoon ground nutmeg	1 cup milk

frosting

3 cups confectioners' sugar	1½ teaspoons rum flavoring
4 tablespoons milk	Several drops red food
	coloring

Sift the flour. Add the baking powder, cocoa, and spices to the flour and sift 2 more times. Add the raisins and walnuts to the flour mixture and mix well. Cream the shortening and sugar until light. Add the eggs and beat well. Add the flour mixture a little at a time alternately with the milk until all the ingredients are combined. Mix well. Refrigerate the dough for several hours or overnight.

Using a rounded teaspoon of dough, form into small balls. Place on a lightly greased cookie sheet 1 inch apart. Bake at 400°F for 10 minutes or until a toothpick inserted in the center of a cookie comes out clean. Remove from the cookie sheet and cool on a cake rack.

When the cookies have cooled completely, make the frosting. Combine the confectioners' sugar, milk, flavoring and food coloring and mix well. Spread the top of each cookie with 1 teaspoon of icing and allow to dry on waxed paper. Store in airtight cookie tins.

MAKES ABOUT 8 DOZEN.

Sicilian iced cookies

ITALY

dough

½ cup margarine	1 teaspoon vanilla
½ cup shortening	2 cups all-purpose flour
½ cup sugar	2 teaspoons baking powder
2 eggs	6 tablespoons milk

icing

2¼ cups sifted confectioners' sugar	A few drops red food coloring
3 tablespoons maraschino cherry liqueur	2 tablespoons warm water
	Colored candy decorettes

Melt the margarine and shortening in a medium saucepan. Remove from the heat and add the sugar. Mix well. Beat the eggs well and add to the mixture. Add the vanilla and mix well. Combine the flour and baking powder. Add to the butter and sugar mixture and stir well. Slowly add the milk and mix to form a stiff dough. Refrigerate the dough several hours or overnight. Drop the mixture by rounded teaspoons onto a greased cookie sheet. Bake at 350°F for 8 to 10 minutes or until lightly browned. Cool on a rack.

When the cookies have cooled completely, make the icing. Place the confectioners' sugar in a small mixing bowl. Make a well in the center. Place the cherry liqueur and the food coloring in the well (use enough to make the frosting a pale pink). Stir the sugar into the liquid to form a very stiff paste. Slowly add the warm water, while stirring, until the mixture is smooth and spreadable. Ice the tops of the cookies and sprinkle with the candy decorettes. Allow to dry on the cake racks. Store in an airtight container.

MAKES 4 DOZEN COOKIES.

Cottage-cheese and pear stacks

POLAND

1 1-pound can pear halves
1 cup all-purpose white flour
½ teaspoon baking soda
¼ teaspoon salt
2 tablespoons granulated sugar
1 egg, beaten
1 cup sour milk
⅓ cup butter, melted
2 cups small-curd cottage cheese

Drain pear halves, reserving liquid for Marmalade Sauce.

Combine flour, baking soda, salt, and sugar. Blend egg and milk; beat into flour mixture until smooth. Pour 1 tablespoon butter into 5½-inch skillet. Add enough batter to cover bottom of pan; brown on both sides. Repeat, using remaining batter. Stack pancakes, spreading cottage cheese between each layer.

Arrange pear quarters, fan-shape, on top of stack. Cut in wedges; serve with Marmalade Sauce.

MAKES 6 SERVINGS.

Marmalade sauce

¾ cup pear syrup
1 cup orange marmalade
1 tablespoon cornstarch
¼ teaspoon mace

Combine all ingredients. Cook until thickened. Serve over Cottage-Cheese and Pear Stacks.

MAKES 1¼ CUPS.

Hot-water chocolate cake

POLAND

2 cups granulated sugar
2 cups all-purpose white flour
¼ cup cocoa
½ teaspoon salt
1 teaspoon soda
½ cup butter
1 cup water
½ cup sour milk
2 eggs, beaten
1 teaspoon vanilla

Combine sugar, flour, cocoa, salt, and soda. Set aside. Bring butter and water to boil. Remove from heat; stir in dry ingredients. Add milk, eggs, and vanilla; mix thoroughly.

Pour cake batter into greased 9 × 13-inch pan. Bake at 375°F for 25 minutes or until a toothpick inserted into center comes out clean. Remove cake from the oven; frost immediately with Chocolate Frosting.

MAKES 24 SERVINGS.

591

Chocolate frosting

⅓ cup half-and-half cream
½ cup butter
⅓ cup cocoa
1 pound powdered sugar
1 teaspoon vanilla
½ cup English walnuts

Combine half-and-half, butter, and cocoa in saucepan. Bring to boil. Add powdered sugar and vanilla; beat until blended. Stir in English walnuts. Spread on cake while frosting and cake are still warm.

Cinnamon cake

POLAND

¾ cup butter
1 cup granulated sugar
1 egg
1½ teaspoons cinnamon
1½ cups all-purpose white flour
1½ cups whipping cream
1 teaspoon vanilla

Cream butter until soft. Gradually add ¾ cup sugar; beat until light and fluffy. Add egg; beat well. Add cinnamon and flour; mix well. Spread about ⅓ of batter on ungreased baking sheet into a rectangle about 10 × 12 inches. Bake in 400°F oven 8 minutes or until lightly browned. Remove from oven; let stand a few minutes. Cut cake into 3 equal rectangles (4 × 10); transfer to cooling rack.
Repeat process twice with remaining batter.
Whip cream until stiff. Fold in ¼ cup sugar and vanilla. Spread a thin layer of whipped cream between each piece of cake. Top with remaining cream; serve immediately.
MAKES 8 SERVINGS.

Easter cake

POLAND

½ cup milk
½ cup granulated sugar
½ teaspoon salt
¼ cup butter
¼ cup warm water
1 package active dry yeast
2 eggs, beaten
2½ cups all-purpose white flour
½ cup chopped almonds
½ cup raisins
½ teaspoon lemon peel
1 cup confectioners' sugar
1 tablespoon milk
Whole candied cherries

Scald milk. Stir in sugar, salt, and butter. Cool to lukewarm. Pour lukewarm water into large bowl. Sprinkle yeast over water; stir until dissolved. Add milk mixture, eggs, and flour; beat vigorously 5 minutes. Cover; let rise in warm place, free from draft, for 1½ hours or until doubled in bulk.
Stir batter down; beat in almonds, raisins, and lemon peel. Pour batter into greased and floured 1½-quart casserole. Let rise for 1 hour. Bake in 350°F oven 50 minutes. Let cool in pan 20 minutes before removing.
Beat together 1 cup confectioners' sugar and 1 tablespoon milk to form glaze. To serve, place cake on serving platter; drizzle glaze on top. Garnish with cherries.
MAKES 8 SERVINGS.

Cheesecake

POLAND

18 ounces cream cheese
⅔ cup zwieback crumbs, packed
1 teaspoon vanilla
5 egg whites
1 cup granulated sugar
1 can fruit pie filling (cherry, pineapple, or apple)

Let cream cheese stand at room temperature until softened. Sprinkle bottom and sides of buttered 8-inch springform pan with zwieback crumbs, pressing any extra crumbs evenly on bottom of pan.
Put cream cheese into mixing bowl. Add vanilla; cream until fluffy. Beat egg whites until foamy. Beat in sugar, ⅓ cup at a time, beating well after each addition. Beat until whites are stiff enough to hold a peak but not dry. Fold gently

into cheese. Turn mixture into springform pan lined with zwieback. Bake at 350°F for 25 minutes. Remove from oven (center will still be soft); let cool away from drafts. When cake is room temperature, chill in refrigerator 4 hours. Remove side of pan. Cut into serving pieces; garnish with fruit filling.
MAKES 12 SERVINGS.

Vanilla ice cream

POLAND

½ cup granulated sugar
4 egg yolks
2 cups half-and-half cream
2 cups whipping cream
2 teaspoons vanilla

Mix sugar and egg yolks in top of double boiler. Pour half-and-half cream on top of egg-yolk mixture. Cook egg-yolk and half-and-half mixture in double boiler until mixture coats spoon. Cool and strain. Add cream and vanilla. Freeze in conventional ice-cream freezer.
MAKES 1½ QUARTS.

Rice pudding w/sour cream

POLAND

1½ cups cold water
1 cup whole milk
1 teaspoon salt
1 cup uncooked rice
1 cup seedless raisins
2 tablespoons butter
2 tablespoons granulated sugar
½ teaspoon nutmeg
1 cup sour cream
¼ cup sugar
1 teaspoon vanilla extract

Combine 1 cup cold water, milk, salt, and uncooked rice in 3-quart saucepan. Place on heated surface; bring mixture to boil. Stir rice once; cover. Turn heat very low; cook for 20 minutes or until water and milk are absorbed. Do not lift lid during cooking.
While rice is cooking, combine remaining ½ cup cold water and raisins. Simmer for 10 min-

utes or until raisins have absorbed their cooking water. Combine cooked rice and raisins. Blend in butter, 2 tablespoons sugar, and nutmeg. Mix well. Pour rice pudding into greased 1-quart mold. Chill.
In chilled bowl, whip sour cream until it stands in soft peaks. Blend in ¼ cup sugar and vanilla. Be careful not to overwhip the sour cream, or butter will result. To serve pudding, slice and top with whipped sour cream.
MAKES 8 SERVINGS.

Baba au rum

POLAND

½ cup milk
⅓ cup butter
1 teaspoon salt
1¼ cups granulated sugar
1 package active dry yeast
¼ cup warm water
2 eggs, beaten
½ teaspoon grated lemon peel
2¼ cups all-purpose white flour
½ cup water
½ cup molasses
½ cup rum
½ cup powdered sugar

Scald milk; add butter, salt, and ¼ cup granulated sugar until melted. Cool to lukewarm. Dissolve yeast in warm water. Add to lukewarm milk; mix well. Stir in beaten eggs and lemon peel. Add flour; beat until smooth. Cover; let rise for 5 hours. Beat down until smooth and elastic.
Fill greased tube pan or Baba mold. Let dough rise uncovered 30 minutes. Bake in 425°F oven 20 minutes or until done. Remove from pan at once.
Combine ½ cup water, 1 cup sugar, and molasses in heavy saucepan. Bring mixture to boil; boil rapidly 10 minutes. Cool mixture slightly; add rum. Place Baba in serving dish; spoon over the rum sauce gradually and gently, allowing the Baba to absorb it. Let stand 24 hours in the refrigerator. To serve, dust Baba with powdered sugar.
MAKES 12 SERVINGS.

Almond torte

POLAND

6 egg yolks
1 cup granulated sugar
1 teaspoon grated lemon rind
2 tablespoons lemon juice
1 teaspoon cinnamon
1 cup ground almonds
¾ cup fine bread crumbs
6 egg whites
¼ teaspoon salt

Beat egg yolks until thick and light in color. Gradually beat in sugar; continue beating until light and fluffy. Add lemon rind, juice, cinnamon, almonds, and bread crumbs; blend well. Whip egg whites and salt until stiff. Fold egg whites carefully into yolk mixture. Pour into greased 8-inch tube pan; bake in 350°F oven 1 hour. Remove from oven; let cool in pan.
MAKES 8 SERVINGS.

Warsaw party torte

POLAND

½ pound almonds, ground
6 tablespoons all-purpose white flour
1 teaspoon cream of tartar
10 egg yolks
1¾ cups granulated sugar
3 teaspoons vanilla
10 egg whites
3 cups whipping cream
1 cup slivered almonds, toasted
12 fresh red raspberries

Combine ground almonds, flour, and cream of tartar. Beat egg yolks until light and fluffy. Gradually beat 1¼ cups sugar into egg yolks; continue to beat until mixture is thick and smooth. Stir in 1 teaspoon vanilla. Fold in flour mixture. Beat egg whites until very stiff. Fold egg whites into egg-yolk mixture.
Line bottom of 10-inch tube pan with wax paper. Pour batter into pan. Bake in 375°F oven 1 hour or until done. Invert cake; cool thoroughly. Remove from pan.

Whip cream, adding ½ cup granulated sugar and 2 teaspoons vanilla at end of whipping period. Place cake, top-side-down, on serving platter; cover center hole with small plastic or cardboard disk. Frost cake with whipped cream. Using pastry tube, decorate edge with whipped-cream flowers. Press toasted almonds around sides of frosted cake. Garnish each whipped-cream flower with a fresh raspberry. Refrigerate torte prior to serving.
MAKES 12 SERVINGS.

Dessert crêpe batter

POLAND

3 eggs, beaten
1½ teaspoons granulated sugar
1¾ cups milk
1½ cups all-purpose white flour
3 tablespoons butter, melted
1 teaspoon vanilla
½ cup butter, melted

Beat eggs until frothy. Combine with sugar and milk; gradually beat into flour. Add 3 tablespoons melted butter and vanilla; beat smooth. (Batter should be quite thin.) Heat 1 tablespoon butter in heavy 5-inch skillet. Pour in just enough batter to cover bottom of pan. Cook until bubbles appear and underside is browned. Turn or flip; lightly brown other side. Continue to make crêpes, heating a teaspoon of butter to sizzling for each crêpe.
Serve crêpes warm with your favorite sauce.
MAKES 2 DOZEN CRÊPES.

Cottage-cheese-filled crêpes

POLAND

1 recipe Crêpe Batter (see Index)
1½ cups dry-curd cottage cheese
1 teaspoon cinnamon
2 egg yolks, beaten
2 tablespoons granulated sugar
1 teaspoon vanilla
3 tablespoons kirsch
¼ cup powdered sugar

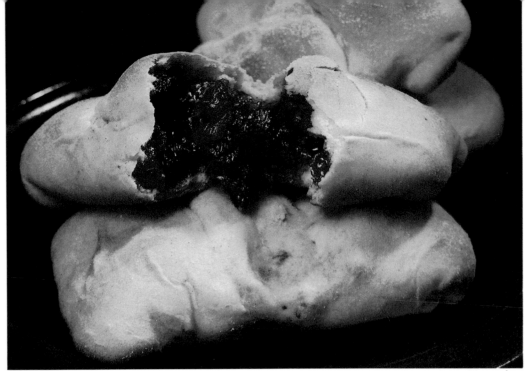

Prepare crêpes as directed. Keep them warm. Rub cottage cheese through a sieve. Mix with cinnamon, egg yolks, granulated sugar, vanilla, and kirsch. Fill crêpes with cottage-cheese mixture; roll them up. To serve, place crêpes on warm serving dish; dust with powdered sugar.
MAKES 2 DOZEN CRÊPES.

Sugar and spice rice

POLAND

1 cup cold water
1 cup whole milk
1 teaspoon salt
1 cup uncooked rice
½ cup butter
½ cup granulated sugar
2 teaspoons cinnamon

Combine water, milk, salt, and uncooked rice in 3-quart saucepan. Bring mixture to boil. Stir rice once; cover. Turn heat very low; cook for 20 minutes or until water and milk are absorbed. Do not uncover while cooking.
Spoon rice into serving dishes; top each serving with 2 tablespoons butter, 2 tablespoons sugar, and ½ teaspoon cinnamon. Serve immediately.
MAKES 4 SERVINGS.

Soft custard

SPAIN

3 eggs
2 egg yolks
½ cup granulated sugar
3 cups milk
2 4-inch cinnamon sticks
6 ladyfingers
Whipped cream

Combine eggs, egg yolks, and sugar. Beat at medium speed with electric mixer 5 minutes or until mixture thickens. Heat milk and cinnamon sticks slowly in heavy saucepan until mixture starts to bubble around edges. *Do not boil.* Remove cinnamon sticks. Beating constantly, slowly pour hot milk into egg mixture in steady stream. Pour mixture into top of double boiler. Cook over boiling water, stirring constantly, 20 to 25 minutes or until thickened. Pour into serving dishes; cover with waxed paper. Refrigerate until cooled.
To serve, garnish each dish with a ladyfinger and whipped cream.
MAKES 6 SERVINGS.

Fried custard squares

SPAIN

1 cup all-purpose flour
3 cups milk
½ teaspoon cinnamon
½ cup granulated sugar
1 teaspoon vanilla
¼ cup butter*
1 egg, beaten
1 cup coffee-cake or sweet-bun crumbs

Pour flour into heavy saucepan. Slowly add 1 cup milk to form smooth paste. Add remaining milk, cinnamon, and sugar. Beat with electric

Almond macaroons

mixer until smooth. Place mixture over heat. Cook on high until mixture boils and thickens. (Stir constantly while cooking, to prevent scorching.) When mixture thickens, remove from flame; beat in vanilla. Pour custard mixture into 8-inch-square cake pan. Chill 5 hours. Remove custard from refrigerator; cut into 2-inch squares. Melt butter in skillet. Coat custard squares with egg, then with crumbs. Fry in butter until golden brown on both sides, about 40 seconds on each side. Serve hot.
MAKES 8 SERVINGS.

*Olive oil may be substituted if you prefer.

Coconut pudding

SPAIN

8 egg yolks
1 cup sugar
½ cup flour
2 cups milk
½ cup dry white wine
1½ cups freshly grated coconut
1 teaspoon vanilla extract
Chopped almonds

Combine egg yolks, sugar, and flour. Beat until creamy. Place milk and wine in double boiler. Heat to boiling. Pour milk mixture slowly into egg mixture, stirring constantly to prevent curdling. Add coconut and vanilla; mix well. Cook over double boiler until mixture thickens and coats wooden spoon. Cover top with waxed paper to prevent scum from forming. Cool in refrigerator.

To serve, spoon into serving dishes; sprinkle with chopped almonds.

596 MAKES 6 TO 8 SERVINGS.

Cinnamon flan

SPAIN

1 cup sugar
2 tablespoons water
4 eggs
1 14-ounce can sweetened condensed milk
1 cup water
½ teaspoon cinnamon
½ teaspoon grated lemon rind

Combine sugar and 2 tablespoons water in heavy, small skillet. Cook, stirring constantly,

Florentines

until caramelized and syrupy. Immediately pour into warm 4-cup buttered mold; tilt to coat bottom and sides of container while sugar is still hot.

Beat eggs well. Add milk, 1 cup water, cinnamon, and lemon peel; mix well. Pour into prepared mold. Place casserole in larger pan containing hot water to level of custard. Bake at 350°F 1 hour or until knife inserted in center comes out clean. Cool completely. Loosen custard with knife; invert on serving platter. Spoon caramel over top.
MAKES 4 TO 6 SERVINGS.

Polish Easter cake

Mint apple crisp

SPAIN

½ cup granulated sugar
½ cup brown sugar
2 eggs, beaten
1 cup all-purpose flour
½ teaspoon salt
2 teaspoons baking powder
1 teaspoon cinnamon
1½ cups cooking apples, peeled, diced
1 teaspoon mint flavoring
½ cup chopped blanched almonds
1 cup table cream

Gradually add sugars to eggs; beat well. Add flour, salt, baking powder, and cinnamon. Fold in apples, mint flavoring, and nuts. Pour into greased 9 × 9-inch pan. Bake in 350°F oven 30 minutes. Serve apple crisp warm with cream.
MAKES 6 SERVINGS.

Honeyed apples

SPAIN

4 medium cooking apples
¼ cup chopped blanched almonds
⅓ cup chopped dried figs
¼ cup butter
¼ cup honey

Core apples. Cut thin line through peeling around center of each apple. Place apples in baking dish. Combine almonds and figs. Fill apple centers with fig and nut mixture. Place 1 tablespoon butter and honey in each apple center. Bake in 375°F oven 45 minutes or until apples are tender but still retain their shape. Baste occasionally with liquid that accumulates on bottom of pan.

Remove apples from oven; gently slip top half of apple peel away. Place apples in serving dish; spoon pan juice over apples. Serve warm.
MAKES 4 SERVINGS.

Strawberries in wine

SPAIN

Fresh fruit is a popular dessert and/or snack in Spain.

24 large, freshly picked strawberries
1 cup dry white wine
Sugar

Remove stems from strawberries; wash thoroughly. Place in shallow dish; cover with wine. Allow to marinate 3 to 4 hours in refrigerator. Remove strawberries from wine (save wine for a punch); arrange on serving tray. Place small bowl of sugar on tray to allow guests to coat strawberries with sugar if desired.
MAKES 4 TO 6 SERVINGS.

Baba au rum

Valencia crêpes

SPAIN

4 eggs
1 cup flour
2 tablespoons sugar
1 cup milk
¼ cup water
1 tablespoon melted margarine
8 Valencia oranges
3 tablespoons kirsch
2 tablespoons Grand Marnier
1 cup sour cream
8 ounces cream cheese, softened
½ cup sugar
Powdered sugar for dusting

Beat eggs with whisk in medium mixing bowl. Gradually add flour and sugar alternately with milk and water, beating until smooth. Beat in margarine. Refrigerate 1 hour before using. Prepare crêpes.

Peel oranges. Cut into segments, cutting between membranes. Slice each segment into 3 to 4 pieces. Sprinkle oranges with kirsch and Grand Marnier. Blend sour cream, cream cheese, and sugar. Fold oranges into cream mixture, saving ½ cup oranges for garnish. Top each crêpe with 2 to 3 tablespoons cheese and orange mixture. Roll up.

Place crêpes on serving platter. Dust with powdered sugar. Garnish with orange slices.
MAKES 6 SERVINGS.

Spanish wings

SPAIN

⅓ cup shortening
⅔ cup sugar
1 tablespoon cold water
2 egg yolks
1 teaspoon freshly grated lemon peel
2 cups flour
¼ teaspoon salt
2 egg whites, unbeaten

Cream shortening and sugar until light and fluffy. Beat in water, egg yolks, and lemon peel. Work flour and salt in with your hands to form smooth dough. Wrap dough in waxed paper; chill.

Pinch off walnut-size piece of dough; roll it into 4- to 5-inch rope. Place on cookie sheet. Fold rope in middle, then fold each end back to meet fold in middle. Pinch together. Brush with egg whites. Bake at 325°F 10 minutes or until cookies just start to turn brown.
MAKES 4 DOZEN CRISP COOKIES.

Danish pastry

DENMARK

2 packages dry yeast
¼ cup lukewarm water
1¾ cups heated milk, cooled to lukewarm
½ cup sugar
½ teaspoon salt
½ teaspoon ground cardamom
7 to 7½ cups flour
2 eggs
1 pound butter or margarine
Raspberry jam

In large bowl dissolve the yeast in lukewarm water. Blend in the milk. Add the sugar, salt, cardamom, and flour sifted together. Add beaten eggs. Add ¼ pound of the butter, either softened or melted. Mix thoroughly (fingers may be used in a kneading motion) and set aside in a covered bowl to rise for 30 minutes.

Roll out the dough on a board (flour is not necessary) into a large rectangle. Dot ⅔ of this dough with a whole stick of butter. Fold the unbuttered ⅓ of the dough over half of the buttered portion. Then fold the remaining ⅓ to make 3 thicknesses. Seal the edges; cover the dough with a sheet of wax paper and a cloth. Let it rise for 20 minutes.

Turn the dough halfway around and repeat the procedure, making sure there are again 3 layers and using another stick of butter. Let the dough rise again for 20 minutes. Turn the dough a third time and roll it out again. This time use the last stick of butter. Seal the edges as before and let it rise for another 20 minutes.

Shape the dough as desired. Crescents, combs,

or envelopes may be used, or you might try the following. Divide the dough in 2 parts. Set aside 1 part. Roll out half of the dough into a rectangle 8 × 12 inches. With a knife cut the dough in strips about ½ inch wide. Curl the dough around itself to form a round Danish. (The size you use depends on the size pastries you prefer.) Put the round circles on an ungreased baking sheet. Put ½ teaspoon of raspberry jam (or your own preference) in the center of each Danish. When the baking sheet is full, set it aside to rise for another 45 minutes. Bake the pastry in a hot oven (450°F) for 15 to 20 minutes. Eat and enjoy.
MAKES 40 OR MORE PASTRIES.

Quick Danish

DENMARK

2 packages dry yeast
¼ cup sugar
1 cup milk
4 cups flour
2 egg yolks
½ teaspoon salt
4 tablespoons butter
Fruit marmalade or preserves for filling
2 extra egg yolks for garnish
Sugar for garnish
Chopped almonds for garnish

Dissolve the yeast and 1 tablespoon of the sugar in 2 tablespoons of warm milk. Let this sit for 10 minutes. Sift the flour. Mix the yeast with the flour, the remainder of the sugar and milk, the egg yolks, and salt. Work this mixture until the dough is smooth and elastic and does not stick to your hands. Cover the well-worked dough and set it aside to rise for at least 15 minutes.
On a floured board roll out the dough to ½ inch thick. Dot it with 4 teaspoons of the butter and fold the dough together. Roll out the dough again, repeating this process until all the butter has been used. Let the dough rest for about 10 minutes.
Roll out the dough for the final time to ½ inch thick. Cut it into 4-inch squares. Place the mar-

malade or preserves in the center of each square and form the dough into horn- or pocket-shaped pieces. Place the pieces on a greased baking sheet. Coat the unbaked pastries with beaten egg yolks; sprinkle with sugar and almonds. Bake them at 400°F for 20 minutes.
MAKES ABOUT 10 PASTRIES.

Cinnamon coffee cake

DENMARK

⅓ cup butter
¾ cup sugar
2 eggs
1 cup flour
¼ cup cornstarch
2 teaspoons baking powder
½ teaspoon salt
½ teaspoon ground cardamom
½ cup milk
topping
⅓ cup sugar
½ teaspoon cinnamon
¼ cup slivered almonds or chopped nuts

Cream the butter and sugar. Add beaten eggs. Sift the dry ingredients together and add them alternately with the milk. Put this in a round, 8-inch well-greased baking pan. Mix the topping ingredients and sprinkle the cake with the mixture. Bake the cake at 375°F for 30 minutes.
MAKES 6 OR MORE SERVINGS.

Christmas crullers

DENMARK

3 eggs
⅓ cup sugar
⅔ cup butter or margarine, melted
¼ teaspoon ground cardamom
Grated rind of 1 lemon
3 tablespoons cream
4 cups flour
Shortening for deep-frying
Confectioners' sugar (optional)

Beat the eggs and sugar together until very light. Stir in the melted butter, cardamom, and lemon rind. Next add the cream and flour. The dough will be quite buttery and easy to handle.

Roll out the dough thin, about ¼ inch. Cut it with a pastry cutter or knife into 1-inch-wide oblongs. Cut a slit into the middle of each oblong and pull one corner through to make a knot. Fry the crullers in deep hot fat until lightly browned. Sprinkle them with powdered sugar if you wish. Store them in a tightly covered container.

MAKES ABOUT 36 CRULLERS.

Danish dollars

DENMARK

12 tablespoons butter
1 cup confectioners' sugar
2 cups flour
½ teaspoon salt
1 cup chopped nuts (hazelnuts preferred)

Cream the butter until it is foamy. Add the powdered sugar and mix well. Sift together the flour and salt and add them to the bowl. Add the chopped nuts. The dough will be stiff.

In waxed paper form the dough into long rolls about 2 inches round. Chill it in the refrigerator for at least 30 minutes. Slice the roll into thin rounds and place them on a greased cookie sheet. (The thinner the slice is, the thinner the finished cookie will be.) Bake them at 325°F for 10 to 15 minutes.

MAKES 40 OR MORE COOKIES.

Apple rings

DENMARK

3 or 4 large apples
2 eggs, separated
2 teaspoons sugar
¼ teaspoon salt
¼ teaspoon ground cardamom
2 tablespoons butter
¾ cup milk
1 cup flour

Peel, core, and slice the apples ½ inch thick. Beat the egg whites until stiff and set them aside. Beat the egg yolks and add the sugar, salt, and

cardamom. Add melted butter, milk, and flour. Beat thoroughly. Fold in the stiffened egg whites.

Dip the apple slices into the batter and drop them at once into deep fat. Fry them until lightly browned. Drain the apples and sprinkle them with sugar. Serve the apple rings warm.

MAKES 12 OR MORE RINGS.

Apple turnovers

DENMARK

1½ cups butter (or margarine)
4 cups flour
½ teaspoon salt
2 packages dry yeast
1 egg
Applesauce for filling

Cut the butter into the flour and salt with 2 knives. The mixture will be slightly lumpy. Mix the yeast in a beaten egg until all yeast is dissolved. Add this to the flour mixture. Knead thoroughly with your hands. Roll out the dough on a floured board. Cut it with a round cutter at least 3 inches in diameter. Put a teaspoonful of applesauce on half of each dough round. Fold over the other half and seal the edges with a fork.

Bake the turnovers on a greased baking sheet at 425°F for 15 to 20 minutes. They may be glazed with your favorite icing when cold.

MAKES 12 OR MORE PASTRIES.

Currant squares

DENMARK

2 eggs, separated
⅔ cup butter
½ cup sugar
¼ cup blanched, ground almonds
Grated rind of 1 lemon
1 cup flour
Chopped almonds, sugar, and currants for topping

Beat the egg whites until stiff and set them aside. In a large bowl cream the butter and sugar, beaten egg yolks, almonds, lemon rind, and flour. Fold in the stiffly beaten egg whites. Pour the mixture into a greased baking pan, spreading it about ½ inch thick. Sprinkle it with the topping mixture. Bake it at 375°F for 10 to 15 minutes. Cut it into small squares while it is still warm.

MAKES 18 OR MORE SQUARES.

Soda cake

DENMARK

½ pound butter
1¼ cups sugar
3 eggs
1½ cups milk
4½ cups flour
2 tablespoons milk
1 teaspoon baking soda
1 teaspoon lemon extract
½ cup currants

white glaze (optional)
1 cup powdered sugar
½ teaspoon lemon extract
3 tablespoons milk

Cream the butter and sugar together. Add well-beaten eggs. Add the milk and flour alternately, beating well after each addition. Mix 2 tablespoons of milk with the baking soda and add this to the cake mixture. Last, add the lemon extract and currants. Pour the mixture into a well-greased loaf pan. Bake it at 350°F for 1 hour. If desired, mix together the white-glaze ingredients and ice the cooled cake with the glaze.

MAKES 8 OR MORE SERVINGS.

Almond cookies

DENMARK

½ pound butter
½ cup sugar
1½ cups flour
¼ cup cornstarch
½ teaspoon baking powder
1 teaspoon cinnamon
1 teaspoon ground cardamom
½ cup chopped almonds
1 egg yolk
2 teaspoons water
Halved blanched almonds for decoration

Cream together the butter and sugar. Sift together the flour, cornstarch, baking powder, and spices. Mix them well with the butter mixture. Last, add the chopped almonds. Chill the dough for at least 2 hours.

Shape the dough into rounds, rolling it between the palms of your hands until it is about the size of a melon ball. Place the balls on a greased baking sheet. Flatten each ball slightly with your thumb or a knife. Brush each ball with egg yolk mixed with 2 teaspoons of water. Decorate each cookie with a nutmeat. Bake them at 375°F for about 10 minutes. The cookies should be golden brown when finished.

MAKES 3 DOZEN COOKIES.

Carrot cake pudding

DENMARK

¼ pound butter
1¼ cups brown sugar
2 eggs
½ teaspoon baking soda dissolved in 1 tablespoon hot water
1 cup grated raw carrots
1 cup seedless raisins
½ cup currants
1 tablespoon finely cut candied lemon peel
1 tablespoon finely cut candied orange peel
1¾ cups flour
2 teaspoons baking powder
½ teaspoon salt
½ teaspoon cinnamon
½ teaspoon nutmeg
¼ teaspoon allspice
¼ teaspoon ground cardamom
1 cup chopped nuts
Whipped cream for topping

Cream the butter and sugar and add beaten eggs and the dissolved baking soda. Add the rest of the ingredients, except the whipped cream, in the order given; mix thoroughly. Pour into a greased mold. Bake at 350°F for 1 hour. Serve the cake hot or cold, topped with whipped cream.

MAKES 8 OR MORE SERVINGS.

Nut cookies

FINLAND

½ pound butter
½ cup sugar
3 cups flour
1 beaten egg
Sugar
Chopped nuts

Cream the butter and ½ cup of sugar until well-blended. Add the flour. Chill this mixture in the refrigerator for at least 2 hours.

Form the mixture into long rolls about ½ inch in diameter. Cut these rolls into 3-inch lengths. Place them on a well-greased cookie sheet. Brush each roll with beaten egg and sprinkle it with nuts and sugar. Bake them at 325°F for 15 minutes or until lightly browned.

MAKES 5 DOZEN COOKIES.

Strawberry snow

FINLAND

2 cups fresh strawberries
Sugar to taste
4 egg whites
¾ cup whipping cream

Sprinkle the strawberries with sugar to taste and crush the berries. Reserve 6 whole berries for decoration.

Beat the egg whites until stiff. Beat the whipping cream until stiff. Gently mix together the berries, whipped cream, and stiff egg whites. Spoon this into dessert bowls. Put 1 whole berry on top of each serving.

MAKES 6 SERVINGS.

Dessert pancake

FINLAND

2 cups milk
1 teaspoon salt
1½ cups flour
2 eggs
2 tablespoons sugar
2 tablespoons butter

Mix the milk, salt, and flour to a smooth batter. Set it aside for 1 hour.

Just before frying, beat the eggs and sugar together and add them to the batter. Melt the butter in a frying pan, greasing the sides as well as the bottom of the pan. Pour the melted butter into the batter, and mix again. Put all the batter into the frying pan. Bake it in the oven at 425°F for about 25 minutes or until golden brown on top. Serve the pancake with raspberry jam.

MAKES 6 SERVINGS.

Sugar and spice rice

Applecake

ICELAND

¼ pound butter
2 cups bread crumbs
1 cup sugar
1 to 1½ cups applesauce

Melt the butter in a frying pan. Brown the bread crumbs lightly and stir in the sugar well. In a deep glass dish or bowl place alternate layers of bread crumbs and applesauce, ending with bread crumbs on top. Chill it. Top the cake with whipped cream if desired.

MAKES 6 SERVINGS.

Apple pie

NORWAY

1 egg
¾ cup sugar
1 teaspoon vanilla
¼ teaspoon salt
1 teaspoon baking powder
½ cup flour

½ cup chopped nuts
1 cup diced apples

With a wooden spoon mix the ingredients in the order given, folding in the nuts and apples last. Put the mixture in an 8-inch greased pie pan. Bake it at 350°F for 30 minutes. Serve the pie warm or cold.

MAKES 6 OR MORE SERVINGS.

Cottage-cheese-filled crepes

Apple cake (pg. 562)

Cream the butter and sugar together. Separate the eggs. Add the egg yolks to the butter and sugar and beat the mixture until it is smooth. Sift the flour and baking powder together. Add them to the mixture alternately with the milk. Fold in the currants and, last, the egg whites, stiffly beaten. Pour it into a greased mold. Bake the cake at 350°F for 1 hour.
MAKES 6 OR MORE SERVINGS.

Fruit in cream

NORWAY

2 apples
2 oranges
2 bananas
1/2 cup sugar
1 cup whipping cream
1/4 cup chopped almonds

Peel all the fruits and cut them in slices or pieces. Sprinkle the sugar over the fruit. Let it stand for 10 minutes. Whip the cream until stiff and fold it into the fruit. Sprinkle the chopped nuts over the top and serve.
MAKES 6 SERVINGS.

Honeyed apples

Currant cake

NORWAY

1/4 pound butter
1 cup sugar
3 eggs
2 cups flour
1 teaspoon baking powder
1 cup milk
1/2 cup currants or raisins

Eggedosis

NORWAY

This is often served in glasses for an eggnog type of drink as well as a dessert.

Valencia crepes

6 egg yolks
2 egg whites
6 tablespoons sugar
Brandy to taste

Beat the egg yolks and whites with an electric mixer until thick and lemon-colored. Add the sugar gradually, continuing to beat. Use sherbet glasses, and place 1 teaspoon of brandy in each. Gently spoon the egg mixture over this.
MAKES 4 TO 6 SERVINGS.

Coffee cakes
NORWAY

¼ pound butter
¾ cup sugar
2 large eggs
½ cup cream
½ cup currants (or raisins)
1 teaspoon ground cardamom
2¼ cups flour
2 teaspoons baking powder

Cream the butter and sugar together. Add well-beaten eggs. Add the cream, currants, cardamom, and flour sifted with baking powder. Grease small muffin tins and fill each cup ⅔ full. Bake at 375°F for 20 minutes.
MAKES 3 DOZEN CAKES.

Fruit w/egg sauce
NORWAY

This egg sauce is sometimes served as a drink or an eggnog in Norway, but is delicious over the fruit.

¾ cup chopped bananas
¾ cup halved seedless grapes
½ cup chopped nuts
1 cup chopped apples or oranges

egg sauce
5 egg yolks
2 egg whites
5 tablespoons sugar
1 tablespoon brandy or rum

Toss the fruits and nuts together in a serving bowl. To make the sauce, whip together the egg yolks, whites, and sugar with an electric mixer at high speed. The mixture will thicken slightly. Beat in the liquor. Pour the sauce over the fruit and chill together, or, if you prefer, serve the fruit in one bowl and the sauce in a sauceboat beside it.
MAKES 4 TO 6 SERVINGS.

Coffee fromage
NORWAY

Fromage does not mean cheese in Scandinavia. It is a rich, molded dessert that can be made a day ahead of serving.

1 envelope gelatin
⅓ cup boiling water
2 cups heavy cream
⅓ cup sugar
⅔ cup cold strong coffee
Whipped cream for garnish (optional)

Dissolve the gelatin in boiling water and set it aside to cool. Whip the cream until it is stiff, folding in the sugar and coffee. Add the cooled gelatin to the whipped-cream mixture and pour it into a mold or individual serving dishes. Chill it until set. Garnish with whipped cream if desired.
MAKES 6 TO 8 SERVINGS.

Pineapple fromage
NORWAY

1 envelope unflavored gelatin
⅓ cup boiling water
4 eggs, separated
1-pound can pineapple, crushed or chunks
½ cup sugar
2 cups heavy cream
½ cup pineapple juice
Whipped cream and pineapple for garnish

Soften the gelatin in the boiling water and set it aside to cool. Beat the egg whites stiff and set them aside. Drain the pineapple from the juice, reserving both. Beat together the egg yolks and sugar at high speed on an electric beater. Add the cream, beaten until it is stiff. Add the juice

607

of the pineapple, the cooled gelatin mixture, and the pineapple fruit. Gently fold in the beaten egg whites.

Put the mixture in a mold and chill it for at least several hours. When ready to serve, unmold the fromage on a serving plate and garnish it with whipped cream and pineapple.

MAKES 6 TO 8 SERVINGS.

Applecake

SWEDEN

¼ pound butter
3 cups bread crumbs
3 tablespoons sugar
2 teaspoons cinnamon
2 cups applesauce
2 tablespoons butter

Melt the butter in a pan. Add the bread crumbs, sugar, and cinnamon and stir until well-mixed and golden brown. Place ⅓ of the bread-crumb mixture in a well-greased deep-dish pie pan. Cover this with 1 cup of the applesauce. Continue to layer with another ⅓ of the bread crumbs and another cup of applesauce. Put the rest of the bread crumbs on top and dot with butter. Bake it at 375°F for 25 minutes. Serve the cake at room temperature.

MAKES 6 TO 8 SERVINGS.

Cardamom cake

SWEDEN

4 cups flour
3 teaspoons baking powder
1 cup sugar
2 teaspoons cardamom
½ teaspoon salt
1 cup cream
¼ pound butter
Slivered almonds
1 teaspoon cinnamon
¼ cup sugar

Sift the flour and baking powder into a large bowl. Add the sugar, cardamom, and salt. Make a well in the center and pour in the cream. Mix

together gently. Add melted and cooled butter and mix all together to a smooth dough.

Make the dough into a loaf shape about 10 inches long. Put it on a greased baking sheet. Sprinkle almond slivers over the top of the dough. Mix the cinnamon and sugar and sprinkle them over the top. Press the topping into the dough with your fingers. Bake it at 400°F for 45 minutes. Allow the cake to cool and then slice it into thick pieces.

MAKES 12 OR MORE SLICES.

Baked apple cake

SWEDEN

2 cups cold water
¼ lemon plus 4 teaspoons lemon juice
4 large, tart cooking apples
½ cup sugar
¼ pound butter (1 stick)
⅔ cup sugar
3 eggs, separated
½ cup ground blanched almonds
Pinch of salt

In a 2-quart saucepan combine the cold water, 2 teaspoons of lemon juice, and the ¼ lemon. Halve, peel, and core each apple, dropping each into the lemon water to prevent discoloration. Stir in ½ cup of sugar. Bring this to a boil. Simmer it uncovered for 8 minutes or until the apples are tender. Drain the apples. Remove the ¼ lemon. Grease a deep pie plate or shallow baking dish. Arrange the apple halves cut-side-down. With an electric beater cream the stick of butter with the ⅔ cup of sugar. Add the egg yolks, 1 at a time, the almonds, and the remaining 2 teaspoons of lemon juice. Beat the egg whites with a pinch of salt until stiff. Gently fold them into the egg-yolk mixture, using a spatula. Pour this over the apples. Bake this at 350°F for 20 minutes or until the surface is golden brown. Serve the cake at room temperature.

MAKES 6 SERVINGS.

Tiger cake

SWEDEN

2¼ cups flour
2 teaspoons baking powder
⅔ cup butter or margarine
1⅓ cups sugar
3 eggs
⅔ cup cream or milk
1 teaspoon vanilla
2 tablespoons cocoa
1 cup chocolate chips (for glaze)
Sliced almonds or other nuts

Measure and sift the flour and baking powder and set them aside. Using an electric beater, cream the butter and sugar. Add unbeaten eggs 1 at a time. Add half of the flour and half of the milk, beating thoroughly after each addition. Add the remainder of the flour and milk, and the vanilla.

Set aside ⅓ of the batter in another bowl. Add the cocoa to this. In a well-greased loaf pan or cake mold put alternate layers of light and dark batter, ending with light batter on top. Gently run a long-tined fork through all the cake batter to form a striped pattern. Bake it at 350°F for 50 to 60 minutes. Allow the cake to cool completely. Melt the chocolate in the top of a double boiler over simmering water. Glaze the top of the cake with melted chocolate and sprinkle with nuts.
MAKES 10 SERVINGS.

Fruit soup

SWEDEN

¾ cup dried apricots
¾ cup dried prunes
6 cups cold water
1 cinnamon stick
2 lemon slices
3 tablespoons quick-cooking tapioca
1 cup sugar
1 tart cooking apple
2 tablespoons raisins
1 tablespoon currants

Soak the apricots and prunes for 30 minutes in cold water in a 3-quart saucepan. Add the cinna-

mon stick, lemon slices, tapioca, and sugar and bring them to a boil. Reduce the heat and cover the pan. Simmer the mixture for 10 minutes, stirring with a wooden spoon to prevent sticking to the pan.

Peel and core the apple and cut it into ½-inch slices. Add the raisins, currants, and apple slices to the saucepan. Simmer for 5 minutes more. Pour the mixture into a serving bowl to cool. Remove the cinnamon stick; cover and refrigerate the soup. This may be served in soup bowls as a dessert.
MAKES 6 TO 8 SERVINGS.

Christmas cookies

SWEDEN

½ pound butter or margarine
1½ cups sugar
2 eggs
3 tablespoons light corn syrup
3 cups flour
½ teaspoon baking soda
½ teaspoon salt
1 teaspoon cinnamon
½ teaspoon ground ginger
½ teaspoon allspice
½ teaspoon ground cloves (light)

Cream the butter and sugar together. Add the eggs and corn syrup. Put 3 cups of flour in a 4-cup measure and add the rest of the ingredients. Put the flour mixture together with the rest, working it into a stiff dough. Wrap the dough in wax paper and refrigerate it for at least 2 hours. On a floured board roll out the dough very thin. Cut it with your favorite cookie cutters. Bake the cookies for 10 minutes at 350°F.
MAKES ABOUT 60 COOKIES.

Swedish pancakes

SWEDEN

3 eggs
2 cups milk
1 cup flour
6 tablespoons butter
½ teaspoon salt

609

With a rotary beater or a whisk, beat the eggs together with ½ cup of milk. Add the flour and beat to a smooth consistency. Beat in the remaining milk. Add the butter, melted, and the salt. The batter will be thick but smooth.

Lightly grease a large iron skillet. (You will only have to grease it once.) Drop the batter 1 tablespoon at a time for each pancake. The pancakes will be about 3 inches round. Turn them after the edges have browned, and cook them for another minute or two. Serve the pancakes with fruit preserves.

MAKES 6 TO 8 SERVINGS.

Apples & whipped cream

MIDDLE EAST

1 cup sugar
1 cup water
16 whole cloves
4 peeled and cored cooking apples
½ cup stiffly whipped heavy cream

Use a saucepan large enough to hold the apples, about 4 quarts. Stir sugar and water together until the sugar is totally dissolved. Insert 4 cloves on the top of each apple. Put the apples, clove-side up, in the syrup and baste. Reduce the heat and allow to simmer for 15 minutes, basting occasionally. When apples are tender, remove from the heat and allow to come to room temperature.

Place apples in individual dessert dishes and cover with a dollop of whipped cream. Pour 1 tablespoon of syrup over all and serve.
MAKES 4 SERVINGS.

Apricot delight

MIDDLE EAST

1 cup dried apricots
1½ cups water
2 tablespoons apricot preserves
⅓ cup sugar
3 slivers lemon peel
½ teaspoon grated orange peel
1 cup heavy cream

1 cup topping of slightly sweetened whipped cream
Chopped nuts for garnish

Combine apricots, water, preserves, sugar, lemon peel, and orange peel in a saucepan. Bring to a boil and then simmer for 25 minutes. Cool and purée in a blender or put through a food mill. Whip the cup of heavy cream until stiff and fold into the cooled mixture. Fill serving glasses with this. Chill.

When ready to serve, top each portion with the slightly-sweetened whipped cream. Garnish with chopped nuts, if desired.
MAKES 4 TO 6 SERVINGS.

Melon & peach delight

MIDDLE EAST

1 medium Persian melon or 2 small cantaloupes
½ teaspoon salt
2 fresh peaches, peeled and cut into ½-inch slices
½ cup sugar
3 tablespoons lemon juice
2 tablespoons rose water

Halve the melon and remove and discard seeds. Using a melon baller, scoop out as many balls as possible. If you prefer, with a knife, cut the fruit into ¾-inch squares, as this uses all of the melon. Put melon into a bowl and squeeze out the juice remaining in the rind. Discard the shells. Sprinkle the fruit with salt.

Prepare the peaches and add to the melon. Dissolve sugar in lemon juice and rose water and pour over the fruit, stirring gently to combine all flavors. Cover and refrigerate until thoroughly chilled. Serve in individual glass dishes.
MAKES 4 TO 6 SERVINGS.

Sweet figs

MIDDLE EAST

4 cups water
1½ cups sugar
Dash of ginger
Dash of cinnamon
1 pound dried figs

Danish dollars

into 4 chilled compotes. Place three figs in each glass and sprinkle with garnish. Chill until time to serve.
MAKES 4 SERVINGS.

Grape compote

MIDDLE EAST

½ cup sugar
3 cups water
½ cup Concord wine
4 cups grapes

Bring sugar and water to a boil and then add the wine. Bring this mixture back to a boil and then remove from heat. Add the grapes to the hot liquid. No further cooking is needed. When the mixture has cooled to room temperature, put in a bowl and chill. Serve from the chilled bowl.
MAKES 6 TO 8 SERVINGS.

Juice of 1 orange and ½ lemon
Pine nuts for garnish

Make a syrup of the water and sugar and add the spices. (Be generous with spices.) Add figs and cook 10 to 15 minutes until the syrup has thickened. Add the fruit juices and remove from heat. Chill. When ready to serve, spoon into dessert dishes and top with pine nuts.
MAKES 4 TO 6 SERVINGS.

Quick Danish

Figs in yoghurt

MIDDLE EAST

Fresh figs, abundant in the Middle East, have a delicious flavor all their own. However, canned figs may be substituted here and will still make an elegant dessert.

12 peeled fresh figs (do not peel canned figs)
½ cup chopped blanched almonds
12 whole blanched almonds
1 cup almond brandy or fruit wine
1 pint yoghurt
1 tablespoon honey
¼ teaspoon vanilla
Crushed, blanched almonds for garnish

Open each fig and stuff with the nuts. Cover the stuffing with 1 whole almond. Place figs in a shallow dish and pour brandy or wine over them to almost cover the fruit. Let figs stand in this marinade for several hours. Then remove figs, reserving the liquid.
Combine the reserved liquid with yoghurt, honey, and vanilla. Divide the mixture and pour

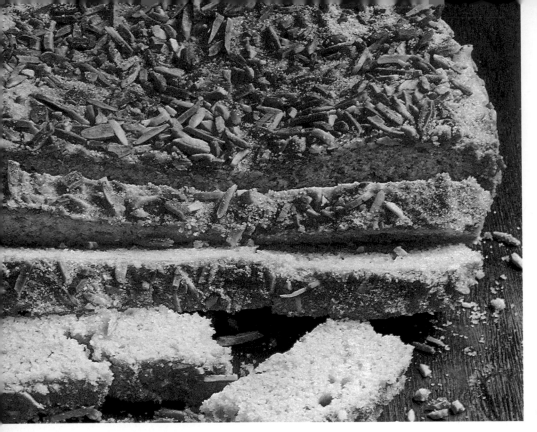

Cardamon cake

Avocado dessert

MIDDLE EAST

4 medium avocados
6 teaspoons lemon juice
¼ cup sugar
3 tablespoons sour cream
1 tablespoon liqueur

Peel and seed ripe avocados and press the meat through a sieve or mash very fine with a fork. Add the remaining ingredients and mix very well. Chill thoroughly. When ready to serve, spoon into dessert dishes and top with extra sour cream, if desired.

MAKES 6 TO 8 SERVINGS.

Egyptian palace bread

MIDDLE EAST

½ pound honey
½ cup margarine
½ cup sugar
1 cup (or more) white bread crumbs

Heat honey, margarine, and sugar in a pan until all are melted and mixed together. Add the bread crumbs stirring constantly until the mixture is one mass, cooking for about 5 to 10 minutes. Put onto a plate and allow to cool, spreading out fairly flat, about ½ inch thick. When cool, cut into individual cakes.

MAKES 4 TO 6 SERVINGS.

Shortbread cookies

MIDDLE EAST

If you have a Syrian "S"-shaped cookie cutter, you can make these into that shape. If not, cut them into rectangles.

1 cup butter
½ cup sugar
4 cups flour
Blanched almonds

Mix butter, sugar, and flour, adding the flour last and gradually so all is well-blended. Pat the dough out onto a floured board. Cut into S-

Applecake (Iceland)

Carrot cake

shapes or rectangles and top each one with a blanched almond. Bake at 350°F for about 30 minutes. Dust with confectioners' sugar, if desired.

MAKES 24 TO 36 COOKIES.

Sweet rice

MIDDLE EAST

This rice is in the dessert section but it is also a pleasant accompaniment to lemon-flavored chicken wings.

5 cups rice
8 cups water
1 cup sugar
2 teaspoons cinnamon
½ teaspoon grated lemon rind
⅓ cup chopped dates
1 cup chopped walnuts
½ cup chopped pine nuts

Place the rice, water, sugar, cinnamon, and lemon rind in a large saucepan. Bring to a boil and then reduce flame to a medium heat. Stirring constantly, allow all to cook for 20 minutes. When rice is tender, add dates and heat through for just 3 more minutes. Place rice in serving bowls and garnish with walnuts and pine nuts.

MAKES 4 TO 6 SERVINGS.

Carrot cake

MIDDLE EAST

1½ cups flour
1½ cups sugar
1 teaspoon baking powder
1 teaspoon salt
½ teaspoon baking soda
½ teaspoon cinnamon
½ teaspoon nutmeg
½ teaspoon ginger
¾ cup cooking oil
3 eggs
3 teaspoons hot water
1 cup cooked, mashed carrots (canned will do)
½ cup walnuts
Powdered sugar
Marzipan carrots (optional)

Mix dry ingredients together in order given. Add cooking oil, eggs, water, and carrots; stir until well-blended. (Use a wooden spoon — it's easier.) Add walnuts. Pour batter into ungreased cake or tube pan. Bake at 350°F for 45 minutes. Dust with powdered sugar and decorate with marzipan carrots, if desired.

MAKES 8 TO 10 SERVINGS.

Date-nut loaf

Date-nut loaf

MIDDLE EAST

3 cups flour
4 tablespoons baking powder
½ cup sugar
1 teaspoon salt
1 cup chopped dates
¼ cup chopped pecans
1 beaten egg
1½ cups milk
2 tablespoons melted butter
Slivered nuts (optional)

Place dry ingredients in a large bowl and add the dates and nuts. Beat egg, milk, and butter together and gradually add to the flour mixture. When all is mixed, turn into a buttered loaf pan and allow to stand for 30 minutes. Then bake at 350°F for about 1½ hours. Cool the loaf on a rack. Decorate with slivered nuts. Slice to serve — the thinner the better.
MAKES ABOUT 10 SLICES.

Quick-&-easy baklava (puff pastry)

MIDDLE EAST

2 packages frozen puff pastry
4 or more tablespoons butter
1 pound coarsely chopped walnuts
1 cup and 2 tablespoons sugar
2 tablespoons lemon juice

Grated lemon peel
3 tablespoons water
1 tablespoon minced peppermint leaves

Knead the dough into a ball and then roll out paper-thin. Melt the butter and grease an 8-inch square baking dish. Line the bottom of the dish with a layer of the thin dough. Brush the top with melted butter and sprinkle some of the nuts on top. Continue layers of dough, butter, and nuts until dish is full (about 6 layers). Cover with a final layer of dough. Bake for 45 minutes at 425°F.

Make a thick syrup of the remaining ingredients in a saucepan. Allow to cool slightly. After the baklava has come out of the oven, pour the glaze over it. Divide into portions with a knife and serve either warm or at room temperature.
MAKES 4 TO 6 SERVINGS.

Arabian orange custard

MIDDLE EAST

½ cup brown sugar
1 tablespoon hot water
2 oranges, peeled and sectioned with membrane removed
6 eggs
¾ cup white sugar
3 cups hot milk
½ teaspoon salt

Butter a baking dish and set aside. Melt the brown sugar in water and cook for 2 minutes. Place the orange sections in the buttered dish and pour the melted sugar over them.

In a bowl, beat the eggs and white sugar together. Gradually add the hot milk and then the salt. Pour this into the dish over the waiting fruit. Place mold in a pan of hot water and bake at 350°F for 50 to 60 minutes. When a knife comes out of the center clean, the custard is done. Allow to cool and then chill for at least 2 hours.
MAKES 6 SERVINGS.

Almond cookies

CHINA

1 cup shortening
1 cup sugar
1 egg, beaten
3 cups sifted flour
1½ teaspoons baking soda
3 tablespoons almond extract
4 tablespoons honey or corn syrup
1 cup blanched almonds

Cream together shortening and sugar. Add egg. Slowly add flour, baking soda, almond extract and honey and blend until smooth. Take a small piece of dough and roll it into a ball. Repeat until all dough is used. Flatten each ball to about ½ inch thickness. Place an almond in the center of each. Bake on greased cookie sheet in preheated 375°F oven for about 15 to 20 minutes.
In China lard is the usual ingredient in Almond Cookies, but you may substitute margarine.
MAKES APPROXIMATELY 4 DOZEN COOKIES.

Sesame cookies

CHINA

1 cup sifted cake flour
½ stick butter
½ cup sugar
¼ teaspoon salt
1 egg
1 egg yolk mixed with 1 tablespoon water
Sesame seeds

Combine flour, butter, sugar, salt, and egg in bowl and knead well until it forms a soft dough. Place on well-floured board and form into long roll about 1½ inches in diameter. Cut into approximately 36 pieces and flatten each with bottom of glass dipped in flour.
Brush one side of cookie with egg-yolk and water mixture. Sprinkle sesame seeds on brushed side and press sesame seeds to cookie. Place on greased cookie sheet and bake at 350°F for 10 to 12 minutes.
MAKES APPROXIMATELY 3 DOZEN COOKIES.

Simple rice dessert

CHINA

1 cup leftover cooked rice
1 cup canned drained fruit, such as pineapple, peaches, mandarin oranges, fruit cocktail
2 cups whipped cream

Mix rice with drained fruit (cut into slices if necessary) and fold in whipped cream. Serve in dessert dishes.
MAKES APPROXIMATELY 4 SERVINGS.

Chinese honey shortbread

CHINA

2½ cups all purpose flour
Pinch of salt
½ cup butter
½ cup honey

In a medium-size bowl, place flour and salt. Mix the butter into the flour with the fingers until mixture is like fine meal. Add the honey gradually and, still working with the fingers, blend until dough is smooth and leaves the side of the bowl. From a piece of cardboard, cut a fan-shaped pattern. Roll out the dough on lightly floured surface to about ¼ inch thick and cut into fan shapes.
Place on baking sheet that has been lightly floured and cut 6 deep slashes lengthwise as shown in picture. Bake in preheated 350°F oven until lightly browned, about 12 minutes.
MAKES APPROXIMATELY 2½ DOZEN "FANS."

Lichees

CHINA

For a totally unique and delightful taste treat, try a dessert of lichees. This is a canned fruit in syrup, usually imported from Hong Kong. They can sometimes be purchased in your local supermarket, for sure at a Chinese food store. Try lichees mixed with other fruits; experiment with different combinations.

ONE CAN OF LICHEES MAKES APPROXIMATELY 4 SERVINGS.

Spiced kumquats

CHINA

1 quart kumquats
3 cups sugar
1 cup vinegar
1 stick cinnamon
1 tablespoon whole cloves
1 tablespoon whole allspice

Wash and slit kumquats; place in pot. Cover with water; bring to boil. Cook 10 minutes; drain.

Combine sugar, vinegar, and 3 cups water in large saucepan; bring to boil. Tie spices in small piece of muslin; drop into syrup. Cook 5 minutes. Add kumquats; cook 10 minutes. Discard spice bag. Let kumquats stand overnight. Bring to boil; cook until syrup is thick. Pack kumquats into hot sterilized jars; cover with syrup. Place lids on jars; screw bands tight. Process jars 10 minutes in boiling water.

MAKES ABOUT 3 PINTS.

Fruit dressing

CHINA

This is delicious poured over any kind of fruit.

1 cup sugar
1 egg, well beaten
Juice and grated rind of 1 orange, 1 lime, and 1 lemon

Combine all ingredients in saucepan and blend well. Cook over medium heat, stirring constantly, until mixture comes to a boil. Boil 1 minute. Remove from heat, cool, and store in refrigerator in covered jar. Serve as an accompaniment to a dessert of fresh fruit.

MAKES APPROXIMATELY 1 PINT OF DRESSING.

Spiced mandarin oranges

CHINA

1 small tangerine (an orange may be substituted)
2 11-ounce cans mandarin oranges
¼ cup water
⅓ cup firmly packed brown sugar
1 2-inch piece of stick cinnamon

Cut the peeling from the tangerine in paper-thin strips. Squeeze the juice and strain. In medium-size saucepan, combine the peeling and juice with the rest of the ingredients. Simmer for 15 minutes.

Remove from heat and remove the peeling and cinnamon. Chill for several hours. Serve in small dessert dishes.

MAKES APPROXIMATELY 4 SERVINGS.

Chinese fruit salad

CHINA

All the fruits in this recipe are available at Oriental food stores. Some may be available at your supermarket.

1 4-ounce jar ginger in syrup, drained
1 11-ounce can lichees in syrup, drained
1 8-ounce can kumquats, drained
1 20-ounce can longans, drained
1 12-ounce can water-lily roots, drained
1 16-ounce can mangos, drained
1 round watermelon, chilled, cut in half, meat and seeds removed, meat cut into balls or cubes
1 18-ounce can white nuts
1 lemon, sliced

Place ginger, lichees, kumquats, longans, lily roots, and mangos in large bowl; mix well. Chill until cold. Cut slice off base of each watermelon half; place each half on serving dish. Place melon balls or cubes back into shells. Spoon mixed fruit on watermelon balls. Serve with nuts and lemon.

MAKES ABOUT 12 SERVINGS.

Fruit cocktail

CHINA

4 cups water
3 tablespoons sugar
1 small can mandarin oranges
3 pineapple slices, quartered
6 canned water chestnuts, sliced
12 strawberries, halved

Place water and sugar in saucepan; heat until sugar dissolves. Remove from heat; cool. Add oranges, pineapple, water chestnuts, and strawberries. Mix gently; chill.
MAKES 2 OR 3 SERVINGS.

Almond delight

CHINA

1 envelope unflavored gelatin
3 tablespoons warm water
1 small can evaporated milk
1¼ cups cold water
6 tablespoons sugar
1 tablespoon almond extract
1 small can mandarin oranges (drain; reserve juice)

Dissolve gelatin in warm water. Heat milk with cold water and sugar to just below boiling. Add gelatin mixture; cool. Add almond extract. Pour into square or rectangular glass dish; refrigerate to set. Cut into squares; float in syrup with mandarin oranges.
MAKES 4 SERVINGS.

Orange syrup

¼ cup sugar
2 cups warm water
1 teaspoon almond extract
Juice from mandarin oranges

Dissolve sugar in water. Add almond extract and juice. Chill before serving. Serve in rice bowls.

Ginger ice cream

CHINA

½ gallon vanilla ice cream
1 cup finely chopped candied ginger

Remove ice cream from carton; place in bowl. Allow to soften. Mix in candied ginger; spoon back into carton. Refreeze ice cream. Let stand in freezer at least 48 hours before serving, giving time for ginger flavor to penetrate ice cream.
MAKES ABOUT 12 SERVINGS.

Fresh-fruit dessert

JAPAN

This is an ideal dessert to enjoy after a Japanese meal. It's especially good after a dinner of Sukiyaki. Use the amount of fruit needed for the number of guests you are serving. Approximate a generous amount per person, for instance 10 to 12 pieces.

Watermelon
Cantaloupe
Bananas
Lime or lemon juice
Grapes
Strawberries
Pineapple

Cut slices of watermelon and cantaloupe into chunks. Slice bananas into about 4 pieces each; sprinkle with lime or lemon juice to prevent darkening. Wash grapes; leave in small bunches. Wash and hull strawberries; leave whole. If using fresh pineapple, cut into bite-size pieces. If canned pineapple is used, you may purchase tidbits, chunks, or slices cut into quarters.
Arrange all fruit attractively on serving platter; serve with a small bowl or pitcher of Fruit Dressing (see Index), to be poured over the fruit.

Dessert yams

JAPAN

1½ pounds yams
Oil
4 tablespoons water
4 tablespoons soy sauce
½ cup sugar
4 tablespoons sesame seeds

Peel yams; cut them into bite-size pieces (irregular shapes). Fry yams in oil until just tender. Remove from oil. In a saucepan combine water, soy sauce, and sugar; simmer together. Put yams into this mixture for about 2 minutes; gently mix. Remove yams to lightly oiled serving platter. Sprinkle with sesame seeds that have been lightly toasted.
MAKES 3 TO 4 SERVINGS.

Fruit bowl

JAPAN

1 can mandarin oranges, drained
1 apple, peeled and sliced
1 banana, sliced and sprinkled with lime or lemon juice
6 dates, cut in half
⅛ cup walnut chips

Place drained mandarin oranges in glass bowl. Combine with apple, banana, and dates. Sprinkle with walnut chips. Serve and enjoy.
MAKES 2 SERVINGS.

Fruit kebabs

JAPAN

Pineapple chunks, canned or fresh
Bananas, cut into large pieces
Mandarin oranges
Brandied peaches, cut into halves, or large pieces
Spiced crab apples, left whole

Skewer fruits or ask your guests to do it for themselves. Cook on hibachi. There is an endless list of fruits suitable for this. Use the fruits that appeal to you and that are available to you. Make approximately 6 to 8 pieces of fruit per serving.

Orange-cup dessert

JAPAN

Oranges with unblemished skin, as many as are needed, 1 per person
Fruit such as:
Pineapple

Orange sections
Grapefruit sections
Bananas
Maraschino cherries
Walnuts

Cut slice from top of orange so that remainder of insides may be scooped out. Combine any of the above fruits, or others of your choice, and spoon into orange shells; refrigerate until serving time. The same thing may be done with grapefruit or bananas, as pictured. If desired, a small amount of your favorite liqueur may be added to the fruit.

Mexican trifle

MEXICO

¼ cup sugar
1 tablespoon cornstarch
¼ teaspoon salt
2 cups milk
2 eggs, slightly beaten
1 teaspoon vanilla
4 cups cubed pound cake
4 tablespoons brandy
4 tablespoons apricot preserves
½ cup whipped cream
1 tablespoon confectioners' sugar
Grated semisweet chocolate
Toasted slivered almonds

Combine sugar, cornstarch, and salt in medium saucepan. Stir in milk until well-blended. Cook over medium heat, stirring constantly, until mixture boils (it will be quite thin). Add a little of the mixture to beaten eggs; beat well. Return to saucepan; cook, stirring constantly, until mixture starts to bubble. Stir in vanilla; cool, covered with waxed paper.
Place cake cubes in glass bowl. Sprinkle with 3 tablespoons of the brandy, and drizzle with preserves. Pour custard over cake cubes. Whip the cream with confectioners' sugar until stiff. Fold in 1 tablespoon brandy. Top the cake and custard with whipped cream. Garnish with grated chocolate and almonds. Cover and chill for several hours before serving.
MAKES 4 TO 6 SERVINGS.

Chinese honey shortbread

Coconut flan

MEXICO

1 cup sugar
2 tablespoons water
4 eggs
1 14-ounce can sweetened condensed milk
1 cup water
1 teaspoon vanilla extract
½ cup flaked coconut

Combine sugar and 2 tablespoons water in small heavy skillet. Cook, stirring constantly, until caramelized and syrupy. Immediately pour into warm 3- to 4-cup buttered mold or casserole; tilt to coat bottom and sides of container while sugar is still hot.

Beat eggs well in medium mixing bowl. Add condensed milk, water, and flavoring; mix well. Pour into prepared mold or casserole; sprinkle with coconut.

Place casserole in a larger pan containing hot water to the level of the custard. Bake at 350°F for 1 hour or until a knife inserted in center of custard comes out clean. Cool mold completely. Loosen custard with a knife; invert on serving platter. Serve with the caramel spooned over each serving.

MAKES 6 SERVINGS.

Sweet fritters

MEXICO

4¾ cups flour
½ cup sugar
¼ teaspoon salt
1 cup water
2 eggs
3 tablespoons rum
Oil for frying
1 teaspoon ground cinnamon
½ cup sugar

Sift flour, sugar, and salt together into large bowl. Beat water, eggs, and rum together. Pour

Orange-cup dessert

into flour mixture; mix to form a stiff dough. Turn out on floured board; knead for 2 minutes or until smooth. Cut into 4 pieces. Roll each piece on floured pastry cloth to a rectangle (10 × 15 inches); cut into strips (2 × 5 inches). Shape by twisting 2 strips together, or cut a 1-inch slit down center of strip and pull 1 end through slit.

Heat oil to 370°F in an electric skillet. Meanwhile, combine cinnamon and sugar in shallow pan. Deep-fry pastries until golden. Drain briefly, dip in cinnamon and sugar, and coat well.

MAKES 40.

Spiced mandarin oranges

Broiled fruit w/cinnamon

MEXICO

3 bananas
½ medium pineapple (or 3 slices canned pineapple)
2 medium apples
½ cup melted butter
½ cup brown sugar
Ground cinnamon

Peel bananas. Peel pineapple; remove core. Cut slices ¾ inch thick. Peel and core apples; slice ¼ inch thick. Place fruits on cookie sheet lined with foil. Brush well with melted butter. Sprinkle with brown sugar and cinnamon. Broil 3 to 4 inches from heat 5 minutes, turning once.

Serve with sour cream or softened vanilla ice cream, flavored with rum.

MAKES 4 TO 6 SERVINGS.

Chinese fruit salad

Fruit bowl

Mocha cherry & nut cookies

1 cup butter
½ cup sugar
2 teaspoons vanilla
2 cups sifted flour
¼ cup unsweetened cocoa
1 tablespoon instant coffee
½ teaspoon salt
1 cup finely chopped pecans
½ cup chopped maraschino cherries
1 box confectioners' sugar

Cream butter, sugar, and vanilla until fluffy. Sift together flour, cocoa, instant coffee, and salt. Gradually add dry ingredients to creamed mixture. Add pecans and cherries. Chill dough. Shape dough into balls, using 1 generous teaspoon of dough for each ball. Place on greased cookie sheets. Bake in 325°F oven 20 minutes. Remove from cookie sheets to cooling racks. While warm, sprinkle with confectioners' sugar.
MAKES 6 DOZEN.

Gelatin dessert

1 tablespoon (1 envelope) unflavored gelatin
½ cup cold pineapple juice
4 egg whites
¼ teaspoon salt
¾ cup sugar
½ teaspoon vanilla
¼ teaspoon almond extract
2 tablespoons chopped maraschino cherries
¼ cup crushed pineapple
⅓ cup chopped blanched almonds
Red and green food coloring as needed

Soften gelatin in cold pineapple juice. Dissolve over hot water. Beat egg whites until foamy, add salt and sugar gradually, and continue beating until soft-peak stage is reached. Add dissolved gelatin to egg whites; beat until thick and of a marshmallow consistency. Add vanilla and almond extract. Divide into 3 parts; color 1 part pink, and add the maraschino cherries; color 1 part green and add pineapple; add chopped almonds to remainder.

Mold in oblong loaf pan, 9½ × 5¼ × 2¾ inches, putting white layer on bottom, then green, then pink, to represent Mexican flag colors. Small individual glass serving cups may be used instead of loaf pan. Let stand until set. Cut in slices; garnish with whipped cream, or serve with a custard sauce.
MAKES 8 SERVINGS.

Coffee dessert

1¼ cups water
¼ cup sugar
2 cloves
1 strip orange peel
1 strip lemon peel
1 small piece cinnamon stick
2 teaspoons instant-coffee powder
1 envelope unflavored gelatin
¼ cup coffee liqueur
Whipped cream or whipped topping

In small saucepan combine water, sugar, cloves, orange peel, lemon peel, and cinnamon stick. Bring to a boil; boil for 2 minutes. Strain; add coffee powder.
Soften gelatin in coffee liqueur. Add hot coffee mixture to gelatin; stir until gelatin is dissolved. Pour into 3 or 4 small molds, rinsed with cold water. Chill overnight. Unmold at serving time by dipping in hot water. Top with whipped cream or whipped topping.
MAKES 3 TO 4 SERVINGS.

Mocha parfait

2 bananas
Juice of 1 lemon (2 tablespoons)
16 walnut halves
½ cup cold heavy whipping cream
½ teaspoon vanilla
2 tablespoons sugar
1½ pints coffee ice cream
Bitter chocolate curls

Peel bananas, slice, and dip slices in lemon juice. Divide bananas among 4 parfait glasses. Top each with 4 walnut halves. Chill the glasses while whipping the cream. Pour whipping cream into small mixing bowl. Add vanilla; whip until stiff, gradually adding sugar while whipping.

At serving time, cube the ice cream; divide it among prepared parfait glasses. Top with whipped cream and chocolate curls.

MAKES 4 SERVINGS.

Cream-cheese turnovers w/ sweet potato, pineapple, & coconut filling or prune filling

MEXICO

cream-cheese pastry

1 cup butter
1 8-ounce package cream cheese
2 cups flour
½ teaspoon salt

sweet potato, pineapple, and coconut filling

1 cup mashed sweet potatoes
1 cup drained crushed pineapple
½ cup sugar
½ teaspoon cinnamon
¾ cup flaked or shredded coconut

prune filling

8 ounces prunes, pitted
⅓ cup sugar
½ teaspoon cinnamon
Dash of nutmeg

Cream butter and cream cheese until smooth. Work in flour and salt until blended. Chill in airtight container at least 6 hours.

Mix potatoes, pineapple, sugar, cinnamon, and coconut in saucepan. Cook over low heat, stirring constantly, until mixture thickens, about 5 to 10 minutes. Cool thoroughly.

Cover prunes with water; boil for 20 minutes or until tender. Purée the prunes. Stir in sugar, cinnamon, and nutmeg. Simmer, stirring, over low heat for 5 minutes. Cool. Makes 1 cup of prune filling.

Divide cream-cheese pastry in half. Prepare on lightly floured surface. Roll dough until ⅛ inch thick. Cut into 3-inch rounds. Place 1 teaspoon filling in center of each round. Moisten edges with water; fold pastry over filling to form a half-moon turnover. Press lightly to seal; crimp edges. Bake on ungreased sheets at 375°F for 18 to 20 minutes. When crisp and golden, remove from oven; place on racks to cool. Pastries may be dipped in a cinnamon and sugar mixture while warm.

MAKES 32.

Note: Each batch of filling is enough for one pastry recipe plus extra, which may be served with meat or fowl as a side dish.

Green tomato pie

MEXICO

6 to 8 medium green tomatoes, peeled and sliced
1 lemon, thinly sliced
2 tablespoons cornstarch
2 tablespoons water
1 cup sugar
2 tablespoons butter
½ teaspoon ground cinnamon
¼ teaspoon salt
1 frozen pie shell and frozen top crust or pie-crust mix

Bring to a boil tomatoes and lemon, then cover and simmer 10 minutes, until tomatoes appear transparent. Combine cornstarch and water; add to tomato mixture. Add sugar, butter, cinnamon, and salt. Stirring constantly, bring to a boil; continue boiling for 1 minute. Remove from heat.

Follow pastry instructions for baking a two-crust pie. Place filling in pie, add top crust, seal, flute edges, and cut steam vents in top crust. Bake at 425°F approximately 35 minutes. This is best served at room temperature.

MAKES 8 SERVINGS.

GLOSSARY

ACHIOTE—the Mexican name given to Annatto, the seeds of a South American Tree. Has a delicate flavor and a dark reddish-orange color. May be purchased ground.

AGAR-AGAR—a gelatin made from seaweed. It is available at Oriental stores.

ANAHEIM CHILIES—canned green chilies grown in California. When seeded, they are only slightly hot. Use with care.

ANCHO CHILIES—large, mild sweet chilies. When dried, they are dark red to brown in color, two to three inches long. Usually available in dried form only; may be stored indefinitely.

ANTIPASTO—usually an assortment of cold appetizers. Translated from Italian, this means "before the meal."

BAKLAVA—a delicious puff pastry often served in the Middle East.

BAMBOO SHOOTS—shoots of the tropical bamboo, which can be purchased canned. Refrigerate in water in covered jar. If water is changed daily, they will keep approximately two weeks.

BARMBRACK—a sweet Irish yeast dough with raisins, currants, etc.

BEAN CURDS—custard-like squares sometimes used as a meat substitute. Can be stored in water in the refrigerator.

BEAN SPROUTS—sprouts of the mung bean. Available canned or, preferably, fresh from the produce department of the supermarket.

BOK CHOY—a variety of Chinese cabbage with smooth white stalks and dark green leaves.

BOUILLABAISSE—a rich seafood stew popular in France.

BOXTY—an Irish bread using both grated and mashed potatoes.

BRATWURST—a type of sausage used in Germany.

BROWN BEAN SAUCE—(miso) a thick, brown sauce made from fermented soy beans, salt, and flour. Comes in jars or tins at Oriental food stores.

BULGUR WHEAT—cracked wheat available in specialty shops and in the gourmet sections of most large supermarkets.

BUNDT—a rich, moist cake that does not require frosting.

BURRITO—a tortilla with a wide variety of fillings, from beans and cheese to leftover tacos filling.

CARDAMOM—an herb of the ginger family used frequently in Scandinavian cooking.

CARRAGEEN—an edible form of dry seaweed, rich in vitamins and noted for its gelling properties. Available in health food or import stores.

CELERIAC ROOT—a variety of celery available in some supermarkets or in specialty stores.

CHALLAH—the traditional Sabbath bread in Jewish homes.

CHIANTI—a well-known red wine, served frequently with Italian meals.

CHILI POWDER—a mixture of powdered chili peppers, spices, and herbs. Test what you buy to find out how hot it is.

CHINESE CABBAGE (also called celery cabbage)—one of the oldest food crops of China; delicious in salads. Wide thick leaves form a long cylindrical head.

CHORIZO—a garlic-flavored pork sausage. Available at Latin American markets.

CILANTRO—leaf coriander, also called Chinese parsley. Available in Oriental and Latin American grocery stores, in dried form.

CLOUD EARS—a black gelatinous fungus that grows on trees, turns gray-brown when dried, and changes to dark brown and expands in size when soaked. When cooked, it has a crisp, crunchy texture. It will keep dried on the shelf indefinitely.

COLCANNON—an Irish main dish served traditionally on Halloween.

COLLOP—a small piece or slice of anything, especially of meat.

COMINO—cumin seed available in spice section of supermarkets. When purchased whole, it must be crushed to release flavor.

CORIANDER—sometimes known as Chinese parsley. A fresh herb used primarily as a garnish. You can substitute chopped scallions.

CRAIBECHAN—A Gaelic word meaning any savory mixture of little bits and pieces.

CREPE—a paper-thin French pancake usually served filled and rolled.

CROISSANT—a delicious French crescent roll served with the meal and sometimes filled with jam for dessert.

CROUTON—a small, crisp square of toasted or fried bread used in soups and salads.

DASHI—a basic fish broth made from dried bonito fish and seaweed. Can be purchased at Oriental specialty stores. Chicken broth can be substituted for it.

DRIED BLACK MUSHROOMS (Chinese mushrooms)—available in some supermarkets and in Oriental food stores. Must be soaked in warm water for 20 to 30 minutes; remove stems and slice.

DRIED SHARKS' FINS—long, translucent threads of dried cartilage from the fins of sharks. Available in Chinese food stores.

DUCK SAUCE (or plum sauce)—a sauce with sweet and pungent flavor made from apricots, plums, chili, sugar, and vinegar.

ENCHILADAS—cornmeal crepes or tortillas rolled around a variety of fillings.

FETA—a white goats-milk cheese, slightly salty in taste and crumbly in texture. Usually packed in jars or cans. Use the brine in which it is cured to pour over the cheese when storing it.

FETTUCCINE—one of the many varieties of pasta used in Italian cooking.

FIDES—long, very thin vermicelli noodles. If necessary, the more common vermicelli can be substituted.

"FIVE-SPICE" POWDER—a powdered blend of Chinese star anise, fennel, cinnamon, clove, and Szechwan pepper. Allspice is a substitute.

FONTINA—A creamy colored cheese that melts easily. If unavailable, substitute a well-aged Swiss or Emmenthaler cheese.

FORCEMEAT—meat, fish, or poultry that has been ground several times and seasoned to taste. Basically Scandinavian.

FROMAGE—a rich, molded dessert used frequently in Scandinavian countries. Also the French word for cheese.

GAZPACHO—a light soup from the Andalusian region of Spain.

GINGERROOT—A "hot" spice made from a knobby brown root. Sold by weight; keeps in the refrigerator for several weeks if wrapped well.

GOLDEN NEEDLES—also known as dried lily flower. Is two to three inches long. Soften in water before cooking, and cut off stem. Available at Oriental stores.

GRAPE-VINE LEAVES—delightful when picked fresh but more commonly found packed in brine in cans and jars. Do not substitute.

GULYAS—refers to a special soup made with paprika.

HIBACHI—a portable Japanese charcoal grill used indoors or outdoors.

HOISIN SAUCE—a thick, sweet, brownish-red sauce made from soybeans, flour, sugar, and spices. Sold in cans; keeps refrigerated in a covered jar for several months.

HONAN—a type of cooking done in northern China, which uses liberal amounts of scallions, garlic, and leeks.

HOUGH—a hearty Irish beef and vegetable soup.

HUMMUS—a Middle Eastern delicacy popular in the West as a dip.

JALAPEÑO PEPPER—a canned, pickled green chili that is very hot. Can be found in most gourmet sections of supermarket.

KABOB—a skewered meat and vegetable dish usually cooked over an open flame.

KAFALOTERI—a hard, grating cheese made from ewe's milk. A well-aged Parmesan or Romano cheese can be used as a substitute.

KASSERI—a semi-hard ewe's milk cheese available in Greek and Italian stores.

KIELBASA—a Polish sausage.

KIFFAL—a small Hungarian cookie.

KOHLRABI—a variety of cabbage, with an edible bulbous stem that resembles a turnip.

KUCHEN—a German coffeecake made of yeast dough base, usually filled with raisins, nuts, etc.

KUGEL—a baked noodle dish with many variations.

LASAGNA—a broad noodle used in Italian dishes.

LEEKS—a member of the onion family consisting of broad leaves that merge into a white bulb at the end.

LESCÓ—a combination of peppers, onions, and tomatoes served with a plain meat dish or used as a sauce.

LICHEES—small oval fruits that can be purchased canned at some supermarkets or in Oriental food stores.

LOVASH—a bread native to Armenia.

MACARONI, TUBULAR—range in size and shape from tiny to enormous tubes in such intricate shapes as seashells, spirals, thin and thick spaghetti, wheels, and many more.

MANDARIN—aristocratic type of cooking done for the royal courts in northern China in the Peking area.

MANICOTTI—one of the many varieties of pasta used in Italy.

MASA HARINA—instant limed corn flour used in making tortillas, tamales, and other Mexican dishes.

MEXICAN CHOCOLATE—bitter chocolate ground with cinnamon and almonds and sweetened with sugar. Substitute semi-sweet chocolate, ounce for ounce, and ½ teaspoon ground cinnamon.

MINESTRONE—an Italian soup including assorted fresh vegetables and topped with Parmesan cheese.

MIRIN—a sweet rice wine or sweet sake available at liquor stores and Oriental specialty stores. Sherry sweetened with sugar may be substituted.

MISO—fermented soy-bean paste available in white or the more flavorful red. Available at Oriental specialty stores.

MIZITHRA—a goat cheese that comes either hard or soft in nature. Sometimes called "the queen" of cheese but usually not available except near a large Greek community.

MONTEREY JACK—a cheese that is creamy white, mild in flavor, and smooth in texture. Substitute Muenster cheese.

MOZZARELLA—a bland white cheese that melts easily. Made from whole or partly skimmed milk. Monterey Jack or Meunster cheese can be substituted.

OLIVES—for Greek cooking, olives are generally black, shriveled, and pickled in brine. Available in most delicatessens.

ORZO—a rice-shaped noodle commonly used in soups. If unavailable, simply substitute rice.

OUZO—the national beverage of Greece, strongly anise-flavored and ranging from 80 to 100 proof. Served straight or with water.

OYSTER SAUCE—thick, brown sauce made from oysters, salt, and soybeans. Available in some supermarkets and in Oriental food stores.

PAELLA—a rice-based favorite known as the dish of Spain.

PALATSCHINKEN—a savory pancake made in Hungary, similar to the French crepe.

PAPRIKA—a mild red condiment used extensively in Hungary. An excellent browning agent for meats and poultry.

PARMESAN and ROMANO—hard grating cheeses that are best when grated just before using.

PASSILLA AND PEQUIN CHILIES—Chilies that are moderately hot and very hot respectively. Crushed red pepper or cayenne may be substituted.

PASTA—collective name applied to over 500 varieties of spaghetti, noodles, macaroni, and like products, which are made from flour, water, and sometimes eggs.

PEPITAS—shelled pumpkin seeds available raw or roasted and salted. Squash seeds may be substituted.

PHYLLO—paper thin pastry used in baking. Generally 16 x 18 inches per sheet, with many sheets to the pound. Must always be covered until ready to use and only worked one sheet at a time. Leftover phyllo should be wrapped well and frozen.

PIEROGI—a favorite dish of Poland, served as a main dish with butter, a dessert, or a French-fried delicacy. Made with a stiff dough, rolled thin, stuffed, and folded like a pocket.

PILAF—a rice dish used in Middle Eastern cooking.

PINE NUTS—generally available in gourmet shops. If you cannot find them, substitute blanched, slivered almonds, browned in butter.

PITA—a flat thin bread used in the Middle East.

PRAWN—edible, shrimp-like animals with a thin, leathery shell.

PROSCIUTTO—a favorite Italian cured ham.

QUARK—a Polish appetizer made of dough wrapped around a filling.

QUESTO BLANCO—a salty, mild Latin American cheese crumbly in texture. Substitute Monterey Jack cheese if unavailable.

RETSINA—Greek wine that can be white, rosé, or red and whose taste must be acquired.

RICE WINE—made from fermented rice. If unavailable, substitute sherry.

RICOTTA—a fresh cheese, soft and creamy in texture and mild in flavor.

RIGATONI—a popular pasta used in Italian cooking.

SAFFLOWER OIL—available in bottles in supermarkets.

SAFFRON—a ground seasoning made from the safflower plant.

SAKE—Japanese rice wine usually served warm for drinking.

SALONIKA PEPPERS—resemble Italian pickled hot peppers. If you cannot obtain the Salonika peppers, substitute the Italian or simply omit them.

SANGRIA—a favorite drink in Spain and a delightful summer cooler worldwide.

SAUERBRATEN—a German main dish using boneless beef roast as a base.

SAVOY CABBAGE—a small, green cabbage with heavily veined leaves. Regular cabbage can be substituted.

SEAWEED STRIPS—paper-thin and black-purple in color. Sold dehydrated at Oriental food stores.

SESAME-SEED OIL—made from roasted sesame seeds and sold in bottles. Available at supermarkets or Oriental food stores.

SMORGASBORD—literally translated means "bread and butter table"; actually, a Scandinavian buffet table including many different foods.

SNOW PEAS—flat, green pea pods with very small peas inside. The entire pod is edible if strings are removed before cooking.

SOFRITO—basic sauce using garlic, onions, sweet green or sweet red peppers, and tomatoes cooked together in olive oil.

SOUFFLÉ—a puffy egg dish native to France, with variations as a main dish or a dessert.

SOY SAUCE—pungent brown liquid made from fermented soy beans, wheat, yeast, and salt.

SPAETZLE—a machine used to press and shape noodles.

STAR ANISE—a dry, brown, licorice-flavored spice, which is available at Oriental food stores.

STOLLEN—a moist, heavy bread usually full of fruits.

STRUDEL—a kind of pastry made of thin dough and usually filled with fruit.

SUGARED GINGER (also called candied ginger)—sold in cellophane bags or boxes at supermarkets and Oriental food stores or gourmet food stores.

SZECHWAN—a type of cooking from the southwest of China, which includes very hot spices in most dishes.

SZECHWAN PEPPERCORNS—brown peppercorns with a very hot flavor. Sold in bulk at Oriental food stores. Substitute black peppercorns.

TACOS—a crisp fried tortilla usually served with a filling covered with sauce.

TAHINA—a sesame-seed paste used in Middle Eastern cooking.

TAMALES—a dough cooked by steaming. Aztec in origin and native to Mexico.

TARAMA—carp roe, a specialty found in gourmet stores in cans and jars.

TEMPURA—a batter used for fried foods in the Orient.

TEQUILA—a popular drink in Mexico and around the world. Made from the maguey cactus and fermented.

TERIYAKI—a sauce used in Japanese cooking for chicken, fish, and meat dishes.

TERRINE—a French name for a cold meatloaf casserole.

TOMATILLO OR TOMATE VERDE—a small, sweet green tomato. It is available canned and is puréed whole. No substitute for this ingredient.

TORTILLAS—thin, unleavened corn cakes baked on a comal or griddle. The bread of Mexico since Aztec times.

TOSTADOS—an open-faced tortilla sandwich, frequently topped with a hot sauce.

TRANSPARENT NOODLES—also called silver threads, cellophane noodles, and translucent noodles. Available in supermarkets or Oriental food stores.

WATER CHESTNUTS—white crunchy bulbs about the size of a walnut. Available in cans. The canned variety will keep (change the water daily) covered in the refrigerator for three to four weeks.

WOK—a conical shaped frying pan with heat center at the bottom. Used for stir frying as well as deep frying.

Index

Index

Index

Index

Index

Index